W9-BZP-952

FTC6–7JBH–3VKQ–CXKE–TG4F

IMPORTANT

HERE IS YOUR REGISTRATION CODE TO ACCESS MCGRAW-HILL PREMIUM CONTENT AND MCGRAW-HILL ONLINE RESOURCES

For key premium online resources you need THIS CODE to gain access. Once the code is entered, you will be able to use the web resources for the length of your course.

Access is provided only if you have purchased a new book.

If the registration code is missing from this book, the registration screen on our website, and within your WebCT or Blackboard course will tell you how to obtain your new code. Your registration code can be used only once to establish access. It is not transferable.

To gain access to these online resources

1. USE your web browser to go to: **www.mhhe.com/patterns**

2. CLICK on "First Time User"

3. ENTER the Registration Code printed on the tear-off bookmark on the right

4. After you have entered your registration code, click on "Register"

5. FOLLOW the instructions to setup your personal UserID and Password

6. WRITE your UserID and Password down for future reference. Keep it in a safe place.

If your course is using WebCT or Blackboard, you'll be able to use this code to access the McGraw-Hill content within your instructor's online course.

To gain access to the McGraw-Hill content in your instructor's WebCT or Blackboard course simply log into the course with the user ID and Password provided by your instructor. Enter the registration code exactly as it appears to the right when prompted by the system. You will only need to use this code the first time you click on McGraw-Hill content.

These instructions are specifically for student access. Instructors are not required to register via the above instructions.

0-07-320915-5 T/A CLOUSE: PATTERNS FOR A PURPOSE: A RHETORICAL READER, 4E

The McGraw-Hill Companies

 Higher Education

Thank you, and welcome to your McGraw-Hill Online Resources.

REGISTRATION CODE
REGISTRATION CODE

The McGraw-Hill Companies

McGraw Hill **Higher Education**

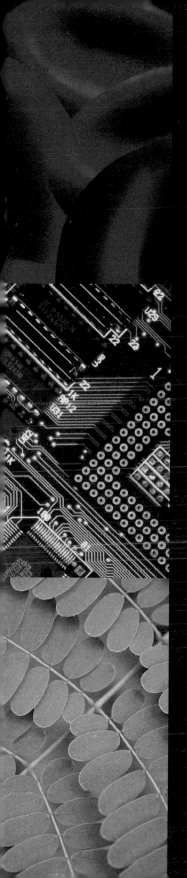

Praise for *Patterns for a Purpose,* Fourth Edition

"Barbara Fine Clouse's *Patterns for a Purpose* is one of the best combination rhetoric-readers I have ever used to teach freshman composition. . . . Simply put, *Clouse gets it right!*"
—J. CHRISTIAN TATU, *WARREN COUNTY COMMUNITY COLLEGE*

"*Patterns for a Purpose* is an outstanding reader with clear, in-depth explanations in the instructional sections, a variety of appropriate essays, and valuable information in the introductions and the post-essay analysis sections."
—LINDA COOPER KNIGHT, *COLLEGE OF THE ALBEMARLE*

"I would describe *Patterns for a Purpose* as an accessible, student-centered text that provides excellent topics for discussion and writing. This text makes the instructor's job easier and the class more interesting for the students."
—CAROL BLEDSOE, *FLORIDA GULF COAST UNIVERSITY*

"*Patterns for a Purpose* is a rhetoric-reader that presents, with clarity and grace, the rhetorical modes in all their overlapping complexity, and the individual distinguishing characteristics of each."
—DIANA CAMERON, *NORTH IOWA AREA COMMUNITY COLLEGE*

". . . *Patterns for a Purpose* presents information in a reader-friendly style and format, and I am sure that students would find it welcoming."
—RITA KRANIDIS, *MONTGOMERY COLLEGE*

"Its accessible format and practical approach make *Patterns for a Purpose* a superb choice for beginning writers."
—DR. ROBERT SAWYER, *EAST TENNESSEE STATE UNIVERSITY*

Patterns for a Purpose

A RHETORICAL READER

Fourth Edition

Barbara Fine Clouse

Boston   Burr Ridge, IL   Dubuque, IA   Madison, WI   New York
San Francisco   St. Louis   Bangkok   Bogotá   Caracas   Kuala Lumpur
Lisbon   London   Madrid   Mexico City   Milan   Montreal   New Delhi
Santiago   Seoul   Singapore   Sydney   Taipei   Toronto

For Denny, with love, admiration, and appreciation

Higher Education

PATTERNS FOR A PURPOSE: A RHETORICAL READER
Published by McGraw-Hill, a business unit of The McGraw-Hill Companies, Inc., 1221
Avenue of the Americas, New York, NY, 10020. Copyright © 2006, 2003, 1999, 1995 by The
McGraw-Hill Companies, Inc. All rights reserved. No part of this publication may be
reproduced or distributed in any form or by any means, or stored in a database or retrieval
system, without the prior written consent of The McGraw-Hill Companies, Inc., including,
but not limited to, in any network or other electronic storage or transmission, or broadcast
for distance learning.

Some ancillaries, including electronic and print components, may not be available to
customers outside the United States.

This book is printed on acid-free paper.

3 4 5 6 7 8 9 0 DOC/DOC 0 9 8 7 6

ISBN-13: 978-0-07-298257-2
ISBN-10: 0-07-298257-8

Editor in Chief: *Emily Barrosse*
Publisher: *Lisa Moore*
Sponsoring Editor: *Christopher Bennem*
Senior Developmental Editor: *Jane Carter*
Marketing Manager: *Lori DeShazo*
Managing Editor: *Jean Dal Porto*
Project Manager: *Ruth Smith*
Lead Designer: *Gino Cieslik*
Interior and Cover Designer:
Maureen McCutcheon
Photo Researcher: *Ruth Mandel*
Photo Research Coordinator: *Natalia C. Peschiera*

Art Editor: *Katherine McNab*
Cover Credit: (*left to right*) © *Royalty
Free/Corbis*, © *Mark L. Stephenson/Corbis*,
© *Gunter Max Photography/Corbis*
Senior Media Producer: *Todd Vaccaro*
Lead Media Project Manager: *Marc Mattson*
Associate Production Supervisor:
Jason I. Huls
Permissions Editor: *Marty Granahan*
Composition: *TechBooks/GTS, York, PA*
Printing: *Four color process on 45 # New Era
Matte*

Credits: The credits section for this book begins on page C-1 and is considered an extension
of the copyright page.

Library of Congress Cataloging-in-Publication Data

Clouse, Barbara Fine.
    Patterns for a purpose : a rhetorical reader/Barbara Fine Clouse.—4th ed.
      p. cm.
    Includes index.
    ISBN 0-07-298257-8 (softcover : alk. paper)
    1. College readers. 2. English language—Rhetoric—Problems, exercises, etc. 3. Report
writing—Problems, exercises, etc. I. Title.
PE1417.C6314 2003
808'.0427—dc22

                               2005041671

The Internet addresses listed in the text were accurate at the time of publication. The
inclusion of a website does not indicate an endorsement by the authors of McGraw-Hill, and
McGraw-Hill does not guarantee the accuracy of the information presented at these sites.

www.mhhe.com

Thematic Contents   xv
Essay Pairs   xxi
Preface   xxiii

CHAPTER 1

Reading Critically

CRITICAL READING   1
Distinguishing Facts from Opinions   2
Making Inferences   3
Synthesizing Information   4
Evaluating Quality   4
Detecting Errors in Logic   5

STRATEGIES FOR CRITICAL READING   8
Approach Your Reading with a Reflective and
    Questioning Attitude   8
Preview the Material   8
Do a First Reading   9
Reread and Study   9
A Sample Marked Essay   11
Keeping a Reading Journal   13

SUMMARIZING   14
The Purpose of Summaries   15
Suggestions for Writing a Summary   15
A Sample Summary   16

SYNTHESIZING   17
The Purpose of Synthesis   17
Suggestions for Synthesizing
    Information   18
A Sample Synthesis   19

STRATEGIES FOR CRITICAL READING OF
VISUAL MATERIAL   21
Charts and Graphs   22
Photographs   23
Advertisements   25

READING SELECTION   28

MORTIMER ADLER
How to Mark a Book   28
The man who helped design the Great Books
Program explains that to really own a book, a
person must write in it.

CHAPTER 2

Planning an Essay and Using the Patterns of Development

CONSIDERING YOUR WRITING
CONTEXT   34
Purpose   34
Audience   35
The Writer's Role   36

GENERATING IDEAS   37
Shaping a Writing Topic   37
Discovering Ideas to Develop Your Topic   42

DEVELOPING A THESIS   45
Location of the Thesis   46
Qualities of an Effective Thesis   47
How to Compose Your Thesis   48

ORDERING IDEAS   50
Outlining   50
The Informal Outline   51
The Outline Tree   52
The Formal Outline   52

USING THE PATTERNS OF
DEVELOPMENT   55

READING SELECTION   58

GAIL GODWIN
The Watcher at the Gates   58
Godwin warns writers about the inner critic, that
restraining voice that interferes with inspiration.

CHAPTER 3

Writing and Rewriting

WRITING YOUR FIRST DRAFT   61
Tips for Drafting   61

ESSAY STRUCTURE   62
The Introduction   62
Body Paragraphs   64
The Conclusion   72
The Title   74

VISUALIZING AN ESSAY   74

REVISING YOUR DRAFT   77
  Tips for Revising   79
  Revising with Peer Review   79

EDITING YOUR DRAFT   83
  Tips for Editing   84

PROOFREADING THE FINAL COPY   85
  *An Essay in Progress: "The Not-so-Ideal
  Male"   85*

READING SELECTION   89

PAUL ROBERTS
How to Say Nothing in 500 Words   89
*With tongue planted firmly in cheek, Roberts
offers writing advice to students.*

CHAPTER 4

Description

THE PATTERN   101

USING DESCRIPTION FOR A PURPOSE   102
  *Description in College, at Work, and in the
  Community   103*

DECIDING ON A DOMINANT
IMPRESSION   104

SUPPORTING DETAILS   105
  Objective and Expressive Details   105
  Descriptive Words   107
  Similes and Metaphors   109

ORGANIZING DETAILS   110

PROCESS GUIDELINES: STRATEGIES
FOR WRITING DESCRIPTION   112

CHECKLIST FOR REVISING
DESCRIPTION   112

ANNOTATED STUDENT ESSAY   114
  The Gendarme   114

*N. SCOTT MOMADAY
**The Homestead on Rainy Mountain
Creek   119**
*In this reverent description of his childhood
home, N. Scott Momaday relates his experience
and expresses his feelings about "sacred
recollections of the mind and heart."*

*New to this edition.

ALFRED KAZIN
My Neighborhood   124
*With vivid description, Kazin expresses his
response to the Brownsville tenement that he
grew up in.*

*RICK BASS
A Winter's Tale   129
*Rick Bass describes winter at his Montana home,
along with its effect on him, entertains at the
same time he relates his experience, expresses
his feelings, and informs the reader.*

ANNIE DILLARD
The Deer at Providencia   135
*Dillard combines description with narration to
relate her experiences with suffering and her
uncertainty about why it exists.*

GRETEL EHRLICH
Struck by Lightning   141
*With images of remarkable power, Ehrlich
combines description and narration to inform
readers about what happened when she was
struck by lightning.*

ALBERTO RIÓS
The Vietnam Wall   149 (poem)
*In this poem, Riós describes the Vietnam Wall
and the effect it has on people.*

ADDITIONAL ESSAY ASSIGNMENTS   152

CHAPTER 5

Narration

THE PATTERN   155

USING NARRATION FOR A PURPOSE   155
  *Narration in College, at Work, and in the
  Community   156*

SUPPORTING DETAILS   158
  Writing Dialogue   159

ORGANIZING DETAILS   160

PROCESS GUIDELINES: STRATEGIES FOR
WRITING NARRATION   162

CHECKLIST FOR REVISING
NARRATION   164

ANNOTATED STUDENT ESSAY   165
  The Family Reunion, Revisited   165

*CHRIS ABANI
The Lottery 169

To relate his experience and express his feelings, Chris Abani narrates a horrific account of mob violence and vigilante justice.

LANGSTON HUGHES
Salvation 173

Langston Hughes uses narration to relate a painful experience: his loss of faith at a revival service.

*WILLIAM GLABERSON
Seeking Justice after a Fatal Spin of the Cylinder 177

William Glaberson's narrative account of teens playing Russian roulette informs the reader of a tragic event.

NATALIE KUSZ
Ring Leader 183

The last thing her friends thought she would do was call attention to her face. With narration and cause-and-effect analysis, the author of this essay explains why she did so—by piercing her nose.

JEAN SHEPHERD
Lost at C 189

Using narration and description a humorist looks back at his high school algebra class to relate his experience, entertain the reader, and inform the reader of some truths about education.

LEE K. ABBOTT
**The View of Me from Mars 199
(short story)**

Abbott's short story is really two stories, one within the other. Both stories inform readers about the nature of lies and forgiveness, using narration, description, and cause-and-effect analysis.

ADDITIONAL ESSAY ASSIGNMENTS 205

CHAPTER 6

Exemplification

THE PATTERN 209

USING EXEMPLIFICATION FOR A PURPOSE 210

Exemplification in College, at Work, and in the Community 211

SUPPORTING DETAILS 212

Hypothetical Examples 213

ORGANIZING DETAILS 214

PROCESS GUIDELINES: STRATEGIES FOR WRITING EXEMPLIFICATION 216

CHECKLIST FOR REVISING EXEMPLIFICATION 217

ANNOTATED STUDENT ESSAY 218

*Food for Thought 218

*CULLEN MURPHY
Lifosuction 223

Using exemplification to inform and entertain, Cullen Murphy illustrates a surprising sin of omission.

TRIP GABRIEL
Computers Help Unite Campuses But Also Drive Some Students Apart 228

Gabriel uses exemplification to inform his audience about the increasing use of computers on college campuses and the pros and cons of that use.

RALPH ELLISON
On Being the Target of Discrimination 234

With examples developed with narration and description, Ellison relates his experience and thereby informs readers of what it was like to grow up when laws prohibited African-Americans from visiting zoos, participating in band concerts, and attending neighborhood schools.

BARBARA EHRENREICH
What I've Learned from Men: Lessons for a Full-Grown Feminist 242

Using exemplification, cause-and-effect analysis, definition, and contrast, Ehrenreich informs readers about the ladylike behavior of women and argues that women should abandon that behavior.

JONATHAN KOZOL
Untouchables 248

Combining exemplification with cause-and-effect analysis, Kozol gives a dramatic account of the real consequences of homelessness to persuade readers that government policy and our own fear are part of the problem.

*TONI CADE BAMBARA
The Lesson 257

Combining exemplification and narration to entertain and inform, the author notes that the most important lessons can be the most painful— and they aren't necessarily learned in school.

ADDITIONAL ESSAY ASSIGNMENTS 264

CHAPTER 7

Process Analysis

THE PATTERN   267

USING PROCESS ANALYSIS FOR A
PURPOSE   268

   Process Analysis in College, at Work, and in
   the Community   269

SUPPORTING DETAILS   270

ORGANIZING DETAILS   272

PROCESS GUIDELINES: STRATEGIES FOR
WRITING A PROCESS ANALYSIS   273

CHECKLIST FOR REVISING A PROCESS
ANALYSIS   276

ANNOTATED STUDENT ESSAY   277

   A Visit to Candyland   277

MIKLÓS VÁMOS
How I'll Become an American   281
Hungarian-born Vámos entertains with a satiric
look at Americans and in the process suggests
areas for improvement. Perhaps the process
analysis will also persuade you that we
Americans should change our ways.

DIANE COLE
Don't Just Stand There   285
Cole informs readers of processes for dealing
with ethnic, racial, and sexist slurs. She also
draws on narration and exemplification to
achieve her purpose.

HENRY LOUIS GATES, JR.
In the Kitchen   291
The author informs readers by explaining several
processes for straightening African-American
hair—and the politics underlying the processes.
He also uses description and definition.

TIMOTHY HARPER
Shoot to Kill   299
As a result of the shootings at Columbine High
School, police rapid-response procedures have
changed. Using process analysis, contrast,
cause-and-effect analysis, and description,
Timothy Harper informs readers about both the
old and new procedures.

JESSICA MITFORD
Behind the Formaldehyde Curtain   307
With description, Mitford tells you more than
you may want to know about the processes of
embalming and burial. Her purpose goes beyond

informing to persuading her readers that
embalming is unnecessary.

*NAOMI SHIHAB NYE
The Traveling Onion   316
Using process analysis and description, Nye will
entertain you as she informs you about the
complex journey the simple onion takes to reach
its place in a stew.

ADDITIONAL ESSAY ASSIGNMENTS   318

CHAPTER 8

Comparison-Contrast

THE PATTERN   323

USING COMPARISON-CONTRAST FOR A
PURPOSE   324

   Comparison-Contrast in College, at Work, and
   in the Community   324

CHOOSING SUBJECTS   326

SUPPORTING DETAILS   327

ORGANIZING DETAILS   328

PROCESS GUIDELINES: STRATEGIES FOR
WRITING COMPARISON-CONTRAST   331

CHECKLIST FOR REVISING COMPARISON-
CONTRAST   333

ANNOTATED STUDENT ESSAY   334

   Teaching a New Dog Old Tricks   334

BRUCE CATTON
Grant and Lee: A Study in Contrasts   338
Catton compares and contrasts the Civil War
generals to inform readers about the nature of
each man.

SUZANNE BRITT
Neat People vs. Sloppy People   344
Sloppy people are morally superior to neat
people, according to this entertaining contrast of
the neat and the sloppy.

*NICHOLAS D. KRISTOF
In Japan, Nice Boys (and Girls) Finish
Together   348
With comparison-contrast and exemplification,
Kristof informs readers about the difference
between the Japanese emphasis on harmony

and the American emphasis on competition. With cause-and-effect analysis, he also explains why Japanese value harmony and the effects of that preference. You will note that he also expresses his feelings *about the two orientations.*

ALICE WALKER
Am I Blue? 353

Walker combines comparison, narration, and description in the story of a horse named Blue. The patterns allow the author to relate part of her experience, inform readers about the nature of animals, and persuade the reader that animals should be treated better.

DEBORAH TANNEN
Squeaky Wheels and Protruding Nails: Direct and Indirect Speech 359

Making important statements indirectly can be a form of polite deference, but it can have deadly consequences. To inform readers of this point, Tannen defines and contrasts direct and indirect communication. She also works to persuade her audience that one style is not better than the other.

ARTHUR L. CAMPA
Anglo vs. Chicano: Why? 368

The author combines contrast with cause-and-effect analysis to inform readers of the cultural differences between Anglos and Chicanos and of the reasons for those differences.

*ROBERT FROST
Fire and Ice 374

In "Fire and Ice," Robert Frost uses comparison-contrast to inform the reader about the dangers of desire and hate.

ADDITIONAL ESSAY ASSIGNMENTS 376

CHAPTER 9

Cause-and-Effect Analysis

THE PATTERN 381

USING CAUSE-AND-EFFECT ANALYSIS FOR A PURPOSE 382

Cause-and-Effect Analysis in College, at Work, and in the Community 382

SUPPORTING DETAILS 384

Avoiding Errors in Logic 385

ORGANIZING DETAILS 386

PROCESS GUIDELINES: STRATEGIES FOR WRITING CAUSE-AND-EFFECT ANALYSIS 387

CHECKLIST FOR REVISING CAUSE-AND-EFFECT ANALYSIS 389

ANNOTATED STUDENT ESSAY 390

Why Athletes Use Steroids 390

DOROTHY SIEGEL
What Is Behind the Growth of Violence on College Campuses? 394

A vice president for student services at Maryland College, Siegel informs readers of the causes of campus violence.

*ANDREW SULLIVAN
Why the M Word Matters to Me 401

Using cause-and-effect analysis, Andrew Sullivan relates his experience as a gay man and expresses his feelings about the importance of gay marriage to persuade readers that such unions should be allowed.

*JAMES SUROWIECKI
Paying to Play 405

James Surowiecki uses cause-and-effect analysis and comparison-contrast to inform readers that music publishers often buy air time to better position their songs on radio play lists and to persuade readers that this practice is flawed.

EYAL PRESS
Fouled Out 410

Using cause-and-effect analysis and exemplification, Press informs readers of what happened when a University of Indiana professor criticized basketball coach Bobby Knight.

BRENT STAPLES
Just Walk on by: A Black Man Ponders His Power to Alter Public Space 416

To inform readers, Brent Staples looks at what causes the perception that black men are threatening. Then he goes on to express how that perception affects him.

CALVIN TRILLIN
It's Just Too Late 422

Calvin Trillin informs readers by narrating the events that caused the death of a teenager.

LESLIE MARMON SILKO
Lullaby 432 (short story)

In this powerful, dark short story, Leslie Marmon Silko combines cause-and-effect analysis with narration to inform readers of the effects of racism on a Navajo family.

ADDITIONAL ESSAY ASSIGNMENTS 440

CHAPTER 10

Classification and Division

THE PATTERN   443

USING CLASSIFICATION AND DIVISION FOR A PURPOSE   444

   Classification and Division in College, at Work, and in the Community   445

THE ORDERING PRINCIPLE FOR CLASSIFICATION AND DIVISION   447

SUPPORTING DETAILS   447

ORGANIZING DETAILS   448

PROCESS GUIDELINES: STRATEGIES FOR WRITING CLASSIFICATION AND DIVISION   451

CHECKLIST FOR REVISING CLASSIFICATION AND DIVISION   451

ANNOTATED STUDENT ESSAY   452

   Strictly Speaking   452

SISSELA BOK
White Lies   455
Are white lies really harmless? With classification and definition, Bok informs readers of the forms these lies take and argues that they may not be as harmless as we think they are.

MARTIN LUTHER KING, JR.
The Ways of Meeting Oppression   459
Civil rights leader Dr. Martin Luther King, Jr., informs readers of the ways to respond to oppression by classifying them, and then he works to persuade his audience that the nonviolent way is the best, using cause-and-effect analysis and definition.

DAVID BODANIS
What's in your Toothpaste?   464
Using division, process analysis, and description, David Bodanis informs the reader that toothpaste is not the appealing product we think it is, and he argues that it may not even be necessary.

WILLIAM ZINSSER
College Pressures   469
Zinsser combines classification, exemplification, and cause-and-effect analysis to inform readers of the kinds of pressures Yale college students face. What is the antidote to stress? Zinsser argues that it rests with the students themselves.

DESMOND MORRIS
Territorial Behaviour   477
A noted zoologist classifies the territorial behavior of humans and with cause-and-effect analysis and exemplifications informs readers about how the behavior helps us reconcile our cooperative and competitive spirits.

DYLAN THOMAS
Do Not Go Gentle into That Good Night   486 (poem)
In his poignant poem, Thomas classifies the ways different kinds of men face death to persuade his father to resist his own death.

ADDITIONAL ESSAY ASSIGNMENTS   488

CHAPTER 11

Definition

THE PATTERN   491

USING DEFINITION FOR A PURPOSE   492

   Definition in College, at Work, and in the Community   493

SUPPORTING DETAILS   494

ORGANIZING DETAILS   495

PROCESS GUIDELINES: STRATEGIES FOR WRITING DEFINITION   497

CHECKLIST FOR REVISING DEFINITION   497

ANNOTATED STUDENT ESSAY   498

   *Why Did the Chicken Cross the Möbius Strip?   498

JUDY BRADY
I Want a Wife   502
Brady's definition informs the reader of the difficulty of the traditional wife's role, and it works to persuade the reader of the unfairness of that role.

*JONATHAN RAUCH
Caring for Your Introvert   506
With definition and contrast, Jonathan Rauch informs readers of the characteristics of an introvert. He also aims to persuade readers that introverts are better than extroverts.

JO GOODWIN PARKER
What Is Poverty?   511
With definition, description, and cause-and-effect analysis, Parker informs the reader of the

true nature of poverty in an effort to persuade her audience to take action against it.

MALCOLM GLADWELL
The Art of Failure   516
Gladwell defines the terms panicking and choking and draws on narration, comparison-contrast, process analysis, and cause-and-effect analysis to inform readers about how panicking and choking lead to failure.

ELIE WIESEL
To Be a Jew   527
A survivor of the Holocaust uses definition and narration to inform readers of what it means to be a Jew, and he uses cause-and-effect analysis to inform about the relationship between Jews and Christians and some of the effects of the Holocaust.

PAT MORA
Immigrants   537 (poem)
In her ironic poem, Pat Mora defines Americans as they are seen by immigrants, and she informs readers of the process some immigrants follow to "Americanize" their children.

ADDITIONAL ESSAY ASSIGNMENTS   539

CHAPTER 12

The Law and Society: A Casebook for Argumentation-Persuasion

THE DIFFERENCE BETWEEN ARGUMENTATION AND PERSUASION   543

PURPOSE AND AUDIENCE   544
Argumentation-Persuasion in College, at Work, and in the Community   544

SUPPORTING DETAILS   546
Logos   546
Pathos   548
Ethos   549
How Logos, Pathos, and Ethos Relate to Purpose and Audience   549

RAISING AND COUNTERING OBJECTIONS   551

THE TOULMIN MODEL   552

INDUCTIVE AND DEDUCTIVE REASONING   553
Induction   553
Deduction   554

ORGANIZING ARGUMENTATION-PERSUASION   555

PROCESS GUIDELINES: STRATEGIES FOR WRITING ARGUMENTATION-PERSUASION   558

CHECKLIST FOR REVISING ARGUMENTATION-PERSUASION   559

ANNOTATED STUDENT ESSAY   560
*Cast Out of Kansas: Music Censorship in Public Libraries   560

SHOULD THE LAW ALLOW CLONING OF EMBRYONIC STEM CELLS?   564

*JEREMY RIFKIN
Why I Oppose Human Cloning   566
Jeremy Rifkin draws on cause-and-effect analysis, narration, and comparison-contrast to persuade readers that therapeutic cloning, is both wrong and dangerous.

*RAYMOND BARGLOW
A Reply to Rifkin   573
Relying on cause-and-effect analysis and comparison-contrast, Raymond Barglow refutes Rifkin's argument against embryonic stem cell research to persuade readers that embryonic stem cell research should be supported.

IS JUSTICE SERVED BY TRYING JUVENILE OFFENDERS AS ADULTS?   580

THE NEW YORK TIMES EDITORIAL
Little Adult Criminals   581
This editorial draws on exemplification and cause-and-effect analysis to persuade its audience that juvenile offenders should not be tried as adults.

LAURENCE STEINBERG
Should Juvenile Offenders Be Tried as Adults?   585
Using definition, contrast, and cause-and-effect analysis, Steinberg argues that young people older than 12 and younger than 16 should be assessed to determine whether they should be tried as juveniles or as adults.

LINDA J. COLLIER
Adult Crime, Adult Time 591
With process analysis *and an* analysis of effects, *Collier* argues *for trying juveniles as adults.*

TIMOTHY ROCHE AND AMANDA BOWER
Young Voices from the Cell 596
The authors use cause-and-effect analysis *and* exemplification *to explain what prompts young boys to kill and how they fare in adult prisons after their convictions.*

WHAT SPEECH DOES THE FIRST AMENDMENT PROTECT ON COLLEGE CAMPUSES? 604

NAT HENTOFF
Free Speech on Campus 605
Using cause-and-effect analysis *and* exemplification, *a writer and journalist argues for the protection of hate speech on college campuses.*

CHARLES R. LAWRENCE III
The Debate over Placing Limits on Racist Speech Must Not Ignore the Damage It Does to Its Victims 612
Using cause-and-effect analysis, *Lawrence aims to persuade his audience that hate speech on campus should not be afforded constitutional protection.*

*HARVEY A. SILVERGLATE AND GREG LUKIANOFF
Speech Codes: Alive and Well at Colleges 617
The authors use exemplification, cause-and-effect analysis, *and* definition *to persuade the readers that campus speech codes, which exist on many campuses, are a serious threat to free speech.*

*HOWARD M. WASSERMAN
Fan Profanity 625
Howard M. Wasserman uses exemplification *and* definition *to inform readers about the kinds of profane speech used by college sports fan. To persuade readers that such speech is protected by the First Amendment, Wasserman draws on* comparison *and* cause-and-effect analysis.

*ROBERT O'NEIL
What Limits Should Campus Networks Place on Pornography? 632
Robert O'Neil uses cause-and-effect analysis *to inform readers about the conflict between free speech and restricting Internet access to pornography. He also argues for a compromise solution to the conflict between free speech advocates who oppose censorship and those who favor restrictions.*

CHAPTER 13

Combining Patterns of Development

PATTERNS FOR A PURPOSE 639

USING THE PATTERNS OF DEVELOPMENT IN YOUR WRITING 640

PROCESS GUIDELINES: STRATEGIES FOR COMBINING PATTERNS 640

ANNOTATED STUDENT ESSAY 642
 The Telephone Is Out; IM Is In 642

*BRAD WHETSTINE
Augustinian Influences 646
Brad Whetstine combines narration, cause-and-effect analysis, description, *and* comparison-contrast *to relate his experience making the decision to give up a welding career for college and to express his feelings about the catalyst for that decision.*

GEORGE ORWELL
A Hanging 650
To relate experience, inform, *and* persuade, *Orwell combines* narration *and* description *in an account of an execution.*

RICHARD RODRIGUEZ
Complexion 657
Rodriguez uses contrast, narration, *and* description *to relate how he was affected by his dark complexion.*

*PAGAN KENNEDY
One Room, 3,000 Brains 662
Using cause-and-effect analysis, description, narration, *and* process analysis, *Pagan Kennedy* informs *readers about the Harvard Brain Tissue Resource Center and the work done there. She also works to* persuade *readers to donate their brains to science and to relate an experience and express the feelings of a brain researcher.*

*ESTHER THORSON
Dissect an Ad 670
Combining division, cause-and-effect analysis, *and* exemplification, *Esther Thorson* informs *readers about the components of televised political advertisements and how they persuade viewers.*

E. B. WHITE
Once More to the Lake 676
After 40 years, White returns to a family vacation spot with his son and comes to a startling

conclusion. To express his feelings and relate his experience, White *combines* description *with* narration *and* comparison-contrast.

CHAPTER 14

Locating, Evaluating, and Drawing on Sources

USING SOURCES   685

LOCATING SOURCES   686

EVALUATING PRINT AND INTERNET SOURCES   689

DRAWING ON SOURCES: PARAPHRASING AND QUOTING   690

INTEGRATING PARAPHRASES AND QUOTATIONS   693

AVOIDING PLAGIARISM   695

DOCUMENTING SOURCES   696

ANNOTATED STUDENT ESSAY   702
  "Divorce as a Violation of Trust"   703

Credits   C-1
Glossary   G-1
Index of Images   I-1
Index of Essays by Purpose   I-3
Index of Student Essays   I-7
Index   I-9

Men and Women

LEE K. ABBOTT
The View of Me form Mars   199

BARBARA EHRENREICH
What I've Learned from Men   242

DEBORAH TANNEN
Squeaky Wheels and Protruding
Nails   359

ANDREW SULLIVAN
Why the *M* Word Matters to Me   401

DESMOND MORRIS
Territorial Behaviour   477

JUDY BRADY
I Want a Wife   502

Marriage and Family

N. SCOTT MOMADAY
The Homestead on Rainy Mountain
Creek   119

LEE K. ABBOTT
The View of Me from Mars   199

JONATHAN KOZOL
Untouchables   248

HENRY LOUIS GATES, JR.
In the Kitchen   291

ALICE WALKER
Am I Blue?   353

ANDREW SULLIVAN
Why the *M* Word Matters to Me   401

CALVIN TRILLIN
It's Just Too Late   422

LESLIE MARMON SILKO
Lullaby   432

JO GOODWIN PARKER
What Is Poverty?   511

RICHARD RODRIGUEZ
Complexion   657

Health, Medicine, Sports, and Recreation

RICK BASS
A Winter's Tale   129

ANNIE DILLARD
The Deer at Providencia   135

JESSICA MITFORD
Behind the Formaldehyde Curtain   307

EYAL PRESS
Fouled Out   410

DAVID BODANIS
What's In Your Toothpaste?   464

DYLAN THOMAS
Do Not Go Gentle into That Good
Night   486

JEREMY RIFKIN
Why I Oppose Human Cloning   566

RAYMOND BARGLOW
A Reply to Rifkin   573

PAGAN KENNEDY
One Room, 3,000 Brains   662

Fitting In

NATALIE KUSZ
Ring Leader   183

TONI CADE BAMBARA
The Lesson   257

HENRY LOUIS GATES, JR.
In the Kitchen   291

ANDREW SULLIVAN
Why the *M* Word Matters to Me   401

CALVIN TRILLIN
It's Just Too Late   422

JONATHAN RAUCH
Caring for Your Introvert   506

PAT MORA
Immigrants   537

TIMOTHY ROCHE AND AMANDA BOWER
Young Voices from the Cell   596

BRAD WHETSTINE
Augustinian Influences   646

RICHARD RODRIGUEZ
Complexion   657

Bias and Discrimination

CHRIS ABANI
The Lottery   169

RALPH ELLISON
On Being the Target of Discrimination   234

BARBARA EHRENREICH
What I've Learned from Men   242

JONATHAN KOZOL
Untouchables   248

MIKLÓS VÁMOS
How I'll Become an American   281

DIANE COLE
Don't Just Stand There   285

HENRY LOUIS GATES, JR.
In the Kitchen   291

ANDREW SULLIVAN
Why the *M* Word Matters to Me   401

BRENT STAPLES
Just Walk on By   416

LESLIE MARMON SILKO
Lullaby   432

JUDY BRADY
I Want a Wife   502

ELIE WIESEL
To Be a Jew   527

NAT HENTOFF
Free Speech on Campus   605

CHARLES R. LAWRENCE
The Debate over Placing Limits on Racist Speech Must Not Ignore the Damage It Does to Its Victims   612

Language and Communication

MORTIMER ADLER
How to Mark a Book   28

GAIL GODWIN
The Watcher at the Gates   58

PAUL ROBERTS
How to Say Nothing in 500 Words   89

TRIP GABRIEL
Computers Help Unite Campuses But Also Drive Some Students Apart   228

DIANE COLE
Don't Just Stand There   285

DEBORAH TANNEN
Squeaky Wheels and Protruding Nails   359

ARTHUR L. CAMPA
Anglo vs. Chicano: Why?   368

SISSELA BOK
White Lies   455

NAT HENTOFF
Free Speech on Campus   605

CHARLES R. LAWRENCE
The Debate over Placing Limits on Racist Speech Must Not Ignore the Damage It Does to Its Victims   612

HARVEY A. SILVERGLATE AND GREG LUKIANOFF
Speech Codes: Alive and Well at Colleges   617

HOWARD M. WASSERMAN
Fan Profanity   625

ROBERT O'NEIL
What Limits Should Campus Networks Place on Pornography?   632

ESTHER THORSON
Dissect an Ad   670

Physical Appearance

NATALIE KUSZ
Ring Leader   183

HENRY LOUIS GATES, JR.
In the Kitchen   291

BRENT STAPLES
Just Walk on By   416

RICHARD RODRIGUEZ
Complexion   657

Attitudes

GRETEL EHRLICH
Struck by Lightning   141

TONI CADE BAMBARA
The Lesson   257

NICHOLAS D. KRISTOF
In Japan, Nice Boys (and Girls) Finish Together   348

ROBERT FROST
Fire and Ice   374

ANDREW SULLIVAN
Why the *M* Word Matters to Me   401

JONATHAN RAUCH
Caring for Your Introvert   506

MALCOLM GLADWELL
The Art of Failure   516

BRAD WHETSTINE
Augustinian Influences   646

Education

JEAN SHEPHERD
Lost at C   189

TRIP GABRIEL
Computers Help Unite Campuses but Also Drive Some Students Apart   228

TONI CADE BAMBARA
The Lesson   257

DOROTHY SIEGEL
What Is Behind the Growth of Violence on College Campuses?   394

EYAL PRESS
Fouled Out   410

WILLIAM ZINSSER
College Pressures   469

NAT HENTOFF
Free Speech on Campus   605

CHARLES R. LAWRENCE
The Debate over Placing Limits on Racist Speech Must Not Ignore the Damage It Does to Its Victims   612

HARVEY A. SILVERGLATE AND GREG LUKIANOFF
Speech Codes: Alive and Well at Colleges   617

HOWARD M. WASSERMAN
Fan Profanity   625

ROBERT O'NEIL
What Limits Should Campus Networks Place on Pornography?   632

BRAD WHETSTINE
Augustinian Influences   646

Memories

N. SCOTT MOMADAY
The Homestead on Rainy Mountain Creek   119

ALFRED KAZIN
My Neighborhood   124

LANGSTON HUGHES
Salvation   173

JEAN SHEPHERD
Lost at C   189

RALPH ELLISON
On Being the Target of Discrimination   234

HENRY LOUIS GATES, JR.
In the Kitchen   291

ELIE WIESEL
To Be a Jew   527

RICHARD RODRIGUEZ
Complexion   657

E. B. WHITE
Once More to the Lake   676

Contemporary Issues

WILLIAM GLABERSON
Seeking Justice After a Fatal Spin of the Cylinder   177

NATALIE KUSZ
Ring Leader   183

CULLEN MURPHY
Lifosuction   223

JONATHAN KOZOL
Untouchables   248

TIMOTHY HARPER
Shoot to Kill   299

JEREMY RIFKIN
Why I Oppose Human Cloning   566

RAYMOND BARGLOW
A Reply to Rifkin   573

NAT HENTOFF
Free Speech on Campus   605

CHARLES R. LAWRENCE
The Debate over Placing Limits on Racist
Speech Must Not Ignore the Damage It
Does to Its Victims   612

HARVEY A. SILVERGLATE AND GREG LUKIANOFF
Speech Codes: Alive and Well at
Colleges   617

HOWARD M. WASSERMAN
Fan Profanity   625

ROBERT O'NEIL
What Limits Should Campus Networks
Place on Pornography?   632

ESTHER THORSON
Dissect an Ad   670

The Law and Justice

CHRIS ABANI
The Lottery   169

WILLIAM GLABERSON
Seeking Justice after a Fatal Spin of the
Cylinder   177

RALPH ELLISON
On Being the Target of
Discrimination   234

ANDREW SULLIVAN
Why the M Word Matters to Me   401

LAURENCE STEINBERG
Should Juvenile Offenders Be Tried as
Adults?   585

LINDA J. COLLIER
Adult Crime, Adult Time   591

TIMOTHY ROCHE AND AMANDA BOWER
Young Voices from the Cell   596

GEORGE ORWELL
A Hanging   650

Places with Special Meaning

N. SCOTT MOMADAY
The Homestead on Rainy Mountain
Creek   119

ALFRED KAZIN
My Neighborhood   124

RICK BASS
A Winter's Tale   129

HENRY LOUIS GATES, JR.
In the Kitchen   291

E. B. WHITE
Once More to the Lake   676

Childhood, Adolescence, Adulthood, and Death

ALFRED KAZIN
My Neighborhood   124

GRETEL EHRLICH
Struck by Lightning   141

ALBERT RIÓS
The Vietnam Wall   149

LANGSTON HUGHES
Salvation   173

JEAN SHEPHERD
Lost at C   189

TIMOTHY HARPER
Shoot to Kill   299

JESSICA MITFORD
Behind the Formaldehyde Curtain   307

ROBERT FROST
Fire and Ice   374

LESLIE MARMON SILKO
Lullaby   432

DYLAN THOMAS
Do Not Go Gentle into That Good
Night   486

LAURENCE STEINBERG
Should Juvenile Offenders Be Tried as
Adults?   585

TIMOTHY ROCHE AND AMANDA BOWER
Young Voices from the Cell   596

RICHARD RODRIGUEZ
Complexion   657

E. B. WHITE
Once More to the Lake   676

Memories of Childhood

N. SCOTT MOMADAY
The Homestead on Rainy Mountain
Creek   119

ALFRED KAZIN
My Neighborhood   124

Relationships between Humans and Animals

GRETEL EHRLICH
Struck by Lightning   141

ALICE WALKER
Am I Blue?   353

Systems of Justice

TIMOTHY ROCHE AND AMANDA BOWER
Young Voices from the Cell   596

GEORGE ORWELL
A Hanging   650

Demonstrations of Courage

GRETEL EHRLICH
Struck by Lightning   141

LESLIE MARMON SILKO
Lullaby   432

Beyond the Classroom

TONI CADE BAMBARA
The Lesson   257

BRAD WHETSTINE
Augustinian Influences   646

Academic Pressures

JEAN SHEPHERD
Lost at C   189

WILLIAM ZINSSER
College Pressures   469

Living in Poverty

JONATHAN KOZOL
Untouchables   248

JO GOODWIN PARKER
What Is Poverty?   511

Living with Oppression

RALPH ELLISON
On Being the Target of Discrimination   234

LESLIE MARMON SILKO
Lullaby   432

Dealing with Discrimination

RALPH ELLISON
On Being the Target of Discrimination   234

DIANE COLE
Don't Just Stand There   285

Reactions to Skin Color

HENRY LOUIS GATES, JR.
In the Kitchen   291

RICHARD RODRIGUEZ
Complexion   657

Men and Women

BARBARA EHRENREICH
What I've Learned from Men   242

PAIRED READINGS

DEBORAH TANNEN
Squeaky Wheels and Protruding Nails   359

Public Space

BRENT STAPLES
Just Walk on By   416

DESMOND MORRIS
Territorial Behaviour   477

Politically Correct Language

DIANE COLE
Don't Just Stand There   285

HARVEY A. SILVERGLATE AND GREG LUKIANOFF
Speech Codes: Alive and Well at
Colleges   617

Communication Styles

DEBORAH TANNEN
Squeaky Wheels and Protruding Nails   359

ARTHUR L. CAMPA
Anglo vs. Chicano: Why?   368

Death and Dying

GRETEL EHRLICH
Struck by Lightning   141

JESSICA MITFORD
Behind the Formaldehyde Curtain   307

Perceptions of People

BRENT STAPLES
Just Walk on By   416

RICHARD RODRIGUEZ
Complexion   657

Everyday Communication

DEBORAH TANNEN
Squeaky Wheels and Protruding Nails   359

SISSELA BOK
White Lies   455

The Meaning of Marriage

LEE K. ABBOTT
The View of Me from Mars   199

ANDREW SULLIVAN
Why the *M* Word Matters to Me   401

Adolescents at Risk

CALVIN TRILLIN
It's Just Too Late   422

TIMOTHY ROCHE AND AMANDA BOWER
Young Voices from the Cell   596

Writing

GAIL GODWIN
The Watcher at the Gates   58

PAUL ROBERTS
How to Say Nothing in 500 Words   89

How We Relate to Each Other

NICHOLAS D. KRISTOF
In Japan, Nice Boys (and Girls) Finish
Together   348

DESMOND MORRIS
Territorial Behaviour   477

PREFACE

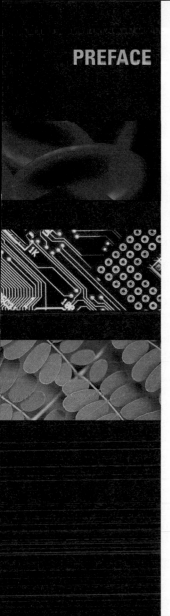

Patterns for a Purpose, Fourth Edition, remains a rhetorical reader that focuses on showing students how to use the rhetorical patterns—either alone or in combination—to achieve a range of writing purposes; it continues to emphasize critical reading and thinking, to offer detailed coverage of the writing process, to provide a rich variety of writing opportunities, to emphasize argumentation and persuasion, and to provide an array of reading selections, both classic and contemporary, that function both as models and as springboards for discussion.

FEATURES FOR A PURPOSE

Among the features that help *Patterns* achieve its goals are

The Connection between Patterns and Purpose

- NEW: A dazzling, new design that uses images to reinforce the interplay between pattern and purpose.

- NEW: "[The Pattern] for a Purpose" sections (e.g., "Description for a Purpose," "Narration for a Purpose," and so on) that explain how to use each pattern to entertain, express feelings, relate experience, inform, or persuade.

- NEW: "[The Pattern] in College, at Work, and in the Community" sections, which explain how to use each pattern to achieve the full range of writing purposes in a variety of contexts important to students.

- NEW: "Using [the Pattern] for a Purpose" assignments after each reading that invite students to use the patterns to achieve a range of writing purposes.

- NEW: Writing assignments that suggest ways of using the patterns.

- Headnotes that point out the patterns used in the reading selections and the purposes they help the writer achieve.

Blending Patterns to Achieve the Writer's Purpose

- NEW: An exciting, new design that reflects the book's greater attention to the mixing of rhetorical patterns.

- NEW: "Noting Combined Patterns" questions following readings with multiple patterns to call students' attention to strategies for combining patterns.
- NEW: A chapter (Chapter 13) that focuses exclusively on combining rhetorical patterns to achieve the full range of writing purposes.
- NEW: "Combining Patterns" assignments after each reading that invite students to write an essay using multiple patterns.
- Multiple essays in each chapter of readings that combine patterns to achieve the writer's purpose and headnotes that point out what patterns are combined and what purpose this combination achieves.

Critical Reading and Thinking

- NEW: Writing assignments that suggest ways to combine patterns.
- Critical reading and thinking instruction in Chapter 1 that focuses on helping students learn to make inferences, synthesize and evaluate information, think logically, and read critically.
- "Reading Closely and Thinking Critically" questions after each reading selection to prompt students to apply the critical reading and thinking skills they learned in Chapter 1.
- Reading selections and writing prompts in Chapter 12, "The Law and Society: A Casebook on Argumentation-Persuasion," that call on students to apply their critical reading and thinking skills to synthesize and evaluate multiple perspectives on controversial issues.

An Emphasis on the Writing Process

- NEW: "Process Guidelines" (in Chapters 4–13) that offer practical strategies for using and combining patterns of development.
- NEW: Twenty-four "Troubleshooting Guides" (in Chapters 4–14) that offer tips for solving common writing problems.
- Procedures for planning an essay, developing a thesis, and drafting, revising, and editing an essay (in Chapter 2–3).
- Illustration of the writing process through a student essay in multiple drafts (in Chapters 2–3).
- Revision checklists (in Chapters 4–13) to help students revise with confidence.

Multiple Writing Prompts—Journal Entries to Essay Assignments

- Twenty additional essay topics at the end of each rhetorical-pattern chapter.
- NEW: In chapters 4–11 and 13, "Examining Visuals" activities that encourage students to explore the pattern.
- For each reading selection, an online writing/discussion prompt, a journal prompt, four or more topics for writing in the pattern for a

variety of purposes, a topic that requires using the pattern in combination with one or more other patterns, a topic that requires synthesizing ideas in multiple readings, and a topic that requires using a primary or secondary source.

- "Consider the Pattern" activities opening Chapters 4–14 that use visuals to prompt brief introductory writing activities.

- "Responding to an Image" topics at the end of each rhetorical chapter that ask students to write in response to a visual image, using the pattern under consideration.

Applying Critical Reading Skills to Visual Texts

- NEW: An explanation of how to read visuals critically (Chapter 1).

- NEW: An explanation of how to use visuals to support a thesis (Chapter 3).

- NEW: Two student essays (in Chapters 3 and 11) that demonstrate the appropriate use of visuals as support.

- NEW: "Examining Visuals" sections in Chapters 4–11 and 13 that provide an image (advertisement, photograph, corporate logo, cartoon, or screenshot) using one of the patterns of development to help students learn to identify patterns and purposes in visuals.

- NEW: Visuals in Chapter 12, "Law and Society: A Casebook for Argumentation-Persuasion," that offer another sense of the issue under consideration.

- "Consider the Pattern" images opening Chapters 4–14 to prompt brief writing activities that get students thinking about the pattern on which the chapter focuses.

- "Responding to an Image" topics closing Chapters 4–11 that provide the basis for writing assignments in the pattern under consideration.

An Emphasis on Argumentation and Persuasion

- Essays in every chapter of readings (except the chapter on description) that are meant to convince readers to think or act in a particular way.

- An in depth study of argumentation-persuasion in the revised Chapter 12; this chapter now includes 11 essays on 3 themes: "Should the Law Allow Cloning of Embryonic Stem Cells?" "Is Justice Served by Trying Juvenile Offenders as Adults?" and "What Speech Does the First Amendment Protect on College Campuses?"

Seventy Professional Selections

- NEW: With twenty new reading selections from writers like N. Scott Momaday, Rick Bass, Chris Abani, Toni Cade Bambara, Naomi Shihab Nye, and Andrew Sullivan, *Patterns for a Purpose* offers more essays than most modes-based readers on the market.

- NEW: A stunning full-color design in which the reading selections are set to resemble the original publication venue, emphasising the fact that the readings come from the real world of magazines, books, and newspapers.

- NEW: "As You Read" prompts at the start of each reading selection that help students stay focused.

- Eight literary selections to provide instructional variety.

- A mix of classic and contemporary essays that focus on themes of interest to students—including classroom violence, gay marriage, stem cell research, radio play lists, and pornography on campus computers—and offer a variety of cultural viewpoints and perspectives.

- Eleven annotated student essays—four of them new—that provide both instruction and realistic models.

ALSO NEW TO THE FOURTH EDITION
Integrated Technology Resources

Powered by *Catalyst 2.0*, the Fourth Edition provides click paths that direct students to special online resources, such as new interactive tutors that help students write papers for different rhetorical purposes and patterns; new tutorials on visual rhetoric; additional resources on authors that appear in the text; guides for avoiding plagiarism and evaluating sources; and many more tools that support students with their writing at every stage of the writing process.

SUPPLEMENTS
Online Learning Center: www.mhhe.com/patterns

Powered by *Catalyst 2.0*, the Premier Online Tool for Writing and Research, the OLC offers

- New interactive writing tutors for different rhetorical purposes and patterns.

- Tutorials on avoiding plagiarism and evaluating sources.

- Over 4,500 grammar exercises with personalized feedback for each response.

- Bibliomaker software for MLA, APA, *Chicago,* and CSE styles of documentation.

- And much more.

Delivered in a new, state-of-the-art course management system featuring online peer-review utilities, a grade book, and communication tools, *Catalyst 2.0* is available free with *Patterns for a Purpose*.

The Instructor's Resource Manual, by Barbara Fine Clouse

This manual includes helpful advice for new teachers and graduate students as well as suggested answers for the questions that follow each reading selection. It is available on the password protected instructor's side of the Online Learning Center: www.mhhe.com/patterns

Teaching Composition Faculty Listserv: www.mhhe.com/comp

Moderated by Chris Anson at the North Carolina State University and offered by McGraw-Hill as a service to the composition community, this listserv brings together senior members of the college composition community with new members—junior faculty, adjuncts, and teaching assistants—in an online newsletter and accompanying discussion group that addresses issues of pedagogy in theory and in practice.

ACKNOWLEDGMENTS

For this new edition, I had the great good fortune to work with an immensely talented team at McGraw-Hill. Jane Carter oversaw the development process with grace and good humor. I am grateful for her insights, gentle guidance, astute judgment, and creative problem-solving—and the fact that she was always there when I needed her, despite her very heavy workload. Also at McGraw-Hill, Christopher Bennem, Lisa Moore, and Carla Samodulski shaped this revision in fundamental ways. They are very wise, and I cannot overstate their influence.

Of course, the evolution of this edition grew out of the previous edition, so I must again acknowledge Carla Samodulski, the development editor for that earlier incarnation. Her impeccable insights and sound counsel inform every chapter of the third edition and, therefore, much of this fourth.

I am indebted to Ruth Mandel and Marty Granahan, who researched the images and provided important, steady guidance for the extensive image package. I must also acknowledge the assistance of student intern, Shona Sequeira, and the help of Meg Botteon, both of whom provided supplemental materials. For guiding the manuscript through the production process with its many details and pressing deadlines, I am grateful to Ruth Smith.

And then there is my development editor, the remarkable Ann Grogg. Patient, brilliant, talented, and knowing, Ann ordered the chaos and brought her infallible instincts and keen perceptions to my ragged drafts. My debt to her is inestimable.

A number of professors offered a wealth of sound advice and thoughtful criticism. I am truly appreciative of the guidance and support offered by the following instructors:

Joseph Alvarez, *Central Piedmont Community College*
Dan Bauer, *Georgia College and State University*
Mary Baumhover, *Western New Mexico University*
Laura Blankenship, *University of Arkansas*

Carol Bledsoe, *Florida Gulf Coast University*

Ellen Burke, *Casper College*

Diana Cameron, *North Iowa Area Community College*

Keith Comer, *Idaho State University*

Linda Cooper Knight, *College of the Albemarle*

Brenda Cornell, *Central Texas College*

Romana Cortese, *Montgomery College*

Bryan P. Davis, *Georgia Southwestern State University*

Nancy Dessommes, *Georgia Southern University*

Betty Freeland, *University of Arkansas at Little Rock*

Judy Haberman, *Phoenix College*

Jamal A. Halawa, *Pine Manor College*

Dan Hannon, *Mount Hood Community College*

Deborah Heller, *Western New Mexico University*

Allan M. Hikida, *Seattle Central Community College*

Michael Hricik, *Westmoreland County Community College*

Mahbub Jamal, *Prince George's Community College*

Josie Kearns, *University of Michigan*

Rita S. Kranidis, *Montgomery College*

Linda LaPointe, *St. Petersburg Junior College*

Kristina Lilleberg, *Minnesota State University*

Robert Lorenzi, *Camden County College*

Larry Marrs, *Rend Lake College*

Frank Mathias, *Polk Community College*

Joseph McCadden, *Burlington Community College*

Kirsten Moreno, *Long Beach City College*

Robert Mugford, *Scottsdale Community College*

Brian T. Murphy, *Burlington County College*

Gary Myers, *Mississippi State University*

Miller Newman, *Montgomery College*

Richard Regan, *Fairfield University*

Melissa Richardson, *Central Texas College*

Robert Sawyer, *East Tennessee State University*

Nancy Sherrod, *Georgia Southern University*

Sandra W. Smith, *Penn State University*

J. Christian Tatu, *Warren County Community College*

Rita Yeasted, *La Roche College*

Finally, my heartfelt thanks goes to my husband, Denny, whose patience and support are unfailing and indispensable.

Barbara Clouse

Patterns for a Purpose

A RHETORICAL READER

Reading Critically

When you read to relax, you can grab a well-plotted novel, put your feet up, and lose yourself in the story as the words wash over you and the tensions of the day melt away. Such reading is one of life's pleasures. Because your goal is to enjoy, it is okay if your mind wanders a bit or if you feel too lazy to look up the meaning of a word. You can go at your own pace and skip pages if you want.

College reading, however, is different. College reading demands more of you because it requires you to stay focused on the material as you consider and evaluate it. College reading requires you to think of the material in light of what you already know and to judge the importance of what you read. College reading requires you to question, draw conclusions, make associations, develop opinions, and support those opinions. In short, college reading requires *critical reading*, the process considered in this chapter.

CRITICAL READING

People sometimes assume that critical reading is finding fault or "criticizing," but this is not so. **Critical reading** involves going beyond what is readily apparent to look beneath the surface and outside the boundaries. It is a careful consideration that includes evaluating the quality and reliability of a piece, drawing conclusions about the significance of the author's ideas and the meaning of the points he or she is making, and discovering connections between new ideas and what you have learned. In short, critical reading is *thoughtful* reading. It involves evaluating and assimilating the ideas you read, whether they are in textbooks, in journals, in newspapers, or on the Internet.

Critical reading is a skill you will draw on repeatedly in college as your instructors ask you to judge the significance of ideas, evaluate data, and consider the difference between theories. For example, your sociology instructor may ask you to read the latest census report and draw conclusions about the nature of the American family. Critical reading is also a skill you are likely to need on the job, as when a supervisor asks you to read a marketing report and evaluate a sales trend or compare the findings of two research studies. Even in your private life, critical reading is important. In an election year, for example, you will read campaign literature, newspaper editorials, and magazine articles to form judgments about candidates in order to vote wisely. Or you may need to research and read opinions about treatments for a medical condition in order to decide on the best course of action.

As you can tell, critical reading is important both in and out of the classroom. You may be wondering, then, what it is that critical readers do. Actually, critical readers do several things. They

- distinguish facts from opinions.
- make inferences.
- synthesize information.
- evaluate quality.

Distinguishing Facts from Opinions

People often assume that anything that appears in print is a fact, but the words on a page or computer screen can represent the writer's opinion instead. **Facts** can be proven or have been proven, but **opinions** are the writer's judgments, interpretations, or beliefs. For example, it is a *fact* that electricity can power automobiles, but it is an *opinion* that electrically powered cars will be commonplace in 10 years. As a critical reader, you must distinguish between facts and opinions and determine whether or not the opinions a writer asserts are well founded and well supported.

Sometimes people think that facts are better than opinions, but they both have their place and importance. For example, scientists seeking to prove a theory must be able to support their case with facts. Opinion is equally important, however, especially once a theory has been established. For what benefit can the theory be applied? How does the theory affect subsequent research? How should the theory influence public policy? The answers to questions such as these are matters of opinion, but the answers are nonetheless important because they can guide the course of future research and the application of the established theory.

Much of the reading you encounter in college will include both facts and opinions. For example, consider this paragraph from the introductory business textbook *Understanding Business* by William Nickels, James McHugh, and Susan McHugh:

> U.S. businesses are rapidly changing their ways of operating to become world-class competitors. The Ford Taurus, the Chrysler minivan, and

the Oldsmobile Aurora are now competitive with the best automobiles in the world. Companies such as Disney, Federal Express, Intel, and Microsoft, as well as many smaller companies, are as good [as] or better than competing organizations anywhere in the world. But businesses have gone beyond simply competing with organizations in other countries by learning to cooperate with international firms. That cooperation has the potential to create rapidly growing world markets that can generate prosperity beyond most people's expectations. The challenge is tremendous, but so is the will to achieve. (16)

Look again at the paragraph. This time the sentences in brackets point out places where fact and opinion are blended.

U.S. businesses are rapidly changing their ways of operating to become world-class competitors. [*It is a fact that some U.S. businesses are changing their operations, but how rapidly that change is occurring is a matter of opinion.*] The Ford Taurus, the Chrysler minivan, and the Oldsmobile Aurora are now competitive with the best automobiles in the world. [*How competitive the Ford, Chrysler, and Oldsmobile cars are can be documented by looking at sales figures, but which cars are the "best automobiles in the world" would, again, be a matter of opinion.*] Companies such as Disney, Federal Express, Intel, and Microsoft, as well as many smaller companies, are as good [as] or better than competing organizations anywhere in the world. But businesses have gone beyond simply competing with organizations in other countries by learning to cooperate with international firms. That cooperation has the potential to create rapidly growing world markets that can generate prosperity beyond most people's expectations. [*Are Microsoft and the other companies mentioned as good as or better than other companies? That is a matter of opinion, although the statement that some businesses are cooperating with international firms can be documented and, therefore, shown to be fact. The possible benefit of that cooperation, however, is an opinion.*] The challenge is tremendous, but so is the will to achieve. [*The size of the challenge and will to achieve are matters of opinion.*]

Critical readers must do more than distinguish between facts and opinions. They must also evaluate the *quality* of the opinions they identify. Some opinions are more valuable than others. Valuable opinions—ones to take seriously—are offered by knowledgeable people, are backed up by solid support, or both. Less valuable opinions—ones to be wary of—are unsupported beliefs or are offered by people with little relevant knowledge or experience.

Making Inferences

Critical readers make inferences. An **inference** is a conclusion drawn on the basis of what a speaker's or writer's information "suggests" rather than "states." Think of making inferences as "reading between the lines." For example, consider this paragraph from "What Is Behind the Growth of

Violence on College Campuses?" (p. 394); an essay that examines the causes of campus violence:

> The same students who sponsor night walks to check the lighting and grounds to increase safety will hold the door open for a stranger entering their residence hall. Despite frequent warnings, students—and even faculty, administrators, and other campus personnel—act less judiciously than they would elsewhere.

In this paragraph, the author *says* that students and campus employees are not as careful on campus as they are in other places. However, readers can *infer* that the author believes that this lack of caution contributes to campus crime, even though that point is not specifically made.

Making inferences is an important part of critical reading. However, conclusions you draw—your reading between the lines—must be supported by evidence. Thus, you cannot infer from the above paragraph that the author believes victims of campus crime get what they deserve because they are not sufficiently careful. As a reader, *you* might feel that way, but you cannot ascribe that idea to the author, based on the evidence in the paragraph.

Synthesizing Information

Synthesis is the process of connecting new information to what you already know. Thus, synthesis involves fitting new information into the larger scheme of your knowledge. When you read or hear a lecture, you can synthesize the information by noting how it supports, refutes, clarifies, illustrates, or calls into question other ideas, observations, or experiences. Say, for example, that you are reading a newspaper article that mentions the shortage of male teachers in elementary schools. If you heard an education professor comment that male elementary school teachers get little respect, you can synthesize your reading with your instructor's lecture by assuming that there may be a cause-and-effect relationship: One reason for the shortage of male elementary school teachers might be that males do not want to teach elementary school because they do not get enough respect for doing so.

In college classes, you will synthesize by relating new ideas to information you have already learned. Thus, your history teacher might ask you to compare some aspect of the Bill of Rights (which you just read about) with some aspect of the Magna Carta (which you studied last term). Even though in your college classes you will usually synthesize by relating new classroom learning to earlier classroom learning, do not hesitate to synthesize ideas in a more personal way as well. For example, if your education instructor lectures on bilingual education and you are an international student, you can relate your instructor's points to your own school experience using English as a second language.

Evaluating Quality

People often think that if something is in print, it must be accurate and it must be good, but this assumption is not true. A great deal of material of dubious quality and questionable truth makes its way into print and onto the Internet. For this reason, critical readers must evaluate the quality of their reading material. As a student, you may feel uncomfortable judging what you read. Perhaps you feel that you do not know enough or are not high enough in the academic "pecking order" to make such judgments. In fact, as a student you should practice critical reading at every opportunity. You are entitled to your opinion, as long as you back it up with evidence for your view. Answering the following questions about reading material can help you form a reasonable judgment.

- **Are the "facts" really facts, or are they opinions?** A point is not a fact just because a writer calls it one. The statement could be an opinion dressed up as a fact. Consider this example: "The fact that science is poorly taught in elementary school helps explain our nation's lack of scientific literacy." *Is* it a fact that science is poorly taught in elementary school? *Is* it a fact that we lack scientific literacy? No, these are opinions, and calling them facts does not make them so.

- **Are the opinions adequately supported?** Opinions backed up by sound reasoning and solid evidence are valuable; opinions offered without any support may not be. For example, an author may offer the opinion that the United States should increase spending for space exploration, but without reasons for doing so, this opinion is not worth much.

- **Is the material current or dated?** If you are reading a biography of Abraham Lincoln, the fact that it was written 20 years ago may not be a problem (unless historians have recently made important new discoveries about Lincoln's life). However, if you are reading about population trends in rural areas, an essay with census information from 1980 will not be as relevant as a piece with census information from 2000.

- **Are the source and author trustworthy?** Consider the author's credentials and possible biases. If you are looking for a balanced view of the issues surrounding handgun control, for instance, the National Rifle Association's website or an essay written by the mother of a student killed in a school shooting may not be the best sources.

- **Is the reasoning logical?** A critical reader discounts material that contains faulty reasoning. The next section will help you recognize errors in logic when you read and avoid them when you write.

Detecting Errors in Logic

You should always be on the lookout for errors in logic. An **error in logic** is a form of faulty reasoning that can lead a person to a false conclusion. Unethical writers use errors in logic intentionally, to mislead or manipulate a reader. However, many writers do not intend to deceive; they use flawed logic without meaning to. In either case, as a critical reader, you should be wary of material that includes errors in logic. As a writer, you should avoid such errors in your own work. Some of the most common errors in logic are explained here.

1. Overgeneralizing. Very little is true all of the time, so be careful of sweeping statements.

> EXAMPLE   The only reason teenagers quit school is to avoid the work. (This may be true for some, but not for all.)

2. Oversimplifying. Most issues worth arguing are complex, so be wary of "quick fix" explanations or solutions.

> EXAMPLE   If women would just stay home to care for their children, we would have no day-care problem in this country. (The issue is not that simple. Many women must work in order to feed their children.)

3. Begging the question. "Begging the question" is basing an argument or conclusion on the truth of a point that has not been proven.

> EXAMPLE   Immature couples who live together do not deserve spousal rights. (Where is the proof that couples who live together are "immature"? To assume they are is to beg the question.)

4. Name calling. Also called an *ad hominem* ("to the man") attack or *mudslinging,* this fallacy involves attacking the people who believe something instead of criticizing their ideas or sticking with issues.

> EXAMPLE   People who oppose school vouchers are bleeding-heart liberals who will destroy this country. (The pros and cons of school vouchers are unrelated to the people who oppose or favor them.)

5. Either–or reasoning. With complex issues, more than two alternatives usually exist.

> EXAMPLE   If we do not ban hand guns, we will have a social crisis on our hands. (What about other alternatives, such as limited gun control or mandatory jail sentences?)

6. Assuming an earlier event caused a later event. This fallacy is also called *post hoc, ergo propter hoc,* which means "after this, therefore because of this." The fact that one event occurred before another does not prove that the first event caused the second.

> EXAMPLE   After homosexual characters began to be featured in television and movies, more people began considering homosexual marriage. (The first event did not necessarily cause the second.)

7. **Attacking or defending an issue on the basis of what was believed or done in the past.** This kind of fallacy would have kept women from getting the vote.

> EXAMPLE   If our grandparents managed without federally subsidized health care, so can we. (Our grandparents lived in a different world.)

8. **Assuming that what is true for one person is true for everybody.**

> EXAMPLE   My cousin and his girlfriend live together without benefit of marriage, and they are just fine. Obviously, marriage is not that important. (What is true for the cousin may not be true for others.)

9. **Playing to general sentiments.** Also called *ad populum,* which means "to the crowd," this fallacy involves winning people over by calling upon commonly held feelings such as patriotism, fear of war, and religious fervor rather than discussing issues.

> EXAMPLE   I would make an excellent senator because I come from humble beginnings and know what it means to work for a living. (This argument appeals to our respect for those who work hard to improve their circumstances. It says nothing about the speaker's political qualifications.)

10. **Falsely indicating that one point follows conclusively from another.** This fallacy is also called *non sequitur,* which means "it does not follow."

> EXAMPLE   Fewer minority students are attending our university this year. Apparently, minorities are losing interest in higher education. (The conclusion does not follow from the first statement. There may be many causes for the decline in enrollment, including the fact that many minority students are attending other colleges.)

11. **Using the "as any fool can see" approach.** Because this approach insults those who disagree, it can alienate readers.

> EXAMPLE   It is apparent to everyone that deer hunting solves many problems. (No, it is not apparent to everyone, or your essay would not be necessary.)

> EXAMPLE   As any reasonable person can see, prison reform is necessary. (Those who disagree are cast as "unreasonable," which is both unfair and likely to alienate some readers.)

12. **Alluding to but not naming authorities.** Careful readers distrust phrases such as "experts agree" or "research shows" because they suggest authority or evidence without naming that authority or evidence.

> EXAMPLE   Studies show that most Americans distrust politicians. (What studies?)

STRATEGIES FOR CRITICAL READING

As you have seen, to be a critical reader, you must read thoughtfully to distinguish facts from opinions, make inferences, synthesize information, and evaluate quality. At times, you may draw conclusions that are different from those of your classmates and other readers, but critical readers often disagree with each other. While you need not agree with others, you must support your views with sound reasoning and evidence.

Sometimes you will be uncertain about the meaning of all or part of what you read, and that uncertainty is acceptable, too. If you are puzzled, say so. Critical reading is often an investigative process, so ask questions of other readers, and ask questions in class. Do some research, if necessary, to learn more about the text you are reading and to discover what other critical readers think. Eventually, things will become clearer to you.

Sometimes you will change your mind about a text. Yesterday you may have made one evaluation, but today you have another. Remember that reading is an ongoing process, and critical readers never dig in their heels and refuse to rethink their ideas in light of new evidence or insights. Your reactions and views can change as you continue to reflect, consider the ideas of other readers in and out of class, and gain experience and knowledge that affect how you synthesize information.

The strategies explained next can help you achieve the many goals of a critical reader.

Approach Your Reading with a Reflective and Questioning Attitude

Critical readers think about what they are reading and ask questions. They consider which ideas are facts and which are opinions. They ponder the significance of points and consider the implications behind the words. They ask themselves how the author's ideas connect with what they already know. They examine the author's credentials, and they evaluate the support offered for opinions. They look for errors in reasoning. They determine whether material is dated. In short, critical readers never automatically accept what they read; they reflect and question in order to draw their own conclusions. As you read the explanation of critical reading strategies that follows, remember that the most important strategy is maintaining a reflective and questioning attitude—all the other strategies are based on that one.

Preview the Material

Previewing the material helps you form preliminary impressions and create a context for your more studied reading, which is to come. To preview, initiate your reflective and questioning attitude by doing the following.

- **Consider the author and title** and what they suggest about the piece. Do you know the author's politics or usual subject matter?

Is the author a newspaper columnist, a humorist, or a political commentator? Think about the title and what hints it gives you. Some titles will tell you more than others.

- **Check out the publication information** (in this book, it is part of the headnote). When and where the essay first appeared will suggest how current the information is and who the original audience was.
- **Read the headnote.** In this text, reading selections are preceded by headnotes that tell something about the author's background and publications, the place the selection first appeared, and the content of the selection. This information can help you draw conclusions and evaluate the reading.
- **Read headings, charts, bold and italicized type, and lists** for clues to content.
- **Read the first paragraph or two and the first sentence of other paragraphs** to learn a little about the tone, subject matter, and organization of the selection.

Do a First Reading

After previewing the reading, you will have a first impression and some expectations about the material—an impression and expectations that may or may not be borne out as you read more closely. To begin that closer examination, read the material through in one sitting, without pausing or laboring over anything. Just relax and get a sense of the author's purpose and major points. If the piece appeals to you, enjoy it without considering exactly what techniques create the appeal. If you encounter unfamiliar words, try to figure them out from their context, or circle them to look up later. If you do not understand a point, push on knowing that you will come back to that idea later and wrestle with it. If the piece is too long to read in one sitting, break it into sections and do separate first readings.

Reread and Study

After your first reading, use your reflective and questioning attitude to crawl back into the reading and look more closely at it to discover as much as you can. Shorter, simpler pieces may require only one rereading, but longer, more complex selections will take two or more rereadings. Keep a pencil or pen in your hand so you can make notes in the margin and underline key passages. You may be accustomed to using a yellow or pink marker to highlight important sections; this technique is more useful for marking important textbook passages to study. For most other materials, critical reading goes better when you can make notes about why certain elements are significant. If you do not own the reading or prefer not to mark the text for other reasons, write your annotations on a separate sheet or in a computer file. Or use removable sticky notes and attach your reactions to the appropriate sections of the text. As you reread and study, the following procedures can be helpful.

- **Look up words that you circled during your first reading and any other vocabulary you are unsure of.** You can write the meanings in the margins as a study aid.
- **Identify the thesis (the main or central point).** If it is stated, place brackets around it or underline it. If the thesis is implied rather than stated, write it out in your own words in the margin or at the end of the reading.
- **Identify the purpose.** Most of the time you cannot ask the author about the purpose of a reading, but clues in the selection will tell you whether the author aims to express feelings, relate experience, entertain the reader, inform the reader, or convince the reader to think or act in a particular way. Write out the purpose or combination of purposes in the margin or at the end of the reading. Then note how well you think the reading achieves the author's purpose. (For a discussion of a writer's purpose, see p. 34.)
- **Underline major points.** As you encounter important ideas that support the thesis, note them for special consideration. However, be careful not to underline too much or the selection will have more words underlined than not. Just mark the major points; leave the examples, clarifying description, and other explanations as they are unless you have a reason to highlight a particular item.
- **Make notations as you reflect and question.** Remember, as a critical reader, you need to distinguish fact from opinion, make inferences, synthesize information, and evaluate quality—all of which is easier to do when you have a pencil or pen in your hand and can make notes in the margins. For example, if you like a passage or strongly agree, place an exclamation point next to it. If you disagree, write "no." If a point goes unsupported, write something like "not proven," or if you do not understand something, write a question mark. Note your important responses any way that is convenient for you, using notations like "clever," "reminds me of psych lecture," "who cares?" and so forth. (For an example of a marked essay, see "Americanization Is Tough on 'Macho'," beginning on page 11.)

As you reread the text, studying it and thinking critically, look for answers to questions like these:

- What is the source of the author's ideas: experience, observation, considered opinion, or research?
- Is the author expressing facts, opinion, or both?
- Is the author's detail adequate and convincing? Does the author support generalizations by showing and not just telling?

- What is the author's purpose? Tone? Intended audience? Role? (See the discussion beginning on page 34.)
- Do you agree or disagree with the author? Do you like or dislike the selection? What does it make you think of?
- Does the selection arouse any strong feelings?
- What is the significance of the selection?

(For an example of answering critical reading questions in a journal, see page 14.)

- **Reconsider any material you did not understand earlier.** If necessary, list questions to ask other readers or your instructor. Consider researching in the library or on the Internet.
- **Reconsider the reading in light of your earlier impressions.** Do you feel the same way you did during your preview and first reading? If not, how has your thinking changed and why?

A Sample Marked Essay

To see what a marked essay can look like, review the following selection marked by a student.

Americanization Is Tough on "Macho"

Rose Del Castillo Guibault

1   What is *macho*? That depends which side of the border you come from.

2   Although it's not unusual for words and expressions to lose their subtlety in translation [the negative connotations of *macho* in this country are troublesome to Hispanics.] *Closest thing to a stated thesis*

3   Take the newspaper descriptions of alleged mass murderer Ramon Salcido. That an insensitive, insanely jealous, hard-drinking, violent Latin male is referred to as *macho* makes Hispanics cringe. *Who is this?*

4   "Es muy macho," the women in my family nod approvingly, describing a man they respect. But in the United States, when women say, "He's so macho," it's with disdain.

5   The Hispanic *macho* is manly, responsible, hardworking, a man in charge, a patriarch. A man who expresses strength through silence. What the Yiddish language would call a *mensch*. *male head of family, sounds like Dad*

6   The American *macho* is a chauvinist, a brute, uncouth, selfish, loud, abrasive, capable of inflicting pain, and sexually promiscuous. *crude* *good description*

7   Quintessential *macho* models in this country are Sylvester Stallone, Arnold Schwarzenegger, and Charles Bronson. In their *pure*

movies, they exude toughness, independence, masculinity. But a closer look reveals their machismo is really violence masquerading as courage, sullenness disguised as silence, and irresponsibility camouflaged as independence.

Interesting—never thought of this before.

If the Hispanic ideal of *macho* were translated to American 8 screen roles, they might be Jimmy Stewart, Sean Connery, and Laurence Olivier.

needs more detail for proof

In Spanish, *macho* enobles Latin males. In English, it 9 devalues them. This pattern seems consistent with the conflicts ethnic minority males experience in this country. Typically the cultural traits other societies value don't translate as desirable characteristics in America.

Examples from other cultures needed.

I watched my own father struggle with these cultural ambiguities. He worked on a farm for twenty years. He laid down miles of irrigation pipe, carefully plowed long, neat rows in fields, hacked away at (recalcitrant) weeds and drove tractors through whirlpools of dust. He stoically worked twenty-hour days during harvest season, accepting the long hours as part of agricultural work. When the boss complained or upbraided him for minor mistakes, he kept quiet, even when it was obvious the boss had erred.

hard to handle

Is complaining a strength or a weakness?

He handled the most mental tasks with pride. At home 11 he was a good provider, helped out my mother's family in Mexico without complaint, and was indulgent with me. Arguments between my mother and him generally had to do with money, or with his stubborn reluctance to share his troubles. He tried to work them out in his own silence. He didn't want to trouble my mother—a course that backfired, because the imagined is always worse than the reality.

This is my idea of macho—males never share worries & fears.

Americans regarded my father as decidedly un-*macho*. His 12 character was interpreted as nonassertive, his loyalty nonambition, and his quietness ignorance. I once overheard the boss's son blame him for plowing crooked rows in a field. My father merely smiled at the lie, knowing the boy had done it, but didn't refute it, confident his good work was well known. But the boss instead ridiculed him for being "stupid" and letting a kid get away with a lie. Seeing my embarrassment, my father dismissed the incident, saying, "They're the dumb ones. Imagine, me fighting with a kid."

Why unions are needed!

I tried not to look at him with American eyes because 13 sometimes the reflection hurt.

well put

Listening to my aunts' clucks of approval, my vision focused 14 on the qualities America overlooked. "He's such a hard worker. So serious, so responsible." My aunts would secretly compliment my mother. The unspoken comparison was that he was not

like some of their husbands, who drank and womanized. My
uncles represented the darker side of *macho*.

Father is meek but strong?

15   In a patriarchal society, few challenge their roles. If men
drink, it's because it's the manly thing to do. If they gamble,
it's because it's how men relax. And if they fool around, well,
it's because a man simply can't hold back so much man! My
aunts didn't exactly meekly sit back, but they put up with these
transgressions because Mexican society dictated this was their
lot in life.

the thing to do, but not the macho thing

16   In the United States. I believe it was the feminist movement of the early '70s that changed *macho's* meaning. Perhaps
my generation of Latin women was in part responsible. I recall
Chicanos complaining about the chauvinistic nature of Latin
men and the notion they wanted their women barefoot, pregnant, and in the kitchen. The generalization that Latin men
embodied chauvinistic traits led to this interesting twist of
semantics. Suddenly a word that represented something positive in one culture became a negative (prototype) in another.

I don't get this.

—*model*

17   The problem with the use of *macho* today is that it's
become an accepted stereotype of the Latin male. And like
all stereotypes, it distorts truth.

interesting; I wish she had explored this more.

18   The impact of language in our society is undeniable. And
the misuse of *macho* hints at a deeper cultural misunderstanding that extends beyond mere word definitions.

This essay really makes me sad for all the men who show strength every day but are seen in a negative light.

Keeping a Reading Journal

You can write your responses to readings in a reading journal, which can
be in either paper or electronic form. Journal writing can enrich the reading experience for several reasons.

- You can pursue your thinking further than you would without the
  benefit of writing.
- The journal provides a convenient place to record responses in
  addition to or instead of the marginal responses written during
  critical reading.
- The journal records thoughts that can later be used in essays.

- You can review earlier entries to note the progression of your ideas and to discover ways to synthesize ideas.
- The journal provides a convenient place to write trial drafts and experiment with ideas.

The reading journal is also a good place to record the answers to critical reading questions such as those on pages 10–11. Here, for example, are answers to these questions for "Americanization Is Tough on 'Macho,'" as they might appear in a journal.

Answers to Questions about "Americanization Is Tough on 'Macho'"

1. What is the source of the author's ideas: experience, observation, or research? *The author's ideas came from personal experience and observation.*

2. Is the author expressing facts, opinions, or both? *The points about the connotation of macho are facts, as are the examples about the father and other relatives. The rest is opinion.*

3. Is the author's detail adequate and convincing? Does the author support generalizations by showing and not just telling? *More detail is needed to prove the point in paragraph 9. At the end, the author needs to explain more about the cultural misunderstandings.*

4. What are the author's purpose, tone, intended audience, and role? *Her purpose is to correct misunderstandings about the meaning of macho and the nature of Latin males. The tone is concerned, serious, and controlled. The audience is non-Hispanics. The author assumes the role of knowledgeable person, educator, and Hispanic.*

5. Do you agree or disagree with the author? Do you like or dislike the selection? What does it make you think of? Does it arouse any strong feelings? *I don't have enough experience around Hispanic males to agree or disagree, but I see little evidence of the stereotyped Hispanic male in the media. I like the essay, especially the parts about the author's family, but I wish there were more details. It makes me sad for a group of men who are very strong but viewed as weak.*

6. What is the significance of the selection? *The essay is important because it aims to increase understanding between cultures and dispel a common misconception. The last paragraph, in part, presents this significance.*

SUMMARIZING

When you write a **summary,** you restate the selection's major ideas using your own style and your own words. A summary should faithfully reflect the original, so you should not add points, interpret, or evaluate the author's ideas, or change the original meaning. Think of a summary as a distillation of the author's most important points. Because a summary includes only the most important points, it is shorter than the original selection.

The Purpose of Summaries

You will have many opportunities to summarize in college. For one thing, summarizing is a valuable study technique because writing out the major points of a reading selection gives you a study guide for that material and helps you learn information.

You may also write summaries for a grade. For example, instructors may ask you to summarize material so they can determine if you have read and understood assignments. On midterms and finals, they may also ask you to summarize reading assignments so they can check your comprehension and retention.

In addition, summaries are frequent components of other kinds of writing. If you are writing a research paper, for example, you will need to summarize information you discover in the library or on the Internet. If you are writing an argumentation essay, you can summarize the major points of an article that states a position you oppose and go on to disagree with those points. If you read something that helps explain a point you want to make in an essay, you can summarize what you read and use it as one of your supporting details. (For help with documenting materials from other sources, see p. 696.)

Suggestions for Writing a Summary

Step 1. Read the material over as many times as necessary in order to understand it. Look up unfamiliar words and get help with any passages you do not understand. (You cannot summarize material you do not understand.)

Step 2. Identify the major points and underline them in the text or list them on a piece of paper. You can omit examples, description, repetition, or explanations that support major points, unless these are necessary for clarification.

Step 3. Draft an opening sentence that mentions the author's name, the title of the piece you are summarizing, and one, two, or three of the following: the thesis, the author's purpose, the author's point of view. Here are some examples:

AUTHOR, TITLE, AND THESIS	In "Americanization Is Tough on 'Macho,'" Rose Del Castillo Guibault explains that Americans have a negative connotation for the word *macho*, and this fact bothers Hispanics, who use the word in a positive sense.
AUTHOR, TITLE, AND PURPOSE	"Americanization Is Tough on 'Macho'" is Rose Del Castillo Guibault's attempt to inform Americans that the negative meaning they ascribe to the term *macho* creates cultural misunderstanding and perpetuates an inaccurate stereotype of Latin males.

Summarizing

If you have trouble expressing all or part of a passage in a different way, imagine yourself talking to a friend and explaining the ideas you just read. Then write the explanation in the words you use to explain the passage. If necessary, you can revise the material later to make it less like speech and more like writing.

AUTHOR,
TITLE, POINT
OF VIEW

In "Americanization Is Tough on 'Macho'" Rose Del Castillo Guibault examines the term *macho* and the stereotype it reflects from a Mexican-American's perspective.

Use present tense verbs with the author's name because the words of the text "live on" in the present: Rose Del Castillo Guibault *explains, notes, says, expresses, examines, believes,* and so forth (not *explained, noted, said, expressed, examined, believed*).

Step 4. Following your opening statement, draft your summary by writing out the major points you underlined or listed. Be sure to express these points in your own distinctive style by using your own wording and sentence structure. If you have trouble rewording a phrase or sentence, you can use the original if you place the borrowed words in quotation marks. Just be careful to use quotations sparingly.

To keep your summary flowing smoothly, use transitions to show how ideas relate to each other. In addition, repeat the author's name with a present tense verb as a transitional device, like this:

Smith explains
Smith further believes
The author goes on to note

A Sample Summary

The following is a sample summary of "Americanization Is Tough on 'Macho,' " which appears on page 11. The annotations in the margin call your attention to some of the summary's key features. Notice that the summary is a single paragraph. Because summaries are condensed versions of readings, they are brief. However, summaries of longer selections or those with many main ideas can be two or more paragraphs.

Summary of "Americanization Is Tough on 'Macho'" by Rose Del Castillo Guibault

[1]In "Americanization Is Tough on 'Macho,'" Rose Del Castillo Guibault [2]explains that Americans have a negative connotation for the word *macho,* and this fact bothers Hispanics, who use the word in a positive sense. [3]While Americans use the term to refer to a man who is a [4]"chauvinist, a brute, uncouth, selfish, loud, abrasive, capable of inflicting pain, and sexually promiscuous," Hispanics use the term respectfully for a male who is [4]"responsible, hardworking, a man in charge, a patriarch." [5]Guibault [2]believes this difference in connotation reflects the fact that in the United States the traits that other cultures prize are not valued by American society. [6]She also believes that during the seventies, the rise of feminism was responsible for *macho* acquiring negative connotations. [7]More than anything, though, Guibault is concerned because Americans' sense of *macho* has become an inaccurate stereotype of the Latin man which contributes to cultural misunderstanding.

[1]Summary opens with a statement that gives the author, title, and thesis of material summarized.
[2]Verb is in the present tense.
[3]First major point is given.
[4]Borrowed words appear in quotation marks.
[5]Next major point is given. Transition repeats the author's name.
[6]Transition is achieved with use of the pronoun.
[7]Transition is achieved with repetition of the author's name and the phrase "more than anything."

SYNTHESIZING

To **synthesize,** use your critical reading strategies to integrate material from two or more sources with each other and with your own ideas. Synthesis involves recording, evaluating, and drawing conclusions about material from multiple sources. For example, if you were writing an essay about social pressure, you would be using synthesis if you incorporated ideas from "The Lottery" (page 169) and from "Salvation" (page 173) about how adults pressure children and related them to an experience you had as a child. You would also be synthesizing if you explained the ideas in two or more essays and went on to argue that the ideas in one of the essays are more valid than the ideas in the other, or if you explained why you disagreed with one or more ideas in the essays. In other words, when you synthesize, you bring material together from multiple sources, but you do more than record what you read (which is summarizing)—you go on to think critically about that material and draw conclusions, see relationships, and make inferences.

The Purpose of Synthesis

Synthesis can help support a thesis. In fact, synthesis is so important to thesis support that you will use it often to inform and persuade in many types of classroom writing. For example, for a paper for a child psychology class about the effects of televised violence on preschoolers, you can inform by mentioning the effects described in several journal articles on the subject.

To stamp the material with your own conclusions, you can indicate which effects are the most significant. To persuade, you could devise a strategy for minimizing the effects of televised violence and argue for its implementation.

Suggestions for Synthesizing Information

Step 1. Be sure you understand everything in all the sources you are dealing with. If necessary, look up words and ask your instructor for clarification.

Step 2. Underline or list the major ideas in each source.

Step 3. Review all of the major ideas and determine how they relate to each other. Answering these five questions can help:

a. Do the ideas in the sources support each other or contradict each other?

b. Do the ideas in the sources form a cause-and-effect relationship?

c. Do the ideas in one source explain or exemplify the ideas in another source?

d. Do the ideas in one source pick up where the ideas in another source end?

e. Do the sources examine the same topic from different perspectives?

Step 4. Decide how you want to use the material in the sources. Answering these five questions can help:

a. Can I use the information to explain something?

b. Can I use the information to prove something?

TROUBLESHOOTING GUIDE

Avoiding Plagiarism

If you have trouble knowing whether what you write is plagiarizing—using source material dishonestly—remember these points:

- For the most part, rewrite the author's ideas in your own words—do not imitate the author's style.

- When you do use the author's words, place them in quotation marks.

- Check the accuracy of your paraphrases and quotations.

- Document your sources with introductions and citations according to the guidelines on documenting sources in Chapter 14.

www.mhhe.com/patterns

For more help with avoiding plagiarism, click on

Research > Avoiding Plagiarism

Research > Incorporating Source Information

c. Can I show how the sources contradict each other or present different perspectives?
d. Can I explain the significance of the information?
e. Can I use the information to support my own experience or observation?

A Sample Synthesis

This essay synthesizes material from the following sources in Chapter 12: "Little Adult Criminals," "Should Juvenile Offenders Be Tried as Adults?" "Adult Crime, Adult Time," and "Young Voices from the Cell." The notes in the margin call your attention to some key features of the synthesis, including quotations, paraphrases, and parenthetical citations, which are discussed in Chapter 14.

Keep Juvenile Offenders in the Juvenile Justice System

[1]Alarmingly, some of our most violent crimes are committed by children and teenagers. Until we determine why that is so and address the causes, we are left with the problem of how to treat these juvenile offenders. Currently, we have one judicial process for adult offenders and a different judicial process for young offenders. Many people oppose that arrangement for violent juvenile offenders, believing that young people who commit murder and other violent crimes should be subject to adult laws in the adult system—adult time for adult crime, it is called. In fact, in many states young, violent offenders are routinely tried and punished as adults. [2]We should discontinue that practice and return young offenders to the juvenile justice system, but it should be a juvenile system that includes extensive psychiatric care.

[3]First, we must ask ourselves why we put young offenders in the adult judicial system in the first place. In some cases, I fear it is a reaction to one of our baser impulses, the desire for revenge. When innocents are murdered, our first impulse is to seek revenge: We want to hurt the murderer. We want to lock the murderer up and throw away the key, so to speak. While understandable, the desire for revenge must be kept in check. We should not satisfy our appetite for revenge by taking 12-year-olds and sentencing them to hopelessly long terms in adult prisons with adult criminals.

Some people maintain that revenge is not the motive, that juveniles who commit violent crimes should be in the adult system because the juvenile system does not serve children well. [4]Linda J. Collier, for example, is an attorney who has worked in the juvenile courts. [5]In "Adult

[1]The writer's ideas provide background and evaluation to lead in to the synthesis.

[2]The thesis.

[3]The paragraph presents the writer's ideas.

[4–5]The introduction credits source. It includes the author's full name and the title of the essay, since this is the first use of the source. The introduction also notes the author's credentials.
[4]Note the transition.
[5]Note the present tense introduction to the quotation from paragraph 7 of Collier's essay.

Crime, Adult Time," she says that the juvenile system [6]"is doing a poor job at treatment as well as punishment"[7](638). [8]She believes the poor showing of the juvenile system is a result of the fact that it was devised to deal with "truants, vandals, and petty thieves," not the young murderers we are seeing today (639). [9]Certainly, problems do exist in the juvenile system, very serious problems. However, the problems cannot be addressed by placing young people in the adult system where sentences are so long that prison officials see no reason to attempt rehabilitation. [10]In "Young Voices from the Cell," Timothy Roche and Amanda Bower report this phenomenon. [11]They cite Robert Johnson, commissioner of Mississippi's Department of Corrections, who says he makes no effort to rehabilitate prisoners who are in for life. He sees no use to it. [9]Life sentences and no rehabilitation are hardly appropriate for many juvenile offenders, even those who have committed murder, because in many cases they are young enough to be treated and returned to society.

[12]For Laurence Steinberg, the answer lies in compromise. In "Should Juvenile Offenders Be Tried as Adults?" he advocates keeping young people 12 and under in the juvenile system (634). [13]Those older than 16 should be placed in the adult system, and those between 12 and 16 should be tested to determine placement (634–635). [14]Unfortunately, this compromise will not work because neither system works well enough to meet the challenges of the violent juvenile offender.

[15]The answer more logically lies with improving the juvenile system. If the system does not work well enough, then legislators need to make the necessary adjustments. Courts should not move young offenders into an adult system that is even less prepared to cope effectively with them. [16]Even Collier expresses surprise that the juvenile system has not been overhauled, especially in light of the increase in juvenile crime (639). As a first step, judges should require intensive, long-term psychiatric care for juveniles convicted of violent crimes. [17]We can assume that juveniles who commit such crimes are emotionally disturbed. [18]Roche and Bower report the assessment of forensic psychiatrist Park Dietz. Dietz interviewed juveniles who opened fire in schools and concludes that the shooters were depressed and angry (647)—obviously, pathologically so. [19]Psychiatrists for Jacob Davis, who shot his girlfriend's ex-lover, say that Davis was "suffering from serious depression with psychotic features" (Roche and Bower, 646). [20]If we treat the pathology, we may be able to

return the juvenile to society as a productive person who does not pose a threat. [21]Granted, the treatment can take a very long time, but the alternative is worse. Eventually, some of these juveniles will be released—as adults who may commit murder. [22]T.J. Solomon, who is currently incarcerated in an adult prison, may be released after serving his 40-year sentence. He has flashbacks, hears screams, and hallucinates (Roche and Bower, 648). [23]He shot his classmates as a mentally ill juvenile. Do we want him on the streets as a mentally ill adult?

[26]Sentencing juveniles as adults may keep young violent offenders off the streets longer, and it may satisfy our desire for revenge, but it does nothing to address the real problems—why young people kill, and how to rehabilitate the killers so they do not murder again. Neither the adult nor the juvenile justice system will address the first issue; only an overhauled juvenile system can address the second.

[27]Works Cited

Collier, Linda J. "Adult Crime, Adult Time." Patterns for a Purpose: A Rhetorical Reader. Ed. Barbara Fine Clouse. 4th ed. New York: McGraw-Hill, 2006, 591–594.

The New York Times. "Little Adult Criminals." Patterns for a Purpose: A Rhetorical Reader. Ed. Barbara Fine Clouse. 4th ed. New York: McGraw Hill, 2006, 581–583.

Roche, Timothy, and Amanda Bower. "Young Voices from the Cell." Patterns for a Purpose: A Rhetorical Reader. Ed. Barbara Fine Clouse. 4th ed. New York: McGraw-Hill, 2006, 596–602.

Steinberg, Laurence. "Should Juvenile Offenders Be Tried as Adults?" Patterns for a Purpose: A Rhetorical Reader. Ed. Barbara Fine Clouse. 4th ed. New York: McGraw-Hill, 2006, 585–589.

[26]Writer concludes with a summary of the argument.

[27]In your synthesis, the "Works Cited" page should begin on a new page.

STRATEGIES FOR READING VISUAL MATERIAL CRITICALLY

You are accustomed to images in magazines and newspapers and on everything from cereal boxes to busses, but more and more, your college reading will have a visual component. Textbooks are using graphs, charts, maps, drawings, and photographs in greater numbers to present and supplement essential material. In addition, instructors are making PowerPoint presentations with images as a key component, and they are directing students to the Internet for information that is often graphically displayed.

All these images are important for the same reason the written word is important: They have a purpose. They entertain, express feelings, relate experience, inform, and persuade, just as the written word does. For example, reproductions of paintings on a museum's Internet site entertain those who view the site; your sister's wedding photos posted to her Web site express the love of the bride and groom; a pie chart in your economics textbook informs you about the distribution of wealth in the United States; and an advertisement in your favorite magazine persuades you to buy a particular headache remedy. Like the written word, visuals can also combine purposes. For example, a political cartoon aims both to entertain you and convince you to think a particular way.

Because visual images are prevalent both in the classroom and beyond, and because these images have a purpose, you should learn to read them critically, using the same techniques you use to assess and interpret the written word. That means you should approach visual material with a reflective and questioning attitude. Distinguish fact from opinion, make inferences, determine reliability, and connect the information to what you already know. In "reading" visual material, consider who created the image, what audience the creator is trying to reach, and why.

Charts and Graphs

Charts and graphs often appear in textbooks, scholarly journals, and popular magazines. As visual representations, charts and graphs convey a great deal of information very succinctly. Line graphs are particularly good for showing how data change over time and how trends progress; pie charts and bar graphs show how items relate to each other. The bar graphs on page 23 show the percentage of people in different demographic groups who voted Democratic in recent presidential elections.

Not only do the graphs convey a great deal of information, but they also allow you to analyze data and draw conclusions. For example, the graphs suggest that Democrats drew their greatest support from blacks, Hispanics, Jews, and the poor. The graphs also allow you to make inferences, such as noting that Democratic support likely comes from city dwellers. The visual depiction of data in graphs and charts can make it easier to determine how to use information. The bar graphs here, for example, suggest the best media markets for placement of campaign ads and the most critical populations to reach out to in order to increase the ranks of the Democratic party.

To read graphs and charts critically, study the data, captions, explanations, or other text that accompanies the image. Then be sure you can answer these questions:

- What point is the graph or chart trying to make?
- What is the source of the information—a newspaper, the government, a university, a private foundation, a corporation, an

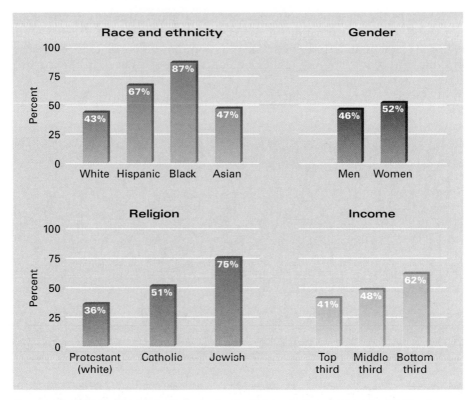

Percentage of Votes Earned by Democratic Candidates in Recent Presidential Elections.

Source: Thomas E. Patterson in *We the People*, 5th ed., New York: McGraw-Hill, 2004, p. 245.

individual researcher? Is the source reliable? Does the source have a particular agenda to promote?

- What is the date of the information? Is it sufficiently current?
- Is there any attempt to mislead? For example, are important time periods or groups omitted?
- What can you infer?
- How do the data and inferences relate to the text? How do they relate to what you already know?

Photographs

Like charts and graphs, photographs have to be studied for what they can reveal. Many photographs are posed, or arranged, for a particular purpose, but even candid shots, which record a particular individual or a particular place and time, can radiate with information and meaning. Keep in mind that the photographs you will encounter in the classroom have been selected by textbook editors or by your instructor for their rich insights into the subject of your course.

Outside the classroom, photographs with a purpose can ignite emotions and speed us to action. A thousand-word newspaper article about children starving in a drought-stricken nation may cause us to sigh in pity, but one photo of a starving child can lead us to put a check in the mail to a relief agency.

Consider, for example, this photograph of a young girl.

Lewis Hine, _Addie Laird, 12 Years Old. Spinner in a Cotton Mill_, North Pownal, Vermont, February 9, 1910. Lewis Hine (1874–1940), American photographer, helped develop the photograph as social commentary. With a mission to inform complacent Americans of the nature and conditions of poverty, he photographed newly arrived immigrants, street life in the big cities, and children at work in the mines and factories of early twentieth-century America. This photograph was taken for the National Child Labor Committee, which aimed to end child labor through federal legislation.

Study this photograph and the caption. What is the purpose of the photograph? How does Hine's choice of subject help him achieve that purpose? Look closely at the young girl. Notice her skinny arms, her soiled pinafore, and her dirty, bare feet. What can you infer from her appearance? What emotion do her face and, especially, her eyes, convey? Hine posed this photograph; the young girl stands in front of the spindles she is tending and looks straight out at us. What message is she sending? How does the information in the caption help you understand the message?

To "read" a photograph, ask yourself questions like these:

- Who took the photograph, and why—for what organization or cause?
- Is the photograph candid or posed?
- Is the image meant to document an event or to arouse emotions? Or does it do both?
- What inferences can you make about the photograph? What message is it intended to convey?
- How does the caption help you understand the photograph?

Critical reading strategies are essential for interpreting visual images. You ask questions similar to those you ask about a written text to determine the purpose and the means by which the purpose is achieved. For contemporary photographs, you may also need to ask if they are likely to have been retouched and how authentic they are.

Advertisements

Learning to read visual material critically is an especially important skill outside the classroom, because we are bombarded with images intended to influence our thinking and behavior. Television and print advertisements are the most prominent examples. Most often such ads try to convince us to buy a particular product. Sometimes, they try to convince us to have positive feelings about the company that manufactures the product or offers a service, such as an energy-company ad that showcases its concern for the environment. Either way, advertisements aim to profit those who sponsor them. The only way to avoid being manipulated by the ads is to learn to read them critically.

Consider, for example, the advertisement on page 26 featuring a photograph of a young mother. Study this advertisement, both the image and the text that accompanies it. What is State Farm's purpose in running the ad? What aspects of the photograph and text help the company achieve its purpose? Notice that the young mother is wearing business clothes, indicating that the primary audience for the ad is working mothers of young children. But the text at the top of the image suggests that all moms are always working. So this ad aims to appeal also to mothers who are not paid to work outside the home. It tells women

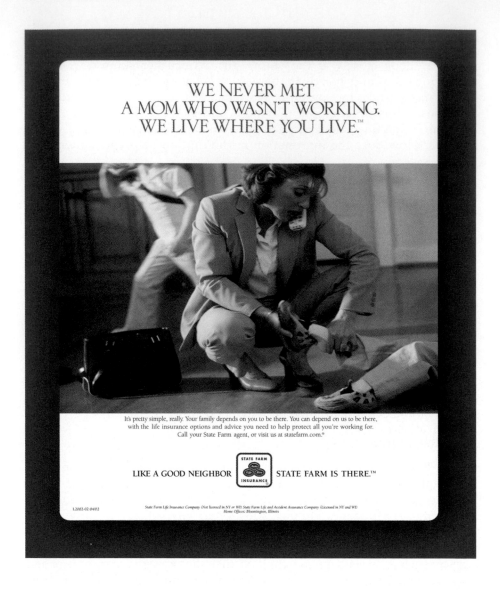

that State Farm understands their needs and can help them meet those needs.

Notice the way color is used in this ad. The only bright color is red, which is used for the company's name and logo, its slogan, and the mother's purse—where her money is kept. Notice the way motion is used in the ad: The boy in the background is on the move, and the mother is talking on the phone while she puts on another child's shoe. Obviously the woman is multitasking, and as a viewer of the ad we have to admire her poise as she capably manages to do many things at once. At the same time, we might see that her life is busy, perhaps even hectic. Does the target audience see themselves in this image? State Farm certainly hopes so.

Advertisements often work by encouraging us to identify emotionally with the individual pictured in the ad. Sometimes the appeal is to an ideal we all cherish—motherhood, in this case. Notice how this ad implies that mothers are essential, always there for their families. And the text explains that just as the family depends on mothers, so mothers can depend on State Farm.

Other advertisements make emotional appeals through symbols of power, pleasure, patriotism, beauty, or sex to sell products and services, to imply, "If you buy our products or services, you, too, will be a competent mother, or a powerful executive, a fun-to-be-with friend, a patriotic American, or a person with sex appeal." To avoid being too easily convinced that you can achieve your ideal by purchasing a product, learn to "read" an advertisement critically by asking yourself questions like these:

- What audience does the advertisement target? Are you in that audience? If not, do you respond favorably to the advertisement anyway?
- What is the purpose of the ad?
- Does the ad appeal more to reason or emotion?
- What does the ad imply?
- How do techniques involving color, size, shape, texture, and lighting highlight the ad's appeal?
- How does the text work with the image to achieve the ad's purpose? Are there slogans or symbols? Testimonials by celebrities? Statistics or research findings?
- Is the ad credible? Can its claims—implied or stated directly—possibly be true?

When you apply your critical reading strategies to advertisements, you are able to take *from* them what information you need without being taken *in* by their manipulations of your emotions and your reasoning. In fact, the critical reading strategies you will practice throughout *Patterns for a Purpose* will help you assess and respond appropriately to everything you read and view—in the college classroom, in your workplace, and in your community.

The following reading selection says something about critical reading. It reinforces and, in some cases, adds to points made in this chapter.

ASSIGNMENT

Read with a pencil or pen in hand, and mark the selection using the strategies for annotation found on page 10. If your instructor directs, form small groups in class and compare the ways you have marked the selection. What similarities and differences do you note? What accounts for the differences?

B A C K G R O U N D : Born in New York City, philosopher and writer Mortimer Adler (1902–2001) taught at the University of Chicago, where he helped develop the Great Books program and where he directed the Institute for Philosophical Research. Although a high school dropout, Adler earned a Ph.D., was an editor for the *Encyclopaedia Britannica,* and wrote widely on philosophy and education. He spent much of his career popularizing the great ideas of Western civilization in works such as *Great Books of the Western World,* 54 vols. (1954 and revised in 1990). He is particularly noted for *How to Read a Book: The Art of Getting a Liberal Education* (1940). The following essay first appeared in the *Saturday Review* in 1940.

www.mhhe.com/patterns

For more information on this author, go to

More resources > Chapter 1 > Mortimer Adler

R E A D I N G   W I T H   A   P U R P O S E : A person cannot truly own a book without writing in it, according to Mortimer Adler, for writing in a book "is not an act of mutilation but of love." Thus, Adler explains that it does not matter how many expensive volumes a person has on display. What matters is whether a person "consumes" the books with a pen or pencil in hand. Although the essay was written over 60 years ago, it still offers sound advice to readers. As you read, try to determine why this essay has remained popular for so long.

HOW TO MARK A BOOK | MORTIMER ADLER

You know you have to read "between the lines" to get the most out of anything. I want to persuade you to do something equally important in the course of your reading. I want to persuade you to "write between the lines." Unless you do, you are not likely to do the most efficient kind of reading.

2   I contend, quite bluntly, that marking up a book is not an act of mutilation but of love.

3   You shouldn't mark up a book which isn't yours. Librarians (or your friends) who lend you books expect you to keep them clean, and you should. If you decide that I am right about the usefulness of marking books, you will have to buy them. Most of the world's great books are available today, in reprint editions, at less than a dollar.

> "Most of the world's great books are available today, in reprint editions, at less than a dollar."

4　There are two ways in which you can own a book. The first is the property right you establish by paying for it, just as you pay for clothes and furniture. But this act of purchase is only the prelude to possession. Full ownership comes only when you have made it a part of yourself, and the best way to make yourself a part of it is by writing in it. An illustration may make the point clear. You buy a beefsteak and transfer it from the butcher's icebox to your own. But you do not own the beefsteak in the most important sense until you consume it and get it into your bloodstream. I am arguing that books, too, must be absorbed in your bloodstream to do you any good.

5　Confusion about what it means to *own* a book leads people to a false reverence for paper, binding, and type—a respect for the physical thing—the craft of the printer rather than the genius of the author. They forget that it is possible for a man to acquire the idea, to possess the beauty, which a great book contains, without staking his claim by pasting his bookplate inside the cover. Having a fine library doesn't prove that its owner has a mind enriched by books; it proves nothing more than that he, his father, or his wife, was rich enough to buy them.

6　There are three kinds of book owners. The first has all the standard sets and best-sellers—unread, untouched. (This deluded individual owns woodpulp and ink, not books.) The second has a great many books—a few of them read through, most of them dipped into, but all of them as clean and shiny as the day they were bought. (This person would probably like to make books his own, but is restrained by a false respect for their physical appearance.) The third has a few books or many—everyone of them dog-eared and dilapidated, shaken and loosened by continual use, marked and scribbled in from front to back. (This man owns books.)

7　Is it false respect, you may ask, to preserve intact and unblemished a beautifully printed book, an elegantly bound edition? Of course not. I'd no more scribble all over a first edition of *Paradise Lost* than I'd give my baby a set of crayons and an original Rembrandt! I wouldn't mark up a painting or a statue. Its soul, so to speak, is inseparable from its body. And the beauty of a rare edition or of a richly manufactured volume is like that of a painting or a statue.

8　But the soul of a book *can* be separated from its body. A book is more like the score of a piece of music than it is like a painting. No great musician confuses a symphony with the printed sheets of music. Arturo Toscanini reveres Brahms, but Toscanini's score of the C-minor Symphony is so thoroughly marked up that no one but the maestro himself can read it. The reason why a great conductor makes notations on his musical scores—marks them up again and again each time he returns to study them—is the reason why you should mark your books. If your respect for magnificent binding or typography gets in the way, buy yourself a cheap edition and pay your respects to the author.

9　Why is marking up a book indispensable to reading? First, it keeps you awake. (And I don't mean merely conscious; I mean wide awake.) In the second place, reading, if it is active, is thinking, and thinking tends to express itself in words, spoken or written. The marked book is usually the thought-through book. Finally, writing helps you remember the thoughts you had, or the thoughts the author expressed. Let me develop these three points.

10   If reading is to accomplish anything more than passing time, it must be active.

> "If reading is to accomplish anything more than passing time, it must be active."

You can't let your eyes glide across the lines of a book and come up with an understanding of what you have read. Now an ordinary piece of light fiction, like say, *Gone With the Wind*, doesn't require the most active kind of reading. The books you read for pleasure can be read in a state of relaxation, and nothing is lost. But a great book, rich in ideas and beauty, a book that raises and tries to answer great fundamental questions, demands the most active reading of which you are capable. You don't absorb the ideas of John Dewey[1] the way you absorb the crooning of Mr. Vallee.[2] You have to reach for them. That you cannot do while you're asleep.

11   If, when you've finished reading a book, the pages are filled with your notes, you know that you read actively. The most famous *active* reader of great books I know is President Hutchins, of the University of Chicago. He also has the hardest schedule of business activities of any man I know. He invariably reads with a pencil, and sometimes, when he picks up a book and pencil in the evening, he finds himself, instead of making intelligent notes, drawing what he calls "caviar factories" on the margins. When that happens, he puts the book down. He knows he's too tired to read, and he's just wasting time.

12   But, you may ask, why is writing necessary? Well, the physical act of writing, with your own hand, brings words and sentences more sharply before your mind and preserves them better in your memory. To set down your reaction to important words and sentences you have read, and the questions they have raised in your mind, is to preserve those reactions and sharpen those questions.

13   Even if you wrote on a scratch pad, and threw the paper away when you had finished writing, your grasp of the book would be surer. But you don't have to throw the paper away. The margins (top and bottom, as well as side), the end-papers, the very space between the lines, are all available. They aren't sacred. And, best of all, your marks and notes become an integral part of the book and stay there forever. You can pick up the book the following week or year, and there are all your points of agreement, disagreement, doubt, and inquiry. It's like resuming an interrupted conversation with the advantage of being able to pick up where you left off.

14   And that is exactly what reading a book should be: a conversation between you and the author. Presumably he knows more about the subject than you do; naturally, you'll have the proper humility as you approach him. But don't let anybody tell you that a reader is supposed to be solely on the receiving end. Understanding is a two-way operation; learning doesn't consist in being an empty receptacle. The learner has to question himself and question the teacher.

> "The learner has to question himself and question the teacher."

---

[1]John Dewey (1859–1952), a philosopher and educator.
[2]Rudy Vallee (1901–1986), a band leader and singer.

He even has to argue with the teacher, once he understands what the teacher is saying. And marking a book is literally an expression of your differences, or agreements of opinion, with the author.

15 There are all kinds of devices for marking a book intelligently and fruitfully. Here's the way I do it:

16 **1.** *Underlining:* of major points, of important or forceful statements.

17 **2.** *Vertical lines at the margin:* to emphasize a statement already underlined.

18 **3.** *Star, asterisk, or other doo-dad at the margin:* to be used sparingly, to emphasize the ten or twenty most important statements in the book. (You may want to fold the bottom corner of each page on which you use such marks. It won't hurt the sturdy paper on which most modern books are printed, and you will be able to take the book off the shelf at any time and, by opening it at the folded-corner page, refresh your recollection of the book.)

19 **4.** *Numbers in the margin:* to indicate the sequence of points the author makes in developing a single argument.

20 **5.** *Numbers of other pages in the margin:* to indicate where else in the book the author made points relevant to the point marked; to tie up the ideas in a book, which, though they may be separated by many pages, belong together.

21 **6.** *Circling of key words or phrases.*

22 **7.** *Writing in the margin, or at the top or bottom of the page, for the sake of:* recording questions (and perhaps answers) which a passage raised in your mind; reducing a complicated discussion to a simple statement; recording the sequence of major points right through the books. I use the end-papers at the back of the book to make a personal index of the author's points in the order of their appearance.

23 The front end-papers are, to me, the most important. Some people reserve them for a fancy bookplate. I reserve them for fancy thinking. After I have finished reading the book and making my personal index on the back end-papers, I turn to the front and try to outline the book, not page by page, or point by point (I've already done that at the back), but as an integrated structure, with a basic unity and an order of parts. This outline is, to me, the measure of my understanding of the work.

24 If you're a die-hard anti-book-marker, you may object that the margins, the space between the lines, and the end-papers don't give you room enough. All right. How about using a scratch pad slightly smaller than the page-size of the book—so that the edges of the sheets won't protrude? Make your index, outlines, and even your notes on the pad, and then insert these sheets permanently inside the front and back covers of the book.

25 Or, you may say that this business of marking books is going to slow up your reading. It probably will. That's one of the reasons for doing it. Most of us have been taken in by the notion that speed of reading is a measure of our intelligence. There is no such thing as

> "There is no such thing as the right speed for intelligent reading."

the right speed for intelligent reading. Some things should be read quickly and effortlessly, and some should be read slowly and even laboriously. The sign of intelligence in reading is the ability to read different things differently according to their worth. In the case of good books, the point is not to see how many of them you can get through, but rather how many can get through you—how many you can make your own. A few friends are better than a thousand acquaintances. If this be your aim, as it should be, you will not be impatient if it takes more time and effort to read a great book than it does a newspaper.

26   You may have one final objection to marking books. You can't lend them to your friends because nobody else can read them without being distracted by your notes. Furthermore, you won't want to lend them because a marked copy is a kind of intellectual diary, and lending it is almost like giving your mind away.

27   If your friend wishes to read your *Plutarch's Lives, Shakespeare,* or *The Federalist Papers,* tell him gently but firmly to buy a copy. You will lend him your car or your coat—but your books are as much a part of you as your head or your heart.

Planning an Essay and Using the Patterns of Development

To become a better tennis player, you play more tennis. But practice alone is not the key to improvement. You must also consider what you *do* when you play tennis, so you adjust your form, vary your technique at the net, try different approach shots, experiment with different rackets, and so forth. To become a better writer, you should do much the same thing by working to improve the procedures you follow when you write. Unfortunately, no one can tell you that certain procedures will guarantee successful writing. Instead, you must experiment a little to discover the procedures that work best for you. This chapter and the next can help with that experimentation. They explain what all writers must pay attention to:

The writing context (identifying purpose, audience, and role).

Generating ideas (discovering what you have to say).

Ordering ideas (determining the progression and relationship of ideas).

Drafting (writing a preliminary version of the essay).

Revising (rewriting to improve content, organization, and expression of ideas).

Editing (finding and correcting errors in grammar and usage).

In addition to explaining context, idea generation, sequencing, drafting, revising, and editing, these chapters present procedures for working on each of these areas. Sample these procedures until you find ones that work well for you, and your writing is sure to improve. Keep in mind, however, that different writers function in different ways, and the procedures that work well for some of your classmates will not necessarily work well for you. Your goal is to find your own effective procedures.

CONSIDERING YOUR WRITING CONTEXT

Successful writers do not plan their writing in a vacuum. Instead, they consider the *context* in which their writing occurs. The **writing context** includes the reason for writing (the writer's *purpose*), who the readers are (the *audience*), and how the writer wants to present himself or herself (the writer's *role*). Together, purpose, audience, and role affect everything the writer does—from idea generation through the final check for typos.

Purpose

Whether you are writing an e-mail to your best friend, preparing a business report, or composing a college essay, you are writing for a reason—and that reason is your **purpose.** In general, the primary purposes for writing are

- To entertain the reader.
- To relate experience and/or express feelings.
- To inform the reader about something interesting or important.
- To persuade the reader to think or act a particular way.

You encounter writing that fulfills these purposes all the time. Dave Barry's books and weekly newspaper column amuse you, so they *entertain*; a friend e-mails you to tell about the frustrations of interviewing for a job in order to *express feelings and relate experience*; the letter you receive explaining the terms of your student health insurance policy *informs* you about the nature of your coverage; and the newspaper editorial about a critical blood shortage tries to *persuade* you to donate blood to the Red Cross.

Your purpose in writing influences your approach. Say, for example, that you are a single parent who wants to write about the child care problems in this country. To entertain your reader, you can write a funny piece about what you went through the day you had to take final examinations and the babysitter canceled. To express your feelings, you can describe how much you worry about whether your children get quality care while you are at work. To inform your reader, you can explain what the child care options are for a single working parent of preschool children. To persuade your reader, you can argue for a federally funded child care program. Of course, you can also combine purposes. For example, you can relate your own experiences and then go on to argue that a federally funded program would make life easier for you and others. Obviously, each of these writings would have a different character because the content would be shaped by your purpose.

Because purpose influences the content and character of writing so profoundly, you should be clear about your purpose at the outset. For help establishing a purpose or combination of purposes, answer these questions:

- Do I need or want to relate ideas, feelings, or experiences to my reader?
- Am I seeking to inform my reader about something?
- Am I trying to entertain my reader?
- Do I need or want to persuade my reader to think or act a particular way?

(For a reminder of the four main purposes, glance at the back inside cover of this book.)

Audience

To write successfully, you must achieve your purpose. However, you cannot achieve your purpose without a clear sense of **audience**—that is, a clear sense of who the reader is and what that reader is like. Suppose you are writing an essay about the pollution in a local river. If the essay were written for your biology class, it might include a great deal of technical information about specific chemical pollutants. However, if the essay were for a letter to your local newspaper, such technical information might overwhelm the average reader of that paper. Now suppose that you are writing to convince your reader to support a school levy that would raise property taxes. If your reader has school-age children, you could argue that the quality of their education will improve if the levy passes. However, if your reader has no children, you may do better to argue that good schools will increase the value of the reader's property.

In some writing classes, you can establish any audience (person or group of people) for your writing because your instructor will assume the role of any reader you designate. Thus, you can say that your audience consists of city council members, your housemates, a co-worker, the head of the Environmental Protection Agency, the professors at your college, your parents, and so forth. In other writing classes, you must consider your classmates and teacher to be your audience. In either case—or in any situation in or out of the classroom—you must identify your audience and the particular characteristics and needs of that audience because this information will influence your approach, your details, your word choice, and almost every decision you make about your writing. Do you need to define a term? That depends on whether your reader is likely to know its meaning. Should you provide an example? That depends on whether your reader requires the clarification. Should you use this sophisticated word or that more common one? That depends on your reader's likely vocabulary. Which of two points will be more persuasive? That may depend on your reader's age, gender, political leanings, or economic situation.

If you need help identifying an audience for your writing, answer the following questions.

Who would enjoy reading my essay?

Who would learn something from my essay?

Who is interested in my topic?

Who should be persuaded to think or act in the way my essay recommends?

Who would find my essay important?

Who needs to hear what I have to say?

Once you have identified your audience, consider your reader's traits and needs, so you do not inadvertently bore, confuse, or annoy your audience and thereby fail to achieve your purpose. How do you assess traits and needs to avoid this outcome? Answering the following questions can help.

- **What does my reader already know about my topic?** The answer to this question can help you decide what your reader needs to know, and it can help you avoid boring your audience by providing information your reader does not need or already has. It can also help you determine the nature and number of clarifying points, such as examples and definitions, to provide.

- **How interested is my reader in what I have to say?** The answer to this question can help you decide how much of your writing should be devoted to capturing the reader's interest or convincing your reader that your topic is important.

- **Does my reader have strong feelings about my topic?** The answer to this question will help you determine whether you must overcome a reader's particular biases or respond to the reader's concerns.

- **How will my reader's age, gender, level of education, income, job, politics, or religion affect his or her reaction to my writing?** The answer to this question will help you decide on appropriate details and language.

When your audience is a diverse group—say, the readers of your local newspaper, the students on your campus, or the members of a large organization—your readers may not have much in common, so you may not be able to assess their needs and traits in a way that yields a single useful profile. In that case, you can identify one or two characteristics that are shared by many members of the group and let that information guide you. For example, if you are writing to working students on your campus, you can think of them as dealing with the stress of juggling courses, studying, and work.

The Writer's Role

In addition to audience and purpose, the role you assume as a writer will influence the character of your writing. Your **role** is the particular way you want to present yourself. For example, a student writing for a teacher will be careful to conform to all the terms of the assignment. An employee writing for a supervisor will adopt the appropriate respectful tone. A friend writing to another friend may be casual and use slang, but a student writing an essay as part of a scholarship competition will not include slang.

To appreciate the significance of the writer's role, consider a report on how to select the right college. A person in the role of a high school counselor will provide an objective set of procedures, but a person in the role of a college admissions counselor may slant the detail to favor his or her school. A person in the role of a student may express the frustrations that are part of the process, but a person in the role of a parent may stress financial concerns.

If the nature of your role is not obvious, consider whether you are writing as one or more of the following.

- Brother, sister, wife, husband, child, parent
- Employer, employee
- Student, tutor, roommate, coach
- Neutral party, authority, interested observer, average person
- Friend, stranger, newcomer
- Young adult, retiree, midde-aged person

GENERATING IDEAS

Perhaps you think that writing is the product of inspiration and that it involves staring at a blank page or computer screen until a brilliant flash of insight sends your pen racing across the page or your fingers flying across the keys. If the inspiration does not strike, perhaps you assume that you cannot write, so you might as well pack it up and go play racquetball. If you think this way, you are not alone—but you are wrong.

Inspiration *does* strike writers on occasion, but most often it does not, and we must rely on other techniques to come up with ideas. Collectively, these other techniques are called *idea generation*. Successful writers use the idea generation techniques described in this chapter to pursue ideas in the absence of inspiration. They use these techniques to shape writing topics and to discover ideas for developing their writing topics.

Shaping a Writing Topic

Many times an instructor will specify your writing topic. In that case, your first priority is to be sure you understand the terms of the assignment so you meet your instructor's expectations. First of all, you must be sure you understand the *kind of paper* called for. Does your instructor want you to take a position and defend it? Summarize an author's ideas? Explain the meaning of a concept? Compare and contrast two essays? Consider, for example, this assignment that could be made in response to "Americanization Is Tough on 'Macho'" (page 11):

> In what ways do movies and television influence our views of how men or women are supposed to behave?

This topic requires you to deal with only one gender; dealing with both is not called for and would result in an unwieldy paper. The topic also requires you to provide examples of specific movies and television programs to illustrate your points.

Now consider this assignment based on the same reading selection:

> Agree or disagree with Rose Del Castillo Guibault's claim that "the American *macho* is a chauvinist, a brute, uncouth, selfish, loud, abrasive, capable of inflicting pain, and sexually promiscuous."

This topic requires a different approach, for you must convince your reader of the validity of your point of view by arguing convincingly.

In addition to understanding the kind of paper required, you must also be sure you understand the *terms of the assignment:* the length; the due date; the necessary manuscript form; the need to have a teacher conference, engage in peer review, or submit an outline; and so forth. If you have questions about the nature of an assigned topic, or if you are having difficulty fulfilling the assignment, speak to your instructor for guidance.

When you are not given a specific topic to respond to, the following idea generation techniques can help you shape a writing topic.

1. Review the journal entries and marginal notes you made during critical reading. (See Chapter 1 on critical reading.) Your comments, questions, and areas of disagreement and agreement may suggest a topic. For example, the marginal note in response to paragraph 7 of "Americanization Is Tough on 'Macho'" could prompt an essay about the image of males presented in action movies.

2. Use a provocative quotation as a topic source. For example, in paragraph 16 of "Americanization Is Tough on 'Macho,'" the author says, "I believe it was the feminist movement of the early '70s that changed *macho's* meaning." This quotation could prompt an essay about the changing meaning of *macho.*

3. Pick a subject treated in a reading and brainstorm. To brainstorm, make a list of every idea that occurs to you and then examine the list for possible topics. For best results, you should not censor yourself. Just list everything that occurs to you without evaluating the worth of the ideas. For example, one student wrote the following list to brainstorm for topics about violence in sports.

fan violence	why athletes are violent
player violence	Are athletes too violent?
causes of violence	Is it violence or aggression?
effects of violence	How can we make sports less violent?
Is the violence justified?	
violence = part of the game	Fans love it.
It's expected.	Players think it's okay.
Is society sick if it likes violence?	Are players violent off the field?
players getting hurt	fans getting hurt

The student ultimately drew his topic from the question "Are players violent off the field?" That question prompted him to write about players being violent on the playing field and nonviolent off the field.

4. Freewrite for about 10 minutes on a subject found in a reading. To freewrite, write nonstop without censoring yourself. Simply record everything that occurs to you without worrying about its quality or about spelling, grammar, or neatness. Do not stop writing for any reason. If you run out of ideas, just write anything: the alphabet, names of family members—anything. Soon new ideas will occur to you, and you can record those. If you like to use a computer, try freewriting with the screen dark. Just turn off your monitor and freewrite "blindfolded." You will have many typing errors, but the freedom that comes from not seeing what you are writing can stimulate your thinking.

The following freewriting was done by a student in response to an essay that argues that female homemakers should not be financially dependent on their husbands. As you review the freewriting, notice that the author did not worry about correctness. Also notice that she allowed herself to write even silly things as she waited for better ideas to surface.

> William Raspberry says women who are homemakers shouldn't be considered as dependant on male breadwinners. Well that's true but aren't male breadwinners dependant on the homemaker too? Could they cope if the woman walked out? I bet not, theird be hell to pay. Let's see what to write, oh the guy would have to pay somme-one to come in and clean and cook and take care of the kiddies. That would be hard and expensive. Let's see what do I think now? Maybe we should pay homemakers a salary. Could that be done? Maybe, or maybe a giant PR campaign to upgrade the image of homemakers—yeah bring Madison Avenue into the act. I agree with Raspberry that women shouldn't be dependant financially if they are homemakers but I know a lot of women who don't mind so I doubt anything will change.

The student's freewriting suggests at least three topics:

- The need to upgrade the image of homemakers
- Paying homemakers for the jobs they do
- Why some women do not mind depending on males

Your freewriting may not yield as many topics, but it is likely to suggest at least one.

5. Examine the subject of a reading from different angles. Answering these questions will help:

a. Does the subject make me think of something else?
b. Why is the subject important?

c. Do I agree or disagree with the author?
d. What interests me about the subject?
e. Can I give the author's ideas a broader or different application?
f. Can I relate the subject to my own experience?

Narrowing Your Topic

If you have trouble working with your writing topic, perhaps that topic is too broad. A topic like "education reform" may seem perfect to you at first because you think there are so many problems with schools today. However, you may also find that you have *too* much to say and don't know where to begin, or that you have too much to say in the specified length. Try narrowing your topic by writing a tree diagram. Place your broad topic on top and "branch off" some ideas, like this:

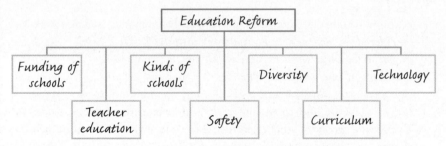

Select a branch that interests you and branch a second time, like this:

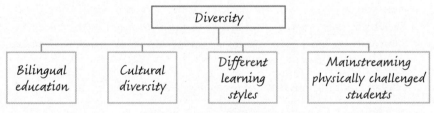

If the topics in your second branching are still too broad, branch again.

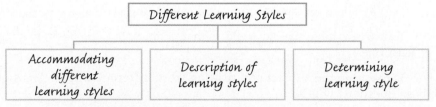

Any of these last branches could make a workable, narrow writing topic.

An Essay in Progress: Shaping a Topic and Identifying Context

To see how idea generation techniques can help you shape a writing topic, examine the following brainstorming list written by a student writer, Jeff, who was working to shape a writing topic based on "Americanization Is Tough on 'Macho'" (page 11).

> sources of American concept of "macho"
> why the concept is wrong (?)
> why Am. don't understand the Latin macho
> nature of concept of "ideal male"
> when this ideal is unreasonable
> nature of concept of "ideal female"
> how this ideal is unreasonable
> cultural conflict over gender roles
> — world scale
> — national scale
> — local scale
> need for more realistic concept of gender roles strong silence vs. aggression

Notice that Jeff felt free to abbreviate and place a question mark next to an idea he was unsure of. During idea generation, use any notations that stimulate your thinking and help you push forward.

After reviewing his brainstorming, Jeff decided his topic would be the nature of the concept of the ideal male. Jeff also decided his purpose would be to inform the reader of the source of misconceptions about the idealized male. His teacher was willing to adopt the role of any reader, so he established his audience as the average, general reader and his role as that of a young, concerned male.

Shaping a Writing Topic and Identifying Context

EXERCISE 2.1

1. Select two subjects from the following list and shape a writing topic from each. For one subject, use brainstorming to shape a topic. For the other subject use freewriting.

   a. MTV   **e.** The image of men or women in the media

   b. Education   **f.** The movie rating system

   c. Television   **g.** Friendship

   d. Automobiles   **h.** Technology

2. For each of the following, set up a writing context by establishing a possible purpose, audience, and role. For example, using the topic the dangers of boxing, your purpose might be to persuade the reader that boxing should be banned; your audience, boxing fans; and your role, concerned citizen.

   a. Topic: a car accident you witnessed.

   b. Topic: a report on the financial health of the local schools.

   c. Topic: the use of pesticides on food grown in the United States.

   d. Topic: the causes of the high divorce rate in the United States.

3. Select one of the writing contexts you created for number 2 and change the context by altering one or more of the elements (audience, purpose, and role). How do you think the change(s) will affect the final essay?

4. Establish a writing context for the topics you generated in response to number 1. Save your work to use in a later exercise.

Discovering Ideas to Develop Your Topic

Once you have a topic, you must discover ideas for developing that topic, ideas compatible with your writing context. Some of the following procedures may help.

1. Write a discovery draft. A discovery draft is not so much a first draft as a first try. It is an effort to identify what you already know about your topic and what you can think of along the way. To write a discovery draft, start writing anything that comes to mind about your topic. Do not worry about anything except recording everything you can think of. If you cannot think of much, you may not know enough about your topic, or you may need to try some other idea generation techniques.

2. Review the journal entries and marginal notes you made during critical reading. They may include ideas for developing your topic. (See Chapter 1 on critical reading.)

3. Write a brainstorming list that focuses on your subject. Like brainstorming for a topic, brainstorming for ideas to develop a topic involves listing every idea that occurs to you. Remember, do not evaluate the worth of your ideas; just write down everything you can think of. Later, you can reject anything unusable. Here is an example of a brainstorming list for one of the topics that emerged from the freewriting on page 39.

Topic: the need to upgrade the image of homemakers

homemakers are the backbone of the family
they work hard
they work long hours, 7 days a week
it would be very expensive to pay people to do everything that homemakers do
homemakers make it possible for other family members to do things
they often do volunteer work that helps schools and society at large
women would feel less like they need outside jobs for fulfillment
nothing is more important than homemaking
we must stop assigning value according to how much money is earned

Because brainstorming is idea generation, its results are preliminary. You need not use everything on the list, and you can add to the list at any time.

4. Try clustering. Clustering helps you generate ideas and see how those ideas relate to each other. To cluster, first write your topic in the center of the page and draw a circle around it. As ideas to develop your topic occur to you, write them down, circle them, and draw lines attaching them to the circled ideas they relate to. Do not censor yourself. Write down everything, regardless of its quality. The following clustering was done for an essay about violence on the playing field.

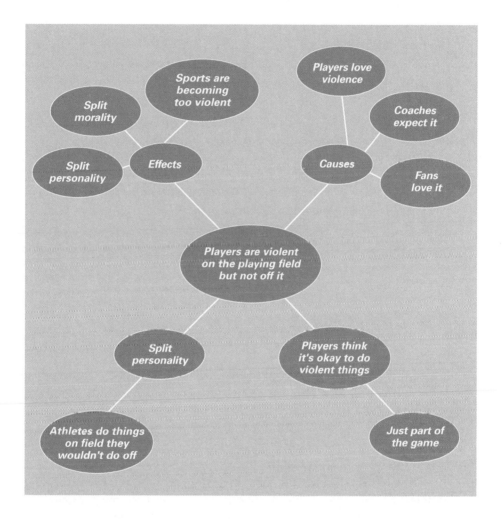

In the final version of the essay, the writer did not use all of the ideas in his clustering also, and he used some ideas that do not appear in the clustering. That is fine because nothing about idea generation is set in stone. Also notice that the writer placed "split personality" in two spots on the clustering. That is also fine. If you are unsure what an idea relates to, jot it down in more than one spot and solve the problem later.

5. **Talk to other people about your topic.** Your classmates, in particular, can suggest ideas for developing your topic.

Using the Internet

If you have trouble generating ideas, try using the Internet.

- *Surf the Internet.* Type a subject into a search engine like one of the following, and scan the titles returned for possible writing topics or ideas for developing a topic.

Alta Vista: www.altavista.com	Yahoo: www.yahoo.com
Google: www.google.com	All the Web: www.alltheweb.com

- *Browse news sites and electronic newspapers and magazines.* Scan one of these popular sites for information on current events, health, business, and entertainment. You might get several writing ideas.

Yahoo news: news.yahoo.com/?u	www.retiesk.com/paper.html
Reuters News Service:	state: www.state.msn.com
www.reuters.com/news.ihtm	USA Today: usatoday.com
Google News: news.google.com	

- *Browse Web sites with links to varied content.* These two sites, in particular, may give you writing ideas:

Science and Technology Daily: scitechdaily.com
Arts and Letters Daily: aldaily.com

www.mhhe.com/patterns

For more help with using the Internet, click on

Research > Using the Internet

6. **Combine techniques.** Begin by freewriting and then try clustering. Or begin with a brainstorming list and then talk to other people. Combine idea generation strategies in any way that suits you.

An Essay in Progress: Discovering Ideas to Develop Your Topic

Student-author Jeff created the cluster on page 45 as a way to discover ideas that would help him develop the topic he generated with the brainstorming list on page 41.

Discover Ideas to Develop Your Topic

1. Select three of the following topics. For each one, generate three ideas that could be used for development. Use a different idea generation technique for each topic.

    Mandatory drug testing of college athletes.

    The ethical issues associated with cloning animals.

    The causes of stress among college students.

    The characteristics of a leader.

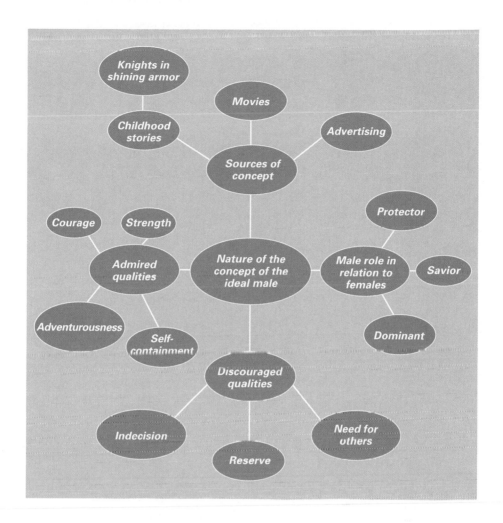

2. Using the idea generation techniques of your choice, discover enough ideas to write a first draft on one of the topics you established a writing context for in number 4 of Exercise 2.1.

DEVELOPING A THESIS

A successful essay has a central point, a main message the writer wants to convey. This central point is the **thesis,** the idea that everything else in the essay pertains to. You can think of the thesis as the controlling idea of an essay. Sometimes you have a good idea of what your thesis is when you first get under way. For example, if your political science instructor asks you to attack or defend the use of lobbyists by corporations and interest groups and you are opposed to them, you already have a sense of your thesis: It will express your opposition to the use of lobbyists. More often, your thesis will emerge as you generate ideas or afterward, when you study the ideas you have generated.

Your thesis should let your reader know the subject of your essay and your assertion about the subject.

SUBJECT	WRITER'S ASSERTION	THESIS
MTV	Parents should limit their children's exposure to it.	Parents should limit their children's exposure to MTV.
practical jokers	There are three kinds.	Careful observation reveals three kinds of practical jokers.
the author's father	He was a strict disciplinarian.	My father was a strict disciplinarian.

A thesis can do more than indicate the subject and the writer's assertion about the subject. It can also note the major points the writer will make in the essay:

SUBJECT	MTV
WRITER'S ASSERTION	Parents should limit their children's exposure to it.
POINTS TO BE MADE	MTV airs sexually explicit material. It demeans people.
THESIS	Parents should limit their children's exposure to MTV because the channel airs sexually explicit material, and it demeans people.

In scientific, technical, business, and some social science writing, thesis statements that indicate major points are fairly common. Especially when the piece of writing is long or technical, such a thesis helps the reader by laying out the architecture of the piece. In your writing class and many humanities courses, however, this kind of thesis can seem boring—particularly for a relatively brief and uncomplicated essay—so use it with caution.

Location of the Thesis

The thesis often appears in the essay's introduction, frequently at the end of that section. However, a thesis can also be in the beginning or middle of the introduction. The following paragraphs illustrate different placements of the thesis, which is underlined as a study aid.

THESIS AT THE BEGINNING

I am always tardy, a habit that creates difficulties for my family and friends. Ever since I was a child, I have tended to get up late, show up for meals late, and leave for school late. I am not sure when I last saw the opening credits for a movie because I typically arrive 10 or 15 minutes into the film. Usually, my friends and family forgive me, but who knows how long they will tolerate my lateness when it causes them so many problems.

THESIS IN THE MIDDLE

We all have personality traits that hurt us as much as they help us. It might be our sense of humor or our dedication to perfection. The quality that hurts me as much as it helps me is my overdeveloped sense of responsibility. Most people would see a sense of responsibility as a positive trait. However, when it is overdone, it can be harmful.

THESIS AT THE END

Have you ever received unwanted credit cards in the mail? Did a credit card company ever offer you such a big line of credit at such a low interest rate that you could not resist the offer? Yes, accepting the cards is tempting, but they come with risks the credit card companies never mention. As a former credit card addict, I can assure you that the dangers of relying on credit are very serious.

In some essays, the thesis is in the last paragraph. This works well when all the detail in the essay builds cumulatively to a conclusion that is the essay's main point. In other essays, the thesis is not stated. Instead, it is strongly implied by the details in the essay. When the thesis is not stated, a critical reader must infer the thesis. (See page 3 on inference.)

Qualities of an Effective Thesis

An effective thesis includes the subject of the essay and the writer's assertion about that subject. In addition, keep the following points in mind as you formulate your thesis statements.

1. Avoid the formal announcement.

    NO   This paper will discuss the reasons the United States needs election reform.

    YES   The United States would benefit from election reform.

    NO   The following essay will explain how to behave during a job interview.

    YES   If you want to land that dream job, follow this advice during the job interview.

    NO   I want to tell you the characteristics of a nuturing family.

    YES   All nurturing families share the same characteristics.

    You will see the formal announcement in some scientific, technical, business, and social science writing, but in composition classes and most of the humanities disciplines, it is considered poor style.

2. Present an assertion that is arguable or in need of explanation rather than a statement of fact.

    NO   Drunk drivers are a menace. (No one will disagree with this statement of fact, so why contruct an essay around it?)

YES	To make the roads safer for everyone, we should suspend the driver's license of anyone convicted of drunk driving. (This thesis presents an arguable point.)
NO	During the Depression my grandmother raised four children by herself. (This is a statement of fact; the essay has nowhere to go from here.)
YES	I have always admired my grandmother's strength and courage during difficult times. (This thesis allows for explanation.)

3. Present a manageable topic; it should not involve more than you can cover adequately in the assigned length of your essay.

| NO | Our system of education is in need of a complete overhaul. (An essay that discusses changes in every aspect of the educational system will be much longer than the standard college essay. If the essay is a reasonable length, the discussion will be superficial.) |
| YES | To be competitive with the rest of the world, we must change the way we teach mathematics. (This thesis presents a topic that can be treated in adequate detail in a manageable length.) |

4. Use specific language; avoid vague words such as *nice, interesting, good, bad,* and *great.*

| NO | Playing high school football was a great experience. |
| YES | Playing high school football taught me self-confidence and the importance of teamwork. |

How to Compose Your Thesis

1. Study the ideas and details you have generated. Does one idea have more points than the others? Does one idea interest you more than the others? Does one idea seem more manageable than the others? The answer to one or more of these questions can lead to a thesis.

2. Engage in additional idea generation, if necessary. If you cannot formulate a thesis, you may not yet have generated enough ideas and details. Try again, this time using a different idea generation technique.

3. Consider your writing context. What do you already know or what can you determine about your audience, purpose, and role that can point you toward a thesis? Say you are writing about the dangers associated with the Internet. If you cannot think of a thesis, identify an audience and go from there. For example, you could establish your audience as teenagers, which could lead you to explain how teens can avoid sexual predators in chat rooms.

4. Allow your early thesis to be preliminary. Although you are learning about the qualities of an effective thesis right now, your first version need not have all those qualities. An imperfect thesis can be revised later. Write an announcement if doing so moves you forward. Later, you can craft a more elegant thesis.

---

www.mhhe.com/patterns

For help with developing a thesis, click on
Writing > Thesis/Central Idea

An Essay in Progress: Composing a Preliminary Thesis

Before drafting a preliminary thesis, Jeff studied his clustering, which appears on page 45. He thought he had many good ideas, but at first he had trouble seeing how the ideas in the main circles branching off his center topic related to each other. He reflected about this and was somewhat frustrated until he considered the ideas in light of his personal dislike of the concept of the ideal male. Then he related the ideas to that dislike and found a unifying thread, which he expressed in this sentence:

The concept of the ideal male is a problem and has no basis.

He rewrote that sentence for clarity and came up with a preliminary thesis he was happy with:

The popular concept of the ideal male is unsuitable in our society.

Next, Jeff considered the thesis in light of his writing context and realized that he wanted to broaden his purpose. Rather than just inform his reader, he also wanted to convince his audience that the concept of the ideal male is misguided.

Composing a Thesis

1. Explain what you can expect to find in an essay with each of the following thesis statements Try to determine the pattern of development (p. 55) and purpose (p. 34) for each essay.

EXAMPLE   The 12-month school year offers several advantages.

EXPLANATION   The essay will mention and explain the effects of the 12-month school year, perhaps to persuade the reader that it is the best academic calendar.

a. Professional athletes are often viewed as heroes.

b. Karate is an excellent sport for school-age children who need to build self-esteem.

c. To find the right job, a person needs a strategy.

d. A good teacher has a sense of humor, a commitment to excellence, and the ability to be flexible.

e. The spring drought will create economic hardships in the Midwest.

2. In the following thesis statements, underline the subject once and the writer's assertion twice. If the major points are included, place brackets around them.

   a. Universities should not have physical education requirements because they delay students' progress and contribute little to students' education.

   b. I was deeply moved by the prayer service held at the war memorial.

   c. Paul Newman's success as a film star is a result of his wise choice of roles, his sex appeal, and his acting talent.

   d. African-American authors Toni Morrison and Maya Angelou have very different writing styles.

   e. Oil and gas well drilling should be banned from residential areas because of the danger to the environment and the problem for homeowners.

3. Indicate whether each thesis is acceptable or unacceptable. If it is unacceptable, state what is wrong with the thesis and rewrite it to make it acceptable.

   a. Regular exercise is important to a person's physical well-being.

   b. *I Love Lucy* is one of the most popular television comedies of all time.

   c. Newspapers are a better source of information about current affairs than network news programs.

   d. The following paragraph will explain why all high school students should take four years of a foreign language.

   e. The current movie rating system is inadequate for a number of reasons.

   f. The entertainment available to Americans is of the poorest quality.

   g. Summer camp is a good experience for children.

4. Return to the idea generation material and topic you developed for number 2 of Exercise 2.2 on page 44. Study that material and develop a thesis from it. Save your work to use in a later exercise.

ORDERING IDEAS

The order in which you present your ideas is important because a reader who cannot follow the sequence will become confused and frustrated. There are many possibilities for ordering ideas. Here are three common ones, which can be used alone or in combination.

1. **Chronological order** arranges details across time. The event that occurred first is written first; the event that occurred second is written second; and so on.

2. **Spatial order** arranges details as they appear across space—front to back, near to far, top to bottom, left to right.

3. **Progressive order** arranges details from the least to the most important, compelling, interesting, representative, surprising, and so on. A progressive order allows for a big finish because the most significant point comes at the end. A variation of progressive order is to begin and end with the strongest points and sandwich everything else in the middle for the strongest possible beginning and ending.

Outlining

With a workable outline in hand, writers often find that drafting goes much more smoothly. However, many people who would benefit from outlining resist it because they are only familiar with the formal outline developed with roman numerals, letters, and numbers. The formal outline is very helpful, especially for long or complex essays. However, less formal and less detailed alternatives are available for simpler papers, and these are also explained in this chapter. You might find one of these works well for you. Choose the outline that best suits your paper: The more complicated the paper, the more detailed the outline should be.

The Scratch Outline

The scratch outline is the least detailed outline. It is simply a list of the major ideas you plan to include in your first draft, written in the order you plan to cover them. Typically, the scratch outline just covers major points with no mention of details for developing those points, so it is not well suited for complicated essays or for writers who must plan in detail before drafting. As an example, here is a scratch outline based, in part, on some of the ideas generated with the clustering on page 43.

> *Preliminary thesis: Even nonviolent people are often violent on the playing field.*
> *Violence is okay because it's part of the game.*
> *A player has to be violent to compete with other players.*
> *Sports is different from the real world, so violence is justified.*
> *Fans want the violence.*

If you brainstormed at the computer, you can turn your brainstorming list into a scratch outline. First delete ideas you do not want to use and add any new ones that occur to you. Then, using your cut-and-paste functions, arrange the ideas in your list in the order you want to treat them in your draft.

The Informal Outline

The informal outline is more detailed than the scratch outline. It includes some details for developing major points and it groups related ideas together, so the writer has a sense of which details will appear together in the same paragraph. Although more detailed than the scratch outline, the informal outline may not be suitable for complex papers or writers who need a fair amount of structure before they draft. An informal outline might look like this:

> *Preliminary thesis: Even nonviolent people are often violent on the playing field.*
> *Violence is okay because it's part of the game.*
>   *Use roommate as example.*
>   *Coaches only play people with killer instinct.*

A player has to be violent to compete with other players.

   Get other guys before they get you.

   If everyone else is violent, you have to be, too.

   Violence is okay if you win the game.

Sports is different from the real world, so violence is justified.

   It's only a game and not part of reality, so it's okay to be violent.

   But the injuries are real.

Fans want the violence.

   Fans cheer for violence.

   They even act violently themselves in the stands.

The Outline Tree

An outline tree, which can be moderately to heavily detailed, allows a writer to see how ideas relate to each other. Many writers appreciate the visual representation the tree provides. To construct an outline tree, write your preliminary thesis at the top of a page and connect ideas with "branches," as the student example on page 53 illustrates.

The Formal Outline

The formal outline allows you to plan your essay in considerable detail. To construct a formal outline, write your preliminary thesis at the top of the page. Then label your major points with roman numerals and your supporting details with capital letters. Details that explain or illustrate supporting details are given numbers. You are probably familiar with the formal outline, which looks something like this:

Preliminary thesis: _____

    I.

       A.

       B.

       C.

   II.

       A.

       B.

          1.

          2.

  III.

       A.

          1.

          2.

          3.

       B.

          1.

          2.

       C.

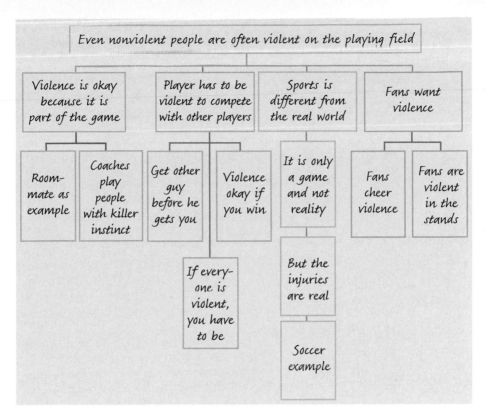

To see how a formal outline plots a draft, review the following formal outline for an essay with this thesis: Nonviolent people can be violent on the playing field.

I. Hurting people is part of the game.
    A. My roommate is gentle off the basketball court and hurtful on the court.
    B. If he didn't hurt others, the coach would bench him.
II. Violence is necessary for winning.
    A. Players feel violence is okay if they win.
        1. In my soccer game, an opposing player intentionally hurt one of our players.
        2. He did it to win.
    B. Players injure others so they don't get hurt themselves.
III. Players think violence is okay because sports are games.
    A. But the violence is real.
    B. The injuries are lasting.
        1. Our soccer goalie missed a month of school.
        2. He still has effects from a violent play.
IV. Fans like violence.
    A. Fans encourage player violence.
    B. Fans are violent themselves.

If you like to compose at the computer, check your word processing program to see if it has outlining capability. If it does, you can develop a formal outline by filling in the various levels. If it does not, develop your own

Writing an Outline

If you have trouble outlining, these tips can help:

- **Refer to your preliminary thesis.** Ideas that don't seem to fit in your outline may not be sufficiently related to your thesis. You may need to eliminate some ideas or adjust your thesis to accommodate them.

- **Consider your context.** Ideas that don't seem to belong may not be appropriate for your purpose, audience, or role. Adjust your ideas or context as necessary.

- **Be flexible.** The outlining process may lead you to reconsider some of your ideas or your thesis. Be ready to add and delete ideas and adjust your thesis in light of new insights.

- **Return to idea generation, if necessary.** If you cannot outline, you may not yet have enough material.

outline form, using roman numerals, letters, and numbers. Save the form as a file you can retrieve whenever you want to outline. To learn more about the mechanics of writing a formal outline, visit Purdue University's Online Writing Lab at owl.english.purdue.edu/handouts/general/gl_outlin.html.

---

www.mhhe.com/patterns

For more help with creating an outline, click on
Writing > Outlines
Writing > Outlining Tutor

An Essay in Progress: Outlining

Using his clustering as a guide (see page 43), student writer Jeff developed the following informal outline. You will notice that Jeff did not use all the ideas from his clustering and that he included ideas that do not appear in the clustering. Writers are always free to make changes as new ideas occur to them.

Preliminary thesis: The popular concept of the ideal male is unsuitable in our society.

The sources of the ideal are ridiculous.

  movie industry

    —highly unrealistic situations

  advertising

    —deceitful industry to begin with

  folktales and childhood stories

    —originated in completely different eras and societies

The admired/discouraged qualities of the ideal are out of place.

  instinctive vs. considered action

    —increasingly complex society

self-containment vs. need for others

　　—increasingly cooperative society

The idealized male's relation to women is archaic.

　protector, savior, rescuer, dominant male

　　—increasing appearance of female equality in all respects

Ordering Ideas

1. For each preliminary thesis statement, indicate whether the order of ideas is likely to be spatial, chronological, or progressive.

    a. The university should offer a study skills seminar as part of its orientation program.

    b. Once the flood waters receded, I discovered the devastation to my apartment.

    c. The movie version of *Lord of the Rings* is better than the book version.

    d. I will always remember the day Julio won the state pole vault championship.

    e. You can learn to change the oil in your car and save money as a result.

    f. At sunset, the flower garden of Municipal Park offers a peaceful retreat.

2. Using the techniques of your choice, generate ideas for an essay with one of the following preliminary thesis statements:

    Americans are too materialistic.

    Americans are not too materialistic.

    Then write an informal outline for the essay.

3. Using the techniques of your choice, generate ideas for an essay with one of the following preliminary thesis statements:

    Our enthusiasm for computers has gone too far.

    Our enthusiasm for computers has not gone too far.

    Then write an outline tree for the essay.

4. Using the thesis and ideas you have from number 4 for Exercise 2.3, write either a formal outline or outline tree. Feel free to add or delete ideas as you see fit. Save your work to use in a later exercise.

USING THE PATTERNS OF DEVELOPMENT

As you generate ideas, compose your thesis, and organize your draft, consider how the patterns of development can help you achieve your writing purpose. As tools, the patterns of development can help you generate ideas and find an effective order for those ideas. The following patterns of development are explained and illustrated throughout this text.

- **Description** (Chapter 4)—using words to explain what something looks, sounds, feels, smells, and/or tastes like (spatial or progressive order often used)
- **Narration** (Chapter 5)—telling a story (chronological order often used)
- **Exemplification** (Chapter 6)—providing examples (progressive order often used)

- **Process analysis** (Chapter 7)—explaining how something works or how it is made or done (chronological order often used)
- **Comparison-contrast** (Chapter 8)—explaining similarities and/or differences (Block pattern or alternating pattern often used)
- **Cause-and-effect analysis** (Chapter 9)—explaining the reasons for an action and/or the results of an action (progressive order often used)
- **Classification-division** (Chapter 10)—grouping items into categories and/or breaking something down into its parts (progressive order often used)
- **Definition** (Chapter 11)—explaining the meaning of a term or concept (progressive order often used)

In addition to using the strategies on pages 37 and 42, you can ask these questions related to the patterns to help shape a writing topic and generate ideas to develop that topic. (You will not be able to answer every question for every writing subject.)

a. Can I describe something related to my subject? (description)

b. Can I tell a story related to my subject? (narration)

c. Can I provide examples that illustrate my subject? (exemplification)

d. Can I explain how my subject works or how it is made or done? (process analysis)

e. What is my subject like? What is it different from? (comparison-contrast)

f. What causes my subject? What are the effects of my subject (cause-and-effect analysis)

g. Can I classify my subject into different categories? Can I break my subject down into parts? (classification-division)

h. What is the meaning of my subject? Are there any terms or concepts I need to define? (definition)

To see how considering the patterns of development can help with idea generation and organization, consider the following chart, developed to discover ideas for an essay about the need to upgrade the image of homemakers.

The Need to Upgrade the Image of Homemakers

PATTERN	IDEA	ORDER
Description	Describe the image of the homemaker that many people have.	While spatial order is often used to describe people and places, progressive order might be used here.
Narration	Tell the story of the time a friend felt embarrassed at a party because she was the only woman who did not work outside the home.	Chronological order is likely.

Exemplification	Give examples of advertisements that show working mothers as the ideal.	Progressive order is possible. Examples could also be grouped by category (per Chapter 10), with ads for makeup in one group, ads for clothing in another, and ads for electronics in a third.
Process analysis	Explain a procedure for upgrading the image of homemakers.	Chronological order would be used if the steps were to be performed in a specific order, progressive order would be used if steps were arranged in order of effectiveness or difficulty.
Comparison-contrast	Contrast the perception of the homemaker with the perception of the woman working outside the home.	Block pattern would be used to make all the points about the homemaker and then all the points about the woman working outside the home. Alternating pattern would be used if one point were made about the homemaker and then one about the woman working outside the home, until all the points were presented.
Cause-and-effect analysis	Explain the effects the current image of the homemaker has on family life.	Progressive order is possible with the most significant effects given last. This order could be combined with grouping by category if effects on relationships are given together, effects on self-esteem are given together, and so on.
Classification-division	Explain the components of the image of the homemaker.	Grouping by category is possible if personality components are given together, physical components given together, and so on. This order could be combined with progressive order if components or groupings are given in order of significance.
Definition	Provide a definition of a *homemaker.*	Progressive order is possible if aspects of the definition are given in order of significance.

www.mhhe.com/patterns

For more help with using the rhetorical patterns, click on
Writing > Paragraph Patterns

In the following essay, Gail Godwin discusses what may be the most difficult aspect of writing: the feeling that one can't write—what some people call lack of inspiration or "writer's block." Godwin understands the problem and has recommendations for dealing with it.

ASSIGNMENT

In a paragraph or two, note what Godwin says that pertains to you as a writer. If nothing pertains to you, explain why. What, if anything, did you learn from Godwin that you will apply to your own writing?

BACKGROUND: Born in Alabama in 1937 and raised in Asheville, North Carolina, Gail Godwin received her journalism degree from the University of North Carolina and her Ph.D. in English from the University of Iowa, where she studied with John Irving and Kurt Vonnegut. She was a journalist and English teacher before becoming a fiction writer. She has won numerous writing awards, including the Simon Guggenhiem Fellowship and the Award in Literature from the American Academy and Institute for Arts and Letters. Godwin is the author of ten novels and two collections of fiction. Three of her novels were nominated for the National Book Award: *The Odd Woman, A Mother and Two Daughters,* and *Violet Clay.* Her novels frequently appear on the *New York Times* best-seller list. Her most recent novel, *Evenings at Five* was published in 2003. "The Watcher at the Gates" originally appeared in the *New York Times Book Review* in 1977.

READING WITH A PURPOSE: All writers—both student and professional—experience writer's block. In "The Watcher at the Gates," Gail Godwin looks at the cause of the block—the "inner critic" that restrains writers if it is not silenced during the early stages of writing, during idea generation and drafting. Godwin explains (and you will learn in the next chapter) that writers should hold the inner critic at bay until they are ready to revise their writing. As you read, consider your own inner critic. How much of a problem is it?

The Watcher at the Gates

GAIL GODWIN

I first realized I was not the only writer who had a restraining critic who lived inside me and sapped the juice from green inspirations when I was leafing through Freud's "Interpretation of Dreams" a few years ago. Ironically, it was my "inner critic" who had sent me to Freud.

I was writing a novel, and my heroine was in the middle of a dream, and then I lost faith in my own invention and rushed to "an authority" to check whether she could have such a dream. In the chapter on dream interpretation, I came upon the following passage that has helped me free myself, in some measure, from my critic and has led to many pleasant and interesting exchanges with other writers.

2 Freud quotes Schiller, who is writing a letter to a friend. The friend complains of his lack of creative power. Schiller replies with an allegory. He says it is not good if the intel-

lect examines too closely the ideas pouring in at the gates. "In isolation, an idea may be quite insignificant, and venturesome in the extreme, but it may acquire importance from an idea which follows it . . . In the case of a creative mind, it seems to me, the intellect has withdrawn its watchers from the gates, and the ideas rush in pell-mell, and only then does it review and inspect the multitude. You are ashamed or afraid of the momentary and passing madness which is found in all real creators, the longer or shorter duration of which distinguishes the thinking artist from the dreamer . . . you reject too soon and discriminate too severely."

3   So that's what I had: a Watcher at the Gates. I decided to get to know him better. I discussed him with other writers, who told me some of the quirks and habits of their Watchers, each of whom was as individual as his host, and all of whom seemed passionately dedicated to one goal: rejecting too soon and discriminating too severely.

4   It is amazing the lengths a Watcher will go to keep you from pursuing the flow of your imagination. Watchers are notori-
ous pencil sharpeners, ribbon changers, plant waterers, home repairers and abhorrers of messy rooms or messy pages. They are compulsive looker-uppers. They are superstitious scaredy-cats. They cultivate self-important eccentricities they think are suitable for "writers." And they'd rather die (and kill your inspiration with them) than risk making a fool of themselves.

5   My Watcher has a wasteful penchant for 20-pound bond paper above and below the carbon of the first draft. "What's the good of writing out a whole page," he whispers begrudgingly, "if you just have to write it over again later? Get it perfect the first time!" My Watcher adores stopping in the middle of a morning's work to drive down to the library to check on the name of a flower or a World War II battle or a line of metaphysical poetry. "You can't possibly go on till you've got this right!" he admonishes. I go and get the car keys.

6   Other Watchers have informed their writers that:

7   "Whenever you get a really good sentence you should stop in the middle of it and go on tomorrow. Otherwise you might run dry."
8   "Don't try and continue with your book till your dental appointment is over. When you're worried about your teeth, you can't think about art."

9   Another Watcher makes his owner pin his finished pages to a clothesline and read them through binoculars "to see how they look from a distance." Countless other Watchers demand "bribes" for taking the day off: lethal doses of caffeine, alcoholic doses of Scotch or vodka or wine.

10   There are various ways to outsmart, pacify or coexist with your Watcher. Here are some I have tried, or my writer-friends have tried, with success:

11   Look for situations when he's likely to be off-guard. Write too fast for him in an unexpected place, at an unexpected time. (Virginia Woolf captured the "diamonds in the dustheap" by writing at a "rapid haphazard gallop" in her diary.) Write when very tired. Write in purple ink on the back of a Master Charge statement. Write whatever comes into your mind while the kettle is boiling and make the steam whistle your deadline. (Deadlines are a great way to outdistance the Watcher.)

12   Disguise what you are writing. If your Watcher refuses to let you get on with your story or novel, write a "letter" instead, telling your "correspondent" what you are going to write in your story or next chapter. Dash off a "review" of your own unfinished opus. It will stand up like a bully to your Watcher the next time he throws obstacles in your path. If you write yourself a good one.

13   Get to know your Watcher. He's yours. Do a drawing of him (or her). Pin it to the wall of your study and turn it gently to the wall when necessary. Let your Watcher feel needed. Watchers are excellent critics after inspiration has been captured; they are dependable, sharp-eyed readers of things already set down. Keep your Watcher in shape and he'll have less time to keep you from shaping. If he's really ruining your whole working day sit down, as Jung did with his personal demons, and write him a letter. On a very bad day I once wrote my Watcher a letter. "Dear Watcher," I wrote, "What is it you're so afraid I'll do?" Then I held his pen for him, and he replied instantly with a candor that has kept me from truly despising him.

14   "Fail," he wrote back.

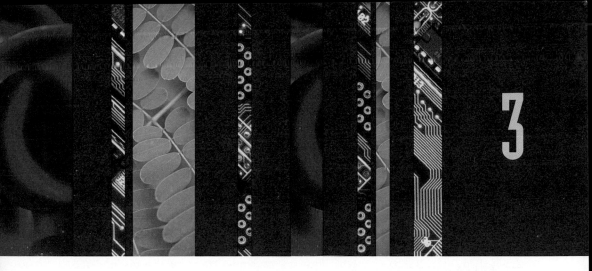

Writing and Rewriting

Once you have a preliminary thesis and outline, you are ready to write your first draft. A **first draft** is your initial attempt to write your ideas in essay form. Because it is a first attempt, your first draft will be rough—and that is fine. In fact, first drafts are supposed to be rough, which is why they are often called *rough drafts*. Later, during **revising,** you can refine your writing.

WRITING YOUR FIRST DRAFT

Many writers expect too much of a first draft. They think they should be able to write one draft, "fix it up" by correcting spelling and punctuation, and be done. However, this is not the way writing usually goes. For most writers, the first draft produces raw material that requires shaping and polishing through multiple drafts. Thus, do not expect perfection; write your ideas the best way you can and be prepared to revise—more than once—after drafting.

Tips for Drafting

- **If you get stuck, move on.** Skip troublesome aspects and go on to sections that are easier to write. If you cannot think of an appropriate word, leave a blank and come back to it later. If you cannot come up with a suitable introduction, begin with your first major point and deal with your opening later. Don't be afraid to draft out of order. Just concentrate on what you *can* write and do not dwell on what you cannot.
- **Use your outline.** Your outline can be a guide and a support system. At the same time, depart from your outline if a better strategy or new idea occurs to you. Remember, inspiration is welcome no matter when it occurs.

- **Write from start to finish in one sitting.** Even if you skip parts, push through to the end to get as much raw material as possible.
- **Write the way you speak.** If you have trouble getting the words down, you may be straining for an academic style. In that case, write your draft the way you would speak it to a friend. You can polish the style later during revision.

ESSAY STRUCTURE

Essays are typically made up of an *introduction, body paragraphs,* and a *conclusion*. Think of the introduction as the beginning of your essay, the body paragraphs as the middle, and the conclusion as the end.

The Introduction

Because first impressions are important, a successful essay begins well. In general, that beginning is a one- or two-paragraph **introduction** aimed at stimulating the reader's interest and, many times, presenting the thesis. You can approach the introduction many ways, some of which are illustrated in the examples that follow. (Notice that the thesis, underlined in these examples, appears as the last sentence of each introduction. Student writers often find this placement convenient. However, as explained on page 46, the thesis can appear elsewhere.)

TELL A STORY (USE NARRATION)
The new kid walked into fourth-period English with his head down. He handed a slip to Mrs. Kuhlins, who announced, "Frankie is our new student, class. I trust that you will make him welcome." With that, Frankie brushed a stray hair out of his eyes and shuffled to a seat in the back. His clothes were hopelessly out of date, and his hair was a mess. But as he passed my desk, our eyes met, and I saw something there. <u>At that moment, I knew there was something special about this new kid.</u>

ESTABLISH YOURSELF AS SOMEONE KNOWLEDGEABLE ABOUT THE SUBJECT
When I was six, I joined a T-ball league and spent a glorious summer at third base. When I was ten, I began playing intramural basketball and learned the pleasures of rebounding and making foul shots. In junior high school, I began running middle distances for the track team and learned the joy of crossing the finish line in one last burst of speed. In high school, I lettered in three sports. <u>As a result of all these years of playing team sports, I have come to realize that there are three kinds of coaches.</u>

PROVIDE HELPFUL BACKGROUND INFORMATION
In 2001, President George W. Bush's education plan, dubbed "No Child Left Behind," created new federal guidelines for teachers, schools, and students. In particular, the plan emphasized school accountability

and penalties for schools that did not help its students achieve specific standards. One of the most immediate effects of "No Child Left Behind" was an increase in testing of students and evaluation of teachers. Today, educators and politicians are divided on the success of the plan. They do, however, agree on one point: <u>The testing program should be more flexible.</u>

EXPLAIN WHY YOUR TOPIC IS IMPORTANT

If you are planning to buy a used car, you can make a very costly mistake. <u>For this reason, you should know what to look for when you examine and test drive an automobile.</u>

DESCRIBE SOMETHING

His belly swelled over his belt line and cascaded toward the bony knees that poked out between the white knee socks and navy blue polyester stretch shorts. His face was twisted into a permanent scowl, and his eyes squinted against the sun until they formed slits. To call roll, he barked each boy's name and checked it off on the clipboard that was never more than arm's reach away. <u>I was only five minutes into seventh-grade gym, but I could tell Mr. Winnikee deserved his reputation as the gym teacher from hell.</u>

DEFINE SOMETHING

A grandmother is supposed to be a white-haired, chubby woman who rolls her stockings below the knees and spends her days knitting scarves and baking cookies for her grandchildren. <u>However, someone forgot to tell my mother's mother all this because, believe me, she is not the typical grandmother.</u>

USE AN INTERESTING OR PERTINENT QUOTATION

Last week at his press conference, the governor said, "It is with regret that I announce a 20 percent cut in subsidies for higher education. I believe, however, that this cut is the least painful way to balance the state budget." <u>The governor is wrong: these cuts will have a catastrophic effect on the people of this state.</u>

Note: Avoid quotations such as "The early bird gets the worm" or "Better late than never." These are clichés more likely to bore than interest a reader.

Do not limit yourself to the approaches explained above, as they are just some common strategies. Additional approaches are given in Chapters 4 through 11, and you will likely come up with your own approaches. Furthermore, when you are writing in different disciplines or in the workplace, specific conventions may apply for introductions. For example, a report for your boss presenting a solution to a personnel problem would likely open with a description of the problem and then move on to your explanation of the solution. In papers for science classes, you may be expected to open with a review of the relevant research on your topic. In papers for business classes, you may be expected to open with your thesis. Always investigate the conventions for the field in which you are writing.

Body Paragraphs

The **body paragraphs,** which form the middle of an essay, prove or explain your thesis. For that reason, you cannot overestimate the importance of body paragraphs because they are the heart of your essay.

Each body paragraph has two parts. One part expresses the paragraph's main idea, the point the paragraph will develop to help support or explain the thesis. That part is the **topic sentence,** which can be specifically stated or strongly implied. The second part includes all the points you make to support, explain, or clarify the topic sentence. Those are the **supporting details.**

The following body paragraph, taken from the final version of Jeff's essay, illustrates these two parts.

Topic sentence (gives main idea of paragraph)

Supporting details (back up the topic sentence by showing it is true)

[Another source of deception is the advertising industry.] Advertisers bombard us every day with powerful male athletes endorsing products. Men are enticed to buy the products because they are led to believe they will be similarly powerful if they do. At one time, Michael Jordan, in all his athletic, superhero grandeur, seduced us into buying Nikes. Now that torch has been passed to the latest basketball phenomenon, LeBron James. Superstars from many sports, including Lance Armstrong, Tiger Woods, and Derek Jeter make us want the shoes with the swoosh, but even more, they make males long for their ability, acclaim, and lifestyles. We buy the shoes hoping to be more like the athletes we envy and then feel inferior because we don't achieve athletic superstardom or any of its trappings. Jason Giambi and Jeff Gordon may have sold a lot of Pepsi, but they also sold the notion that the ideal male has the strength and physique to hit a baseball out of the park or drive a race car at 100 m.p.h. Most males can't do that, so we feel inferior, less than the ideal. Advertising sends two messages: You should buy this product because this man should be your idol, and if you want to be a "real man," you should have the athletic prowess, physique, and other characteristics of a sports star.

In a successful essay, body paragraphs have *adequate supporting detail,* and they have *relevant supporting detail.* These points are discussed next.

Adequate Supporting Detail

You cannot expect your reader to believe what you say just because you say it. You must explain and prove your points convincingly. To do so, think of your thesis and each of your topic sentences as a **generalization,** a broad statement that asserts that something is true in most cases or in every case. To have *adequate supporting detail,* you must back up every generalization, including your thesis and every topic sentence, with enough detail to prove or explain it to your reader's satisfaction.

If, for instance, you write that your roommate is a practical joker, you have made a generalization. You then must prove that generalization with examples of your roommate's practical jokes. If you say that Chez Paris is the most beautiful restaurant in town, you are making a generalization and must support it with descriptive details, showing why you find it beautiful. If you say that schoolchildren should not be grouped by ability because such grouping discourages achievement, you must explain that generalization by showing how grouping by ability discourages achievement. A good way to remember the need to provide adequate detail is to remind yourself that a writer must "show and not just tell." You can show and not just tell if you first state a generalization, and then go on to give specific points to prove or support that generalization.

To appreciate the need to show and not just tell, and to see how a writer can move from the general to the specific, contrast the following two drafts. Draft A does not support generalizations, but draft B does—by moving from the general to the specific. The specific points are underscored.

DRAFT A

Dr. Garcia is a dedicated teacher. She is concerned about students and always willing to give a struggling young scholar extra attention. In addition, she takes pains to include everyone in class discussions, even the shy students who ordinarily do not participate. Particularly impressive is the personal interest she takes in each of her students. No wonder her class is always one of the first to fill up every semester.

DRAFT B

Dr. Garcia is a dedicated teacher. She is concerned about students and always willing to give a struggling young scholar extra attention. Last week, for example, two students were having trouble finding topics for their research papers, so Dr. Garcia met them at the library and helped them explore the possibilities. In addition, she takes pains to include everyone in class discussions, even the shy students who ordinarily do not participate. One way she does this is to ask people their opinions on subjects under discussion. That way, they do not have to worry about giving a wrong answer. Another way she brings students into discussions is to plan group work so students can talk to each other in more comfortable, smaller groups.

Particularly impressive is the personal interest Dr. Garcia takes in each of her students. Everyone writes a journal, and from the journals Dr. Garcia learns about her students' interests, successes, problems, and family life. Because she comes to know her students so well, she can talk to them about things important to them, which creates a bond between student and teacher. As a result, all her students come to understand that Dr. Garcia cares about them. No wonder her class is always one of the first to fill up every semester.

Relevant Supporting Detail

Supporting details must be *relevant,* which means they must be clearly related to the thesis. Most readers will grow annoyed when details are not related to the matter at hand. If you want to argue for the elimination of the physical education requirement at your school, you would not mention that it would also be a good idea to eliminate the foreign language requirement. When you read the following draft, you will notice the distraction created by one sentence that presents irrelevant detail.

> Many universities are altering their teacher education curricula to require prospective teachers to get into the classroom as soon as possible, even in the freshman year. These future teachers observe, tutor, and in general get the feel of a teacher's responsibilities. The plan is a good one because students can decide early on if they are suited to teaching and change their majors if necessary. In the more traditional curriculum, an education major waits until the junior or senior year to get into the classroom, when it can be too late to change majors without serious inconvenience and expense. Many students in all programs change majors and problems are to be expected. Certainly it makes sense to move prospective teachers into the classroom as early as possible, so the plan should catch on.

You probably found the next to last sentence annoying and distracting because it is not related closely enough to the matter at hand. To avoid such irrelevant detail in your own writing, outline carefully to be sure everything you write is related to the thesis.

Using the Patterns of Development to Convey Supporting Details

Your supporting details can come from your own experience and observation, as well as from what you learn in the classroom and as a result of reading, watching television, listening to the radio, or surfing the Internet. If necessary and appropriate, you can use facts, statistics, and opinions of experts, some of which you may find in this book and some of which you can research in the library and on the Internet. If you do use such material, be sure to check Chapter 14 for information on paraphrasing, quoting, and documenting source material. In addition, Chapter 1 offers advice for summarizing and synthesizing ideas from sources.

Most of the rest of this book explains various forms your supporting details can take. These forms, called *patterns of development,* are description, narration, exemplification, process analysis, comparison-contrast, cause-and-effect analysis, definition, and classification-division. You can use these patterns—alone or in combination—to organize and present your supporting details.

Each pattern of development is treated in its own chapter; however, the inside front cover of this book also gives a brief explanation of each pattern.

Take a look now at that information and refer to it whenever a particular pattern is mentioned and you are unsure of its nature.

So you can see how the patterns of development can help you prove your thesis and achieve your purpose, here are examples of how each pattern could support the thesis used earlier in the chapter, that Dr. Garcia is a dedicated teacher.

DESCRIPTION	give details that show how Dr. Garcia looks and acts
NARRATION	tell a story about a time Dr. Garcia helped a student
EXEMPLIFICATION	give examples of ways Dr. Garcia shows interest in students
PROCESS ANALYSIS	explain Dr. Garcia's process for using groups to help students learn
COMPARISON-CONTRAST	compare and/or contrast Dr. Garcia with other teachers to show how good she is
CAUSE-AND-EFFECT ANALYSIS	explain the effects of one or more of Dr. Garcia's teaching methods
DEFINITION	define a "good teacher" and show how Dr. Garcia conforms to that definition
CLASSIFICATION-DIVISION	classify all the ways Dr. Garcia helps students

You would not use all these patterns in a single essay, but they do provide options to consider as you develop your supporting details.

Combining the Patterns of Development

To achieve their purpose and meet their readers' needs, writers sometimes use a single pattern of development. Frequently, though, they combine two or more patterns. Essays with multiple patterns often are developed by a dominant pattern with a few paragraphs organized by one or more other patterns. Sometimes, multiple patterns are combined in roughly equal amounts. In the next chapters, you will read both essays that rely primarily on a single pattern and ones that combine multiple patterns to achieve their purpose. In addition, Chapter 13 focuses solely on essays that combine patterns. In your own writing, your purpose and audience will determine whether you use one or more patterns. To see how patterns can be combined in a single paragraph, read again this excerpt from the final version of Jeff's essay and notice the use of both exemplification and cause-and-effect analysis.

Another source of deception is the advertising industry. Advertisers bombard us every day with powerful male athletes endorsing products. Men are enticed to buy the products because they are led to believe they will be similarly powerful if they do. At one time, Michael Jordan, in all his athletic, superhero grandeur, seduced us into buying Nikes. Now that torch

Cause-and-effect analysis Advertisers cause males to envy sports superstars, a feeling that leads males to buy the products athletes endorse and ultimately, to feel inferior.

Exemplification James, Jeter, Woods, are examples of athletes who endorse products and make males feel inferior. Nike shoes and Pepsi are examples of products advertised.

has been passed to the latest basketball phenomenon, LeBron James. Superstars from many sports, including Lance Armstrong, Tiger Woods, and Derek Jeter make us want the shoes with the swoosh, but even more, they make males long for their ability, acclaim, and lifestyles. We buy the shoes hoping to be more like the athletes we envy and then feel inferior because we don't achieve athletic superstardom or any of its trappings. Jason Giambi and Jeff Gordon may have sold a lot of Pepsi, but they also sold the notion that the ideal male has the strength and physique to hit a baseball out of the park or drive a race car at 100 m.p.h. Most males can't do that, so we feel inferior, less than the ideal. Advertising sends two messages: You should buy this product because this man should be your idol, and if you want to be a "real man," you should have the athletic prowess, physique, and other characteristics of a sports star.

---

www.mhhe.com/patterns

For more help with writing using rhetorical patterns, click on
Writing > Paragraph Patterns

Organizing Body Paragraphs

Each body paragraph typically focuses on one main idea, to support or explain the thesis. (A main idea that requires considerable explanation can be the focus of more than one body paragraph.) When the main idea of a body paragraph is written rather than implied, it is expressed in a topic sentence. The **topic sentence** is a generalization that must be developed with adequate, relevant supporting details.

You may find it easiest to compose body paragraphs that begin with a topic sentence followed by the supporting details meant to explain or prove the idea in that topic sentence. If you were writing an essay with the thesis "Dr. Garcia is a dedicated teacher," for example, your essay might have three body paragraphs, each beginning with a version of one of these topic sentences:

Dr. Garcia makes sure every student is relaxed in class.

Dr. Garcia is always willing to give students extra help.

Dr. Garcia takes a personal interest in each of her students.

Notice that each of these topic sentences is relevant to the thesis. Similarly, the supporting details in each body paragraph should be relevant to the topic sentence of that paragraph. Thus, the first body paragraph would include only details about helping students relax, the second only details about providing students with extra help, and the third only details about taking a personal interest in students.

Coherence

To have **coherence,** the supporting details in your body paragraphs, and the body paragraphs themselves, must connect to each other in ways your reader can easily understand and follow. Four strategies can help you achieve coherence.

Use Transitional Words and Phrases

These words and phrases signal the relationship between ideas. The chart that follows lists and illustrates transitions.

Transition Chart

RELATIONSHIP	TRANSITIONS	EXAMPLE
addition	also, and, too, in addition, furthermore, first, further	The apartment has all the features I want. In addition, the rent is low.
time	now, then, before, after, earlier, later, soon, finally, first, next	First, measure the flour. Then add it to the butter and eggs.
space	near, next to, away from, beside, inside, on the left, on the right, along-side, behind	Go two blocks west to the light. On the right is the park.
comparison	similarly, likewise, in the same way, in like manner	The mayor will recommend some layoffs. Similarly, she will not approve any new hirings.
contrast	however, in contrast, but, still, on the contrary, neverthe-less, yet	The House will pass the jobs bill. However, the Senate will vote it down.
cause and effect	since, because, so, as a result, consequently, thus, therefore, hence	Because half the students are sick with the flu, school will be closed.
emphasis	indeed, in fact, surely, certainly, without a doubt	Everyone enjoys Dr. Hill's class. In fact, it is always the first to close.
illustration	for example, for instance, specifically, in particular	Counting fat grams is a good way to diet. Dana, for example, lost a pound a week that way.
summary or clarification	in summary, in conclusion, in brief, in short, in other words, all in all	The President has vetoed the spending bill. In short, he will not raise taxes.

Repeat Words or Ideas

Repeating key words or ideas can help a writer achieve coherence and improve the flow of writing. Here are two examples:

REPEATING A WORD	Chronic fatigue <u>syndrome</u> is becoming more widely recognized in the medical community and therefore more frequently diagnosed. This <u>syndrome</u> is so debilitating that its sufferers often cannot work.
REPEATING AN IDEA	<u>A group of volunteer parents is now working cooperatively with school authorities</u> to introduce more extracurricular activities into the schools and to begin a drug awareness program. <u>These worthy efforts</u> will no doubt improve the quality of education in our township.

Use Synonyms

Another way to achieve coherence is to use a synonym for a word or idea mentioned earlier, as in these two sentences:

The workers expressed their <u>dissatisfaction</u> with management's latest wage offer. Their <u>discontent</u> may well lead to a strike.

Use Sentences that Look Backward and Forward

You can make an effective transition from one paragraph to another—and thereby achieve coherence—by beginning with a sentence that looks back to something in the previous paragraph and forward to an idea in the one coming up. Assume, for example, that you have just written a paragraph about the fact that Dr. Garcia gives students extra help, and you are about to write a paragraph about how she makes students feel comfortable in class. You could write one of these sentences to connect the two paragraphs.

looking back   looking forward

[In addition to giving students extra help,] [Dr. Garcia always makes them feel comfortable in class.]

looking back

[Dr. Garcia does more than provide extra help to those in need;]

looking forward

[she also makes sure that everyone feels comfortable in class.]

---

www.mhhe.com/patterns

For more help with paragraph coherence, click on

Writing > Coherence

When to Paragraph

Typically, writers begin a new body paragraph each time they move to a new main idea to support the thesis. However, if you have a great deal to say about one point, you can break up the discussion into two or more paragraphs. If you have a point that deserves special emphasis, you can place it in its own paragraph, or if you have an extended example or narration (a story), you can set it off by placing it in its own paragraph.

Tone

Speakers can use tone of voice to help convey feelings and meaning. Similarly, writers can establish a *tone* for their writing. **Tone** is the writer's attitude or feelings toward the reader or the subject. The tone can be angry, sarcastic, serious, preachy, argumentative, conciliatory, hurtful, playful, earnest, scornful, hostile, enthusiastic, neutral, and so forth.

Most often, tone is established by the words you choose to convey supporting details. Notice, for example, how word choice creates the different tones in the following sentences on the same subject.

ANGRY AND JUDGMENTAL TONE	Many so-called citizens who are too tight-fisted to invest in the future of our children refuse to vote for the school levy.
NEUTRAL TONE	A significant number of citizens hesitate to pass the school levy and thereby increase their taxes.

www.mhhe.com/patterns

For more help with tone, click on
Editing > Word Choice

Using Visual Material for Support

You are accustomed to encountering visual material in your reading. Newspapers and magazines, textbooks, Web pages, journal articles, reports at work—much of what you read is accompanied by photos, charts, graphs, illustrations, and other images. In Chapter 1, you learned that this visual material needs to be "read" critically, in the same way you read written text.

Technological advances make it so much easier for you to include visual material in your writing. With the Internet, you can locate and import images; with digital photography, you can insert photos into documents; and with computer programs, you can create graphs from data you supply. Before you include visual materials, however, ask your instructor whether you may use them in your submissions. If yes, follow your instructor's guidelines. In addition, keep these points in mind:

- **Use images *only* when they help explain, illustrate, or prove a point.** Visual material should support the text, not be a substitute for it. Never use visual material to pad a piece of writing that is too short. But do select visuals if they can amplify or complement what you have written.
- **Consider your audience and purpose.** Make sure the visuals you select suit your audience and help fulfill your purpose. A complicated

Using Images in Classroom Writing

If you have trouble selecting or integrating images into your writing, consider this advice:

- Select or create your visual material only after writing your first draft. That way, you can be certain this material supplements the written text, fulfills your writing purpose, and meets the needs of your audience.

- Place the visual as close as possible to the material it supports. If design and layout considerations prevent that, add a cross-reference for the reader, such as: "The chart on page 3 shows how different people will benefit from the tax cut."

- If you use an image from another source, provide proper credit. Refer to Chapter 14 for information on evaluating and documenting source materials.

diagram explaining how plants turn carbon dioxide into oxygen might confuse a ten-year-old, but a simple flow chart might work perfectly. If you import visual material from another source, remember that it was developed for a different writer's purpose and audience, so evaluate it carefully. Its tone must be in keeping with your tone. A humorous cartoon may not be appropriate for a research paper examining spousal abuse, but a bar graph showing the frequency of spousal abuse by age group may be informative.

- **Consider the quality of the visual.** An image of poor quality or a graph that is difficult to decipher will detract from your writing. Select or prepare visual material that is attractive, easy to read, and easy to understand. Make sure the color, font, spacing, and other features are appropriate for your paper.

- **Write the caption carefully.** Most images require captions. Take this opportunity to guide your reader's interpretation. Provide the reader background information about the creator of the image or the purpose for which it was created. Establish the authority or reliability of the image by indicating its source and/or date. See the caption for the Lewis Hine photograph in Chapter 1 (p. 24) for an example of the way caption information can guide interpretation.

The Conclusion

The **conclusion,** the last sentences or paragraph that provides closure, is an important part of a successful essay because it influences the reader's final, lasting impression. No matter how strong your introduction and body paragraphs are, if your ending is weak, your reader will come away from the essay feeling let down.

Many approaches for concluding an essay are possible. If your essay is long, with many ideas, you can summarize your main points as a helpful reminder to your reader. However, if your essay is brief and the ideas are easily remembered, summarizing is not a good idea because it will bore rather than help a reader.

Repeating the thesis or another important idea is an effective way to conclude an essay when the repetition provides emphasis or dramatic effect. Be careful, though. The repetition will bore a reader if it fails to provide drama or emphasis. Sometimes, writers delay the thesis until the conclusion because they want to build up to it.

Another common technique is to introduce a new but related idea in the conclusion. The idea must be clearly related to the rest of the essay to avoid dismaying the reader with new material that seems unconnected to the topic. Finally, writers often craft effective conclusions by combining approaches.

Other approaches to the conclusion are illustrated below. In addition, the introductory Sections in Chapters 4 through 11 suggest ways to handle conclusions.

DRAW A CONCLUSION FROM THE INFORMATION IN THE ESSAY (THIS ILLUSTRATION IS FROM AN ESSAY ABOUT THE EFFECTS OF DIVORCE.)

Recent evidence suggests that the children of divorced parents suffer a number of difficulties, regardless of their age at the time of the divorce. For this reason, parents who stay together "for the sake of the children" may be doing the right thing.

PRESENT THE FINAL, MOST IMPORTANT POINT (THIS ILLUSTRATION IS FROM AN ESSAY ARGUING AGAINST CENSORSHIP.)

The most compelling reason to oppose censorship is the threat it poses to our First Amendment rights. Once we limit free speech, we establish a climate that permits the chipping away at our freedoms until our rights are severely curtailed.

OFFER A SOLUTION TO A PROBLEM MENTIONED IN THE ESSAY (THIS ILLUSTRATION IS FROM AN ESSAY THAT EXPLAINS PROBLEMS ASSOCIATED WITH COLLEGE ATHLETICS.)

College athletics will remain controversial until we reform the system dramatically. Perhaps the most honest thing to do is to hire the athletes to play and pay them salaries. If they want to use their paychecks to pay for tuition, fine. If not, they can just be university employees. The fans will still turn out to see the teams, regardless of whether the players are student athletes or professional athletes.

CALL YOUR READERS TO ACTION (THIS ILLUSTRATION IS FROM AN ESSAY ARGUING FOR INCREASING THE SALARY OF TEACHERS.)

To improve the quality of education, we must increase teachers' salaries to make them compatible with those in business and industry. Only then will we attract the best people to the profession. Thus, we must support school levies that fund pay increases and lobby boards of education to do whatever it takes to increase teachers' salaries.

Drafting Introductions and Conclusions

If you have trouble drafting your introduction keep it short. Begin with your preliminary thesis and move on. During revising, you can add details to stimulate interest. Similarly, an effective conclusion can be brief, even one or two sentences. If you are stuck for a closing, end with your final point and improve the conclusion during revision, if necessary.

www.mhhe.com/patterns

For more help with writing introductions and conclusions,

Writing > Introductions
Writing > Conclusions

LOOK TO THE FUTURE (THIS ILLUSTRATION IS FROM AN ESSAY EXPLAINING THE EFFECTS OF THE ROUTE 8 BYPASS.)

Once the Route 8 bypass is built, our area will become a major crossroads. In ten years, our economy will be flourishing from the business and commerce that will result from our strategic location, and our tax base will broaden to the benefit of our schools and infrastructure.

LEAVE YOUR READER WITH A FINAL IMPRESSION (THIS ILLUSTRATION IS FROM AN ESSAY ON DISCRIMINATION AGAINST OVERWEIGHT PEOPLE.)

Our society discriminates against overweight people, and it's a shame. Many capable people never get a chance to show what they can do because of our narrow-mindedness.

The Title

Although the title is the first thing a reader sees, many people compose it last because a good title often suggests itself after the essay is written. There are many ways to approach the title. Sometimes a clever or funny title is a good way to pique your reader's interest. However, not everyone can be clever or funny, so it is fine to write a title that suggests the content of the essay, like "What Is Poverty?" which is in this book. Sometimes an intriguing title like "The Watcher at the Gates" (which also appears in this book) can stimulate a reader's interest. Avoid a title that presents your thesis. If your title is "Capital Punishment Is Inhumane," you will tip your hand too soon. Also, avoid very broad titles that do not suggest your content. "Television" is too broad, but "The Effects of Television Violence" is fine.

VISUALIZING AN ESSAY

The essay structure explained in this chapter is not the only one—or even the best one in all circumstances—and many of the essays in this text will illustrate departures from this structure. Nonetheless, this structure is a very serviceable one, so you can use it in many writing situations. To review the structure and help you visualize it, examine this graphic representation.

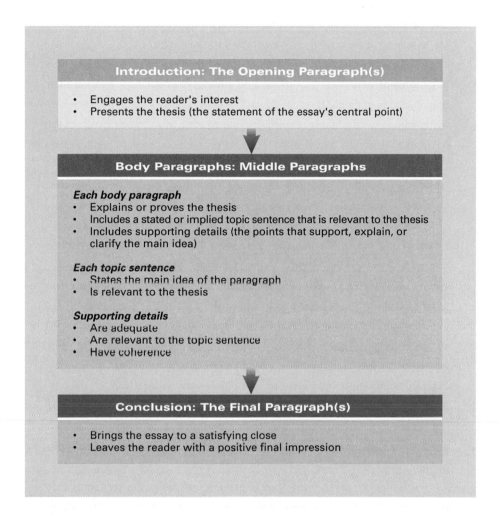

Introduction: The Opening Paragraph(s)

- Engages the reader's interest
- Presents the thesis (the statement of the essay's central point)

Body Paragraphs: Middle Paragraphs

Each body paragraph
- Explains or proves the thesis
- Includes a stated or implied topic sentence that is relevant to the thesis
- Includes supporting details (the points that support, explain, or clarify the main idea)

Each topic sentence
- States the main idea of the paragraph
- Is relevant to the thesis

Supporting details
- Are adequate
- Are relevant to the topic sentence
- Have coherence

Conclusion: The Final Paragraph(s)

- Brings the essay to a satisfying close
- Leaves the reader with a positive final impression

An Essay in Progress: Drafting

Using his informal outline as a guide (see page 54), Jeff wrote the first draft that appears on the next page. You will notice that Jeff departed from his outline at times, which is fine. Writers should always be open to new ideas and ways of organizing their material. Knowing that he would polish the draft during revision, Jeff concentrated on writing his ideas down as best he could without laboring over anything. Notice that Jeff realized some problems while drafting and wrote reminders to himself in brackets about revisions to make.

The Not-So-Ideal Ideal Male

We, the people of the United States of America, are being bullied, tricked, 1
and led astray by products of our own culture. We are being fed falsehoods,
and we digest them happily, but we are being poisoned. Our own culture—our
own heritage and popular society—is feeding us misinformation; we are being
led to believe in an absurd concept of the ideal male. [fix intro.]

The root of the inappropriateness of this idealization lies in the nature 2
of its main perpetuators—the movie and advertising industries, and folktales
and childhood stories. The most obvious of these sources is the movie industry, which produces totally unrealistic plots typically having (perhaps subtly,
but still) superhuman males as heroes. We watch these movies and feel that
this is what our men are supposed to be like. [give examples] The cartoon-
ish action movies are generally the most extreme, and these are targeted at
the most vulnerable audience—teenage boys who are ready to become men.
They see these heroes on the screen and see visions of themselves in ten
years. This is tragic. An equally prevalent but less glaring source of deception is the advertising industry. They bombard us every day with quick
scenes of powerful, intimidating male atheletes endorsing their products.
[give examples] The message is this: you should buy this product because
this man should be your idol. Physical dominance is put in the spotlight
as much as the product. A third projector of this concept comes from our
heritage, and that is its problem. Folktales and childhood stories are usually
legends that have been passed down through generations of people.
Nobody even remembers how long ago they were created. That is precisely
the trouble. Triumphant men like Robin Hood originated in an entirely different society; they are heroes of the distant past, and they do not befit the
present.

The problem these unsuitable sources of the ideal male present is that 3
their admired and discouraged qualities are out of place. In action movies
and folk tales, the hero wins the battle because his instincts are flawless.
He knows just where every attacker will be in a battle, and he knows by
sight which fair maiden will be faithful to him. But in the real world today,
how often does a man fend off a small mob in hand-to-hand combat or
choose his wife from a lineup of beautiful princesses? To apply the power
of understatement—rarely. In our highly complex, and civilized, society, the
considered decision is more important then the instinctive or rash one. Also,
the men of advertising, movies, and legends are loners. Their great strength

stems from the fact that they need no one else to help them accomplish their goals. Again, this clashes with modern society. Our world is becoming increasingly cooperative on all levels—from interpersonal to international. A realistic man knows that the help of others is esential in achieving his dream.

4   Finally, the men these sources give us often are deplorable in their relations to women. Many times the entire purpose of the movie, advertisement, or tale is for the hero to "get" the woman. He is almost invariably her protector, savior, or unrepellable lover. In a world in which possibly the characteristic of modern history is the rise of women nearer and nearer to equality, how can the ideal man have this type of relationship with women? The answer is simple: he is not the ideal man.

Drafting

EXERCISE 3.1

1. Refer to the thesis statements and supporting details you used for numbers 2 and 3 of Exercise 2.4 on page 55. For each thesis and set of supporting details, do the following:

    a. Decide on a possible approach to the introduction and explain why the approach is a good one.

    b. Write two topic sentences that could open two body paragraphs.

    c. Decide on a possible approach to the conclusion and explain why the approach is a good one.

2. Using the material you have from number 4 of Exercise 2.4 (and adding and deleting ideas as you wish), write a first draft.

REVISING YOUR DRAFT

Revising is shaping and refining your draft until it is ready for your reader. Most experienced writers will tell you that revising is the heart of their writing processes and that it is time-consuming. Unfortunately, many inexperienced writers believe that revision simply involves changing a few words, adding a comma here and there, and checking spellings. In truth, when you revise you should completely rethink your essay to be sure everything in it suits your purpose, audience, and role. To that end, revision requires you to consider the aspects of your draft covered in the following checklist and make changes as necessary. As you look over the checklist, you can tell that revision takes in quite a bit. Thus, you will often write multiple drafts until you are satisfied that your essay is reader-ready. And because you have so much to consider, the first rule of revision is *be sure to allow plenty of time.*

Revision Checklist

FOR YOUR THESIS (see page 45), be sure:

1. ____ Your essay has a clearly stated or strongly implied thesis.
2. ____ Your thesis is not a statement of fact.
3. ____ Your thesis can be treated in a manageable length.
4. ____ Your thesis is not a formal announcement and that it is expressed in specific language.
5. ____ Your thesis allows you to achieve your purpose and is geared toward your reader's traits and needs.
6. ____ Your thesis is compatible with your role.

FOR YOUR INTRODUCTION (see page 62), be sure:

1. ____ Your introduction makes a good first impression.
2. ____ Your introduction is suited to your purpose, audience, and role.

FOR YOUR SUPPORTING DETAILS (see page 64), be sure:

1. ____ All your details are suited to your purpose, audience, and role.
2. ____ Your details are in a logical order and arranged in body paragraphs.
3. ____ Each body paragraph has a clearly stated or strongly implied topic sentence.
4. ____ All your details are relevant to the thesis and appropriate topic sentence.
5. ____ You have enough details to support the thesis and each topic sentence.
6. ____ Transitions move the reader smoothly from idea to idea and from paragraph to paragraph.
7. ____ You avoid errors in logic (p. 5).

FOR YOUR CONCLUSION (see page 72):

8. ____ Your essay comes to a satisfying finish.
9. ____ Your conclusion is appropriate to your purpose, audience, and role.

FOR EFFECTIVE EXPRESSION, be sure:

1. ____ Unnecessary words are eliminated.
2. ____ All your ideas are clearly expressed.
3. ____ Specific words are substituted for vague ones.
4. ____ Words are compatible with your tone.
5. ____ Tired expressions (clichés) such as "cold as ice" are rewritten.
6. ____ Choppy or singsong prose is eliminated.

FOR YOUR TITLE (see page 74), be sure:

1. ____ Your title suggests the content of the essay without being too broad.
2. ____ Your thesis is not given in the title.

Tips for Revising

- **Allow plenty of time** because revising is time-consuming. Pace your work so you will have a period of several days to revise.
- **Remember your writing context.** Every evaluation of your draft and every change you make should be done with your audience, purpose, and role in mind. However, because idea generation is ongoing, you may decide to change some aspect of the context as you revise.
- **Revise in stages** by considering one or two of the revision concerns at a time. (Use the revision checklist to be sure you consider everything.) As an alternative, revise one or two paragraphs at a time. Be sure to take a break whenever you get tired.
- **Return to idea generation or adjust your thesis, if necessary.** If you have trouble coming up with adequate detail, try one of the idea generation techniques covered on pages 37–44 to develop more material. If that does not work, reconsider your thesis. Should you broaden it or refocus it to have enough to say?
- **Revise typed copy** because you are less likely to overlook problems in type than in your own handwriting or on the computer screen.
- **Avoid editing,** which comes later. If you deal with spelling, grammar, punctuation, and such, you will be distracted and unable to focus on revision concerns.
- **In Microsoft Word, use Track Changes.** Located on the dropdown "Tools" menu on your toolbar, Track Changes allows you to revise while preserving the original draft. Your changes will not become permanent until and unless you want them to, so you can easily return to and restore all or part of your earlier work.

www.mhhe.com/patterns

For more help with revising using your computer, click on
Writing > Using Computers

Revising with Peer Review

Because feedback can be so helpful to writers, you should always consider asking other people to read your drafts, react, and suggest changes. In fact, your instructor may arrange for you and your classmates to exchange drafts. When you find readers on your own, be sure to use *reliable readers,* people who know the qualities of effective writing and who will not hesitate to offer constructive criticism. It makes no sense to ask a friend for help if that friend has not yet taken a writing course, nor is it useful to ask people who always hesitate to tell you what they really think. Also, use more than one reader, so you have the advantage of multiple perspectives and so you can look for consensus. Remember, though, that you have the final say. Rather than accepting everything your readers offer, consider their reactions critically and revise accordingly.

If you have particular concerns about your draft, you can ask your readers to read and react just to those concerns. Ask them to tell you what they think of your introduction, help you think of another example to support a point in paragraph 4, help you clarify an idea, and so forth. Otherwise, ask your readers to use the revision checklist on page 78 as a guide to reacting to your draft.

When readers help you, always return the favor by offering to react to *their* drafts. When it is your turn to respond, follow these guidelines.

- **Comment on strengths and weaknesses.** Offering praise alone makes a writer feel good but does little to help that writer improve a draft. Offering criticism alone is demoralizing.
- **Put your responses in writing.** That way, the writer has a record to refer to. (If you are given an electronic copy of a draft and you use Microsoft Word, you can insert comments using the Comment feature of the program, located in the drop down "Insert" menu on the toolbar.)
- **Be specific.** Rather than say, "Paragraph 2 is unclear," write "In paragraph 2, I do not understand why you say that men experience discrimination in the workplace."
- **Offer suggestions.** When you comment on a weakness, suggest a revision strategy, like this: "If you could give an example of discrimination against males in the workplace, I would be able to accept your point more readily."

www.mhhe.com/patterns

For more help with revising, click on
Writing > Drafting and Revising

An Essay in Progress: Writing a Second Draft

Jeff knew some of the changes needed in his first draft and indicated them on the draft in brackets. (See pages 76–77.) Before revising to compose a second draft, Jeff reread his first draft and considered his bracketed comments. In addition, he sought responses from two classmates and his teacher. He was reassured to discover that his readers' reactions to the draft were very similar to his own. As a result, he felt confident in his ability to judge his writing accurately. The teacher's response, which helped guide Jeff's revision, appears here.

Jeff,

Your draft held my interest every step of the way. I was particularly taken by the energy in your writing. You feel very strongly about your topic. You even seem passionate about it. Your energy and your honest emotions really propelled me forward, and I am hoping you can retain that spirit in your revision. I'd take a careful look at the introduction, though. It's a place where your emotion creates a problem. The introduction makes you seem very angry, even a bit out of control, so it is a little off-putting, especially in the opening. Remember, you want your reader to see you as a reasonable, thoughtful person. Anger is fine, but you don't want to appear more emotional than thoughtful. You indicate that you want to work on your intro; I think softening the angry tone will help considerably.

Your thesis is very clear, so I have no trouble determining your focus, and you make excellent points in paragraph 2. These points can go a long way to support your thesis, but right now you have too many main ideas in one paragraph (movies, advertising, and folktales and stories). You noted yourself that you need specific examples, and I agree. Perhaps if you give each of your main points its own body paragraph, you could more easily incorporate your examples.

You state important ideas in your last body paragraph. I was particularly intrigued by your contrast of the loner not being well adapted to today's cooperative environment—very astute. In fact, all of your points are interesting and significant.

I look forward to your revision. One last thing, though: Your last paragraph brings up your final points and is rather like a body paragraph. Do you feel the need for a separate conclusion? Frankly, I'm not sure because your final sentence provides some closure. Think about it and maybe get some other opinions.

Jeff's Second Draft

1   On the movie screen, characters played by actors like Bruce Willis, Arnold Schwarzenegger, Tom Cruise, and Pierce Brosnan are men of action and resolve. They depict the ideal male that men strive to be but can never achieve. However, the truth is that men are being tricked and led astray by these characterizations. We are being led to believe in an absurd image of the ideal male, not just in movies, but in advertising and childhood stories.

The introduction is less angry. The thesis now indicates three of the main points to be discussed.

2   An obvious perpetrator of this idealization is the movie industry, which produces totally unrealistic plots typically having (perhaps subtly but still) superhuman males as heroes. We watch these movies and feel that this is what our men are supposed to be like. Arnold slams through walls and saves the beautiful woman from the jaws of death and The Rock does away with bad guys by singlehandedly fighting an entire

The first body paragraph now discusses only one main idea. Two examples have been added for support.

compound and throwing himself through a pillar. Granted, the cartoon-ish action movies are generally the most extreme, but these are targeted at the most vulnerable audience—teenage boys who are ready to become men. They see these heroes on the screen and see visions of themselves in ten years. This is tragic because the boys can never be what movie action heroes are.

An equally prevalent but less glaring source of deception is the advertising industry. They bombard us every day with quick scenes of pow-erful, intimidating male atheletes endorsing their products. Michael Jordan who everybody worshipped in his superathlete glory made us want Nikes and now LeBron James does the same. But at the same time the image makes males want to be an athlete like them but that can never be. Sports superstars like Derek Jeter and Jason Giambi sell products, but they sell more. Physical dominance is in the spotlight as much as the product, but how likely is it that the average viewer can attain such physical domi-nance? Advertising sends two messages. One is to buy the product, but the more harmful one is that to be a "real man" you must look and per-form like a star athelete. Once again, the male is left feeling inadequate.

A third projector of this concept comes from our heritage, and that is the source of the problem. Folktales and childhood stories are usually legends that have been passed down through generations. Triumphant men like Robin Hood, Sir Lancelot, and Davy Crockett originated in an entirely different society; they are heroes of the distant past, and they do not befit the present. As legends, they risked their lives for the under-dog, but their feats are impossible to emulate, so males exposed to these stories are made to feel inadequate.

The ideal men depicted in advertising, movies, and legends are loners. Their great strength stems from the fact that they need no one else to help them accomplish their goals. For example, the Marlboro man always rides out alone; the action hero single handedly saves the day. Again, this clashes with modern society because it leads men to wall themselves off from others. Also, our world is becoming more coopera-tive on all levels. The loner will not succeed in the workplace where col-laboration is increasingly valued.

Finally, the men these sources give us are often deplorable to women. Many times the entire purpose of the movie, advertisement, or tale is for the hero to "get" the woman. He is almost invariably her protector, savior, or unrepellable lover. In a world in which possibly the main characteristic of modern history is the rise of women to equality, how can the ideal man have this type of relationship with women? The answer is simple: he cannot because except in advertising, movies, and folktales, he is not the ideal male.

Revising the Draft

1. Read the first draft that follows and then make four suggestions you think the author should consider during revising.

   ### IS TODAY'S ATHLETE A GOOD SPORT?

   I have been playing soccer for a long time and I can see that players are playing much more violently now than they used to. Players will do anything to win, even stuff they would never consider doing off the field. I think that today's athlete is one person on the field and another person off the field.

   Players think that hurting someone is okay because it's just part of the game. My roommate, for example, is a real gentle guy until he gets on the basketball court, then he's rough and ready and violent. If he didn't play that way, the coach would keep him on the bench.

   Many players say they have to be violent to beat the other players. They don't feel they've done anything wrong as long as they win. In one of my soccer games, for example, an opposing player intentionally spiked the sweeper and cheated to get the goal.

   A lot of times, players justify violence by saying "it's only a game" and not reality. Yes, it's a game but the injuries are real and can cause a lot of problems and pain. For example, a player on my soccer team missed a month of school as a result of an opposing player who knocked him into the goal. I'm sure the player didn't think twice about the consequences of his actions.

   Unfortunately, fans love the violence. The more violence, the more cheering. They're violent in the stands, too.

   The violence must stop and players should be penalized for it. Otherwise, people will get hurt more and more.

2. Revise the draft you wrote in response to number 2 of Exercise 3.1 on page 77.

EDITING YOUR DRAFT

Editing is finding and correcting mistakes in grammar, spelling, punctuation, capitalization, and usage. Finding and eliminating such errors is important because a reader can lose confidence in a writer if the essay has many errors, and if you undermine your reader's confidence, you may fail to achieve your purpose for writing. To be efficient, do most or all of your editing after you revise. Why look for errors in sentences that you ultimately strike during revision?

Tips for Editing

- **Know the kinds of mistakes you typically make and be on the lookout for them.** For example, if spelling is a problem for you, pay particular attention to this aspect of your draft.
- **Learn the rules.** You cannot edit effectively if you do not know the rules. Buy a good handbook of grammar and usage at your college bookstore, consult it as needed, and learn the rules for matters that cause you problems.
- **Use computer grammar and spell checks with caution.** These tools are not foolproof. For example, they will not tell you whether you have substituted *here* for *hear.*
- **Trust your instincts.** If you have a feeling that something is wrong, the odds are good that a problem exists—even if you cannot give the problem a name or figure out a solution at the moment.
- **Think like your reader.** Identify the characteristics of your reader and then read your draft the way someone with those characteristics would. Think about where such a reader might need more information and where he or she might lose interest. Then revise accordingly.
- **Edit print copy.** You are less likely to overlook errors in print copy than on the computer screen. At the same time, be aware that computer-generated print material often looks so professional that you can be fooled into overlooking problems and mistakes.

www.mhhe.com/patterns

For more help with editing your work, click on
Editing
and select from the many subtopics available.

Making Revising and Editing Decisions

If you have trouble knowing what changes to make, try the following:

- **Leave your work for at least a day** to gain some objectivity about your draft. After a break, you will be better able to identify material to revise and edit.
- **Read your work aloud** to listen for problems you have overlooked visually. Be careful, though, to read exactly what is on the page, not what you intended to write.
- **Point to each word with a pen or pencil** and linger over it for a second or two. This procedure will prevent you from building the kind of speed that can lead you to overlook errors.
- **Place a ruler under each line as you edit** to block out other material and prevent it from distracting you.

TROUBLESHOOTING GUIDE

PROOFREADING THE FINAL COPY

After editing, use your computer to type your essay into the proper form for your reader. Then, check carefully for typing errors. Read very slowly, lingering over each word and punctuation mark, so you do not build up too much speed and miss something. If your instructor permits, neatly ink in corrections; otherwise, type in the correction and print a new copy.

An Essay in Progress: The Final Copy

Below is the final version of the essay that Jeff wrote in response to "Americanization Is Tough on 'Macho'" (page 11). (The notes in the margin point out some key features of the essay.) You have already viewed the idea generation (pages 41 and 45), outlining (page 54), and two of the drafts (pages 76 and 81) that preceded this final copy. Between the second draft and the final version, Jeff wrote two additional drafts in the course of revising and editing. In those drafts, he added more detail and improved his word choice.

The Not-So-Ideal Male

1   First there was Errol Flynn; then there was John Wayne; after him came Bruce Willis, Sylvester Stallone, Jean-Claude Van Damme, and Arnold Schwarzenegger. Now we have Pierce Brosnan, Tom Cruise, Russell Crowe, Denzel Washington—and the most recent entry, The Rock. These men of action and resolve are the celluloid depictions of the ideal male. They are the model that men strive for, but the goal they can never achieve. They are the men that women want but never find (off the big screen, that is). They are the reason men feel inferior. The image of these movie action heroes is one reason men feel inferior, but it is not the only reason. The truth is that we are being led to believe in an absurd image of the ideal male, and the source of this image is not just movies; it is also advertising and childhood stories.

2   An obvious contributor to the falsehood is the movie industry, which produces unrealistic plots with superhuman male heroes. Arnold (pre-governor days) slammed through brick walls and snatched the beautiful woman from the jaws of death. The Rock does away with the bad guys by singlehandedly fighting an entire compound of evil-doers and throwing himself through a support pillar. Dangling on a wire, Tom Cruise breaks into an impenetrable government agency, scales mountains of heart-stopping heights, and clings to the top of a speeding train without ever losing his cool or mussing his hair. As 007, Pierce Brosnan

The introduction engages the reader's interest by providing background information and specific examples.

The thesis presents the subject as the image of the ideal male and the writer's assertion that the image is absurd. The thesis also notes main points to be covered (movies, advertising, and childhood stories).

The topic sentence presents a generalization about the movie industry. The examples in the paragraph provide support.

From the beginning, the tone (one of strong feeling and concern) is clear.

stays similarly unruffled as he saves the world, gets the beautiful, aloof woman, and escapes from no fewer than 10 near death experiences— and that's just ten mintues after the opening credits roll. Even aging Harrison Ford performs superhuman heroics worthy of a much younger action hero, including hanging from the back of a 747 jetliner flying at top speed. We watch these movies and feel that this is what men are supposed to be like. Granted, cartoonish action movies are generally the most extreme, but they appeal to the most vulnerable audience— teenage boys. Adolescent males see in these screen heroes visions of what they should be like when they become men. The goal is, of course, unattainable, so males feel inadequate because they do not perform remarkable deeds or look like this image of The Rock in "The Scorpion King."

The Rock in *The Scorpion King* (2002; dir. Chuck Russell)

3   Another source of deception is the advertising industry. Advertisers bombard us every day with powerful male athletes endorsing products. Men are enticed to buy the products because they are led to believe they will be similarly powerful if they do. At one time, Michael Jordan, in all his athletic, superhero grandeur, seduced us into buying Nikes. Now that torch has been passed to the latest basketball phenomenon, LeBron James. Superstars from many sports, including Lance Armstrong, Tiger Woods, and Derek Jeter make us want the shoes with the swoosh, but even more, they make males long for their ability, acclaim, and lifestyles. We buy the shoes hoping to be more like the athletes we envy and then feel inferior because we don't achieve athletic superstardom or any of its trappings. Jason Giambi and Jeff Gordon may have sold a lot of Pepsi, but they also sold the notion that the ideal male has the strength and physique to hit a baseball out of the park or drive a race car at 100 m.p.h. Most males can't do that, so we feel inferior, less than the ideal. Advertising sends two messages: You should buy this product because this man should be your idol, and if you want to be a "real man," you should have the athletic prowess, physique, and other characteristics of a sports star.

4   A third perpetrator of the misconception is folktales and childhood stories, legends that have been passed down through generations. Triumphant men who confront danger and risk their lives for the underdog are everywhere in our myths, and they cause males to feel inadequate. The likes of Robin Hood, Sir Lancelot, and Davy Crockett originated in an entirely different time and society; they are heroes of the past who do not befit the present, yet their legendary (and impossible to emulate) feats shape the psyches of males. The tradition continues into more recent times, as Superman, Batman, and Spiderman fight injustice, rescue the weak, and generally contribute to the notion that real men are action figures.

5   The ideal men depicted in advertising, movies, and legends are loners. Their strength stems from the fact that they need no one to help them accomplish their goals. The Marlboro man always rides out alone; the action hero single-handedly saves the day. This fact causes problems for males who try to live up to the perceived ideal. It leads them to wall themselves off from others, depriving themselves of enjoyable, satisfying relationships. Further, our world is becoming increasingly cooperative on

"Another source of deception" provides coherence by linking the paragraph to the introduction. The topic sentence is the first sentence.

Supporting details are developed with cause-and-effect analysis and examples. The paragraph would benefit from more detail on how advertisers perpetuate the false image of the ideal male.

The topic sentence indicates that the body paragraph will focus on folktales and childhood stories. The words "a third perpetrator of the misconception" provide coherence.

Paragraph development includes specific examples. Some readers may feel the need for more details.

The topic sentence presents a generalization about the depiction of men as loners. Coherence is achieved with the words "the ideal men."

Paragraph development includes cause-and-effect analysis.

all levels—from interpersonal to international. A successful male knows that the help of others is essential to achieving his dream and that collaboration is increasingly valued in the workplace. The loner may not perform as well on the job.

The conclusion provides closure by presenting a final point and leaving the reader with a final impression. Coherence is achieved with the transition "finally."

Finally, the unfortunate image of the ideal male perpetrated by 6 advertising, movies, and myth damages relations with women. Many times the point of the movie, advertisement, or tale is that the male hero "gets" the woman. He is almost invariably her protector, savior, or unrepellable lover. In a world whose defining characteristic is the advancement of women nearer and nearer to equality, how can the ideal man have such a relationship with women? The answer is simple: he cannot. Indeed, once outside the worlds of advertising, movies, and folktales, he is not the ideal male.

Work Cited

Photograph is documented as explained in Chapter 14.

The Rock as The Scorpion King. Photofest. 2002, New York.

In the following reading, Paul Roberts gives advice to writers.

In a paragraph or two, compare and contrast your writing process with one or more procedures explained in the reading. If you wish, you can also compare and contrast some aspect of your writing style with the style depicted in the essay.

BACKGROUND: Paul Roberts (1917–1967) was a teacher, a linguist, and textbook author. His writing books include *English Syntax* (1954) and *Patterns of English* (1956). "How to Say Nothing in 500 Words" comes from Roberts's best known book, *Understanding English* (1958).

READING WITH A PURPOSE: Although written almost 50 years ago, "How to Say Nothing in 500 Words" is one of the most frequently anthologized essays in first-year composition readers because it says so much about writing that remains true to this day. (You will notice the author's use of the masculine "he" to refer to the instructor and student, who could be either male or female. At the time the essay was written, using "he" was the conventional way to refer to groups that included both genders.) The essay's lively style makes this a most entertaining piece, but do not be fooled—Roberts is very serious about his advice to writers. As you read, think about whether you know many student writers who behave the way Roberts describes.

How to Say Nothing in 500 Words

PAUL ROBERTS

NOTHING ABOUT SOMETHING

It's Friday afternoon, and you have almost survived another week of classes. You are just looking forward dreamily to the weekend when the English instructor says: "For Monday you will turn in a five-hundred-word composition on college football."

2 Well, that puts a good big hole in the weekend. You don't have any strong views on college football one way or the other. You get rather excited during the season and go to all the home games and find it rather more fun than not. On the other hand, the class has been reading Robert Hutchins in the anthology and perhaps Shaw's "Eighty-Yard Run," and from the class discussion you have got the idea that the instructor thinks college football is for the birds. You are no fool, you. You can figure out what side to take.

3 After dinner you get out the portable typewriter that you got for high school graduation. You might as well get it over with and enjoy Saturday and Sunday. Five hundred words is about two double-spaced pages with normal margins. You put in a sheet of paper, think up a title, and you're off:

Why College Football Should Be Abolished

4 College football should be abolished because it's bad for the school and also bad for the players. The players are so busy practicing that they don't have any time for their studies.

5   This, you feel, is a mighty good start. The only trouble is that it's only thirty-two words. You still have four hundred and sixty-eight to go, and you've pretty well exhausted the subject. It comes to you that you do your best thinking in the morning, so you put away the typewriter and go to the movies. But the next morning you have to do your washing and some math problems, and in the afternoon you go to the game. The English instructor turns up too, and you wonder if you've taken the right side after all. Saturday night you have a date, and Sunday morning you have to go to church. (You shouldn't let English assignments interfere with your religion.) What with one thing and another, it's ten o'clock Sunday night before you get out the typewriter again. You make a pot of coffee and start to fill out your views on college football. Put a little meat on the bones.

Why College Football Should Be Abolished

6   In my opinion, it seems to me that college football should be abolished. The reason why I think this to be true is because I feel that football is bad for the colleges in nearly every respect. As Robert Hutchins says in his article in our anthology in which he discusses college football, it would be better if the colleges had race horses and had races with one another, because then the horses would not have to attend classes. I firmly agree with Mr. Hutchins on this point, and I am sure that many other students would agree too.

7   One reason why it seems to me that college football is bad is that it has become too commercial. In the olden times when people played football just for the fun of it, maybe college football was all right, but they do not play football just for the fun of it now as they used to in the old days. Nowadays college football is what you might call a big business. Maybe this is not true at all schools, and I don't think it is especially true here at State, but certainly this is the case at most colleges and universities in America nowadays, as Mr. Hutchins points out in his very interesting article. Actually the coaches and alumni go around to the high schools and offer the high school stars large salaries to come to their colleges and play football for them. There was one case where a high school star was offered a convertible if he would play football for a certain college.

8   Another reason for abolishing college football is that it is bad for the players. They do not have time to get a college education, because they are so busy playing football. A football player has to practice every afternoon from three to six, and then he is so tired that he can't concentrate on his studies. He just feels like dropping off to sleep after dinner, and then the next day he goes to his classes without having studied and maybe he fails the test.

(Good ripe stuff so far, but you're still a hundred and fifty-one words from home. One more push.)

9   Also I think college football is bad for the colleges and the universities because not very many students get to participate in it. Out of a college of ten thousand students only seventy-five or a hundred play football, if that many. Football is what you might call a spectator sport. That means that most people go to watch it but do not play it themselves.

(Four hundred and fifteen. Well, you still have the conclusion, and when you retype it, you can make the margins a little wider.)

10   These are the reasons why I agree with Mr. Hutchins that college football should be abolished in American colleges and universities.

11   On Monday you turn it in, moderately hopeful, and on Friday it comes back marked "weak in content" and sporting a big "D."

12   This essay is exaggerated a little, not much. The English instructor will recognize it as reasonably typical of what an assignment on college football will bring in. He knows that nearly half of the class will contrive in five hundred words to say that college football is too commercial and bad for the players. Most of the other half will inform him that college football builds character and prepares one for life and brings prestige to the school. As he reads paper after paper all saying the same thing in almost the same words, all bloodless, five hundred words dripping out of nothing, he wonders how he allowed himself to get trapped into teaching English when he might have had a happy and interesting life as an electrician or a confidence man.

13   Well, you may ask, what can you do about it? The subject is one on which you have few convictions and little information. Can you be expected to make a dull subject interesting? As a matter of fact, this is precisely what you are expected to do. This is the writer's essential task. All subjects, except sex, are dull until somebody makes them interesting. The writer's job is to find the argument, the approach, the angle, the wording that will take the reader with him. This is seldom easy, and it is particularly hard in subjects that have been much discussed: College Football, Fraternities, Popular Music, Is Chivalry Dead?, and the like. You will feel that there is nothing you can do with such subjects except repeat the old bromides. But there are some things you can do which will make your papers, if not throbbingly alive, at least less insufferably tedious than they might otherwise be.

AVOID THE OBVIOUS CONTENT

14   Say the assignment is college football. Say that you've decided to be against it. Begin by putting down the arguments that come to your mind: it is too commercial, it takes the students' minds off their studies, it is hard on the players, it makes the university a kind of circus instead of an intellectual center, for most schools it is financially ruinous. Can you think of any more arguments just off hand? All right. Now when you write your paper, *make sure that you don't use any of the material on this list*. If these are the points that leap to your mind, they will leap to everyone else's too, and whether you get a "C" or a "D" may depend on whether the

instructor reads your paper early when he is fresh and tolerant or late, when the sentence "In my opinion, college football has become too commercial," inexorably repeated, has brought him to the brink of lunacy.

15   Be against college football for some reason or reasons of your own. If they are keen and perceptive ones, that's splendid. But even if they are trivial or foolish or indefensible, you are still ahead so long as they are not everybody else's reasons too. Be against it because the colleges don't spend enough money on it to make it worth while, because it is bad for the characters of the spectators, because the players are forced to attend classes, because the football stars hog all the beautiful women, because it competes with baseball and is therefore un-American and possibly Communist inspired. There are lots of more or less unused reasons for being against college football.

16   Sometimes it is a good idea to sum up and dispose of the trite and conventional points before going on to your own. This has the advantage of indicating to the reader that you are going to be neither trite nor conventional. Something like this:

17   We are often told that college football should be abolished because it
        has become too commercial or because it is bad for the players. These
        arguments are no doubt very cogent, but they don't really go to the
        heart of the matter.

Then you go to the heart of the matter.

TAKE THE LESS USUAL SIDE

18   One rather simple way of getting interest into your paper is to take the side of the argument that most of the citizens will want to avoid. If the assignment is an essay on dogs, you can, if you choose, explain that dogs are faithful and lovable companions, intelligent, useful as guardians of the house and protectors of children, indispensable in police work—in short, when all is said and done, man's best friends. Or you can suggest that those big brown eyes conceal, more often than not, a vacuity of mind and an inconstancy of purpose; that the dogs you have known most intimately have been mangy, ill-tempered brutes, incapable of instruction; and that only your nobility of mind and fear of arrest prevent you from kicking the flea-ridden animals when you pass them on the street.

19   Naturally, personal convictions will sometimes dictate your approach. If the assigned subject is "Is Methodism Rewarding to the Individual?" and you are a pious Methodist, you have really no choice. But few assigned subjects, if any, will fall in this category. Most of them will lie in broad areas of discussion with much to be said on both sides. They are intellectual exercises and it is legitimate to argue now one way and now another, as debaters do in similar circumstances. Always take the side that looks to you hardest, least defensible. It will almost always turn out to be easier to write interestingly on that side.

20   This general advice applies where you have a choice of subjects. If you are to choose among "The Value of Fraternities" and "My Favorite High School Teacher" and "What I Think About Beetles," by all means plump for the beetles. By the time

the instructor gets to your paper, he will be up to his ears in tedious tales about the French teacher at Bloombury High and assertions about how fraternities build character and prepare one for life. Your views on beetles, whatever they are, are bound to be a refreshing change.

21   Don't worry too much about figuring out what the instructor thinks about the subject so that you can cuddle up with him. Chances are his views are no stronger than yours. If he does have convictions and you oppose them, his problem is to keep from grading you higher than you deserve in order to show he is not biased. This doesn't mean that you should always cantankerously dissent from what the instructor says; that gets tiresome too. And if the subject assigned is "My Pet Peeve," do not begin, "My pet peeve is the English instructor who assigns papers on 'my pet peeve.'" This was still funny during the War of 1812, but it has sort of lost its edge since then. It is in general good manners to avoid personalities.

SLIP OUT OF ABSTRACTION

22   If you will study the essay on college football . . . you will perceive that one reason for its appalling dullness is that it never gets down to particulars. It is just a series of not very glittering generalities: "football is bad for the colleges," "it has become too commercial," "football is a big business," "it is bad for the players," and so on. Such round phrases thudding against the reader's brain are unlikely to convince him, though they may well render him unconscious.

23   If you want the reader to believe that college football is bad for the players, you have to do more than say so. You have to display the evil. Take your roommate, Alfred Simkins, the second-string center. Picture poor old Alfy coming home from football practice every evening, bruised and aching, agonizingly tired, scarcely able to shovel the mashed potatoes into his mouth. Let us see him staggering up to the room, getting out his econ textbook, peering desperately at it with his good eye, falling asleep and failing the test in the morning. Let us share his unbearable tension as Saturday draws near. Will he fail, be demoted, lose his monthly allowance, be forced to return to the coal mines? And if he succeeds, what will be his reward? Perhaps a slight ripple of applause when the third-string center replaces him, a moment of elation in the locker room if the team wins, of despair if it loses. What will he look back on when he graduates from college? Toil and torn ligaments. And what will be his future? He is not good enough for pro football, and he is too obscure and weak in econ to succeed in stocks and bonds. College football is tearing the heart from Alfy Simkins and, when it finishes with him, will callously toss aside the shattered hulk.

24   This is no doubt a weak enough argument for the abolition of college football, but it is a sight better than saying, in three or four variations, that college football (in your opinion) is bad for the players.

25   Look at the work of any professional writer and notice how constantly he is moving from the generality, the abstract statement, to the concrete example, the facts and figures, the illustration. If he is writing on juvenile delinquency, he does not just tell you that juveniles are (it seems to him) delinquent and that (in his opinion) something should be done about it. He shows you juveniles being delinquent,

tearing up movie theatres in Buffalo, stabbing high school principals in Dallas, smoking marijuana in Palo Alto. And more than likely he is moving toward some specific remedy, not just a general wringing of the hands.

26   It is no doubt possible to be *too* concrete, too illustrative or anecdotal, but few inexperienced writers err this way. For most the soundest advice is to be seeking always for the picture, to be always turning general remarks into seeable examples. Don't say, "Sororities teach girls the social graces." Say "Sorority life teaches a girl how to carry on a conversation while pouring tea, without sloshing the tea into the saucer." Don't say, "I like certain kinds of popular music very much." Say, "Whenever I hear Gerber Spinklittle play 'Mississippi Man' on the trombone, my socks creep up my ankles."

GET RID OF OBVIOUS PADDING

27   The student toiling away at his weekly English theme is too often tormented by a figure: five hundred words. How, he asks himself, is he to achieve this staggering total? Obviously by never using one word when he can somehow work in ten.

28   He is therefore seldom content with a plain statement like "Fast driving is dangerous." This has only four words in it. He takes thought, and the sentence becomes:

In my opinion, fast driving is dangerous.

Better, but he can do better still:

In my opinion, fast driving would seem to be rather dangerous.

If he is really adept, it may come out:

In my humble opinion, though I do not claim to be an expert on this complicated subject, fast driving, in most circumstances, would seem to be rather dangerous in many respects, or at least so it would seem to me.

Thus four words have been turned into forty, and not an iota of content has been added.

29   Now this is a way to go about reaching five hundred words, and if you are content with a "D" grade, it is as good a way as any. But if you aim higher, you must work differently. Instead of stuffing your sentences with straw, you must try steadily to get rid of the padding, to make your sentences lean and tough. If you are really working at it, your first draft will greatly exceed the required total, and then you will work it down, thus:

It is thought in some quarters that fraternities do not contribute as much as might be expected to campus life.
Some people think that fraternities contribute little to campus life.

The average doctor who practices in small towns or in the country must toil night and day to heal the sick.
Most country doctors work long hours.

When I was a little girl, I suffered from shyness and embarrassment in the presence of others.

I was a shy little girl.

It is absolutely necessary for the person employed as a marine fireman to give the matter of steam pressure his undivided attention at all times.

The fireman has to keep his eye on the steam gauge.

30   You may ask how you can arrive at five hundred words at this rate. Simply. You dig up more real content. Instead of taking a couple of obvious points off the surface of the topic and then circling warily around them for six paragraphs, you work in and explore, figure out the details. You illustrate. You say that fast driving is dangerous, and then you prove it. How long does it take to stop a car at forty and at eighty? How far can you see at night? What happens when a tire blows? What happens in a head-on collision at fifty miles an hour? Pretty soon your paper will be full of broken glass and blood and headless torsos, and reaching five hundred words will not really be a problem.

CALL A FOOL A FOOL

31   Some of the padding in freshman themes is to be blamed not on anxiety about the word minimum but on excessive timidity. The student writes, "In my opinion, the principal of my high school acted in ways that I believe every unbiased person would have to call foolish." This isn't exactly what he means. What he means is, "My high school principal was a fool." If he was a fool, call him a fool. Hedging the thing about with "in-my-opinion's" and "it-seems-to-me's" and "as-I-see-it's" and "at-least-from-my-point-of-view's" gains you nothing. Delete these phrases whenever they creep into your paper.

32   The student's tendency to hedge stems from a modesty that in other circumstances would be commendable. He is, he realizes, young and inexperienced, and he half suspects that he is dopey and fuzzy-minded beyond the average. Probably only too true. But it doesn't help to announce your incompetence six times in every paragraph. Decide what you want to say and say it as vigorously as possible, without apology and in plain words.

33   Linguistic diffidence can take various forms. One is what we call *euphemism*. This is the tendency to call a spade "a certain garden implement" or women's underwear "unmentionables." It is stronger in some eras than others and in some people than others but it always operates more or less in subjects that are touchy or taboo: death, sex, madness, and so on. Thus we shrink from saying "He died last night" but say instead "passed away," "left us," "joined his Maker," "went to his reward." Or we try to take off the tension with a lighter cliché: "kicked the bucket," "cashed in his chips," "handed in his dinner pail." We have found all sorts of ways to avoid saying *mad*: "mentally ill," "touched," "not quite right upstairs," "feeble-minded," "innocent," "simple," "off his trolley," "not in his right mind." Even such a now plain word as *insane* began as a euphemism with the meaning "not healthy."

34　Modern science, particularly psychology, contributes many polysyllables in which we can wrap our thoughts and blunt their force. To many writers there is no such thing as a bad schoolboy. Schoolboys are maladjusted or unoriented or misunderstood or in need of guidance or lacking in continued success toward satisfactory integration of the personality as a social unit, but they are never bad. Psychology no doubt makes us better men or women, more sympathetic and tolerant, but it doesn't make writing any easier. Had Shakespeare been confronted with psychology, "To be or not to be" might have come out, "To continue as a social unit or not to do so. That is the personality problem. Whether 'tis a better sign of integration at the conscious level to display a psychic tolerance toward the maladjustments and repressions induced by one's lack of orientation in one's environment or—" But Hamlet would never have finished the soliloquy.

35　Writing in the modern world, you cannot altogether avoid modern jargon. Nor, in an effort to get away from euphemism, should you salt your paper with four-letter words. But you can do much if you will mount guard against those roundabout phrases, those echoing polysyllables that tend to slip into your writing to rob it of its crispness and force.

BEWARE OF THE PAT EXPRESSION

36　Other things being equal, avoid phrases like "other things being equal." Those sentences that come to you whole, or in two or three doughy lumps, are sure to be bad sentences. They are no creation of yours but pieces of common thought floating in the community soup.

37　Pat expressions are hard, often impossible, to avoid, because they come too easily to be noticed and seem too necessary to be dispensed with. No writer avoids them altogether, but good writers avoid them more often than poor writers.

38　By "pat expressions" we mean such tags as "to all practical intents and purposes," "the pure and simple truth," "from where I sit," "the time of his life," "to the ends of the earth," "in the twinkling of an eye," "as sure as you're born," "over my dead body," "under cover of darkness," "took the easy way out," "when all is said and done," "told him time and time again," "parted the best of friends," "stand up and be counted," "gave him the best years of her life," "worked her fingers to the bone." Like other clichés, these expressions were once forceful. Now we should use them only when we can't possibly think of anything else.

39　Some pat expressions stand like a wall between the writer and thought. Such a one is "the American way of life." Many student writers feel that when they have said that something accords with the American way of life or does not they have exhausted the subject. Actually, they have stopped at the highest level of abstraction. The American way of life is the complicated set of bonds between a hundred and eighty million ways. All of us know this when we think about it, but the tag phrase too often keeps us from thinking about it.

40　So with many another phrase dear to the politician: "this great land of ours," "the man in the street," "our national heritage." These may prove our patriotism or give a clue to our political beliefs, but otherwise they add nothing to the paper except words.

COLORFUL WORDS

41   The writer builds with words, and no builder uses a raw material more slippery and elusive and treacherous. A writer's work is a constant struggle to get the right word in the right place, to find that particular word that will convey his meaning exactly, that will persuade the reader or soothe him or startle or amuse him. He never succeeds altogether—sometimes he feels that he scarcely succeeds at all—but such successes as he has are what make the thing worth doing.

42   There is no book of rules for this game. One progresses through everlasting experiment on the basis of ever-widening experience. There are few useful generalizations that one can make about words as words, but there are perhaps a few.

43   Some words are what we call "colorful." By this we mean that they are calculated to produce a picture or induce an emotion. They are dressy instead of plain, specific instead of general, loud instead of soft. Thus, in place of "Her heart beat," we may write "Her heart *pounded, throbbed, fluttered, danced.*" Instead of "He sat in his chair," we may say, "He *lounged, sprawled, coiled.*" Instead of "It was hot," we may say, "It was *blistering, sultry, muggy, suffocating, steamy, wilting.*"

44   However, it should not be supposed that the fancy word is always better. Often it is as well to write "Her heart beat" or "It was hot" if that is all it did or all it was. Ages differ in how they like their prose. The nineteenth century liked it rich and smoky. The twentieth has usually preferred it lean and cool. The twentieth-century writer, like all writers, is forever seeking the exact word, but he is wary of sounding feverish. He tends to pitch it low, to understate it, to throw it away. He knows that if he gets too colorful, the audience is likely to giggle.

45   See how this strikes you: "As the rich, golden glow of the sunset died away along the eternal western hills, Angela's limpid blue eyes looked softly and trustingly into Montague's flashing brown ones, and her heart pounded like a drum in time with the joyous song surging in her soul." Some people like that sort of thing, but most modern readers would say, "Good grief," and turn on the television.

COLORED WORDS

46   Some words we would call not so much colorful as colored—that is, loaded with associations, good or bad. All words—except perhaps structure words—have associations of some sort. We have said that the meaning of a word is the sum of the contexts in which it occurs. When we hear a word, we hear with it an echo of all the situations in which we have heard it before.

47   In some words, these echoes are obvious and discussable. The word *mother*, for example, has, for most people, agreeable associations. When you hear *mother* you probably think of home, safety, love, food, and various other pleasant things. If one writes, "She was like a mother to me," he gets an effect which he would not get in "She was like an aunt to me." The advertiser makes use of the associations of *mother* by working it in when he talks about his product. The politician works it in when he talks about himself.

48   So also with such words as *home, liberty, fireside, contentment, patriot, tenderness, sacrifice, childlike, manly, bluff, limpid.* All of these words are loaded with favorable associations that would be rather hard to indicate in a straightforward definition.

There is more than a literal difference between "They sat around the fireside" and "They sat around the stove." They might have been equally warm and happy around the stove, but *fireside* suggests leisure, grace, quiet tradition, congenial company, and *stove* does not.

49   Conversely, some words have bad associations. *Mother* suggests pleasant things, but *mother-in-law* does not. Many mothers-in-law are heroically lovable and some mothers drink gin all day and beat their children insensible, but these facts of life are beside the point. The thing is that *mother* sounds good and *mother-in-law* does not.

50   Or consider the word *intellectual*. This would seem to be a complimentary term, but in point of fact it is not, for it has picked up associations of impracticality and ineffectuality and general dopiness. So also with such words as *liberal, reactionary, Communist, socialist, capitalist, radical, schoolteacher, truck driver, undertaker, operator, salesman, huckster, speculator*. These convey meanings on the literal level, but beyond that—sometimes, in some places—they convey contempt on the part of the speaker.

51   The question of whether to use loaded words or not depends on what is being written. The scientist, the scholar, try to avoid them; for the poet, the advertising writer, the public speaker, they are standard equipment. But every writer should take care that they do not substitute for thought. If you write, "Anyone who thinks that is nothing but a Socialist (or Communist or capitalist)," you have said nothing except that you don't like people who think that, and such remarks are effective only with the most naive readers. It is always a bad mistake to think your readers more naive than they really are.

COLORLESS WORDS

52   But probably most student writers come to grief not with words that are colorful or those that are colored but with those that have no color at all. A pet example is *nice*, a word we would find it hard to dispense with in casual conversation but which is no longer capable of adding much to a description. Colorless words are those of such general meaning that in a particular sentence they mean nothing. Slang adjectives, like *cool* ("That's real cool") tend to explode all over the language. They are applied to everything, lose their original force, and quickly die.

53   Beware also of nouns of very general meaning, like *circumstances, cases, instances, aspects, factors, relationships, attitudes, eventualities*, etc. In most circumstances you will find that those cases of writing which contain too many instances of words like these will in this and other aspects have factors leading to unsatisfactory relationships with the reader resulting in unfavorable attitudes on his part and perhaps other eventualities, like a grade of "D." Notice also what "etc." means. It means "I'd like to make this list longer, but I can't think of any more examples."

THE RAILWAY ENGINE—The locomotive is the most perfect of machines. It approaches nearer to the spiritual and physical combination of the human machine than any other. In it we behold the steam engine 'unchained to the rock, and unfettered to the soil.'
Scientific American 1851.

Description

The steam locomotive shown on the facing page was one of the most important machines of the 19th and early 20th centuries because it gave Americans mobility, connected the coasts, and stimulated the economy. Select a machine important in our time and write a paragraph description of it.

THE PATTERN

What happens when you encounter a striking landscape, hear a moving song on the radio, smell a peculiar scent in your apartment, taste a delightful dessert in a restaurant, or touch a velvety sweater in a store? Like most people, you probably want to share the experience with others, so you find yourself saying things like

"Quick, come see this!"

"You've got to listen to this song."

"Do you smell that?"

"Here, you have to have a bite of this cake."

"Oh, feel how soft this sweater is."

Writers have the same impulse. They want to share their sensory impressions, so they use words to create mental pictures that will help their readers experience a bit of what they did.

When writers use words to create mental pictures, they are writing **description.** To appreciate how description can allow writers to convey sensory impressions, consider this sentence, taken from a newspaper description of Tennessee's Reelfoot Lake:

> Shaggy cypress trees jut from dark waters where white waterlilies as big as dinner plates bloom.

Can you picture that scene? You can probably picture it more clearly than you would with this less descriptive sentence:

> Trees grow out of the lake at the point where large waterlilies bloom.

The first sentence shows the power of words to create mental pictures, which is a primary purpose of description: using words to move your reader to mentally see, hear, smell, taste, and touch in a particular manner. In a similar way, writers can use words to convey how it feels to experience a situation or emotion, as is the case in this example from "My Neighborhood" (page 124):

> Everything beginning at Blake Avenue would always wear for me some delightful strangeness and mildness.

---

www.mhhe.com/patterns

For more help with description, click on
Writing > Paragraph Patterns
Writing > Writing Tutor: Description

USING DESCRIPTION FOR A PURPOSE

Description can entertain, convey feelings, relate experience, inform, and persuade. When people on vacation want to share their good times, for example, they often write description on postcards to *relate their experience* and *express* to friends and relatives back home how they see and react to the beautiful vistas, local cuisine, and interesting people they encounter. Newspaper and magazine columnists often use description to *entertain* their readers, as Rick Bass does in his beautiful description of a Montana winter on page 129. On the job, people can use description to *inform* a reader. For example, the public relations director of your university might include description of your campus in your college catalog to inform prospective students about what the campus is like. Description can also be an important component of writing meant to *persuade.* Because well-written description can move a reader's emotions, it is often used to convince a reader to think or act a particular way. A travel agent trying to persuade people to take a Caribbean cruise might write a letter to clients describing the luxurious ship and breathtaking ports of call to get them excited about the trip and convince them to send a deposit.

Although it can serve a variety of purposes, description is most often expressive, so it most often helps writers share their perceptions. As human beings, we have a compelling desire to connect with other people by sharing our experiences with them. Description helps us do that. In addition, because well-written description can be beautiful and therefore pleasurable to read, a secondary purpose of description is often to entertain.

Since description helps the reader form mental pictures, writers often rely on it to add interest and vividness. That is, description helps writers do more than just *tell* that something is true; it allows them to *show* that something is true. For this reason, writers often combine description with other patterns of development. For example, suppose you are writing an explanation of how to make the perfect spaghetti sauce (this would be *process analysis*, an explanation of how something is made). If you tell your reader to pick only the best tomatoes, you might go on to describe how those tomatoes look, feel, and smell, so your reader knows how to select them. Now suppose you are telling a story about the time you wrecked your uncle's classic car (this would be *narration*). You might include a vivid description of what the car looked like after the wreck to help your reader appreciate how badly the car was damaged.

Description in College, at Work, and in the Community

One mark of an educated person is the ability to observe closely and assess the significance of what is observed. Thus, in your college classes, you will frequently be asked to observe, describe, and evaluate. For example, in an art history course, you might be asked to describe two paintings by Van Gogh to show their similarities and differences. In a music appreciation course, you might be asked to describe a Chopin nocturne to explain the technique the performer used. In an advertising course, you might be required to describe an ad for a particular product to learn about persuasive strategies. In your history courses, you might be asked to describe conditions after events such as wars, coups, economic reversals, and social reforms to assess their effects. In a biology lab, you might need to describe organs after dissection in order to understand their characteristics, and in a psychology lab, you might need to describe the behavior of a mouse following a particular experiment to learn about the effects of certain stimuli. In a fashion design class, you might need to describe classic Gucci designs, and in a dental hygiene class, you might need to describe the appearance of a healthy bicuspid.

You will also find description in most of your textbooks, whatever discipline you are studying. Here, for example, is description taken from an American history textbook:

> Europeans seemed, by the Indians' standards, grotesquely over-dressed. Indeed, European fashion was ill suited to the environment between the Chesapeake and the Caribbean. Elizabethan gentlemen

strutted in silk stockings attached with garters to padded, puffed knee breeches, topped by long-sleeved shirts and tight quilted jackets called "doublets." Men of lesser status wore coarse woolen hose, canvas breeches, shirts, and fitted vests known as "jerkins"; when at work, they donned aprons of dressed leather. Women wore gowns with long, full skirts, low-cut bodices, aprons, and hosiery held up by garters. Ladies went about in silk and wore hoods and mantles to ward off the sun, while the rest dressed in flannels or canvas and covered their heads with linen caps or coifs. Both sexes favored long hair, and men sported mustaches and beards. (Davidson, et al., *Nation of Nations*)

Notice how the textbook author uses description both to give readers a clear picture of what the first European settlers looked like and to add interest to the narrative.

Beyond the classroom, you will likely use description. For example, description is common in workplace writing. Real estate agents describe properties in classified advertisements, and police officers describe crime scenes in crime reports. Psychologists describe their patients' demeanors in therapy notes, and scientists describe specimens before and after experiments. Nurses describe patients' appearances in medical charts, and insurance adjusters describe the condition of cars after accidents.

Description is also helpful in community-based writing. For instance, assume you are writing a letter to the editor of your campus newspaper to persuade students to recycle soda cans. You might describe the appearance of the campus quad littered with used aluminum cans. Or assume you are e-mailing friends asking them to volunteer their time at a homeless shelter. You could create sympathy by describing the conditions of those forced to live on the street.

DECIDING ON A DOMINANT IMPRESSION

If you describe something small and uncomplicated, such as a chair, you can probably describe all its features. However, if you are describing something larger or more complex, including all of its features would be difficult for you and overwhelming to your reader. To keep complex descriptions manageable, settle on a **dominant impression** (one notable quality) and write only those details that express that impression.

The quality is not "dominant" because it is the most significant or noticeable feature of what you are describing. The quality is dominant because it is the characteristic your description will focus on—it is "dominant" in your essay. For example, suppose you decide to describe the house you grew up in. Do you *really* want the task of describing all aspects of that house? Probably not. For most purposes, you can cut the job of describing your house down to a manageable size by choosing only those details that convey some opinion you have of the house. Once you decide on that opinion, you have the dominant impression, and you can safely ignore details that do not convey that impression.

Let's say the house you grew up in was an architectural nightmare, cluttered, but nonetheless cheerful. You can settle on one of those characteristics for your dominant impression. If you decided to convey the impression that the house was an architectural nightmare, you would describe the sagging porch and leaky roof rather than the beauty of the stained glass windows in the dining room. If you decided to convey how cluttered the house was, you would describe the collection of glass bottles that covered every tabletop, but not the crisply starched and pressed curtains. If you decided to convey the cheerfulness of the house, you would describe the sun flooding the front room, but not the tattered sofa. You can also form a dominant impression from more than one quality, if doing so still gives you a manageable writing task. You could, for example, describe your house as rundown but cheerful. In that case, you would describe the sagging porch and the leaky roof as well as the beautiful stained glass windows and starched, pressed curtains.

SUPPORTING DETAILS

Supporting details in a description essay should give your reader a clear mental image of your subject. In addition, they should convey your dominant impression of your subject and establish why you have formed that impression. The strategies explained next will help you write supporting details that accomplish these goals.

Objective and Expressive Details

Objective details give a factual, impartial, unemotional account of your subject, whereas **expressive details** present a more subjective, personal, or emotional view. A bank appraiser describing a piece of property would use objective details because his or her personal opinion about the property is not relevant. However, an advertising executive writing a description of a new car would use expressive detail to create an emotional appeal that will persuade the consumer to buy the car. Notice the difference between objective and expressive details in these examples, taken from readings in this chapter.

OBJECTIVE DETAILS   The siding [of the store] consists of rough sawn boards nailed vertically; the cracks between the boards are covered with equally rough battens. The silver steel roof is the Gendarme's most prominent feature. The raised ribs running the length of it, from the spouting to the ridge, provide a sense of purpose to the structure that is lost among the rest of its components. One small window on the side and one door in front permit a meager amount of natural light into the interior. Off to the side, a sign announcing the name of the store hangs from a pole; it is faded with age and almost hidden from view behind the branches of a small tree. (From "The Gendarme," page 114)

EXPRESSIVE DETAILS

Winter lacks the pyrotechnics of spring, the brute, strapping joy of summer, the old sugary nostalgia of autumn. It's just cold and elegant, monochromatic, somnolent. (From "A Winter's Tale," page 129)

Whether expressive or objective, descriptive details are **sensory details** (details that pertain to the senses: sight, sound, taste, smell, and touch). Sometimes a writer will use only one sense—typically sight—and other times a writer will appeal to several senses.

To see how writers can appeal to the five senses, consider the following sentences taken from essays in this book.

SIGHT

The clarity, the lucidity, of the ice is not the memorable thing. . . . this clear, clean ice will retain bands of colors within it, ribbons of cobalt, extraterrestrial in hue. . . . But the ice glows with those space-blue ribbons, just beneath the slick surface. ("A Winter's Tale," page 129)

SOUND

I remember the air whistling around me as I ran, the panicky thud of my bones in my sneakers. ("My Neighborhood," page 124)

TASTE

With our fingers we pulled soft fragments of [the cooked fish] from its sides to our plates, and ate; it was delicate fish-flesh, fresh and mild. Someone found the roe, and I ate of that too—it was fat and stronger, like egg yolk, naturally enough, and warm. ("The Deer at Providencia," page 135)

SMELL

I guess I remembered clearest of all the early mornings, when the lake was cool and motionless, remembered how the bedroom smelled of the lumber it was made of and the wet woods whose scent entered through the screen. ("Once More to the Lake," page 676)

TOUCH

To walk meant lifting each leg up by the thigh, moving it forward with my my hands, setting it down. The earth felt like a peach that had split open in the middle; one side moved up while the other side moved down and my legs were out of rhythm. The ground rolled the way it does during an earthquake . . . (From "Struck by Lightning," page 141)

Descriptive Words

Whether you are writing objective or expressive description, choose your words carefully. This does *not* mean that you should dash for the dictionary or thesaurus to find as many big words as possible. While these sources can be helpful, relying on them too heavily can lead you to write an overbearing sentence like this one:

> The pulchritudinous rose imparted delightful olfactory sensations upon me.

This sentence illustrates two problems that can occur when writers abandon their own natural styles and pile on words taken from the thesaurus and dictionary: The writing becomes stiff, pretentious, and unnatural, and the reader has a hard time understanding.

You can always turn to a dictionary or thesaurus when you are stuck, but usually you can write effective description with words you already know. The key is to use *specific* nouns, verbs, and modifiers rather than general ones because specific words are more descriptive. *General words* give readers a broad sense of what you are referring to, while *specific words* offer them a narrower, more focused meaning. The following list will help you see the difference between general and specific words.

GENERAL NOUNS	SPECIFIC NOUNS
car	Ford Taurus
sweater	cardigan
shoe	Nike Shox
class	Physics 103
meat	filet mignon
magazine	*Newsweek*

GENERAL VERBS	SPECIFIC VERBS
walk	stroll
spoke	shouted
look	glance
went	raced

GENERAL MODIFIERS	SPECIFIC MODIFIERS
nice	elegant
awesome	overwhelming
terrible	frightening
bad	gaudy

To develop effective descriptive language, expect to work through a series of refinements as you revise your drafts.

FIRST DRAFT	The house stood in the shadow of the huge tree.
REVISION **1**	The huge tree cast a shadow over the house.
REVISION **2**	The enormous poplar cast a shadow over the house.
REVISION **3**	The enormous poplar cast an eerie shadow over the house.

As you refine your descriptions in stages, look for opportunities to substitute specific nouns, verbs, and modifiers for more general words. Consider this sentence for example.

The tree moved in the wind.

The nouns are *tree* and *wind*. As a first refinement, you might make *tree* more specific:

The <u>poplar</u> moved in the wind.

Now you might make the verb *moved* more specific:

The poplar <u>swayed</u> in the wind.

Next, you might add specific modifiers:

The <u>newly planted</u> poplar swayed in the <u>gusting</u> wind.

Eventually, striving for specific nouns, verbs, and modifiers might lead you to rewrite the entire sentence to make it more active and vivid.

The gale-force wind whipped the branches of the young poplar.
Mother's favorite poplar was whipped by the powerful gusts.

How you describe the tree and the wind will depend upon the mental picture you want to create. However, a little description can go a long way. Do not overwhelm your reader by stringing together too many modifiers, or you will create an overburdened sentence like this one:

The emaciated, spindly, waxen old man stared vacantly into the barren, colorless hallway as his bony, arthritic, pale fingers played absently with the beige fringes of the faded blue bedspread.

When you do have highly descriptive sentences, balance them with less descriptive ones so your reader is not overwhelmed. For example, consider this passage from "Struck by Lightning," where a highly descriptive sentence is followed by a less descriptive one:

On the face of the mountain, a mile ahead, hard westerly gusts and sudden updrafts collided, pulling black clouds apart. Yet the storm looked harmless.

Avoiding Clichés

If you have trouble finding and eliminating clichés (overused expressions like "sadder but wiser" and "the last straw"), the following suggestions may be helpful.

1. To identify clichés in your own writing, look for similes (see below) that are not original—ones you have heard before, like these:

   cold as ice   **free as a bird**   **crazy like a fox**   **dark as night**

2. To eliminate a cliché that is a simile, rewrite the simile in a new way. Here's an example from paragraph 2 of "The Gendarme" on page 114:

   FIRST DRAFT: **Some sit on the railing like ducks in a row . . .**
   REVISION: **Some perch like chickens on the railing . . .**

   If you cannot rewrite the simile in a new way, rewrite without the simile:

   FIRST DRAFT: **Some sit on the railing like ducks in a row . . .**
   REVISION: **Some sit on the railing shoulder to shoulder.**

3. Not all clichés are similes, and not all similes are clichés. To become more familiar with clichés, visit this Web site and browse the cliché lists: www.clichesite.com

www.mhhe.com/patterns

For more help with avoiding clichés, click on
Editing > Clichés, Slang, Jargon, Colloquialisms

www.mhhe.com/patterns

For more help with descriptive vocabulary, click on
Editing > Adjectives and Adverbs
Learning > Links to Dictionary and Thesauri

Similes and Metaphors

Writers often use similes and metaphors in description because they help create mental images. A **simile** uses the words *like* or *as* to compare two things that are not usually seen as similar. Here is an example of a simile taken from "My Neighborhood" (page 124). In it, the smell and touch of lots that the author calls "fields" are compared to an open door with the word *as:*

> The smell and touch of those "fields," with their wild compost under the billboards of weeds, goldenrod, bricks, goat droppings, rusty cans,

empty beer bottles, fresh new lumber, and damp cement, lives in my mind as Brownsville's great open door, the wastes that took us through to the west.

A **metaphor** compares two items not usually seen as similar, but without *like* or *as*. In this metaphor from "Struck by Lightning" (page 141), the author compares her state of semiconsciousness to being submerged in an ocean:

Deep in an ocean. I am suspended motionless. The water is gray. . . . My arms are held out straight, cruciate, my head and legs hang limp. Nothing moves. . . . There are no shadows or sounds.

ORGANIZING DETAILS

An essay developed with description will often include a thesis that mentions both what is being described and the dominant impression. Here are two examples:

I was always embarrassed by the rundown house I grew up in. (*The house will be described; the dominant impression is "rundown."*)

At noon, the park comes alive with businesspeople taking a midday break from the pressures of work. (*The park at noon will be described; the dominant impression is that it is alive with the activity of business-people.*)

The thesis of a descriptive essay can be implied rather than stated. (See page 47 on the implied thesis.) If your thesis is implied, be sure the cumulative effect of your descriptive details gives your reader a clear sense of your dominant impression.

To order your descriptive details, ask yourself what arrangement will best help you convey your dominant impression and achieve your purpose for writing the description. Often, you will opt for a *spatial order,* especially when you are describing a room or other contained space where it is logical to move from front to back, left to right, top to bottom, and so on. If you describe the rundown house you grew up in, for example, you can begin at the front door and move clockwise through the rooms on the first floor. Other times, a *progressive order* will serve your purpose, particularly when your description is meant to persuade your reader to think or act a particular way. A real estate agent trying to convince people to buy the house you grew up in would probably describe the best features last to leave the reader with the strongest possible final impression of the place. *Chronological order* is another option in which you describe a place as if you were moving through it. Say you want to describe the house you grew up in as it was when you returned there last Thanksgiving. You could arrange the details according to what you noticed first, second, and so on as you entered and moved through the house.

VISUALIZING A DESCRIPTIVE ESSAY

The following chart can help you visualize the structure for a descriptive essay. Like all good models, however, this one can be altered as needed.

Introduction

- Creates interest in what is being described
- Can state the thesis, which indicates what is being described and the dominant impression

First Body Paragraph

- Begins the focus on the dominant impression
- Includes objective or expressive details or both
- Includes specific words and sensory details
- May include similes and metaphors
- Arranges details in a suitable order, which may be spatial, chronological, or progressive

Next Body Paragraph

- Continues the description by focusing on the dominant impression
- Includes objective or expressive details or both
- Includes specific words and sensory details
- May include similes and metaphors
- Arranges details in a suitable order, which may be spatial, chronological, or progressive

Next Body Paragraphs

- Continue until the description is complete
- Focus on the dominant impression, include objective and/or expressive details, specific words, sensory details, and possibly similes and metaphors
- Arrange details in a suitable order, which may be spatial, chronological, or progressive

Conclusion

- Provides a satisfying finish
- Leaves the reader with a positive final impression

PROCESS GUIDELINES: STRATEGIES FOR WRITING DESCRIPTION

1. **Selecting a Topic.** You need not worry about finding a magnificent, dramatic, or unusual subject to describe. Concentrate on finding a topic and settling on a dominant impression that will allow you to write vivid descriptions that convey the significance of your subject and help you achieve a particular purpose. Also, try to describe something you can visit and observe, such as a doctor's waiting room, a bus station, a popular campus gathering place, or a restaurant with a theme decor. When you visit the spot, take notes about sensory details to make drafting easier. If you describe a subject from memory, such as a childhood haunt, your high school cafeteria, or a tree house you used to have, be sure the memory is fresh enough to allow you to come up with vivid, specific details.

2. **Establishing a Dominant Impression.** If you have trouble settling on a dominant impression, list all the emotions your subject arouses in you and all the reactions you have to your subject. Then choose one of those feelings or reactions as your dominant impression. You need not choose your strongest reaction. You can select the one you find most interesting or surprising, or the one you think you can write about the best.

3. **Drafting.** When you write your first draft, be as descriptive as you can comfortably be, but do not labor too long over individual sentences or particular words. Descriptive language often does not come easily; choosing specific nouns, verbs, and modifiers takes time and often involves a series of revisions, so do not expect too much too soon. When you revise, you can shape your descriptive language to get it just right.

4. **Revising.** Remember to use specific words to show rather than tell. Instead of writing "The child looked tired," be specific about how the child acted: "Little Alfie rubbed his fists into his eyes and stretched his mouth into a wide yawn." Also, revise vague words like *good, nice, awful, terrible, cool, bad,* and *great.* Aim for more specific alternatives. Instead of "bad food," revise to get "over-seasoned, stringy steak"; instead of "awful headache," revise to get "throbbing headache."

Checklist for Revising Description

Be sure:

_____ Details work together to convey a single dominant impression.

_____ Nouns, verbs, and modifiers are specific and appeal to the appropriate senses.

_____ Less descriptive sentences follow highly descriptive sentences.

_____ Details work to fulfill your purpose or combination of purposes.

_____ Details are arranged in a suitable order, indicated by topic sentences and transitions, as needed.

Using the Dictionary, Thesaurus, and OneLook Reverse Dictionary

If you have trouble finding the right descriptive word, a dictionary or thesaurus can help. But be aware of the connotations—the implied or secondary meanings—of words you take from these sources because synonyms are not always interchangeable. While *stern* is a synonym for *fierce*, you would not write that you encountered a stern bear in the woods.

www.mhhe.com/patterns

For links to online dictionaries and thesauri, click on
Learning > Links to Dictionary and Thesauri

If you have a concept in mind, but can't think of the word or phrase you want, use OneLook Reverse Dictionary at www.onelook.com/reverse-dictionary.shtml. You can use this site to find a word if you already know the definition, get a list of related concepts and words, and answer identification questions.

Student author Ralph Mitchell uses expressive and objective detail to describe a one-of-a-kind store. After writing this essay, Ralph posted it on The Gendarme's Web site www.seneca-rocks.com/gendarme.html. After you read, you will have an opportunity to evaluate this essay.

The Gendarme

Paragraph 1
The thesis (first sentence) notes what is being described (The Gendarme) and the dominant impression (it is one of a kind). Objective description creates visual images of the store and includes a simile (the store is like Shangri-La).

In an obscure corner of West Virginia, near the triangular intersection of state routes 28, 55, and 33, stands the climbing store known as The Gendarme; it is a one-of-a-kind establishment. Few of the people passing by on the nearby road are even aware of its presence. Like the mythical city of Shangri-La, it exists beyond the realm of the casual traveler; to find it takes purpose. Tucked away behind Buck Harper's General Store and the Rocks View Restaurant, its construction mimics the small barns and outbuildings of the local inhabitants. The siding consists of rough sawn boards nailed vertically; the cracks between the boards are covered with equally rough battens. The silver steel roof is the Gendarme's most prominent feature. The raised ribs running the length of it, from the spouting to the ridge, provide a sense of purpose to the structure that is lost among the rest of its components. One small window on the side and one door in front permit a meager amount of natural light into the interior. Off to the side, a sign announcing the name of the store hangs from a pole; it is faded with age and almost hidden from view behind the branches of a small tree.

Paragraph 2
The topic sentence (sentence 1) indicates that the paragraph's focus is the porch. Supporting details are largely objective descriptions appealing to sight. Notice the simile ("Some perch like chickens").

The porch is cluttered with an odd assortment of chairs and benches. An aluminum lawn chair, its nylon seat hanging in tatters, sits dejectedly next to a log bench suspended from four crooked legs of various diameters. Its top hewn flat, it appears almost as an afterthought. The porch posts are tied together with a wooden railing that, judging from the amount of wear, must be used as seating also. Ashtrays, the origin of which cannot be discerned, are strewn haphazardly about. Some perch like chickens on the railing; others hunker down among the jetsam strewn about the floor, fighting for a space of their own. In the center, an old cable reel, battered, burned, carved, and stained, presides over the collection—the remnants of someone's snack still adorning its top. Pushed back against the wall to the left of the door sits a corroded aluminum box about six feet long, three feet deep, and two feet high. Stenciled on the front in official looking letters are the words, "For Emergency Use Only. Stokes Litter." Covering the top of the box are bundles of firewood neatly bound and labeled "$3." A large bulletin board is handily fastened to the wall above the firewood. Covering its face are a multitude of notes, advertisements, and Park Service notices. One note reads, "To whom it may concern: Wasp nest located above the crux of Soler, use caution if climbing this route." Another offers climbing shoes for sale "cheap." A third, tattered and faded, makes a person wonder if Jennifer ever did meet Steve at the base of Old Man's route. A Park Service notice, advising of cliff closures due to the Peregrine Falcon nesting season, hangs off to the right. Immediately to the right of the notice is the door.

Once inside, a person is immediately struck by the incredible 3 amount of climbing paraphernalia clinging to the walls and counters. The sight of this immediately sets the climber salivating and probably is about as comprehensible to the nonclimber as implements used for brain surgery are to a plumber. Towards the back of the store, a collection of used and outdated equipment hangs from the wall. In any other sport, they would reside in a Hall of Fame or a museum—icons behind glass, to be revered, out of touch to all. But here they typify the innocence of the sport, where the pioneers and the legends remain accessible to even the meekest among their brethren.

Holding court behind the cash register stands John Markwell: pur- 4 veyor of fine climbing gear and finer advice. The twinkle in his eye as he talks to a customer reveals the nature of someone who truly enjoys what he is doing. A head of graying hair seems to be his only concession to the passing years, for his trim, athletic build speaks of someone years younger. He first started his business out of the back of a Volkswagen bus in the mid-60s. He was a brilliant visionary or damned lucky, as few could have foreseen the dramatic growth of the sport in the subsequent years. He lives in a fine brick home several doors back up the road, one of the seven or eight that comprise the little community of

Mouth of Seneca. After living here for over 20 years, he is still regarded with suspicion by the locals. His children, however, participate fully as members of the community, after having spent their entire lives as playmates of the local children.

Paragraph 5
The paragraph opens with a transition ("Towards dusk") signaling chronological order.

Towards dusk, the climbers begin filtering into the parking area 5 across the street from Harper's General Store. Stepping gingerly over a flattened rattlesnake, they pause (no doubt wondering about the sanctity of their tents pitched nearby) then continue down the community's only alley onto the porch of the Gendarme, settling into whatever seating is still available. One climber, wearing brightly colored clothing and a rebellious haircut, stands talking animatedly. His arms gesticulate wildly, for he remains full of adrenaline from the day's climb. Another sits in a chair tipped back against the wall, hands folded across his chest, eyeing with apparent amusement the actions of the rest of the group. None is a permanent resident of the area. Most are from town and cities all over the eastern United States, and several have traveled from the West and from other countries as well. They are drawn here by the nearby climbing and the opportunity to renew old friendships and establish new ones.

Paragraph 6
The topic sentence (sentence 1) indicates that the paragraph's focus will be conversation. Mitchell emphasizes the dominant impression by noting the unique range of discussion topics.

The conversation begins as an anarchic free-for-all then gradually 6 forms into a common subject, with everyone offering his or her own insight. The topics could include anything: from yesterday's epic climbs to tomorrow's projects, from the terminal ballistics of the newly adopted FBI 40 caliber sidearm to the amount of iguana guano produced by a pet iguana in a week. As the night turns to early morning, the group reluctantly disbands, returning to their tents to pass the remainder of the night in relative quiet.

Paragraph 7
The conclusion provides closure by explaining the significance of The Gendarme and by highlighting its special role.

Previous generations each laid claim to a unique edifice to serve 7 as a focal point for their social interaction. During the 1940s, the General Store served this purpose. Later generations used the drugstore soda fountain, the drive-up root beer stand, and fast food restaurants. In today's age of the car phone, e-mail, and fax, social boundaries no longer are defined by physical limits, such as a neighborhood or a town, but by common interests and goals. The Gendarme stands as a contemporary version of a social centerpoint for one small segment of society: the climbing community.

PEER REVIEW

Responding to "The Gendarme"

Evaluate "The Gendarme" by responding to these questions:

1. Does the essay hold your interest? Why or why not?
2. What do you think of the thesis? Why?
3. Does the author use objective details well? Does he use expressive details well? Explain and cite examples to support your view.
4. What do you think of the author's word choice? Why? Cite an example to support your view.
5. Are the details arranged in a suitable order? Explain.
6. What are the chief strengths of the essay? Why do you find these features strong?
7. Mention one revision you would like to see. How will that revision improve the essay and help the author achieve his purpose?

- What dominant impression do each of the Google logos present?
- For what purpose do you think Google adapts its logo for different occasions or circumstances?
- How do you think Google users respond to these logos?

BACKGROUND: Poet, playwright, novelist, and artist, N. Scott Momaday was born in Lawton, Oklahoma, in 1934. He lived at his grandparents' house on the Kiowa Indian reservation until he was a year old, when he moved to Arizona with his parents, who taught on Indian reservations. In Arizona, Momaday learned about Navajo, Apache, and Pueblo Indian traditions in addition to his own Kiowa traditions. Active in a number of activities to preserve Indian culture, Momaday is a founding trustee of the National Museum of the American Indian. His works include *House Made of Dawn* (1968), for which he won the Pulitzer prize; *The Way to Rainy Mountain* (1968), to which Momaday refers in paragraph 5 of the essay; *The Ancient Child* (1989); *In the Presence of the Sun* (1991); and *The Native Americans: Indian Country* (1993). "The Homestead on Rainy Mountain Creek" is an essay from *The Man Made of Words* (1997).

THE PATTERN AND ITS PURPOSES: In "The Homestead on Rainy Mountain Creek," N. Scott Momaday uses *objective description* to **relate his experience** and **share his feelings** about his childhood home and the people who were part of his formative years. Although Momaday does not use much emotional language, he still manages to convey his reverence and affection for the homestead and for Kiowa culture.

The Homestead on Rainy Mountain Creek
N. SCOTT MOMADAY

The house and arbor stand on a rise on the plain east of the town of Mountain View. A little to the north and west are the Washita River and Rainy Mountain Creek. A few miles to the south and west is Rainy Mountain itself, scarcely a mountain, rather a knoll or a hummock. But in a way it is a singular feature in the immedi-

As you read Ask yourself how Momaday conveys his feelings for his homestead without using much emotional language.

ate landscape. From the top of Rainy Mountain you can see a long way in any direction. It is said that when the Kiowas camped on this ground, it inevitably rained, thus the name. At the base of the mountain is the ruin of the old Rainy Mountain School, which my grandmother, Aho, attended as a young girl. Nearby is the Rainy Mountain Baptist Church and the cemetery in which many of my forebears are buried.

2   The house was built in 1913, the year my father was born. He was in fact born while the house was under construction, in a tepee close to where the arbor now stands, on the corner closest to the well. And in that house and arbor he grew up with his sister, Clara, and his brothers, James, Lester, and Ralph.

3   My grandfather, Mammedaty, was greatly respected by all who knew him. For one thing, he was a successful farmer. The Kiowas, who migrated to the southern plains from the north, were a nomadic tribe of hunters; they never had an agrarian tradition. In my grandfather's day, when only a generation before the old roving life of the buffalo hunter had been intact, the Kiowas did not take easily to farming. Their land was fertile, but they preferred to lease it to white farmers. Mammedaty was an exception. He worked hard, and he saw that his sons worked hard. He made a good life for himself and his family.

4   I never knew my grandfather. He died in 1933, the year before I was born. But I feel I knew him. His powerful presence was discernible in his wife and children,

in the homestead on Rainy Mountain Creek, and in the countless stories I was told about him. All my life he has been an inspiration to me. His grandfather was the great chief Lone Wolf, and his grandmother was Kau-au-ointy, a Mexican captive who raised a great herd of cattle and became a prominent figure in the tribe. His mother, Keahdinekkeah, loved him above all others, I am told, and when he died she had him buried in a bronze casket, over which she placed her favorite shawl.

5   My grandmother, Aho, was the principal force in the homestead when I was a child. She was a beautiful and gracious woman, and she presided over family affairs with great generosity and goodwill. She was in her middle fifties when I was born, and she died at the age of eighty-five. About the time of her death I was writing *The Way to Rainy Mountain,* and in that writing I retraced the migration route of the Kiowas from western Montana to Oklahoma. My pilgrimage ended at my grandmother's grave. The introduction to *The Way to Rainy Mountain* is in large measure an evocation of my grandmother's spirit, and for this reason among others that book is my favorite of my works.

6   The house seems small to me now, but when I was a child it was grand and full of life. Aho and my uncle Jimmy, who never married, were always there. There were frequent reunions when my aunt Clara and my other uncles, Lester and Ralph, my cousins, and my parents and I convened to rejoice in the institution of our family. There were frequent visitors, kinsmen who brought greetings from, and news of, friends and relatives. We were always glad to see them. They would stay for days, according to the Kiowa notion of a proper visit.

7   It was not until later that I became aware of the real significance of these reunions and visitations. They were matters of ancient tradition and necessity. In the heyday of the plains culture, the tribe was composed of bands, each one going its own way. The essential integrity of the tribe was maintained by means of a kind of institutionalized visiting, whereby persons and families would venture abroad to pay visits, to keep intact a whole network of news and trade. This communion was of course a principal function of the annual Sun Dance as well.

8   The visitors I liked best, besides the children of my own age, were the old people, for they were exotic. They wore their hair in braids, both men and women, they spoke only Kiowa, and they imaged for me the bygone and infinitely exciting time of the centaurs, the warriors, and the buffalo hunters.

9   Among the visitors in my father's day was the old man Koi-khanhodle, "Dragonfly," who to pay his respects every morning would get up before dawn, paint his face, and go out to pray aloud to the rising sun. I have stood on the red earth just east of the house where Koi-khan-hodle stood; I have seen across the plain to the edge of the world; and there I have seen the sun rise. And it was for me the deity that it was for Dragonfly. In that image is concentrated for me the great mystery of the Sun Dance, the long migration of the Kiowas to their destiny, and the tenure of my people on this continent, a tenure of many thousands of years.

10   When I was a child there was a red barn a little to the north and east of the house, near the place where Koi-khan-hodle made his prayer. I loved to play in the barn, which seemed a great cavern of possibility. There, in the dim light, lay

a box of bones, the bones of a horse. The horse, called "Gudal-san" never lost a race. That its bones should be kept long after its death seems entirely appropriate in the context of the plains culture. The Kiowas owned more horses *per capita* than any other tribe on the Great Plains. There is no story of the Kiowa without the horse.

11   Off the southwest corner of the house, near the kitchen steps, was the storm cellar. On the surface it was an earthen mound supported by concrete or cement, I believe, with a large wooden trapdoor at the end nearer the house, slanted at perhaps twenty or thirty degrees. Beneath this door concrete steps led down into a small, subterranean room outfitted with a bench, and little if anything else. In the springtime, when storms raged on the plains, my mother would take me and a kerosene lamp down into that gravelike room in which the earth had a smell that I have never known elsewhere. With the wind roaring and rain—sometimes ear-splitting hail—pounding at the door, my mother would read to soothe her frayed nerves, and I would fall asleep in spite of the fury. My father, who had a Kiowa indifference to such weather, could not be bothered to join us.

12   The arbor was the center of summer. When the weather turned hot we lived in the arbor. It was a sizable frame building, open and screened on all sides, so that the air could move through it freely. It was basically one great room, though a small kitchen extended from the northwest corner. When it rained, water came in from the roof and all around. There was a large table in the middle of the red earthen floor, large enough to seat a dozen people easily. Along the south and east walls were broad wooden benches. On these we slept at night. Along the north wall were cabinets in which were kept dishes and flatware, an ice box (I loved to go with my father to Mountain View, where we bought great blocks of ice), and a shelf on which were a bucket of water and a dipper for drinking and two or three metal basins for washing. When I was old and strong enough, I drew water from the well and carried it to its place on the shelf. There was no plumbing in those days, and no electricity. We walked to the outhouse, and we lighted the nights with kerosene lamps.

13   Most of the Kiowas in the vicinity, including my grandmother, were members of the Rainy Mountain Baptist Church congregation. There were prayer meetings in the arbor on summer nights, and these were wonderful occasions. The older people came in their finery, and they brought good food in abundance. They sang hymns in Kiowa, they gave testimony to their faith in the rich oratory of the Native American oral tradition—and they visited. The children played outside in the lamplight that fell upon the grass, caught up in the sheer excitement of communion, celebration, festivity. I can still hear the singing and the laughter and the lively talk floating on the plain, reaching away to the dark river and the pecan grove, reaching perhaps to Rainy Mountain and the old school and cemetery.

14   Home. Homestead. Ancestral home. If I close my eyes, I can see Dragonfly there beyond the hedge. I can see my young parents walking toward the creek in the late afternoon, a coppery light on the path. I can hear my grandmother's voice in the rooms of the house and in the cool corners of the arbor. And these are sacred recollections of the mind and heart.

1. What is the primary reason the homestead on Rainy Mountain Creek is important to Momaday?

2. Why did Momaday feel that he knew his grandfather, even though he died before Momaday was born?

3. Momaday's grandfather, unlike most Kiowas at the time, was a good farmer. Why didn't the grandfather's contemporaries take to farming very readily? What does it say about Momaday's grandfather that he *did* become a good farmer? Do the answers to these questions have anything to do with assimilation and cultural persistence? Why or why not?

4. As a child, Momaday's favorite visitors included the elderly, whom he found to be "exotic" (paragraph 8). As an adult, is Momaday still likely to consider these visitors to be exotic? Why or why not?

5. When Momaday watched the sun rise across the plain, "it was for [him] the deity that it was for Dragonfly" (paragraph 9). Explain why that is the case.

EXAMINING STRUCTURE AND STRATEGY

1. In your own words, write out the thesis of the essay. Be sure to include the dominant impression.

2. Paragraphs 9, 10, and 11 do more than describe aspects of Momaday's homestead. What else do they do? How do these paragraphs help the author achieve his purpose for writing?

3. Although the description is largely objective, Momaday still conveys emotion. How does he convey how he feels about his homestead and his family?

4. Why does Momaday use so much objective description? How does it help him achieve his purpose for writing?

5. What kind of order does Momaday use for the details in paragraphs 1 and 12? Does he use this order anywhere else in the essay?

6. What words describe the tone of the essay? (See page 71 on tone.)

CONSIDERING LANGUAGE AND STYLE

1. Why does Momaday use "Homestead" rather than "Home" in the essay's title?

2. Momaday's closing paragraph begins "Home. Homestead. Ancestral home." What progression do you notice in these sentence fragments? What point do they make?

3. Consult a dictionary if you are unsure of the meaning of any of these words: *hummock* (paragraph 1), *agrarian* (paragraph 3), *centaurs* (paragraph 8).

FOR DISCUSSION IN CLASS OR ONLINE

Does the Kiowa tradition for reunions and visits make sense for Americans today? Would it work? Does it appeal to you? Explain your views. If your instructor so directs, post your response to your class Web site.

WRITING ASSIGNMENTS

1. **In your journal.** In a page or two, explain how connected you feel to your ancestors. If you feel a connection, explain how it is made. If you do not feel a connection, explain why not.

2. **Using description for a purpose.** The purposes in the assignments are possibilities. You may establish whatever purposes you like, within your instructor's guidelines.

   • If you recently visited a place you knew as a child—or if you can do so now— describe the place to convey your feelings upon revisiting it.

   • Momaday notes that the house seems small to him now. To express your feelings and relate your experience, describe a place that seems small to you but that seemed large when you were a child.

   • To express your feelings, relate experience, and perhaps inform, describe someone you consider "exotic" or that you once thought of as exotic.

   • To express your feelings, relate experience, and perhaps inform, describe one aspect of your childhood home (the yard, the kitchen, your bedroom, the porch, and so on) to relate the importance of your family or your cultural heritage.

3. **Combining patterns.** Use description to describe someone who is or was important to you and cause-and-effect analysis to explain why the person is or was important. (Cause-and-effect analysis is explained in Chapter 9.)

4. **Connecting the readings.** Momaday has very strong feelings about his childhood surroundings, as does Alfred Kazin, as he expresses in "My Neighborhood" (page 124). Explain how each author views his childhood environment and then go on to draw one or more conclusions about how we are shaped by place.

5. **Drawing on sources.** Interview someone from a culture other than your own, perhaps an international student or someone else born in another country. Ask that person about some ceremony, ritual, or custom from his or her culture. You might ask about weddings, funerals, child-rearing customs, holiday celebrations, or school customs. Then write an essay describing the ritual, custom, or ceremony that you learned about.

BACKGROUND: A prolific writer of literary criticism and autobiographical works and a popular teacher and lecturer, Alfred Kazin (1915–1998) was born in New York City. Educated at City College and Columbia University, Kazin became known for *On Native Grounds* (1942), a classic study of modern American prose. He was a masterful wordsmith who often wrote reminiscences of the immigrant Jewish neighborhood where he grew up. He also edited volumes of works by the important American authors Herman Melville, F. Scott Fitzgerald, Theodore Dreiser, and Nathaniel Hawthorne. In 1989, he published *Our New York*, a look at New York City that he produced with photographer David Finn. "My Neighborhood" is an excerpt from his autobiographical *A Walker in the City* (1951).

THE PATTERN AND ITS PURPOSES: In "My Neighborhood," you will notice that Alfred Kazin uses both *expressive description* and *objective description* to do more than just *describe* the particulars of his childhood neighborhood in Brownsville, New York; he also **expresses the conflicting feelings** he had about the block he grew up on and the world beyond it, and he **relates some of his experiences** in the neighborhood. Perhaps his conflicting feelings are best summed up in this sentence from the selection: "There was a tremor of pleasure at one place; I held my breath in nausea at another" (paragraph 4).

My Neighborhood
ALFRED KAZIN

The block: *my* block. It was on the Chester Street side of our house, between the grocery and the back wall of the old drugstore, that I was hammered into the shape of the streets. Everything beginning at Blake Avenue would always wear for me some delightful strangeness and mildness, simply because it was not of my block, *the* block, where the clang of your head sounded against the pavement when you fell in a fist fight, and the rows of storelights on each side were pitiless, watching you. Anything away from the block was good: even a school you never went to, two blocks away; there were vegetable gardens in the park across the street. Returning from "New York," I would take the longest routes home from the subway, get off a station ahead of our own, only for the unexpectedness of walking through Betsy Head Park and hearing gravel crunch under my feet as I went beyond the vegetable gardens, smelling the sweaty sweet dampness from the pool in summer and the dust on the leaves as I passed under the ailanthus trees. On the block itself everything rose up only to test me.

> **As you read**
> Notice the artistry of Kazin's precise, evocative word choice and reflect on your own feelings about the neighborhood you grew up in.

2   We worked every inch of it, from the cellars and the backyards to the sickening space between the roofs. Any wall, any stoop, any curving metal edge on a billboard sign made a place against which to knock a ball; any bottom rung of a fire escape ladder a goal in basketball; any sewer cover a base; any crack in the pavement a "net" for the tense sharp tennis that we played by beating a soft ball back and forth with our hands between the squares. Betsy Head Park two blocks away would always feel slightly foreign, for it belonged to the Amboys and the Bristols and the Hopkinsons as much as it did to us. *Our* life every day was fought out on

the pavement and in the gutter, up against the walls of the houses and the glass fronts of the drugstore and the grocery, in and out of the fresh steaming piles of horse manure, the wheels of passing carts and automobiles, along the iron spikes of the stairway to the cellar, the jagged edge of the open garbage cans, the crumbly steps of the old farmhouses still left on one side of the street.

3   As I go back to the block now, and for a moment fold my body up again in its narrow area—there, just there, between the black of the asphalt and the old women in their kerchiefs and flowered housedresses sitting on the tawny kitchen chairs— the back wall of the drugstore still rises up to test me. Every day we smashed a small black viciously hard regulation handball against it with fanatical cuts and drives and slams, beating and slashing at it almost in hatred for the blind strength of the wall itself. I was never good enough at handball, was always practicing some trick shot that might earn me esteem, and when I was weary of trying, would often bat a ball down Chester Street just to get myself to Blake Avenue. I have this memory of playing one-o'-cat by myself in the sleepy twilight, at a moment when everyone else had left the block. The sparrows floated down from the telephone wires to peck at every fresh pile of horse manure, and there was a smell of brine from the delicatessen store, of egg crates and of the milk scum left in the great metal cans outside the grocery, of the thick white paste oozing out from behind the fresh Hecker's Flour ad on the metal signboard. I would throw the ball in the air, hit it with my bat, then with perfect satisfaction drop the bat to the ground and run to the next sewer cover. Over and over I did this, from sewer cover to sewer cover, until I had worked my way to Blake Avenue and could see the park.

4   With each clean triumphant ring of my bat against the gutter leading me on, I did the whole length of our block up and down, and never knew how happy I was just watching the asphalt rise and fall, the curve of the steps up to an old farmhouse. The farmhouses themselves were streaked red on one side, brown on the other, but the steps themselves were always gray. There was a tremor of pleasure at one place; I held my breath in nausea at another. As I ran after my ball with the bat heavy in my hand, the odd successiveness of things in myself almost choked me, the world was so full as I ran—past the cobblestoned yards into the old farmhouses, where stray chickens still waddled along the stones; past the little candy store where we went only if the big one on our side of the block was out of Eskimo Pies; past the three neighboring tenements where the last of the old women sat on their kitchen chairs yawning before they went up to make supper. Then came Mrs. Rosenwasser's house, the place on the block I first identified with what was farthest from home, and strangest, because it was a "private" house; then the fences around the monument works, where black cranes rose up above the yard and you could see the smooth gray slabs that would be cut and carved into tombstone, some of them already engraved with the names and dates and family virtues of the dead.

5   Beyond Blake Avenue was the pool parlor outside which we waited all through the tense September afternoons of the World's Series to hear the latest scores called off the ticker tape—and where as we waited, banging a ball against the bottom of the wall and drinking water out of empty Coke bottles, I breathed the chalk off the cues and listened to the clocks ringing in the fire station across the street. There was

an old warehouse next to the pool parlor; the oil on the barrels and the iron staves had the same rusty smell. A block away was the park, thick with the dusty gravel I liked to hear my shoes crunch in as I ran round and round the track; then a great open pavilion, the inside mysteriously dark, chill even in summer; there I would wait in the sweaty coolness before pushing on to the wading ring where they put up a shower on the hottest days.

6   Beyond the park the "fields" began, all those still unused lots where we could still play hard ball in perfect peace—first shooing away the goats and then tearing up goldenrod before laying our bases. The smell and touch of those "fields," with their wild compost under the billboards of weeds, goldenrod, bricks, goat droppings, rusty cans, empty beer bottles, fresh new lumber, and damp cement, lives in my mind as Brownsville's great open door, the wastes that took us through to the west. I used to go round them in summer with my cousins selling near-beer to the carpenters, but always in a daze, would stare so long at the fibrous stalks of the goldenrod as I felt their harshness in my hand that I would forget to make a sale, and usually go off sick on the beer I drank up myself. Beyond! Beyond! Only to see something new, to get away from each day's narrow battleground between the grocery and the back wall of the drugstore! Even the other end of our block, when you got to Mrs. Rosenwasser's house and the monument works, was dear to me for the contrast. On summer nights, when we played Indian trail, running away from each other on prearranged signals, the greatest moment came when I could plunge into the darkness down the block for myself and hide behind the slabs in the monument works. I remember the air whistling around me as I ran, the panicky thud of my bones in my sneakers, and then the slabs rising in the light from the street lamps as I sped past the little candy store and crept under the fence.

7   In the darkness you could never see where the crane began. We liked to trap the enemy between the slabs and sometimes jumped them from great mounds of rock just in from the quarry. A boy once fell to his death that way, and they put a watchman there to keep us out. This made the slabs all the more impressive to me, and I always aimed first for that yard whenever we played follow-the-leader. Day after day the monument works became oppressively more mysterious and remote, though it was only just down the block; I stood in front of it every afternoon on my way back from school, filling it with my fears. It was not death I felt there— the slabs were usually faceless. It was the darkness itself, and the wind howling around me whenever I stood poised on the edge of a high slab waiting to jump. Then I would take in, along with the fear, some amazement of joy that I had found my way out that far.

READING CLOSELY AND THINKING CRITICALLY

1.   Kazin's feelings about his neighborhood and the territory beyond his neighborhood contrast with each other. Describe this contrast.

2.   Kazin has conflicting feelings about his neighborhood. Describe those conflicting feelings. Describe Kazin's conflicting feelings about the world beyond his neighborhood.

3. As an adult returning to his old neighborhood, how does Kazin feel about the block he grew up on? Cite evidence to support your view.
4. When Kazin says, "We worked every inch of it [his block]" (paragraph 2), what do you think he means?
5. Why was Kazin so drawn to the monument works?
6. Since it is at the edge of the neighborhood, the monument works can be taken as the bridge from Kazin's neighborhood to the outside, a bridge from the known to the unknown. With this in mind, interpret the last two sentences of the selection.

EXAMINING STRUCTURE AND STRATEGY

1. Very early in the essay—in the first two paragraphs, in fact—Kazin conveys the idea that his neighborhood was a harsh, difficult place. Cite three or four sensory details that help convey this idea.
2. Kazin uses both objective and expressive description (see page 105). Cite an example of each that you particularly like. Why do these descriptions appeal to you?
3. To which of the five senses does Kazin's description appeal? Cite an example of description that appeals to each sense you name.
4. Which paragraphs begin with topic sentences? What purpose do these topic sentences serve?
5. Part of Kazin's purpose is to convey the conflicting feelings he had about his neighborhood. How does the description of the monument works in paragraph 7 help him achieve that purpose?
6. Do you think a reader must be familiar with urban life in order to appreciate "My Neighborhood"? Why or why not?

CONSIDERING LANGUAGE AND STYLE

1. "My Neighborhood" opens with a four-word sentence fragment. What effect does this beginning have on the reader?
2. Consult a dictionary if you are unsure of the meaning of any of these words: *tawny* (paragraph 3), *fanatical* (paragraph 3), *brine* (paragraph 3), *ticker tape* (paragraph 5), *near-beer* (paragraph 6).
3. Which of the words in number 2 are obsolete (relevant to a much earlier time)? Explain.

FOR DISCUSSION IN CLASS OR ONLINE

Although Kazin enjoyed aspects of his neighborhood, he found life on the block harsh, difficult, and confining; although he longed for the world beyond because he found it milder, he feared the uncertainty of the outside. How do you explain Kazin's ambivalent feelings? Are they normal? Do young people commonly experience such conflicting feelings regardless of where they are raised? With your classmates, consider the answers to these questions. If your instructor so directs, post your response to your class Web site.

1. **In your journal.** Write out your most vivid memory of your childhood neighborhood and the positive and/or negative emotions this memory stirs in you. Also, try to explain why you feel the way you do.

2. **Using description for a purpose.** The purposes given in the assignments are possibilities. You may establish whatever purposes you like, within your instructor's guidelines.

    *   To express your feelings and relate your experience, do what Kazin does and describe the neighborhood where you grew up. Your description should convey whether you liked the neighborhood, disliked the neighborhood, or had conflicting feelings about it.

    *   To express your feelings and relate your experience and/or to inform, describe any place that raises conflicting emotions in you—your house or apartment, a doctor's office, a hospital, or your parents' home, for example. Select details that convey these conflicting emotions.

    *   Part of Kazin's description focuses on the games he played as a child. Describe a common childhood game. You can include the place where it was played and the people it was played with if you like. Your purpose is to convey what the game means to children and what they learn as a result of playing.

3. **Combining patterns.** Describe a place that had a significant impact on you (Little League fields, your high school gym, your best friend's bedroom, for example) and use cause-and-effect analysis to explain how the place affected you.

4. **Connecting the readings.** Both "My Neighborhood" and "The Homestead on Rainy Mountain Creek" (page 119) include descriptions of places where the authors played. Describe a place where you played as a child and convey the feelings you have or had for that place. If you like, you can explain to what extent the place has shaped who you are now.

5. **Drawing on sources.** At one time, most sports were only for the rich, but baseball attracted people from all walks of life. League players were usually from the working class, and because African-Americans were barred from professional teams, they formed their own league. (Eventually, Jackie Robinson joined the Brooklyn Dodgers, leading the way by desegregating a major league baseball team. Other teams soon followed the Dodgers' lead.) Baseball is mentioned several times in "My Neighborhood" and was clearly important to young Kazin. Describe the features of baseball that might have appealed to city-dwellers of the 1930s, who, like Kazin, lived during the Great Depression. In addition to your own thinking, you may get ideas from *Baseball: An Illustrated History* by Geoffrey C. Ward and Ken Burns or from these Web sites devoted to baseball history: www.baseball-links.com/links/history, www.baseballhalloffame.org/history, www.pbs.org/kenburns/baseball/players.

BACKGROUND: Born in Fort Worth, Texas, in 1958, Rick Bass became fascinated by nature early, in part because his father was a geologist. Bass himself went on to become an oil and gas geologist. His experiences prospecting for new wells in the South and Southwest formed the basis for his book *Oil Notes* (1989). Eventually, love of nature drew Bass to Yaak Valley, Montana, where he now works to save the remaining acres of roadless land. Primarily a nature writer, Bass has also won awards for fiction. His fiction includes the novel *Where the Sea Used to Be* (1988) and a number of short story collections, including *The Hermit's Story* (2002). Bass's nonfiction works include *The New Wolves* (1998), *Brown Dog of the Yaak: Essays on Art and Activism* (1999), and *Colter: The True Story of the Best Dog I Ever Had* (2000). "A Winter's Tale" first appeared in *The Atlantic Monthly* (January 2000).

COMBINED PATTERNS AND THEIR PURPOSES: In "A Winter's Tale," Rick Bass uses both objective and expressive detail to *describe* winter at his Montana home and its effect on him to **relate his experience** and **express his feelings.** Because his expressive description is so evocative, you may also be **entertained** by the essay, and if you know little about winter in Montana, you may also be **informed.** Despite the essay's title, Bass opens by saying that he doesn't have "a specific Winter's tale." He does, nonetheless, *narrate* a tale to **inform** the reader of why winter is so memorable to him.

A WINTER'S TALE

RICK BASS

When I consider whether anything memorable or extraordinary has happened to me up here in the Montana winter, I come up lacking. I don't have a specific winter's tale. Or if I ever had one, it has been wiped clean from the slate; no memory or even hint of a memorable winter event exists. It's as if all the winters of my life have hypnotized me, committing my memory to snowmelt, to runoff.

As you read Notice Bass's use of both objective and expressive details.

2   Mostly I remember the ephemera of winter—the regular details, hypnotic and soothing in their repetition and their steadfast predictability, which give a peculiar sweetness to the so-short days, the steadiness of the non-events. It's possible that I'm sleeping through most of winter's memorability. (Often in January and February I sleep ten hours a night; I'm exhausted by five in the evening, wobbly by six, longing for the pillow by seven, and snoring by eight.) But I don't think so. I don't be-

> "I don't believe that it's in winter's nature to live by big events."

lieve that it's in winter's nature to live by big events. Winter lacks the pyrotechnics of spring, the brute, strapping joy of summer, the old sugary nostalgia of autumn. It's just cold and elegant, monochromatic, somnolent. Animals are asleep or gone south. I might hear a lone raven croak or caw, and the integrity of that sound, so isolate, can seem almost shattering. For a moment I nearly awaken—such crispness, amid a time of all-other mutedness, lures my heart up and out of its sleepy resting time. But then the raven is gone. I listen to the cloth-cutting sound of its heavy wingbeats, and then even that is gone, and it doesn't call again.

3   I remember the sounds in town in early winter, as the trucks go driving

past with their rattling, clanking tire chains. But I'm not sure that's memorable.

4   I remember the sight of a swarm of mayflies hatching along the river during a snowstorm, when the temperature was right around freezing: mayflies rising and disappearing into a descending curtain of snow.

5   I remember the way the house gets warmer in the middle of the night when it's snowing—as if someone had laid another blanket over me. I remember what it's like to wake briefly, feel that extra warmth, know without having to look out the window that the snow has begun again, and then go back to sleep.

6   I remember walking outside one day in midwinter, when my skin was already dry and tight—going from 60° indoors to −45° outside. When the cold air hit my face, my skin contracted so quickly that the thin skin on the bridge of my nose split, as if a fine knife had been drawn across it, and a spray of blood leaped out from that split.

7   What I remember about winters past is the sweet and complete loneliness, and the deep rest of down time. The incredible, unyielding slowness. The purple, snow-laden skies dense over the twin humps of Roderick Butte outside my kitchen window: the same view every day.

8   The routine: up early, eat a bowl of oatmeal, drive my older daughter to school, return home, fix coffee, head out to the cabin to work, shuffling through the new snow, usually ankle-deep. Such stillness: to remember color or sound at that time of year, one must go into the imagination.

9 Build a fire in the wood stove. Work for three or four hours. Go back to the house. Only a few hours of light left, just enough time to put on snowshoes or cross-country skis and set out for a short trip, which is a necessary thing every day, no matter what the weather—necessary for the beauty, but also to keep the blood flowing, to keep cabin fever at bay. Down in the depths of winter a fine line distinguishes euphoria from despair for the unpracticed or the extravagant. One has to move carefully, slowly, as if on thin ice above a deep emotional chasm.

10 While I'm out on snowshoes or skis, even with my heart pounding and my blood running strong, I find that I'll nonetheless fall back into trances, into winter states of near-hypnosis. I can stare for long moments at the stark white of an aspen tree against the day's new snow, with more falling, or at the ice scallop where a deer bedded down, the warmth of its body melting its shape into fallen snow, the cast as yet un-filled by the oncoming snow. And I can be made inexplicably happy by such staring.

11 Time to push on, gliding on the skis. Not going anywhere, and not running from anything. Just going.

* * *

12 My wife and I have two young daughters, and I worry as I age that they will soon find us, or me, exceedingly boring. I worry that I will hold them back with my staid, sleepy pleasure in the world; that my stodginess might somehow rub off on them; that my will-ingness to postpone the pursuit of true excitement in favor of a quiet evening at home with a book, or a short walk in the woods, may in some vague way be keep-ing them from unfettered joy.

13 I don't always feel that way. But in winter it's more pronounced; their hearts beat so fast, and mine beats so slowly.

14 Once, something happened that I guess I could call memorable—though someone else might find it unexcep-tional.

15 Our house looks out on a large, per-fectly round marsh. We live tucked be-neath dense forests of spruce and fir and larch, but the marsh has only sky above it—one of the few openings in the dense forest.

16 Once or twice each winter a chinook will blow through, melting the snow in the marsh and turning it into a pond; and then, following the chinook, the cold will return, freezing the pond crack-ling solid, perfect for skating. In any winter weather we ski or sled on the frozen marsh. I attach the sled to my waist with a rope and gallop around and around like a horse, giving the girls rides, glorying at being, for a little while, out from under the beautiful shroud of the forest. But in the cold spells follow-ing those chinooks we skate, and be-cause the ice is so new, so quickly refor-mulated, it is strangely clear. We can see the bent, yellowing marsh grass folded down below that clear ice, but we aren't in danger: the ice is solid, and even if it weren't, the marsh is rarely more than a foot deep.

17 The clarity, the lucidity, of the ice is not the memorable thing. We've discov-ered that at dusk—even after the sun has gone down behind the buttes—this clear, clean ice will retain bands of color within it, ribbons of cobalt, extraterres-trial in hue. We have no idea where the color is coming from. No sunlight is left in the sky—just the ghost light of dusk. But the ice glows with those space-blue

ribbons, just beneath the slick surface. We've never seen the color anywhere else. It seems trapped in the ice, desiring

> We've never seen the color anywhere else."

to get out. We can see it only at dusk, and it's there for only a day or two. Then the snow returns and buries it.

18   The memorable thing is this: that swirling cobalt gives us extra energy, extra strength. The children are always joyful, but out there on that clear ice I can skate with them and pull them on the sled all day long, on into the dusk, and into the gloom of winter-evening light, long past supper, leaping, sliding, running, jumping. Out on that cobalt pond another alchemy seems to take place just above the ice: I feel the same age as the children, and do not tire, and the leaps of my heart are in perfect lockstep with theirs.

19   Later that night, after supper, because the ice is smooth and perfect, I go back out to skate on it by starlight, and to watch the winter stars, so fierce and bright. It's twenty below or colder, but the stars are so much more brilliant, the atmosphere is so clear, at that temperature, and that great opening in the sky above the marsh is exhilarating.

20   I hope the children remember those times. They are memorable to me.

21   I have no other tales beyond that. Have I slept through winter always? Have I missed something? I don't believe that I have.

READING CLOSELY AND THINKING CRITICALLY

1. In paragraph 1, Bass says he has no "specific winter's tale" because he can think of nothing "extraordinary" that has happened. How does the essay prove him correct? How does it prove him incorrect?

2. How does Bass feel about his Montana winters? Why does he feel that way?

3. In paragraph 10, Bass notes that he is happy staring at an aspen tree or the imprint of a deer in the snow. Why does staring make him happy?

4. What is the alchemy that Bass refers to in paragraph 18? Why does he use the word *alchemy*?

5. Answer the two questions that Bass asks in the conclusion.

EXAMINING STRUCTURE AND STRATEGY

1. Bass includes both objective and expressive details. Cite an example of each. Do you think he should have limited himself to just one or the other kind of detail? Why or why not?

2. What is Bass's dominant impression? Cite three examples of expressive description that effectively conveys that impression and explain why the examples are effective.

3. Why does Bass end paragraph 7 by making a point that the view from his kitchen window is "the same view every day" and then begin paragraph 8 with "The routine"?

NOTING COMBINED PATTERNS

1. Where does the narration of the tale actually begin? Why is that narration delayed to this point?
2. Bass really pairs two narrations in his essay. What are they?
3. Why do the asterisks appear before paragraph 12? How would the essay be different if the asterisks were omitted?

CONSIDERING LANGUAGE AND STYLE

1. **Verbal irony** occurs when an author says one thing but really means another, often opposite point. What verbal irony occurs in "A Winter's Tale"?
2. Bass uses a number of sentence fragments (incomplete sentences). What is the effect of the sentence fragments in paragraphs 8 and 9?
3. Bass's description includes both similes and metaphors (see page 109). Cite an example of each and explain how they help the author achieve his writing purposes.
4. Consult a dictionary if you are unsure of the meaning of any of these words: *ephemera* (paragraph 2), *pyrotechnics* (paragraph 2), *somnolent* (paragraph 2), *staid* (paragraph 12), *stodginess* (paragraph 12) *chinook* (paragraph 16), *alchemy* (paragraph 18).

FOR DISCUSSION IN CLASS OR ONLINE

Why does Bass feel so energized when he is skating on cobalt ice? Is it "alchemy" (paragraph 18), or is there another explanation? Share your conclusions with your classmates, and if your instructor directs, post them to your class Web site.

WRITING ASSIGNMENTS

1. **In your journal.** Does the kind of winter Bass describes appeal to you? In a page or so, explain why or why not.
2. **Using description for a purpose.** The purposes given in the assignments are possibilities. You may establish whatever purposes you like, within your instructor's guidelines.
   - Describe your favorite season to express your feelings and/or relate your experience. Be sure to include a dominant impression and details that explain why the season is so pleasant for you.
   - In paragraph 18, Bass says that skating on the blue ice makes him feel young. To relate your experience and/or express your feelings, describe something that makes you feel younger or older than you are.
   - In paragraph 2, Bass refers to the "ephemera of winter." To entertain your reader, describe one or more of the ephemera of another season, or describe one or more of the ephemera of winter. As an alternative, describe the "pyrotechnics of spring" (paragraph 2) or of some other season.

3. **Combining patterns.**
   - Using description and narration (explained in Chapter 5), tell your own winter's tale— or tell a spring, summer, or fall tale.
   - Describe an activity associated with a particular season, such as raking leaves, shoveling snow, swimming, or planting a garden. Use process analysis (explained in Chapter 7) to explain how the activity is performed.
4. **Connecting the readings.** One theme of "A Winter's Tale" is youth and age, a theme also apparent in "Once More to the Lake" (page 676). Using the ideas in those essays, along with your own experience and observation, discuss how adults are influenced by their views of childhood. How are you influenced by your view of childhood?
5. **Drawing on sources.** "A Winter's Tale" paints a vivid picture of winter in Yaak Valley, Montana. Assume you work for the Montana Tourism Bureau, and write copy for a brochure about winter in Montana, in order to entice people to travel to the state between January and March. As a starting point, consider the essay and look at some Montana travel guides, such as *Frommer's Montana and Wyoming* by Don Laine and Barbara Laine. Online, visit www.wintermt.com for information.

BACKGROUND: Both a writer and a teacher of writing (at Wesleyan University in Connecticut); Annie Dillard has been a columnist for *The Living Wilderness* and a contributing editor for *Harper's* magazine. Born in 1945, Dillard won a Pulitzer Prize in 1975 for her first book of prose, *The Pilgrim at Tinker Creek,* a collection of observations about the beauty and violence of the natural world near her Virginia home. Dillard's other works include poetry; *For the Time Being* (1999), a personal narrative; *Encounters with Chinese Writers* (1984), a work about her visit to China as part of a United States cultural delegation; *The Writing Life* (1989), a narrative about the writing process; and a book of essays, *Teaching a Stone to Talk* (1982). "The Deer at Providencia," is from *Teaching a Stone to Talk.*

www.mhhe.com/patterns

For more information on this author, go to

More resources > Chapter 4 > Annie Dillard

COMBINED PATTERNS AND THEIR PURPOSES: "The Deer at Providencia" is a *description* of the torment of a deer. This description is a powerful component of Dillard's *narration* (story) about the suffering of humans and animals. The weaving of the descriptive and narrative elements allows Dillard to **relate her experience** in the Ecuadorian jungle and **express her feelings** of uncertainty.

The Deer at Providencia
ANNIE DILLARD

There were four of us North Americans in the jungle, in the Ecuadorian jungle on the banks of the Napo River in the Amazon watershed. The other three North Americans were metropolitan men. We stayed in tents in one riverside village, and visited others. At the village called Providencia we saw a sight which moved us, and which shocked the men.

As you read
Think about the suffering people and animals experience. How much of that suffering is avoidable?

2   The first thing we saw when we climbed the riverbank to the village of Providencia was the deer. It was roped to a tree on the grass clearing near the thatch shelter where we would eat lunch.

3   The deer was small, about the size of a whitetail fawn, but apparently full-grown. It had a rope around its neck and three feet caught in the rope. Someone said that the dogs had caught it that morning and the villagers were going to cook and eat it that night.

4   This clearing lay at the edge of the little thatched-hut village. We could see the villagers going about their business, scattering feed corn for hens about their houses, and wandering down paths to the river to bathe. The village headman was our host; he stood beside us as we watched the deer struggle. Several village boys were interested in the deer; they formed part of the circle we made around it in the clearing. So also did four businessmen from Quito who were attempting to guide us around the jungle. Few of the very different people standing in this circle had a common language. We watched the deer, and no one said much.

5   The deer lay on its side at the rope's very end, so the rope lacked slack to let it rest its head in the dust. It was "pretty," delicate of bone like all deer, and thin-skinned for the tropics. Its skin looked virtually hairless, in fact, and almost translucent, like a membrane. Its neck was no thicker than my wrist; it was rubbed open on the rope, and gashed. Trying to paw itself free of the rope, the deer had scratched its own neck with its hooves. The raw underside of its neck showed red stripes and some bruises bleeding inside the muscles. Now three of its feet were hooked in the rope under its jaw. It could not stand, of course, on one leg, so it could not move to slacken the rope and ease the pull on its throat and enable it to rest its head.

6   Repeatedly the deer paused, motionless, its eyes veiled, with only its rib cage in motion, and its breaths the only sound. Then, after I would think, "It has given up; now it will die," it would heave. The rope twanged; the tree leaves clattered; the deer's free foot beat the ground. We stepped back and held our breaths. It thrashed, kicking, but only one leg moved; the other three legs tightened inside the rope's loop. Its hip jerked; its spine shook. Its eyes rolled; its tongue, thick with spittle, pushed in and out. Then it would rest again. We watched this for fifteen minutes.

7   Once three young native boys charged in, released its trapped legs, and jumped back to the circle of people. But instantly the deer scratched up its neck with its hooves and snared its forelegs in the rope again. It was easy to imagine a third and then a fourth leg soon stuck, like Brer Rabbit and the Tar Baby.

8   We watched the deer from the circle, and then we drifted on to lunch. Our palm-roofed shelter stood on a grassy promontory from which we would see the deer tied to the tree, pigs and hens walking under village houses, and black-and-white cattle standing in the river. There was even a breeze.

9   Lunch, which was the second and better lunch we had that day, was hot and fried. There was a big fish called *doncella*, a kind of catfish, dipped whole in corn flour and beaten egg, then deep fried. With our fingers we pulled soft fragments of it from its sides to our plates, and ate; it was delicate fish-flesh, fresh and mild. Someone found the roe, and I ate of that too—it was fat and stronger, like egg yolk, naturally enough, and warm.

10   There was also a stew of meat in shreds with rice and pale brown gravy. I had asked what kind of deer it was tied to the tree; Pepe had answered in Spanish, "*Gama*." Now they told us this was *gama* too, stewed. I suspect the word means merely game or venison. At any rate, I heard that the village dogs had cornered another deer just yesterday, and it was this deer which we were now eating in full sight of the whole article. It was good. I was surprised at its tenderness. But it is a fact that high levels of lactic acid, which builds up in muscle tissues during exertion, tenderizes.

11   After the fish and meat we ate bananas fried in chunks and served on a tray; they were sweet and full of flavor. I felt terrific. My shirt was wet and cool from swimming; I had had a night's sleep, two decent walks, three meals, and a swim— everything tasted good. From time to time each one of us, separately, would look beyond our shaded roof to the sunny spot where the deer was still convulsing in the dust. Our meal completed, we walked around the deer and back to the boats.

12   That night I learned that while we were watching the deer, the others were watching me.

13   We four North Americans grew close in the jungle in a way that was not the usual artificial intimacy of travelers. We liked each other. We stayed up all that night talking, murmuring, as though we rocked on hammocks slung above time. The others were from big cities: New York, Washington, Boston. They all said that I had no expression on my face when I was watching the deer—or at any rate, not the expression they expected.

14   They had looked to see how I, the only woman, and the youngest, was taking the sight of the deer's struggles. I looked detached, apparently, or hard, or calm, or focused, still. I don't know. I was thinking. I remember feeling very old and energetic. I could say like Thoreau that I have traveled widely in Roanoke, Virginia. I have thought a great deal about carnivorousness; I eat meat. These things are not issues; they are mysteries.

15   Gentlemen of the city, what surprises you? That there is suffering here, or that I know it?

16   We lay in the tent and talked. "If it had been my wife," one man said with special vigor, amazed, "she wouldn't have cared *what* was going on; she would have dropped *everything* right at that moment and gone in the village from here to there to there, she would not have *stopped* until that animal was out of its suffering one way or another. She couldn't *bear* to see a creature in agony like that."

17   I nodded.

18   Now I am home. When I wake I comb my hair before the mirror above my dresser. Every morning for the past two years I have seen in that mirror, beside my sleep-softened face, the blacked face of a burnt man. It is a wire-service photograph clipped from a newspaper and taped to my mirror. The caption reads: "Alan McDonald in Miami hospital bed." All you can see in the photograph is a smudged triangle of face from his eyelids to his lower lip; the rest is bandages. You cannot see the expression in his eyes; the bandages shade them.

19   The story, headed MAN BURNED FOR SECOND TIME, begins:

> "Why does God hate me?" Alan McDonald asked from his hospital bed.
> "When the gunpowder went off, I couldn't believe it," he said. "I just couldn't believe it. I said, 'No, God couldn't do this to me again.'"

He was in a burn ward in Miami, in serious condition. I do not even know if he lived. I wrote him a letter at the time, cringing.

20   He had been burned before, thirteen years previously, by flaming gasoline. For years he had been having his body restored and his face remade in dozens of operations. He had been a boy, and then a burnt boy. He had already been stunned by what could happen, by how life could veer.

21   Once I read that people who survive bad burns tend to go crazy; they have a very high suicide rate. Medicine cannot ease their pain; drugs just leak away, soaking the sheets, because there is no skin to hold them in. The people just lie there and weep. Later they kill themselves. They had not known, before they were burned, that the world included such suffering, that life could permit them personally such pain.

22   This time a bowl of gunpowder had exploded on McDonald.

"I didn't realize what had happened at first," he recounted. "And then I heard that sound from 13 years ago. I was burning. I rolled to put the fire out and I thought, 'Oh God, not again.'

"If my friend hadn't been there, I would have jumped into a canal with a rock around my neck."

His wife concludes the piece, "Man, it just isn't fair."

23   I read the whole clipping again every morning. This is the Big Time here, every minute of it. Will someone please explain to Alan McDonald in his dignity, to the deer at Providencia in his dignity, what is going on? And mail me the carbon.

24   When we walked by the deer at Providencia for the last time, I said to Pepe, with a pitying glance at the deer, *"Pobrecito"*—"poor little thing." But I was trying out Spanish. I knew at the time it was a ridiculous thing to say.

READING CLOSELY AND THINKING CRITICALLY

1. In your own words, write a sentence or two that expresses the thesis of "The Deer of Providencia."

2. Describe the way the men react to the deer. How is their reaction different from Dillard's? Why are the men surprised by Dillard's reaction to the deer?

3. Why does Dillard note (in paragraph 10) that high levels of lactic acid tenderize meat?

4. What view of women is referred to in paragraphs 15 and 16?

5. Do you agree with Dillard that *"Pobrecito"* ("poor little thing") was a ridiculous thing for her to say as she walked by the deer? Explain.

6. Why do you think that Dillard kept the picture and article about Alan McDonald?

EXAMINING STRUCTURE AND STRATEGY

1. What approach does Dillard take to her introduction (see page 62)?

2. Dillard writes of the deer at Providencia and of Alan McDonald. What do these two have in common? That is, how is it possible to discuss both in the same essay? How does each discussion relate to Dillard's purpose?

3. Which of the descriptive paragraphs are developed primarily with objective detail and which with expressive detail?

4. What attitude toward the deer is Dillard's audience likely to have? How is the reader likely to react to the deer's plight? How does Dillard respond to her audience's probable reaction? How does her response further her purpose?

NOTING COMBINED PATTERNS

1. Which paragraphs are developed primarily with description?
2. Which paragraphs are developed primarily with narration (storytelling)?

CONSIDERING LANGUAGE AND STYLE

1. Dillard uses descriptive language to portray the deer as fragile. Cite two examples of such language.
2. What is significant about the name of the village (Providencia)?
3. Consult a dictionary if you are unsure of the meaning of any of these words: *watershed* (paragraph 1), *thatch* (paragraph 2), *translucent* (paragraph 5), *spittle* (paragraph 6), *promontory* (paragraph 8), *carnivorousness* (paragraph 14).

FOR DISCUSSION IN CLASS OR ONLINE

With your classmates, consider this question: Do you see a difference between the suffering of the deer and the suffering of Alan McDonald? If so, explain what that difference is. If not, explain why. If your instructor so directs, post your response to your class website.

WRITING ASSIGNMENTS

1. **In your journal.** At one time, killing animals for food was a necessity, but many people claim that we no longer need to do so, that vegetarianism eliminates the need for animals to suffer and die for us. Attack or defend the killing of animals for food.
2. **Using description for a purpose.** The purposes given in the assignments are possibilities. You may establish whatever purposes you like, within your instructor's guidelines.
   - Like Dillard, describe an animal engaged in some activity. For example, you could describe a kitten at play, a cat washing itself, a dog chasing a ball, or fish swimming in a tank. Use expressive detail to entertain your reader (if the activity is a pleasant one), to relate the animal's experience, and to inform your reader about the animal's level of comfort.
   - If you have experienced considerable pain, describe what you went through. For example, you can describe having a broken leg, a migraine headache, or a sports injury. Your purpose can be to relate your experience, to express your feelings about it, and/or to inform your reader of what the experience was like.
   - To entertain and perhaps inform your reader, describe an animal in its natural habitat or its common surroundings. For example, you can describe a squirrel on the campus commons, a monkey in the zoo, a dog in your yard, or a cat in a pet store.
3. **Combining patterns.** Like Dillard, narrate a story that teaches something about life. Include a considerable amount of description.
4. **Connecting the readings.** Do you think we do enough to reduce suffering in the world? Explain your view. The information in "The Deer at Providencia," "Untouchables" (page 248), and "What Is Poverty?" (page 511), may give you some ideas.

5. **Drawing on sources.** Part of "The Deer at Providencia" focuses on the tremendous suffering endured by Alan McDonald. Many people believe that those who are suffering and who have little or no chance to recover should be allowed to request euthanasia, sometimes called "mercy killing." Many others believe that euthanasia is wrong. To examine this controversial issue, summarize the chief arguments on both sides of the euthanasia debate. Use description to provide examples that support either or both sides. If you need a starting point, look up *euthanasia* in the *Social Sciences Index* and the *Humanities Index*. These volumes, located in your library's reference room, will direct you to articles on the subject. If you prefer to use the Internet, type in the keyword *euthanasia* into your favorite search engine. Your search results will lead you to a number of helpful sites.

BACKGROUND: Novelist, poet, and essayist, Gretel Ehrlich was born in California and attended Bennington College, UCLA Film School, and the New School for Social Research. She is multitalented, having been a journalist, documentary filmmaker, poet, and fiction writer. Annie Dillard, who wrote "The Deer at Providencia" (page 135), calls Ehrlich's writing "vivid, tough, and funny." Ehrlich decided to live in Wyoming after going there to make a film. She is noted for writing poetically about the vast Wyoming landscapes. Strong and capable (as the following selection reveals), Ehrlich did ranch work, sheep herding, and cattle branding. A prolific author, she has published in the *New York Times, Atlantic, Time,* and *Harper's.* She has received awards from the National Endowment for the Arts and the Wyoming Council for the Arts. Ehrlich's books include *The Solace of Open* Spaces (1985), *Heart Mountain* (1988), *Drinking Dry Clouds: Stories from Wyoming* (1991), *A Match to the Heart: One Woman's Story of Being Struck by Lightning* (1994), and *Questions of Heaven: The Chinese Journeys of an American Buddhist* (1997). "Struck by Lightning" is taken from *A Match to the Heart.*

www.mhhe.com/patterns

For more information on this author, go to

More resources > Chapter 4 > Gretel Ehrlich

COMBINED PATTERNS AND THEIR PURPOSES: To **express her feelings,** Gretel Ehrlich *describes* what it was like when she was struck by lightning. Although Ehrlich uses some *objective description,* she relies much more heavily on *expressive description.* Pay particular attention to the images throughout the piece, as they are among the richest and most provocative in this chapter. Notice, too, that as Ehrlich uses *narration* to **relate her experience,** she moves back and forth in time.

Struck by Lightning
GRETEL EHRLICH

Deep in an ocean. I am suspended motionless. The water is gray. That's all there is, and before that? My arms are held out straight, cruciate, my head and legs hang limp. Nothing moves. Brown kelp lies flat in mud and fish are buried in liquid clouds of dust. There are no shadows or sounds. Should there be? I don't know if I am alive, but if not, how do I know I am dead? My body is leaden, heavier than gravity. Gravity is done with me. No more sinking and rising or bobbing in currents. There is a terrible feeling of oppression with no oppressor. I try to lodge my mind against some boundary, some reference point, but the continent of the body dissolves . . .

As you read
Try to determine why Ehrlich moves her readers back and forth in time.

2   A single heartbeat stirs gray water. Blue trickles in, just a tiny stream. Then a long silence.

3   Another heartbeat. This one is louder, as if amplified. Sound takes a shape: it is a snowplow moving grayness aside like a heavy snowdrift. I can't tell if I'm moving, but more blue water flows in. Seaweed begins to undulate, then a whole kelp forest rises from the ocean floor. A fish swims past and looks at me.

Another heartbeat drives through dead water, and another, until I am surrounded by blue.

4   Sun shines above all this. There is no pattern to the way its glint comes free and falls in long knives of light. My two beloved dogs appear. They flank me like tiny rockets, their fur pressed against my ribs. A leather harness holds us all together. The dogs climb toward light, pulling me upward at a slant from the sea.

5   I have been struck by lightning and I am alive.

6   Before electricity carved its blue path toward me, before the negative charge shot down from cloud to ground, before "streamers" jumped the positive charge back up from ground to cloud, before air expanded and contracted producing loud pressure pulses I could not hear because I was already dead, I had been walking.

7   When I started out on foot that August afternoon, the thunderstorm was blowing in fast. On the face of the mountain, a mile ahead, hard westerly gusts and sudden updrafts collided, pulling black clouds apart. Yet the storm looked harmless. When a distant thunderclap scared the dogs, I called them to my side and rubbed their ears: "Don't worry, you're okay as long as you're with me."

8   I woke in a pool of blood, lying on my stomach some distance from where I should have been, flung at an odd angle to one side of the dirt path. The whole sky had grown dark. Was it evening, and if so, which one? How many minutes or hours had elapsed since I lost consciousness, and where were the dogs? I tried to call out to them but my voice didn't work. The muscles in my throat were paralyzed and I couldn't swallow. Were the dogs dead? Everything was terribly wrong: I had trouble seeing, talking, breathing, and I couldn't move my legs or right arm. Nothing remained in my memory—no sounds, flashes, smells, no warnings of any kind. Had I been shot in the back? Had I suffered a stroke or heart attack? These thoughts were dark pools in sand.

9   The sky was black. Was this a storm in the middle of the day or was it night with a storm traveling through? When thunder exploded over me, I knew I had been hit by lightning.

10   The pain in my chest intensified and every muscle in my body ached. I was quite sure I was dying. What was it one should do or think or know? I tried to recall the Buddhist instruction regarding dying—which position to lie in, which direction to face. Did the "Lion's position" taken by the Buddha mean lying on the left or the right? And which sutra to sing? Oh yes, the Heart Sutra . . . gaté, gaté, paragaté . . . form and formlessness. Paradox and cosmic jokes. Surviving after trying to die "properly" would be truly funny, but the chances of that seemed slim.

11   Other words drifted in: how the "gateless barrier" was the gate through which one passes to reach enlightenment. Yet if there was no gate, how did one pass through? Above me, high on the hill, was the gate on the ranch that led nowhere, a gate I had mused about often. Now its presence made me smile. Even when I thought I had no aspirations for enlightenment, too much effort in that direction was being expended. How could I learn to slide, yet remain aware?

12   To be struck by lightning: what a way to get enlightened. That would be the joke if I survived. It seemed important to remember jokes. My thinking did not seem connected to the inert body that was in such terrible pain. Sweep the mind

of weeds, I kept telling myself—that's what years of Buddhist practice had taught me . . . But where were the dogs, the two precious ones I had watched being born and had raised in such intimacy and trust? I wanted them with me. I wanted them to save me again.

13 It started to rain. Every time a drop hit bare skin there was an explosion of pain. Blood crusted my left eye. I touched my good hand to my heart, which was beating wildly, erratically. My chest was numb, as if it had been sprayed with novocaine. No feeling of peace filled me. Death was a bleakness, a grayness about which it was impossible to be curious or relieved. I loved those dogs and hoped they weren't badly hurt. If I didn't die soon, how many days would pass before we were found, and when would the scavengers come? The sky was dark, or was that the way life flew out of the body, in a long tube with no light at the end? I lay on the cold ground waiting. The mountain was purple, and sage stirred against my face. I knew I had to give up all this, then my own body and all my thinking. Once more I lifted my head to look for the dogs but, unable to see them, I twisted myself until I faced east and tried to let go of all desire.

14 When my eyes opened again I knew I wasn't dead. Images from World War II movies filled my head: of wounded soldiers dragging themselves across a field, and if I could have laughed—that is, made my face work into a smile and get sounds to discharge from my throat—I would have. God, it would have been good to laugh. Instead, I considered my options: either lie there and wait for someone to find me—how many days or weeks would that take?—or somehow get back to the house. I calmly assessed what might be wrong with me—stroke, cerebral hemorrhage, gunshot wound—but it was bigger than I could understand. The instinct to survive does not rise from particulars; a deep but general misery rollercoasted me into action. I tried to propel myself on my elbows but my right arm didn't work. The wind had swung around and was blowing in from the east. It was still a dry storm with only sputtering rain, but when I raised myself up, lightning fingered the entire sky.

15 It is not true that lightning never strikes the same place twice. I had entered a shower of sparks and furious brightness and, worried that I might be struck again, watched as lightning touched down all around me. Years before, in the high country, I'd been hit by lightning: an electrical charge had rolled down an open meadow during a fearsome thunderstorm, surged up the legs of my horse, coursed through me, and bounced a big spark off the top of my head. To be struck again—and this time it was a direct hit—what did it mean?

16 The feeling had begun to come back into my legs and after many awkward attempts, I stood. To walk meant lifting each leg up by the thigh, moving it forward with my hands, setting it down. The earth felt like a peach that had split open in the middle; one side moved up while the other side moved down and my legs were out of rhythm. The ground rolled the way it does during an earthquake and the sky was tattered book pages waving in different directions. Was the ground liquifying under me, or had the molecular composition of my body deliquesced? I struggled to piece together fragments. Then it occurred to me that my brain was torn and that's where the blood had come from.

17 I walked. Sometimes my limbs held me, sometimes they didn't. I don't know how many times I fell but it didn't matter because I was making slow progress toward home.

18 Home—the ranch house—was about a quarter of a mile away. I don't remember much about getting there. My concentration went into making my legs work. The storm was strong. All the way across the basin, lightning lifted parts of mountains and sky into yellow refulgence and dropped them again, only to lift others. The inside of my eyelids turned gold and I could see the dark outlines of things through them. At the bottom of the hill I opened the door to my pickup and blew the horn with the idea that someone might hear me. No one came. My head had swollen to an indelicate shape. I tried to swallow—I was so thirsty—but the muscles in my throat were still paralyzed and I wondered when I would no longer be able to breathe.

19 Inside the house, sounds began to come out of me. I was doing crazy things, ripping my hiking boots off because the bottoms of my feet were burning, picking up the phone when I was finally able to scream. One of those times, someone happened to be on the line. I was screaming incoherently for help. My last conscious act was to dial 911.

20 Dark again. Pressing against sore ribs, my dogs pulled me out of the abyss, pulled and pulled. I smelled straw. My face was on tatami. I opened my eyes, looked up, and saw neighbors. Had they come for my funeral? The phone rang and I heard someone give directions to the ambulance driver, who was lost. A "first responder," an EMT from town who has a reputation with the girls, leaned down and asked if he could "touch me" to see if there were any broken bones. What the hell, I thought. I was going to die anyway. Let him have his feel. But his touch was gentle and professional, and I was grateful.

21 I slipped back into unconsciousness and when I woke again two EMTs were listening to my heart. I asked them to look for my dogs but they wouldn't leave me. Someone else in the room went outside and found Sam and Yaki curled up on the porch, frightened but alive. Now I could rest. I felt the medics jabbing needles into the top of my hands, trying unsuccessfully to get IVs started, then strapping me onto a backboard and carrying me out the front door of the house, down steps, into lightning and rain, into what was now a full-blown storm.

22 The ambulance rocked and slid, slamming my bruised body against the metal rails of the gurney. Every muscle was in violent spasm and there was a place on my back near the heart that burned. I heard myself yell in pain. Finally the EMTs rolled up towels and blankets and wedged them against my arms, shoulders, hips, and knees so the jolting of the vehicle wouldn't dislodge me. The ambulance slid down into ditches, struggled out, bumped from one deep rut to another. I asked to be taken to the hospital in Cody, but they said they were afraid my heart might stop again. As it was, the local hospital was thirty-five miles away, ten of them dirt, and the trip took more than an hour.

23 Our arrival seemed a portent of disaster—and an occasion for comedy. I had been struck by lightning around five in the afternoon. It was now 9:00 P.M. Nothing at the hospital worked. Their one EKG machine was nonfunctional, and jokingly

the nurses blamed it on me. "Honey, you've got too much electricity in your body," one of them told me. Needles were jammed into my hand—no one had gotten an IV going yet—and the doctor on call hadn't arrived, though half an hour had elapsed. The EMTs kept assuring me: "Don't worry, we won't leave you here." When another nurse, who was filling out an admission form, asked me how tall I was, I answered: "Too short to be struck by lightning."

24   "Electrical injury often results in ventricular fibrillation and injury to the medullary centers of the brain. Immediately after electric shock patients are usually comatose, apneic, and in circulatory collapse . . ."

25   When the doctor on call—the only doctor in town, waddled into what they called the emergency room, my aura, he said, was yellow and gray—a soul in transition. I knew that he had gone to medical school but had never completed a residency and had been barred from ER or ICU work in the hospitals of Florida, where he had lived previously. Yet I was lucky. Florida has many lightning victims, and unlike the doctors I would see later, he at least recognized the symptoms of a lightning strike. The tally sheet read this way: I had suffered a hit by lightning which caused ventricular fibrillation—cardiac arrest—though luckily my heart started beating again. Violent contractions of muscles when one is hit often causes the body to fly through the air: I was flung far and hit hard on my left side, which may have caused my heart to start again, but along with that fortuitous side effect, I sustained a concussion, broken ribs, a possible broken jaw, and lacerations above the eye. The paralysis below my waist and up through the chest and throat—called kerauno-paralysis—is common in lightning strikes and almost always temporary, but my right arm continued to be almost useless. Fernlike burns—arborescent erythema—covered my entire body. These occur when the electrical charge follows tracings of moisture on the skin—rain or sweat—thus the spidery red lines.

26   "Rapid institution of fluid and electrolyte therapy is essential with guidelines being the patient's urine output, hematocrit, osmolality, central venous pressure, and arterial blood gases . . . "

27   The nurses loaded me onto a gurney. As they wheeled me down the hall to my room, a front wheel fell off and I was slammed into the wall. Once I was in bed, the deep muscle aches continued, as did the chest pains. Later, friends came to visit. Neither doctor nor nurse had cleaned the cuts on my head, so Laura, who had herded sheep and cowboyed on all the ranches where I had lived and whose wounds I had cleaned when my saddle horse dragged her across a high mountain pasture, wiped blood and dirt from my face, arms, and hands with a cool towel and spooned yogurt into my mouth.

28   I was the only patient in the hospital. During the night, sheet lightning inlaid the walls with cool gold. I felt like an ancient, mummified child who had been found on a rock ledge near our ranch: bound tightly, unable to move, my dead face tipped backwards toward the moon.

29   In the morning, my regular doctor, Ben, called from Massachusetts, where he was vacationing, with this advice: "Get yourself out of that hospital and go somewhere else, anywhere." I was too weak to sign myself out, but Julie, the young woman who had a summer job on our ranch, retrieved me in the afternoon. She helped me get dressed in the cutoffs and torn T-shirt I had been wearing, but there were no shoes, so, barefoot, I staggered into Ben's office, where a physician's assistant kindly cleansed the gashes in my head. Then I was taken home.

30   Another thunderstorm slammed against the mountains as I limped up the path to the house. Sam and Yaki took one look at me and ran. These dogs lived with me, slept with me, understood every word I said, and I was too sick to find them, console them—even if they would have let me.

31   The next day my husband, who had just come down from the mountains where he worked in the summer, took me to another hospital. I passed out in the admissions office, was loaded onto a gurney, and taken for a CAT scan. No one bothered to find out why I had lost consciousness. Later, in the emergency unit, the doctor argued that I might not have been struck by lightning at all, as if I had imagined the incident. "Maybe a meteor hit me," I said, a suggestion he pondered seriously. After a blood panel and a brief neurological exam, which I failed—I couldn't follow his finger with my eyes or walk a straight line—he promptly released me.

32   "Patients should be monitored electrocardiographically for at least 24 hours for significant arrhythmias which often have delayed onset . . . "

33   It was difficult to know what was worse: being in a hospital where nothing worked and nobody cared, or being alone on an isolated ranch hundreds of miles from decent medical care.

34   In the morning I staggered into the kitchen. My husband, from whom I had been separated for three months, had left at 4:00 A.M. to buy cattle in another part of the state and would not be back for a month. Alone again, it was impossible to do much for myself. In the past I'd been bucked off, stiff and sore plenty of times but this felt different: I had no sense of equilibrium. My head hurt, every muscle in my body ached as if I had a triple dose of the flu, and my left eye was swollen shut and turning black and blue. Something moved in the middle of the kitchen floor. I was having difficulty seeing, but then I did see: a rattlesnake lay coiled in front of the stove. I reeled around and dove back into bed. Enough tests of character. I closed my eyes and half-slept. Later, when Julie came to the house, she found the snake and cut off its head with a shovel.

35   My only consolation was that the dogs came back. I had chest pains and all day Sam lay with his head against my heart. I cleaned a deep cut over Yaki's eye. It was half an inch deep but already healing. I couldn't tell if the dogs were sick or well, I was too miserable to know anything except that Death resided in the room: not as a human figure but as a dark fog rolling in, threatening to cover me; but the dogs stayed close and while my promise to keep them safe during a thunderstorm had proven fraudulent, their promise to keep me alive held good.

READING CLOSELY AND THINKING CRITICALLY

1. What is Ehrlich describing in paragraphs 1–3? Should the reader take the passage literally? Why or why not?

2. Paragraph 2 opens with "A single heartbeat stirs gray water," and paragraph 3 opens with "Another heartbeat." What is Ehrlich conveying with these sentences?

3. What were the author's primary concerns after she regained consciousness? What do these concerns suggest about the kind of person she is?

4. In paragraph 14, Ehrlich says that when she regained consciousness at one point, "Images from World War II movies filled [her] head." Why do you think these images occurred to her?

5. Ehrlich's husband leaves her for a month shortly after she returns from the hospital. Ehrlich notes this fact without comment. What does this information suggest?

6. Despite her dire circumstances, Ehrlich manages to have a sense of humor about her predicament. Evidence of her sense of humor appears in paragraphs 12, 20, 23, and 31. What do these humorous details reveal about the author?

EXAMINING STRUCTURE AND STRATEGY

1. Read paragraph 1 aloud, and then read paragraph 7 aloud. How do these two paragraphs differ in the way they sound? Why does Ehrlich use such different styles?

2. The movement from paragraph 7 to paragraph 8 is abrupt because it occurs without a transition or repetition. Do you think Ehrlich intended the movement between these paragraphs to jolt the reader? Explain.

3. What purpose do the quotations in paragraphs 24, 26, and 32 serve?

NOTING COMBINED PATTERNS

1. Ehrlich's descriptions fall into four main categories: descriptions of the weather, descriptions of her body after the lightning strike, descriptions of being unconscious and semiconscious, and descriptions of the hospital. Cite one description you particularly like from each category and do the following:

    a. Underline the specific words.

    b. Identify the description as objective or expressive.

    c. Explain why you like the description.

    d. Explain how the description helps Ehrlich achieve her purpose for writing.

2. Ehrlich does not begin her narration with the lightning strike and then move sequentially to the time she began to recover at home. Instead, she uses a variation of chronological order by including *flashbacks* between time periods. Explain how she uses the flashback technique. How does this technique help Ehrlich achieve her purpose?

CONSIDERING LANGUAGE AND STYLE

1. Paragraphs 1, 2, and 20 include intentional *sentence fragments* (sentence parts punctuated as sentences). How does Ehrlich use these fragments?

2. Read paragraph 6 aloud. What effect does Ehrlich create by repeating clauses that begin with *before*?

3. Explain the similes in paragraphs 16 and 35. Explain the metaphor in paragraph 16. What do these figures of speech contribute to the essay? (Similes and metaphors are explained on page 109.)

4. Consult a dictionary if you are unsure of the meaning of any of these words: *cruciate* (paragraph 1), *paradox* (paragraph 10), *deliquesced* (paragraph 16), *refulgence* (paragraph 18), *tatami* (paragraph 20), *portent* (paragraph 23), *gurney* (paragraph 27)

FOR DISCUSSION IN CLASS OR ONLINE

Did Ehrlich demonstrate courage after she was struck by lightning? Explain. Did she display more than one kind of courage? If so, what were these different kinds? With your classmates, answer these questions. If your instructor so directs, post your answers to your class Web site.

WRITING ASSIGNMENTS

1. **In your journal.** Using the information in the selection, explain the kind of person you think Ehrlich is. Would you like to be more like her? Why or why not?

2. **Using description for a purpose.** The purposes given in the assignments are possibilities. You may establish whatever purposes you like, within your instructor's guidelines.
   - In paragraph 7, Ehrlich describes an approaching thunderstorm. To entertain your reader, describe the time just before or after a particular weather event: a spring shower, an ice storm, a thunderstorm, a tornado, a hurricane, a flash flood, or some other occurrence.
   - If you have been in the hospital, relate your experience and/or express your feelings by describing one room you were in.
   - Describe a doctor or dentist's office to persuade your reader that these offices are (or are not) designed with patients in mind.

3. **Combining patterns.** Combine description and narration to tell about a time you were ill or injured. Like Ehrlich, describe what the injury or illness felt like.

4. **Connecting the readings.** Ehrlich's relationship with her dogs is very close. In "Am I Blue?" (page 353), Alice Walker tells of her relationship with a horse. Using the information in these essays, along with your own experience and observation, discuss the relationship between humans and animals. You may need to use an idea generation technique to narrow this topic to something manageable. (See page 37.)

5. **Drawing on sources.** Living an outdoor life in Wyoming, Ehrlich was particularly vulnerable to being hit by lightning. However, lightning strikes and other natural disasters can occur in any part of the world. Your area may be susceptible to a particular kind of natural disaster—if, for example, you live on the West Coast, you may have experienced earthquakes. What natural disasters have occurred in your area? What can you do to avoid being hurt should one occur? For ideas, try visiting the Federal Emergency Management Agency's preparedness Web site at *www.fema.gov/pte/prep.htm.* If possible, also try looking at the index or Web site for your local paper to find out about disasters that may have struck your area in the past.

BACKGROUND: Alberto Ríos was born in 1952 to a Guatemalan father and an English mother. He grew up in Nogales, Arizona, on the Mexican border. The winner of many writing awards, including the prestigious Walt Whitman Award of the Academy of American Poets in 1981 and the Western States Book Award in 1984, Ríos received a Bachelor of Arts from the University of Arizona in 1974 and an MFA in creative writing from the same institution in 1979. His many books include *The Lime Orchard Woman: Poems* (1988), *Pig Cookies and Other Stories* (1995), *The Curtain of Trees: Stories* (1999), *Capirotada: A Nogales Memoir* (1999), and *Smallest Muscle in the Human Body* (2002). His poetry has been set to music, and he has been featured in the documentary *Birthwrite: Growing Up Hispanic*. "The Vietnam Wall" was first published in *The Lime Orchard Woman* (1988).

COMBINED PATTERNS AND THEIR PURPOSE: In "The Vietnam Wall," Alberto Ríos *describes* the Vietnam Veterans Memorial in Washington, D.C., and **expresses** his reaction to it. As only a poet can, Ríos evokes images of deceptive simplicity, creating vivid mental pictures with only a few descriptive words. You may be struck by the clarity of the images, particularly those created by Ríos's similes and metaphors. As the poem approaches its conclusion, note the use of *contrast* to underscore the mood around the memorial.

The Vietnam Wall
ALBERTO RÍOS

As you read
Think about whether people who have seen the Vietnam Veterans Memorial will respond to the poem differently from those who have not seen it.

I
Have seen it
And I like it: The magic,
The way like cutting onions
It brings water out of nowhere.   5
Invisible from one side, a scar
Into the skin of the ground
From the other, a black winding
Appendix line.
    A dig.   10
    An archaeologist can explain.
The walk is slow at first
Easy, a little black marble wall
Of a dollhouse,
A smoothness, a shine   15
The boys in the street want to give.
One name. And then more
Names, long lines, lines of names until
They are the shape of the U.N. building
Taller than I am: I have walked   20
Into a grave.

And everything I expect has been taken away, like that, quick:
    The names are not alphabetized.
    They are in the order of dying,
    An alphabet of—somewhere—screaming.   25
I start to walk out. I almost leave
But stop to look up names of friends,
My own name. There is somebody
Severiano Riós.
Little kids do not make the same noise   30
Here, junior high school boys don't run
Or hold each other in headlocks.
No rules, something just persists
Like pinching on St. Patrick's Day
Every year for no green.   35
    No one knows why.
Flowers are forced
Into the cracks
Between sections.
Men have cried   40
At this wall.
I have
Seen them.

Vietnam Veterans Memorial

CONSIDERING THE POEM

1. What magic is associated with the Vietnam Wall?
2. What effect does the wall have on children? Why does it have that effect?
3. What dominant impression does the description convey?
4. Riós describes the wall as "a scar/into the skin of the ground." Why do you think he uses this metaphor? What other similes and metaphors does he use?
5. What element of contrast appears in the poem? How does that contrast help Riós achieve his purpose?

WRITING ASSIGNMENTS

1. **In your journal.**
   - Record your reaction to "The Vietnam Wall." Why do you react the way you do?
   - Just to see what happens, write a draft of a poem about a place that stirs emotion in you or others.
2. **Using description for a purpose.** To relate your experience and express your feelings, describe a monument, shrine, gravesite, or tourist attraction you have visited. Your dominant impression should be the mood the place creates. If you prefer, your purpose can be to persuade readers to visit the site. The purposes in the assignment are a possibility. You may establish whatever purpose you like, within your instructor's guidelines.
3. **Drawing on sources.** Ask three people who have visited the Vietnam Veterans Memorial to read the poem and comment on their reaction to it. (If you have visited the wall, you can be one of those people.) Then ask three people who have not visited the wall to do the same. Is a reader's reaction to the poem affected by whether he or she has visited the memorial? Write your findings and any conclusions you draw from them.

See page 112 for strategies for writing description and for a revising checklist.

ADDITIONAL ESSAY ASSIGNMENTS

1. Describe a place you go to relax: a park, a spot on campus, the gym, or the zoo, for example. Try to convey why the place helps you unwind.

2. Describe a favorite nightspot, someplace people go to have fun. Try to convey the sense that people are enjoying themselves.

3. Describe a view from a window, using expressive detail to convey a dominant impression.

4. Describe a store where you frequently shop, using objective detail to convey to what extent the store's features meet the needs of its customers.

5. Describe a place where you enjoy spending leisure time: a bowling alley, the student union, a shopping mall, a porch, a theater, or a basketball court, for example. Use expressive detail to convey why the place appeals to you.

6. Describe the room you liked best in the house you grew up in. Your dominant impression will be how the room made you feel.

7. Describe a place during a holiday celebration. For example, you could describe your parents' dining room at Thanksgiving, Main Street during the Christmas season, or a park on Independence Day.

8. Describe your favorite vacation spot, using expressive detail to convey why you enjoy this place.

9. Describe a winter scene, a fall scene, a spring scene, or a summer scene.

10. Describe one of your classrooms. Try to convey whether or not the room is conducive to learning.

11. Describe your bedroom. Use expressive detail to reveal what the bedroom says about you.

12. Describe a room after a party has been held there.

13. Using objective detail, describe the place where you work to show whether or not your work environment is pleasant.

14. Describe part of an amusement park.

15. Describe your favorite restaurant to persuade other people to try it.

16. Describe the neighborhood you grew up in to share a portion of your past with your reader.

17. Describe a scene at a sporting event.

18. Describe a rock concert for someone who has never been to one.

19. Describe a painting or sculpture you enjoy.

20. **Description in context:** Assume that you are a student employee in your campus admissions office. As part of its recruiting efforts, the director of admissions is putting together a large, glossy brochure that presents information about the school. You have been asked to contribute to the brochure by photographing a favorite campus spot and writing a description of it. Visit a suitable spot, decide on a dominant impression, and develop your description. Keep in mind that your purpose is to present the campus attractively so that potential students will want to attend your school.

You have learned that a descriptive essay often conveys a dominant impression. Visual images also convey impressions. Consider the Great Seal of the United States, which is reproduced here. What impressions of the United States does the seal convey? Is the seal a good symbol for the country? Why or why not?

Library of Congress Prints and Photographs Division
Washington, D.C. 20540 USA Library of Congress,
LC-USZ 62-474.

Narration

Tell a story that explains what led up to the event depicted in the picture on the opposite page. Let your imagination fly.

THE PATTERN

Everyone likes a good story. We go to movies for good stories, we read books for good stories, and we gravitate toward people at parties who tell good stories. We tell them to our children before they go to sleep and to our friends when we happen to meet them in a store or on a street corner. Another name for a story is a **narration,** and this chapter will discuss writing effective narration.

USING NARRATION FOR A PURPOSE

Obviously, a narration can *entertain* because a good story can amuse readers and help them forget about themselves for a time. Romance novels and detective fiction are two popular types of stories that provide escapist entertainment. Narration can do more than entertain, however. Say, for example, that for many years you visited your grandfather at a retirement home every week, and as a result you learned much about such facilities.

To *express your feelings* about retirement homes *and relate your experience* with them, you could narrate an account of your final visit with your grandfather. For this purpose, you would tell what happened during the visit and how the events made you feel. To *inform* your reader about the benefits of retirement homes, you could narrate an account of a typical day for your grandfather, pointing out the advantages he enjoyed because he lived at the retirement home. To *persuade* your reader to volunteer at a retirement home, you could narrate an account of one or more of your own experiences as a volunteer and the benefits you and the residents enjoyed as a result.

A brief narration, called an **anecdote,** is often useful as a secondary pattern in other essays. For example, in an *exemplification* essay, an anecdote can be an example. If you want to illustrate your mother's courage, you can include a moving anecdote about the time she fended off an attack by a mugger. A *comparison-contrast* that notes the differences between two mayoral candidates can include a telling anecdote about the time you met both candidates at a League of Women Voters meeting. A *cause-and-effect analysis* that explains the effects of the treatment of juveniles in the courts can include a powerful anecdote from the newspaper about a young offender who was jailed with adults for a long period because he could not afford a good lawyer. A *process analysis* that explains how to surf can tell the story of the time you broke your leg because you failed to follow a procedure you mention in the essay.

---

www.mhhe.com/patterns

For more help with narration, click on
Writing > Paragraph Patterns
Writing > Writing Tutor: Narration

Narration in College, at Work, and in the Community

Narration is important in many kinds of college writing. For instance, a history paper on the events leading up to the Holocaust can tell the story of "The Night of the Broken Glass," when Jewish homes and businesses were looted and destroyed. A political science paper can narrate an account of the events following the close election of 2000. In writing courses, students relate their personal experiences, and in journalism classes, students write newspaper-style accounts of current events or campus happenings.

Brief narrations, or anecdotes, are particularly useful for illustrating a point. If you write a paper for an education class and argue that people with learning disabilities do not get appropriate support in the classroom, you might tell the story of the time a learning-disabled friend was ignored in a high school algebra class. In a paper for a criminal justice class, you could support your point that judges should give out harsher penalties by telling the story of an offender who was repeatedly released, only to commit more crimes.

Narration is a frequent component of textbooks in most disciplines. Here, for example, is an excerpt from a section of an introduction to psychology text that focuses on sleep and dreams:

> The crowd roared as running back Donald Dorff, age 67, took the pitch from his quarterback and accelerated smoothly across the artificial turf. As Dorff braked and pivoted to cut back over a tackle, a huge defensive lineman loomed in his path. One hundred twenty pounds of pluck, Dorff did not hesitate. But let the retired grocery merchandiser from Golden Valley, Minnesota, tell it:
>
> "There was a 280-pound tackle waiting for me, so I decided to give him my shoulder. When I came to, I was on the floor in my bedroom. I had smashed into the dresser and knocked everything off it and broke the mirror and just made one heck of a mess. It was 1:30 A.M." (Long, 1987, p. 787).
>
> Dorff, it turned out, was suffering from a rare condition afflicting some older men. The problem occurs when the mechanism that usually shuts down bodily movement during dreams does not function properly. People suffering from the malady have been known to hit others, smash windows, punch holes in walls—all while fast asleep. (Feldman, *Understanding Psychology*)

In this example, the textbook author uses narration to illustrate a particular kind of sleep disturbance and how serious its consequences can be. Because the narration comes at the beginning of the section on sleep and dreams and because it is a very interesting story, the narration also creates interest in the discussion to come. Notice how dialogue and description help create that interest.

Narration is also a component of workplace writing. Police officers write crime reports, and insurance investigators write accident reports, both of which narrate sequences of events. Physical therapists and nurses write narrative accounts of their patients' progress, and teachers narrate events for disciplinary reports. Supervisors write narrative accounts of employees' actions for individual personnel files, and company officials use narration to report on the company's performance during the fiscal year for its stockholders.

Outside school and work, you already use narration often and will continue to do so. You may narrate events in your life in letters and e-mail you write to friends and in your diary or journal entries. If you are a recording secretary for an organization, you will write narrative minutes of meetings. In fact, anecdotes appear in all kinds of writing. For example, if you write to a company to complain about a pair of shoes that wore out prematurely, you could narrate an account of what happened when you wore the shoes to work. If you are speaking at a dinner honoring a friend, you could illustrate that friend's kindness with an anecdote about the time she helped a stranger search for his lost dog.

SUPPORTING DETAILS

Your narration should make a point, and your point is tied to your purpose. Without focusing on your point and purpose, you can go off on a narrative tangent, which will cause your readers to scratch their heads and wonder why they are reading your essay. Thus, you should choose supporting details that help your readers see the point of your narration. Say, for example, that you are narrating an account of being accused of shoplifting at the mall. If your point is that sales personnel accused you because you appeared to be poor, and your purpose is to inform your reader that salespeople are biased against the poor, you would emphasize your appearance—your dirty hair and face, torn jeans, oversized T-shirt, and so forth. However, if your point is that you suffered public humiliation and your purpose is to relate an experience and express your feelings, then you may want to emphasize your appearance less than the people who stared at you when you were stopped and accused.

A narration usually includes the answers to the **journalist's questions** *who? what? when? where? why?* and *how?* The narrative explains *who* was involved, *what* happened, *when* it happened, *where* it happened, *why* it happened, and *how* it happened. Of course, you may not need to include the answers to each of these questions in every narrative you write, but they are a good starting point for generating ideas. Also, you might emphasize different answers in different narrations. Thus, in some stories you might pay more attention to *who* was involved, but in other stories, you might consider *when* the event happened more significant and treat the time element in more detail. To decide which journalist's questions to emphasize, carefully consider the point of your narration and your purpose.

---

www.mhhe.com/patterns

For more help with supporting details, click on

Writing > Prewriting > Use Five Methods

In addition to the answers to the journalist's questions, narration often includes descriptive detail. When a person's appearance is important to the story, that person will be described; when locale, or scene, is important, a place will be described. For example, in "Lost at C," (page 189), Jean Shepherd uses description to set the scene for his narration:

> Schwartz smiled wanly. And Helen Weathers giggled—until she saw, at the same moment I did, a tall, square man standing motionless at the blackboard. He had a grim blue jaw and short, kinky black crew-cut hair. His eyes were tiny ball bearings behind glasses with thick black rims. He wore a dark, boxy suit that looked like it was made of black sandpaper. The bell rang and the door closed behind us. I joined the crowd around his desk who were putting registration cards into a box. I did likewise.

Now would be a good time to review the information on using specific words for description on page 107.

If your reader needs additional information to appreciate the story, you can provide background information or an explanation. For example, in "Salvation" (page 173), the author provides this explanation to help the reader understand why he was in church the night the story takes place:

> There was a big revival at my Auntie Reed's church. Every night for weeks there had been much preaching, singing, praying, and shouting, and some very hardened sinners had been brought to Christ, and the membership of the church had grown by leaps and bounds. Then just before the revival ended, they held a special meeting for children, "to bring the young lambs to the fold." My aunt spoke of it for days ahead. That night, I was escorted to the front row and placed on the mourner's bench with all other young sinners, who had not yet been brought to Jesus.

Writing Dialogue

Dialogue can advance the story and make it more vivid. To appreciate what dialogue can add, consider the difference between these sentences; the first one was taken from "Lost at C" (page 189).

1. "Why, Schwartz, what seems to be troubling you?" I asked with irony, vigorously working the salt shaker.
2. In an ironic manner, I asked Schwarz what was troubling him, while I vigorously worked the salt shaker.

The dialogue makes the first version more lively, vivid, and interesting.

When you write dialogue, follow the conventions for capitalizing and punctuating **quotations,** a speaker's or writer's exact words. The conventions for punctuating quotations are illustrated here, and you can use these examples as models. (Pay particular attention to the location of quotation marks, commas, periods, question marks, and capital letters.) For other situations, consult a writing handbook.

www.mhhe.com/patterns

For more help with quotation marks, click on

Editing > Quotation Marks

When the Quotation Comes Before the Speaker or Writer is Mentioned

1. "Most people overestimate their ability to handle threatening situations," the police officer explained.
2. "How will price controls affect foreign trade?" the senator asked.

When the Quotation Comes After the Speaker or Writer is Mentioned

1. The police officer explained, "Most people overestimate their ability to handle threatening situations."

Paragraphing and Dialogue

If you have trouble paragraphing to identify speakers when you write dialogue, use the convention of beginning a new paragraph each time a different person speaks. The paragraph indentation signals the change in speaker, as illustrated by this passage from "Lost at C" (page 189):

> "Boy, look at the stuff kids study these days," the old man said with wonder as he hefted my algebra textbook in his bowling hand and riffled through the pages.
>
> "What's all this X and Y stuff?" he asked.
>
> "Yeah, well, it ain't much," I muttered as coolly as I could, trying to recapture some of the old élan.
>
> "Whaddaya mean, ain't much?" His eyes glowed with pride at the idea that his kid has mastered algebra in only one day.
>
> "Abstract mathematics, that's all it is."

If one person speaks for more than a paragraph, begin that speaker's new paragraphs with quotation marks, but use closing quotation marks at the end of the quotation only, not at the end of each paragraph.

2. The senator asked, "How will price controls affect foreign trade?"

3. Do you believe the senator asked, "How will price controls affect foreign trade"? [The entire sentence, not just the quoted words, forms a question.]

When the Quotation Comes Both Before and After the Speaker or Writer is Mentioned

1. "Most people," the police officer explained, "overestimate their ability to handle threatening situations." [The words that come before the speaker or writer is mentioned *do not* form a complete sentence.]

2. "Most people overestimate their ability to handle threatening situations," the police officer explained. "They mistakenly believe they can talk themselves out of danger." [The words that come before the speaker or writer is mentioned *do* form a complete sentence.]

3. "Should online auctions be regulated," asked Delia, "or is the business sufficiently self-regulating?" [The words that come before and after the speaker or writer is mentioned are two parts of a compound sentence.]

ORGANIZING DETAILS

If you've ever listened to someone tell a story and drone on and on, you know how important it is to select narrative details carefully to avoid boring your reader with unnecessary information. Choose carefully which *who? what? when? where? why?* and *how?* questions to answer, and be careful not to include insignificant details or over-emphasize minor points. In other words, one key to a successful narration is pacing.

One way to communicate the point of your narration is to express it in a thesis, such as the following:

> After my recent experience with a credit card company, I realize that college students should be cautious about accepting those bank cards they get in the mail. (*The narration is about the writer's experience with a credit card company, and the point is that students should be careful about accepting the credit cards that are mailed to them.*)

If a stated thesis will disturb the flow of your story, you can imply rather than state your thesis, but be sure your reader can infer your point from the details you have included. (For more on implied thesis, see page 47.) Another alternative is to state the point at the end of the narration, so it forms the conclusion of your essay. For example, in "Salvation" (page 173), Langston Hughes tells a story about attending a revival service when he was 12. He concludes his narration with a statement of the story's significance, which reads, in part:

> I didn't believe there was a Jesus any more, since he didn't come to help me.

Arranging narrative details usually involves placing the events in **chronological order.** Most often this means beginning with the first event, moving to the second, on to the third, and so on. Variations of this pattern are possible, however. For some stories, you may want to begin at the end or in the middle, then shift back to the beginning, using **flashback.**

Say, for example, you want to narrate an account of a car accident you were involved in. You could begin with the first event and move forward to the last event, like this:

> A year ago, I was on my way to pick up my girlfriend, looking forward to a pleasant dinner. As I approached the intersection at Fifth and Grove, the light turned yellow, but I figured I had plenty of time to slide through.

After this opening, you would narrate an account of the accident and then go on to tell about its aftermath.

You could also begin at the end and flash back to the beginning, like this:

> As I walked out of my last physical therapy session, I thought about how remarkable it is that I can walk at all. An accident nine months earlier had left me in critical condition with a smashed pelvis.

From here, you would flash back to the beginning and narrate an account of the accident and all the events leading up to the time you walked out of your last physical therapy session.

You could also begin in the middle of the chronology, like this:

> I remember waking up in the hospital with my parents and sister at my side. Mom was crying and Dad looked worried. In an instant the pain overwhelmed me and I could not remember what happened. Then all at once I remembered the accident.

From this point in the middle, you would flash back to the beginning and narrate an account of the accident. You would then move chronologically through the events until you reached the last event, walking out of your final physical therapy session.

To signal chronological order, move smoothly through your time sequence, and help your reader follow the events in your narrative, you can use *transitions* such as the following:

at first	later	second
at the same time	meanwhile	soon
in the meantime	next	the next day

Because a story is told in chronological order, the time sequence provides a clear structure, so the reader often does not need the organizational signposts provided by topic sentences. For this reason, writers of narrations tend to leave them out.

VISUALIZING A NARRATIVE ESSAY

The chart on the facing page can help you visualize the structure for a narrative essay. Like all good models, however, this one can be altered as needed.

PROCESS GUIDELINES: STRATEGIES FOR WRITING NARRATION

1. *Selecting a Topic.* Pick a story that you want to tell for a reason. Rather than tell a story for the sake of telling a story, have a purpose in mind: to entertain, express feelings, relate experience, inform, or persuade.

2. *Establishing the Point.* Write out a statement of the point of your narration. You can use a version of this statement as your thesis or imply your point through your choice of details.

3. *Generating Ideas.* List the answers to the *who? what? when? where? why?* and *how?* questions. Decide which of these answers should be emphasized, based on your audience and purpose. Also, identify important features about the people and scenes of your story. Look for points in the narration where you may want to add these descriptive details.

4. *Drafting.* As you write your first draft, concentrate on getting all the events down on paper or on your computer screen and answering all the appropriate journalist's questions. During revision you can consider using flashback and adding description, transitions, and other elements of an effective essay.

Introduction

- Creates interest in the story
- States the thesis, which may indicate the point of the story

First Body Paragraph

- Begins the story
- Answers the appropriate journalist's questions
- May include description
- May include background information or explanation
- May include dialogue
- Arranges details in chronological order, which may include flashback

Next Body Paragraph

- Continues the story
- Answers the appropriate journalist's questions
- May include description
- May include background information or explanation
- May include dialogue
- Arranges details in chronological order, which may include flashback

Next Body Paragraphs

- Continue until the story is complete
- Answer the appropriate journalist's questions; may include description, background information or explanation, and dialogue
- Arrange details in chronological order, which may include flashback

Conclusion

- Provides a satisfying finish
- May state the point of the narration if not done elsewhere

5. *Revising.* Consider adding dialogue to make your narrative more vivid, and decide whether to describe people or scenes. Does the narration make a readily identifiable point? Read your draft aloud; if you hear any abrupt shifts, consider whether transitions are needed.

Avoiding Tense Shifts

If you have trouble maintaining tense in narration, edit carefully. A distorted time sequence can confuse your reader. The most common tense shifts in narration occur when the writer moves between the past and present tense inappropriately, like this:

INAPPROPRIATE TENSE SHIFT FROM PAST TO PRESENT	**I walked into the classroom and found a seat in the back. As soon as I sit down, Luis cracks a joke.**
CORRECTION	**I walked into the classroom and found a seat in the back. As soon as I sat down, Luis cracked a joke.**

When you write dialogue, moving between the past tense and present tense can be appropriate.

APPROPRIATE TENSE SHIFT	**Katrina announced, "I am quitting my job and joining the Peace Corps."**

www.mhhe.com/patterns

For more help with verb tense, click on
Editing > Verbs and Verbals

Checklist for Revising Narration

Be sure:

_____ The journalist's questions are answered and appropriately emphasized.

_____ Descriptions of people and scenes are included when they are important.

_____ Dialogue is included where it can advance the narrative and make it more vivid.

_____ Background information required by your reader is included.

_____ Your narration's point is easily determined.

_____ Extraneous details are deleted.

_____ Details are arranged in a chronological or other suitable order.

_____ Transitions help your reader follow the chronology or other order.

In the following essay, student writer Robbie Warnock shares an account of the annual family reunion and comes to see the event differently now than in the past. After you read, you will have an opportunity to evaluate this essay.

The Family Reunion, Revisited

1   Once a year, with the regularity of Old Faithful, scores of people claiming to be my kin[1] would storm my hometown. The brood did not appear gradually, but as a veritable deluge of eccentricity, and often senility. The family's elders, in their twenty-year-old gas guzzlers, circled the town like vultures, finally "nesting" at the community center. As the rusty doors squeaked open in protest, I could almost hear John Williams's "Imperial March" blasting dirgelike through my mind. It was time for the annual family reunion, and I dreaded it as much as a trip to the dentist because to a youngster like me, everyone was as old as Methuselah and as quirky as Larry, Moe, and Curly.

2   Every woman present was clad in a floral spring dress, each with a distinct pattern.[2] Most of the botanical togs reeked of mothballs. This pungent aroma was the only thing that held the bees attracted by the dress at bay. The men, on the other hand, looked like reject golfers or court jesters in their mismatched clothes of many colors. After each example of Henry Ford's worst nightmare had ejected the people crammed inside, the center's double doors were opened, and the celebration commenced.

3   Food is a major love for my family, which explains why portliness is the status quo.[3] At the reunion, long wooden tables, like those in Hrothgar's meadhall, were laden with all types of dishes. However, an elderly matriarch of the clan became discontented with the same old food served every year. To ease the monotony, she created the "Annual Odd Recipe Contest," the goal of which was to create the most appetizing dish from the most bizarre ingredients.

4   I was present at the inception of this contest, albeit reluctantly. Along with the down-home staples, fried chicken and chocolate layer cake, I sampled a curious-looking green and purple casserole. Immediately, I fell victim to Aunt Frankie's infamous "Eggplant and Kudzu Surprise." Upon tasting the foul abomination, I fled to the nearest

Paragraph 1
The introduction provides background and tells what and *when.* The thesis is the last sentence. The subject is the annual reunion, and the writer's view is that he dreaded it. Note the descriptive language. Did the cliché disturb you?

Paragraph 2
This paragraph centers on *who?* by describing the people involved.

Paragraph 3
Description and specific word choice add interest and vitality.

Paragraph 4
This paragraph flashes back to the more distant past.

McDonald's and vowed never to consume another bite even remotely connected with the old crone.

Paragraphs 5 and 6
Each paragraph begins with a transitional phrase. Details emphasize *who?* and *what?* The vivid description continues.

After eating the wonderful meal of poultry and vegetation, the fam- 5 ily would seek[5] amusement. Refusing to simply converse the evening away, the motley crew would begin to square dance. Recovering from whatever odd recipe I had unwittingly subjected myself to, I would glance inside to view a plethora of octogenarians tramping and stomping in a futile attempt at dancing. Then the entertainment took a nosedive. Uncle Oliver produced a set a bagpipes and unleashed a sonic aberration akin to the sound produced when a few dozen cats are run over slowly by a bulldozer.

After the musical torture, the group underwent a schism. The men 6 ditched their[6] wives and each group would nestle in a separate corner and settle down enough to actually begin conversations unrelated to food. Now the talk focused on the past. At just the right moment, Uncle Oliver presented a hundred or so bags, each sealed, labeled, and containing a piece of debris from the family homeplace. As he presented these heirlooms, he recited a stentorian lecture on the "sacred domicile." Each member of the family then received a fragment of the house.

Paragraph 7
The conclusion presents the last event and the point of the narration (the reunion served an important purpose). The last paragraph also answers *why?*

Stomach churning, ears smarting, and bearing a Ziploc bag con- 7 taining a burnt bit[7] of shingle, I returned home at the end of the day, praising God for deliverance. Today, I see things differently, however. Rather than eccentricity, I see love and a memorial to past times. The would-be Scotsman Oliver wanted the kids to cherish their heritage. I now regret my impatience and impudence because I realize that the reunion was an annual link between the past and the present. I now realize that the past is a treasure and the key to the future. For one more chance to remember and relive those times, I would square dance, listen to bagpipes, and even choke down kudzu.

Responding to "The Family Reunion, Revisited"

Evaluate "The Family Reunion, Revisited" by responding to these questions:

1. Does the narration hold your interest? Why or why not?
2. Does the story support the writer's point? Explain.
3. What do you think of the tone of the narration? (See page 71 on tone.)
4. Is the word choice effective? Should the writer revise for more effective word choice?
5. Does the writer use description effectively? Explain.
6. Is anything unclear?

Copyright © King Features Syndicate.

- In which panel does the narration begin?
- For what purpose does Curtis tell his story?
- Is Curtis using narration responsibly?
- How well does Curtis assess his audience?

BACKGROUND: Born in Nigeria, award-winning poet and novelist Chris Abani teaches at Antioch University in Los Angeles and is a visiting professor at the University of California, Riverside. Abani was jailed as a political prisoner three times in Nigeria for his writing and theater work. His first incarceration was in 1985, two years after his first novel was published, on the grounds that the book inspired a failed coup against the government. Abani's novels are *Masters of the Board* (1985), *Sirocco* (1987), and *GraceLand* (2004). His plays are *Room at the Top* (1983) and *Song of a Broken Flute* (1990). Abani's poetry collections are *Kalakuta Republic* (2001) and *Daphne's Lot* (2003). "The Lottery" first appeared in the "Lives" section of *The New York Times Magazine* (February 2004).

THE PATTERN AND ITS PURPOSES: Abani's narration begins pleasantly enough, but it takes a chilling turn. The author *narrates* the account of justice gone awry both to **relate his experience** in Nigeria and to **inform** the reader about the nature of mob violence. It's a difficult story, but one that will grab and hold your attention.

THE LOTTERY | CHRIS ABANI

Even though it was a wet, rainy afternoon, I was glad my aunt had taken me to the market with her. Even her religious fanaticism, which sometimes prompted her to proselytize, embarrassingly, to complete strangers, wasn't enough to deaden my good mood. The rainy season in Nigeria was my favorite even as a 10-year-old. It had something to do with the light. It was crisp, like a new bank note or a thing washed and starched. And then there was the way everything smelled.

As you read
Think about how people respond to various kinds of social pressure, particularly pressure from peers adults, and crowds.

2   I inhaled deeply. The scent was a balanced mix of wet earth and the dry roughness of rope. There was continuity to that smell, as if it were the essence of the land itself. I closed my eyes for a moment. Other scents in the market broke through the smell of wet earth—the throat-burning sharpness of peppers, dried fish, the animal-funk of goats and chickens.

3   Suddenly, a lone voice screamed one word over and over: "Thief! Thief! Thief!" It was picked up slowly, as if the

> "Suddenly, a lone voice screamed one word over and over: 'Thief! Thief! Thief!' "

drizzle that afternoon had dampened the scent of blood. My aunt froze and faced the sound, nose sniffing the air like a lioness sensing prey. A man's voice, tired and breathless, tried to counter the rising chant with a feeble retort: "It's a lie! It's a lie!"

4   I drew nearer to my aunt, confused and more than a little afraid, but she shook off my clutching hand. Her head turned like an antenna seeking a signal. The sound of a chase grew closer—desperate, pounding feet and shouts. A man with a wild expression came around a corner and nearly knocked over a stall. Young men were almost on his heels, followed some distance behind by a larger cluster. The man ran past us, and it seemed as if I could see the pores in his skin. As he pushed past, my aunt slapped him across the face. He flinched but didn't stop; he was headed for the courtyard in the middle of the

market, where the retired elders sat daily to dispense justice. I imagined the man bursting into the clearing, cries of "Sanctuary, sanctuary!" breaking from his lips. The council of elders was the highest court in my community, besides, of course, the civil system. It arbitrated on everything from murder to marital disputes, and its authority was never questioned. I felt certain the man would be safe there.

5   This was the mob justice I had read about in the newspaper editorials that my father made my homework. Rife with condemnations of the mob lynchings that were becoming the norm in the 70s, the editorials pointed out that these victims of vigilante justice received no trials and that the crimes they were accused of were never investigated. The editorials went a step further to suggest that most of those killed this way were probably innocent. But in the terror of that moment, editorials were of little use to the man running for his life and would do little to placate the angry horde. My aunt dragged me along behind the crowd that swept past us.

6   The man stood in the middle of the clearing facing the elders while the crush of people pressed around them. In the center of this sacred space, the sole elder to stand up and call for tolerance was booed and pelted with rotten fruit. He sat down quickly and turned his face away. I was sure that the man was about to be lynched. How could

"I was sure that the man was about to be lynched."

the crowd ignore the elder's intervention? And why didn't the other elders speak out?

7   The mob was oddly silent; its loud breathing filled the space. The accused man began to beg, but people were too busy picking up stones and tree branches, anything that could be used as a weapon. A young man broke through the crowd carrying an old rubber tire and a metal can. He hung the tire from the accused's neck. This singular action ended the man's pleas for mercy. Resigned, he sobbed softly, mumbling inaudibly, but he didn't move as the young man emptied the contents of the can onto him. The young man smiled and talked as he went about his task: "You see why crime doesn't pay? I am doing this for you, you know. If you burn here, you won't burn in hell. God is reasonable."

8   Finishing, he held up a box of matches. The crowd roared. The elder who had tried intervening spoke again, but nobody listened. Someone called out, "Bring the children forward so that they can learn." My aunt hustled me to the front. Next to me stood a girl. Her face was impassive; I was ashamed at my fear. I never saw the match fall, but I felt the heat as the man erupted into a sheet of flame, burning like a lighthouse in the drizzly haze. "Watch," my aunt said as I tried to turn away from the writhing figure.

9   As the man burned, people began to file past him in an orderly manner like the offertory line in the Catholic church I attended. As they walked past, they spat on the incandescent figure. My aunt spat. I looked away, hand held over my nose at the smell of burning flesh, horrified that it reminded me of kebabs. "Spit," she snapped, rapping me on the head with her knuckles. I spat.

READING CLOSELY AND THINKING CRITICALLY

1. The essay's title does not prepare readers for the essay's content. Explain the significance of the title. Why do you think Abani chose it?
2. In paragraph 6, Abani asks how the crowd could disregard the elder who intervened, and he also asks why the other elders did not intervene as well. Answer these questions.
3. What point does the narration make?
4. In paragraph 1, Abani mentions that his aunt was a religious fanatic. Is that detail important? Why or why not?
5. Young Abani drew close to his aunt in fear, yet she "shook off [his] clutching hand" (paragraph 4). Why does she do this?
6. What is the significance of the fact that young Abani spat on the victim?

EXAMINING STRUCTURE AND STRATEGY

1. Does Abani answer all of the journalist's questions? Which ones does he emphasize? How does that emphasis help him achieve his writing purpose?
2. Which paragraphs provide background information? Is that information helpful? Explain.
3. What purpose does the detail in paragraph 3 serve? The detail in paragraph 7? In paragraph 8? Should Abani have included more detail in these paragraphs? Why or why not?
4. In paragraph 2, Abani focuses on the smells in the marketplace. Why is the description of smell important in this essay?
5. Abani's essay ends with the last event in the narration. Does the essay end effectively? Explain.

CONSIDERING LANGUAGE AND STYLE

1. What similes appear in paragraphs 1, 3, 4, 8, and 9? What do you think of these similes and why?
2. To appreciate the brisk pacing (movement) and narrative power that derives, in part, from that pacing, read paragraphs 3 and 4 aloud. What do you notice?
3. Consult a dictionary if you are unsure of the meaning of any of these words: *proselytize* (paragraph 1), *rife* (paragraph 5), *vigilante* (paragraph 5), *offertory* (paragraph 9), *incandescent* (paragraph 9).

FOR DISCUSSION IN CLASS OR ONLINE

The time depicted in "The Lottery" was one of political unrest in Nigeria, a time of coups, revolutionaries, and extreme factionalism. Is the kind of mob pressure seen in the essay strictly a function of those circumstances, or are we all capable of succumbing to mob pressure, regardless of the political climate? Explain your view.

1. **In your journal.** How did you react when you read the "The Lottery"? Why did you react that way? Would you recommend the story to a friend? Why or why not?

2. **Using narration for a purpose.** The purposes given in the assignments are possibilities. You may establish whatever purposes you like, within your instructor's guidelines.

    *   To relate your experience and perhaps express your feelings, narrate an account of a time you went along with the crowd despite your better judgment. Explain why you did so and whether you would do so again in similar circumstances. If there is something to learn from your experience, your purpose can also be to inform your reader of that lesson.

    *   To relate your experience and perhaps express your feelings, narrate an account of a time you pressured a person to do something against his or her will. Explain why you did so and whether you would do so again in similar circumstances. If there is something to learn from your experience, your purpose can also be to inform your reader of that lesson.

    *   Narrate an account of a time justice was not served or something unfair occurred. The event might have taken place in the classroom, on the playing field, in the workplace, or in any other environment. Your purpose can be to relate your experience or inform your reader of a lesson or of the nature of justice. You might also want to convince your reader to think or act a particular way in response to the injustice or lack of fairness.

3. **Combining patterns.** Explain the nature and effect of *peer pressure* by defining it and narrating one or more illustrative anecdotes. (See Chapter 11 for information on writing definition.)

4. **Connecting the readings.** In both "The Lottery" and "Salvation" (page 173) children feel coerced by adults to behave in uncomfortable ways. In both cases, the adults believe they are acting in the child's best interests. Discuss to what extent adults should have the authority to impose their moral and ethical standards on young people and to what extent young people should be permitted to act in accordance with their own sense of moral and ethical beliefs.

5. **Drawing on sources.** In the 1960s, psychologist Stanley Milgram performed a now-classic experiment related to obedience. Read about the experiment in just about any introductory psychology textbook or by typing "Stanley Milgram" into your favorite search engine. Then explain the nature of the experiment, its outcome, what it teaches, and how it relates to events in "The Lottery."

BACKGROUND: Born in Joplin, Missouri, Langston Hughes (1902–1967) was a prolific poet, playwright, critic, newspaper columnist, and fiction writer. In all, 47 volumes bear his name. His work has been translated into a dozen languages, earning him an international reputation unparalleled by most other African-American authors of his time. Hughes was committed to writing about racial themes, particularly the everyday life of African Americans and pride in African heritage. He also wrote about democracy and patriotism. As a newspaper columnist, Hughes created a character called "Simple," an uneducated African American who had conversations with a better educated but less sensitive African-American acquaintance. His many works include *Simple Speaks His Mind* (1950), the first of four volumes of short stories, *Montage of a Dream Deferred* (1951), a collection of poetry, and *Ask Your Mamma: 12 Moods for Jazz* (1961), a collection of poetry inspired by the civil rights movement. The following selection is from Hughes's autobiographical *The Big Sea* (1940).

THE PATTERN AND ITS PURPOSES: In "Salvation," Langston Hughes employs *narration* to **relate an experience** that changed his life dramatically and to **express** the disillusionment he felt as a result of that experience. As you read, pay attention to how Hughes gives the reader background and builds tension.

Salvation

LANGSTON HUGHES

I was saved from sin when I was going on thirteen. But not really saved. It happened like this. There was a big revival at my Auntie Reed's church. Every night for weeks there had been much preaching, singing, praying, and shouting, and some very hardened sinners had been brought to Christ, and the membership of the church had grown by leaps and bounds. Then just before the revival ended, they held a special meeting for children, "to bring the young lambs to the fold." My aunt spoke of it for days ahead. That night, I was escorted to the front row and placed on the mourner's bench with all other young sinners, who had not yet been brought to Jesus.

As you read
Ask yourself what pressures led Hughes to take the action that he did.

2   My aunt told me that when you were saved you saw a light, and something happened to you inside! And Jesus came into your life! And God was with you from then on! She said you could see and hear and feel Jesus in your soul. I believed her. I had heard a great many old people say the same thing and it seemed to me they ought to know. so I sat there calmly in the hot, crowded church, waiting for Jesus to come to me.

3   The preacher preached a wonderful rhythmical sermon, all moans and shouts and lonely cries and dire pictures of hell, and then he sang a song about the ninety and nine safe in the fold, but one little lamb was left out in the cold. Then he said: "Won't you come? Won't you come to Jesus? Young lambs, won't you come?" and he held out his arms to all us young sinners there on the mourner's bench. And the little girls cried. And some of them jumped up and went to Jesus right away. But most of us just sat there.

4   A great many old people came and knelt around us and prayed, old women with jet-black faces and braided hair, old men with work-gnarled hands. And the church sang a song about the lower lights are burning, some poor sinners to be saved. And the whole building rocked with prayer and song.

5   Still I kept waiting to *see* Jesus.

6   Finally all the young people had gone to the altar and were saved, but one boy and me. He was a rounder's son named Westley. Westley and I were surrounded by sisters and deacons praying. It was very hot in the church, and getting late now. Finally Westley said to me in a whisper. "God damn! I'm tired o' sitting here. Let's get up and be saved." So he got up and was saved.

7   Then I was left all alone on the mourner's bench. My aunt came and knelt at my knees and cried, while prayers and songs swirled all around me in the little church. The whole congregation prayed for me alone, in a mighty wail of moans and voices. And I kept waiting serenely for Jesus, waiting, waiting—but he didn't come. I wanted to see him, but nothing happened to me. Nothing! I wanted something to happen to me, but nothing happened.

8   I heard the songs and the minister saying. "Why don't you come? My dear child, why don't you come to Jesus? Jesus is waiting for you. He wants you. Why don't you come? Sister Reed, what is this child's name?"

9   "Langston," my aunt sobbed.

10   "Langston, why don't you come? Why don't you come and be saved? Oh, Lamb of God! Why don't you come?"

11   Now it was really getting late. I began to be ashamed of myself, holding everything up so long. I began to wonder what God thought about Westley, who certainly hadn't seen Jesus either, but who was now sitting proudly on the platform, swinging his knickerbockered legs and grinning down at me, surrounded by deacons and old women on their knees praying. God had not struck Westley dead for taking his name in vain or for lying in the temple. So I decided that maybe to save further trouble, I'd better lie, too, and say that Jesus had come, and get up and be saved.

12   So I go up.

13   Suddenly the whole room broke into a sea of shouting, as they saw me rise. Waves of rejoicing swept the place. Women leaped in the air. My aunt threw her arms around me. The minister took me by the hand and led me to the platform.

14   When things quieted down, in a hushed silence, punctuated by a few ecstatic "Amens," all the new young lambs were blessed in the name of God. Then joyous singing filled the room.

15   That night, for the last time in my life but one—for I was a big boy twelve years old—I cried. I cried, in bed alone, and couldn't stop. I buried my head under the quilts, but my aunt heard me. She woke up and told my uncle I was crying because the Holy Ghost had come into my life, and because I had seen Jesus. But I was really crying because I couldn't bear to tell her that I had lied, that I had deceived everybody in the church, that I hadn't seen Jesus, and that now I didn't believe there was a Jesus any more, since he didn't come to help me.

READING CLOSELY AND THINKING CRITICALLY

1. What does young Langston Hughes expect to happen at the revival? What happens instead?
2. How was Hughes affected by what happened at the revival?
3. What do you think Hughes means in the first two sentences of the narration?
4. Why does young Langston pretend to see Jesus and be saved? Do you think he was right or wrong to pretend to be saved? What would you have done in his place? Explain.
5. How do you think young Langston's aunt would have reacted if he had told her the truth about why he was crying?
6. **Situational irony** occurs when events happen in ways that are contrary to expectations. What situational irony occurs in "Salvation"?

EXAMINING STRUCTURE AND STRATEGY

1. Do the first two sentences of "Salvation" make an effective opening? Explain why or why not.
2. Where does Hughes explain the point of the narration?
3. Hughes includes description of people and events in his narration. Cite two examples of this description and explain how it helps Hughes achieve his purpose.
4. Hughes incorporates just a bit of dialogue in the story. What purpose does that dialogue serve?
5. Which of the *who? what? when? where? why?* and *how?* questions does Hughes emphasize the most?
6. To help the reader recognize and follow the chronological order, Hughes opens several of his paragraphs with transitions that signal time order (see page 69). Which paragraphs open with transitions, and what are those transitions?
7. In addition to telling his story, Hughes offers some explanation. What is explained and where does this explanation occur?

CONSIDERING LANGUAGE AND STYLE

1. What metaphor appears in paragraph 13? (See page 109 on metaphors.) What does this metaphor contribute to the description that appears in the essay?
2. Paragraph 12 is only four words long. Explain the effect created by this four-word paragraph. What would be lost if the four words were moved to the end of paragraph 11?
3. Consult a dictionary if you are unsure of the meaning of any of these words: *revival* (paragraph 1), *dire* (paragraph 3), *rounder* (paragraph 6), *deacons* (paragraph 6), *knickerbockered* (paragraph 11), *ecstatic* (paragraph 14).

FOR DISCUSSION IN CLASS OR ONLINE

With your classmates, consider these questions: What do you think would have happened if young Langston had not pretended to see Jesus and be saved? How would his aunt have reacted? How would Westley have reacted? If your instructor so directs, post your responses to your class Web site.

1. **In your journal.** Tell about a time you pretended to believe something. What was your motivation?

2. **Using narration for a purpose.** The purposes given in the assignments are possibilities. You may establish whatever purposes you like, within your instructor's guidelines.

   - In paragraph 2, Hughes explains that he believed his aunt when she described what it was like to be saved. However, his experience did not conform to his aunt's description. To relate your experience, express your feelings, and perhaps entertain, tell a story about a time when you were led to expect something, but it did not happen. If there is a lesson to be learned from you narration, your purpose can also be to inform.

   - Hughes says that he pretended to see Jesus "to save further trouble." To relate your experience, express your feelings, and perhaps entertain, narrate an account of a time you or someone you know did something to avoid trouble or inconvenience. Explain the outcome.

   - Hughes felt pressured to see Jesus and be saved. To relate your experience, express your feelings, and perhaps inform, narrate an account of a time you or someone you know was pressured to think or behave a particular way. Explain how you or the other person responded to the pressure.

   - The religious community and a family member pressured 12-year-old Hughes to see Jesus and be saved. Pick one organization, institution, or group—a congregation, a class, the family, the community, a peer group, and so on—and narrate a story that reveals one or more pressures it exerts on us. Your purpose is to convince your reader that the pressure is a positive one or a negative one.

3. **Combining patterns.** Narrate a story about a traumatic experience you had when you were young. Use cause-and-effect analysis to explain the impact the event had on you. (Cause-and-effect analysis is explained in Chapter 9.)

4. **Connecting the readings.** Young people do not lead the carefree life many people think they do. Instead, they are often struggling to deal with a variety of pressures from many sources. Using the information in "Salvation" and "Lost at C" (page 189), along with your own experience and observation, discuss the pressures young people face.

5. **Drawing on sources.** The Harlem Renaissance was an important period in the literary history of the United States because it changed the character of African-American literature. Write an essay that explains what the Harlem Renaissance was and how it affected literature, and use narration to show Langston Hughes's place in the movement. If you need a starting point, you can find articles in the *MLA International Bibliography of Books and Articles on Modern Language and Literature.* You can also find information in *Black American Literature: A Critical History.* Online, *http://www.nku.edu/~diesmanj/harlem.html* and at *http://bv.channel.aol.com* has helpful information and links to other relevant sites.

BACKGROUND: William Glaberson writes for *The New York Times* on a wide range of legal issues. In the past, his articles have dealt with sexual harrassment, military tribunals for accused terrorists, perjury, constitutional challenges to gun control, and criminal justice proceedings. "Seeking Justice after a Fatal Spin of the Cylinder" first appeared in *The New York Times* as "Court Stories: Seeking Justice after a Fatal Spin of the Cylinder" (April 2001).

THE PATTERN AND ITS PURPOSES: In "Seeking Justice after a Fatal Spin of the Cylinder," William Glaberson *narrates* two stories: an account of the death of a teenager and an account of the civil trial that followed. Both narrations **inform** readers about what happened and why, but Glaberson may also have a **persuasive** purpose in mind as well.

Seeking Justice after a Fatal Spin of the Cylinder

WILLIAM GLABERSON

INDIANA, Pa.—There was one round in the cylinder.

2 It was prom night at Marion Center High School in rural western Pennsylvania. Sean Miller was a senior, but he was not going to the dance.

As you read
Think about the verdict you would have rendered had you been on the jury.

He and Carl Kellar, a ninth grader, were with Leila Dudek, another freshman; the three were listening to one CD over and over again in Carl's tiny basement bedroom. They were the only ones in the house.

3 Early in the evening Carl went upstairs, grabbed the keys from where they were hidden on top of the family's gun cabinet and took out his father's .357 Magnum.

4 It was Sean who first spun the cylinder of the revolver, put the eight-inch barrel to his head and pulled the trigger. Much later he would admit he took no chances because he could see where the cartridge with the bullet landed in the cylinder after each spin.

5 That spring night came alive at a civil trial here last month that told an unusually detailed story of guns and teenage bluster. The trial came and went with little notice in this small town 60 miles east of Pittsburgh. But in a simply furnished courtroom here it raised the kinds of moral questions with no easy answers that are often on the dockets of courts across America.

6 The Russian roulette was a performance of sorts for the benefit of Leila.

7 "I was just trying to impress her," Sean testified.

8 She testified, too. "It went click," she said. She was terrified, she said.

9 Sean spun the cylinder and put the gun to his head again.

10 Click.

11 He spun it again. This time he handed the revolver to Carl, who, Leila testified, could not see the back of the cylinder.

12 It was a dare, she said. "It looked," she told

the jurors, "like he was gesturing for him to do the same thing." Then she heard the blast.

13 Every day in courtrooms across the country, people grapple with the endless variety of human evil, nobility, error, stupidity and bravery. Because the oath to tell the truth is taken seriously by some people in courtrooms, from the biggest cities to the smallest towns, courtroom battles can offer unusually clear snapshots of American life—even the parts that stubbornly defy explanation.

14 For four days in March in the Court of Common Pleas of Indiana County, a jury heard the civil suit of Carl's mother, Patricia A. Kellar, against Sean T. Miller, who is now 23. In Judge Gregory A. Olson's courtroom, the crack of that revolver was described so many times it seemed almost to break the silence of the two families facing off.

15 The suit claimed Sean was negligent in prodding Carl to his death on May 26, 1995. In court, the Kellars' lawyer, Victor H. Pribanic of White Oak, Pa., said Sean "took the life of Carl Kellar as surely as if he had pulled the trigger himself."

16 But Sean's lawyer, W. Alan Torrance Jr. of Pittsburgh, said the case hinged on "personal responsibility." Sean did a "dumb thing" that night, he said, but it was Carl who had pulled the trigger that final time.

17 The suit asked for millions of dollars in damages. But a few days before the trial began, Mrs. Kellar, who is 39, said she wanted as much as anything to unravel the mysteries of that night. Sean and Leila lied at first about the events leading up to Carl's death, so she was left struggling with confusion as well as loss.

18 "I'd like to know what happened that night," Mrs. Kellar said a few days before the trial, sitting next to her husband, John, in their modest ranch house where their son had died.

19 During questioning by the state police the night of the shooting, Sean and Leila left out any mention of Russian roulette. After they had all looked at the gun, they said, Carl had suddenly and inexplicably shot himself.

20 Sean Miller was never charged with a crime. So when the trial began on March 19, it became something of an inquest into the teenage world that is hidden from parents. It

also shed light on corners of a story that for six years had remained dark.

21 As the older of the two, Mr. Pribanic argued, Sean had power over Carl. Ms. Dudek testified, "Sometimes he got real bossy with him."

22 Mr. Pribanic called Mr. Miller to the stand. Now a square-jawed young man with darting blue eyes, he simmered as Mr. Pribanic led him through a series of admissions.

23 Yes, he had lied to the police that night.

24 "I was afraid of what people were going to think" if they concluded he had provoked Carl to point the gun at his head. Yes, he had asked Leila to lie, too.

25 The police had received anonymous phone calls after Carl's death saying that Mr. Miller had played Russian roulette before. They had called him in for another interview a month later. Then he admitted that he had spun the cylinder and pulled the trigger too that night; that he had begun the game.

26 Mr. Miller told the jurors he had watched where the round was before he had pulled the trigger. "I assumed he would catch onto what I was doing," he said of Carl. But "it didn't cross my mind that he was going to do that."

27 Then Mr. Pribanic asked Mr. Miller to recall for the jurors what he had said about Carl in pretrial testimony. He had called him "the kid" and had suggested he would "follow me around like a dog."

28 There were a lot things he had said that he wished he could change, Mr. Miller told the jurors.

29 As the central witness in the case, Sean Miller was an enigma. He was clearly furious to be defending a lawsuit but inexplicably cool as a witness. His fingers never trembled and his voice was always firm.

30 "Somewhat cocky," one of the jurors, Wendell Marsh, would say later in an interview.

31 Mr. Miller never said he was sorry his friend had died. "I don't think he has a lot of conscience involved," another juror, Marian Urish, would say.

32 When he was not on the stand, Mr. Miller sat in the front row, often with his mother. While seated in front of the jurors, the two clasped hands almost every minute. Sometimes they were joined by his father, who owns a construction company, and his brother, Josh, a college student.

33 Behind the Millers sat a gray-haired man from their homeowners insurance company, which would have to pay any verdict up to the policy's limit of $100,000. In a courtroom with few strangers, his presence was never explained to the jurors.

34 On the other side of the courtroom, in the front row, Mrs. Kellar sat. Usually, she was with her husband, a machine operator at a coal mine, who had adopted her two children from an earlier marriage. Carl's sister, now 23, and her husband, were with them, and behind them, sometimes as many as a dozen family members.

35 In the hallways of the quiet courthouse, the Millers and the Kellars shunned each other.

36 Inside the courtroom, Mr. Pribanic, a former Pittsburgh prosecutor, sketched the Sean of six years ago as a sinister 17-year-old who used a dangerous image to manipulate younger friends.

37 He called two wiry young men, now 21 and 22, who had been Carl's classmates. They testified that shortly before the night Carl died, Sean had cajoled them to play Russian roulette with his father's revolver.

38 When they refused, one of the young men, Richard L. Smith, testified, Sean made a macabre counteroffer, saying, "Why don't we point it out toward the field and act as if it were us in front of the bullet."

39 Mr. Miller told the jurors that conversation had never happened. But he admitted he had slipped the pins out of the hinges of his father's gun cabinet, removed a revolver and shot into the field that afternoon.

40 As described by witnesses, Carl was a young man with ambition: a high school football player who was in R.O.T.C. He was interested in the Air Force. Though he was almost six feet tall, he had written in a school essay just before he died that he wished to be bigger so that he could have had a chance of playing football at Penn State. "For a car," he wrote, "I want a Corvette."

41 But the dead boy, like the one who lived, did not escape the attacks that are part of legal battle. Mr. Torrance dwelled on the fact that Carl had had his own guns and a hunting rifle, as many boys around here do, as well as a bow and arrow and a collection of knives. Sean's younger brother Josh testified that Carl was a daredevil dirtbike rider and said he had once seen him

courting danger by "car surfing," riding on the roof of a moving vehicle.

42 Mr. Torrance brought in an adolescent psychiatrist, David R. Burns of Philadelphia, to say that Carl might have been a certain type of high-risk adolescent boy who believes "that the dangers they know about don't apply to them."

43 Just after noon on Thursday, March 22, the case went to the jury—seven men and five women from this county where coal mining dominated for decades. Guns here, as in much of America, are not a political issue, they are a part of life. When Judge Olson asked 34 potential jurors whether they or family members had firearms at home, only one did not raise her hand.

44 Four hours after they began deliberations, the jurors sent a note inquiring about a question on the verdict form that asked whether Carl "knowingly and voluntarily accepted the specific risk that caused his death." If they answered "yes," Carl's family would lose.

45 Later, jurors would say they had been divided six to six on that threshold question. At that moment, each side could still have won.

46 Mr. Pribanic said the jurors unnerved him partly because they did not glance over at Mrs. Kellar. After they had left the courtroom, he went in search of Mr. Torrance and the gray-haired man from the insurance company.

47 When he found them in the court's law library, he said later, they seemed as rattled as he was by the jurors' question. The gray-haired man, he said, was already on the phone to the insurance company asking for authorization to settle the case. Court filings show that before the trial the company had offered $100,000. Both sides agreed to keep the new settlement offer secret. But other lawyers said that under the circumstances of the case it was probably only modestly more than $100,000.

48 After six years of waiting, the settlement was reached in an instant. But it happened so fast that the jurors completed their deliberations first, three of them said in interviews. Sean was negligent, their verdict would have said. He had helped cause Carl's death.

49 But Carl was more at fault, 70 percent responsible for his own death, the jurors found, for pulling the trigger. Had the jurors delivered their verdict, the Kellars would not have collected damages.

50 "They were both responsible for what happened," said Nolan Blystone, a juror.

51 When it was over, the Millers sat in the hall. In obvious relief, Sean and his brother shared some private joke. Sean smiled widely, looking boyish for the first time in a week in court.

52 Mrs. Kellar was subdued about the settlement her lawyer had advised her to accept. "I learned more than what I knew" about what happened that night, she said.

53 Out in the hall after six years, the two families still did not speak to each other.

2. In paragraph 5, Glaberson refers to the Kellar's lawsuit as raising "the kinds of moral questions with no easy answers." Do you agree? Why or why not?

3. Why did the Kellars offer the Millers a settlement? Why did the Millers accept the settlement offer?

4. Do the courtroom battle and the shooting offer "snapshots of American life" (paragraph 13)? What do the snapshots look like?

5. If you were on the jury, what would your verdict be? Why?

EXAMINING STRUCTURE AND STRATEGY

1. Does the opening sentence/paragraph of the narration create an effective beginning? Why or why not?

2. Which of the journalist's questions are emphasized? Why does Glaberson focus more on the answers to those questions?

3. What purpose does the dialogue serve in the narration? Do you think Glaberson should have used more dialogue? Explain.

4. Paragraph 29 includes description of Sean Miller. Why does Glaberson include that description? Would anything be lost if the description were omitted?

5. Many of the paragraphs in "Seeking Justice after a Fatal Spin of the Cylinder" are brief; some are just a single sentence. What is the purpose of these short paragraphs? Does the length of the paragraphs have anything to do with the essay's original appearance in *The New York Times*? Explain.

6. Does the last sentence/paragraph create an effective conclusion? Explain.

CONSIDERING LANGUAGE AND STYLE

1. Cite three examples of specific word choice. How does the specific word choice help the author achieve his purpose for writing?

2. Consult a dictionary if you are unsure of the meaning of any of these words: *Russian roulette* (paragraph 6), *inexplicably* (paragraphs 19, 29), *inquest* (paragraph 20), *enigma* (paragraph 29).

FOR DISCUSSION IN CLASS OR ONLINE

At the end of the essay, did you feel that justice was served? With your classmates, discuss why or why not. If your instructor so directs, post your responses to your class Web site.

WRITING ASSIGNMENTS

1. **In your journal.** Do you think high school students would benefit from reading "Seeking Justice after a Fatal Spin of the Cylinder"? In a page or so, explain why or why not.

2. **Using narration for a purpose.** The purposes given in the assignments are possibilities. You may establish whatever purposes you like, within your instructor's guidelines.

    • The teenagers in "Seeking Justice after a Fatal Spin of the Cylinder" engaged in risky behavior. Because the outcome was tragic, the narration can be taken as a cautionary tale. To inform readers and convince them to avoid a specific risky behavior, narrate a story that is a cautionary tale.

- To relate your experience and perhaps express your feelings, tell a story about a time you did something just to impress another person.
- If you have participated in the legal system as a witness, jury member, plaintiff, defendant, observer, or member of youth court, narrate a story that relates your experience.
- To inform your reader, and perhaps relate your experience and express your feelings, narrate a story about a time justice was—or was not—served.

3. **Combining patterns.** Define "personal responsibility" (paragraph 16), and narrate a story that illustrates the concept. (See Chapter 11 on writing definition.)

4. **Connecting the readings.** Using the information in "Should Juvenile Offenders Be Tried as Adults?" (page 585), in "Adult Crime, Adult Time" (page 591), and in "Seeking Justice after a Fatal Spin of the Cylinder," discuss what kind of punishment juveniles should receive if they handle guns in dangerous or illegal ways.

5. **Drawing on sources.** Many aspects of our legal system are currently being debated, including the death penalty, DNA testing, racial bias, detaining political prisoners and suspected terrorists, and executing the mentally retarded. Select one of these issues or another one of your choice and discuss why that issue is significant. Your purpose is not to argue for or against capital punishment, plea bargaining, and so forth; rather, your purpose is to explain why the issue *matters*. For ideas, you can consult keywords related to your topic, such as "capital punishment" and "DNA Testing" in the *Social Sciences Index* or visit the "Issues & Action" Section at *http://dailynews.yahoo.com/h/pl.*

B A C K G R O U N D :   Natalie Kusz is the author of the memoir *Road Song* (1990) and of essays published in *Harper's, Threepenny Review, McCall's, Allure* (where "Ring Leader" was first published in 1990), and other periodicals. Her work has earned, among others, a Whiting Writer's Award, a Pushcart Prize, and fellowships from the NEA, the Bush Foundation, and the Bunting Institute of Radcliffe College. A former faculty member of Bethel College and Harvard University, she now teaches in the MFA (master of fine arts) program at Eastern Washington University.

C O M B I N E D   P A T T E R N S   A N D   T H E I R   P U R P O S E S : In "Ring Leader," Natalie Kusz **relates her experience** as an unconventional adolescent and adult and **expresses her feelings** about her physical appearance. Using *narration,* she tells something about herself, first as a high school student and then as a college teacher. Using *cause-and-effect analysis,* she explains what led her to get her nose pierced and the results of that action.

RING LEADER

| NATALIE KUSZ

I was thirty years old when I had my right nostril pierced, and back-home friends fell speechless at the news, lapsing into long telephone pauses of the sort that June Cleaver would employ if the Beave had ever called to report, "Mom, I'm married. His name's Eddie." Not that I resemble a Cleaver or have friends who wear pearls in the shower, but people who have known me the longest would say that for me to *draw* attention to my body rather than to work all out to *repel* it is at least as out of character as the Beave's abrupt urge for his-and-his golf ensembles. A nose ring, they might tell you, would be my last choice for a fashion accessory, way down on the list with a sag-enhancing specialty bra or a sign on my butt reading "Wide Load."

2   The fact is, I grew up ugly—no, worse than that, I grew up unusual, that unforgivable sin among youth. We lived in Alaska, where, despite what you might have heard about the Rugged Individualist, teenagers still adhere to the universal rules of conformity: If Popular Patty wears contact lenses, then you will by gum get contacts too, or else pocket

As you read Notice the humor in the essay. Try to determine what purpose that humor serves.

"The fact is, I grew up ugly— no, worse than that, I grew up unusual, that unforgivable sin. . . ."

those glasses and pray you can distinguish the girls' bathroom door from the boys'. The bad news was that I had only one eye, having lost the other in a dog attack at age seven; so although contacts, at half the two-eyed price, were easy to talk my parents into, I was still left with an eye patch and many facial scars, signs as gaudy as neon, telling everyone, "Here is a girl who is Not Like You." And Not Like Them, remember, was equivalent to Not from This Dimension, only half (maybe one third) as interesting.

3   The rest of my anatomy did nothing to help matters. I come from a long line of famine-surviving ancestors—on my father's side, Polish and Russian, on my mother's, everything from Irish to French Canadian—and thus I have an excellent, thrifty, Ebenezer Scrooge of a metabolism. I can ingest but a single calorie, and before quitting time at the

Scrooge office, my system will have spent that calorie to replace an old blood cell, to secrete a vital hormone, to send a few chemicals around the old nervous system, and still have enough left over to deposit ten fat cells in my inner thigh—a nifty little investment for the future, in case the Irish potato famine ever recurs. These metabolic wonders are delightful if you are planning a move to central Africa, but for an American kid wiggling to Jane Fonda* as if her life depended on it (which, in high school, it did), the luckiest people on earth seemed to be anorexics, those wispy and hollow-cheeked beings whose primary part in the locker room drama was to stand at the mirror and announce, "My God, I disgust myself, I am *so fat*." While the other girls recited their lines ("No, Samantha, don't talk like that, you're beautiful, you really *are!*"), I tried to pull on a gym shirt without removing any other shirt first, writhing inside the cloth like a cat trapped among the bedsheets.

4   Thus, if you add the oversized body to the disfigured face, and add again my family's low income and my second-hand wardrobe, you have a formula for pure, excruciating teenage angst. Hiding from public scrutiny became for me, as for many people like me, a way of life. I

"Hiding from public scrutiny became . . . a way of life."

developed a bouncy sense of humor, the kind that makes people say, "That Natalie, she is always so *up*," and keeps them from probing for deep emotion. After teaching myself to sew, I made myself cheap versions of those Popular Patty clothes or at least the items (*never* halter tops, although this was the seventies) that a large girl could wear with any aplomb. And above all, I studied the other kids, their physical posture, their music, their methods of blow-dryer artistry, hoping one day to emerge from my body, invisible. I suppose I came as close to invisibility as my appearance would allow, for if you look at the yearbook photos from that time, you will find on my face the same "too cool to say 'cheese'" expression as on Popular Patty's eleven-man entourage.

5   But at age thirty, I found myself living in the (to me) incomprehensible politeness of America's Midwest, teaching at a small private college that I found suffocating, and anticipating the arrival of that all-affirming desire of college professors everywhere, that professional certification indicating you are now "one of the family": academic tenure. A first-time visitor to any college campus can easily differentiate between tenured and nontenured faculty by keeping in mind a learning institution's two main expectations: (1) that a young professor will spend her first several years on the job proving herself indispensable (sucking up), working to advance the interests of the college (sucking up), and making a name for herself in her field of study (sucking up); and (2) that a senior, tenured professor, having achieved indispensability, institutional usefulness, and fame will thereafter lend her widely recognized name to the school's public relations office, which will use that name to attract prospective new students and faculty, who will in turn be encouraged to call on senior professors for the purpose of asking deep, scholarly questions

---

*Jane Fonda's exercise videos were very popular in the 1980s and early 1990s.

(sucking up). Thus, a visitor touring any random campus can quickly distinguish tenured faculty persons from non-tenured ones simply by noting the habitual shape and amount of chapping of their lips.

6   I anticipated a future of senior-faculty meetings with academia's own version of Popular Patty—not a nubile, cheerleading fashion plate, but a somber and scholarly denture wearer who, under the legal terms of tenure, cannot be fired except for the most grievous unprofessional behavior, such as igniting plastique under the dean's new Lexus. When that official notice landed in my In box, my sucking-up days would be over. I would have arrived. I would be family.

7   I couldn't bear it. In addition to the fact that I possessed all my own teeth, I was unsuited to Become As One with the other tenured beings because I was by nature boisterous, a collector of Elvis memorabilia, and given to not washing my car—in short, I was and always would be from Alaska.

8   Even in my leisure hours, my roots made my life of that period disorienting. Having moved to the immaculate Midwest from the far-from-immaculate wilderness, I found myself incapable of understanding, say, the nature of cul-de-sacs, those little circles of pristine homes where all the children were named Chris, and where all the parents got to vote on whether the Johnsons (they were all Johnsons) could paint their house beige. I would go to potluck suppers where the dishes were foreign to me, and twelve people at my table would take a bite, savor it with closed eyes, and say, "Ah, Tater Tot casserole. Now *that* takes me back." It got to the point where I felt defensive all the time, professing my out-of-townness whenever I was

mistaken for a local, someone who understood the conversational subtexts and genteel body language of a Minnesotan. Moreover, I could never be sure what I myself said to these people with my subtextual language or my body. For all I knew, my posture during one of those impossible kaffeeklatsches proclaimed to everyone, "I am about to steal the silverware," or "I subscribe to the beliefs of Reverend Sun Myung Moon."

9   I grew depressed. Before long, I was feeling nostalgic for Alaskan eccentricities I had avoided even when I had lived

"Before long, I was feeling nostalgic for Alaskan eccentricities. . . ."

there—unshaven legs and armpits, for example, and automobiles held together entirely by duct tape. I began decorating my office with absurd and nonprofessional items: velvet paintings, Mr. Potato Head, and a growing collection of snow globes from each of the fifty states. Students took to coming by to play with Legos, or to blow bubbles from those little circular wands, and a wish started to grow in my brain, a yearning for some way to transport the paraphernalia around with me, to carry it along as an indication that I was truly unconventional at heart.

10   So the week that I received tenure, when they could no longer fire me and when a sore nose would not get bumped during the course of any future sucking-up maneuver, I entered a little shop in the black-leather part of town and emerged within minutes with my right nostril duly pierced. The gesture was, for me, a celebration, a visible statement that said, "Assume nothing. I might be a

punk from Hennepin Avenue, or a belly dancer with brass knuckles in my purse." Polite as was the society of that region, my colleagues never referred to my nose, but I could see them looking and wondering a bit, which was exactly the thing I had wanted—a lingering question in the minds of the natives, the possibility of forces they had never fathomed.

11   After this, my comfort level changed some, and almost entirely for the better. I had warned my father, who lived with me those years, that I was thinking of piercing my nose. When I arrived home that day and the hole was through the side instead of the center—he had expected, I found out, a Maori-style bone beneath the nostrils—he looked at me, his color improved, and he asked if I wanted chicken for dinner. So that was all fine. At school, students got over their initial shock relatively quickly, having already seen the trailer-park ambience of my office, and they became less apt to question my judgment on their papers; I could hear them thinking, She looks like she must understand *something* about where I'm coming from. And my daughter—this is the best part of all—declared I was the hippest parent she knew, and decided it was O.K. to introduce me to her junior high friends; even Cool Chris—the Midwestern variety of Popular Patty—couldn't boast a body-pierced mom.

12   I have since moved away from Minnesota, and old friends (those of the aforementioned June Cleaver–type stunned silence) have begun to ask if I have decided to stop wearing a nose stud now that my initial reason for acquiring it has passed. And here, to me, is the interesting part: the answer, categorically, is no. Nonconformity, or something like it, may have been the initial reason behind shooting a new hole through my proboscis, but a whole set of side effects, a broad and unexpected brand of liberation, has provided me a reason for keeping it. Because the one-eyed fat girl who couldn't wear Popular Patty's clothes, much less aspire to steal her boyfriends, who was long accustomed to the grocery-store stares of adults and small children ("Mommy, what happened to that fat lady's face?"), who had learned over the years to hide whenever possible, slathering her facial scars with cover stick, is now—am I dreaming?—in charge. I have now, after all, deliberately chosen a "facial flaw," a remarkable aspect of appearance. Somehow now, the glances of strangers seem less invasive, nothing to incite me to nunhood; a long look is just that—a look—and what of it? I've invited it, I've made room for it, it is no longer inflicted upon me against my will.

READING CLOSELY AND THINKING CRITICALLY

1.   Why does Kusz get her nose pierced?

2.   What were the various reactions to the author's pierced nose? Why did people react the way they did?

3.   In paragraph 2, Kusz says that among youth, looking unusual is worse than being ugly. What does she mean?

4.   Did Kusz fit in as a faculty member? Explain.

5. Kusz felt self-conscious about her appearance, and that self-consciousness influenced her behavior. How did it influence her behavior as an adolescent? As an adult?

EXAMINING STRUCTURE AND STRATEGY

1. How does Kusz use flashback? How does the flashback help the author achieve her purpose?
2. What words describe the tone of the essay? (See page 71 on tone.)
3. What purpose does the humor in the essay serve? How does that purpose compare to the purpose humor served in the author's life?

NOTING COMBINED PATTERNS

1. Where does Kusz use cause-and-effect analysis? (Cause-and-effect analysis is explained in Chapter 9).
2. Do you consider "Ring Leader" a cause-and-effect analysis with elements of narration, or a narration with elements of cause-and-effect analysis? Explain.

CONSIDERING LANGUAGE AND STYLE

1. In paragraph 1, Kusz refers to characters from "Leave It to Beaver," a popular television program of the late 50s and early 60s that depicted middle-class whites in an overly wholesome way. June Cleaver was the ideal wife and mother. Her son Beaver was an all-American child. Friend Eddie was a troublemaker. How does Kusz use these references?
2. Explain the metaphor and simile that appear in paragraph 3. How does Kusz use these figures of speech?
3. Consult a dictionary if you are unsure of the meaning of any of these words: *angst* (paragraph 4), *aplomb* (paragraph 4), *entourage* (paragraph 4), *nubile* (paragraph 6), *plastique* (paragraph 6), *cul-de-sacs* (paragraph 8), *kaffeeklatsches* (paragraph 8), *ambience* (paragraph 11), *proboscis* (paragraph 12).

FOR DISCUSSION IN CLASS OR ONLINE

Body piercing and tattooing have become popular in recent years, particularly among young people. With your classmates, discuss why you think these practices are so popular. If your instructor so directs, post your responses to your class Web site.

WRITING ASSIGNMENTS

1. **In your journal.** When you were in high school, how did you feel about your appearance? To what extent did that feeling affect your behavior then, and how does it affect you now? Answer in a page or two.

2. **Using narration for a purpose.** The purposes given in the assignments are possibilities. You may establish whatever purposes you like, within your instructor's guidelines.

   - To relate your experience and perhaps express your feelings, narrate a story that reveals something about what high school was like for you.

   - In paragraph 4, Kusz refers to teenage angst. If you suffered from teenage angst, write a narration that tells about a time you experienced it. Your purpose is to express your feelings and relate your experience.

   - Narrate a story that reveals you or someone you know as unconventional to inform your reader about the nature of the person who is your subject.

   - Tell a story about a time you did not fit in to relate your experience and perhaps express your feelings.

3. **Combining patterns.** Kusz notes that in addition to being affected by her physical appearance, she was shaped by living in Alaska. Use narration and cause-and-effect analysis to tell a story that illustrates how you were affected by the town or neighborhood where you grew up. If you like, you can also explain why the town affected you the way it did. (Cause-and-effect analysis is explained in Chapter 9.)

4. **Connecting the readings.** Discuss the connection between our self-concepts and how we feel about our appearance. To what extent does how we think we look affect how we feel about ourselves? In addition to the ideas in "Ring Leader," the ideas in "Am I Blue?" (page 353) may be helpful.

5. **Drawing on sources.** Many people have body image problems because they look in the mirror and do not like what they see, even though they look perfectly fine. Some people speculate that the impossible standard of beauty presented in magazine and television advertisements contributes to body image problems. Study a sampling of advertisements in magazines and on television and then agree or disagree with this speculation. You can also look in the *Social Sciences Index* under the heading "body image."

B A C K G R O U N D : Noted humorist Jean Shepherd (1929–1999) began as a standup comic and went on to be an author, an off-Broadway actor with four one-man shows to his credit, and a radio and television personality in Cincinnati, Philadelphia, Detroit, and New York, where he became a cult favorite. Shepherd wrote for *The Village Voice,* and he contributed award-winning fiction to *Playboy.* You may know the popular movie *A Christmas Story,* based on his memoir *In God We Trust, All Others Pay Cash* (1996). Like the piece reprinted here, his work usually treats growing up in America's heartland with humor and insight. "Lost at C" is taken from Shepherd's humorous book *Fistful of Fig Newtons* (1973).

C O M B I N E D   P A T T E R N S   A N D   T H E I R   P U R P O S E S : In "Lost at C," Jean Shepherd employs *narration* and *description* to **relate the memory of an experience** in his high school algebra class and **express** his **feelings** about that experience. At the same time, he **entertains** the reader with his characteristic humor and **informs** by pointing out some unfortunate truths about American education. Because Shepherd's humor has such wide appeal, "Lost at C" can be enjoyed by almost any mature reader.

Lost at C

JEAN SHEPHERD

Miss Snyder stood at the blackboard and hurled the first harpoon of the season: "You freshmen who are with us today are already enrolled for the courses you will be required to take. Here are your program cards." She dealt out 3 × 5-inch blue cards, which were handed back to the freshmen. Each card was neatly lined into eight periods, and after each period was the name of a teacher, a subject, and a classroom. One period was labeled LUNCH, another STUDY, and so on. Every minute of my day was laid out for me. So much for my dreams of freedom.

As you read
Think about how Shepherd uses exaggeration.

2   "Freshmen, this is your first day in high school. You are no longer in grade school. If you work hard, you will do well. If you don't you will regret it. You are here to learn. You are not here to play. Remember this and remember it well: *What you do here will follow you all through life."* She paused dramatically. In the hushed silence, I could hear Rukowski wheezing ahead of me. None of this, of course, affected him. Anyone who could block the way he could block would have no trouble getting through life.

3   "Your first class will begin in five minutes. Any questions?" No one raised a hand.

4   I sat there pawing in the chute, anxious to begin my glorious career of learning. No more would I fake my way. A new era was about to begin. The bell rang. The starting gate slammed open.

5   I had thundered a couple of hundred feet through the hall with the mob before it hit me that I had no idea where the hell I was supposed to go. As the crowd surged around me, I struggled to read my program card. All I could make out was Room 127. I had only a minute to make it, so I battled my way down a flight of stairs. Then: 101, 105, 109, 112, 117—127, just in time. Already the classroom was three-quarters filled. Ahead of me, running interference, was Rukowski, trying his

luck at this course, I later learned, for the third time in as many semesters. Getting his shoulder into it, he bulled his way through the door, buffeting aside a herd of spindly little freshmen. It was Schwartz, good old Schwartz, and Flick and Chester and Helen Weathers. My old gang! Even poor old Zynzmeister. Whatever it was, I would not have to go through it alone.

6   "Hi, Schwartz!"

7   Schwartz smiled wanly. And Helen Weathers giggled—until she saw, at the same moment I did, a tall, square man standing motionless at the blackboard. He had a grim blue jaw and short, kinky black crew-cut hair. His eyes were tiny ball bearings behind glasses with thick black rims. He wore a dark, boxy suit that looked like it was made of black sandpaper. The bell rang and the door closed behind us. I joined the crowd around his desk who were putting registration cards into a box. I did likewise.

8   "All right. Settle down. Let's get organized." The man's voice had a cutting rasp to it, like a steel file working on concrete. "We sit alphabetically in this class. As up here in front to my right. Get going."

9   I trudged behind Schwartz and Helen Weathers toward the dim recesses in the back of the classroom. Well, at least I'd be among friends. It was about a quarter of a mile to the front of the room, but I sat bolt upright in my seat, my iron determination intact. No more faking it.

10   "Class, my name is Mr. Pittinger." He was the first male teacher I had ever had. Warren G. Harding was peopled entirely by motherly ladies like Mrs. Bailey and Miss Shields. Mr. Pittinger was a whole new ball game. And I still had no idea what he taught. I would soon find out.

11   "If you work in this class, you'll have no trouble. If you don't, I promise you nothing."

12   I leaned forward at my desk, scribbling madly in my notebook: *class my name is mr. pittinger if you work you will have no trouble if you don't i promise you nothing . . .*

13   I figured if you wrote everything down there'd be no trouble. Every classroom of my life had been filled with girls on the Honor Roll who endlessly wrote in mysterious notebooks, even when nothing seemed to be going on. I never knew what the hell they were writing, so I took no chances. I figured I'd write everything.

14   "Braaghk." Mr. Pittinger cleared his gravelly throat.

15   *braaaghk,* I scribbled, *brummph.* You never know, I thought, it might appear on the exam.

16   He turned, picked up a piece of chalk, and began to scrawl huge block letters on the blackboard.

17   A–L—the chalk squeaked decisively—G–E–B–R–A. I copied each letter exactly as he'd written it.

18   "That is the subject of this course," he barked.

19   Algebra? What the hell is that?

20   "Algebra is the mathematics of abstract numbers."

21   I gulped as I wrote this down.

22   "I will now illustrate."

23   Pittinger printed a huge Y on the blackboard and below it an enormous X. I doggedly followed suit in my notebook. He then put equal signs next to the X and the Y.

24   "If Y equals five and X equals two, what does the following mean?"

25   He wrote out: $X + Y = ?$

26   Black fear seized my vitals. How could you add Xs and Ys? I had enough trouble with nines and sevens!

27   Already the crowd in front of the room were waving their hands to answer Pittinger's question. The class wasn't thirty seconds old and I was already six weeks behind. I sank lower in my seat, a faint buzzing in my ears. Instinctively I began to weave. I knew it was all over. Out of the corner of my eye I saw that Schwartz, next to me, had hunched lower and begun to emit a high, thin whimpering sound. Helen Weathers had flung up a thin spray of sweat. Chester's skin had changed to the color of the cupboards in the back of the room. And from behind me I could hear the faint, steady click of Zynzmeister's rosary.

28   Second by second, minute by minute, eon by eon that first algebra class droned on. I couldn't catch another word that was said, and by the time Mr. Pittinger wrote the second equation on the board, I was bobbing and weaving like a cobra and sending out high-voltage thought rays. A tiny molten knot of stark terror hissed and simmered in the pit of my stomach. I realized that for the first time in my school life, I had run into something that was completely opaque and unlearnable, and there was no way to fake it.

29   Don't call on me, Don't call on me, Don't call on me . . .

30   That night I ate my meatloaf and red cabbage in sober silence as the family yapped on, still living back in the days when I was known to all of them as the smartest little son of a bitch to ever set foot on Cleveland Street.

31   "Boy, look at the stuff kids study these days," the old man said with wonder as he hefted my algebra textbook in his bowling hand and riffled through the pages.

32   "What's all this X and Y stuff?" he asked.

33   "Yeah, well, it ain't much," I muttered as coolly as I could, trying to recapture some of the old élan.

34   "Whaddaya mean, ain't much?" His eyes glowed with pride at the idea that his kid has mastered algebra in only one day.

35   "Abstract mathematics, that's all it is."

36   The old man knew he'd been totally outclassed. Even my mother stopped stirring the gravy for a few seconds. My kid brother continued to pound away at the little bbs of Ovaltine that floated around on the top of his milk.

37   That night sleep did not come easily. In fact, it was only the first of many storm-tossed nights to come as, algebra class by algebra class, my terror grew. All my other subjects—history, English, social studies—were a total breeze. My years of experience in fakery came into full flower. In social studies, for example, the more you hoked it up, the better the grades. On those rare occasions when asked a question, I would stand slowly, with an open yet troubled look playing over my thoughful countenance.

38   "Mr. Harris, sir," I would drawl hesitantly, as though attempting to unravel the perplexity of the ages, "I guess it depends on how you view it—objectively, which, naturally, is too simple, or subjectively, in which case many factors such as a changing environment must be taken into consideration, and . . ." I would trail off.

39   Mr. Harris, with a snort of pleasure, would bellow: "RIGHT! There are many diverse elements, which . . ." After which he was good for at least a forty-minute solo.

40   History was more of the same, and English was almost embarrassingly easy as, day after day, Miss McCullough preened and congratulated herself before our class. All she needed was a little ass-kissing and there was no limit to her applause. I often felt she regretted that an A+ was the highest grade she could hand out to one who loved her as sincerely and selflessly as I did.

41   Every morning at eight-thirty-five, however, was another story. I marched with leaden feet and quaking bowels into Mr. Pittinger's torture chamber. By the sixth week I knew, without the shadow of a doubt, that after all these years of dodging and grinning, I was going to fail. Fail! No B, no gentleman's C—Fail. F. The big one: my own Scarlet Letter. Branded on my forehead—F, for Fuckup.

42   There was no question whatever. True, Pittinger had not yet been able to catch me out in the open, since I was using every trick of the trade. But I knew that one day, inevitably, the icy hand of truth would rip off my shoddy facade and expose me for all the world to see.

43   Pittinger was of the new school, meaning he believed that kids, theoretically motivated by an insatiable thirst for knowledge, would devour algebra in large chunks, making the final examination only a formality. He graded on performance in class and total grasp of the subject, capped off at the end of the term with an exam of brain-crushing difficulty from which he had the option of excusing those who rated A+ on classroom performance. Since I had no classroom performance, my doom was sealed.

44   Schwartz, too, had noticeably shrunken. Even fat Helen had developed deep hollows under her eyes, while Chester had almost completely disappeared. And Zynzmeister had taken to nibbling Communion wafers in class.

45   Christmas came and went in tortured gaiety. My kid brother played happily with his Terry and the Pirates Dragon Lady Detector as I looked on with the sad indulgence of a withered old man whose youth had passed. As for my own presents, what good did it do to have a new first baseman's mitt when my life was over? How innocent they are, I thought as I watched my family trim the tree and scurry about wrapping packages. Before long, they will know. They will loathe me. I will be driven from this warm circle. It was about this time that I began to fear—or perhaps hope—that I would never live to be twenty-one, that I would die of some exotic debilitating disease. Then they'd be sorry. This fantasy alternated with an even better fantasy that if I did reach twenty-one, I would be blind and hobble about with a white cane. Then they'd really be sorry.

46   Not that I'd given up without a struggle. For weeks, in the privacy of my cell at home, safe from prying eyes, I continued trying to actually learn something about algebra. After a brief mental pep rally—This is simple. If Esther Jane Alberry can

understand it, any fool can do it. All you gotta do is think. THINK! Reason it out!—I would sit down and open my textbook. Within minutes, I would break out in a clammy sweat and sink into a funk of nonunderstanding, a state so naked in its despair and self-contempt that it was soon replaced by a mood of defiant truculence. Schwartz and I took to laughing contemptuously at those boobs and brown-noses up front who took it all so seriously.

47 The first hints of spring began to appear. Birds twittered, buds unfurled. But men on death row are impervious to such intimations of life quickening and reborn. The only sign of the new season that I noticed was Mr. Pittinger changing from a heavy scratchy black suit into a lighter-weight scratchy black suit.

48 "Well, it won't be long. You gonna get a job this summer?" my old man asked me one day as he bent over the hood of the Olds, giving the fourth-hand paint job its ritual spring coat of Simonize.

49 "Maybe. I dunno," I muttered. It wouldn't be long, indeed. Then he'd know. Everybody would know that I knew less about algebra than Ralph, Mrs. Gammie's big Airedale, who liked to pee on my mother's irises.

50 Mr. Pittinger had informed us that the final exam, covering a year's work in algebra, would be given on Friday of the following week. One more week of stardom on Cleveland Street. Ever since my devastating rejoinder at the dinner table about abstract mathematics, my stock had been the hottest in the neighborhood. My opinions were solicited on financial matters, world affairs, even the infield problems of the Chicago White Sox. The bigger they are, the harder they fall. Even Ralph would have more respect than I deserved. At least he didn't pretend to be anything but what he was—a copious and talented pee-er.

51 Wednesday, two days before the end, arrived like any other spring day. A faint breeze drifted from the south, bringing with it hints of long summer afternoons to come, of swung bats, of nights in the lilac bushes. But not for such as me. I stumped into algebra class feeling distinctly like the last soul aboard the *Titanic* as she was about to plunge to the bottom. The smart-asses were already in their seats, laughing merrily, the goddamn A's and B's and C's and even the M's. I took my seat in the back, among the rest of the condemned. Schwartz sat down sullenly and began his usual moan. Helen Weathers squatted toadlike, drenched in sweat. The class began, Pittinger's chalk squeaked, hands waved. The sun filtered in through the venetian blinds. A tennis ball pocked back and forth over a net somewhere. Faintly, the high clear voices of the girls' glee club sang, "Can you bake a cherry pie, charming Billy?" Birds twittered.

52 My knot of fear, by now an old friend, sputtered in my gut. In the past week, it had grown to roughly the size of a two-dollar watermelon. True, I had avoided being called on even once the entire year, but it was a hollow victory and I knew it. Minute after minute inched slowly by as I ducked and dodged, Pittinger firing question after question at the class. Glancing at my Pluto watch, which I had been given for Christmas, I noted with deep relief that less than two minutes remained before the bell.

53 It was then that I made my fatal mistake, the mistake that all guerrilla fighters eventually make—I lost my concentration. For years, every fiber of my being, every

instant in every class, had been directed solely at survival. On this fateful Wednesday, lulled by the sun, by the gentle sound of the tennis ball, by the steady drone of Pittinger's voice, by the fact that there were just two minutes to go, my mind slowly drifted off into a golden haze. A tiny mote of dust floated down through a slanting ray of sunshine. I watched it in its slow, undulating flight, like some microscopic silver bird.

54 "You're the apple of my eye, darling Billy . . . I can bake a cherry pie . . . "

55 A rich maple syrup warmth filled my being. Out of the faint distance, I heard a deadly rasp, the faint honking of disaster.

56 For a stunned split second, I thought I'd been jabbed with an electric cattle prod. Pittinger's voice, loud and commanding, was pronouncing my name. He was calling on ME! Oh, my God! With a goddamn minute to go, he had nailed me. I heard Schwartz bleat a high, quavering cry, a primal scream. I knew what it meant: If they got him, the greatest master of them all, there's no hope for ANY of us!

57 As I stood slowly at my seat, frantically bidding for time, I saw a great puddle forming around Helen Weathers. It wasn't all sweat. Chester had sunk to the floor beneath his desk, and behind me Zynzmeister's beads were clattering so loudly I could hardly hear his Hail Marys.

58 "Come to the board, please. Give us the value of C in this equation."

59 In a stupor of wrenching fear, I felt my legs clumping up the aisle. On all sides the blank faces stared. At the board—totally unfamiliar territory to me—I stared at the first equation I had ever seen up close. It was well over a yard and a half long, lacerated by mysterious crooked lines and fractions in parentheses, with miniature twos and threes hovering above the whole thing like tiny barnacles. Xs and Ys were jumbled in crazy abandon. At the very end of this unholy mess was a tiny equal sign. And on the other side of the equal sign was a zero. Zero! All this crap adds up to nothing! Jesus Christ! My mind reeled at the very sight of this barbed-wire entanglement of mysterious symbols.

60 Pittinger stood to one side, arms folded, wearing an expression that said, At last I've nailed the little bastard! He had been playing with me all the time. He knew!

61 I glanced back at the class. It was one of the truly educational moments of my life. The entire mob, including Schwartz, Chester, and even Zynzmeister, were grinning happily, licking their chops with joyous expectation of my imminent crucifixion. I learned then that when true disaster strikes, we have no friends. And there's nothing a phony loves more in this world than to see another phony get what's coming to him.

62 "The value of C, please," rapped Pittinger.

63 The equation blurred before my eyes. The value of C. Where the hell was it? What did a C look like, anyway? Or an A or a B, for that matter. I had forgotten the alphabet.

64 "C, please."

65 I spotted a single letter C buried deep in the writhing melange of Ys and Xs and umlauts and plus signs, brackets, and God knows what all. One tiny C. A torrent of sweat raged down my spinal column. My jockey shorts were soaked and sodden with the sweat and stink of execution. Being a true guerrilla from years of

the alphabetical ghetto, I showed no outward sign of panic, my face stony: unyielding. You live by the gun, you die by the gun.

66 "C, please." Pittinger moodily scratched at his granite chin with thumb and forefinger, his blue beard rasping nastily.

67 "Oh my darling Billy boy, you're the apple of my eye . . ."

68 Somewhere birds twittered on, tennis racquet met tennis ball. My moment had finally arrived.

69 Now, I have to explain that for years I had been the leader of the atheistic free-thinkers of Warren G. Harding School, scoffers all at the Sunday School miracles taught at the Presbyterian church: unbelievers.

70 That miracle stuff is for old ladies, all that walking on water and birds flying around with loaves of bread in their beaks. Who can believe that crap?

71 Now, I am not so sure. Ever since that day in Pittinger's algebra class I have had an uneasy suspicion that maybe something mysterious is going on somewhere.

72 As I stood and stonily gazed at the enigmatic Egyptian hieroglyphics of that fateful equation, from somewhere, someplace beyond the blue horizon, it came to me, out of the mist. I heard my voice say clearly, firmly, with decision:

73 "C . . . is equal to three."

74 Pittinger staggered back; his glasses jolted down to the tip of his nose.

75 "How the hell did you know?!" he bellowed hoarsely, his snap-on bow tie popping loose in the excitement.

76 The class was in an uproar. I caught a glimpse of Schwartz, his face pale with shock. I had caught one on the fat part of the bat. It was a true miracle. I had walked on water.

77 Instantly, the old instincts took over. In a cool, level voice I answered Pittinger's rhetorical question.

78 "Sir, I used empirical means."

79 He paled visibly and clung to the chalk trough for support. On cue, the bell rang out. The class was over. With a swiftness born of long experience, I was out of the room even before the echo of the bell had ceased. The guerrilla's code is always hit and run. A legend had been born.

80 That afternoon, as I sauntered home from school, feeling at least twelve and a half feet tall, Schwartz skulked next to me, silent, moody, kicking at passing frogs. I rubbed salt deep into his wound and sprinkled a little pepper on for good measure. Across the street, admiring clusters of girls pointed out the Algebra King as he strolled by. I heard Eileen Akers's silvery voice clearly: "There he goes. He doesn't say much in class, but when he does he makes it count." I nodded coolly toward my fans. A ripple of applause went up. I autographed a few algebra books and walked on, tall and straight in the sun. Deep down I knew that this was but a fleeting moment of glory, that when I faced the blue book exam it would be all over, but I enjoyed it while I had it.

81 With the benign air of a baron bestowing largess upon a wretched serf, I offered to buy Schwartz a Fudgesicle at the Igloo. He refused with a snarl.

82 "Why, Schwartz, what seems to be troubling you?" I asked with irony, vigorously working the salt shaker.

83 "You phony son of a bitch. You know what you can do with your goddamn Fudgesicle."

84 "Me, a phony? Why would you say an unkind thing like that?"

85 He spat viciously into a tulip bed. "You phony bastard. You studied!"

86 Inevitably, those of us who are gifted must leave those less fortunate behind in the race of life. I knew that, and Schwartz knew it. Once again I had lapped him and was moving away from the field, if only for a moment.

87 The next morning, Thursday, I swaggered into algebra class with head high. Even Jack Morton, the biggest smart-ass in the class, said hello as I walked in. Mr. Pittinger, his eyes glowing with admiration, smiled warmly at me.

88 "Hi, Pit," I said with a casual flip of the hand. We abstract mathematicians have an unspoken bond. Naturally, I was not called on during that period. After all, I had proved myself beyond any doubt.

89 After class, beaming at me with the intimacy of a fellow quadratic equation zealot, Mr. Pittinger asked me to stay on for a few moments.

90 "All my life I have heard about the born mathematical genius. It is a well-documented thing. They come along once in a while, but I never thought I'd meet one, least of all in a class of mine. Did you always have this ability?"

91 "Well . . ." I smiled modestly.

92 "Look, it would be pointless for you to waste time on our little test tomorrow. Would you help me grade the papers instead?"

93 "Gosh, Pit, I was looking forward to taking it, but if you really need me, I'll be glad to help." It was a master stroke.

94 "I'd appreciate it. I need somebody who really knows his stuff, and most of these kids are faking it."

95 The following afternoon, together, we graded the papers of my peers. I hate to tell you what, in all honesty, I had to do to Schwartz when I marked his pitiful travesty. I showed no mercy. After all, algebra is an absolute science and there can be no margin for kindness in matters of the mind.

READING CLOSELY AND THINKING CRITICALLY

1. Why was Shepherd so happy to encounter his friends in school?

2. What reason does Shepherd give for being called on the last day of class? Is that the real reason? Explain.

3. Discuss the meaning of the title. Explain Shepherd's play on words.

4. How would you characterize the tone of "Lost at C"? (See page •• for an explanation of tone.)

5. Make a list of words and phrases that describe the kind of student Shepherd was in his first year of high school. Make another list of words and phrases, this time to describe the kind of teacher Mr. Pittinger was.

6. "Lost at C" is an amusing story, but like all good humor, it points to important truths while it amuses. Cite three humorous passages in the essay that suggest truths.

EXAMINING STRUCTURE AND STRATEGY

1. How does the opening paragraph set the tone of the essay and give the reader an idea of what is in store?
2. Shepherd often uses exaggeration for its comic effect. For example, in paragraph 15, to show that he took notes on the teacher's every utterance, Shepherd says he wrote down "Braaaghk." Cite two other examples of exaggeration for comic effect.
3. Does Shepherd state or imply the point of his narration? What is that point?
4. **Situational irony** occurs when something happens that runs counter to what was expected. Explain the situational irony in the conclusion.

NOTING COMBINED PATTERNS

Shepherd uses a considerable amount of description in "Lost at C." Cite three examples of description that you find effective, and underline the specific nouns, verbs, and modifiers. Explain how the description helps Shepherd achieve his purpose.

CONSIDERING LANGUAGE AND STYLE

1. What metaphors does Shepherd create in paragraphs 4 and 5? (See page 109 on metaphors.) Do you find these metaphors appropriate? Why or why not?
2. Why do you think Shepherd uses so much dialogue in "Lost at C"? What does the dialogue add to the essay?
3. Consult a dictionary if you are unsure of the meaning of any of these words: *élan* (paragraph 33), *funk* (paragraph 46), *truculence* (paragraph 46), *impervious* (paragraph 47), *intimations* (paragraph 47), *Simonize* (paragraph 48), *melange* (paragraph 65), *umlauts* (paragraph 65), *empirical* (paragraph 78), *largess* (paragraph 81).

FOR DISCUSSION IN CLASS OR ONLINE

How do Shepherd and his friends compare to today's high school students? Cite the chief similarities and differences. If your instructor so directs, post your answers to your class Web site.

WRITING ASSIGNMENTS

1. **In your journal.** In a page or so, discuss your own experiences with high school math and whether or not those experiences have had an enduring influence on you.
2. **Using narration for a purpose.** The purposes given in the assignments are possibilities. You may establish whatever purposes you like, within your instructor's guidelines.
    - Write a narrative account of a time you were lost and confused. The narration can be humorous to entertain your reader, if you like.
    - To relate you experience, write a narrative account of a time you faked your way through a situation. Explain why you felt you had to pretend and what the consequences were. If you learned anything, inform your reader of what you learned.

- In paragraph 61, Shepherd says that "when true disaster strikes, we have no friends." Write a narration to convince your reader that this statement is (or is not) true.

- To relate your experience and express your feelings, write a narrative account of a time you enjoyed a "moment of glory" (paragraph 80).

3. **Combining patterns.** Is anything that Shepherd says about teachers, students, high school, and the education system still true today? Use anecdotes and other examples to support your assertion. (See Chapter 6 for information on exemplification.)

4. **Connecting the readings.** "Salvation," (page 173) "Lost at C," and "Lifosuction" (page 223) give accounts of people who are not being truthful. Explain what you think prompts people to be phonies. Also note how prevalent you think fakery is and what its consequences are.

5. **Drawing on sources.** The media continue to report that the math skills of American students lag behind those of their counterparts in many other countries. In some reports, American seniors come in last. Many people think that proficiency testing will improve students' performance in mathematics and other subjects. What do you think? Explain whether or not proficiency testing is a good idea. For information, you can consult the *Educational Resources Information Center* in your library reference room. This bibliography of education resources is also available online at http://ericir.syr.edu.

BACKGROUND: Born in 1947, award-winning author Lee K. Abbott is director of the master of fine arts program in creative writing at Ohio State University. He has also taught at Rice University, Yale University, and Colorado College. Abbott has written numerous collections of short stories, including *Wet Places at Noon* (1997) and *It's Only Rock and Roll: An Anthology of Rock and Roll Short Stories* (1998). "The View of Me from Mars" was originally published in Abbott's collection, *Dreams and Distant Lives* (1990). Abbott's work has appeared in *Harper's, Ploughshares,* and *Kenyon Review.* One of his stories was included in *The Best American Short Stories, 1984.* One critic compares Abbott to Jean Shepherd, whose work also appears in this chapter (see page 189): "Like Shepherd, Lee Abbott writes hilarious stories about common human heartbreak and fractured families . . . ."

COMBINED PATTERNS AND THEIR PURPOSES: In "The View of Me from Mars," Lee K. Abbott *narrates* two stories, one within the other. As you read, look for *description,* which creates vivid scenes, and *cause-and-effect analysis* (an explanation of the reasons for and the consequences of an event). Abbott himself claims that his stories are not meant to teach: "I don't write to instruct anybody about anything. I've got nothing to tell people that they didn't already know by the time they got to be fourteen." Nonetheless, you may find that in addition to **entertaining**, the story **informs** because it makes specific points about human behavior.

The View of Me from Mars
LEE K. ABBOTT

A week before I became a father, which now seems like the long ago and far away fairy tales happen in, I read a father-child story that went straight at the surprise one truth between children and parents is. It was called "Mirrors," and had an end, to the twenty-three-year-old would-be know-it-all I was, that literally threw me back in my chair—an end, sad somehow and wise, which held that it is now and then necessary for the child, in ways mysterious with love, to forgive the parent.

As you read
Decide what Abbott's main point is.

2   In "Mirrors" the child was a girl, though it could have been a boy just as easily, whose father—a decent man, we have to believe—takes her to the sideshow tent at a one-horse and one-elephant circus in the flatlands of Iowa or Nebraska or Kansas. She's seven or eight at this time, and—as we have all begged for toys or experiences it can be, I see now, our misfortune to receive—she begs and begs to see the snake charmer and the tattooed lady, the giant and the dwarf. He gives in, the girl decides much later, because of his decency; or he gives in, as my own father might say, because he's too much a milk-and-cookies sort of fool to understand that in that smelly, ill-lit tent is knowledge it is a parent's duty often to deny or to avoid. It is a good moment, I tell you, this moment when they pay their quarters and go in, one person full of pride, the other sucking on cotton candy, the sad end of them still pages and pages away.

3   In that tent—a whole hour I think—walking from little stage to little stage, the girl is awestruck and puzzled and, well, breath-taken, full of questions about where these people, these creatures, live and what they do when they're not standing in

front of a bunch of hayseeds and would it be possible to get a face, a tattoo, printed on her knee. "Can I touch?" she asks. "Do they talk?" A spotlight comes on, blue and harsh, and nearby, in a swirl of cigarette smoke and field dust, are two little people, Mr. and Mrs. Tiny, gussied up like a commodore and his society bride; another light snaps on, yellow this time and ten paces away, and there stands a man—"A boy," the barker tells us, "only eighteen and still growing!"—who's already nine feet tall, his arms long as shovels, nothing in his face about his own parents or what he wants to be at twenty-five. These are clichés, my smart wife, Ellen Kay, tells me ("Sounds too artsy-fartsy," her exact words were when I read the thing to her), but in the story I remember, these are the exhibitions girl and man pass by—the girl Christmas Eve impatient, the man nervous—before they come to the main display, which is, in "Mirrors," a young woman, beautiful and smooth as china, who has no arms and no legs.

4   The father, complaining that he's grubby-feeling and hot, wants to get out, but his daughter, her heart hammering in her ears, can't move. As never before, she's conscious of her own hands and feet, the wonders they are. She's aware of smells— breath and oil and two-dollar cologne—and of sounds—a gasp here, a whisper there, exclamations that have in them ache and horror and fear. "C'mon," the father says, taking her elbow. But onstage, businesslike as a banker, the woman—"The Human Torso," the barker announces, "smart like the dickens"—is drinking water, the glass clamped against her neck by her shoulder; is putting on lipstick; is writing her name with a brush between her teeth; is, Lordy, about to type—with her chin maybe—a letter to a Spec 4 with the Army in Korea, her boyfriend.

5   Outside, the midway glittering and crowded with Iowans going crosswise, the girl, more fascinated than frightened (though the fright is coming), asks how that was done. The father has a Lucky Strike out now, and the narrator—seven or eight but on the verge of learning that will stay with her until seventy or eighty—realizes he's stalling. He's embarrassed, maybe sick. He says "Howdy" to a deadbeat he'd never otherwise talk to. He says he's hungry, how about a hot dog, some buttered popcorn? He's cold, he says, too cold for September. "How?" she says again, pulling at his sleeve a little and watching his face go stiff and loose in a way that has her saying to herself, "I am not scared. No, I am not." And then he says what the narrator realizes will be his answer—sometimes comic, often not—for all thereafter that astounds or baffles and will not be known: "Mirrors, it's done with mirrors."

6   There's a pause here, I remember, six sentences that tell what the weather is like and how, here and there, light bulbs are missing and what the girl's favorite subjects are in school. "What?" she thinks to ask, but doesn't. "It's an illusion," he says, his voice squeaky the way it gets when he talks about money they don't have much of. "A trick, like magic." Part of her—the part that can say the sum of two plus two, and that A is for Apple, B is for Boy—knows that mirrors have nothing to do with what she's seen; another part—this the half of her that will remember this incident forever and ever—knows that mirrors have nothing to do with what she's seen; another part—this the half of her that will remember this incident forever and ever—knows that her father, now as strange to her as the giant and the dwarf, is lying.

7   His hand is working up and down, and his expression says, as lips and eyes and cheeks will, that he's sorry, he didn't mean for her to see that, she's so young. Something is trembling inside her, a muscle or a bone. One-Mississippi, she says to herself. Two-Mississippi. Over there sits a hound dog wearing a hat and somewhere a shout is going up that says somebody won a Kewpie doll or a stuffed monkey, and up ahead, creaking and clanking, the Tilt-A-Whirl is full of people spinning round and round goggle-eyed. Her father has a smile not connected to his eyes—another lie—and his hand out to be held, and going by them is a fat lady who lives on Jefferson Street and a man with a limp who lives on Spruce. Her father seems too hairy to her now, and maybe not sharp-minded enough, with a nose too long and knobby. She tells herself what she is, which is a good dancer and smart about which side the fork goes on and who gets introduced first when strangers meet; and what she is not, which is strong enough to do pull-ups and watchful about who goes where and why. She is learning something, she thinks. There is being good, she thinks. And there is not. There is the truth, she thinks. And there is not.

8   And so, in the climax of what I read years and years ago, she says, her hands sticky and her dress white as Hollywood daylight, "Yes, mirrors, I thought so"— words that, years and years ago, said all I thought possible about lies and love and how forgiveness works.

9   In this story, which is true and only two days old and also about forgiveness, I am the father to be read about and the child is my son, Stuart Eliot Polk, Jr. (called "Pudge" in and out of the family); he's a semifat golfer—"linksman," he insists the proper term is—and honor student who will at the end of this summer go off to college and so cease to be a citizen in the sideshow tent my big house here in El Paso now clearly is. Yes, forgiveness—particularly ironic in that, since my graduation years ago from Perkins Seminary at SMU, it has been my job to say, day after day after day, the noises that are "It will get better" and "We all make mistakes" to a thousand Methodists who aim to be themselves forgiven and sent home happy. There is no "freak" here, except the ordinary one I am, and no storybook midway, except my modern kitchen and its odd come and go.

10   I am an adulterer—an old-fashioned word, sure, but the only one appropriate to the ancient sin it names; and my lover—a modern word not so full of terror and guilt and judgment as another—was, until two days ago, Terri Ann Mackey, a rich, three-times-married former Zeta Tau Alpha Texas girl who might one day make headlines for the dramatic hair she has or the way she can sing Conway Twitty tunes. In every way likable and loud and free-minded, she has, in the last four years, met me anywhere and everywhere—in the Marriott and Hilton hotels, in the Cavern of Music in Juarez, even at a preachers' retreat at the Inn of the Mountain Gods near Ruidoso in southern New Mexico's piney forests. Dressed up in this or that outfit she sent away for or got on a trip to Dallas, she has, to my delight and education, pretended to be naughty as what we imagine the Swedish are or nice as Snow White; she has pretended, in a hundred rented rooms, to be everything I thought my wife was not—daring and wicked, heedless as a tyrant. Shameful to say, it seems we have always been here, in this bright desert cowtown, now far-flung and fifty percent ticky-tacky, drinking wine and fornicating and then hustling

home to deceive people we were wed to. Shameful to say, it seems we have always been playing the eyes' version of footsy—her in pink and cactus yellow in a pew in the middle of St. Paul's, me in the pulpit sermonizing about parables and Jesus and what welfare we owe the lost and poor and beaten down.

11   "Yes," my wife, Ellen Kay, would answer when I told her I was at the Stanton Street Racquet Club playing handball with a UTEP management professor named Red Walker. "Go change," she'd say, herself lovely and schoolgirl trim as that woman I'd collapsed atop a half-hour before. "I phoned," she'd say, "Mrs. Denbo said you were out." Yes, I'd tell her. I was in the choir room, hunting organ music that would inspire and not be hokey; I was in the library, looking up what the Puritan Mathers had written about witchcraft and gobbledygook we are better off without; I was taking a drive in my Volvo, the better to clear my head so I could get to the drafting of a speech for the Rotarians, or the LULAC Club of Ysleta, or the Downtown Optimists. "You work too hard," she'd say, "let's go to Acapulco this year." And I'd head to my big bedroom, the men I am, the public one amazed by his private self—the first absolutely in love with a blonde continental-history major he'd courted at the University of Texas in 1967; the second still frazzled by what, in the afternoon, is made from deceit and bednoise and indecency. And until two days ago, it was possible to believe that I knew which was which, what what.

12   "Where were you?" Ellen Kay said, making (though too violently, I think now) the tuna casserole I like enough to eat twice a year. "I called everywhere," she said. "It was as if you didn't exist." Upset, her hair spilling out of the French roll she prefers, she said more, two or three paragraphs whose theme was my peculiar behavior and the sly way I had lately and what time I was supposed to be somewhere and was not; and suddenly, taking note of the thump-thump my heart made and how one cloud in the east looked like a bell, I stood at the sink, steadily drinking glass after glass of water, trying to put some miles between me and her suspicions. Terri Ann Mackey Cruz Robinson Cross was all over me, my hands and my thighs and my face; and, a giant step away, my wife was asking where I'd been. "You were going to call," Ellen Kay said. "You had an appointment, a meeting." I had one thought, which was about the bricked-up middle of me, and another, which was about how like TV this situation was. "I talked to Bill Watson at the bank," she said. "He hasn't seen you for a week, ten days. I called—" And her wayward husband had a moment then, familiar to all cheaters and sorry folks, when he thought he'd tell the truth; a moment, before fear hit him and he got a 3-D vision of the cheap world he'd have to live in, when he thought to make plain the creature he was and the no-account stage he stood upon.

13   "I was at the golf course," I said, "watching Pudge. They have a match tomorrow." The oven was closed, the refrigerator opened. "Which course?" she said. Forks and knives had been brought out, made a pile of. "Coronado Hills," I said. "Pudge is hitting the ball pretty good." She went past me a dozen times, carrying the plates and the bread and the fruit bowl, and I tried to meet her eyes and so not give away the corrupt inside of me. I thought of several Latin words—*bellum* and *verus* and *fatum*—and the Highland Park classroom I learned them in. "All right," she said, though by the dark notes in her voice it was clear she was going to ask Pudge if

he'd seen me there, by the green I'd claimed to have stood next to, applauding the expert wedge shot I'd seen with my very own eyes.

14 As in the former story of illusions and the mess they make crashing down, there is a pause here, one of two; and you are to imagine now how herky-jerky time moved in our house when Pudge drove up and came in and said howdy and washed his hands as he'd been a million times told. You are to imagine, too, the dinner we picked at and our small talk about school and American government and what money does. While time went up and down, I thought about Pudge the way evil comic-book Martians are said to think about us: I was curious to know how I'd be affected by what, in a minute or an hour, would come from the mouth of an earthling who, so far as I knew, had never looked much beyond himself to see the insignificant dust ball he stood upon. I saw him as his own girlfriend, Traci Dixon, must: polite, fussy as a nun, soft-spoken about everything except golf and how it is, truly, a full-fledged sport.

15 Part of me—that eye and ear which would make an excellent witness at an auto wreck or similar calamity—flew up to one high corner of the room, like a ghost or an angel, and wondered what could be said about these three people who sat there and there and there. They were Democrats who, in a blue moon, liked what Reagan did; they had Allstate insurance and bank books and stacks of paper that said where they were in the world and what business they conducted with it; they played Scrabble and Clue and chose to watch the news Dan Rather read. The wife, who once upon a time could run fast enough to be useful in flag football, now used all her energy to keep mostly white-collar rednecks from using the words "nigger" and "spic" in her company; the son, who had once wanted to be an astronaut or a Houston brain surgeon, now aimed to be the only Ph.D. in computer science to win the Masters at Augusta, Georgia; and the father—well, what was there to say about a supposedly learned man for whom the spitting image of God, Who was up and yonder and everywhere, was his own father, a bent-over and gin-soaked cattle rancher in Midland, Texas? I hovered in that corner, distant and disinterested, and then Ellen Kay spoke to Pudge, and I came rushing back, dumb and helpless as anything human that falls from a great height.

16 "Daddy says you had a good round this afternoon," Ellen Kay began. "You had an especially nice wedge shot, he says." She was being sneaky, which my own sneaky self admired; and Pudge quit the work his chewing was, a little confusion in his round, smart face. He was processing, that machine between his ears crunching data that in no way could ever be, and for the fifteen seconds we made eye contact I wanted him to put aside reason and logic and algebra and see me with his guts and heart. On his lip he had a crumb that, if you didn't tell him, would stay until kingdom come; I wanted him to stop blinking and wrinkling his forehead like a first-year theater student. The air was heavy in that room, the light coming from eight directions at once, and I wanted to remind him of our trip last January to the Phoenix Open and that too-scholarly talk we'd had about the often mixed-up relations between men and women. I had a picture of me throwing a ball to him, and of him catching it. I had a picture of him learning to drive a stick shift, and of him so carefully mowing our lawn. Oddly, I thought about fishing, which

I hate, and bowling, which I am silly at, and then Ellen Kay, putting detergent in the dishwasher, asked him again about events that never happened, and I took a deep breath I expected to hold until the horror stopped.

17   Here is that second pause I spoke of—that moment, before time lurches forward again, when the eye needs to look elsewhere to see what is ruined, what not. Pudge now knew I was lying. His eyes went here and there, to the clock above my shoulder, to his mother's overwatered geranium on the windowsill, to his mostly empty plate. He was learning something about me—and about himself too. Like his made-up counterpart in "Mirrors," he was seeing that I, his father, was afraid and weak and damaged; and like the invented daddy in that story I read, a daddy whose interior life we were not permitted to see, I wanted my own child, however numbed or shocked, to forgive me for the tilt the world now stood at, to say I was not responsible for the sad magic trick our common back-and-forth really is. "Tell her," I said. I had in mind a story he could confirm—the Coke we shared in the clubhouse, a corny joke that was heard, and the help I tried to be with his short game—a story that had nowhere in it, two days ago, a father cold and alone and small.

CONSIDERING THE SHORT STORY

1. What point can be taken from "The View of Me from Mars"? Where in the story is that point expressed?

2. Both the narrator and the father in "Mirrors" tell lies. How are the lies different? Is one of the lies more justifiable than the other? Explain.

3. In paragraph 17, the narrator says his son "was learning something about me—and about himself too." What was the son learning?

4. What do you think the title of Abbott's short story means?

5. Writers use cause-and-effect analysis to explain the reasons something happens and the consequences of that event. How does Abbott use cause-and-effect analysis?

WRITING ASSIGNMENTS

1. **In your journal.**
    - In a page or so, consider whether the father in "Mirrors" did the right thing in lying to his daughter.
    - Do you think the narrator's son should have lied for his father? Explain your view.

2. **Using narration for a purpose.** To relate your experience and express your feelings— or for another purpose—tell about a time you learned something positive or negative about a parent or another authority figure.

3. **Combining patterns.** Tell about a time you lied or were lied to. Explain the causes and/or effects of the lie. As an alternative, tell about a time you needed forgiveness or a time you forgave someone.

See pages 162 and 164 for strategies for writing narration and for a revision checklist.

1. Narrate an account of an event that caused you to change your view of someone or something.

2. Narrate an account of an embarrassing moment that you or someone you know suffered. If you wish, make the narration humorous.

3. Narrate an account of a childhood memory. If possible, include description and dialogue.

4. Tell the story of a time when things did not go as you expected them to. Be sure to indicate the point of the narration.

5. Tell the story of an event that marked a turning point in your life. Be sure to indicate how you were affected by this event.

6. Narrate an account of a happy birthday or holiday celebration. Try to include dialogue and description.

7. Tell the story of a time when you displayed or witnessed courage.

8. Tell the story of an athletic event in which you were involved. Be sure to indicate the point of the narration.

9. Tell the story of a disappointment someone you know experienced. Be sure to indicate the point of the narration.

10. Tell a story that shows that people can be cruel (or kind).

11. Tell a story that shows that we rely heavily on technology.

12. Tell the story of a time that you or someone you know overcame an obstacle. Be sure to indicate the point of the narration.

13. Tell the story of a time when hard work did (or did not) pay off.

14. Tell a story about a school experience you have had. Be sure to indicate the point of the narration.

15. Tell a story that reveals a personality trait of someone. For example, if you have a friend who is reckless, tell a story that illustrates that recklessness. Try to use description and dialogue.

16. Tell a story that shows that things are not always what they seem.

17. Tell a story that shows that some modern device (the car, the DVD player, the computer, the microwave, for example) is more trouble than it is worth. If you like, you can make the narration humorous.

18. Tell a story that shows we should be careful of what we wish for because we may get it.

19. Narrate an account of a difficult decision that you had to make. Be sure to indicate the effect the decision had on you.

20. **Narration in context.** Assume that you are contributing a piece for a "My Life" column in your campus newspaper. The piece will be a narration about a first-time experience: the first time you drove a car, a first kiss, your first day of college, your first job, your first time away from home, and so on. Your column should indicate the effect the experience had on you. If you want, you can make the narration humorous. To come up with ideas, list all the "firsts" you can think of.

The man in the car is smiling, but he probably won't be for long. Narrate an account of how he discovers where his briefcase is and what happens when he does.

"THEY SPEND MOST OF THEIR WAKING HOURS CLICKING."

6

Exemplification

CONSIDER THE PATTERN

The cartoon on the facing page points out that we can spend much of our days in front of screens, clicking away to get what we want or find what we need. To illustrate that point, list examples of activities we can accomplish by sitting in front of our televisions or computers. Here are two activities to get you started: getting news reports and buying books.

THE PATTERN

"Can you give me an example?" How many times have you asked that question? Like most people, you probably ask for examples often—and for good reason, because nothing clarifies a point better. Usually, examples clarify by making the general more specific or by showing that something is true. To understand how examples work to clarify, consider this statement:

> Living in a high-tech society has its drawbacks.

To clarify that general statement, specific examples can be added, like this:

> Living in a high-tech society has its drawbacks. For example, our devices have become so complicated that many people can no longer operate them. I don't know anyone who can program a DVD recorder or figure out how to get the message light to stop blinking on an answering machine after a power outage.

In addition to clarifying points, specific examples can keep your writing interesting. In "What I've Learned from Men" (page 242), Barbara Ehrenreich uses examples for that purpose in this passage, which comments on the belief she once held that men could teach her little:

> What else would we possibly want to learn from them [men]? How to interrupt someone in mid-sentence as if you were performing an act of conversational euthanasia? How to drop a pair of socks three feet from an open hamper and keep right on walking? How to make those weird guttural gargling sounds in the bathroom?

To make the point that for years she mistakenly believed she had little to learn from men, she does not just ask, "What else would we possibly want to learn from them?" She creates interest and humor by adding questions as examples of how little she once thought men could teach her.

Examples can also help you persuade your reader. In "Untouchables" (page 248), Jonathan Kozol uses examples to convince his audience that the government treats the homeless cruelly:

> In several cities it is a crime to sleep in public; in some, armrests have been inserted in the middle of park benches to make it impossible for homeless people to lie down. In others, trash has been defined as "public property," making it a felony to forage in the rotted food.

When you use specific examples (specific instances) to clarify a point, add interest, or persuade, you are using **exemplification**.

www.mhhe.com/patterns

For more help with using examples, click on
Writing > Paragraph Patterns
Writing > Writing Tutor > Exemplification

USING EXEMPLIFICATION FOR A PURPOSE

Because examples are so important for clarification, adding interest, and persuasion, writers rely on them all the time, even when they use other patterns of development. Thus, you will see examples in essays developed largely with cause-and-effect analysis, process analysis, comparison-contrast, and other patterns or combination of patterns. Say, for instance, that you are using cause-and-effect analysis to explain why sexually active teenagers often do not use birth control. Once you note that teenagers may not always understand when and how pregnancy can occur, you can illustrate with an example you read of a 15-year-old who became pregnant because she thought she was "safe" since it was her first sexual experience.

Although examples are often a part of essays developed with any pattern or combination of patterns, exemplification also can form the primary pattern of development to help you entertain, relate experience and express feelings, inform, and persuade.

Regardless of your purpose for using exemplification, your examples will support, clarify, or explain a **generalization,** which is a statement of something you consider to be true in your own life or in a broader context. For example, if you want to write about your college experience in a way that would *entertain* your reader, you could give examples of your humorous mishaps on campus to support the generalization that your first week of college was a comedy of errors. You can also use examples to *express feelings and relate experience.* For example, in "On Being the Target of Discrimination" (page 234), Ralph Ellison relates the pain he felt and the difficulty he endured to explain the generalization that as a child he faced racial discrimination. He does so by providing examples of discrimination he experienced. Examples can help you *inform* a reader as well. In his essay, Jonathan Kozol gives examples of what the homeless experience in order to support the generalization that the homeless are treated unfairly and thereby inform his audience about their miserable plight. Finally, examples can *persuade* your reader. To persuade your reader to support tax incentives for businesses relocating to your area, you can provide examples to support the generalization that other communities benefited when they offered similar incentives.

Exemplification in College, at Work, and in the Community

You will use exemplification in most of your academic writing, including essay examinations and required papers. Assignments that direct you to "explain and illustrate . . . ," "define and provide examples of . . . ," and "cite illustrations to show that . . . ," are requiring you to use examples. In a world history class, you may be asked to explain and illustrate the role of women in ancient Egypt. In a political science class, you may argue for or against gun control legislation, and to do so you may cite examples of murder rates in countries that either have or lack such legislation. In an education class, you might be called upon to argue against proficiency exams by citing examples of problems such tests cause or fail to address. In a marketing class, you might be asked to define and illustrate target marketing, and in a biology class, you might be asked to define and illustrate natural selection.

Because examples clarify points so well, they help students understand important concepts. For that reason, you will encounter examples frequently in all your textbooks, as in this excerpt from an introduction to business textbook:

> Business is perhaps the most crucial institution of civil society.
> For its own well-being, business depends on its employees being
> active in politics, law, churches, arts, charities, and so on. For example, some folks at the General Electric plastics division helped their
> community while developing their own team-building skills. Rather
> than heading to a resort hotel to participate in some isolated team-
> building activities, the group went into the neighborhood surround-
> ing their offices and helped rebuild the community, barn-raising

style. The result back on the job was a sense of team camaraderie that proved as lasting as the buildings that were rebuilt. (Nickels, McHugh, and McHugh, *Understanding Business*)

Notice that the textbook author uses examples twice. The first time, he gives examples of the kinds of civic institutions a business needs its employees to be involved in: "politics, law, churches, arts, charities, and so on." The second time, he gives a more extended example to illustrate civic involvement more specifically and to illustrate how the involvement helps a business: rebuilding a neighborhood around the business improved both the neighborhood and the employees' camaraderie. For students trying to learn material, such clear examples aid understanding by making general concepts very specific.

Workplace writing also requires examples. Job application letters highlight examples of accomplishments: "As an intern in a local advertising agency, I learned a great deal about copywriting, including how to target an audience, how to assess that audience, and how to write colorfully yet succinctly." Written job descriptions state and illustrate responsibilities: "The regional sales manager supports the sales staff in any way needed. The support can include providing budget funds for travel, visiting important clients, and brainstorming for marketing ideas." Performance evaluations give examples of workplace behavior: "Lee is unreliable. He consistently arrives late, leaves early, and reports off sick."

Examples are also an important part of writing outside the classroom and workplace. If you are writing to persuade a friend to vote for a particular candidate, you might provide examples of that person's accomplishments: "Grace Wang is a sound fiscal manager. She has been financial vice president for First Asset Mortgage Company for 12 years, and she has successfully managed the investments of Park Street Church for 10 years." When you write a condolence note to a person who lost a loved one, you can share an example of your memories of the deceased: "Whenever I talked to Juan, he always made me laugh." If you place a classified ad for a garage sale, you might give examples of your wares to attract certain kinds of customers: "Children's toys, including Star Wars figures, Hot Wheels cars, and numerous board games."

SUPPORTING DETAILS

The examples you use to support a generalization can come from a variety of sources: personal experience, observation, general knowledge, class lectures, reading research, and so forth. In "Untouchables" (page 248), for instance, Jonathan Kozol's examples of the trials of the homeless come from *research* and *observation*—he interviewed many homeless people to get his information. In "What I've Learned from Men" (page 242) Barbara Ehrenreich gives an example of an encounter she had with a professor, an encounter from her own *experience*, to illustrate that at one time she was too "ladylike." In "Computers Help Unite Campuses but Also Drive Some

Students Apart" (page 228) Trip Gabriel *observes* attendance at campus gathering places to illustrate how much time students spend in front of computer screens. If you wanted to illustrate that people lie about unimportant things, you could do so with examples taken from a recent psychology *class lecture* you attended about why people lie.

Examples can take many forms. Sometimes an example is a simple explanation. For example, Jonathan Kozol makes this statement in "Untouchables":

> Several cities have devised unusual measures to assure that homeless people will learn quickly that they are not welcome.

His clarifying examples, which follow the statement, are simple explanations:

> Several cities have devised unusual measures to assure that homeless people will learn quickly that they are not welcome. In Laramie, Wyoming, they are given one night's shelter. On the next morning, an organization called "The Good Samaritan Fund" gives them one-way tickets to another town. The college town of Lancaster, Ohio, offers homeless families one-way tickets to Columbus.

An example can also take the form of a narration. In "Untouchables," Jonathan Kozol tells the story of how a financially secure man became homeless. This narrative illustrates that even middle-class people can suffer reversals that lead to the loss of their homes.

Sometimes examples take the form of description. For example, if you wanted to illustrate that people do not care about cleaning up the planet, you could describe the litter in a public park and the pollution of a local river.

You may be wondering how many examples you should use; there is no one number that applies in all instances. The appropriate number of examples to use is a decision you should make based upon audience and purpose. How much does your audience know about your topic? How difficult is the material? The less your readers know and the more challenging the material, the more examples your readers may require. Are you attempting to persuade your readers to think or act a particular way? If so, you may need more examples than if you want to entertain.

Examples can be brief or extended, and sometimes the length of your examples factors into your decision about how many to use. If your examples are extended, you may be able to use fewer than you would if your examples were brief. For example, in "On Being the Target of Discrimination" (page 234), Ralph Ellison provides only three examples of his personal experience of racism, but each one is richly detailed. Your goal is to provide enough examples in enough detail to achieve your purpose.

Hypothetical Examples

Sometimes writers use **hypothetical examples.** These are not drawn from any single observation or experience of the writer but are created from what the writer knows *could* happen, based on common knowledge, past experience, past observation, and logic. To be effective, hypothetical examples must be plausible, and they must not be overused. For example, say that you wanted to illustrate that advertisements make drinking beer look cool. Rather than point to specific advertisements, you could say something like this:

> Beer advertisements make it seem that beer drinkers have more fun. The ads show beautiful people frolicking on the beach, playing volleyball, sitting by a campfire, and laughing away the hours. Other ads show beautiful people bundled in ski clothes, nestled by the fire, listening to jazz.

The examples in the above passage are not from specific beer ads. They are hypothetical. However, they are sufficiently like real advertisements to be effective. In other words, to be effective, a hypothetical example must be representative enough of reality that it *could* happen.

ORGANIZING DETAILS

In an essay developed primarily with exemplification, the thesis can embody the generalization that your examples will prove or clarify. For example, consider the thesis of "What I've Learned from Men":

> After more than a decade of consciousness-raising, assertiveness training, and hand-to-hand combat in the battle of the sexes, we're [women] still too ladylike.

The rest of the essay provides examples of ways women are too ladylike; that is, it provides examples of ladylike behaviors that cause problems. Many times, the clarifying examples can be introduced with topic sentences, like this one from "What I've Learned from Men":

> The essence of ladylikeness is a persistent servility masked as "niceness."

Following this topic sentence, Ehrenreich notes several instances of women's ladylike niceness casting them in servile roles.

The order in which you present your examples should be carefully considered. For a **progressive order,** arrange your examples from the least to the most compelling. As an effective alternative, place your two strongest examples first and last, with the others in between. Progressive order is particularly effective for a persuasive purpose because it provides a strong final impression with its convincing example at the end.

Sometimes **chronological** (time) **order** is effective. For example, if you want to illustrate that a particular politician's record is problematic, you could do so with examples arranged in chronological order from the time the politician took office up to the present.

On occasion, **a spatial order** is desirable. If, for example, you want to demonstrate that your campus presents obstacles for the physically disabled, you could move across campus space (maybe north to south) giving examples of physical barriers.

VISUALIZING AN EXEMPLIFICATION ESSAY

The following chart can help you visualize the structure for an exemplification essay. Like all good models, however, this one can be altered as needed.

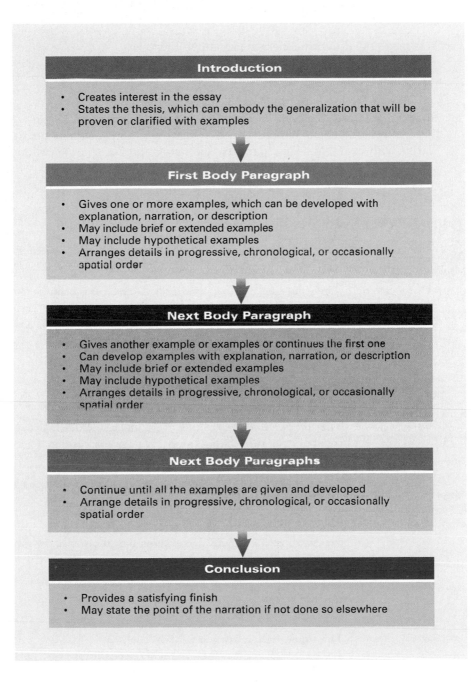

Introduction

- Creates interest in the essay
- States the thesis, which can embody the generalization that will be proven or clarified with examples

First Body Paragraph

- Gives one or more examples, which can be developed with explanation, narration, or description
- May include brief or extended examples
- May include hypothetical examples
- Arranges details in progressive, chronological, or occasionally spatial order

Next Body Paragraph

- Gives another example or examples or continues the first one
- Can develop examples with explanation, narration, or description
- May include brief or extended examples
- May include hypothetical examples
- Arranges details in progressive, chronological, or occasionally spatial order

Next Body Paragraphs

- Continue until all the examples are given and developed
- Arrange details in progressive, chronological, or occasionally spatial order

Conclusion

- Provides a satisfying finish
- May state the point of the narration if not done so elsewhere

PROCESS GUIDELINES: STRATEGIES FOR WRITING EXEMPLIFICATION

1. **Selecting a Topic.** For a generalization to clarify with examples, fill in the blanks in one of these sentences:

   _____ is the best (worst) _____ I know.

   _____ is the most (least) _____ I know.

   You may end up with generalizations like these:

   > Television advertising is the most manipulative form of communication I know.

   > Nurses are the least appreciated professionals I know.

2. **Shaping a Thesis.** The sentences you develop when you fill in the blanks provide generalizations you can shape into thesis statements to clarify with examples. For example, you can shape the generalization

TROUBLESHOOTING GUIDE

Introducing Examples in a Series

If you have trouble introducing examples in a series using *such as* or *including,* follow these guidelines:

1. Use a comma before—but not after—these words. Do not use a colon.

   YES   The teacher had many innovative ideas, including collaborative test-taking, morning yoga instruction, and self-grading.

   NO   The teacher had many innovative ideas including, collaborative test-taking, morning yoga instruction, and self-grading.

   NO   The teacher had many innovative ideas, including: collaborative test-taking, morning yoga instruction, and self-grading.

2. Use a colon if the words before that colon are an independent clause (a word group that can stand alone as a sentence).

   YES   The union had many grievances: mandatory overtime, lack of layoff procedures based on seniority, and suspension of pay raises.

   YES   The union had many grievances, such as mandatory overtime, lack of layoff procedures based on seniority, and suspension of pay raises.

   NO   The union had many grievances, such as: mandatory overtime, lack of layoff procedures based on seniority, and suspension of pay raises.

"Television advertising is the most manipulative form of communication I know" into the thesis "Television advertisements use manipulative techniques to persuade people to buy products they do not need." You can then support that thesis by giving examples of manipulative advertisements for unnecessary products.

3. **Generating Ideas.** To generate examples for supporting details, you can ask yourself these questions:
   a. What have I experienced that illustrates my generalization?
   b. What have I observed that illustrates my generalization?
   c. What have I read that illustrates my generalization?
   d. What have I learned in school that illustrates my generalization?
   e. What stories can I tell to illustrate my generalization?
   f. What can I describe to illustrate my generalization?

4. **Organizing Details.** List all the examples you will use and number them in the order you will present them.

5. **Drafting.** Write your draft using your numbered list as a scratch outline. Do not worry about polished prose now. Just write your ideas any way you can; you can refine later.

6. **Revising.** Ask a classmate or friend who has good judgment about writing to read your draft and evaluate whether you have enough examples and have included the right amount of detail for each.

Checklist for Revising Exemplification

Be sure:

_____ The generalization is clearly stated in a thesis or is strongly implied.

_____ Examples clarify the generalization and/or show that it is true.

_____ Examples are suited to your audience and purpose.

_____ You have enough examples developed in enough detail.

_____ Hypothetical examples, if you use them, are plausible.

_____ Examples are arranged in a progressive or other suitable order.

In the following essay, student author Shona Sequeira uses exemplification for three purposes: to convince the reader that American food qualifies as "cuisine," to inform the reader that American food reflects American society, and to entertain the reader. After reading, you will have an opportunity to evaluate the essay.

Food for Thought

Paragraph 1
The introduction engages interest with an opening question, by noting what people who disagree with the writer believe, and with specific word choice. The thesis (formed by the last three sentences) presents the generalization to be proven with examples: America does have a cuisine that is tasty and a reflection of American culture. The clever opening suggests one purpose is to entertain.

American cuisine? The connoisseurs of Europe scoff at the term, 1 thinking it an oxymoron. Far Eastern food snobs turn up their finely trained noses at the very idea. Americans themselves are often apologetic for what they believe to be, in the aftertaste of swank French sauces and robustly scented Thai treats, their insignificant culinary heritage. Tempting price discounts on American foods (super-size a meal for 99 cents, for example) are the most obvious manifestation of this apologetic posture, as though Americans are telling the world that if what they feed themselves cannot be labeled "cuisine," at least it can be cheap. As an Indian who was raised in the United Arab Emirates and who has traveled in parts of Europe and the Far East, I have sampled a variety of fine cuisines. However, after coming to the United States to attend college two years ago, I can tell you that American cuisine does indeed exist. It is a flavorsome force to reckon with—rich, varied, and oh-so-sinfully-good! And most significant of all, American cuisine reflects American society.

Paragraph 2
The topic sentence is the second sentence. The focus of the paragraph is that American food is varied. Examples include types of cookies, bread, and pies. Are these enough examples? Notice that the first sentence helps link American cuisine to American society.

American society is diverse, unparalleled in its rich variety of peo- 2 ple. American food has its own unparalleled variety because a country with such diverse people requires an array of food choices. Contrary to popular belief, American food is not restricted to hamburgers, hot dogs, and French fries (excuse me, *freedom* fries). In fact, American cuisine offers the consumer a greater and more tantalizing array of choices than most international culinary traditions have been able to cook up over centuries. For instance, ask for a Chinese fortune cookie and you will always get the same bland thing (often containing the same fortune, too). On the other hand, request an American cookie, and you can be showered with hundreds of delectable options, including oatmeal raisin, double chocolate chip, macadamia pecan delight, and coconut brownie. The same holds true for bread (white, brown, rye, whole wheat, whole meal, speckled, low-carb), ice-cream, which comes in a palate-boggling selection of flavors, toppings, textures, fat content, and serving styles, and good old American pie (savory, fruity, cream, ice cream, double-crust, single-crust and deep dish).

The United States is a land of immigrants, who not only came here 3 tired, poor, and yearning to breathe freely but with the food of their native lands. Just as the immigrants assimilated into American society, their food became a rich part of American cuisine. However, American cooks did not merely appropriate other countries' traditional delicacies but often improved these cuisines in notable ways. For instance, although it is true that pizza harbors Italian origins, the skimpy little versions they try to sell you in Rome just do not hold a candle to Domino's generous, gooey, thickly crusted, double-cheese offerings.

Given the surplus of wealth in the United States, Americans can 4 afford many leisure activities, and they want snack food to complement that leisure. With snacks, as with so much of American culture, there is an embarrassment of riches. What other cuisine can offer such palate-pleasing choices as pretzels and peanuts, baked and fried chips, chocolate-coated raisins and butter-drenched popcorn? All these foods are manufactured in hundreds of models (pretzels, for example, come salty, garlicky, cinnamon-sprinkled, jalapeño-flavored, chocolate-coated, sugar-covered, twisted, knotted, heart-shaped, and straight). The fact that people everywhere, from South America to Far East Asia, are now proudly munching on Pringles is testimony not only to American food's great taste and accessibility, but to its solid status as a recognized world cuisine.

Unfortunately, American leisure has, in part, created the fattest cit- 5 izenry on the planet, a fact that has spawned an entire American cuisine subset that includes low-fat chips, diet popcorn, reduced-fat ice cream, fat-free dessert bars, low-carb cookies, and Slim Fast shakes. Entire industries with their own food lines have sprung up to deal with American obesity. The Jenny Craig, LA Weight Loss, and Weight Watchers

Paragraph 3
The second and third sentences form the topic sentence. The focus is on assimilation and improvement of immigrants' cuisines. Notice that one example is developed with description and contrast. Also notice the humor and that the first sentence helps link American cuisine to American society.

Paragraph 4
The topic sentence is the first sentence. It includes both the focus of the paragraph and the linking of American society and American food. The examples are lists of representative foods. Here and throughout the essay, the word choice is specific and descriptive.

Paragraph 5
The topic sentence is the first sentence. Repeating "leisure" creates transition by referring to the focus of the previous paragraph. The examples are lists. Notice the humor. In addition to entertaining, the essay has a persuasive and informational purpose.

Paragraph 6
The topic sentence is the third sentence. The first two sentences link American cuisine to American society. Notice the specific details and that the tone remains lighthearted.

Paragraph 7
The topic sentence is the second sentence. The focus is on the innovation of using the same foods for different meals. Does the paragraph include enough examples? Notice that the first two sentences help link American cuisine to American society and that the transition "above all" indicates that the most compelling example comes last.

product lines include heavenly sounding entrées, tantalizing desserts, and satisfying snack items so the overweight can still enjoy their food. Yes, even those who shouldn't eat very much have their own special cuisine because America is, after all, the land of equal opportunity where no person will be discriminated against on the basis of race, creed, or body type.

Americans enjoy gadgets and accoutrements for specific activities 6 which explains the need for so many kinds of athletic footwear: tennis shoes, basketball shoes, baseball shoes, running shoes, cross-training shoes, aerobics shoes, and even walking shoes. This American desire for activity-specific items is also reflected in the country's cuisine. Thus, different foods are available for different pastimes. Just as snack food satisfies the cravings of the couch potato watching reruns of *The Simpsons,* the Starbucks "Frappuccino," with its frothy charms and fancy flavors, is the must-have accessory for walking around town in flip flops and khakis. Hot dogs are for ball park outings, Ramen noodles and Easy Mac provide quick meals for college students sick of cafeteria food, Cup-a-Soup feeds busy office workers lunching at their desks, trail mix is perfect for hikers needing energy on-the-go, and protein bars provide a quick nutritional boost for those engaged in any activity that won't let them stop long enough to sit down and eat.

Above all, Americans are innovators who are always looking for 7 new ways to carry out tasks and who harbor an admirable attitude for "thinking outside the box." When it comes to cuisine, too, Americans often think outside the box, turning food for one meal into food for another. Breakfast staples are turned into substantial dinner meals, and dinner foods into breakfast fare. This explains why, even with trays of gleaming meatloaf and gravy (which is to American cuisine what curry is to Indian cuisine and sushi is to Japanese) sitting idle in the college cafeteria hot line, students still flock to the cereal counter. It's Cheerios for an entrée and Fruit Loops for dessert. If you aren't up for chicken pot pie for dinner tonight, you can always rely on a ham and cheese omelet instead, even if you had one for breakfast this morning. Or perhaps breakfast wasn't eggs at all, but the pizza (now cold) you were supposed to have eaten the previous night.

Although snobs in other countries may turn up their noses at the notion of American cuisine, Americans should be as proud of their food as they are of their culture. After all, their food reflects their culture. If other countries find American food so repellent, then why do they welcome so many McDonalds, Pizza Huts, Burger Kings, and Taco Bells on their soil?

Paragraph 8
The conclusion refers to the idea in the introduction (people in other countries disparage American cuisine). The writer also gets her own jab in at those who disparage American cuisine.

PEER REVIEW

Responding to "Food for Thought"

Evaluate "Food for Thought" by responding to these questions:

1. Does the essay hold your interest? Why or why not?
2. What do you think of the thesis? Why?
3. Are the examples good ones? Does the essay include enough examples? Explain.
4. Are the examples arranged in a suitable order? Explain.
5. What do you think of the author's word choice? Cite examples to support your opinion.
6. What are the chief strengths of the essay? Why do you find these features strong?
7. Mention one revision you would like to see. How will that revision improve the essay and help the author achieve her purpose?

Copyright © The New-Yorker Collection 2002. Roz Chast from cartoonbank.com. All Rights Reserved.

- What generalization do the examples of "important" books support?
- Why did the cartoonist choose these particular examples?
- Does she include enough examples to support her generalization?
- What audience is likely to find the examples funny?

BACKGROUND: A frequent writer for *The Atlantic Monthly,* Cullen Murphy has been its managing editor since 1985. Murphy began his magazine career in the production department of *Change,* a magazine devoted to higher education. Later, he became an editor of the *Wilson Quarterly* and wrote for *Harper's.* Murphy also writes *Prince Valiant,* the comic strip drawn by his father, which appears in newspapers around the world. Murphy's essays are on a broad range of topics, including religion, language, and social science. He often writes about popular culture and has penned essays on ventriloquism, eating habits, and the items we save. Murphy's books include *Rubbish! The Archaeology of Garbage* (1992), which he co-authored with William Rathj; *Just Curious* (1995), a collection of his essays from *The Atlantic Monthly* and *Harper's;* and *The Word According to Eve: Women and the Bible in Ancient Times and Our Own* (1998). "Lifosuction" first appeared in *The Atlantic Monthly* (February 2002) in Murphy's regular "Innocent Bystander" column.

THE PATTERN AND ITS PURPOSES: In "Lifosuction," Cullen Murphy uses *examples* to **inform** readers about a form of lying somewhat common among public figures, a form that may surprise you. While largely informational, the essay also aims to **entertain,** which you may not realize until the end.

LIFOSUCTION | CULLEN MURPHY

Thomas M. Menino, the mayor of Boston, is not a flashy fellow. He gets tongue-tied easily, as many of us do, and he lacks the aura of a Willie Brown or a Rudolph Giuliani.[1] But he is a tribune of the city's neighborhoods and working people, and he was elected to a third term last fall with more than 70 percent of the vote.

2   One of the few clouds to darken his campaign, and it was a small one, came a couple of weeks before the election, when *The Boston Globe* alleged that Menino had committed a familiar political transgression—tweaking his résumé in a manner inconsistent with the facts. Menino, the *Globe* observed, "has long cultivated an image of himself as a neighborhood kid who spurned college and made good instead by dint of hard work and shrewd politicking." The newspaper now disclosed that Menino had indeed earned a college degree—an associate's degree from Chamberlayne

As you read Notice that Murphy is sometimes serious and sometimes humorous, sometimes formal and sometimes informal.

Junior College. The degree isn't mentioned in any of the mayor's official biographies. When a reporter asked Menino about this achievement, Menino replied, "You're just trying to dig up dirt on me."

3   We are all familiar with the more usual résumé-padding story, whereby a public figure incorporates credentials or accomplishments to which he or she has no honest claim. A recent case in point is that of the Pulitzer Prize–winning historian Joseph Ellis, whose anecdotes about military service in Vietnam, offered repeatedly in his Mount Holyoke classroom, turned out to be untrue. There have been many others. The Mayan peasant woman who is presented in the widely acclaimed and supposedly autobiographical book *I, Rigoberta Menchú* (1984) appears to have invented many of the central details of her personal history. Two years ago the civil-rights leader Paul Parks, an African-American veteran of World War II, was presented with an award by the Berlin chapter of

[1]Willie Brown was mayor of San Francisco, and Rudolph Giuliani was mayor of New York City.

B'nai B'rith[2] for his role in the liberation of Dachau[3]—a role, as it happens, that no one can document and that all evidence contradicts. The actress Sandra Bullock once claimed to have been voted "Girl Most Likely to Brighten Your Day" in high school, though in fact she wasn't.

4 Everyone agrees that this kind of cosmetic makeover is wrong. But what about lifosuction—the removal from one's biography of innocuous yet somehow unsightly elements that happen to be true? It is a common procedure. Musicians, for instance, have a powerful incentive to make sure that public pose and personal background are appropriately in sync. Jim Morrison, of The Doors, who fashioned himself into an icon of anarchy and self-destruction, never took pains to point out that he was the son of an admiral. During the past decade a cadre of rap musicians, black and white, have presented personal histories presumptively rooted in the violent bleakness of the streets but in truth often rooted in the bedroom communities of New York and Los Angeles. The street cred[4] of the white rapper Vanilla Ice diminished rapidly in the face of allegations involving an affluent suburban high school in Dallas and the birth name Robert Van Winkle.

5 Lifosuction is often attempted when issues of class are on the line. Bill O'Reilly, the television talk-show pugilist and the host of *The O'Reilly Factor*, has stated, "I understand working-class Americans. I'm as lower-middle-class as they come." *The Washington Post* has noted that O'Reilly grew up in not-exactly-working-class Westbury, Long Island; went to a private college without benefit of financial aid; and holds master's degrees from Boston University and Harvard. (Also, the "used car" he drives is a Lexus.) The television commentator and newspaper columnist Mike Barnicle imbues his opinions with the rough-and-tumble attitude of blue-collar Boston. He does not dateline his work "Lincoln," where he actually lives, a wealthy suburb that once made a local road into a one-way street to deter entry by people from an adjacent, working-class town.

"Rather than discourage lifosuction, perhaps, we should encourage people to subtract even more of themselves from public view than they currently do."

6 Humble origins can be a political asset. William Henry Harrison waged the first presidential campaign with a log-cabin-to-White-House theme; Harrison's supporters ridiculed his opponent, Martin Van Buren, for wearing ruffled shirts and taking baths. In truth Harrison was himself a wealthy man, from a distinguished Virginia family. In acutely class-conscious England the pressure on Labour politicians to biovac any sign of privilege has long been intense. Harold Wilson, the Oxford-educated former Prime Minister, cultivated working-class eating habits. In public he smoked a pipe, rather than the more aristocratic cigars he preferred. In the late 1980s a

---

[2]B'nai B'rith is an organization that works to promote charitable and political causes of interest to Jews.

[3]Dachau was a Nazi concentration camp.

[4]"Cred" is short for "credibility."

Labour member of Parliament named Michael Meacher, now Tony Blair's Environment Minister, wished it to be inferred that he was a son of the soil. Then a newspaper pointed out that Meacher's father was actually an accountant who merely had retired to a farm, and suggested that Meacher came from a middle-class background. Middle class! Meacher sued the newspaper for libel. (He lost.)

7   Another person seeking identification with the rural proletariat is Subcomandante Marcos, the leader of the Zapatista National Liberation Army in the Mexican state of Chiapas. Photographs always show him wearing a ski mask. Some legends held him to be a former priest, others a veteran guerrilla fighter trained by the Cubans and the Soviets. He turned out to be the son of a prosperous Mexican furniture retailer. He studied sociology and philosophy at the National Autonomous University of Mexico and went on to earn a graduate degree and teach in a Mexican university. His ski mask is probably from Orvis.[5]

8   It's easy to raise an eyebrow at lifosuction, but hard to be censorious. We all permit ourselves some degree of cosmetic suppression, and we are ambivalent about the ethics. Philosophers and theologians send mixed signals. The Sermon on the Mount cautions against hiding your light under a bushel, and an ancient philosophical tradition warns that wrongdoing can take the form of *not* doing—there are sins of omission as well as of commission. But another long tradition,

---

[5]Orvis is the country's oldest mail order retailer. It specializes in clothing and gear for outdoor sports and activities.

also going back to antiquity, justifies the sparing disbursement of truth—an "economy of truth," to use the artful locution—in certain circumstances. Edmund Burke once observed, "I do not impute falsehood to the government, but there has been a considerable economy of truth." He characterized economies of truth as "a sort of temperance."

9   Rather than discourage lifosuction, perhaps, we should encourage people to subtract even more of themselves from public view than they currently do. Book publishers may complain about a glut of memoirs, but they continue to publish truckloads of them. Every week thousands of people place personal ads in newspapers and magazines—small masterpieces of selective revelation. Millions of people have distilled themselves into personal Web pages.

10   A case can be made, then, for turning the bio-vac up to "high." To be sure, there may be the occasional gruesome accident. With a moment's inattention the assault on unwanted ripples of biography could cause entire personas—*pfflttt*—to be suddenly sucked into oblivion. Some may see that as too great a risk. I see it as a sort of temperance.

READING CLOSELY AND THINKING CRITICALLY

1.   According to Murphy, why do people engage in lifosuction?

2.   Murphy says, "It's easy to raise an eyebrow at lifosuction, but hard to be censorious." What does he mean? How serious does Murphy think lifosuction is? How can you tell?

3.   Murphy says that lifosuction involves the removal of "innocuous" biographical elements. Do the examples he uses illustrate the removal of *harmless* elements? Explain.

4.   Why do so many of Murphy's examples deal with the removal of privilege?

5.   Menino's comment to the reporter, given at the end of paragraph 2, is surprising—even ironic. Why?

EXAMINING STRUCTURE AND STRATEGY

1.   In your own words, write out the generalization/thesis that the examples support. Where in the essay is that idea best expressed?

2.   What is the tone of the essay? Is the tone consistent throughout? (See page 71 for an explanation of tone.)

3.   How do the examples in paragraph 3 contrast with the examples in the rest of the essay? How does that contrast help the author achieve his writing purpose?

4.   In which paragraphs does Murphy introduce examples with a topic sentence? Are the topic sentences helpful to the reader? Why or why not?

5.   How does Murphy organize his examples?

CONSIDERING LANGUAGE AND STYLE

1.   *Lifosuction* is a coined word. Explain how it is made up. Do you find the term clever? Why or why not?

2. Murphy is both serious and satiric, formal and informal in the essay. Cite examples of these contrasts.

3. Consult a dictionary if you are unsure of the meaning of any of these words: *tribune* (paragraph 1), *dint* (paragraph 2), *cadre* (paragraph 4), *pugilist* (paragraph 5), *proletariat* (paragraph 7).

FOR DISCUSSION IN CLASS OR ONLINE

Do you agree that Mayor Menino's omission of his college degree was only a small cloud "to darken his campaign" (paragraph 2)? Is omitting details as serious as adding them? Explain. If your instructor so directs, post your response to your class Web site.

WRITING ASSIGNMENTS

1. **In your journal.** Murphy says, "We all permit ourselves some degree of cosmetic suppression" (paragraph 8). In a page or so, tell about your own cosmetic suppressions and your reasons for them.

2. **Using exemplification for a purpose.** The purposes in the assignments are possibilities. You may establish whatever purposes you like, within your instructor's guidelines.

   * Like the public figures in "Lifosuction," we all have public personas—images of ourselves that we like to project. To inform and perhaps entertain, use examples to illustrate the ways people present and protect their public images.

   * "Lifosuction" illustrates that less is sometimes more. To inform and perhaps entertain, illustrate one or more other instances of less being more.

   * Murphy says that our society is "ambivalent about the ethics" of lifosuction (paragraph 8). State and illustrate one or more other situations about which our ethics are ambivalent. You might consider drug use among athletes; getting out of unpleasant responsibilities, such as jury duty; or pilferage, such as taking office supplies. Argue whether or not we should be ambivalent about these situations.

   * Lifosuction is a sin of omission. To inform and perhaps entertain, explain and illustrate one or more other sins of omission. If you like, you can also argue that the sin is more (or less) serious than commonly believed.

3. **Combining patterns.** Paragraphs 4, 6, and 7 include examples of musicians and politicians who used lifosuction to help create an image. Describe the image of either musicians or politicians and give examples of people who illustrate the image. You can narrow to include particular kinds of musicians, such as rap singers or boy bands, or to include particular kinds of politicians, such as liberals or conservatives. Description is explained in Chapter 4.

4. **Connecting the readings.** Both "Lifosuction" and "Salvation" (page 173) deal with dishonesty. How prevalent in our society are the kinds of dishonesty depicted in these essays? How prevalent is dishonesty in general? Does the dishonesty represent a moral decline in this country? State and defend your views.

5. **Drawing on sources.** Collect the personal ads in your local newspaper and in any publications you subscribe to that have them, along with some personal Web pages. Analyze the words those who place these ads use to describe themselves. What might some of the words—such as "robust" or "hearty"—really mean? Then use these examples to discuss how people select words to present themselves in the best possible light.

BACKGROUND: Newspaper columnist Trip Gabriel graduated from Middlebury College in 1977. Currently, he is the editor of the "Style" section of the *New York Times,* the section of the newspaper devoted to popular trends. He has written essays for numerous publications, including *Rolling Stone,* for which he was a contributing editor, *Vanity Fair,* and *Outside.* Gabriel often writes about computers, but he has also written about personal coaching, television, vinyl records, and other popular culture topics and social trends. The essay reprinted here first appeared in the *New York Times* (1996).

THE PATTERN AND ITS PURPOSE: Trip Gabriel uses *examples* in "Computers Help Unite Campuses but Also Drive Some Students Apart" in order to **inform** readers of the *New York Times* about the advantages and disadvantages of computers for college students.

Computers Help Unite Campuses But Also Drive Some Students Apart

TRIP GABRIEL

Hanover, N.H.—Through a plug in his dorm room, Arthur Desrosiers, a Dartmouth College sophomore, pursues all the preoccupations of undergraduate life without leaving his chair: he questions professors, fishes for dates, browses the library catalogue, orders in pizza

As you read Consider whether the author presents an evenhanded view.

and engages in 2 A.M. bull sessions on the meaning of it all.

2   Using the campus E-mzail system, known as Blitzmail, he sometimes trades a series of back-and-forth messages with his two roommates—even though they are sitting just a few feet away.

3   "I guess you could say you're pretty addicted if you're having a long Blitzmail conversation

with your roommate, and you happen to be sitting right there in the same room," Mr. Desrosiers said.

4   Anyone who has not visited a college campus lately might be in for a jolt. Across the country, computer networks are cinching even tighter the already inward-looking communities typical of campuses, transforming the social and academic life of today's students.

5   Dormitory lounges are being carved up for

clusters of computers, student unions are declining as gathering places, and computer-wired dorm rooms are becoming, in some cases, high-tech caves. Some scholars say "plug per pillow" campuses are undermining the ideal of a residential college as a melting pot where people from different social and regional backgrounds meet.

6   Prof. James Banning, an environmental psychologist at Colorado State University who surveyed some 100 university housing officers last year, remarked: "Universities are saying, 'Oh, my God, they're in their rooms. How can we ever build a sense of community in this building if they don't come out?' "

7 Dartmouth, one of the most academically competitive colleges in the country, has long had a reputation for encouraging computer use by students. It now has the new distinction of being one of the most e-mail-intensive, delivering about 250,000 electronic messages a day to 5,000 students and 3,000 faculty and staff members, or more than 30 messages apiece.

8 At public terminals all over the campus (to keep students from having to return to their rooms), 5 to 10 students line up as if at a cash machine, observing rules of Blitzmail etiquette like not reading over the shoulder of the person at the screen. In the Thayer dining hall recently, Stephanie Waddell, a senior studio art major, read a Blitz request from a male friend that began, "Need a date."

9 James Hunnicutt, a junior English major who was next in line, received five messages from his mother in Charlotte, N.C., asking about his law school plans, a note from a high school girlfriend at a college in Oregon and a message from his roommate vetoing the idea of a party in their room.

10 Most students say Blitzmail is convenient and indispensable on campus and gives them an easy way to stay in touch with family and high school friends. But Mark Shahinian, a junior history major, complained that it encouraged one-line electronic bantering while inhibiting meaningful communication.

11 He compared Blitzmail relationships to the brief encounters typical of those at fraternity parties, which play a big role on the isolated New Hampshire campus. "Blitzmail has a bit of that casualness—knowing a lot of people but not all that well," he said.

12 Computer technology has come to higher education in many forms, including World Wide Web sites where art professors create digitized galleries, custom software for teaching human anatomy, and "smart" classrooms with a computer for each student to teach engineering or writing. Many college guides now give campuses a "wired rating."

13 After building momentum for a decade, the wired campus has reached critical mass and will soon be unavoidable,

said Kenneth C. Green, the director of the Campus Computing Survey, which collects data annually from 650 colleges and universities.

14 More than half of all residential campuses in the United States have network connections in dormitory rooms, according to the latest survey, released this year. The number of classes using e-mail to supplement academic discussions and professors' office hours grew to 20 percent in 1995 from 8 percent in 1994. The number that use specialized educational software rose to 18 percent from 12 percent.

15 Mr. Green, a visiting scholar at the Claremont Graduate School, said that even though there were "a lot of questions about the pedagogical value" of computer technology, academia had largely accepted it, and that there were apparently no efforts to counter any antisocial side effects of systems like Blitzmail.

16 Paradoxically, it is electronic mail, one of the most mundane and least-examined of computer applications, that is probably having the most profound effect on campuses.

17 "E-mail is like the god of every college student,"

said Abigail Butler, who graduated from Vassar College this year with a major in French and political science. "People probably spend easily three hours a day sending and receiving messages. It's the No. 1 way that romances go on at colleges. It's like the dating game online."

18   Jeremy Edberg, an undergraduate at the University of California at Berkeley who said he spent 10 hours a day online, said that almost all his conversations with professors were now by e-mail. Just about the only time he visits them in person, he said, is to try to persuade them to change a grade.

19   "Students don't meet at rathskellers[1] and hamburger joints and in dorm rooms anymore," said Clifford Stoll, a former researcher at Harvard University and the author of *Silicon Snake Oil: Second Thoughts on the Information Highway* (Doubleday, 1995). "Instead, they poke their heads into computers for hours on end.

20   "We're turning colleges into a cubicle-directed electronic experience and denying the importance of learning to work closely with other students and professors, and developing social adeptness," Mr. Stoll said.

21   Professor Banning, the scholar studying dorm life, said that since going to Colorado State in 1978, he had noticed that students were spending more time in their rooms. A once-crowded restaurant across from the residence halls closed three years ago and has not reopened.

22   "It's kind of odd to think of a restaurant space that's been vacant for three years across from where about 3,000 students live," he said.

23   But the image of students sitting trancelike in front of computers, cut off from the grit of life, is exaggerated, other experts say. "A certain sector of undergraduates, especially adolescent males," has always focused obsessively on narrow interests, said Steven W. Gilbert, the director of technology projects for the American Association for Higher Education. "Sometimes it's fixing hot rods. Sometimes it's the Internet. I would bet you wouldn't find any more doing it now than 20 years ago."

24   To judge by a recent Friday night at Dartmouth, Blitzmail has hardly killed off rathskellers and other gathering places. There were good crowds at Queer Club, a dance presented by the campus gay and lesbian alliance, and off campus at the Dirt Cowboy Cafe, where students sipped carrot juice and cappuccinos.

25   At the same time, many dorm room windows emitted a bluish glow, the light of a computer screen with a student's head buried in it. A few students said Blitzmail contributed to a feeling of alienation.

26   Enthusiasts of e-mail praise it as a virtual office system in which students can question professors about courses at any time, and shy students and those for whom English is a second language have a better chance to be heard.

27   David G. Brown, the provost of Wake Forest University and a professor of economics, said that e-mail had not isolated him from students.

28   "It's increased the face-to-face communica-

---

[1]A restaurant below street level

tion I've had with my students at least fivefold," he said. "Because we're in communication every day, we feel that we're a group ready to help one another, not only over the network but in person."

29 This fall, Wake Forest, a private university with 3,700 undergraduates in Winston-Salem, N.C., distributed I.B.M. lap-top computers to all its approximately 940 freshmen, paid for with part of a $3,000 tuition increase. It is part of a sweeping Wake Forest plan to use network technology to change the ways students work and communicate.

30 Professor Brown's freshman economics seminar is already a paperless course that students attend with their lap-top computers, which are all linked together. The professor might ask them to write a one-sentence summary of an economic topic like opportunity cost, what is given up when a choice is made, then electronically forward it to the others.

31 For homework, he might have students search the Internet for a news article demonstrating opportunity cost, write a short essay about it and then send it to him

by e-mail with a picture obtained from the Louvre museum Web site demonstrating opportunity cost. Back in class, essays and pictures spark discussion.

32 Professor Brown and others who are enthusiastic about wired campuses insist that the cart of technology is being pulled by the horse of learning, rather than the reverse.

33 But there is concern that the unequal distribution of technology between rich and poor campuses will create a system of computer haves and have-nots. Public universities and two-year community colleges are typically less wired because of the high costs. Bringing fiber-optic cable into dormitories and faculty offices for a network can cost millions of dollars. Fitting a classroom with 20 computers and a projection system costs as much as $100,000.

34 Paradoxically, the highest-tech learning of all—the delivery of lectures over computer screens or cable television, called distance learning—is the subject of the most serious experimentation at cash-strapped public universities. The American Federation of Teachers, in a report this year critical of the sterility of

distance learning, noted, "All our experience as educators tells us that teaching and learning in the shared human spaces of a campus are essential to the undergraduate experience."

35 But the nature of those shared spaces seems to be changing.

36 At Vassar, students chat electronically between dorm rooms using screen names.

37 "One woman, an English major, met a physics major who quoted Shakespeare to her, and it was love at first Broadcast," said Ms. Butler, the recent Vassar graduate, who was known on the network as Snow White. "I've also known people who sat home Friday and Saturday nights, Broadcasting back and forth to people they know only by nicknames, while the rest of the world was going by.

38 "After a while, it starts to be really unfulfilling," she said. "Every Broadcast conversation with someone new is the same for the first 20 messages, finding out who they are. It's easier to just meet someone. You learn how much of a difference it makes to see someone in person and actually talk to them."

READING CLOSELY AND THINKING CRITICALLY

1. According to Gabriel, what are the chief advantages and disadvantages of extensive use of e-mail and the Internet on college campuses?
2. Does Gabriel give a balanced presentation of both the advantages and disadvantages of e-mail and the Internet? Can you tell what Gabriel's own leanings are? Explain.
3. In paragraph 16, Gabriel says, "Paradoxically, it is electronic mail, one of the most mundane and least-examined of computer applications, that is probably having the most profound effect on campuses." Explain what you think he means.
4. How does computer technology threaten to create a divide between public universities and community colleges on one side and private colleges on the other side?
5. What is the American Federation of Teachers' criticism of distance learning? Do you agree? Explain why or why not.

EXAMINING STRUCTURE AND STRATEGY

1. Is the thesis of the essay stated or implied? If it is stated, where is it? If it is implied, write it out in your own words.
2. What are the sources of Gabriel's examples?
3. Gabriel's examples focus on the experience of people at Dartmouth. Are these examples representative enough to appeal to readers not on the Dartmouth campus? Explain.
4. Does Gabriel use enough examples in enough detail to achieve his purpose? Explain.
5. How does Gabriel begin his essay? Is this opening effective for reaching the intended audience? Why or why not? How does Gabriel end the essay? Does that ending help Gabriel achieve his purpose? Explain.

CONSIDERING LANGUAGE AND STYLE

1. What two metaphors appear in paragraph 5? (Metaphors are explained on page 109.) What do the metaphors reveal about Gabriel's belief about his subject matter?
2. What simile appears in paragraph 8? (Similes are explained on page 109.) What idea does that simile express?
3. Consult a dictionary if you are unsure of the meaning of any of these words: *digitized* (paragraph 12), *critical mass* (paragraph 13), *pedagogical* (paragraph 15), *paradoxically* (paragraph 16), *mundane* (paragraph 16).

FOR DISCUSSION IN CLASS OR ONLINE

Consider these questions: Do computers and e-mail unite campuses or drive students apart? Are students enriched by involvement in virtual communities or deprived of important face-to-face contact? If your class has a Web site, has it enhanced your ability to communicate with other students and understand the course material? If your instructor so directs, post your response to your class Web site.

WRITING ASSIGNMENTS

1. **In your journal.** In a page or two tell about your own experiences with campus e-mail and the Internet. To what extent do they mirror the examples in the essay?

2. **Using exemplification for a purpose.** The purposes in the assignments are possibilities. You may establish whatever purposes you like, within your instructor's guidelines.

    *   In paragraph 8, Gabriel refers to Blitzmail etiquette. To inform your reader, explain and illustrate the etiquette associated with e-mail or with instant messaging. As an alternative, explain and illustrate the etiquette for another campus activity: dorm behavior, dating, interacting with a professor, and so forth.

    *   If you have experience with distance learning or with a paperless classroom, use examples to inform a reader who does not have that experience what it is like.

    *   In general, do you think technology enables people to come together more than ever, or has it led to greater isolation? Use examples to argue your view.

    *   Use examples to relate your experience with and express your feelings about one of the following: cell phones, Internet chat rooms, instant messaging, MCP players, or digital cameras. Your purpose can also be to entertain.

3. **Combining patterns.** In paragraphs 10 and 11, Mark Shahinian, a junior history major, says that e-mail communication lacks meaning and depth. He compares e-mail relationships to "the brief encounters typical of those at fraternity parties." Classify the various kinds of relationships and encounters students have on campus. Use examples to illustrate each kind. (Classification is explained in Chapter 10.)

4. **Connecting the readings.** Two essays in this book deal with free speech on campus: "Free Speech on Campus" (page 605), and "The Debate over Placing Limits on Racist Speech Must Not Ignore the Damage It Does to Its Victims" (page 612). Drawing on these essays, along with Trip Gabriel's essay, consider whether or not e-mail and Internet speech should be censored on campus. You might consider Web sites sponsored by hate groups; e-mail that expresses racial, ethnic, or gender bias; pornographic sites; or sites that explain how to make bombs.

5. **Drawing on sources.** Interview 8–10 students on your campus, striving for a mix of majors and class ranks. Learn how much these students rely on computers for socializing, how successfully they use them to socialize, and where they use them. Then write a report explaining the benefits and/or drawbacks of computers on your campus social life.

BACKGROUND: Best known for his 1952 novel *Invisible Man,* which explores racial stereotypes, Ralph Ellison (1914–1994) was born in Oklahoma. His father died in an accident when Ellison was three, forcing his mother to become an apartment house custodian—events reflected in the autobiographical essay reprinted here. Music was Ellison's first creative outlet, and his love of music is also noted in the essay. In fact, at one time Ellison hoped to become a professional musician. He studied music at Tuskegee Institute but left before graduation when confusion about his scholarship left him without sufficient tuition money. He traveled to New York City and joined the Federal Writers' Project. Among the African-American authors that he met was Langston Hughes, whose work appears on page •••. After the publication of *Invisible Man,* Ellison enjoyed considerable popularity and was a sought-after speaker and teacher. He taught at a number of colleges, including New York University, Rutgers, and Yale. Ellison's essays have been collected in *Going to the Territory* (1986) and *Collected Essays* (1995). You may have read about the 1999 publication of *Juneteenth,* a novel Ellison's literary executor prepared from more than 2,000 pages of drafts that Ellison wrote. "On Being the Target of Discrimination" first appeared in a special *New York Times Magazine* supplement called "A World of Difference" in 1989.

www.mhhe.com/patterns

For more information on this author, go to

More resources > Chapter 6 > Ralph Ellison

COMBINED PATTERNS AND THEIR PURPOSES: Using *exemplification,* Ralph Ellison **relates three of his experiences** with racial discrimination when he was a child growing up in Oklahoma. He also **expresses the feelings** he had at the time of the experiences and afterward. Each of the examples developed with *narration* and *description* also **informs** the reader about the nature of the United States during the time of the so-called separate-but-equal laws.

ON BEING THE TARGET OF DISCRIMINATION

RALPH ELLISON

It got to you first at the age of six, and through your own curiosity. With kindergarten completed and the first grade ahead, you were eagerly anticipating your first day of public school. For months you had been imagining your new experience and the children, known and unknown, with whom you would study and play. But the physical framework on your imagining, an elementary school in the process of construction, lay close at hand on the block-square site across the street from your home. For over a year

As you read
Try to determine how Ellison views race relations.

you had watched it rise and spread in the air to become a handsome structure of brick and stone, then seen its broad encircling grounds arrayed with seesaws, swings, and baseball diamonds. You had imagined this picture-book setting as the scene of your new experience, and when enrollment day arrived, with its grounds astir with bright colors and voices of kids like yourself, it did, indeed, become the site of your very first lesson in public schooling—though not within its classrooms, as you had imagined, but well outside its walls. For while located within a fairly mixed neighborhood this new public school was exclusively for whites.

"For while located within a fairly mixed neighborhood this new public school was exclusively for whites."

2   It was then you learned that you would attend a school located far to the south of your neighborhood, and that reaching it involved a journey which took you over, either directly or by way of a viaduct which arched head-spinning high above, a broad expanse of railroad tracks along which a constant traffic of freight-cars, switch engines, and passenger trains made it dangerous for a child to cross. And that once the tracks were safely negotiated you continued past warehouses, factories, and loading docks, and then through a notorious red-light district where black prostitutes in brightly colored housecoats and Mary Jane shoes supplied the fantasies and needs of a white clientele. Considering the fact that you couldn't attend school with white kids this made for a confusion that was further confounded by the giggling jokes which older boys whispered about the district's peculiar form of integration. For you it was a grown-up's mystery, but streets being no less schools than routes to schools, the district would soon add a few forbidden words to your vocabulary.

3   It took a bit of time to forget the sense of incongruity aroused by your having to walk *past* a school to get *to* a school, but soon you came to like your school, your teachers, and most of your schoolmates. Indeed, you soon enjoyed the long walks and anticipated the sights you might see, the adventures you might encounter, and the many things not taught in school that could be learned along the way. Your school was not nearly so fine as that which faced your home but it had its attractions. Among them its nearness to a park, now abandoned by whites, in which you picnicked and played. And there were the two tall cylindrical fire escapes on either wing of its main building down which it was a joy to lie full-length and slide, spiraling down and around three stories to the ground—providing no outraged teacher was waiting to strap your legs once you sailed out of its chute like a shot off a fireman's shovel. Besides, in your childish way you were learning that it was better to take self-selected risks and pay the price than be denied the joy or pain of risk-taking by those who begrudged your existence.

4   Beginning when you were four or five you had known the joy of trips to the city's zoo, but one day you would ask your mother to take you there and have her sigh and explain that it was now against the law for Negro kids to view the animals. Had someone done something bad to the animals? No. Had someone tried to steal them or feed them poison? No. Could white kids still go? Yes! So why? Quit asking questions, it's the law and only because some white folks are out to turn this state into a part of the South.

5   This sudden and puzzling denial of a Saturday's pleasure was disappointing and so angered your mother that later, after the zoo was moved north of the city, she decided to do something about it. Thus one warm Saturday afternoon with you and your baby brother dressed in your best she took you on a long streetcar ride which ended at a strange lakeside park, in which you found a

crowd of noisy white people. Having assumed that you were on your way to the integrated cemetery where at the age of three you had been horrified beyond all tears or forgetting when you saw your father's coffin placed in the ground, you were bewildered. But now as your mother herded you and your brother in to the park you discovered that you'd come to the zoo and were so delighted that soon you were laughing and babbling as excitedly as the kids around you.

6   Your mother was pleased and as you moved through the crowd of white parents and children she held your brother's hand and allowed as much time for staring at the cages of rare animals as either of you desired. But once your brother began to tire she herded you out of the park and toward the streetcar line. And then it happened.

7   Just as you reached the gate through which crowds of whites were coming and going you had a memorable lesson in the strange ways of segregated-democracy as instructed by a guard in civilian clothes. He was a white man dressed in a black suit and a white straw hat, and when he looked at the fashion in which your mother was dressed, then down to you and your brother, he stiffened, turned red in the face, and stared as though at something dangerous.

8   "Girl," he shouted, "where are your *white* folks!"

9   "*White* folks," your mother said, "What white folks? I don't *have* any white folks, I'm a Negro!"

10   "Now don't you get smart with me, colored gal," the white man said, "I mean where are the white folks you come *out* here with!"

11   "But I just told you that I didn't come here with any white people,"

your mother said, "I came here with my boys . . ."

12   "Then what are you doing in this park," the white man said.

13   And now when your mother answered you could hear the familiar sound of anger in her voice.

14   "I'm here," she said, "because I'm a *taxpayer,* and I thought it was about time that my boys have a look at those animals. And for that I didn't *need* any *white* folks to show me the way!"

15   "Well," the white man said, "*I'm* here to tell you that you're breaking the law! So now you'll have to leave. Both you and your chillun too. The rule says no niggers is allowed in the zoo. That's the law and I'm enforcing it!"

16   "Very well," your mother said, "we've seen the animals anyway and were on our way to the streetcar line when you stopped us."

17   "That's fine," the white man said, "and when that car comes you be sure that you get on it, you hear? You and your chillun too!"

18   So it was quite a day. You had enjoyed the animals with your baby brother and had another lesson in the sudden ways good times could be turned into bad when white people looked at your color instead of *you.* But better still, you had learned something of your mother's courage and were proud that she had broken an unfair law and stood up for her right to do so. For while the white man kept staring until the streetcar arrived she ignored him and answered your brother's questions about the various animals. Then the car came with its crowd of white parents and children, and when you were entrained and rumbling home past the fine lawns and houses your mother gave way to a gale of laughter; in which, hesi-

tantly at first, and then with assurance and pride, you joined. And from that day the incident became the source of a family joke that was sparked by accidents, faux pas, or obvious lies. Then one of you was sure to frown and say, "Well, I think you'll have to go now, both you and your chillun too!" And the family would laugh hilariously. Discrimination teaches one to discriminate between discriminators while countering absurdity with black (Negro? Afro-American? African-American?) comedy.

19   When you were eight you would move to one of the white sections through which you often passed on the way to your father's grave and your truly last trip to the zoo. For now your mother was the custodian of several apartments located in a building which housed on its street floor a drug store, a tailor shop, a Piggly Wiggly market, and a branch post office. Built on a downward slope, the building had at its rear a long driveway which led from the side street past an empty lot to a group of garages in which the apartments' tenants stored their cars. Built at an angle with wings facing north and east, the structure supported a servant's quarters which sat above its angle like a mock watchtower atop a battlement, and it was there that you now lived.

20   Reached by a flight of outside stairs, it consisted of four small rooms, a bath, and a kitchen. Windows on three of its sides provided a view across the empty frontage to the street, of the back yards behind it, and of the back wall and windows of the building in which your mother worked. It was quite comfortable but you secretly disliked the idea of your mother living in service and missed your friends who now lived far away. Nevertheless, the neighborhood was pleasant,

served by a sub-station of the street-car line, and marked by a variety of activities which challenged your curiosity. Even its affluent alleys were more exciting to explore than those of your old neighborhood, and the one white friend you were to acquire in the area lived nearby.

21   This friend was a brilliant but sickly boy who was tutored at home, and with him you shared your new interest in building radios, a hobby at which he was quite skilled. Your friendship eased your loneliness and helped dispel some of the mystery and resentment imposed by segregation. Through access to his family, headed by an important Episcopalian minister, you learned more about whites and thus about yourself. With him you could make comparisons that were not so distorted by the racial myths which obstructed your thrust toward self-perception; compare their differences in taste, discipline, and manners with those of Negro families of comparable status and income; observe variations between your friend's boyish lore and your own, and measure his intelligence, knowledge, and ambitions against your own. For you this was a most important experience and a rare privilege, because up to now the prevailing separation of the races had made it impossible to learn how you and your Negro friends compared with boys who lived on the white side of the color line. It was said by word of mouth, proclaimed in newsprint, and dramatized by acts of discriminatory law that you were inferior. You were barred from vying with them in sports and games, competing in the classroom or the world of art. Yet what you saw, heard, and smelled of them left irrepressible doubts. So you ached for objective proof, for a fair field of testing.

> "It was said by word of mouth, proclaimed in newsprint, and dramatized by acts of discriminatory law that you were inferior."

22   Even your school's proud marching band was denied participation in the statewide music contests so popular at the time, as though so airy and earth-transcending an art as music would be contaminated if performed by musicians of different races.

23   Which was especially disturbing because after the father of a friend who lived next door in your old neighborhood had taught you the beginner's techniques required to play valved instruments you had decided to become a musician. Then shortly before moving among whites your mother had given you a brass cornet, which in the isolation of the servant's quarters you practiced hours on end. But you yearned to play with other musicians and found none available. Now you lived less than a block from a white school with a famous band, but there was no one in the neighborhood with whom to explore the mysteries of the horn. You could hear the school band's music and watch their marching, but joining in making the thrilling sounds was impossible. Nor did it help that you owned the scores to a few of their marches and could play with a certain facility and fairly good tone. So there, surrounded by sounds but unable to share a sound, you went it alone. You turned yourself into a one-man band.

24   You played along as best you could with the phonograph, read the score to *The Carnival of Venice* while listening to Del Steigers executing triple-tongue variations on its themes; played the trumpet parts of your bandbook's marches while humming in your head the supporting voices of horns and reeds. And since your city was a seedbed of Southwestern jazz you played Kansas City riffs, bugle calls, and wha-wha-muted imitations of blues singer's pleas. But none of this made up for your lack of fellow musicians. And then, late one Saturday afternoon when your mother and brother were away, and when you had dozed off while reading, you awoke to the nearby sound of live music. At first you thought you were dreaming, and then that you were listening to the high school band, but that couldn't be the source because, instead of floating over building tops and bouncing off wall and windowpane, the sounds you heard rose up, somewhat muffled, from below.

25   With that you ran to a window which faced the driveway, and looking down through the high windowpane of the lighted post office you could see the metal glint of instruments. Then you were on your feet and down the stairs, keeping to the shadows as you drew close and peeped below. And there you looked down upon a room full of men and women postal workers who were playing away at a familiar march. It was like the answer to a silent prayer because you could tell by the sound that they were beginners like yourself and the covers of the thicket of bandbooks revealed that they were of the same set as yours. For a while you listened and hummed along, unseen but shaking with excitement in the dimming twilight. And then, hardly before the idea formed in your head, you were skipping up the stairs to grab your cornet, lyre, and bandbook and hurtling down again to the drive.

26   For a while you listened, hearing the music come to a pause and the sound of the conductor's voice. Then came a rap on a music stand and once again the music. And now turning to the march by the light from the window, you snapped score to lyre, raised horn to lip, and began to play; at first silently tonguing the notes through the mouthpiece and then, carried away with the thrill of stealing a part of the music, you tensed your diaphragm and blew. And as you played, keeping time with your foot on the concrete drive, you realized that you were a better cornetist than some in the band and grew bold in the pride of your sound. Now in your mind you were marching along a downtown street to the flying of flats, the tramping of feet, and the cheering of excited crowds. For at least by an isolated act of brassy cunning you had become a member of the band.

27   Yes, but unfortunately you then let yourself become so carried away that you forgot to listen for the conductor's instructions which you were too high and hidden to see. Suddenly the music faded and you opened your ears to the fact that you were now rendering a lonely solo in the startled quietness. And before you could fully return to reality there came the sound of table legs across a floor and a rustle of movement ending in the appearance of a white startled face in the opened window. Then you heard a man's voice exclaim, "I'll be damn, it's a little nigger!" whereupon you took off like a quail at the sound of sudden shotgun fire.

28   Next thing you knew, you were up the stairs and on your bed, crying away in the dark your guilt and embarrassment. You cried and cried, asking yourself how could you have been so lacking in pride as to shame yourself and your entire race by butting in where you weren't wanted. And this just to make some amateur music. To this you had no answers but then and there you made a vow that it would never happen again. And then, slowly, slowly, as you lay in the dark, your earlier lessons in the absurd nature of racial relations came to your aid. And suddenly you found yourself laughing, both at the way you'd run away and the shock you'd caused by joining unasked in the music.

29   Then you could hear yourself intoning in your eight-year-old's imitation of a white Southern accent. "Well boy, you broke the law, so you have to go, and that means you and your chillun too!"

READING CLOSELY AND THINKING CRITICALLY

1.   In paragraph 1, Ellison says that the new school was the site of his "first lesson in public schooling." What was that lesson?

2.   What is the "peculiar form of integration" that Ellison mentions in paragraph 2? What other "peculiar form[s] of integration" can you think of?

3.   After his move to a new house, Ellison made friends with a white boy. Why was that friendship important to Ellison?

4.   Although the incident at the zoo was a painful one, it became an ongoing joke for Ellison's family. Explain why.

5. What do you think the author means when he writes, "Discrimination teaches one to discriminate between discriminators" (paragraph 18)?

6. Ellison has definite views on race relations and definite reactions to being the target of discrimination. What are those views and reactions?

EXAMINING STRUCTURE AND STRATEGY

1. Does Ellison use enough examples? Explain.

2. In what order does Ellison arrange his examples? Is this order effective? Why or why not?

3. Ellison does not directly refer to himself. Rather than use "I," he uses "you," even though the essay is autobiographical. Why do you think the author uses "you" instead of "I"?

4. How do you think an audience who has not lived during the time when segregation was legal is likely to react to the essay? How do you think Ellison wants them to react? How did *you* react?

5. The photograph on page 265 is a visual illustration of life in the United States during the time when separate-but-equal laws were considered constitutional. Are the examples in the "On Being the Target of Discrimination" sufficiently vivid, or would the essay benefit from the inclusion of photos like this one? Explain.

NOTING COMBINED PATTERNS

1. In paragraph 2, Ellison offers a detailed description of the journey African-American students took to their school. How does this description help the author achieve his purpose?

2. How does Ellison use narration to achieve his writing purpose?

CONSIDERING LANGUAGE AND STYLE

1. In paragraph 18, Ellison refers to "black comedy." What is "black comedy" (sometimes called "black humor")? Explain the word play involving the term "black comedy" at the end of the paragraph.

2. The noun *refrain* is a musical term. (If you do not know its meaning, look it up.) "On Being the Target of Discrimination" has a refrain of sorts. What is it?

3. Consult a dictionary if you are unsure of the meaning of any of these words: *viaduct* (paragraph 2), *red-light district* (paragraph 2), *Mary Jane shoes* (paragraph 2), *incongruity* (paragraph 3), *faux pas* (paragraph 18), *affluent* (paragraph 20), *irrepressible* (paragraph 21).

FOR DISCUSSION IN CLASS OR ONLINE

In paragraph 21, Ellison explains that he learned more about himself by learning more about his white friend and his family. Consider to what extent our knoweldge of ourselves is a function of what we know about other people. If your instructor so directs, post your response to your class Web site.

WRITING ASSIGNMENTS

1. **In your journal.** Write about an incident of discrimination or other injustice you have experienced, witnessed, or heard about. You need not limit yourself to racial discrimination, you can discuss discrimination against or injustice toward the mentally or physically disabled, a gender, a nationality, and so forth.

2. **Using exemplification for a purpose.** The purposes in the assignments are possibilities. You may establish whatever purposes you like, within your instructor's guidelines.

   - When Ellison writes that "streets [are] no less schools than routes to schools" (paragraph 2), he is observing that much education occurs outside of schoolroom walls. Use examples to relate your own experiences outside of school to support Ellison's observation. Explain what you learned and how you learned it.

   - To relate your experience, illustrate "the sudden ways good times [can] be turned into bad" (paragraph 18).

   - Write an essay with the title "On Being _____." (Fill in the blank with some circumstance of your life—being tall or short, a single parent, an adult learner, an only child, a student athlete, and so forth.) To relate your experience and express your feelings, illustrate what life is or was like for you.

3. **Combining patterns.** Despite his fierce desire to do so, circumstance denied Ellison the opportunity to play in a band. Tell a story that is an example of a time you were unable to do something that you yearned to do. Use cause-and-effect analysis (explained in Chapter 9) to note how you were affected by your inability to participate.

4. **Connecting the readings.** In "The Ways of Meeting Oppression" (page 459), Martin Luther King, Jr., writes that oppressed people deal with their oppression in one of three ways. Discuss the ways young Ralph Ellison and his mother deal with oppression. Do their methods fit any of King's categories? Are their methods effective?

5. **Drawing on sources.** Jim Crow laws, instituted in the 1880s and allowed to continue into the 1960s, were state laws—upheld by the U.S. Supreme Court—that created race-based segregation. The laws allowed segregated restaurants, hospitals, buses, schools, public institutions, water fountains, and other public and private facilities.

   Assume that you have been asked to contribute an essay on the Jim Crow era to a local high school newspaper in honor of Black History Month. Your audience will be young people who may not be familiar with this period of American history, and your purpose will be to bring the experience of African Americans under Jim Crow laws vividly to life. There are many Web sites rich in narratives, pictures, and historical information about Jim Crow and the fight for civil rights. An excellent place to start is the Library of Congress African American Odyssey Web site at *http://memory.loc.gov/ammem/aaohtml/exhibit/aointro.html*. You might also check *Africana* or *The Encyclopedia of African-American Culture and History* in your campus library, and you can interview people over 60 for their memories.

BACKGROUND: Born in Butte, Montana, in 1941, award-winning political essayist and social activist Barbara Ehrenreich has lent her support to many progressive causes, including the women's movement. She comes from a science background, having earned her Ph.D. in biology from Rockefeller University. After teaching college for a time, she turned to writing. She is a social critic whose sometimes scathing commentaries have appeared in *The Nation, Harpers, Z Magazine, Atlantic Monthly, New York Times Magazine, TV Guide,* and *Mother Jones.* Ehrenreich also writes regularly for *The Progressive* and *Time.* A popular guest on television programs, Ehrenreich has appeared on both "Good Morning America" and "Today." She is the author of several books, including two collections of essays, *The Worst Years of Our Lives* (1990) and *The Snarling Citizen* (1995). Her most recent book is *Nickel and Dimed: On (Not) Getting by in America* (2001). "What I've Learned from Men" first appeared in *Ms.* in 1985.

www.mhhe.com/patterns

For more information on this author, go to

More resources > Chapter 6 > Barbara Ehrenreich

COMBINED PATTERNS AND THEIR PURPOSES: In "What I've Learned from Men," Barbara Ehrenreich combines *exemplification* with *cause-and-effect analysis, definition, contrast,* and *narration* to **inform** her audience about a problem she thinks women have: they are too "ladylike." She goes on to **persuade** her readers that women should become more like men—that is, tougher and more assertive. Although the essay originally appeared in 1985 in a magazine aimed at women, it has relevance today for both male and female readers.

WHAT I'VE LEARNED FROM MEN: LESSONS FOR A FULL-GROWN FEMINIST

BARBARA EHRENREICH

For many years I believed that women had only one thing to learn from men: how to get the attention of a waiter by some means short of kicking over the table and shrieking. Never in my life have I gotten the attention of a waiter, unless it was an off-duty waiter whose car I'd accidentally scraped in a parking lot somewhere. Men, however, can summon a maître d' just by thinking the word "coffee," and this is a power women would be well-advised to study. What else would we possibly want to learn from them? How to interrupt someone in midsentence as if you were performing an act of conversational euthanasia? How to drop a pair of socks three feet from an open hamper and keep right on walking? How to make those weird guttural gargling sounds in the bathroom?

As you read
Think about what it means to be "ladylike."

2   But now, at mid-life, I am willing to admit that there are some real and useful things to learn from men. Not from all men—in fact, we may have the most to learn from some of the men we like the least. This realization does not mean that my feminist principles have gone soft with age: what I think women could learn from men is how to get *tough*. After more than a decade of consciousness-raising, assertiveness training, and hand-to-hand combat in the battle of the sexes, we're still too ladylike. Let me try that again—we're just too *damn* ladylike.

3   Here is an example from my own experience, a story that I blush to recount. A few years ago, at an international conference held in an exotic and luxurious setting, a prestigious professor invited me to his room for what he said would be an intellectual discussion on matters of theoretical importance. So far, so good. I showed up promptly. But only minutes into the conversation—held in all-too-adjacent chairs—it emerged that he was interested in something more substantial than a meeting of minds. I was disgusted, but not enough to overcome 30-odd years of programming in ladylikeness. Every time his comments took a lecherous turn, I chattered distractingly; every time his hand found its way to my knee, I returned it as if it were something he had misplaced. This went on for an unconscionable period (as much as 20 minutes); then there was a minor scuffle, a dash for the door, and I was out—with nothing violated but my self-esteem. I, a full-grown feminist, conversant with such matters as rape crisis counseling and sexual harassment at the workplace, had behaved like a ninny—or, as I now understand it, like a lady.

4   The essence of ladylikeness is a persistent servility masked as "niceness." For example, we (women) tend to assume that it is our responsibility to keep everything "nice" even when the person we are with is rude, aggressive, or emotionally AWOL. (In the above example, I was so busy taking responsibility for preserving the veneer of "niceness" that I almost forgot to take responsibility for myself.) In conversations with men, we do almost all the work: sociologists have observed that in male-female social interactions it's the woman who throws out leading questions and verbal encouragements ("So how did you *feel* about that?" and so on) while the man, typically, says "Hmmmm." Wherever we go, we're perpetually smiling—the on-cue smile, like the now-outmoded curtsy, being one of our culture's little rituals of submission. We're trained to feel embarrassed if we're praised, but if we see a criticism coming at us from miles down the road, we rush to acknowledge it. And when we're feeling aggressive or angry or resentful, we just tighten up our smiles or turn them into rueful little moues. In short, we spend a great deal of time acting like wimps.

5   For contrast, think of the macho stars we love to watch. Think, for example, of Mel Gibson facing down punk marauders in "The Road Warrior" . . .

> "Think, for example, of Mel Gibson facing down punk marauders in 'The Road Warrior.'"

John Travolta swaggering his way through the early scenes of "Saturday Night Fever" . . . or Marlon Brando shrugging off the local law in "The Wild One." Would they simper their way through tight spots? Chatter aimlessly to keep the conversation going? Get all clutched up whenever they think they might—just might—have hurt someone's feelings? No, of course not, and therein, I think, lies their fascination for us.

6   The attraction of the "tough guy" is that he has—or at least seems to have—what most of us lack, and that is an aura of power and control. In an article, feminist psychiatrist Jean Baker Miller writes that "a woman's using self-determined power for herself is equivalent to selfishness [and] destructiveness—an equation

that makes us want to avoid even the appearance of power." Miller cites cases of women who get depressed just when they're on the verge of success—and of women who do succeed and then bury their achievement in self-deprecation. As an example, she describes one company's periodic meetings to recognize outstanding salespeople: when a woman is asked to say a few words about her achievement, she tends to say something like, "Well, I really don't know how it happened. I guess I was just lucky this time." In contrast, the men will cheerfully own up to the hard work, intelligence, and so on, to which they owe their success. By putting herself down, a woman avoids feeling brazenly powerful and potentially "selfish"; she also does the traditional lady's work of trying to make everyone else feel better ("She's not really so smart, after all, just lucky").

7   So we might as well get a little tougher. And a good place to start is by cutting back on the small acts of deference that we've been programmed to perform since girlhood. Like unnecessary smiling. For many women—waitresses, flight attendants, receptionists—smiling is an occupational requirement, but there's no reason for anyone to go around grinning when she's not being paid for it. I'd suggest that we save our off-duty smiles for when we truly feel like sharing them, and if you're not sure what to do with your face in the meantime, study Clint Eastwood's expressions—both of them.

8   Along the same lines, I think women should stop taking responsibility for every human interaction we engage in. In a social encounter with a woman, the average man can go 25 minutes saying nothing more than "You don't say?" "Izzat so?" and, of course,

"Hmmmm." Why should we do all the work? By taking so much responsibility for making conversations go well, we act as if we had much more at stake in the encounter than the other party—and that gives him (or her) the power advantage. Every now and then, we deserve to get more out of a conversation than we put into it: I'd suggest not offering information you'd rather not share ("I'm really terrified that my sales plan won't work") and not, out of sheer politeness, soliciting information you don't really want ("Wherever did you get that lovely tie?"). There will be pauses, but they don't have to be awkward for *you*.

9   It is true that some, perhaps most, men will interpret any decrease in female deference as a deliberate act of hostility. Omit the free smiles and perky conversation-boosters and someone is bound to ask, "Well, what's come over *you* today?" For most of us, the first impulse is to stare at our feet and make vague references to a terminally ill aunt in Atlanta, but we should have as much right to be taciturn as the average (male) taxi driver. If you're taking a vacation from smiles and small talk and some fellow is moved to inquire about what's "bothering" you, just stare back levelly and say, the international debt crisis, the arms race, or the death of God.

10   There are all kinds of ways to toughen up—and potentially move up—at work, and I leave the details to the purveyors of assertiveness training. But Jean Baker Miller's study underscores a fundamental principle that anyone can master on her own. We can stop acting less capable than we actually are. For ex-

"We can stop acting less capable than we actually are."

ample, in the matter of taking credit when credit is due, there's a key difference between saying "I was just lucky" and saying "I had a plan and it worked." If you take the credit you deserve, you're letting people know that you were confident you'd succeed all along, and that you fully intend to do so again.

11   Finally, we may be able to learn something from men about what to do with anger. As a general rule, women get irritated; men get *mad*. We make tight little smiles of ladylike exasperation; they pound on desks and roar. I wouldn't recommend emulating the full basso profundo male tantrum, but women do need ways of expressing justified anger clearly, colorfully, and when necessary, crudely. If you're not just irritated, but *pissed off*, it might help to say so.

12   I, for example, have rerun the scene with the prestigious professor many times in my mind. And in my mind, I play it like Bogart. I start by moving my chair over to where I can look the professor full in the face. I let him do the chattering, and when it becomes evident that he has nothing serious to say, I lean back and cross my arms, just to let him know that he's wasting my time. I do not smile, neither do I nod encouragement. Nor, of course, do I respond to his blandishments with apologetic shrugs and blushes. Then, at the first flicker of lechery, I stand up and announce coolly, "All right, I've had enough of this crap." Then I walk out—slowly, deliberately, confidently. Just like a man.

13   Or—now that I think of it—just like a woman.

READING CLOSELY AND THINKING CRITICALLY

1.   What three things has Barbara Ehrenreich learned from men?

2.   Why do you think that Ehrenreich "blush[es] to recount" the story of her encounter at the conference? Do you think she has good reason to blush? Explain.

3.   Why wasn't Ehrenreich more assertive with the lecherous professor?

4.   Why do you think some women get depressed when "they're on the verge of success," and why do others "bury their achievement in self-deprecation" (see paragraph 6)?

5.   Using the evidence in the essay, write a one- or two-sentence definition of *lady* or *ladylike* that reflects Ehrenreich's meaning of one of these terms.

EXAMINING STRUCTURE AND STRATEGY

1.   Ehrenreich delays her thesis until paragraph 2. Which sentence presents that thesis? The material before the thesis is humorous. How does the humor help her achieve her purpose? Do you think that beginning a discussion of a serious topic in an amusing way is an effective strategy?

2.   What paragraph marks Ehrenreich's move from an informative to a persuasive purpose?

3.   How would you describe Ehrenreich's original audience (see the headnote on page 242)? Was this audience likely to be receptive to her message? Explain.

1. What is the function of the narrative example in paragraph 3? Does this example clarify by showing that something is true, by making the general specific, or both? What contrast does the example set up? (Contrast, discussed in Chapter 8, points out differences.) What other paragraphs include contrast?

2. Brief examples appear in paragraphs 4, 5, 6, 7, 8, and 10. How do these examples help the author achieve her purpose? Which paragraph provides a definition of *ladylikeness* and *lady?* What is the purpose of that definition? (Definition, which explains the meaning of something, is discussed in Chapter 11.)

3. Paragraphs 6, 9, and 10 include cause-and-effect analysis. (Cause-and-effect analysis, which explains the causes and/or effects of something, is explained in Chapter 9.) How does this analysis help the author achieve her purpose?

CONSIDERING LANGUAGE AND STYLE

1. What connotations does the word *lady* have for most people? What connotations does it have in "What I've Learned from Men"?

2. How does the language in the last two sentences echo Ehrenreich's thesis and create closure?

3. Consult a dictionary if you are unsure of the meaning of any of these words: *maître d'* (paragraph 1), *euthanasia* (paragraph 1), *guttural* (paragraph 1), *lecherous* (paragraph 3), *unconscionable* (paragraph 3), *veneer* (paragraph 4), *rueful* (paragraph 4), *taciturn* (paragraph 9), *purveyors* (paragraph 10).

FOR DISCUSSION IN CLASS OR ONLINE

What do you think "What I've Learned from Men" has to offer to male readers? Do you think the essay is relevant today? Explain why you think as you do. If your instructor so directs, post your response to your class Web site.

WRITING ASSIGNMENTS

1. **In your journal.** Compose a one- or two-paragraph narration to illustrate what Ehrenreich should have done when she was in the company of the lecherous professor.

2. **Using exemplification for a purpose.** The purposes in the assignments are possibilities. You may establish whatever purposes you like, within your instructor's guidelines.

   - Write an essay with the title, "What I've Learned from _____." Fill in the blank with the name of a teacher, a boss, a coach, a member of the clergy, a relative, and so on. To relate your experience and to inform, give examples to illustrate the lessons you learned from the person's behavior.

   - Ehrenreich writes about what women can learn from men. To inform, turn the tables and write about what men can learn from women. Use examples to illustrate your points. If you want to make your essay humorous, your purpose can be to entertain.

   - Do you agree with Ehrenreich? Using illustrations to support your stand, persuade your reader that Ehrenreich is right (or wrong).

3. **Combining patterns.** Select something about yourself you would like to change. Perhaps you are impulsive, a procrastinator, short-tempered, easily intimidated, or afraid to take risks. Give examples of times you exhibited the behavior and explain a process for changing the behavior. (Process analysis is explained in Chapter 7.)

4. **Connecting the readings.** In "Computers Help Unite Campuses but Also Drive Some Students Apart" (page 228), Trip Gabriel notes the decline in face-to-face communication on wired campuses. Consider Gabriel's points along with those of Ehrenreich and then discuss the ways less assertive students might respond to distance learning, paperless classrooms, and e-mail communication.

5. **Drawing on sources.** For two or three days, observe the way male and female students behave in the classroom. Pay attention to such things as how they speak, what they say, how many questions they ask, how often they are called upon, where they sit, how they interact with the instructor, and how they interact with classmates. Then write an essay that notes and gives examples of similarities in and differences between the way male and female students behave in the classroom.

BACKGROUND: Born in 1936, Harvard University graduate Jonathan Kozol has taught in both college and public schools. In 1967, he was teaching in a poor section of Boston when he was fired for teaching a Langston Hughes poem to fourth graders. (See page ••• for an essay by Langston Hughes.) A description of his first year of teaching appears in his *Death at an Early Age: The Destruction of the Hearts and Minds of Negro Children in Boston Public Schools* (1967). The book, for which he won the first of his two National Book Awards, champions education reform. Kozol has always combined his teaching with activism. For example, when he taught at South Boston High School, he set up a storefront learning center that became a model nationwide. In 1985, Kozol spent the winter interviewing people in a homeless shelter in New York. From that experience came *Rachel and Her Children: Homeless Families in America* (1988), an account of the struggles of America's homeless. "Untouchables" is an excerpt from that book. Kozol has also written *Savage Inequalities: Children in America's Schools* (1991), *Amazing Grace: The Lives of Children and the Conscience of a Nation* (1995), and *Ordinary Resurrections* (2000).

COMBINED PATTERNS AND THEIR PURPOSES: In "Untouchables," Jonathan Kozol combines graphic *exemplification* with an explanation of the *causes and effects* of homelessness to **inform** his reader about the plight of the homeless. In addition, Kozol works to **persuade** the reader that government policy and the general public are part of the problem.

Untouchables

JONATHAN KOZOL

Richard Lazarus, an educated, thirty-six-year-old Vietnam veteran I met two days after Thanksgiving in the subway underneath [New York's] Grand Central station, tells me he had never been without a job until the recent summer. In July he underwent the loss of job, children and wife, all in a single stroke. As in almost all these situations, it was the simultaneous occurrence of a number of emergencies, any of which he might sustain alone but not all at the same time, that suddenly removed him from his home.

As you read Try to determine why Kozol believes the government and the public are part of the problem of homelessness.

2   "Always, up until last summer, I have found a job that paid at least $300. Now I couldn't find a job that paid $200. When I found an opening at a department store they said that I was overqualified. If someone had asked me a year ago who are the homeless, I would not have known what to reply. Now I know the answer. They are people like myself. I went to Catholic elementary school. I had my secondary education in a private military school. I joined the service and was sent to Thailand as an airman." He has a trade. It's known as "inventory data processing." He had held a single job in data processing for seven years until last summer when the company shut down, without a warning, and moved out of state.

3   "When the company left I could find nothing. I looked everywhere. I got one job for two months in the summer. Part-time, as a security guard in one of the hotels for homeless families."

4   When I ask which one it was, he says the Martinique. "I clocked the floors for fire check. From the top floor to the lobby I swore to myself; rat infested, roach infested, drug infested, filth infested, garbage everywhere, and little children

playing in the stairs. Innocent people, women, children, boxed in by their misery. Most people are permitted to make more than one mistake. Not when you're poor."

5   In September he was sick. "I was guarding homeless people and I didn't have a home. I slept in Washington Square and Central Park." He's living now in a run-down hotel operated in conjunction with the Third Street Shelter on the Bowery. "When you come in at night the guards wear gloves. They check you with a metal detector. They're afraid to touch me."

6   While we talk we watch an old man nearby who is standing flat and motion-less against the wall, surrounded by two dozen bright red shopping bags from Macy's. Every so often, someone stops to put a coin into his hand. I notice the care with which the people drop their coins, in order that their hands do not touch his. When I pass that spot some hours later he will still be there. I'll do the same. I'll look at his hand—the fingers worn and swollen and the nails curled in like claws—and I will drop a quarter and extract my hand and move off quickly . . .

7   Many homeless people, unable to get into shelters, frightened of disease or vio-lence, or else intimidated by the regulations, look for refuge in such public places as train stations and church doorways.

8   Scores of people sleep in the active subway tunnels of Manhattan, inches from 600-volt live rails. Many more sleep on the ramps and station platforms. Go into the subway station under Herald Square on a December night at twelve o'clock and you will see what scarce accommodations mean at the rockbottom. Emerging from the subway, walk on Thirty-second Street to Penn station. There you will see another form of scarce accommodations: Hot-air grates in the area are highly prized. Homeless people who arrive late often find there is no vacancy, even in a cardboard box over a grate.

9   A man who's taken shelter from the wind that sweeps Fifth Avenue by sleep-ing beneath the outstretched arms of Jesus on the bronze doors of St. Patrick's Cathedral tells a reporter he can't sleep there anymore because shopkeepers feel that he is hurting business. He moves to the south side of the church where he will be less visible.

10   Stories like these are heard in every state and city of the nation. A twenty-year-old man in Florida tells me that he ran away when he was nine years old from a juvenile detention home in Michigan. He found that he was small enough to slip his body through the deposit slot of a Good Will box. Getting in was easy, he explains, and it was warm because of the clothes and quilts and other gifts that peo-ple dropped into the box. "Getting out," he says, "was not so easy. I had to reach my arms above my head, grab hold of the metal edge, twist my body into an S, and pull myself out slowly through the slot. When I was fourteen I was too big to fit into the slot. I believe I am the only person in America who has lived for five years in a Good Will box."

11   Thousands of American people live in dumpsters behind restaurants, hotels, and groceries. A woman describes the unimaginable experience of being awakened in the middle of a winter's night by several late-arriving garbage trucks. She nearly drowned beneath two tons of rotting vegetables and fruit.

12   A thirty-four-year-old man in Chicago found his sanctuary in a broken trash compactor. This offered perhaps the ultimate concealment, and the rotting food which generated heat may have protected him against the freezing weather of Chicago. One night, not knowing that the trash compactor had in his absence been repaired, he fell asleep. When the engine was turned on, he was compressed into a cube of refuse.

13   People in many cities speak of spending nights in phone booths. I have seen this only in New York. Public telephones in Grand Central Station are aligned in recessed areas outside the main concourse. On almost any night before one-thirty, visitors will see a score of people stuffed into these booths with their belongings. Even phone-booth vacancies are scarce in New York City. As in public housing, people are sometimes obliged to double up. One night I stood for an hour and observed three people—man, woman, and child—jammed into a single booth. All three were asleep.

14   Officials have tried a number of times to drive the homeless from Grand Central Station. In order to make conditions less attractive, benches have been removed throughout the terminal. One set of benches has been left there, I am told, because they have been judged "historic landmarks." The terminal's 300 lockers, used in former times by homeless people to secure their few belongings, were removed in 1986. Authorities were forced to justify this action by declaring them, in the words of the city council, "a threat to public safety." Shaving, cleaning of clothes, and other forms of hygiene are prohibited in the men's room of Grand Central. A fast-food chain that wanted to distribute unsold donuts in the terminal was denied the right to do so on the grounds that this would draw more hungry people.

15   At one-thirty every morning, homeless people are ejected from Grand Central. Many have attempted to take refuge on the ramp that leads to Forty-second Street. The ramp initially provided a degree of warmth because it was protected from the street by wooden doors. The station management responded to this challenge in two ways. First, the ramp was mopped with a strong mixture of ammonia to produce a noxious smell. When the people sleeping there brought cardboard boxes and newspapers to protect them from the fumes, the entrance doors were chained wide open. Temperatures dropped some nights to ten degrees.

16   In a case that won brief press attention in December 1985, an elderly woman who had been living in Grand Central on one of the few remaining benches was removed night after night during the weeks preceding Christmas. On Christmas Eve she became ill. No ambulance was called. At one-thirty the police compelled her to move to the ramp outside. At dawn she came inside, climbed back on bench number 9 to sleep, and died that morning of pneumonia.

17   At Penn Station, fifteen blocks away, homeless women are denied use of the bathroom. Amtrak police come by and herd them off each hour on the hour. In June of 1985, Amtrak officials issued this directive to police: "It is the policy of Amtrak to not allow the homeless and undesirables to remain . . . Officers are encouraged to eject all undesirables . . . Now is the time to train and educate them that their presence will not be tolerated as cold weather sets in." In an internal memo, according to CBS, an Amtrak official later went beyond this language and asked flatly: "Can't we get rid of this trash?"

18   In a surprising action, the union representing the police resisted this directive and brought suit against Penn Station's management in 1986. Nonetheless, as temperatures plunged during the nights after Thanksgiving, homeless men and women were ejected from the station. At 2:00 A.M. I watched a man about my age carry his cardboard box outside the station and try to construct a barricade against the wind that tore across Eighth Avenue. The man was so cold his fingers shook and, when I spoke to him, he tried but could not answer.

19   Driving women from the toilets in a railroad station raises questions that go far beyond the issue of "deterrence." It may surprise the readers to be told that many of these women are quite young. Few are dressed in the familiar rags that are suggested by the term "bag ladies." Some are dressed so neatly and conceal their packages and bags so skillfully that one finds it hard to differentiate them from commuters waiting for a train. Given the denial of hygienic opportunities, it is difficult to know how they are able to remain presentable. The sight of clusters of police officials, mostly male, guarding a women's toilet from its use by homeless females does not speak well for the public conscience of New York.

20   Where do these women defecate? How do they bathe? What will we do when, in her physical distress, a woman finally disrobes in public and begins to urinate right on the floor? We may regard her as an animal. She may by then begin to view herself in the same way.

21   Several cities have devised unusual measures to assure that homeless people will learn quickly that they are not welcome. In Laramie, Wyoming, they are given one night's shelter. On the next morning, an organization called "The Good Samaritan Fund" gives them one-way tickets to another town. The college town of Lancaster, Ohio, offers homeless families one-way tickets to Columbus.

22   In a number of states and cities, homeless people have been murdered, knifed, or set on fire. Two high school students in California have been tried for the knife murder of a homeless man whom they found sleeping in a park. The man, an unemployed house painter, was stabbed seventeen times before his throat was slashed.

23   In Chicago a man was set ablaze while sleeping on a bench in early morning, opposite a popular restaurant. Rush-hour commuters passed him and his charred possessions for four hours before someone called police at noon. A man who watched him burning from a third-floor room above the bench refused to notify police. The purpose was "to get him out," according to a local record-store employee. A resident told reporters that the problem of the homeless was akin to that of "nuclear waste."

24   In Tucson, where police use German shepherds to hunt for the homeless in the skid-row neighborhoods, a mayor was recently elected on the promise that he'd drive the homeless out of town. "We're tired of it. Tired of feeling guilty about these people," said an anti-homeless activist in Phoenix.

25   In several cities it is a crime to sleep in public; in some, armrests have been inserted in the middle of park benches to make it impossible for homeless people to lie down. In others, trash has been defined as "public property," making it a felony to forage in the rotted food.

26   Grocers in Santa Barbara sprinkled bleach on food discarded in their dumpsters. In Portland, Oregon, owners of some shops in redeveloped Old Town have designed slow-dripping gutters (they are known as "drip lines") to prevent the homeless from attempting to take shelter underneath their awnings.

27   Harsher tactics have been recommended in Fort Lauderdale. A city council member offered a proposal to spray trash containers with rat poison to discourage foraging by homeless families. The way to "get rid of vermin," he observed, is to cut their food supply. Some of these policies have been defeated, but the inclination to sequester, punish and conceal the homeless has attracted wide support.

28   "We are the rejected waste of the society," said Lazarus. "They use us, if they think we have some use, maybe for sweeping leaves or scrubbing off graffiti in the subway stations. They don't object if we donate our blood. I've given plasma. That's one way that even worthless people can do something for democracy. We may serve another function too. Perhaps we help to scare the people who still have a home— even a place that's got no heat, that's rat infested, filthy. If they see us in the streets, maybe they are scared enough so they will learn not to complain. If they were thinking about asking for a better heater or a better stove, they're going to think twice. It's like farmers posting scarecrows in the fields. People see these terrifying figures in Penn Station and they know, with one false step, that they could be here too. They think: 'I better not complain.'

29   "The problem comes, however, when they try to find a place to hide us. So it comes to be an engineering question: waste disposal. Store owners certainly regard us in that way. We ruin business and lower the value of good buildings. People fear that we are carriers of illness. Many times we are. So they wear those plastic gloves if they are forced to touch us. It reminds me of the workers in the nuclear reactors. They have to wear protective clothing if they come in contact with the waste. Then you have state governors all over the United States refusing to allow this stuff to be deposited within their borders. Now you hear them talking about dumping toxic waste into the ocean in steel cans. Could they find an island someplace for the homeless?"

30   His question brings back a strange memory for me. In Boston, for years before the homeless were identified as a distinguishable category of the dispossessed, a de facto caste of homeless people dwelt in a vast public housing project built on a virtual island made, in part, of landfill and linked only by one access road to the United States. Columbia Point, adjacent to a camp for prisoners of war in World War II, was so crowded, violent and ugly that social workers were reluctant to pay visits there, few shop owners would operate a business, and even activists and organizers were afraid to venture there at night. From the highway to Cape Cod, one could see the distant profile of those highrise structures. A friend from California asked me if it was a prison. He told me that it looked like Alcatraz. I answered that it was a housing project. The notion of shoving these people as far out into the ocean as we can does bring to mind the way that waste-disposal problems sometimes are resolved.

31   New York has many habitable islands. One of those islands has already earned a place in history as the initial stopping point for millions of European refugees

who came to the United States in search of freedom. One reason for their temporary isolation was the fear that they might carry dangerous infection. New York's permanent refugees are carriers of every possible infection; most, moreover, have no prospering relatives to vouch for them, as earlier generations sometimes did, in order to assure that they will not become a burden to the state. They are already regarded as a burden. An island that served once as quarantine for aliens who crowded to our shore might serve this time as quarantine for those who huddle in train stations and in Herald Square.

32   Lazarus may not be paranoid in speaking of himself as human waste; he may simply read the headlines in the press. "I just can't accommodate them," says the owner of a building in midtown Manhattan. The mayor of Newark, where a number of homeless families have been sent from New York City, speaks of his fear that displaced families from New York might be "permanently dumped in Newark." He announces a deadline after which they will presumably be dumped back in New York.

33   New Yorkers, according to the *New York Times*, "are increasingly opposing [city] attempts to open jails, shelters for the homeless, garbage incinerators" in their neighborhoods. The *Times* reports the city has begun to "compensate communities" that will accept "homeless shelters and garbage-burning generating plants."

34   Do homeless children have some sense of this equation?

35   "Be not forgetful to entertain strangers," wrote Saint Paul, "for thereby some have entertained angels unawares." But the demonology that now accrues to homeless people, and the filth with which their bodies soon become encrusted, seem to reassure us that few of these strangers will turn out to have been angels in disguise.

36   When homeless infants die in New York City, some are buried not in New York itself but on an island in an unmarked grave. Homeless mothers therefore live with realistic fears that they may lose their infants to anonymous interment. Another fear is that their child may be taken from them at the hour of birth if they should be homeless at the time. Hundreds of babies taken by the state for this and other reasons—often they are very ill and sometimes drug addicted—remain in hospitals, sometimes for months or even years, before a foster home is found. Some of these "boarder babies," as they are described, have been kept so long that they have learned to walk and, for this reason, must be tethered in their cribs. Infants held in hospitals so long, physicians tell us, are likely to grow retarded. Some, even after many months, have not been given names. Like their homeless parents in the city's shelters, they remain bed numbers.

37   Many of these children do in time find homes, though most end up in dismal institutions where conditions are no better and often a great deal worse than those they would have faced had they been left with their own parents. Mayor Koch attempted in 1986 to establish a group home for six or seven of these babies in a small house on a quiet street in Queens. Unknown vandals set the house on fire. "Afraid of Babies in Queens," the *New York Times* headlined its editorial response.

38   It seems we *are* afraid of homeless children, not only in Queens but everywhere in the United States. It is hard to know exactly what it is we fear (the children themselves, the sickness they may carry, the adolescents they will soon become if they

survive, or the goad to our own conscience that they represent when they are visible, nearby); but the fear is very real. Our treatment of these children reaffirms the distancing that now has taken place. They are not of us. They are "the Other."

39   What startles most observers is not simply that such tragedies persist in the United States, but that almost all have been well documented and that even the most solid documentation does not bring about corrective action. Instead of action, a common response in New York, as elsewhere, is the forming of a "task force" to investigate. This is frequently the last we hear of it. Another substitute for action is a press event at which a city official seems to overleap immediate concerns by the unveiling of a plan to build a thousand, or a hundred thousand, homes over the course of ten or twenty years at an expense of several billion dollars. The sweep of these announcements tends to dwarf the urgency of the initial issue. When, after a year or so, we learn that little has been done and that the problem has grown worse, we tend to feel not outrage but exhaustion. Exhaustion, however, as we have seen, turns easily to a less generous reaction.

40   "I am about to be heartless," wrote a columnist in *Newsweek* in December 1986. "There are people living on the streets . . . turning sidewalks into dormitories. They are called the homeless . . . Often they are called worse. They are America's living nightmare . . . They have got to go."

41   The author notes that it is his taxes which pay for the paving and the cleaning of the streets they call their home. "That makes me their landlord. I want to evict them."

42   A senior at Boston University sees homeless people on the streets not far from where he goes to class. He complains that measures taken recently to drive them from the area have not been sufficiently aggressive: "I would very much like to see actions more severe . . . ." Perhaps, he admits, it isn't possible to have them all arrested, though this notion seems to hold appeal for him; perhaps "a more suitable middle ground" may be arrived at to prevent this "nauseating . . . element" from being permitted to "run free so close to my home."

43   "Our response," says one Bostonian, "has gone from indifference to pitying . . . to hatred." I think this is coming to be true and that it marks an incremental stage in our capacity to view the frail, the ill, the disposed, the unsuccessful not as people who have certain human qualities we share but as an outcast entity. From harsh deterrence to punitive incarceration to the willful cutting off of life supports is an increasingly short journey. "I am proposing triage of a sort, triage by self-selection," writes Charles Murray. "The patient always has the right to fail. Society always has the right to let him."

44   Why is it that writings which present these hardened attitudes seem to prevail so easily in public policy? It may be that kindly voices are more easily derided. Callous attitudes are never subject to the charge of being sentimental. It is a recurrent theme in *King Lear*, writes Ignatieff[1] that "there is a truth in the brutal simplicities of the merciless which the more complicated truth of the merciful is helpless to refute."

---

[1] A noted scholar who has written on the homeless.

A rich man, he observes, "never lacks for arguments to deny the poor his charity. 'Basest beggars' can always be found to be 'in the poorest things superfluous.'"

45 "They are a nightmare. I evict them. They will have to go."

46 So from pity we graduate to weariness; from weariness to impatience; from impatience to annoyance; from annoyance to dislike and sometimes to contempt.

READING CLOSELY AND THINKING CRITICALLY

1. According to Kozol, what are the prevailing attitudes toward the homeless?
2. To what extent are government officials and the general public part of the problem of homelessness?
3. In paragraph 38, Kozol says that we are afraid of homeless children. What are we afraid of?
4. Are any examples particularly moving? Which ones? Why do they affect you the way they do?
5. Has your perception of the homeless changed as a result of reading "Untouchables"? Explain.

EXAMINING STRUCTURE AND STRATEGY

1. "Untouchables" lacks a stated thesis, but you can still identify the implied thesis. Write out that implied thesis.
2. In addition to the opening paragraphs, much of the essay illustrates the plight of the homeless. Cite at least five paragraphs that serve this purpose.
3. Which paragraphs illustrate government indifference to the homeless?
4. Which paragraphs illustrate the public's indifference to or fear of the homeless?

NOTING COMBINED PATTERNS

1. The opening five paragraphs are an extended example. What pattern of development is used for the example? What purposes does the example serve?
2. From paragraph 17 to the end of the essay, examples appear with cause-and-effect analysis. (Cause-and-effect analysis explains the causes or effects of something; see Chapter 9.) According to these paragraphs, what causes people to treat the homeless the way they do?

CONSIDERING LANGUAGE AND STYLE

1. The title of the essay is a reference to one aspect of India's caste system. Research where the untouchables fit into the Indian caste system and then explain why Kozol's reference to this caste is fitting.

2. Kozol tells the story of Richard Lazarus; however, in the introduction to his book, he notes that he has changed the names of those he writes of. Why do you think Kozol chose the name "Lazarus"? Is the name appropriate? Explain.

3. Consult a dictionary if you are unsure of the meaning of any of these words: *Bowery* (paragraph 5), *sanctuary* (paragraph 12), *refuse* (paragraph 12), *noxious* (paragraph 15), *skid-row* (paragraph 24), *foraging* (paragraph 27), *vermin* (paragraph 27), *de facto* (paragraph 30), *Alcatraz* (paragraph 30), *demonology* (paragraph 35), *interment* (paragraph 36), *goad* (paragraph 38), *triage* (paragraph 43).

FOR DISCUSSION IN CLASS OR ONLINE

What do homelessness and our reaction to the homeless say about us? Why do we fear and scorn the homeless? If your instructor so directs, post your answers to your class Web site.

WRITING ASSIGNMENTS

1. **In your journal.** Lazarus says that the homeless are "the rejected waste of the society" (paragraph 28). In a page or so, explain what you think Lazarus means and go on to note whether you think his assessment is correct.

2. **Using exemplification for a purpose.** The purposes in the assignments are possibilities. You may establish whatever purposes you like, within your instructor's guidelines.
   - Kozol notes that people fear the homeless. Think about someone or something that you fear. To relate your experience and express your feelings, use examples to illustrate how you react to your fear. You can also explain the cause of your fear.
   - The homeless are not the only "untouchables" in our society. Pick another group that is often feared or scorned. To inform and perhaps convince your reader to treat the group differently, give examples of our treatment of the group.
   - Were there any "untouchables" in your high school (any people feared or scorned)? If so, pick one of these groups or one of these people and use examples to inform about how they were treated and, perhaps, why.

3. **Combining patterns.** Homelessness is a problem in society at-large. Identify a problem that currently exists in your campus society. Give examples of the problem so your reader understands its nature and seriousness. Then, using process analysis (explained in Chapter 7), explain a procedure for solving the problem or lessening its negative effects.

4. **Connecting the readings.** Using "What Is Poverty?" (page 511) and "Untouchables" to stimulate your thinking, describe our attitudes toward the poor and explain how our attitudes contribute to the problem of poverty and homelessness.

5. **Drawing on sources.** Pick a particular group of people to which you do not belong (for example, athletes, international students, adult learners, a particular minority, part-time students, or student employees). Interview at least three members of that group and then write an essay that explains what life is like for group members. Use examples to illustrate your points.

BACKGROUND: Toni Cade Bambara (1939–1995) created television documentaries and wrote short stories and novels before losing her battle with colon cancer. She was a social activist who worked to improve the living conditions of urban minorities and heighten awareness of racial and social injustice. Bambara lived in Harlem until she was ten, and she considered her time in that community to be a prime influence on her writing. Of her writing, Bambara said in a 1982 interview: "When I look back at my work with any little distance, the two characteristics that jump out at me is one, the tremendous capacity for laughter, but also a tremendous capacity for rage." Bambara's works include the anthologies *The Black Woman* (1970) and *Tales and Stories for Black Folks* (1971). Her short story collections include *Gorilla, My Love* (1972)—from which "The Lesson" was taken—and *The Seabirds Are Still Alive* (1977). Her novels are *The Salt Eaters* (1980), *If Blessing Comes* (1987), and *Raymond's Run* (1990) and *Deep Sightings and Rescue Missions* (1996). *Those Bones Are Not My Child* (1999) were published posthumously.

www.mhhe.com/patterns

For more information on this author, go to

More resources > Chapter 6 > Toni Cade Bambara

COMBINED PATTERNS AND THEIR PURPOSES: As a short story, "The Lesson," is a *narration* meant to **entertain**. However, this is a short story with a message: Bambara is **informing** the reader about unequal distribution of wealth and using her story to **persuade** the reader that the inequity is wrong. *Exemplification* is an important pattern in the story, as the narration is about an illustration of an important life lesson.

The Lesson
TONI CADE BAMBARA

Back in the days when everyone was old and stupid or young and foolish and me and Sugar were the only ones just right, this lady moved on our block with nappy hair and proper speech and no makeup. And quite naturally we laughed at her, laughed the way we did at the junk man who went about his business like he was some big-time president and his sorry-ass horse his secretary. And we kinda hated her too, hated the way we did the winos who cluttered up our parks and pissed on our handball walls and stank up our hallways and stairs so you couldn't halfway play hide and seek without a goddamn gas mask. Miss Moore was her name. The only woman on the block with no first name. And she was black as hell, cept for her feet, which were fish-white and spooky. And she was always planning these boring-ass things for us to do, us being my cousin, mostly, who lived on the block cause we all moved North the same time and to the same apartment then spread out gradual to breathe. And our parents would yank our heads into some kinda shape and crisp up our clothes so we'd be presentable for travel with Miss Moore, who always looked like she was going to church, though she never did. Which is just one of things the grownups talked about when they talked behind her back like a dog. But when she came calling with some sachet

As you read
The story is told from the point of view of a child. Think how the child's perspective helps the author achieve her purpose.

she'd sewed up or some gingerbread she'd made or some book, why then they'd all be too embarrassed to turn her down and we'd get handed over all spruced up. She'd been to college and said it was only right that she should take responsibility for the young ones' education, and she not even related by marriage or blood. So they'd go for it. Specially Aunt Gretchen. She was the main gofer in the family. You got some ole dumb shit foolishness you want somebody to go for, you send for Aunt Gretchen. She been screwed into the go-along for so long, it's a blood-deep natural thing with her. Which is how she got saddled with me and Sugar and Junior in the first place while our mothers were in a la-de-da apartment up the block having a good ole time.

2 So this one day Miss Moore rounds us all up at the mailbox and it's puredee hot and she's knockin herself out about arithmetic. And school suppose to let up in summer I heard, but she don't never let up. And the starch in my pinafore scratching the shit outta me and I'm really hating this nappy-head bitch and her goddamn college degree. I'd much rather go to the pool or to the show where it's cool. So me and Sugar leaning on the mailbox being surly, which is a Miss Moore word. And Flyboy checking out what everybody brought for lunch. And Fat Butt already wasting his peanut-butter-and-jelly sandwich like the pig he is. And Junebug punchin on Q.T.'s arm for potato chips. And Rosie Giraffe shifting from one hip to the other waiting for somebody to step on her foot or ask her if she from Georgia so she can kick ass, preferably Mercedes'. And Miss Moore asking us do we know what money is, like we a bunch of retards. I mean real money, she say, like it's only poker chips or monopoly papers we lay on the grocer. So right away I'm tired of this and say so. And would much rather snatch Sugar and go to the Sunset and terrorize the West Indian kids and take their hair ribbons and their money too. And Miss Moore files that remark away for next week's lesson on brotherhood, I can tell. And finally I say we oughta get to the subway cause it's cooler and besides we might meet some cute boys. Sugar done swiped her mama's lipstick, so we ready.

3 So we heading down the street and she's boring us silly about what things cost and what our parents make and how much goes for rent and how money ain't divided up right in this country. And then she gets to the part about we all poor and live in the slums, which I don't feature. And I'm ready to speak on that, but she steps out in the street and hails two cabs just like that. Then she hustles half the crew in with her and hands me a five-dollar bill and tells me to calculate 10 percent tip for the driver. And we're off. Me and Sugar and Junebug and Flyboy hangin out the window and hollering to everybody, putting lipstick on each other cause Flyboy a faggot anyway, and making farts with our sweaty armpits. But I'm mostly trying to figure how to spend this money. But they all fascinated with the meter ticking and Junebug starts laying bets as to how much it'll read when Flyboy can't hold his breath no more. Then Sugar lays bets as to how much it'll be when we get there. So I'm stuck. Don't nobody want to go for my plan, which is to jump out at the next light and run off to the first bar-b-que we can find. Then the driver tells us to get the hell out cause we there already. And the meter reads eight-five cents. And I'm stalling to figure out the tip and Sugar say give him a dime. And I decide he don't need it bad as I do, so later for him. But then he tries

to take off with Junebug foot still in the door so we talk about his mama something ferocious. Then we check out that we on Fifth Avenue and everybody dressed up in stockings. One lady in a fur coat, hot as it is. White folks crazy.

4   "This is the place," Miss Moore say, presenting it to us in the voice she uses at the museum. "Let's look in the windows before we go in."

5   "Can we steal?" Sugar asks very serious like she's getting the ground rules squared away before she plays. "I beg your pardon," say Miss Moore, and we fall out. So she leads us around the windows of the toy store and me and Sugar screamin, "This is mine, that's mine, I gotta have that, that was made for me, I was born for that," till Big Butt drowns us out.

6   "Hey, I'm goin to buy that there."

7   "That there? You don't even know what it is, stupid."

8   "I do so, he say punchin on Rosie Giraffe. "It's a microscope."

9   "Whatcha gonna do with a microscope, fool?"

10   "Look at things."

11   "Like what, Ronald?" ask Miss Moore. And Big Butt ain't got the first notion. So here go Miss Moore gabbing about the thousands of bacteria in a drop of water and the somethinorother in a speck of blood and the million and one living things in the air around us is invisible to the naked eye. And what she say that for? Junebug go to town on the "naked" and we rolling. Then Miss Moore ask what it cost. So we all jam into the window smudgin it up and the price tag say $300. So then she ask how long'd take for Big Butt and Junebug to save up their allowances. "Too long," I say, "Yeh," adds Sugar, "Outgrown it by that time." And Miss Moore say no, you never outgrow learning instruments. "Why, even medical students and interns and," blah, blah, blah. And we ready to choke Big Butt for bringing it up in the first damn place.

12   "This here costs four hundred eighty dollars," say Rosie Giraffe. So we pile up all over her to see what she pointin out. My eyes tell me it's a chunk of glass cracked with something heavy, and different-color inks dripped into the splits, then the whole thing put into a oven or something. But for $480 it don't make sense.

13   "That's a paperweight made of semi-precious stones fused together under tremendous pressure," she explains slowly, with her hands doing the mining and all the factory work.

14   "So what's a paperweight?" asks Rosie Giraffe.

15   "To weigh paper with, dumbbell," say Flyboy, the wise man from the East.

16   "Not exactly," say Miss Moore, which is what she say when you warm or way off too. "It's to weigh paper down so it won't scatter and make your desk untidy." So right away me and Sugar curtsy to each other and then to Mercedes who is more the tidy type.

17   "We don't keep paper on top of the desk in my class," say Junebug, figuring Miss Moore crazy or lyin one.

18   "At home, then," she say. "Don't you have a calendar and pencil case and a blotter and a letter-opener on your desk at home where you do your homework?" And she know damn well what our homes look like cause she nosys round in them every chance she gets.

19   "I don't even have a desk," say Junebug. "Do we?"

20   "No. And I don't get no homework neither," say Big Butt.

21   "And I don't even have a home," say Flyboy like he do at school to keep the white folks off his back and sorry for him. Send this poor kid to camp posters, is his specialty.

22   "I do," says Mercedes. "I have a box of stationery on my desk and a picture of my cat. My godmother bought the stationery and the desk. There's a big rose on each sheet and the envelopes smell like roses."

23   "Who wants to know about your smelly-ass stationery," say Rosie Giraffe fore I can get my two cents in.

24   "It's important to have a work area all your own so that . . . "

25   "Will you look at this sailboat, please," say Flyboy, cuttin her off and pointin to the thing like it was his. So once again we tumble all over each other to gaze at this magnificent thing in the toy store which is just big enough to maybe sail two kittens across the pond if you strap them to the posts tight. We all start reciting the price tag like we in assembly. "Handcrafted sailboat of fiberglass at one thousand one hundred ninety-five dollars."

26   "Unbelievable," I hear myself say and am really stunned. I read it again for myself just in case the group recitation put me in a trance. Same thing. For some reason this pisses me off. We look at Miss Moore and she lookin at us, waiting for I dunno what.

27   "Who'd pay all that when you can buy a sailboat set for a quarter at Pop's, a tube of glue for a dime, and a ball of string for eight cents? It must have a motor and whole lot else besides," I say. "My sailboat cost me about fifty cents."

28   "But will it take water?" say Mercedes with her smart ass.

29   "Took mine to Alley Pond Park once," say Flyboy. "String broke. Lost it. Pity."

30   "Sailed mine in Central Park and it keeled over and sank. Had to ask my father for another dollar."

31   "And you got the strap," laugh Big Butt. "The jerk didn't even have a string on it. My old man wailed on his behind."

32   Little Q.T. was staring hard at the sailboat and you could see he wanted it bad. But he too little and somebody'd just take it from him. So what the hell. "This boat for kids, Miss Moore?"

33   "Parents silly to buy something like that just to get all broke up," say Rosie Giraffe.

34   "That much money it should last forever," I figure.

35   "My father'd buy it for me if I wanted it."

36   "Your father, my ass," say Rosie Giraffe getting a chance to finally push Mercedes.

37   "Must be rich people shop here," say Q.T.

38   "You are a very bright boy," say Flyboy. "What was your first clue?" And he rap him on the head with the back of his knuckles, since Q.T. the only one he could get away with. Though Q.T. liable to come up behind you years later and get his licks in when you half expect it.

39   "What I want to know is," I says to Miss Moore though I never talk to her, I wouldn't give the bitch that satisfaction, "is how much a real boat costs? I figure a thousand'd get you a yacht any day."

40   "Why don't you check that out," she says, "and report back to the group?" Which really pains my ass. If you gonna mess up a perfectly good swim day least you could do is have some answers. "Let's go in," she say like she got something up her sleeve. Only she don't lead the way. So me and Sugar turn the corner to where the entrance is, but when we get there I kinda hang back. Not that I'm scared, what's there to be afraid of, just a toy store. But I feel funny, shame. But what I got to be shamed about? Got as much right to go in as anybody. But somehow I can't seem to get hold of the door, so I step away for Sugar to lead. But she hangs back too. And I look at her and she looks at me and this is ridiculous. I mean, damn, I have never ever been shy about doing nothing or going nowhere. But then Mercedes steps up and then Rosie Giraffe and Big Butt crowd in behind and shove, and next thing we all stuffed into the doorway with only Mercedes squeezing past us, smoothing out her jumper and walking right down the aisle. Then the rest of us tumble in like a glued-together jigsaw done all wrong. And people lookin at us. And it's like the time me and Sugar crashed into the Catholic church on a dare. But once we got in there and everything so hushed and holy and the candles and the bowin and the handkerchiefs on all the drooping heads, I just couldn't go through with the plan. Which was for me to run up to the altar and do a tap dance while Sugar played the nose flute and messed around in the holy water. And Sugar kept givin me the elbow. Then later teased me so bad I tied her up in the shower and turned it on and locked her in. And she'd be there till this day if Aunt Gretchen hadn't finally figured I was lyin about the boarder taking a shower.

41   Same thing in the store. We all walkin on tiptoe and hardly touchin the games and puzzles and things. And I watched Miss Moore who is steady watchin us like she waitin for a sign. Like Mama Drewery watches the sky and sniffs the air and takes note of just how much slant is in the bird formation. Then me and Sugar bump smack into each other, so busy gazing at the toys, 'specially the sailboat. But we don't laugh and go into our fat-lady bump-stomach routine. We just stare at that price tag. Then Sugar ran a finger over the whole boat. And I'm jealous and want to hit her. Maybe not her, but I sure want to punch somebody in the mouth.

42   "Watcha bring us here for, Miss Moore?"

43   "You sound angry, Sylvia. Are you mad about something?" Givin me one of them grins like she tellin a grown-up joke that never turns out to be funny. And she's lookin very closely at me like maybe she plannin to do my portrait from memory. I'm mad, but I won't give her that satisfaction. So I slouch around the store bein very bored and say, "Let's go."

44   Me and Sugar at the back of the train watchin the tracks whizzin by large then small then gettin gobbled up in the dark. I'm thinkin about this tricky toy I saw in the store. A clown that somersaults on a bar then does chin-ups just cause you yank lightly as his leg. Cost $35. I could see me askin my mother for a $35 birthday clown. "You wanna who that costs what?" she'd say, cocking her head to the side to get a better view of the hole in my head. Thirty-five dollars could buy new bunk beds for Junior and Gretchen's boy. Thirty-five dollars and the whole household could go visit Granddaddy Nelson in the country. Thirty-five dollars would pay for the

rent and the piano bill too. Who are these people that spend that much for performing clowns and $1,000 for toy sailboats? What kinda work they do and how they live and how come we ain't in on it? Where we are is who we are, Miss Moore always pointin out. But it don't necessarily have to be that way, she always adds then waits for somebody to say that poor people have to wake up and demand their share of the pie and don't none of us know what kind of pie she talkin about in the first damn place. But she ain't so smart cause I still got her four dollars from the taxi and she sure ain't gettin it. Messin up my day with this shit. Sugar nudges me in my pocket and winks.

45 Miss Moore lines up in front of the mailbox where we started from, seem like years ago, and I got a headache for thinkin so hard. And we lean all over each other so we can hold up under the draggy-ass lecture she always finishes us off with at the end before we thank her for borin us to tears. But she just looks at us like she readin tea leaves. Finally she say, "Well, what did you think of F.A.O. Schwartz?"

46 Rosie Giraffe mumbles, "White folks crazy."

47 "I'd like to go there again when I get my birthday money," says Mercedes, and we shove her out the pack so she has to lean on the mailbox by herself.

48 "I'd like a shower. Tiring day," say Flyboy.

49 Then Sugar surprises me by sayin, "You know, Miss Moore, I don't think all of us here put together eat in a year what that sailboat costs." And Miss Moore lights up like somebody goosed her. "And?" she say, urging Sugar on. Only I'm standin on her foot so she don't continue.

50 "Imagine for a minute what kind of society it is in which some people can spend on a toy what it would cost to feed a family of six or seven. What do you think?"

51 "I think," say Sugar pushing me off her feet like she never done before, cause I whip her ass in a minute, "that this is not much of a democracy if you ask me. Equal chance to pursue happiness means an equal crack at the dough, don't it?" Miss Moore is besides herself and I am disgusted with Sugar's treachery. So I stand on her foot one more time to see if she'll shove me. She shuts up, and Miss Moore looks at me, sorrowfully I'm thinkin. And somethin weird is going on, I can feel it in my chest.

52 "Anybody else learn anything today?" lookin dead at me. I walk away and Sugar has to run to catch up and don't even seem to notice when I shrug her arm off my shoulder.

53 "Well, we got four dollars anyway," she says.

54 "Uh hunh."

55 "We could go to Hascombs and get half a chocolate layer and then go to the Sunset and still have plenty money for potato chips and ice-cream sodas."

56 "Uh hunh."

57 "Race you to Hascombs," she say.

58 We start down the block and she gets ahead which is O.K. by me cause I'm going to the West End and then over to the Drive to think this day through. She can run if she want to and even run faster. But ain't nobody gonna beat me at nuthin.

1. What lesson is Miss Moore teaching the children?

2. Why does Miss Moore feel it is her responsibility to educate the children in her neighborhood? Do you agree that it is her responsibility? Explain.

3. When Sylvia is about to enter the store, she hesitates. Why? What is she thinking and feeling?

4. How does telling the story through the point of view of a child help Bambara achieve her writing purpose?

5. Bambara carefully duplicates the dialect of her characters. (A **dialect** is a variety of language with a distinctive word choice, grammar, and pronunciation.) What does the dialect contribute to the story?

WRITING ASSIGNMENTS

1. **In your journal.** Although the story is about childhood in the 1950s, the lesson is still relevant, as the gap between our nation's rich and poor remains a great one. In a page or two, tell about one or more of your observations about this gap.

2. **Using exemplification for a purpose.** What does Miss Moore mean when she says, "Where we are is who we are"? To inform your reader, give one or more examples to illustrate the meaning. The purpose in the assignment is a possibility. You may establish whatever purpose you like, within your instructor's guidelines.

3. **Combining patterns.**
   - Select one of the characters in the story, and, drawing on evidence in the text, write a description of that person's personality that presents and illustrates his or her main characteristic(s).
   - Tell a story about a time someone tried to teach you an important life lesson and compare and contrast (explained in Chapter 8) that person with Miss Moore.

See pages 216 and 217 for strategies for writing exemplification and for a revising checklist.

1. Use examples to show that the life of a teenager is not an easy one.
2. Use examples to prove that advertisements cause people to want things that they do not really need.
3. Use examples to show that life has its surprising moments.
4. Use examples to show that our society does [or does not] worship youth.
5. Use examples to illustrate the benefits or drawbacks of computers or some other form of technology.
6. Form a generalization about the way some group is depicted on television (women, police officers, the elderly, teenagers, or fathers, for instance) and provide examples to illustrate that generalization. Evaluate the accuracy of the depiction.
7. Provide examples to illustrate the fact that appearances can be deceiving.
8. Use examples to show that advertisements can mislead the consumer.
9. Use illustrations to persuade your reader that sometimes a lie is better than the truth.
10. Provide humorous examples to illustrate Murphy's First Law ("What *can* go wrong, *will* go wrong").
11. Provide examples to show that people are at their worst when they are behind the wheels of their cars.
12. Use examples to persuade your reader that athletics have (or have not) assumed excessive importance in this country.
13. Use examples to persuade your reader that the American family is [or is not] changing for the better.
14. Use examples to persuade your reader that the U.S. education system is in need of a major overhaul.
15. Use examples to illustrate the best characteristics of your favorite teacher.
16. Use examples to illustrate the fact that sometimes people can surprise you.
17. Use examples to illustrate some aspect of the relationship you had with your best friend when you were growing up.
18. Provide examples to illustrate the fact that jealousy can be a destructive emotion.
19. Provide examples to illustrate the fact that people make their own luck.
20. **Exemplification in context:** Assume that your local Parents-Teachers Association (PTA) has asked families and schools to consider a month-long ban on television viewing for school-age children. The organization's goal is to get children away from their television sets and engaged in "more worthwhile" activities, such as reading, interacting with family members, studying, playing sports, enjoying hobbies, and so forth. A public forum is being held to look at the advantages and disadvantages of the proposal. Write a position paper to be distributed at the forum, a paper in which you support or attack the moratorium by offering illustrations to convince people that television has negative (or positive) effects on children.

In 1896, the Supreme Court ruled in *Plessy v. Ferguson* that a Louisiana law requiring whites and blacks to ride in separate railroad cars was legal. This ruling provided federal protection for the separate but equal laws that enabled so much of segregation. In its 1954 decision in *Brown v. Board of Education of Topeka,* the Supreme Court determined that racially segregated schools were not constitutional. That decision doomed separate but equal laws. "On Being the Target of Discrimination" on page 234 describes and illustrates life between the *Plessy* and *Brown* decisions. If you were including that essay in a lesson for a history class about the era of segregation, why do you think it would be a good idea to also include the following photo? What does it exemplify? What would students learn from it that they might not understand in the same way from Ellison's essay by itself? Explain.

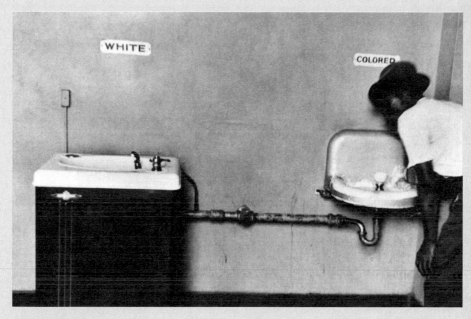

Separate but Equal?

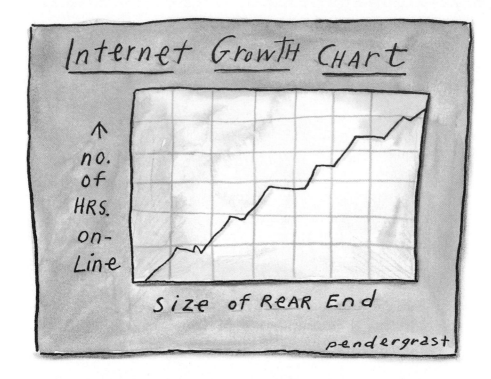

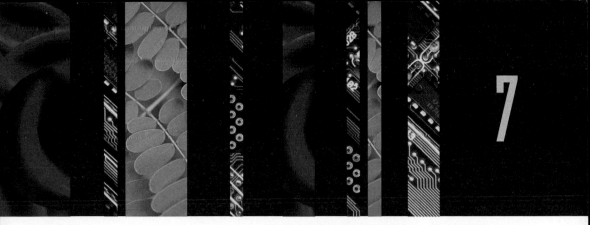

7

Process Analysis

CONSIDER THE PATTERN

In a short paragraph, explain the process implied in the cartoon on the facing page. What point is the cartoonist making?

THE PATTERN

A **process analysis** explains how something works, how something is made, or how something is done. There are two kinds of process analyses:

- The directional process analysis.
- The explanatory process analysis.

A **directional process analysis** gives the steps in a procedure the reader may want to perform. For example, when you buy a watch, the accompanying instruction booklet explains how to set the time, how to change the battery, and how to work the alarm. Each of these explanations is a directional process analysis. When you consult a recipe to prepare a new dish, you are reading and following a directional process analysis. Similarly, if you apply for a scholarship, the instructions for completing the application are a directional process analysis.

An **explanatory process analysis** is a bit different. Like a directional process analysis, it tells how something works, how something is made, or how something is done, but the procedure explained will *not* be performed by the reader. Explanatory process analyses are also common. Your biology textbook explains how plants convert carbon dioxide to oxygen with the process of photosynthesis. Since no reader will engage in photosynthesis, the process analysis is purely explanatory, meant to increase understanding. Similar explanations of how an internal combustion engine works, how natural selection occurs, and how rivers become polluted are examples of explanatory process analyses.

---

www.mhhe.com/patterns

For more help with process analysis, click on
Writing > Writing Tutor > Process Analysis

USING PROCESS ANALYSIS FOR A PURPOSE

A directional process analysis can *inform* a reader how to perform a particular procedure or process. For example, a process analysis that explains how to install a computer program serves this informational purpose. A directional process analysis can also inform a reader who wants to discover a better or different way to do something. For example, you already know how to study, but you still might be interested in a process analysis essay with the title "Six Steps to More Efficient Studying" because the essay may help you save time and improve your grades by showing you an even better way. An explanatory process analysis can inform a reader who desires

TROUBLESHOOTING GUIDE

Using Imperative and Declarative Sentences

If you have trouble keeping your approach consistent in a process analysis, remember the difference between imperative and declarative sentences. An imperative sentence gives a directive. Its subject is *you*, which can be stated or unstated. A declarative sentence makes a statement. Its subject, which is stated, can be any noun or pronoun. Use imperative sentences with directional process analyses and declarative sentences with explanatory process analyses. The following examples for process analyses about bread baking illustrate the difference:

IMPERATIVE SENTENCES (FOR DIRECTIONAL PROCESS ANALYSIS):	**Dissolve the yeast in the water and let it sit for 10 minutes. In a big bowl, combine the water/yeast, milk, sugar, salt and oil.**
DECLARATIVE SENTENCES (FOR EXPLANATORY PROCESS ANALYSIS):	**Yeast eats sugar, and from the sugar it creates alcohol and carbon dioxide gas. The carbon dioxide gas gives bread its texture, and the alcohol flavors the bread.**

a better understanding of how a procedure works. This is the case with "Behind the Formaldehyde Curtain" (page 307), which explains how a body is prepared for burial. The author assumes you are not reading her essay because you want to go out and embalm a body. You are reading it because you are curious about how this process is performed and you want to learn about it.

Finally, an explanatory process analysis can inform a reader about the beauty, difficulty, or complexity of a process so the reader can better appreciate it. For example, say that you are a distance runner. If you want your reader to appreciate the rigor and discipline that go into running a cross-country race, you can describe the process of running that race to impress the reader with its difficulty.

In addition to informing a reader, a process analysis can *entertain*. In "How I'll Become an American" (page 281), for example, the author entertains with a humorous account of how Americans behave.

A process analysis can also *express feelings and relate experience*. For example, assume one of your happiest childhood memories is of your annual fishing trips with your grandfather. You could relate part of that experience by explaining how you and your grandfather prepared for the trip and by noting the special ways you interacted during the process.

Finally, a process analysis can *persuade* a reader. For example, if you want to convince your reader that current gun registration procedures are inadequate, you can explain the registration process and point out its flaws. If you want to persuade your reader to use a particular computer security system, you can explain how the system works and point out its superior features.

Process Analysis in College, at Work, and in the Community

You are likely to use both directional and explanatory process analyses in much of your college writing. An obvious use of directional process analysis is for biology, chemistry, and physics lab reports, where you must explain the process you followed to complete various experiments. In a marketing class, an examination question might require you to write a directional process analysis to explain how to conduct a consumer survey. A report you write for a computer science class would use directional process analysis to explain how to develop a certain kind of computer program. In an art class, you would write a directional process analysis if you were to explain how to mix paints to achieve a desired effect.

Similarly, you will often write explanatory process analyses. For example, for a geology midterm exam you may need to explain how erosion occurs; for a political science exam you may need to explain how the electoral college works; for a psychology class, you may need to write a research paper that explains how children acquire language.

Process analysis—particularly explanatory process analysis—is a common component in textbooks of all kinds. Here, for example, is an excerpt from an introductory psychology textbook. It explains the classic experiments that Russian psychologist Ivan Pavlov performed to learn about a form of learning called *classical conditioning,* which occurs when an organism is trained or "conditioned" to produce a response not ordinarily associated with a particular stimulus.

> To demonstrate and analyze classical conditioning, Pavlov conducted a series of experiments (Pavlov, 1927). In one, he attached a tube to the salivary gland of a dog, allowing him to measure precisely the amount of salivation that occurred. He then sounded a tuning fork and, just a few seconds later, presented the dog with meat powder. This pairing, carefully planned so that exactly the same amount of time elapsed between the presentation of the sound and the meat powder, occurred repeatedly. At first the dog would salivate only when the meat powder itself was presented, but soon it began to salivate at the sound of the tuning fork. In fact, even when Pavlov stopped presenting the meat powder, the dog still salivated after hearing the sound. The dog had been classically conditioned to salivate to the tone. (Feldman, *Understanding Psychology*).

In the textbook, the process analysis helps students understand that an animal (in this case, a dog) can be conditioned to produce a response (salivating) that is normally unrelated to the stimulus (the sound of the tuning fork). The process analysis helps students better remember the concept of classical conditioning by helping them visualize the concept in action.

Beyond the classroom, process analysis can be an important component of workplace communications. A restaurant manager might send a memo to employees with an explanatory process analysis that describes how food poisoning occurs. Human resource managers send memos explaining procedures for using vacation days, physical therapists write out instructions for performing exercises, and safety officers write out procedures for emergency evacuations of buildings. To help a colleague with online research, you might write an explanation of how to use a specific kind of search engine.

Process analysis is also important to writing you do in the community. When you write out directions to your home or another location, you are writing a directional process analysis. If you e-mail a friend about how to install a computer firewall to protect against viruses, you are writing a directional process analysis, as you are if you send a letter to the editor urging people to donate blood by explaining how simple the procedure is.

SUPPORTING DETAILS

Because a process analysis explains how something is made, how something works, or how something is done, the primary detail will be the steps in the process. Sometimes, you will find it necessary to go on to explain *how* a particular step is performed. For example, in "Don't Just Stand There" (page 285), Diane Cole describes how to deal with racial, ethnic, and sexist remarks. At one point she tells what to do when the remark occurs at a large meeting or public talk, and then she goes on to explain *how* to perform the step:

> At a large meeting or public talk, you might consider passing the speaker a note . . . You could write, "You may not realize it, but your remarks were offensive because . . ."

At times, you may want to explain *why* a step is performed so your reader appreciates the importance of the step. For example, assume you are explaining the best job application procedure, and you mention that you should follow every interview with a letter of thanks that also reaffirms your interest in the position. To help your reader appreciate the importance of this step, you can explain that the letter marks you as someone who is courteous and as someone who follows through—two qualities that can help you land the job.

If you need to clarify a step to be sure your reader understands, an example may help. In this excerpt from "Don't Just Stand There," notice that the author uses an example to clarify how the host of a gathering can control the behavior of guests:

> If you, yourself, are the host, you can exercise more control; you are, after all, the one who sets the rules and the tone of behavior in your home. Once, when Professor Kahn's party guests began singing offensive, racist songs, for instance, he kicked them all out, saying "You don't sing songs like that in my house!" And, he adds, "they never did again."

If you think your reader might perform a step incorrectly or might perform an unnecessary step, you can explain what *not* to do and why. For example, in "Don't Just Stand There," the author cautions the reader not to deal with offensive remarks by embarrassing a person publicly:

> But in general, psychologists say, shaming a person in public may have the opposite effect of the one you want: The speaker may deny his offense all the more strongly in order to save face.

If a particular part of the process can be troublesome, you can point that out to the reader, as Jessica Mitford does in "Behind the Formaldehyde Curtain":

> Proper placement of the body requires a delicate sense of balance. It should lie as high as possible in the casket, yet not so high that the lid, when lowered, will hit the nose. On the other hand, we are cautioned, placing the body too low creates the impression that the body is in a box.

Description can be an important element of a process analysis when you want your reader to visualize some aspect of the process in order to better appreciate it. (See Chapter 4 for more information on writing description.) In "In the Kitchen," (page 291), for example, Henry Louis Gates, Jr., explains how his mother used to straighten the hair of her African-American clients and includes this description:

> Mama would stroke that red-hot iron—which by this time had been in the gas fire for half an hour or more—slowly but firmly through their hair, from scalp to strand's end. It made a scorching, crinkly sound, the hot iron did, as it burned its way through kink, leaving in its wake straight strands of hair, standing long and tall but drooping over at the ends, their shape like the top of a heavy willow tree.

If your reader is unlikely to understand specialized vocabulary, your process analysis may include definition, as in this excerpt from "In the Kitchen," which defines a potentially unfamiliar use of *kitchen*:

> But the word has another meaning, and the kitchen that I'm speaking of is the very kinky bit of hair at the back of your head, where your neck meets your shirt collar.

Deciding whether or not to define specific terms requires an understanding of who your audience is and what your reader knows. For that reason, careful audience assessment is important.

ORGANIZING DETAILS

The thesis for a process analysis can mention the process to be explained:

> A person should take great care when choosing a personal physician. (*Thesis indicates that the essay will explain how to choose a personal physician.*)

In addition to mentioning the process, the thesis can also explain why it is important to understand the process:

> To avoid making a costly mistake, follow this procedure when you shop for a car. (*Thesis indicates that the process is important because it can save the reader money.*)

If you do not mention the importance of the process in the thesis, you can do so elsewhere in the essay. In "Don't Just Stand There," Diane Cole uses her fourth paragraph to explain why it is important to know a process for dealing with racial and ethnic insults:

> But left unchecked, racial slurs and offensive ethnic jokes "can poison the atmosphere," says Michael McQuillan, adviser for racial/ethnic affairs for the Brooklyn borough president's office. "Hearing these remarks conditions us to accept them; and if we accept these, we can become accepting of other acts."

If you want your reader to know why you are qualified to describe the process, you can give your credentials in your introduction. For example, if you are explaining an efficient note-taking system you have devised, you can explain that you have made the dean's list every term since you started using the system.

If completing the process requires particular materials, make note of that fact early, perhaps even in the first paragraph. If, for example, you are explaining how to build a bookcase, note the lumber sizes, tools, and other materials needed.

When the steps in the process must be performed in a particular order, details are arranged in a **chronological** (or time) order. To help your reader follow the chronological order, transitions like these can help:

First, you must . . .

Next, be careful to . . .

Now, you can . . .

After that, try . . .

Finally, you should . . .

If you need to mention what *not* to do so your reader does not make a mistake or misunderstand a step, include this information at the point in the process when the confusion can occur. If you need to define a term, do so the first time the term is used. Finally, if you need to explain why a step is performed, do so when the step is given.

PROCESS GUIDELINES: STRATEGIES FOR WRITING A PROCESS ANALYSIS

1. **Selecting a Topic.** Select a process you know well so you are not struggling for detail or presenting the process incompletely.

2. **Establishing a Purpose.** To establish your purpose, ask yourself these questions:
   - Am I writing a directional process analysis to inform my audience so my reader can perform the process?
   - Am I writing an explanatory process analysis to inform a reader who will not perform the process?
   - Do I want my reader to appreciate the beauty, difficulty, or complexity of the process?
   - Do I want to entertain my reader? Do I want to relate part of my experience or express my feelings about something associated with the process?
   - Do I want to convince my reader that the process is a better way to do something?
   - Do I want to show my reader the flaws in a specific process and suggest ways in which that process might be improved?

3. **Assessing Your Audience.** To assess your audience, ask yourself whether your reader appreciates the importance of the process, understands any part of the process, or would find any of the steps difficult to perform or understand. In addition, consider why your reader might be interested in the process.

VISUALIZING A PROCESS ANALYSIS ESSAY

The following chart can help you visualize the structure for a process analysis. Like all good models, however, this one can be altered as needed.

Introduction

- Creates interest in the essay
- Can explain why you are qualified to explain the process
- Can note what materials, if any, are needed
- States the thesis, which mentions the process to be explained and may note why it is important to understand the process

First Body Paragraph

- Gives the first step in the process
- May explain how the step is performed, why the step is performed, and what not to do
- May clarify the step or point out a troublesome aspect
- May include description or definition of specialized vocabulary
- Arranges details in chronological order

Next Body Paragraph

- Gives the next step in the process
- May explain how the step is performed, why the step is performed, and what not to do
- May clarify the step or point out a troublesome aspect
- May include description or definition of specialized vocabulary
- Arranges details in chronological order

Next Body Paragraphs

- Give remaining steps in the process
- Arrange details in progressive, chronological, or occasionally spatial order

Conclusion

- Provides a satisfying finish
- May state the point of the narration if not done so elsewhere

4. **Generating Ideas.** List every step in the process in the order it is performed. Then write a statement that explains the importance of the process.

5. **Drafting.** With your list of steps as a guide, write out the process. Try to visualize the process as you are describing it. Are you providing enough information? Do the steps follow a logical order? Try to include a statement that indicates the importance of understanding the process. If you wish, this statement can be your thesis.

6. **Revising.** Be sure you are not stating the obvious or explaining how to do something the reader already knows how to do. For example, if you are explaining how to use a particular search engine, you do not need to tell your reader to turn on the computer. Be sure to define any specialized terms.

www.mhhe.com/patterns

For more help with pronouns, click on

Editing > Pronouns
Editing > Pronoun-Antecedent Agreement

Avoiding Person Shifts

If you have trouble knowing when to use *you* and *your*, remember that these words refer to the reader. If you use one of these pronouns to refer to a noun or to yourself—that is, if you are *not* referring to the reader—you create a problem called *person shift*.

PERSON SHIFT: **Women often overestimate their ability to handle dangerous situations. For example, women think they can talk themselves out of a confrontation, but you should always remember that your first step should be to walk—or run—away.**

CORRECTION: **Women often overestimate their ability to handle dangerous situations. For example, women think they can talk themselves out of a confrontation, but they should always remember that their first step should be to walk—or run—away.**

Checklist for Revising a Process Analysis

Be sure to:

_____ Explain how steps are performed, if necessary.

_____ Mention what not to do, if necessary.

_____ Explain why steps are performed, if necessary.

_____ Provide clarifying examples, if needed.

_____ Describe, as necessary.

_____ Define terms your reader may not understand.

_____ Point out troublesome aspects of the process.

_____ Indicate the importance of understanding the process.

_____ Avoid stating the obvious.

_____ Use transitions to indicate sequence.

The following student essay is an informational process analysis that says as much about the joy of performing the process as it does about how to perform the process. After you read, you will have an opportunity to evaluate this essay.

A Visit to Candyland

You may have been to the supermarket around Christmastime and seen a gingerbread house kit. It probably involved graham-cracker slabs meant to be stuck together with thick white frosting and decorated with gumdrops. In my family, making gingerbread houses is a long-standing tradition, and one that involves far more than simply slapping some cookies and frosting together. Each year, in early December, we decide on a theme and go on to create an elaborate gingerbread structure that reflects the season and our interests. Our cardinal rule in gingerbread house making often comes as a surprise to the friends who visit to marvel at our creations: absolutely everything in the gingerbread house must be edible, and not only edible, but tasty.

We begin by coming up with a concept. One year, it was a crèche scene with Mary, Joseph, the baby Jesus, and various animals, shepherds, and angels. Another year, it was a covered bridge under snow, with a horse-drawn carriage. Once we've decided on a theme, we might visit the library or go on the Internet to find visual ideas we can incorporate into our design. Then, after we've done some preliminary sketches, we make a pattern, measuring carefully with a ruler to make sure each piece will fit with the others. These pattern pieces are drawn onto thin paper and then precisely cut out with sharp scissors. We've found it helps to note on each pattern piece how many need to be made—a roof, for example, is usually made of two equal rectangles, and only one pattern piece is needed.

The next step is to make the gingerbread. We use an old family recipe that produces a sturdy but extremely tasty gingerbread cookie, flavored with molasses, cinnamon, ground cloves, and lots of ginger. In order to make a really tough cookie, many cups of flour have to be incorporated into the batter. Once all the flour has been added, the dough is so dense it's almost impossible to stir, so we hand it off to my father, whose arms are the strongest. After the dough is finished it has to sit in

Paragraph 1
The introduction gives background information. The thesis is not stated but the paragraph suggests a focus on making gingerbread houses.

Paragraph 2
The paragraph gives the first two steps in the process. The details include examples of the first step and information on how the second step is performed.

Paragraph 3
The topic sentence (the first sentence) gives the next step in the process. Detail is included on why part of the step is performed.

the refrigerator for a time period ranging from several hours to a week. This cooling period makes the dough easier to handle and the finished cookie even tougher.

Paragraph 4
The topic sentence (the first sentence) gives the next step in the process. Notice the transition, "once that's done."

Once the dough is ready to bake, it's time to make the pieces of 4 the house. We do this by rolling out the dough onto sheets of tinfoil. We try to avoid handling the dough too much—if it gets warm before it goes into the oven, it loses some of its resilience. The dough is rolled until it's a little less than a quarter of an inch thick. Then we place the pattern pieces onto the rolled dough. Using a small knife, we cut around the pattern piece, discarding the excess dough. After we've cut out the windows on the wall pieces, we fill the holes with broken bits of hard candy. In the oven, these candy pieces melt and harden, forming what looks like stained glass. Once that's done, we slide the tinfoil with the cookie pieces on it onto a cookie sheet and put them into the oven.

Paragraph 5
The paragraph opens with the transition "seven to ten minutes later." The paragraph also notes a troublesome aspect of the process.

Seven to ten minutes later, the cookies are done, and we slide them 5 onto wire racks to cool. After they've cooled, we peel off the tinfoil backing and admire the colored light through the little stained-glass windows. Now we're ready for the hardest part of the whole process: putting the house together. Frosting is simply not tough enough for the elaborate structures we make, so instead we use melted sugar. We sprinkle regular granulated sugar into a wide, flat pan and heat it over a medium-high flame. In a few minutes it forms a glossy, dark-brown liquid. The ends of the gingerbread pieces that are to be stuck together have to be dipped very quickly into the melted sugar and then speedily and precisely joined to their intended mates. If this process is done too quickly, there may not be enough sugar to make the pieces stick, or we may stick them on at the wrong angle. If it's done too slowly, the sugar can harden, its sticking powers completely lost. When my brothers and I were little, we were not allowed to participate in the melted-sugar operation, but now we've developed the necessary manual dexterity and nerves of steel.

Paragraph 6
The topic sentence (the first sentence) gives the next step and includes a transition.

Now the house is assembled and ready for everyone's favorite 6 stage: decoration. We make frosting out of butter, confectioner's sugar, and food coloring, and add a base coat to the parts of the house that seem to need it, like the roof. We generally leave the sides bare, because the dark brown gingerbread is such a pretty color, but we add details with frosting piped out of a wax-paper tube. Then we add decorations. In the past we've used raisins, cinnamon sticks, star anise, nuts, and, of course, many different kinds of candy. Necco wafers, broken in half, make particularly good shingles.

When we're finished, we've usually consumed a substantial quantity of decorations, spoonfuls of frosting, and cookie scraps. Naturally we make gingerbread men to live in the house, but their lifespans tend to be extremely short—sometimes they don't even get frosted. We're too full to do anything but sit and admire our handiwork. A few days later, however, we host our annual holiday party, where the final part of the tradition comes into play. The youngest child at the event (apart from babies, of course) is handed an orange suspended from a red satin ribbon. This is the gingerbread wrecking ball, and it's swung at the house until total destruction has been achieved. We're always sorry to see the house ruined, but then we have the pleasure, along with our guests, of eating our annual masterpiece.

Paragraph 7
The conclusion provides closure by explaining what is done with the gingerbread house. It also highlights a family tradition.

PEER REVIEW

Responding to "A Visit to Candyland"

Evaluate "A Visit to Candyland" by responding to these questions:

1. Does the essay hold your interest? Why or why not?
2. Are the introduction and conclusion effective? Explain.
3. Is the essay a directional or an explanatory process analysis? If it is the former, could you perform the process after reading the essay? If it is the latter, do you understand and appreciate the process after reading the essay?
4. What do you think of the author's word choice? Why? Cite an example to support your view.
5. What are the chief strengths of the essay? Why do you find these features strong?
6. Mention one revision you would like to see. How will that revision improve the essay or help the author achieve his purpose?

- Does the photograph depict a directional or explanatory process analysis?
- Does the photograph increase your appreciation of the process depicted?
- Does the photograph show all of the steps in the process?
- What purpose do you think the photographer had in mind for this image?

BACKGROUND: Miklós Vámos was born in 1950 in Hungary, where he was also educated. An author of short stories, novels, and screenplays, he has also been a contributor to *Harper's,* the *Atlantic Monthly,* and the *New York Times,* as well as the Eastern European correspondent for *The Nation.* Vámos has taught screenwriting, playwriting, and theater at several American universities, including Yale, Connecticut College, Southern Connecticut State University, and the College of Staten Island. He was also the literary consultant to the Hungarian studio that produced the Oscar-winning movie *Mephisto.* "How I'll Become an American" first appeared in the *New York Times* in 1989.

THE PATTERN AND ITS PURPOSES: Miklós Vámos uses *process analysis* to take an ironic look at Americans, and the resulting portrait is not very flattering. Although **entertaining,** the essay also **informs** the reader that Americans have some unattractive qualities and exhibit some unattractive behaviors. As a result, Vámos aims to **persuade** us to change some of our ways.

How I'll Become an American

MIKLÓS VÁMOS

I have been Hungarian for 38 years. I'll try something else for the next 38. I'll try to be American, for instance. North American, I mean. As an American, I'll speak English fluently. I'll make American mistakes instead of Hungarian mistakes and I'll call them slang.

As you read
Think about how much of Vámos's characterization you agree with.

2 As an American, I'll have a credit card. Or two. I'll use and misuse them and have to pay the fees. I'll apply for other cards right away. Golden Visa. Golden American. Golden Gate. And I'll buy a car, a great American car. Then I'll sell my car and buy a smaller West German car because it's reliable and doesn't use so much gaso-line. Later, I'll sell it and buy a smaller Japanese car with a computer aboard. Then I'll sell it and buy a camper. When I sell the camper I'll buy a bicycle.

3 As an American, I'll buy a dog. And a cat. And a goat. And a white whale. And also some big stones as pets.[1]

4 I'll live in my own house. It will be mine, except for the 99 percent mortgage. I'll sell my house and buy a condo. I'll sell my condo and buy a mobile home. I'll sell my mobile home and buy an igloo. I'll sell my igloo and buy a tent. As an American, I'll be clever: I'll sell my igloo and buy a tent when I move to Florida from Alaska.

5 Anyway, I'll move a lot. And I'll buy the best dishwasher, microwave, dryer and hi-fi in the world—that is, the U.S.A. I'll have warranty for all—or my money back. I'll use automatic toothbrushes, egg boilers and garage doors. I'll call every single phone number starting 1-800.

6 I'll buy the fastest food I can get and I'll eat it very slowly because I'll watch TV during the

[1] A reference to pet rocks, which were novelty items popular for a time in the 1980s.

meals. Of course, I'll buy a VCR. I'll watch the taped programs and then retape. Sometimes I'll retape first.

7   As an American, I'll have an answering machine, too. The outgoing message will promise that I'll call you back as soon as possible, but it won't be possible soon.

8   If I answer the phone as an exception, I'll tell you that I can't talk now because I have a long-distance call on the other line, but I'll call you back as soon as possible (see above).

9   And I'll get a job. I'll always be looking for a better job, but I won't get the job I want. I'll work really hard since as an American I wanna be rich. I'll be always in a hurry: Time is Money. Unfortunately, my time won't be worth as much money as my bosses' time. Sometimes I will have some time and I still won't have enough money. Then I'll start to hate the wisdom of this saying.

10   As an American, sometimes I'll be badly depressed. I'll be the patient of 12 psychiatrists, and I'll be disappointed with all of them. I'll try to change my life a little bit. I'll try to exchange my wives, my cars, my lovers, my houses, my children, my jobs and my pets.

11   Sometimes, I'll exchange a few dollars into other currencies and I'll travel to Europe, Hawaii, Tunisia, Martinique and Japan. I'll be happy to see that people all over the world are jealous of us Americans.

12   I'll take at least 2,000 snapshots on each trip. I'll also buy a video camera and shoot everywhere. I'll look at the tapes, photos and slides, and I'll try to remember my experiences when I have time and am in the mood. But I won't have time or be in the mood because I'll get depressed again and again.

13   I'll smoke cigarettes. Then I'll be afraid of cancer and I'll stop. I'll smoke cigars. And opium. I'll take a breather and then try LSD and heroin and cocaine and marijuana. To top it all off: crack. I'll try to stop then but I won't be able.

14   I'll call 1-800-222-HELP. If nothing helps, I'll have some gay experiences. And swing. And if I am still unhappy I'll make a final effort: I'll try to read a book. I'll buy some best sellers. I'll prefer James A. Michener.[2] My second favorite will be the "How to Be Rich in Seven Weeks." I'll try to follow this advice in seven years.

15   I'll always be concerned about my health as an American. I won't eat anything but health food until I get ill. From time to time, I'll read in the paper that I should stop eating meat, sugar, bread, fiber, grains, iron, toothpaste, and that I should stop drinking milk, soda, water, acid rain. I'll try to follow this advice, but then I'll read in the paper that I should do it the other way around.

16   I'll be puzzled. "Hey, I don't even know what cholesterol is!" Yet I'll stick to decaf coffee, sugar-free cookies, salt-free butter and lead-free gasoline. I'll believe that proper diet and exercise make life longer. I'll go jogging every day until I am mugged twice and knocked down three times. Then I'll just exercise in my room, but it will also increase my appetite. I'll go on several diets, and little by little I'll reach 200 pounds.

17   As an American, I'll buy a new TV every time a larger screen appears on the market. In the end, the screen will be larger than

---

[2]Popular American writer (1907–1997) of historical fiction.

the room. It will be difficult to put this enormous TV into my living room; thus, I will put my living room into the TV. Anyway, my living room will look very much like the living rooms you can see on the screen. My life won't differ from the lives you can see in the soaps: nobody will complain. I won't complain either. I'll always smile.

18 After all, we are Americans, aren't we?

READING CLOSELY AND THINKING CRITICALLY

1. The thesis of "How I'll Become an American" is implied rather than stated. In your own words, write out the thesis. Why do you think the author chose not to write out a thesis?
2. What is Vámos saying about the American attitude toward possessions?
3. Does Vámos believe that Americans are typically content with their lives? Explain.
4. How does Vámos evaluate the mental health of Americans?
5. What is the author saying about the American attitude toward fitness?
6. List words and phrases that describe Americans as Vámos sees them.

EXAMINING STRUCTURE AND STRATEGY

1. **Verbal irony** occurs when the author says one thing but really means the opposite. What verbal irony appears in the essay?
2. Why doesn't Vámos present the steps in the process in chronological order?
3. At what points does Vámos tell why a step is performed?
4. At what points does Vámos tell how a step is performed?
5. Vámos uses a great deal of exaggeration in the essay. Cite an example of that exaggeration. How does the exaggeration help him achieve his purpose?

CONSIDERING LANGUAGE AND STYLE

1. Vámos uses many short sentences, some sentence fragments, contractions, and slang. Why does he use such constructions and diction? What effect is created as a result?
2. What effect does Vámos create with the repetition of "As an American"?
3. Consult a dictionary if you are unsure of the meaning of these words: *LSD* (paragraph 13), *acid rain* (paragraph 15).

FOR DISCUSSION IN CLASS OR ONLINE

Explain how much of Vámos's characterization is accurate and how much is inaccurate, being sure to note why you believe as you do. Do you think Vámos is fair to Americans? Why or why not? If your instructor so directs, post your responses on your class Web site.

WRITING ASSIGNMENTS

1. **In your journal.** "How I'll Become an American" was written in 1989. Do you think your reaction to the essay is similar to or different from the average reader's reaction in 1989? Explain.

2. **Using process analysis for a purpose.** The purposes in the assignments are possibilities. You may establish whatever purposes you like, within your instructor's guidelines.

   - To inform and persuade, write a process analysis with the title "How to Become an American," but make your portrait of Americans a flattering one. If you like, you can create emphasis by repeating "As an American. . . ."

   - To entertain and perhaps persuade, explain the process for becoming a student, an instructor, an athlete, a sorority woman or fraternity man, or some other campus "type." Try your hand at verbal irony.

   - To entertain and perhaps inform or persuade, write an essay with the title, "How to Become a/an _____." (Fill in the blank with something other than a campus "type.") Try your hand at verbal irony.

3. **Combining patterns.** Explain the process a newcomer to the United States can follow in order to fit in as quickly as possible, and use examples to illustrate the steps in the process. (Exemplification is explained in Chapter 6.) If you like, you can limit your discussion to how to fit in within a particular context, such as school, a shopping mall, a grocery store, a football game, and so on. You can use verbal irony if you wish.

4. **Connecting the readings.** How do the Americans depicted in "How I'll Become an American" compare and contrast to the Americans depicted in "The Lesson" on page 257? Note the similarities and differences and go on to discuss how you think the children and Miss Moore would react to Vámos's essay.

5. **Drawing on sources.** Find out about the process for becoming a U.S. citizen and then write up the steps as an explanatory process analysis. After explaining the process, discuss whether or not you think the process should be changed and why. You can learn about becoming a citizen at www.uscitizenship.info/index.htm or by looking it up in an encyclopedia in your library's reference room.

BACKGROUND: Born in Baltimore, Maryland, in 1952, Diane Cole attended Radcliffe College and Johns Hopkins University. In addition to serving as a contributing editor to *Psychology Today,* she has written for *The Wall Street Journal,* the *Washington Post,* the *New York Times, Parents, Newsweek, Ms.,* and *Glamour.* Her writing topics frequently include psychology and women's careers. Cole's books include *Hunting the Headhunters: A Woman's Guide* (1988), *After Great Pain: A New Life Emerges* (1992), and, with Scott Wetzler, *Is It You or Is It Me? How We Turn Our Emotions Inside Out and Blame Each Other* (1998). "Don't Just Stand There" was first published in 1989 in a *New York Times* supplement called *A World of Difference,* which was part of a campaign against bigotry sponsored by the Anti-Defamation League of B'nai B'rith, a Jewish fraternal order.

THE PATTERN AND ITS PURPOSES: Have you ever been unsure how to respond to a bigoted remark? If so, "Don't Just Stand There" can help because Diane Cole uses *process analysis* to **inform** her audience about how to react to bigoted comments and jokes. At the same time, she makes her readers more sensitive to the hurtful nature of such slurs and **persuades** them to take action when they hear them.

DON'T JUST STAND THERE | DIANE COLE

It was my office farewell party, and colleagues at the job I was about to leave were wishing me well. My mood was one of ebullience tinged with regret, and it was in this spirit that I spoke to the office neighbor to whom I had waved hello every morning for the past two years. He smiled broadly as he launched into a long, rambling story, pausing only after he delivered the punch line. It was a very long pause because, although he laughed, I did not: This joke was unmistakably anti-Semitic.

As you read Cole uses a great many quotations in the essay. Consider how they help achieve her purpose for writing.

2 I froze. Everyone in the office knew I was Jewish; what could he have possibly meant? Shaken and hurt, not knowing what else to do, I turned in stunned silence to the next well-wisher. Later, still angry, I wondered, what else should I—could I—have done?

3 Prejudice can make its presence felt in any setting, but hearing its nasty voice in this way can be particularly unnerving.

We do not know what to do and often we feel another form of paralysis as well: We think, "Nothing I say or do will change this person's attitude, so why bother?"

4 But left unchecked, racial slurs and offensive ethnic jokes "can poison the atmosphere," says Michael McQuillan, adviser for racial/ethnic affairs for the Brooklyn borough president's office. "Hearing these remarks conditions us to accept them; and if we accept these, we can become accepting of other acts."

5 Speaking up may not magically change a biased attitude, but it can change a person's behavior by putting a strong message across. And the more messages there are, the more likely a person is to change that behavior, says Arnold Kahn, professor of psychology at James Madison University, Harrisonburg, Va., who makes this analogy: "You can't keep people from smoking in *their* house, but you can ask them not to smoke in *your* house."

6 At the same time, "Even if the other party ignores or discounts what you say,

people always reflect on how others perceive them. Speaking up always counts," says LeNorman Strong, director of campus life at George Washington University, Washington, D.C.

" 'Speaking up always counts.' ... "

7   Finally, learning to respond effectively also helps people feel better about themselves, asserts Cherie Brown, executive director of the National Coalition Building Institute, a Boston-based training organization. "We've found that, when people felt they could at least in this small way make a difference, that made them more eager to take on other activities on a larger scale," she says. Although there is no "cook-book approach" to confronting such remarks—every situation is different, experts stress—there are some effective strategies.

8   *When the "joke" turns on who you are—as a member of an ethnic or religious group, a person of color, a woman, a gay or lesbian, an elderly person, or someone with a physical handicap—shocked paralysis is often the first response. Then, wounded and vulnerable, on some level you want to strike back.*

9   Lashing out or responding in kind is seldom the most effective response, however. "That can give you momentary satisfaction, but you also feel as if you've lowered yourself to that other person's level," Mr. McQuillan explains. Such a response may further label you in the speaker's mind as thin-skinned, someone not to be taken seriously. Or it may up the ante, making the speaker, and then you, reach for new insults—or physical blows.

10   "If you don't laugh at the joke, or fight, or respond in kind to the slur," says Mr. McQuillan, "that will take the person by surprise, and that can give you more control over the situation." Therefore, in situations like the one in which I found myself—a private conversation in which I knew the person making the remark—he suggests voicing your anger calmly but pointedly: "I don't know if you realize what that sounded like to me. If that's what you meant, it really hurt me."

11   State how *you* feel, rather than making an abstract statement like, "Not everyone who hears that joke might find it funny." Counsels Mr. Strong: "Personalize the sense of 'this is how I feel when you say this.' That makes it very concrete"—and harder to dismiss.

12   Make sure you heard the words and their intent correctly by repeating or rephrasing the statement: "This is what I heard you say. Is that what you meant?" It's important to give the other person the benefit of the doubt because, in fact, he may *not* have realized that the comment was offensive and, if you had not spoken up, would have had no idea of its impact on you.

13   For instance, Professor Kahn relates that he used to include in his exams multiple-choice questions that occasionally contained "incorrect funny answers." After one exam, a student came up to him in private and said, "I don't think you intended this, but I found a number of those jokes offensive to me as a woman." She explained why. "What she said made immediate sense to me," he says. "I apologized at the next class, and I never did it again."

14   But what if the speaker dismisses your objection, saying, "Oh, you're just being sensitive. Can't you take a joke?" In that case, you might say, "I'm not so sure about that, let's talk about that a

little more." The key, Mr. Strong says, is to continue the dialogue, hear the other person's concerns, and point out your own. "There are times when you're just going to have to admit defeat and end it," he adds, "but I have to feel that I did the best I could."

15 When the offending remark is made in the presence of others—at a staff meeting, for example—it can be even more distressing than an insult made privately.

16 "You have two options," says William Newlin, director of field services for the Community Relations division of the New York City Commission on Human Rights. "You can respond immediately at the meeting, or you can delay your response until afterward in private. But a response has to come."

17 Some remarks or actions may be so outrageous that they cannot go unnoted at the moment, regardless of the speaker or the setting. But in general, psychologists say, shaming a person in public may have the opposite effect of the one you want: The speaker will deny his offense all the more strongly in order to save face. Further, few people enjoy being put on the spot, and if the remark really was not intended to be offensive, publicly embarrassing the person who made it may cause an unnecessary rift or further misunderstanding. Finally, most people just don't react as well or thoughtfully under a public spotlight as they would in private.

18 Keeping that in mind, an excellent alternative is to take the offender aside afterward: "Could we talk for a minute in private?" Then use the strategies suggested above for calmly stating how you feel, giving the speaker the benefit of the doubt, and proceeding from there.

19 At a large meeting or public talk, you might consider passing the speaker a note, says David Wertheimer, executive director of the New York City Gay and Lesbian Anti-Violence Project: You could write, "You may not realize it, but your remarks were offensive because . . ."

20 "Think of your role as that of an educator," suggests James M. Jones, Ph.D., executive director for public interest at the American Psychological Association. "You have to be controlled."

21 Regardless of the setting or situation, speaking up always raises the risk of rocking the boat. If the person who made the offending remark is your boss, there may be an even bigger risk to consider: How will this affect my job? Several things can help minimize the risk, however. First, know what other resources you may have at work, suggests Caryl Stern, director of the A World of Difference—New York City campaign: Does your personnel office handle discrimination complaints? Are other grievance procedures in place?

22 You won't necessarily need to use any of these procedures, Ms. Stern stresses. In fact, she advises, "It's usually better to try a one-on-one approach first." But simply knowing a formal system exists can make you feel secure enough to set up that meeting.

23 You can also raise the issue with other colleagues who heard the remark: Did they feel the same way you did? The more support you have, the less alone you will feel. Your point will also carry more validity and be more difficult to shrug off. Finally, give your boss credit—and the benefit of the doubt: "I know you've worked hard for the company's affirmative action programs, so I'm sure you didn't realize what those remarks sounded like to me as well as the others at the meeting last week . . ."

24   If, even after this discussion, the problem persists, go back for another meeting, Ms. Stern advises. And if that, too, fails, you'll know what other options are available to you.

25   *It's a spirited dinner party, and everyone's having a good time, until one guest starts reciting a racist joke. Everyone at the table is white, including you. The others are still laughing, as you wonder what to say or do.*

"The others are still laughing, as you wonder what to say or do."

26   No one likes being seen as a party-pooper, but before deciding that you'd prefer not to take on this role, you might remember that the person who told the offensive joke has already ruined your good time.

27   If it's a group that you feel comfortable in—a family gathering, for instance—you will feel freer to speak up. Still, shaming the person by shouting, "You're wrong" or "That's not funny!" probably won't get your point across as effectively as other strategies. "If you interrupt people to condemn them, it just makes it harder," says Cherie Brown. She suggests trying instead to get at the resentments that lie beneath the joke by asking open-ended questions: "Grandpa, I know you always treat everyone with such respect. Why do people in our family talk that way about black people?" The key, Ms. Brown says, "is to listen to them first, so they will be more likely to listen to you."

28   If you don't know your fellow guests well, before speaking up you could turn discreetly to your neighbors (or excuse yourself to help the host or hostess in the kitchen) to get a reading on how they felt, and whether or not you'll find support for speaking up: "I know you probably didn't mean anything by that joke, Jim, but it really offended me . . ." "It's important to say that *you* were offended—not state how the group that is the butt of the joke would feel. "Otherwise," LeNorman Strong says, "you risk coming off as a goody-two-shoes."

29   If you yourself are the host, you can exercise more control; you are, after all, the one who sets the rules and the tone of behavior in your home. Once, when Professor Kahn's party guests began singing offensive, racist songs, for instance, he kicked them all out, saying, "You don't sing songs like that in my house!" And, he adds, "they never did again."

30   *At school one day, a friend comes over and says, "Who do you think you are, hanging out with Joe? If you can be friends with those people, I'm through with you!"*

31   Peer pressure can weigh heavily on kids. They feel vulnerable and, because they are kids, they aren't as able to control the urge to fight. "But if you learn to handle these situations as kids, you'll be better able to handle them as an adult," William Newlin points out.

32   Begin by redefining to yourself what a friend is and examining what friendship means, advises Amy Lee, a human relations specialist at Panel of Americans, an intergroup-relations training and educational organization. If that person from a different group fits your requirement for a friend, ask, "Why shouldn't I be friends with Joe? We have a lot in common." Try to get more information about whatever stereotypes or resentments lie beneath your friend's statement. Ms. Lee suggests: "What makes you think they're so different

from us? Where did you get that information?" She explains: "People are learning these stereotypes from somewhere, and they cannot be blamed for that. So examine where these ideas come from." Then talk about how your own experience rebuts them.

33 Kids, like adults, should also be aware of other resources to back them up: Does the school offer special programs for fighting prejudice? How supportive will the principal, the teachers, or other students be? If the school atmosphere is volatile, experts warn, make sure that taking a stand at that moment won't put you in physical danger. If that is the case, it's better to look for other alternatives.

34 These can include programs or organizations that bring kids from different backgrounds together. "When kids work together across race lines, that is how you break down the barriers and see that the stereotypes are not true," says Laurie Meadoff, president of CityKids Foundation, a nonprofit group whose programs attempt to do just that. Such programs can also provide what Cherie Brown calls a "safe place" to express the anger and pain that slurs and other offenses cause, whether the bigotry is directed against you or others.

35 In learning to speak up, everyone will develop a different style and a slightly different message to get across, experts agree. But it would be hard to do better than these two messages suggested by teenagers at CityKids: "Everyone on the face of the earth has the same intestines," said one. Another added, "Cross over the bridge. There's a lot of love on the streets."

READING CLOSELY AND THINKING CRITICALLY

1. According to Cole, why is it important to respond to racial, ethnic, and sexist slurs?
2. Why does Cole say it is best not to laugh at racial slurs and offensive ethnic jokes?
3. When a person makes an offensive remark, why is it best not to shame that person publicly?
4. Cole offers procedures to help children deal with bigotry. Why do you think she includes information for children?
5. Did you learn anything as a result of reading "Don't Just Stand There"? If so, explain what you learned.

EXAMINING STRUCTURE AND STRATEGY

1. Which sentence is Cole's thesis because it presents the process under consideration?
2. Cite three paragraphs that explain what not to do and why. Which paragraph presents a troublesome aspect of the process?
3. Cole includes a considerable number of quotations. What do you think these quotations contribute? Do they help the author achieve her purpose? Explain.

NOTING COMBINED PATTERNS

1. How does the narration in paragraphs 1 and 2 help Cole achieve her purpose?
2. Cole frequently uses exemplification. Cite at least three examples and explain how they help Cole achieve her purpose.

CONSIDERING LANGUAGE AND STYLE

1. Cole uses first- and second-person pronouns (I, we, you, me, us). Why does she use these pronouns rather than third-person pronouns (he, she, they)?
2. Paragraphs 8, 25, and 30 are set off with extra spacing and italics. Why?
3. Consult a dictionary if you are unsure of the meaning of any of these words: *ebullience* (paragraph 1), *tinged* (paragraph 1), *anti-Semitic* (paragraph 1), *rift* (paragraph 17), *volatile* (paragraph 33).

FOR DISCUSSION IN CLASS OR ONLINE

Is any of the advice in the essay "easier said than done"? Explain why or why not. If your instructor so directs, post your response to your class Web site.

WRITING ASSIGNMENTS

1. **In your journal.** Write about a time when you overheard a racial, sexist, or ethnic slur. How did you respond and why did you respond that way? After reading Cole's essay, do you think you could have handled yourself differently? Explain.
2. **Using process analysis for a purpose.** The purposes in the assignments are possibilities. You may establish whatever purposes you like, within your instructor's guidelines.
   - Select a hurtful behavior (for example, classroom cheating, lying, or teenage drinking) and to inform your reader, describe a process for dealing with it.
   - Select a bothersome behavior that is not harmful (for example, talking in theaters, rudeness by salespeople, channel-switching by the person with the remote control, or inattentive table servers). To inform your reader, explain a process for dealing with the behavior.
   - Inform your reader and relate your experience by explaining your own procedure for dealing with ethnic, sexist, and/or racial slurs.
3. **Combining patterns.** Racial, ethnic, gender, and other forms of bias are current facts of life. Using cause-and-effect analysis (explained in Chapter 9), explain how you think bias originates in people or why people and society allow the bias to persist. Then use process analysis to explain what you think can be done to address the bias.
4. **Connecting the readings.** Summarize the positions of Diane Cole in "Don't Just Stand There" and Nat Hentoff in "Free Speech on Campus" (page 605). Then indicate which author you agree with and why.
5. **Drawing on sources.** Research the policy and procedure for handling discrimination and harassment at either your college or your workplace. Explain whether or not the policy and procedure are satisfactory and why.

BACKGROUND: Born in 1950 in West Virginia, Henry Louis Gates, Jr., taught at Yale, Cornell (where he was the first African-American male to hold an endowed chair), and Duke before joining the faculty of Harvard as the director of the W.E.B. DuBois Institute for Afro-American Research. He is also the chair of Harvard's Afro-American Studies Department. His many honors and grants include a MacArthur Foundation "genius grant" (1981), and a mention as one of *Time* magazine's "25 Most Influential Americans" (1997). Gates's book of critical theory, *The Signifying Monkey: Towards a Theory of Afro-American Literary Criticism* (1989) earned him the American Book Award and brought him great public attention. A prolific author, Gates has written many volumes of literary criticism. He has also written *Colored People: A Memoir* (1994); *The Future of the Race* (1996); and with Cornel West, *Thirteen Ways of Looking at a Black Man* (1997). His most recent work is *African American Lives* (2004), which he edited with Evelyn Higgenbotham. "In the Kitchen" first appeared in 1994 in *The New Yorker,* a weekly magazine of literature, commentary, and in-depth reporting as well as entertainment reviews and listings for New York City.

www.mhhe.com/patterns

For more information on this author, go to

More resources > Chapter 7 > Henry Louis Gates, Jr.

COMBINED PATTERNS AND THEIR PURPOSES: "In the Kitchen" is part memoir, part political statement. In the essay, Henry Louis Gates Jr., uses *process analysis, definition,* and *description* to **inform** the reader of several processes African Americans used to straighten their hair, including the one he remembers his mother performing on her clients. At the same time, Gates asks readers to consider the political significance of *why* African Americans altered their appearance. As Gates explains the processes, he also **relates his own experience** observing his mother, and he **expresses his feelings** about what people went through to straighten their hair.

IN THE KITCHEN

HENRY LOUIS GATES, JR.

We always had a gas stove in the kitchen, in our house in Piedmont, West Virginia, where I grew up. Never electric, though using electric became fashionable in Piedmont in the sixties, like using Crest toothpaste rather than Colgate, or watching Huntley and Brinkley rather than Walter Cronkite.[1] But not us: gas, Colgate, and good ole Walter Cronkite, come what may. We used gas partly out of loyalty to Big Mom, Mama's Mama, because she was mostly blind and still loved to cook, and could feel her way more easily with gas than with electric. But the most important thing about our gas-equipped kitchen was that Mama used to do hair there. The "hot comb" was a fine-toothed iron instrument with a long wooden handle and a pair of iron curlers that opened

As you read Think about the ways things have changed—and the ways they have not— since the time of the essay.

---

[1]Chet Huntley and David Brinkley were the anchors of the "Huntley-Brinkley Report," a nightly news program on NBC that ran from 1956 to 1970. Walter Cronkite anchored "The CBS Evening News" from 1962 to 1981.

and closed like scissors. Mama would put it in the gas fire until it glowed. You could smell those prongs heating up.

2   I liked that smell. Not the smell so much, I guess, as what the smell meant for the shape of my day. There was an intimate warmth in the women's tones as they talked with my Mama, doing their hair. I knew what the women had been through to get their hair ready to be "done," because I would watch Mama do it to herself. How that kink could be transformed through grease and fire into that magnificent head of wavy hair was a miracle to me, and still is.

3   Mama would wash her hair over the sink, a towel wrapped around her shoulders, wearing just her slip and her white bra. (We had no shower—just a galvanized tub that we stored in the kitchen—until we moved down Rat Tail Road into Doc Wolverton's house, in 1954.) After she dried it, she would grease her scalp thoroughly with blue Bergamot hair grease, which came in a short, fat jar with a picture of a beautiful colored lady on it. It's important to grease your scalp real good, my Mama would explain, to keep from burning yourself. Of course, her hair would return to its natural kink almost as soon as the hot water and shampoo hit it. To me, it was another miracle how hair so "straight" would so quickly become kinky again the second it even approached some water.

"It's important to grease your scalp . . . to keep from burning yourself."

4   My Mama had only a few "clients" whose heads she "did"—did, I think, because she enjoyed it, rather than for the few pennies it brought in. They would sit on one of our red plastic kitchen chairs, the kind with the shiny metal legs, and brace themselves for the process. Mama would stroke that red-hot iron—which by this time had been in the gas fire for half an hour or more— slowly but firmly through their hair, from scalp to strand's end. It made a scorching, crinkly sound, the hot iron did, as it burned its way through kink, leaving in its wake straight strands of hair, standing long and tall but drooping over at the ends, their shape like the top of a heavy willow tree. Slowly, steadily, Mama's hands would transform a round mound of Odetta kink into a darkened swamp of everglades. The Bergamot made the hair shiny; the heat of the hot iron gave it a brownish-red cast. Once all the hair was as straight as God allows kink to get, Mama would take the well-heated curling iron and twirl the straightened strands into more or less loosely wrapped curls. She claimed that she owed her skill as a hairdresser to the strength in her wrists, and as she worked her little finger would poke out, the way it did when she sipped tea. Mama was a southpaw, and wrote upside down and backward to produce the cleanest, roundest letters you've ever seen.

5   The "kitchen" she would all but remove from sight with a handheld pair of shears, bought just for this purpose. Now, the kitchen was the room in which we were sitting—the room where Mama did hair and washed clothes, and where we all took a bath in that galvanized tub. But the word has another meaning, and the kitchen that I'm speaking of is the very kinky bit of hair at the back of your head, where your neck meets your shirt collar. If there was ever a part of your

African past that resisted assimilation, it was the kitchen. No matter how hot the iron, no matter how powerful the chemical, no matter how stringent the mashed-potatoes-and-lye formula of a man's "process," neither God nor woman nor Sammy Davis, Jr., could straighten the kitchen. The kitchen was permanent, irredeemable, irresistible kink. Unassimilably African. No matter what you did, no matter how hard you tried, you couldn't de-kink a person's kitchen. So you trimmed it off as best you could.

6   When hair had begun to "turn," as they'd say—to return to its natural kinky glory—it was the kitchen that turned first (the kitchen around the back, and nappy edges at the temples). When the kitchen started creeping up the back of the neck, it was time to get your hair done again.

7   Sometimes, after dark, a man would come to have his hair done. It was Mr. Charlie Carroll. He was very light-complected and had a ruddy nose—it made me think of Edmund Gwenn, who played Kris Kringle in "Miracle on 34th Street." At first, Mama did him after my brother, Rocky, and I had gone to sleep. It was only later that we found out that he had come to our house so Mama could iron his hair—not with a hot comb or a curling iron but with our very own Proctor-Silex steam iron. For some reason I never understood, Mr. Charlie would conceal his Frederick Douglass-like[2] mane under a big white Stetson hat. I never saw him take it off except when he came to our house, at night, to have his hair pressed. (Later, Daddy would tell us about Mr. Charlie's most prized piece of knowledge, something that the man would only confide after his hair

had been pressed, as a token of intimacy. "Not many people know this," he'd say, in a tone of circumspection, "but George Washington was Abraham Lincoln's daddy." Nodding solemnly, he'd add the clincher: "A white man told me." Though he was in dead earnest, this became a humorous refrain around our house—"a white man told me"—which we used to punctuate especially preposterous assertions.)

8   My mother examined my daughters' kitchens whenever we went home to visit, in the early eighties. It became a game between us. I had told her not to do it, because I didn't like the politics it suggested—the notion of "good" and "bad" hair. "Good" hair was "straight," "bad" hair kinky. Even in the late sixties, at the height of Black Power, almost nobody could bring themselves to say "bad" for good and "good" for bad. People still said that hair like white people's hair was "good," even if they encapsulated it in a disclaimer, like "what we used to call 'good.'"

9   Maggie would be seated in her high chair, throwing food this way and that, and Mama would be cooing about how cute it all was, how I used to do just like Maggie was doing, and wondering whether her flinging her food with her left hand meant that she was going to be left-handed like Mama. When my daughter was just about covered with Chef Boyardee Spaghetti-O's, Mama would seize the opportunity: wiping her clean, she would tilt Maggie's head to one side and reach down the back of her neck. Sometimes Mama would even rub a curl between her fingers, just to make sure that her bifocals had not deceived her. Then she'd sigh with satisfaction

---

[2]Frederick Douglass (1818–1895), prominent abolitionist and writer.

and relief: No kink . . . yet. Mama! I'd shout, pretending to be angry. Every once in a while, if no one was looking, I'd peek, too.

10   I say "yet" because most black babies are born with soft, silken hair. But after a few months it begins to turn, as inevitably as do the seasons or the leaves on a tree. People once thought baby oil would stop it. They were wrong.

11   Everybody I knew as a child wanted to have good hair. You could be as ugly as homemade sin dipped in misery and still be thought attractive if you had good hair. "Jesus moss," the girls at Camp Lee, Virginia, had called Daddy's naturally "good" hair during the war. I know that he played that thick head of hair for all it was worth, too.

12   My own hair was "not a bad grade," as barbers would tell me when they cut it for the first time. It was like a doctor reporting the results of the first full physical he has given you. Like "You're in good shape" or "Blood pressure's kind of high—better cut down on salt."

13   I spent most of my childhood and adolescence messing with my hair. I definitely wanted straight hair. Like Pop's. When I was about three, I tried to stick a wad of Bazooka bubble gum to that straight hair of his. I suppose what fixed that memory for me is the spanking I got for doing so: he turned me upside down, holding me by my feet, the better to paddle my behind. Little *nigger,* he had shouted, walloping away. I started to laugh about it two days later, when my behind stopped hurting.

"I definitely wanted straight hair. Like Pop's."

14   When black people say "straight," of course, they don't usually mean literally straight—they're not describing hair like, say, Peggy Lipton's (she was the white girl on "The Mod Squad"), or like Mary's of Peter, Paul & Mary fame; black people call that "stringy" hair. No, "straight" just means not kinky, no matter what contours the curl may take. I would have done *anything* to have straight hair—and I used to try everything, short of getting a process.

15   Of the wide variety of techniques and methods I came to master in the challenging prestidigitation of the follicle, almost all had two things in common: a heavy grease and the application of pressure. It's not an accident that some of the biggest black-owned companies in the fifties and sixties made hair products. And I tried them all, in search of that certain silken touch, the one that would leave neither the hand nor the pillow sullied by grease.

16   I always wondered what Frederick Douglass put on *his* hair, or what Phillis Wheatley[3] put on hers. Or why Wheatley has that rag on her head in the little engraving in the frontispiece of her book. One thing is for sure: you can bet that when Phillis Wheatley went to England and saw the Countess of Huntingdon she did not stop by the Queen's coiffeur on her way there. So many black people still get their hair straightened that it's a wonder we don't have a national holiday for Madame C. J. Walker, the woman who invented the process of straightening kinky hair. Call it Jheri-Kurled or call it "relaxed," it's still fried hair.

17   I used all the greases, from sea-blue Bergamot and creamy vanilla Duke (in its

---
[3]Phillis Wheatley (1753–1784), poet who wrote the first book published by an African American.

clear jar with the orange-white-and-green label) to the godfather of grease, the formidable Murray's. Now, Murray's was some *serious* grease. Whereas Bergamot was like oily jello, and Duke was viscous and sickly sweet, Murray's was light brown and *hard.* Hard as lard and twice as greasy, Daddy used to say. Murray's came in an orange can with a press-on top. It was so hard that some people would put a match to the can, just to soften the stuff and make it more manageable. Then, in the late sixties, when Afros came into style, I used Afro Sheen. From Murray's to Duke to Afro Sheen: that was my progression in black consciousness.

18 We used to put hot towels or washrags over our Murray-coated heads, in order to melt the wax into the scalp and the follicles. Unfortunately, the wax also had the habit of running down your neck, ears, and forehead. Not to mention your pillowcase. Another problem was that if you put two palmfuls of Murray's on your head your hair turned white. (Duke did the same thing.) The challenge was to get rid of that white color. Because if you got rid of the white stuff you had a magnificent head of wavy hair. That was the beauty of it: Murray's was so hard that it froze your hair into the wavy style you brushed it into. It looked really good if you wore a part. A lot of guys had parts *cut* into their hair by a barber, either with the clippers or with a straight-edge razor. Especially if you had kinky hair—then you'd generally wear a short razor cut, or what we called a Quo Vadis.

19 We tried to be as innovative as possible. Everyone knew about using a stocking cap, because your father or your uncle wore one whenever something really big was about to happen, whether sacred or secular: a funeral or a dance, a wedding or a trip in which you confronted of-ficial white people. Any time you were trying to look really sharp, you wore a stocking cap in preparation. And if the event was really a big one, you made a new cap. You asked your mother for a pair of her hose, and cut it with scissors about six inches or so from the open end—the end with the elastic that goes up to the top of the thigh. Then you knotted the cut end, and it became a beehive-shaped hat, with an elastic band that you pulled down low on your forehead and down around your neck in the back. To work well, the cap had to fit tightly and snugly, like a press. And it had to fit that tightly because it *was* a press: it pressed your hair with the force of the hose's elastic. If you greased your hair down real good, and left the stocking cap on long enough, voilà: you got a head of pressed-against-the-scalp waves. (You also got a ring around your forehead when you woke up, but it went away.) And then you could enjoy your concrete do. Swore we were bad, too, with all that grease and those flat heads. My brother and I would brush it out a bit in the mornings, so that it looked—well, "natu-ral." Grown men still wear stocking caps especially older men, who generally keep their stocking caps in their top drawers, along with their cufflinks and their see-through silk socks, their "Maverick" ties, their silk handkerchiefs, and whatever else they prize the most.

20 A Murrayed-down stocking cap was the respectable version of the process, which, by contrast, was most definitely not a cool thing to have unless you were an entertainer by trade. Zeke and Keith and Poochie and a few other stars of the high-school basketball team all used to get a process once or twice a year. It was expensive, and you had to go somewhere like Pittsburgh or D.C. or

Uniontown—somewhere where there were enough colored people to support a trade. The guys would disappear, then reappear a day or two later, strutting like peacocks, their hair burned slightly red from the lye base. They'd also wear "rags"—cloths or handkerchiefs—around their heads when they slept or played basketball. Do-rags, they were called. But the result was straight hair, with just a hint of wave. No curl. Do-it-yourselfers took their chances at home with a concoction of mashed potatoes and lye.

21   The most famous process of all, however, outside of the process Malcolm X describes in his "Autobiography," and maybe the process of Sammy Davis, Jr.,[4] was Nat King Cole's process. Nat King Cole[5] had patent-leather hair. That man's got the finest process money can buy, or so Daddy said the night we saw Cole's TV show on NBC. It was November 5, 1956. I remember the date because everyone came to our house to watch it and to celebrate one of Daddy's buddies' birthdays. Yeah, Uncle Joe chimed in, they can do shit to his hair that the average Negro can't even *think* about—secret shit.

22   Nat King Cole was *clean*. I've had an ongoing argument with a Nigerian friend about Nat King Cole for twenty years now. Not about whether he could sing—any fool knows that he could—but about whether or not he was a handkerchief head for wearing that patent-leather process.

23   Sammy Davis, Jr.'s process was the one I detested. It didn't look good on him. Worse still, he liked to have a fried strand dangling down the middle of his forehead, so he could shake it out from the crown when he sang. But Nat King Cole's hair was a thing unto itself, a beautifully sculpted work of art that he and he alone had the right to wear. The only difference between a process and a stocking cap, really, was taste; but Nat King Cole, unlike, say, Michael Jackson, looked *good* in his. His head looked like Valentino's head in the twenties, and some say it was Valentino the process was imitating. But Nat King Cole wore a process because it suited his face, his demeanor, his name, his style. He was as clean as he wanted to be.

24   I had forgotten all about that patent-leather look until one day in 1971, when I was sitting in an Arab restaurant on the island of Zanzibar surrounded by men in fezzes and white caftans, trying to learn how to eat curried goat and rice with the fingers of my right hand and feeling two million miles from home. All of a sudden, an old transistor radio sitting on top of a china cupboard stopped blaring out its Swahili music and started playing "Fly Me to the Moon," by Nat King Cole. The restaurant's din was not affected at all, but in my mind's eye I saw it: the King's magnificent sleek black tiara. I managed, barely, to blink back the tears.

---

[4]Sammy Davis, Jr. (1925–1990), African-American singer, actor, and dancer.
[5]Nat King Cole (1919–1965), African-American singer and musician.

READING CLOSELY AND THINKING CRITICALLY

1.   Why is Gates so interested in the process his mother used to straighten hair? Why does he find that process and other hair-straightening processes important enough to write an essay about them?

2. Why did African Americans endure the difficult process of straightening their hair? Why have many people discontinued the practice in more recent years?
3. Why does Gates check his daughter's hair for kink? Why does he do so only when no one is looking?
4. What is the "patent-leather" look? Why did it suit Nat King Cole?
5. Why did Gates have to "blink back the tears" when he heard a Nat King Cole recording in Zanzibar?

EXAMINING STRUCTURE AND STRATEGY

1. Paragraph 18 includes information about why a step was performed and problems associated with a step. Why does Gates include this information?
2. Why do you think Gates titled his essay "In the Kitchen" rather than "Straightening Hair"?

NOTING COMBINED PATTERNS

1. Gates includes quite a bit of description in the essay. For example, paragraph 1 describes the hot comb; paragraph 4 includes description in the explanation of the hair-straightening process; paragraph 17 describes hair grease. What does the extensive use of description suggest about Gates's intended audience? How does it help the author achieve his purpose with that audience?
2. Which paragraphs include definition? How does the definition help Gates achieve his purpose?
3. Gates describes the processed hair of entertainers Nat King Cole and Sammy Davis, Jr., but he does not explain the process they used to achieve their hairstyles. Why not?

CONSIDERING LANGUAGE AND STYLE

1. Gates often uses specific product names. For example, he uses *Bergamot* (paragraph 3), *Murray's* (paragraph 17), and *Afro Sheen* (paragraph 17), rather than "hair grease" or "hair product." Why do you think he uses specific product names?
2. Gates describes Nat King Cole as "clean," but he does not explain his use of the term. Using evidence in the essay for clues, what do you think he means by "clean"?
3. Consult a dictionary if you are unsure of the meaning of any of these words: *galvanized* (paragraphs 3, 5), *southpaw* (paragraph 4), *assimilation* (paragraph 5), *circumspection* (paragraph 7), *refrain* (paragraph 7), *prestidigitation* (paragraph 15), *sullied* (paragraph 15), *viscous* (paragraph 17), *voilà* (paragraph 19).

FOR DISCUSSION IN CLASS OR ONLINE

Some employers require their employees to conform to specific standards of appearance. They may specify no facial hair, no dreadlocks, no long hair on males, no tattoos, or no body piercing. Consider whether such requirements are fair and appropriate. If your instructor so directs, post your response on your class Web site.

1. **In your journal.** To what extent have the times since Gates's childhood changed and to what extent have they stayed the same? Answer in a page or two.

2. **Using process analysis for a purpose.** The purposes in the assignments are possibilities. You may establish whatever purposes you like, within your instructor's guidelines.

   - To relate your experience, express your feelings, and perhaps entertain, explain a process you endure in order to meet society's standard of beauty: shaving, dying your hair, applying makeup, dieting, exercising, getting a permanent, using a hairpiece or wig, and so on.

   - To inform and perhaps persuade, explain the process whereby people decide what looks "good" and what looks "bad." If you like, consider one or more of the following: advertising, parental influence, peer influence, sports figures, the music industry, movies, or television.

   - To inform, write a directional process analysis that will help people avoid being manipulated by society's standards of beauty.

   - To relate your experience, express your feelings, and perhaps entertain, explain a process for purchasing something that affects your appearance, such as clothes, makeup, hair care products, or skin care products.

3. **Combining patterns.** Tell about a time you tried to look a particular way in order to be more like another person or group. Explain the process you followed. For example, in high school, you may have tried to look more like the cheerleaders or more like the football players, or even like a favorite rock star. At work, you may have tried to look more like your supervisor. Use cause-and-effect analysis (explained in Chapter 9) to explain what motivated you and how you were affected by your attempt.

4. **Connecting the readings.** Discuss one way people are affected by their childhood contexts. For ideas, you can draw on your own experience, along with "In the Kitchen" and "My Neighborhood" (page 124).

5. **Drawing on sources.** Hairstyles have always changed with the times, but one thing has remained constant: For much of history, people have cut, colored, curled, straightened, and otherwise forced their hair into unnatural styles and colors. Why are people so obsessed with hair? How far will we go to alter our hair's natural looks? For ideas, you can go to *www.google.com* and type in the keywords, "history of hairstyles," or in your library's reference room check the *Reader's Guide to Periodical Literature* or the *Encyclopedia of Popular Culture* under the heading "hairstyles."

BACKGROUND: Timothy Harper is a prolific freelance writer who has won a number of awards. He writes on a remarkable range of subjects, including politics, economics, business, law, art, health, family, education, medicine, and technology. This variety of subjects has allowed him to publish in a surprising array of publications, including *The Atlantic Monthly, Reader's Digest, Time, Glamour, Seventeen, Delta Sky, Metropolitan Home, Cooking Light, Advertising Age, Medical Economics,* the *American Bar Association Journal,* and the *New York Times.* He has also written several books, including *Cracking the New European Markets* (1992), *Moscow Madness* (1999), and *Doing Good* (2001). From 1974 to 1984, Harper worked for the Associated Press and covered a number of important national stories. He earned a law degree from the University of Wisconsin and currently teaches at Columbia University Graduate School of Journalism. "Shoot to Kill" first appeared in *The Atlantic Monthly* in October 2000.

COMBINED PATTERNS AND THEIR PURPOSE: In "Shoot to Kill," Timothy Harper uses *process analysis* to **inform** his audience about how the 1999 shootings at Columbine High School changed the emergency response procedures of police departments around the country. As you read, notice that Harper explains more than one process. Notice, too, that he combines those process analyses with *contrast* and *cause-and-effect analysis.* You will even find an element of *description* in the piece.

SHOOT TO KILL

TIMOTHY HARPER

His ears ringing from gunfire, his uniform damp with sweat, his breath labored and acrid-tasting from the gunpowder in the air, Officer Larry Layman ran heavily down a hallway toward an insistent *pop-pop-pop*. A gunman was running through a school shooting children, and Layman was chasing him. Layman rounded a corner, holding his gun in front of him with two stiff arms, and stopped dead. The gunman stood facing him, with an arm around a hostage's neck and a gun held to the hostage's head. "Drop your gun or I'll blow his head off!" the gunman screamed. Layman, a police officer for more than half his fifty years, had been trained always to drop his gun at a moment like this. Now he fired.

2   This was only a training exercise. But the point of this training is something radically new and different, and it is unsettling for Larry Layman, his fellow officers in Peoria, Illinois, and thousands of other law-enforcement officers across the country. Historically, the police in the United States have employed a standard response when confronted with armed suspects in schools, malls, banks, post offices, and other heavily populated buildings. The first officers to arrive never rushed in. Instead they set up perimeters and controlled the scene. They tried to contain the suspects, and called in a rigorously trained Special Weapons and Tactics (SWAT) team. The SWAT team arrived, assumed positions to keep the suspects pinned down, and negotiated with them until they surrendered. SWAT teams stormed buildings only when necessary to save lives, such as when hostages were being executed one by one.

3   Today, however, police officers are setting aside traditional tactics. They are being taught to enter a building if they are the first to arrive at the scene, to

> **As you read**
> Decide how the author feels about police officers.

chase the gunman, and to kill or disable him as quickly as possible. This sweeping change in police tactics—variously called rapid-response, emergency-response, or first-responder—is a direct result of the shootings that occurred at Columbine High School, in Littleton, Colorado, on April 20 of last year,[1] which was the worst in a series of shootings in schools across the United States in the 1990s. Two students armed with bombs and guns invaded Columbine and wandered through the school, firing indiscriminately. Twelve students and a teacher died, and twenty-three other students were wounded. The shooters took their own lives.

4   The first 911 call from Columbine that day came at 11:19 A.M. Nearly all the victims were shot during the next seventeen minutes, according to a reconstruction released a year later by the Jefferson County Sheriff's Department. The report noted that a deputy sheriff reached the scene at 11:23, four minutes after the call. Many more officers—eventually nearly a thousand of them—quickly converged on the school. But the first policemen to go in—a five-man SWAT team, moving cautiously—did not enter the school until 12:06, forty-three minutes after the first officers had arrived. The two shooters killed themselves at 12:08. Some of the wounded were not brought out until after 3:00 P.M. The teacher, reportedly, died from loss of blood before the paramedics reached him.

5   Fifteen families of Columbine victims have filed lawsuits against Jefferson County, and several of those suits claim that lives could have been saved if the police had entered the school sooner. The consensus among law-enforcement

"The consensus among law-enforcement authorities across the country is that Columbine was handled by the book—but that the book should be rewritten."

authorities across the country is that Columbine was handled by the book—but that the book should be rewritten. The traditional police response was designed for dealing with trapped bank robbers, angry husbands, or disgruntled employees—not with disaffected teenagers running through a school killing as many people as possible.

6   Larry Glick, the executive director of the National Tactical Officers Association, says that Columbine almost immediately became a seminal event in the history of police training and tactics. Most of the nation's 17,000 police agencies, he says, especially the roughly 2,000 agencies with fifty or more officers, have instituted new rapid-response training programs in the past year. These programs are intended to train all police officers—not just SWAT teams—to respond swiftly and aggressively if they are among the first officers on the scene. Glick's association, with 37,000 members from 3,500 participating police agencies, teaches SWAT specialists to retrain their fellow officers, including everyday patrolmen like Larry Layman.

7   "The time line of the violence—from the time the shooting begins until it's over—is short," Glick says. "Traditional police responses just may not cut it." Typically, he says, an officer arrives on the

[1]1999.

scene within three or four minutes, but it takes thirty to sixty minutes to muster a SWAT team. Under the new training, the first four or five officers on a scene, no matter what their rank or experience, form a "contact team" and go in. "Their sole purpose is to move right to the shooter and stop him, using whatever force is necessary," Glick says. The contact team is supposed to pursue gunmen, pressure them to keep moving, and prevent them from taking over populated areas. (The Columbine killers seized the school library, where they killed ten and wounded twelve of their victims.)

8   The training simulates the horror and confusion of a Columbine-style shooting. Bombs explode. Water gushes from broken pipes and rains down from sprinkler systems. The lights go off. Trainers acting like madmen fire "simunitions"—nonlethal bullets that splatter paint on contact—at the trainees. Other trainers, acting as innocent bystanders or wounded victims, run toward the officers, pleading for help. Officers were traditionally trained to help the wounded and evacuate bystanders. Now they are taught to step over the wounded, push bystanders aside, and keep pursuing the shooters. In the past SWAT marksmen were expected to put a shooter down. Now every officer is instructed to "take the shot if you have it." Glick acknowledges that the fear of lawsuits is one factor behind the new tactics. "Do lawsuits drive training?" he says. "Absolutely. But the bottom line is that this training can save lives."

9   The day after Columbine, municipal officials and police chiefs across the nation asked their SWAT team leaders, "If it had happened here, what would have been the result?" They received answers similar to the one that Sergeant Jeff Adams, a longtime SWAT team leader and trainer in Peoria, gave: "The same thing would have happened here." Adams and other trainers for Peoria's Special Response Team (which, he says, was renamed because "SWAT" emphasizes weapons) went through their own retraining last winter. In March they began passing along the new tactics to each of Peoria's 235 active officers. "Columbine was a wakeup call," Adams says.

10   Under the Peoria Police Department's new rapid-response protocol, the first officer on the scene of a Columbine-style shooting waits until three others arrive to form a contact team. Officers in a smaller group or alone would not have 360-degree coverage, Adams says, and Rambo-style freelancing would confuse communications and increase the chances of "blue on blue" casualties: police officers shooting each other. The contact team forms a diamond, with a point, two flanks, and a rear guard handling radio communications. The team enters the building and moves through it as quickly as possible; team members maintain their relative positions so that they can see and hear each other. In a large building a second team may go in, either to help track down the shooters or to rescue bystanders and the wounded.

11   Adams says that gunmen are less likely to fire at innocent bystanders if they are shooting at pursuing police officers. "We train them to move to the sound of gunfire," he says. "Shooting scenes are very chaotic and stressful. You experience sensory overload. Every time you hear a gun-shot, assume someone has been wounded. Try to take ground, and isolate the shooter. If the shooter decides to commit suicide by police, we'll oblige. The person making the decision on how it

will end is the bad guy. We're just reacting." Adams says, however, that "deadly force imperatives" have not changed for the Peoria police. "We teach that you should shoot what you know, not what you think you know. That man with a gun in his hand who steps out of a doorway may be a plainclothes police officer or a school security guard. Or maybe a teacher who brought a gun to school."

12 Neither trainees nor trainers doubt that the new tactics heighten the risks that police officers must accept in the line of duty. "Most officers fit into a rescue role better than an attack role," Adams acknowledges. His message to reluctant trainees in Peoria is grim: "You are a police officer. No one wants to do this. But you swore an oath of office. Your oath of office promises to serve and protect. Let's say it's your wife or children in there. What do you want me to do?" Adams has had to pull aside a couple of officers who were having difficulty with the training. "What you're seeing is terrible," he said to them. "That's why we've got to stop it."

> "Adams has had to pull aside a couple of officers who were having difficulty with the training."

13 To David Klinger, a former police officer who is now a professor of criminology at the University of Missouri at St. Louis, the unease caused by the new training is understandable. "It points up how most policemen don't ever think of using force, deadly force," he says. "It's not something officers contemplate. But now they have to contemplate it. It goes against the doctrines that we've been teaching officers for a long time. It's not

going to be easy. The answer is to train more, and to let officers know that ninety-nine percent of the time they should still wait, but that in some circumstances waiting is wrong."

14 So far rapid-response training has encountered little public opposition, but Klinger expects that will change the first time the police kill a suspect instead of capturing him, or the first time an officer firing at a suspect hits an innocent person instead. "We're going to have to come to the conclusion in our society that in some situations the police need to shoot people," he says. "Regardless of the outcome, we have to accept that, even knowing that mistakes are possible. It's an incredibly complex situation in an incredibly dynamic environment."

15 The Peoria Police Department conducted its training in a department store that had gone out of business. Larry Layman and his fellow trainees wore and carried standard equipment, including bulletproof vests. The only special items employed in the exercise were simunitions, carried by the officers as well as by the trainers, and hockey-style helmets with clear-plastic visors. After lectures and videos explaining the new tactics, Layman and the three other officers in his contact team were sent into a "live" exercise. They were told that one or more gunmen were running rampant in a school. Layman was the team's point man when the trainer shouted "Go!"

16 "It was instant chaos," Layman recalls. He heard gunfire down the hall, and began moving quickly, almost running, toward it. A man shot him and then disappeared around a corner. Layman felt the pain in his arm, glanced at the splotch of red paint, and knew he'd have a bruise later. He kept jogging, making sure he didn't get too far ahead

of his team. "The trainers told us we couldn't quit, even if we were hit," he said. "We had to keep going."

17   Layman stepped over people who were lying on the floor, playing wounded students. They moaned that they were hurt, clutched at his legs, and begged him to stop and help them. One man, playing a terrified but unhurt student, leaped from a doorway and grabbed him. Layman wrestled the man away and pushed him toward his trailing teammates, who in turn pushed the man behind them and told him to run back down the hallway to the exit. Another man leaped from a doorway, but this one fired at Layman's team. Others, with guns blazing, attacked from behind or sniped at the officers from doorways. When the contact team's blue-paint simunitions struck the attackers squarely on their vests or helmets, the gunmen stepped aside. They were out of the exercise.

18   One gunman stayed just ahead of Layman, shooting and then ducking around corners as Layman chased him and fired back. Often during his career Layman had considered switching to one of the high-powered semiautomatics that many younger officers now carry. Maybe a .45-caliber or a 9mm, maybe a fifteen-shot rapid-fire Glock. At that moment, however, he was glad to have his old .38, the six-shooter he had been carrying for twenty-six years. Younger policemen laughed at his weapon and called it an underpowered antique, but it felt like an old friend in his hands as he fired all six shots and reloaded on the run, again and again. "In the old days, if you had to shoot your gun, they taught you to fire in a burst of two shots and then assess," Layman says. "You'd pause. Then another burst of two, and assess again. In this new training they teach you that if you are going to shoot your gun, you empty it."

19   When he came upon the suspect holding the gun to the hostage's head, Layman's initial impulse was to drop his gun. "That's what you were always taught—drop the gun, just like on the TV shows," he says. "Now they teach you to shoot. They say if you don't shoot, the hostage is probably going to die anyway." Most of the gunman's body was shielded by the hostage, but Layman did not hesitate. He took the shot. Blue paint exploded against the gunman's helmet. "Only about a quarter of this bad guy's head was visible, but I hit it," Layman says, marveling. "I surprised myself. At the end of the chase I was able to hit a target. I was able to stay focused and just keep shooting."

20   His clean head shot ended the exercise. The whole thing had taken barely three minutes, but it had seemed like three hours to Layman. He accepted muted congratulations on his shot, and then sat with his contact team in a debriefing room. Layman was panting and exhausted. He was having trouble hearing in the aftermath of the gunfire. His muscles ached as his adrenaline level returned to normal. He was going to be sore all over, and black and blue where he'd been shot in the arms and legs. The trainers went over what Layman and his team had done well, and reviewed the instances in which they had been "killed." The trainers and the contact team talked for twenty minutes about what the officers could or should do differently in a live situation.

21   "Okay, you guys, good job," the officer overseeing the training finally said. "Now let's do it again."

22   Layman groaned. He grudgingly strapped his vest and helmet back on, and reloaded his gun. "You can't imagine

the fatigue from a shoot-'em-up scenario like that," he says. A few minutes later he and his team were in a different part of the old department store, with a different layout and different shooters. This time they were the second team in, the rescue team. Their job was to follow the contact team, direct unhurt people toward a safe exit, and get the wounded out. "Triage is a big part of it," Layman says. "You have to make immediate decisions about who to take out, who to stop and help. It's tragic, but if several people are down, you go to the first one, and if that person is going to die, you go on to the next one."

23   A couple of nights later, nursing his aches and pains with a light beer and a cheap cigar, Layman confessed that the training unnerved him. "It's so different from what we've always been taught. It's contrary to what's become almost instinct for us," he told me. He said he's also uncertain whether all police officers can or should be put into rapid-response situations. "The first cops running into that building are going to be beat cops. If it's a school or an office building, it's probably going to be daytime during the week. The cops with the most seniority work days— the old cops, like me. A lot of older cops are just putting in their time until retirement. They don't sit around talking about police tactics. They talk about where

they're going to live in Florida, or the fishing trips they're going to take in Wisconsin. I let myself get out of shape over the years, and there are other fat old doughnut-eating cops who are worse than me. I wouldn't want to go into a situation like Columbine with those guys, and I wouldn't blame another cop for not wanting to go in with me. It scares me."

24   At the same time, he says, he's glad he had the training. "Even the thought of it is terrifying, but as long as the nuts are out there, we have to prepare for them," he says. He would welcome more training, but doubts that his department, or any other, can adequately train every single police officer for a Columbine-style shooting. "The new training doesn't come close to what would be needed," he says. "To be really prepared for something like that, we would need to be trained almost weekly."

25   Two months after that rapid-response training session, Layman told me that it had helped motivate him to get into better shape. He began working out more, and went on a diet. He managed to lose twenty-five pounds. "The whole experience has been a real reminder of what cops are supposed to be able to do," he says. "I pray to God I'm never in a situation like that, but if I am, I want to be able to do my part."

READING CLOSELY AND THINKING CRITICALLY

1.   Why are some families of Columbine victims suing Jefferson County?

2.   Why have rapid-response police procedures changed as a result of the Columbine shootings?

3.   How have rapid-response police procedures changed since the Columbine shootings?

4.   What aspect of the new rapid-response procedures do some police officers find troubling? Why?

5.   How does the author feel about police officers? How can you tell?

EXAMINING STRUCTURE AND STRATEGY

1. The original audience of "Shoot to Kill" was the readers of *The Atlantic Monthly,* a magazine of literature, reviews of the arts, political commentary, and in-depth reporting. Readers are likely to share the magazine's politically liberal view point. Are the title and opening paragraph likely to engage the interest of the readers of that magazine? Explain.
2. Harper uses many direct quotations. How do these quotations help the author achieve his purpose?
3. Harper does not specifically state the importance of the processes he explains. Does he need to? Why or why not?

NOTING COMBINED PATTERNS

1. Harper uses several patterns of development in "Shoot to Kill." Where does process analysis appear? Where do you find contrast? Where is cause-and-effect analysis used?
2. Paragraph 8 includes description. What does the description add to the essay, and how does it help Harper achieve his purpose?

CONSIDERING LANGUAGE AND STYLE

1. Read the first sentence of the essay aloud. Why is the sentence so effective?
2. In paragraph 10, Harper refers to "Rambo-style freelancing." What does the phrase mean? Explain the reference to "Rambo."
3. Consult a dictionary if you are unsure of the meaning of these words: *converged* (paragraph 4), *disaffected* (paragraph 5), *seminal* (paragraph 6), *muster* (paragraph 7), *protocol* (paragraph 10), *rampant* (paragraph 15), *triage* (paragraph 22).

FOR DISCUSSION IN CLASS OR ONLINE

What kind of person would make a good police officer in today's society? Specifically what traits should the person have? What traits should he or she *not* have? If your instructor so directs, post your response to your class Web site.

WRITING ASSIGNMENTS

1. **In your journal.** Do you think the families of the Columbine victims should sue Jefferson County? Give the reasons for your view in a page or so.
2. **Using process analysis for a purpose.** The purposes in the assignments are possibilities. You may establish whatever purposes you like, within your instructor's guidelines.
   - If you have ever done anything with some risk associated with it (white-water rafting, rock climbing, putting shingles on a roof), explain the process to relate your experience, express your feelings, and perhaps inform. Be sure to communicate the danger associated with the process.

- To relate your experience, express your feelings, and perhaps inform, explain a process you perform with some reluctance (for example, administer your own insulin shots, wash the dog, fire an employee, or discipline a child).
- School children face a number of risks other than from shootings. For example, they can be at risk from students who push drugs, gangs who encourage violence, kidnappers on the way to school, and peer groups that party with alcohol. To inform, explain a process that will help school children deal with one of the risks they face.

3. **Combining patterns.** Use process analysis to tell about something you do differently now than you did in the past. Contrast (explained in Chapter 8) the current and previous processes. Consider, for example, past and present holiday celebrations, college and high school study techniques, or correspondence you handled by letters that you now handle by e-mail.

4. **Connecting the readings.** Discuss one or more reasons for violent incidents that occur in our schools (including colleges if you wish), or discuss one or more effects of that violence, or discuss one or more ways to reduce the violence. In addition to your own ideas, you can draw on "Shoot to Kill" and "What Is Behind the Growth of Violence on College Campuses?" on page 394.

5. **Drawing on sources.** One theory advanced to explain why young people shoot their classmates and teachers suggests that the shooters suffer from the effects of being bullied in school. Consider what schools can do to deal effectively with bullying. For ideas, you can look up "bullying" in *Education Index* in your library. On the Internet, type the keyword *bullying* in your favorite search engine.

BACKGROUND: One of six daughters, Jessica Mitford (1917–1996) was born in England to aristocratic parents, but she never took to the aristocratic way of life. Eventually, she moved to California, became a U.S. citizen, joined the Communist Party, and held a number of jobs, including working as executive secretary for the Civil Rights Congress and teaching sociology at San Jose State University. After resigning from the Communist Party in 1958, Mitford devoted her time to writing, achieving fame as an investigative journalist who exposed corruption and excess in such American institutions as the funeral, television, prison, and diet industries. For her efforts, *Time* magazine dubbed her the "Queen of the Muckrakers." (A *muckraker* searches out and exposes misconduct.) Mitford's works include *Kind and Unusual Punishment: The Prison Business* (1979); *Poison Penmanship* (1979), a collection of her articles from the *Atlantic Monthly, Harper's,* and other magazines; and two volumes of autobiography. "Behind the Formaldehyde Curtain" is taken from Mitford's first investigative study, the 1963 exposé of the funeral business, *The American Way of Death.* Denounced by the funeral industry, the book was very successful and formed the basis of a television documentary.

www.mhhe.com/patterns

For more information on this author, go to

More resources > Chapter 7 > Jessica Mitford

COMBINED PATTERNS AND THEIR PURPOSES: In "Behind the Formaldehyde Curtain, "Jessica Mitford **argues** that the funeral industry extracts money for unnecessary services. At the same time, she **informs** the reader, by explaining the *process* of embalming. The excerpt also includes graphic *description* that is sometimes shocking.

Behind the Formaldehyde Curtain

JESSICA MITFORD

The drama begins to unfold with the arrival of the corpse at the mortuary.

2   Alas, poor Yorick.[1] How surprised he would be to see how his counterpart of today is whisked off to a funeral parlor and is in short order sprayed, sliced, pierced, pickled, trussed, trimmed, creamed, waxed, painted, rouged, and neatly dressed—transformed from a common corpse into a Beautiful Memory Picture. This process is known in the trade as embalming and restorative art, and is so universally employed in the United States and Canada that the funeral director does it routinely, without consulting corpse or kin.[2] He regards as eccentric those few who are hardy enough to suggest that it might be dispensed with. Yet no law requires embalming, no religious doctrine commends it, nor is it dictated by considerations of health, sanitation, or

As you read Think how Mitford reveals her attitude about her subject.

---

[1] The reference is to Hamlet's graveyard speech to Horatio about Yorick, who was buried but not embalmed.

[2] The Federal Trade Commission now requires that families be informed that embalming is optional.

even of personal daintiness. In no part of the world but in Northern America is it widely used. The purpose of embalming is to make the corpse presentable for viewing in a suitably costly container; and here too the funeral director routinely, without first consulting the family, prepares the body for public display.

3   Is all this legal? The processes to which a dead body may be subjected are after all to some extent circumscribed by law. In most states, for instance, the signature of next of kin must be obtained before an autopsy may be performed, before the deceased may be cremated, before the body may be turned over to a medical school for research purposes; or such provision must be made in the decedent's will. In the case of embalming, no such permission is required nor is it ever sought. A textbook, *The Principles and Practices of Embalming,* comments on this: "There is some question regarding the legality of much that is done within the preparation room." The author points out that it would be most unusual for a responsible member of a bereaved family to instruct the mortician, in so many words, to "embalm" the body of a deceased relative. The very term *embalming* is so seldom used that the mortician must rely upon custom in the matter. The author concludes that unless the family specifies otherwise, the act of entrusting the body to the care of a funeral establishment carries with it an implied permission to go ahead and embalm.

4   Embalming is indeed a most extraordinary procedure, and one must wonder at the docility of Americans who each year pay hundreds of millions of dollars for its perpetuation, blissfully ignorant of what it is all about, what is done, how it is done. Not one in ten thousand has any idea of what actually takes place. Books on the subject are extremely hard to come by. They are not to be found in most libraries or bookshops.

5   In an era when huge television audiences watch surgical operations in the comfort of their living rooms, when, thanks to the animated cartoon, the geography of the digestive system has become familiar territory even to the nursery school set, in a land where the satisfaction of curiosity about almost all matters is a national pastime, the secrecy surrounding embalming can, surely, hardly be attributed to the inherent gruesomeness of the subject. Custom in this regard has within this century suffered a complete reversal. In the early days of American embalming, when it was performed in the home of the deceased, it was almost mandatory for some relative to stay by the embalmer's side and witness the procedure. Today, family members who might wish to be in attendance would certainly be dissuaded by the funeral director. All others, except apprentices, are excluded by law from the preparation room.

6   A close look at what does actually take place may explain in large measure the undertaker's intractable reticence concerning a procedure that has become his major *raison d'être.*[3] Is it possible he fears that public information about embalming might lead patrons to wonder if they really want this service? If the funeral men are loath to discuss the subject outside the trade, the reader may, understandably, be equally

---

[3]French phrase meaning "reason for existence."

loath to go on reading at this point. For those who have the stomach for it, let us part the formaldehyde curtain . . .

7   The body is first laid out in the undertaker's morgue—or rather, Mr. Jones is reposing in the preparation room—to be readied to bid the world farewell.

8   The preparation room in any of the better funeral establishments has the tiled and sterile look of a surgery, and indeed the embalmer-restorative artist who does his chores there is beginning to adopt the term *dermasurgeon* (appropriately corrupted by some mortician-writers as "demi-surgeon") to describe his calling. His equipment, consisting of scalpels, scissors, augers, forceps, clamps, needles, pumps, tubes, bowls, and basins, is crudely imitative of the surgeon's, as is his technique, acquired in a nine- or twelve-month post-high-school course in an embalming school. He is supplied by an advanced chemical industry with a bewildering array of fluids, sprays, pastes, oils, powders, creams, to fix or soften tissue, shrink or distend it as needed, dry it here, restore the moisture there. There are cosmetics, waxes, and paints to fill and cover features, even plaster of Paris to replace entire limbs. There are ingenious aids to prop and stabilize the cadaver: a Vari-Pose Head Rest, the Edwards Arm and Hand Positioner, the Repose Block (to support the shoulders during the embalming), and the Throop Foot Positioner, which resembles an old-fashioned stocks.

9   Mr. John H. Eckels, president of the Eckels College of Mortuary Science, thus describes the first part of the embalming procedure: "In the hands of a skilled practitioner, this work may be done in a comparatively short time and without mutilating the body other than by slight incision—so slight that it scarcely would cause serious inconvenience if made upon a living person. It is necessary to remove the blood, and doing this not only helps in the disinfecting, but removes the principal cause of disfigurements due to discoloration."

10   Another textbook discusses the all-important time element: "The earlier this is done, the better, for every hour that elapses between death and embalming will add to the problems and complications encountered . . ." Just how soon should one get going on the embalming? The author tells us, "On the basis of such scanty information made available to this profession through its rudimentary and haphazard system of technical research, we must conclude that the best results are to be obtained if the subject is embalmed before life is completely extinct—that is, before cellular death has occurred. In the average case, this would mean within an hour after somatic death." For those who feel that there is something a little rudimentary, not to say haphazard, about this advice, a comforting thought is offered by another writer. Speaking of fears entertained in early days of premature burial, he points out, "One of the effects of embalming by chemical injection, however, has been to dispel fears of live burial." How true; once the blood is removed, chances of live burial are indeed remote.

11   To return to Mr. Jones, the blood is drained out through the veins and replaced by embalming fluid pumped in through the arteries. As noted in *The Principles and Practices of Embalming,* "every operator has a favorite injection and drainage point—a fact which becomes a handicap only if he fails or refuses to forsake his favorites when conditions demand it." Typical favorites are the carotid artery, femoral artery,

jugular vein, subclavian vein. There are various choices of embalming fluid. If Flextone is used, it will produce a "mild, flexibility rigidity. The skin retains a velvety softness, the tissues are rubbery and pliable. Ideal for women and children." It may be blended with B. and G. Products Company's Lyf-Lyk tint, which is guaranteed to reproduce "nature's own skin texture . . . the velvety appearance of living tissue." Suntone comes in three separate tints: Suntan; Special Cosmetic Tint, a pink shade "especially indicated for female subjects"; and Regular Cosmetic Tint, moderately pink.

12   About three to six gallons of a dyed and perfumed solution of formaldehyde, glycerin, borax, phenol, alcohol, and water is soon circulated through Mr. Jones, whose mouth has been sewn together with a "needle directed upward between the upper lip and gum and brought out through the left nostril," with the corners raised slightly "for a more pleasant expression." If he should be bucktoothed, his teeth are cleaned with Bon Ami and coated with colorless nail polish. His eyes, meanwhile, are closed with flesh-tinted eye caps and eye cement.

13   The next step is to have at Mr. Jones with a thing called a trocar. This is a long, hollow needle attached to a tube. It is jabbed into the abdomen, poked around the entrails and chest cavity, the contents of which are pumped out and replaced with "cavity fluid." This done, and the hole in the abdomen sewn up, Mr. Jones's face is heavily creamed (to protect the skin from burns which may be caused by leakage of the chemicals), and he is covered with a sheet and left unmolested for a while. But not for long—there is more, much more, in store for him. He has been embalmed, but not yet restored, and the best time to start the restorative work is eight to ten hours after embalming, when the tissues have become firm and dry.

14   The object of all this attention to the corpse, it must be remembered, is to make it presentable for viewing in an attitude of healthy repose. "Our customs require the presentation of our dead in the semblance of normality . . . unmarred by the ravages of illness, disease, or mutilation," says Mr. J. Sheridan Mayer in his *Restorative Art.* This is rather a large order since few people die in the full bloom of health, unravaged by illness and unmarked by some disfigurement. The funeral industry is equal to the challenge: "In some cases the gruesome appearance of a mutilated or disease-ridden subject may be quite discouraging. The task of restoration may seem impossible and shake the confidence of the embalmer. This is the time for intestinal fortitude and determination. Once the formative work is begun and affected tissues *are* cleaned or removed, all doubts of success vanish. It is surprising and gratifying to discover the results which may be obtained."

15   The embalmer, having allowed an appropriate interval to elapse, returns to the attack, but now he brings into play the skill and equipment of sculptor and cosmetician. Is a hand missing? Casting one in plaster of Paris is a simple matter. "For replacement purposes, only a cast of the back of the hand is necessary; this is within the ability of the average operator and is quite adequate." If a lip or two, a nose, or an ear should be missing, the embalmer has at hand a variety of restorative waxes with which to model replacements. Pores and skin textures are simulated by stippling with a little brush, and over this cosmetics are laid on. Head off? Decapitation cases are rather routinely handled. Ragged edges are trimmed, and head

joined to torso with a series of splints, wires, and sutures. It is a good idea to have a little something at the neck—a scarf or a high collar—when time for viewing comes. Swollen mouth? Cut out tissue as needed from inside the lips. If too much is removed, the surface contour can easily be restored by padding with cotton. Swollen necks and cheeks are reduced by removing tissue through vertical incisions made down each side of the neck. "When the deceased is casketed, the pillow will hide the suture incisions . . . as an extra precaution against leakage, the suture may be painted with liquid sealer."

16   The opposite condition is more likely to present itself—that of emaciation. His hypodermic syringe now loaded with massage cream, the embalmer seeks out and fills the hollowed and sunken areas by injection. In this procedure the backs of the hands and fingers and the under-chin area should not be neglected.

17   Positioning the lips is a problem that recurrently challenges the ingenuity of the embalmer. Closed too tightly, they tend to give a stern, even disapproving expression. Ideally, embalmers feel, the lips should give the impression of being ever so slightly parted, the upper lip protruding slightly for a more youthful appearance. This takes some engineering, however, as the lips tend to drift apart. Lip drift can sometimes be remedied by pushing one or two straight pins through the inner margin of the lower lip and then inserting them between the two front upper teeth. If Mr. Jones happens to have no teeth, the pins can just as easily be anchored in his Armstrong Face Former and Denture Replacer. Another method to maintain lip closure is to dislocate the lower jaw, which is then held in its new position by a wire run through holes which have been drilled through the upper and lower jaws at the midline. As the French are fond of saying, *il faut souffrir pour être belle.*[4]

18   If Mr. Jones has died of jaundice, the embalming fluid will very likely turn him green. Does this deter the embalmer? Not if he has intenstinal fortitude. Masking pastes and cosmetics are heavily laid on, burial garments and casket interiors are color-correlated with particular care, and Jones is displayed beneath rose-colored lights. Friends will say "How *well* he looks." Death by carbon monoxide, on the other hand, can be rather a good thing from the embalmer's viewpoint: "One advantage is the fact that this type of discoloration is an exaggerated form of a natural pink coloration." This is nice because the healthy glow is already present and needs but little attention.

19   The patching and filling completed, Mr. Jones is now shaved, washed, and dressed. Cream-based cosmetic, available in pink, flesh, suntan, brunette, and blond, is applied to his hands and face, his hair is shampooed and combed (and, in the case of Mrs. Jones, set), his hands manicured. For the horny-handed son of toil special care must be taken; cream should be applied to remove ingrained grime, and the nails cleaned. "If he were not in the habit of having them manicured in life, trimming and shaping is advised for better appearance—never questioned by kin."

20   Jones is now ready for casketing (this is the present participle of the verb "to casket"). In this operation his right shoulder should be depressed slightly "to turn

---

[4]You have to suffer to be beautiful.

the body a bit to the right and soften the appearance of lying flat on the back." Positioning the hands is a matter of importance, and special rubber positioning blocks may be used. The hands should be cupped slightly for a more lifelike, relaxed appearance. Proper placement of the body requires a delicate sense of balance. It should lie as high as possible in the casket, yet not so high that the lid, when lowered, will hit the nose. On the other hand, we are cautioned, placing the body too low "creates the impression that the body is in a box."

21   Jones is next wheeled into the appointed slumber room where a few last touches may be added—his favorite pipe placed in his hand or, if he was a great reader, a book propped into position. (In the case of little Master Jones a Teddy bear may be clutched.) Here he will hold open house for a few days, visiting hours 10 A.M. to 9 P.M.

22   All now being in readiness, the funeral director calls a staff conference to make sure that each assistant knows his precise duties. Mr. Wilber Kriege writes: "This makes your staff feel that they are a part of the team, with a definite assignment that must be properly carried out if the whole plan is to succeed. You never heard of a football coach who failed to talk to his entire team before they go on the field. They have drilled on the plays they are to execute for hours and days, and yet the successful coach knows the importance of making even the bench-warming third-string substitute feel that he is important if the game is to be won." The winning of *this* game is predicated upon glass-smooth handling of the logistics. The funeral director has notified the pallbearers whose names were furnished by the family, has arranged for the presence of clergyman, organist, and soloist, has provided transportation for everybody, has organized and listed the flowers sent by friends. In *Psychology of Funeral Service* Mr. Edward A. Martin points out, "He may not always do as much as the family thinks he is doing, but it is his helpful guidance that they appreciate in knowing they are proceeding as they should . . . The important thing is how well his services can be used to make the family believe they are giving unlimited expression to their own sentiment."

23   The religious service may be held in a church or in a chapel of the funeral home; the funeral director vastly prefers the latter arrangement, for not only is it more convenient for him but it affords him the opportunity to show off his beautiful facilities to the gathered mourners. After the clergyman has had his say, the mourners queue up to file past the casket for a last look at the deceased. The family is *never* asked whether they want an open-casket ceremony; in the absence of their instruction to the contrary, this is taken for granted. Consequently well over 90 percent of all American funerals feature the open casket—a custom unknown in other parts of the world. Foreigners are astonished by it. An English woman living in San Francisco described her reaction in a letter to the writer:

> I myself have attended only one funeral here—that of an elderly fellow worker of mine. After the service I could not understand why everyone was walking towards the coffin (sorry, I mean casket), but thought I had better follow the crowd. It shook me rigid to get there and find the casket open and poor old Oscar lying there in his brown tweed suit, wearing

a suntan makeup and just the wrong shade of lipstick. If I had not been extremely fond of the old boy, I have a horrible feeling that I might have giggled. Then and there I decided that I could never face another American funeral—even dead.

24   The casket (which has been resting throughout the service on a Classic Beauty Ultra Metal Casket Bier) is now transferred by a hydraulically operated device called Porto-Life to a balloon-tired, Glide Easy casket carriage which will wheel it to yet another conveyance, the Cadillac Funeral Coach. This may be lavender, cream, light green—anything but black. Interiors, of course, are color-correlated, "for the man who cannot stop short of perfection."

25   At graveside, the casket is lowered into the earth. This office, once the prerogative of friends of the deceased, is now performed by a patented mechanical lowering device. A "Lifetime Green" artificial grass mat is at the ready to conceal the sere earth, and overhead, to conceal the sky, is a portable Steril Chapel Tent ("resists the intense heat and humidity of summer and the terrific storms of winter . . . available in Silver Gray, Rose, or Evergreen"). Now is the time for the ritual scattering of earth over the coffin, as the solemn words "earth to earth, ashes to ashes, dust to dust" are pronounced by the officiating cleric. This can today be accomplished "with a mere flick of the wrist with the Gordon Leak-Proof Earth Dispenser. No grasping of a handful of dirt, no soiled fingers. Simple, dignified, beautiful, reverent! The modern way!" The Gordon Earth Dispenser (at $5) is of nickel-plated brass construction. It is not only "attractive to the eye and long wearing"; it is also "one of the 'tools' for building better public relations" if presented as "an appropriate non-commercial gift" to the clergyman. It is shaped something like a saltshaker.

26   Untouched by human hand, the coffin and the earth are now united.

27   It is in the function of directing the participants through this maze of gadgetry that the funeral director has assigned to himself his relatively new role of "grief therapist." He has relieved the family of every detail, he has revamped the corpse to look like a living doll, he has arranged for it to nap for a few days in a slumber room, he has put on a well oiled performance in which the concept of *death* has played no part whatsoever—unless it was inconsiderately mentioned by the clergyman who conducted the religious service. He has done everything in his power to make the funeral a real pleasure for everybody concerned. He and his team have given their all to score an upset victory over death.

READING CLOSELY AND THINKING CRITICALLY

1.   In paragraph 6, Mitford says that her essay will "part the formaldehyde curtain." What do you think she means? Is the phrase effective? Explain.

2.   According to Mitford, what is the real purpose of embalming? What is the ostensible (for appearances) purpose?

3.   What are the steps in the embalming process?

4. Why do you think Mitford names the corpse "Mr. Jones"?
5. How would you describe Mitford's attitude toward the mortuary business?
6. Who would you judge to be the original, intended audience for Mitford's exposé? Why?
7. According to Mitford, why do morticians keep the embalming process secret?

EXAMINING STRUCTURE AND STRATEGY

1. What is the thesis of "Behind the Formaldehyde Curtain"?
2. What process does Mitford explain?
3. Mitford begins her explanation of a process in paragraph 7. What is the purpose of the first six paragraphs?
4. Mitford employs a considerable amount of **verbal irony** (saying one thing but suggesting another). For example, in paragraph 2 she refers to the casket as "a suitably costly container," but she does not really think the cost appropriate. Cite two or three other examples of verbal irony. What purpose does the irony serve? How does it reveal the author's attitude toward her subject?

NOTING COMBINED PATTERNS

The description in "Behind the Formaldehyde Curtain" is graphic and, at times, shocking. How does this graphic description help Mitford achieve her persuasive purpose?

CONSIDERING LANGUAGE AND STYLE

1. How would you describe the tone of "Behind the Formaldehyde Curtain"? (See page 71 on tone.) Cite examples to support your view.
2. Mitford opens with a reference to burial and its preparation as "drama." In what ways is the metaphor of the drama sustained in the essay? (See page 110 on metaphors.)
3. Consult a dictionary if you are unsure of the meaning of any of these words: *bereaved* (paragraph 3), *docility* (paragraph 4), *perpetuation* (paragraph 4), *intractable* (paragraph 6), *raison d'être* (paragraph 6), *augers* (paragraph 8), *entrails* (paragraph 13), *stippling* (paragraph 15), *queue* (paragraph 23), *hydraulically* (paragraph 24).

FOR DISCUSSION IN CLASS OR ONLINE

A **euphemism** is a polite or indirect substitute for an unpleasant expression. Mitford notes a number of euphemisms common in the funeral industry. For example, in paragraph 7, she refers to a body "reposing in the preparation room" rather than "dead on a slab in the embalming chamber." With some classmates, cite other euphemisms that appear. Explain what effect these euphemisms have on perceptions of death and burial. If your instructor so directs, post your response on your class Web site.

1. **In your journal.** What did you think of the funeral industry before reading the selection? Have your views of death and the funeral industry changed after reading it? Were your views influenced at all by the graphic description in the essay? Explain in a page or two.

2. **Using process analysis for a purpose.** The purposes in the assignments are possibilities. You may establish whatever purposes you like, within your instructor's guidelines.

   • Select a process that you think is unnecessary or faulty, and to inform your reader, explain how that process works. Like Mitford, use verbal irony and description to convey your attitude toward the process.

   • To inform and perhaps relate your experience, write a graphic description of a grisly or unpleasant process (for example, baiting a fishing hook, cleaning a fish, dissecting a frog, and so on).

   • To convince your reader that there is a better way, devise and describe a funeral and burial process that you think is superior to anything you are currently aware of. As you explain the steps in the process, note why they are superior to existing rituals.

3. **Combining patterns.** If you have experienced the ritual associated with death because someone you know died, use process analysis and description to explain and describe the ritual and cause-and-effect analysis (explained in Chapter 9) to give your reaction to the ritual. Note whether you found the ritual comforting, depressing, confusing, frightening, and so on—and why. In addition, use description to give the reaction of other people who experienced the ritual.

4. **Connecting the readings.** A euphemism tries to make a harsh reality less distressing by substituting a more pleasant expression for an unpleasant one. Consider the euphemisms in the selection and any others you can think of. (For example, *a waiting room* in a doctor's office is a *reception area;* a dentist does not *pull* a tooth but *performs an extraction;* and, a patient experiences *discomfort,* never *pain.*) Then, decide whether Sissela Bok should add the category of euphemisms to her classification of white lies in "White Lies" on page 455. Explain why or why not.

5. **Drawing on sources.** Explain one or more of the funeral customs of a culture you are unfamiliar with. To find this information, check "funeral rites and ceremonies" in the *Social Sciences Index* in your library, or on the Internet, type the key phrase "funeral customs" into your favorite search engine.

BACKGROUND: Award-winning poet, essayist, short story writer, children's author, and teacher, Naomi Shihab Nye was born in 1952 to an American mother and Palestinian father. She grew up in St. Louis, Jerusalem, and San Antonio. She has traveled to the Middle East and Asia for the United States Information Agency promoting international goodwill through the arts. Drawing on her Palestinian-American heritage and her extensive travels, Nye often writes about the shared humanity of diverse people. Her work has appeared in publications throughout North America, Europe, and the Middle and Far East. Nye's collections of poems include *Red Suitcase* (1994), *Fuel* (1998), and *Is This Forever, or What?: Poems and Paintings from Texas* (2004). "The Traveling Onion" is from Nye's 1986 collection, *Yellow Glove.*

COMBINED PATTERNS AND THEIR PURPOSES: In "The Traveling Onion," Naomi Shihab Nye uses *process analysis* and *description* to **inform** readers of how an onion makes its way into a stew. At the same time, Nye is helping the reader to a fresh appreciation of something so familiar it is taken for granted. As is often true of poetry, the artistry of the piece **entertains** the reader.

The Traveling Onion
NAOMI SHIHAB NYE

It is believed that the onion originally came from India. In Egypt it was an object of worship—why I haven't been able to find out. From Egypt the onion entered Greece and on to Italy, thence into all of Europe.

—Better Living Cookbook

As you read
The poem notes two processes. Try to identify both of them.

When I think how far the onion has traveled
just to enter my stew today, I could kneel and praise
all small forgotten miracles,
crackly paper peeling on the drainboard,
pearly layers in smooth agreement,   5
the way knife enters onion, straight
and onion falls apart on the chopping block,
a history revealed.
And I would never scold the onion
for causing tears.   10
It is right that tears fall
for something small and forgotten.
How at meal, we sit to eat,
commenting on texture of meat or herbal aroma
but never on the translucence of onion,   15
now limp, now divided,
or its traditionally honorable career:
For the sake of others,
disappear.

CONSIDERING THE POEM

1. What two processes does the poem refer to?
2. What are the "small forgotten miracles" to which the speaker refers?
3. What is it about the onion that is "honorable"? Would the same trait in a human being be honorable? Why or why not?
4. An excerpt from *Better Living Cookbook* appears before the poem. What purpose does that excerpt serve?

NOTING COMBINED PATTERNS

1. How does Nye use description in "The Traveling Onion"?
2. Does the description help the author achieve her purpose for writing? Explain.

WRITING ASSIGNMENTS

1. **In your journal.**
   - Write a list of other "small forgotten miracles." Do the items in your list have anything in common?
   - Nye shows an ordinary item—the onion—in a new perspective. Where do new perspectives come from? Tell about a time you received—or achieved—a new perspective.
2. **Using process analysis for a purpose.** To inform and perhaps entertain, explain a process for preparing a fruit or vegetable. Do so in a way likely to increase your audience's appreciation for the food. The purpose in the assignment is a possibility. You may establish whatever purpose you like, within your instructor's guidelines.
3. **Combining patterns.** Describe an item commonly taken for granted and a process associated with that item. For example, you can describe your running shoes and how they help a runner perform or the toolbar at the top of your computer screen and how it helps you work efficiently.
4. **Connecting the readings.** Discuss the role of food in family life. For ideas, you can draw on your own experience, "The Traveling Onion," and "A Visit to Candyland" (page 277).

See pages 273 and 276 for strategies for writing a process analysis and for a revising checklist.

1. Explain a process you know that other people should know so they can cope with an emergency: for instance, how to administer CPR, how to administer first aid to someone badly cut, what to do if a tornado strikes, what to do if fire breaks out in the home, or how to rescue a drowning person. Your purpose is to inform your reader.

2. Select a process you perform well (for example, making pizza, wrapping gifts, throwing a surprise party, or planting a garden) and describe it so that your reader can learn how to do it. Your essay should discuss why it is important or even simply pleasurable to learn this process.

3. Explain a process that was an important part of your childhood: catching fireflies, preparing for Halloween, decorating the Christmas tree, planting a garden with your parents, and so forth.

4. Explain a process that will help your reader save money, such as how to buy a used car, how to save money on groceries, how to buy clothes at a thrift shop, how to find bargains at flea markets, or how to buy presents for less.

5. If you have a hobby, such as collecting baseball cards or keeping exotic fish, explain some process associated with that process: evaluating the worth of a baseball card or putting together a tropical fish tank, for example. Let your pleasure at performing the process show.

6. If you play a sport well, explain some process associated with that sport: shooting a foul shot, sliding into home plate, and so on. Let your pleasure at performing the process show.

7. Rewrite "A Visit to Candyland" as a series of instructions.

8. To entertain your reader, write a humorous explanation of a process: how to flunk a test, how to make a bad impression on a date, how to irritate a teacher, how to make a bad impression on a job interview, or how to be a slob. Use verbal irony, if appropriate.

9. Explain how some mechanical device works: a DVD player, a cell phone, a compact disk, a computer, and so on.

10. To inform your reader, explain how something common—such as paper, decaffeinated coffee, or a baseball—is made. If necessary, do some research to learn about the process. (Consult Chapter 14 on how to handle material taken from sources.)

11. To convince your reader that people suffer unfairly to conform to society's concept of beauty, explain a process they go through.

12. Explain the wedding ritual for the religious, ethnic, or cultural group you belong to. Your purpose is to relate your experience and inform your reader. Try to use description to make aspects of the process as vivid as possible. As an alternative, explain the ritual for some other life cycle event.

13. Explain some process for improving relationships between people: how to fight fairly, how to communicate better, how to respect differences, how to offer constructive criticism, and so on.

14. To entertain your reader, write a humorous explanation of how to procrastinate.

15. To help a student who is away from home for the first time, explain how to do laundry. Use examples and keep the tone lighthearted.

16. Explain a way to perform a process to convince your reader that your procedures are better. For example, you can explain a better way to study, a better way to clean a room, a better way to shop, or a better way to plan a party.

17. To inform college students, explain a process for coping with stress.

18. To entertain your reader, explain how to survive adolescence. You may write from a parent's or child's point of view.

19. Explain how to relax.

20. **Process Analysis in Context:** Assume that your college is putting together a handbook for first-year students to help them adjust to school and be successful. As an experienced student, you have been asked to contribute to the handbook by describing an important academic survival skill: taking notes, taking an examination, getting along with a difficult roommate, reading a textbook, studying for finals, and so on. Be sure your process analysis is written in such a way that it is genuinely useful to a new student.

The following page, from the instruction manual for a computer printer, explains how to complete the first step in operating the printer: loading the paper. Explain how the images and words come together to help users perform the process. You might consider some of these questions: What purpose do the pictures serve? What purpose do the words serve? How important are each of these elements? Could you perform the process if the instructions included only the words? What if it included only the pictures?

Step One: Load the paper

You can load up to 100 sheets of paper (depending on thickness).

1 Place the paper against the right side of the sheet feeder, with the print side facing you.

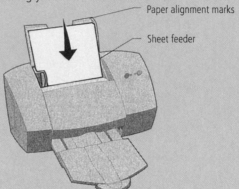

Paper alignment marks

Sheet feeder

2 Squeeze the release tab and the paper guide together and slide the paper guide to the edge of the paper.

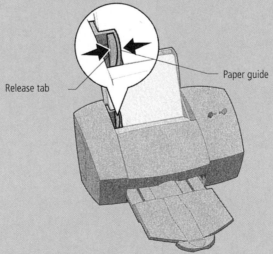

Paper guide

Release tab

THE WAY WE REMEMBER IT......
...THE WAY IT WAS...

McKay — JULY, 1978

① THE OLD STONE FIREPLACE. BURNED CHEAP, AVAILABLE WOOD. RADIATED HEAT.

② YOU BURNED UP IN FRONT - YOU FROZE IN BACK.

③ THE ROMANTIC COAL OIL LAMP.

④ THAT BROUGHT ON THE THICK LENSE GLASSES.

⑤ BEAUTIFUL, COOL, GREEN FORESTS. CLEAN AIR. SPARKLING WATERS.

⑥ SPIDERS, GNATS, RATS, SNAKES --- THINGS!

Comparison-Contrast

CONSIDER THE PATTERN

On page 322, the contrast in "The Way We Remember It . . . The Way It Was" demonstrates that we often idealize the past by focusing on the positives and forgetting the negatives. To demonstrate this fact, write a paragraph that contrasts how something was and how some people remember it. For example, you can contrast the problems associated with staying in touch with people before computers and with the romanticized notions some people have about the advantages of snail mail.

THE PATTERN

Comparison points out similarities; **contrast** points out differences; **comparison-contrast** points out both similarities and differences. Because comparison-contrast allows us to examine the features of two or more subjects, it is an important component of decision making. Should you buy a notebook computer or upgrade your current desktop? Is this political candidate better for the country or is that one? Will the job in Seattle make me happier than the one in Houston? Will the anthropology course be more interesting than the psychology course? To decide, you compare and contrast the merits of the two computers, the two candidates, the two jobs, and the two courses. Comparison-contrast is so integral to decision making that you engage in it many times each day.

USING COMPARISON-CONTRAST FOR A PURPOSE

In addition to helping you make decisions, comparison-contrast can help a writer *inform* a reader about the nature of something that is not well understood. For example, to explain rugby to a reader who knows little about the sport, you could compare and contrast it with the better-known game of football. Comparison-contrast can also help you inform by clarifying the nature of *both* subjects under consideration. For example, to help the reader understand the virtues and limitations of both direct and indirect communication styles, Deborah Tannen compares and contrasts both styles in "Squeaky Wheels and Protruding Nails: Direct and Indirect Speech." (page 359). Another way comparison-contrast can inform is by providing new insight into something already familiar. In this case, the purpose of the comparison-contrast is to sharpen the reader's awareness or appreciation. For example, you already know a fair amount about both horses and people, but after reading Alice Walker's comparison-contrast in "Am I Blue?" (page 353), you are likely to have fresh insight into the nature of both.

In addition to informing, comparison-contrast can allow the writer to *express feelings and relate experience*. To relate the effects of your parents' divorce and express your feelings about it, for example, you could contrast your life before and after the divorce to reveal the impact the event had on you.

By showing that one subject is superior to the other, comparison-contrast also can work to persuade a reader to think or act a particular way. For instance, to convince a reader to vote for a particular candidate, you could contrast that candidate with the opposition to show that your choice is better.

An amusing comparison-contrast will entertain a reader—often at the same time it informs, relates experience, expresses feelings, or persuades. Suzanne Britt's "Neat People vs. Sloppy People" (page 344) is such a piece. Its humorous contrast of neat and sloppy people entertains at the same time it expresses some of Britt's feelings about these distinct types and argues for the superiority of sloppiness.

Comparison-Contrast in College, at Work, and in the Community

Comparison-contrast has many uses in the classroom. Often you will use it to clarify and evaluate the nature of two subjects. In a political science class, you could be asked to compare and contrast two political ideologies such as socialism and communism. In a music appreciation class, you could be asked to compare and contrast the techniques of two composers; in a literature class, you could be asked to compare and contrast the symbolism in two poems; and in a cultural anthropology class, you could be asked to compare and contrast the marriage rituals in two cultures.

You are also likely to use comparison-contrast to show the superiority of one of the subjects. For example, in a clinical psychology class, you might compare and contrast two treatments for depression to show which one is better; in an advertising class, you might compare and contrast two advertising campaigns to determine which one is more effective; and in a history class, you might compare and contrast two World War II generals to determine who was the better strategist.

Because comparison-contrast clarifies ideas and concepts by showing how they are similar to and different from other ideas and concepts, textbook authors use it often. Here is an example from an American history textbook. This section of the text discusses Native-American and European dress, focusing on European reaction to Native American clothing.

> Europeans interpreted the simplicity of Indian dress in two different ways. Some saw the lack of clothing as evidence of "barbarism." André Thevet, a shocked French visitor to Brazil in 1557, voiced this point of view when he attributed nakedness to simple lust. If the Indians could weave hammocks, he sniffed, why not shirts? But other Europeans viewed unashamed nakedness as the Indians' badge of innocence. As remnants of a bygone "golden age," they believed, Indians needed clothing no more than government, laws, regular employment, or other corruptions of civilization. (Davidson et al., *Nation of Nations*)

The passage contrasts two European interpretations of Native-American dress to help students appreciate how divergent opinions were. However, the passage continues, this time using contrast to clarify how wrong both of the divergent opinions were:

> In fact, Indians were no more "naked" than they were without trade, politics, employment, or religion. While the simplest tribes of the Caribbean and Brazil wore little, the members of more advanced Indian cultures in Central and North America clothed themselves with animal pelts sewn into mantles and robes, breechclouts, leggings, and moccasins. They wrought bird feathers into headdresses and ear decorations and fashioned reptile skins into belts and pouches. Even more formidably clad were the Eskimos of the far North, who dressed head to foot in sealskin suits with waterproofed seams, turning the furry side inward for warmth in the winter and outward in the summer.

The textbook authors could have described Native-American dress without including the contrast between European opinions and actual Native-American cultural practice, but including the contrast makes the point that Europeans misunderstood the people and cultures they encountered in the new world.

Comparison-contrast is also a frequent component of writing on the job. For example, professionals often write reports that compare such things as computer systems and phone systems in order to recommend a particular purchase. A construction manager may compare two bid proposals from general contractors to determine which company to award a building project to, and a caterer might compare several menus, themes, and decorations for a reception to help a client make a selection.

Outside the classroom and workplace, you will have many opportunities to use comparison-contrast as part of your decision-making process. For a particularly difficult choice such as choosing which job to take, try writing out a comparison of the items. Not only does writing stimulate your thinking and lead you to ideas that might not otherwise occur to you, but it also gives you something concrete to study as you mull over the choice. If you are a member of an organization, you might use comparison-contrast in a committee report evaluating different fund-raising projects or membership campaigns. If you move to a new city and want to describe your new neighborhood to a friend in your former town, comparing it to your old neighborhood can help your friend better visualize where you now live.

CHOOSING SUBJECTS

The subjects you choose for comparison-contrast should allow you to cite comparisons and contrasts that go beyond trivial points. Do not compare and contrast the bicycle and automobile, for example, if you can note only the number of wheels and speed of travel. However, you can use these subjects if you have a fresh approach, perhaps comparing and contrasting the lifestyles associated with using each vehicle as a principal mode of transportation.

In general, the subjects you choose to compare and contrast should be from the same category, or general type of thing or idea. Thus, you can compare and contrast two kinds of computers, two weight-loss programs, two poems, two mayors, and so forth. If your purpose is to entertain, however, you may be able to compare and contrast subjects from different categories. A political satirist, for example, might compare a former president of the United States to Ronald McDonald, and a campus humor columnist might compare studying for exams and preparing for war.

The comparison of subjects from different categories is an **analogy.** With an analogy, you can compare subjects from different categories if they have compelling similarities or ones that shed light on one or both subjects. For example, author Robert Jastrow once compared the human brain with a computer because the two subjects, although from different categories, function similarly in a number of ways. The analogy helped the reader better understand how both subjects work. Other analogies might be comparing the human eye to a camera or comparing an ant colony to New York City.

SUPPORTING DETAILS

Because mentioning every possible point of comparison and contrast is undesirable—if not impossible—you must select your details with regard to your purpose for writing. Say, for instance, that you are comparing and contrasting public and private schools. If your purpose is to convince your reader that public schools are better, then you might mention that the ethnic diversity often found in these schools can teach students more about people and their cultural heritage. If your purpose is to relate your experiences in these schools, you can tell which school you were happier in and why. If your purpose is to inform, you might discuss the academic programs in each kind of school so parents can make up their own minds about which is better for their children. If your purpose is to entertain, you can give humorous portraits of the students and teachers in each kind of school.

Your audience will also influence the points you choose to compare and contrast. Say you are contrasting public and private schools to persuade your reader to increase support of public schools. If your audience includes politicians, and you do not want them to support legislation increasing funding to private schools, you can contrast enrollments in the two kinds of schools to show that more voters send children to public schools than to private ones. However, if your audience includes parents, and you want them to send their children to public rather than private schools, you can compare and contrast extracurricular activities to show that students have more options in public schools.

In addition to purpose and audience, a sense of balance will influence your selection of details. Most times, any point you make about one of your subjects should also be made about the other subject. Thus, if you are comparing and contrasting public and private schools and you discuss the teachers in public school, you should also discuss the teachers in private school; if you discuss course offerings in public school, you should also discuss course offerings in private school, and so on. You may notice that the authors in this chapter do not always adhere strictly to this principle of balance. An author can depart from this principle only if the essay does not become a random collection of points about the subjects. That is, if you do not maintain enough balance, your essay will not be a comparison-contrast.

Although you are likely to discuss the same points about each of your subjects, you need not do so in equal detail. A point can be discussed in more detail for one subject than for the other. For example, if you are contrasting online classrooms and traditional classrooms, you could make the point that in traditional classrooms, teachers can read facial expressions and body language to determine whether students understand a point. Then you could give examples of expressions and posture that signal understanding and those that signal confusion. When you discuss the same point for online classrooms, you can simply write that online instructors do not have the opportunity to read expressions and body language; further explanation may not be required.

Sometimes writers fall into the trap of stating the obvious. Avoid making self-evident statements, which could bore and alienate your reader. If, for example, you are contrasting online and traditional classrooms, you need not mention that students in online classrooms require computer access, but students in traditional classrooms do not.

Comparison-contrast may include other patterns of development. For example, to compare and contrast the techniques of two artists, you would probably describe the styles of each person. Examples are also a frequent component of comparison-contrast, particularly when a point of comparison or contrast requires clarification. For instance, if you were comparing two political candidates, and you stated that they both favored progressive legislation, you could clarify and support that point of comparison with an example. You could note that both candidates voted for a bill that would provide tax credits for working parents with children in day care centers.

Because a story can serve as an example, narration can be a part of comparison-contrast. Say that you want to compare and contrast your relationship with two friends. To show the differences in the way you interact with each person, you can tell the story of the time the three of you went away for the weekend.

Process analysis, too, can form part of comparison-contrast. For example, to contrast the styles of two baseball coaches, you could explain the process each one follows to motivate players.

ORGANIZING DETAILS

The thesis for a comparision-contrast essay can present the subjects under consideration and indicate whether these subjects will be compared, contrasted, or both compared and contrasted. Consider, for example, this thesis from "Neat People vs. Sloppy People":

> Neat people are lazier and meaner than sloppy people.

This thesis notes that the subjects under consideration are neat people and sloppy people, and it also indicates that the subjects will be contrasted. Now consider these two thesis statements:

> Islam and Christianity have more in common than most people realize.
>
> Smith and Jones have different political philosophies, but they implement those philosophies with similar styles, so the differences between the men are not readily apparent.

The first thesis indicates that the essay will compare Islam and Christianity to make an important point about both religions. Notice that purpose is a component of the thesis—the informational purpose is made clear. The second thesis indicates that politicians Smith and Jones will be both compared and contrasted. Again, the informational purpose is apparent—the thesis will make the point that the similarities between the two politicians mask their differences.

Ordering detail in a comparison-contrast essay requires some thought. One possible arrangement is the **block pattern** whereby all the points about one subject are made (in a block), then all the points about the other subject are made (in a second block.) To appreciate how the block arrangement works, look at the following outline for an essay contrasting political candidates Smith and Jones. Notice that balance is achieved by discussing the same points for both subjects. Also notice that the points are discussed in the same order for both subjects.

I. Smith
   A. Believes in states funding their own health care plans
   B. Believes in supporting education with a state income tax
   C. Wants to form a task force to study lake pollution
II. Jones
   A. Believes the federal government should fund health care
   B. Believes in supporting education with a property tax
   C. Believes lake pollution is not a priority

A second possible arrangement for the details of comparison-contrast is the **alternating pattern,** whereby a point is made for one subject, then for the other. A second point is made for the first subject, then for the other. This alternating pattern continues until all the points are made for both subjects. An outline for an essay contrasting Smith and Jones could look like this if the alternating pattern were used:

I. View on financing health care
   A. Smith believes states should fund their own plans
   B. Jones believes the federal government should fund a plan
II. View on financing education
   A. Smith believes in a state income tax
   B. Jones believes in a property tax
III. View on lake pollution
   A. Smith wants to form a task force to study pollution
   B. Jones believes pollution is not a priority

Although comparison-contrast can be arranged using a block or an alternating pattern, the two strategies are not interchangeable. In general, the block method works better for essays with fewer points of comparison or contrast that are not extensively developed because the reader is not forced to remember many ideas about the first subject while reading about the second. When you have many points to discuss, or points that are very detailed, you can easily lose track of them with the block method, and your reader can easily get lost.

An alternating pattern is usually a better choice for an essay with many points of comparison and contrast or an essay with extensively developed ideas because readers can keep track of the ideas more easily. However, the points must be well developed, or you risk creating a "ping-pong" effect as you switch back and forth between subjects.

If you are both comparing and contrasting, you can organize by treating similarities first and differences next. Or you can reverse this order.

VISUALIZING A COMPARISON-CONTRAST ESSAY

The following chart can help you visualize either the block or alternating structure for a comparison-contrast essay. Like all good models, however, this one can be altered as needed.

Introduction

- Creates interest in the essay
- States the thesis, which mentions the subjects being considered and may indicate whether the subjects will be compared, contrasted, or both

First Body Paragraph(s)

- In a block pattern, make and explain all the points about the first subject
- In an alternating pattern, make and explain a point about the first subject, and then make and explain the same point for the second subject
- Discuss the same points for both subjects, but not necessarily in the same amount of detail
- May include any other patterns of development

Next Body Paragraph(s)

- In a block pattern, make and explain all the points about the second subject
- In an alternating pattern, make and explain the next point about the first subject and then make and explain the same point for the second subject, continuing this way until all points are made
- Discuss the same points for both subjects, but not necessarily in the same amount of detail
- May include any other patterns of development

Conclusion

- Provides a satisfying finish
- May state the point of the narration if not done so elsewhere

Using Transitions in Comparison-Contrast

If you have trouble moving smoothly from point to point or subject to subject, use transitions:

TO SHOW SIMILARITY	similarly, likewise, in similar fashion, in like manner, in the same way

Smith believes in tax reform. Similarly, Jones wants to close tax loopholes.

TO SHOW CONTRAST	however, on the other hand, conversely, in contrast

Smith favors tax reform. However, Jones believes current tax laws are adequate.

Repetition of key words, particularly when combined with transitions, can also help you move smoothly between points and maintain coherence.

Smith believes in tax reform. However, tax reform is equally important to Jones, who wants to close tax loopholes.

Smith favors tax reform. Such reform is not a priority for Jones, though, because he believes current tax laws are adequate.

PROCESS GUIDELINES: STRATEGIES FOR WRITING COMPARISON-CONTRAST

1. **Selecting a Topic.** Try explaining the similarities between two things usually considered different or the differences between two things thought of as alike. For example, you could discuss the similarities between madness and genius or the differences between getting a degree and getting an education. Be sure to select subjects from the same category.

2. **Establishing a Purpose.** To establish your purpose, answer these questions:
   - Do I want to inform readers about the nature of something not well understood?
   - Do I want to clarify the nature of one or both subjects?
   - Do I want to offer a new insight into something familiar?
   - Do I want to convince my reader that one subject is better than the other?
   - Do I want to express feelings or relate experience?
   - Do I want to entertain my reader?

3. **Assessing Your Audience.** To assess your audience, determine how much your reader knows about your subjects and how interested your reader is likely to be in your subjects.

4. **Writing a Thesis.** Write out an early version of your thesis in a sentence that names your subjects, indicates whether you will compare, contrast, or both, and suggests your purpose.

5. **Generating ideas.** Try these techniques if you need help thinking of ideas:

   a. List every similarity you can think of or every difference (whichever is appropriate for your topic). Study the list and eliminate ideas not suited to your audience and purpose.

   b. Ask yourself these questions about the points on your list: Should I describe anything? Should I tell a story? Should I explain a process? Should I provide examples?

6. **Organizing.** Organizing comparison-contrast requires careful planning, so even if you do not ordinarily write detailed outlines, consider doing so for this essay, using a block or alternating pattern.

7. **Revising.** Ask a friend whose judgment about writing you trust to read your draft and note anything that is unclear and any places where you are not moving smoothly from point to point or from subject to subject.

Using Modifiers in Comparison-Contrast

If you have trouble using modifers (adjectives and adverbs) correctly to compare and contrast, this explanation may be helpful.

Modifiers have *comparative forms* and *superlative forms.* Use the comparative form to compare or contrast two items and the superlative form to compare and contrast more than two items.

BASE FORM	COMPARATIVE FORM	SUPERLATIVE FORM
fast	faster	fastest
unusual	more unusual	most unusual
good	better	best
bad	worse	worst

NO	Both cities have low unemployment rates, but Charleston has the *best* average income.
YES	Both cities have low unemployment rates, but Charleston has a *better* average income. [only two cities]
NO	Of all the tutors observed, the writing center tutors were *friendlier.*
YES	Of all the tutors observed, the writing center tutors were *friendliest.* [more than two tutors]

Checklist for Revising Comparison-Contrast

Be sure

_____ You have a sound basis for considering your subjects side by side and that your subjects are from the same category.

_____ Your thesis presents your subjects and notes whether they will be compared, contrasted, or both.

_____ Your details suit your audience and purpose.

_____ You have discussed the same points for both subjects—or if you haven't, that the lack of balance does not create a problem.

_____ You have avoided stating obvious comparisons and contrasts.

_____ You have used a block or alternating pattern to best advantage.

_____ You have used transitions and repetition to move from point to point and subject to subject.

Annotated Student Essay

The student author of "Teaching a New Dog Old Tricks" contrasts her dog Rufus with an electronic dog. You will have no trouble recognizing the writer's opinion about electronic pets. After you read, you will have an opportunity to evaluate this essay.

Teaching a New Dog Old Tricks

Paragraph 1
The introduction creates interest with background information and some description. The thesis, the last sentence, gives the subjects and notes that differences will be discussed.

When I was eight, I got the perfect interactive toy: a new puppy. 1 Rufus was a scrawny mutt with big floppy ears and unsteady legs, but I couldn't have loved him more if he'd been a champion show dog. I considered myself very lucky; some of my friends begged for a pet and were told it would be too messy, too expensive, or too high-maintenance. It seems that many of today's children have found a way to counter these objections. Poo-Chi, an interactive puppy robot made by the Japanese toy manufacturer Sega Toys, took second place on a list of the best-selling toys of 2000 (Bloomberg A57). Although its creators claim the robot mimics some of the engaging qualities of a real puppy, I don't think Poo-Chi would have made an adequate substitute for Rufus.

Paragraph 2
Details, which include information from sources, are given in an alternating pattern.

Poo-Chi, priced at between $20 and $30, is one of several robot 2 dogs on the market, including the $1,500 Sony Aibo, which "can recognize about 50 words, bark, dance, move [its] ears and take pictures with a camera mounted on [its] nose" (Barnes C1). Rufus, born in the local pound, came free to a good home (ours). Of course, there are highly bred puppies that cost as much as or more than the Aibo, but there will always be good-natured mutts and strays that, for no money at all, can learn a range of tricks, skills, and behaviors that would put the Aibo, let alone the simpler Poo-Chi, to shame. Like Poo-Chi, Rufus could interact with others of his kind, but unlike Poo-Chi, Rufus had special friends among the dogs he knew, and knew by smell when one of his friends had been somewhere.

Paragraph 3
Details include description. The alternating pattern continues.

For all Rufus' scruffiness, he did have a coat of warm, glossy light- 3 brown fur, big, wet brown eyes, and a lolling pink tongue. Poo-Chi is made out of two-tone plastic; one of its colors is silver and the other is purple, blue, or another un-doglike hue. The Poo-Chi I examined in a recent visit to a toy store was designed to resemble a bulldog, but in general the toy's appearance is extremely stylized. It looks like what it is: a dog-shaped robot. When my father brought him home from the pound, Rufus was about a foot tall, and he soon grew much bigger. Poo-Chi is around five inches tall, and, naturally, will never grow. One of my favorite things to do with Rufus was roughhouse with him and pet him; I don't think rolling on the floor with a little plastic robot would be nearly as fun.

Rufus was certainly cuddly and playful, but he was also extremely messy. It took us several months to get him housetrained, and even after he learned to wait for his walk he would still knock over his food bowl, trample mud on the kitchen floor, and leave hair on the couch. Despite its name, Poo-Chi will never need to be taken for a walk or fed, and no one will ever need to clean up after it. Its plastic surface can be wiped clean with a damp cloth—no sloppy tub or hose baths needed. Rufus ate like a horse, and my parents sometimes complained about all the dog food they had to buy for him. Poo-Chi runs on batteries, which can last for several weeks before they need to be changed. The silver plastic "bone" packaged with Poo-Chi might get lost, but it won't be because Poo-Chi buried it in the back yard.

Poo-Chi, claims Tiger Electronics, which introduced the toy to the United States, "is so lifelike, he needs love." The manufacturers used biorhythm technology to "create realistic emotional responses that adapt and change as you play with [Poo-Chi]" (Willman E-2). These responses are somewhat limited; Poo-Chi's eyes flash red or green stars when it is happy, half-circles when it is asleep, and so on. It can sing, stand, or sit, but it can't walk. Rufus, by contrast, leaped and wagged his tail when he was happy, flopped on the floor and snored when sleeping, and displayed dozens of other emotions and states of being in complex ways. When I left each morning for school, Rufus would stand by the door and howl, and when I returned he was dizzy with excitement. Poo-Chi may need love, but it probably won't scratch grooves into the front door if you leave it alone for too long.

Ten-year-old Kurt Roeder, one of the first Chicagoans to play with a Poo-Chi, reported, "They're really fun. They sing songs, and they're usually happy" (Fitch). Rufus yodeled and barked, but he didn't sing songs, and he wasn't always happy. It's understandable that some chil-

Paragraph 4
The paragraph opens with a transitional sentence. Notice the humor in the paragraph.

Paragraph 5
The point of contrast is emotions. Notice the specific word choice.

Paragraph 6
The essay concludes with the final point of contrast: emotional attachment to a living creature vs. a replaceable toy. Source material is included.

dren, not to mention their parents, would opt for a pet that is entertaining, inexpensive, and easy to take care of, but I hope that those with enough space, time, and money will consider paying a visit to the pound. Still, in doing so, they'd be taking a big risk: getting attached to a unique and irreplaceable pet with a finite lifespan. Fortunately, Rufus lived a long and happy life, but I was miserable when he finally passed away last year. If my pet had been Poo-Chi, I could simply have gone to the store and picked up another one.

Works Cited

Barnes, Julian E. "As Visions of E-Toys Danced in Their Heads." New York Times 11 Nov. 2000: C1.

Bloomberg News Service. "Old Favorites Led Holiday Toy Sales." Newsday 8 Feb. 2001: A57.

Fitch, Jessica Madore. "Hoping to Be Top Dog." Chicago Sun-Times 3 May 2000. 31 March 2001 <http://www.suntimes.com/output/business/poochi03.html>.

Willman, Martha L. "Bark Versus Byte." Los Angeles Times 3 Feb. 2000: E2.

PEER REVIEW

Responding to "Teaching a New Dog Old Tricks"

Evaluate "Teaching a New Dog Old Tricks" by responding to these questions:

1. Does the essay hold your interest? Why or why not?
2. Are the introduction and conclusion effective? Why or why not?
3. Do the supporting details adequately develop the thesis? Explain.
4. Is the source material effective? Explain.
5. Is the alternating pattern a suitable organization? Why or why not?
6. Is the word choice effective? Explain.
7. What do you like best about the essay?
8. What change or changes would you advise the writer to make?

- What comparison or comparisons are implied by this movie still from *Spiderman* (2002), which starred Tobey Maguire as both the action hero and his alter ego—the mild-mannered Peter Parker?
- What contrast or contrasts are implied?
- Do the comparisons and contrasts you noted help explain the popularity of the Spiderman character? The Spiderman movies?

BACKGROUND: Born in Michigan and educated at Oberlin College until World War I interrupted his studies, historian Bruce Catton—pronounced "Cayton"—(1899–1978), was an authority on the Civil War. He became fascinated by the subject as a child when he heard the stories of the war veterans living in his community. He published extensively on the Civil War, including the Pulitzer Prize-winning book *A Stillness at Appomattox* (1953). Before turning full-time to literary work, Catton was a newspaper reporter in Boston and Cleveland and a public official. His work with the War Production Board during World War II led to his first major book, *The War Lords of Washington* (1948). In 1954, Catton became the editor of *American Heritage* magazine, a position he held until his death. Catton's books on the military history of the Civil War include *Mr. Lincoln's Army* (1951), *Glory Road* (1952), *This Hallowed Ground* (1956), *Grant Moves South* (1960), *Grant Takes Command* (1969), *The Centennial History of the Civil War* (3 vol., 1961–65), and *Prefaces to History* (1970). For his achievements, President Gerald Ford awarded Catton the Medal of Freedom. "Grant and Lee: A Study in Contrasts" was first published in *The American Story* (1956), a collection of essays by historians.

www.mhhe.com/patterns

For more information on this author, go to

More resources > Chapter 8 > Bruce Catton

THE PATTERN AND ITS PURPOSE: In "Grant and Lee: A Study in Contrasts," Bruce Catton *compares and contrasts* the Civil War's most important military officers to **inform** the reader that each man's personality reflected the side he represented. However, Catton does more than inform; he makes history come alive for the reader.

Grant and Lee: A Study in Contrasts
BRUCE CATTON

When Ulysses S. Grant and Robert E. Lee met in the parlor of a modest house at Appomattox Court House, Virginia, on April 9, 1865, to work out the terms for the surrender of Lee's Army of Northern Virginia, a great chapter in American life came to a close, and a great new chapter began.

As you read Determine how Catton makes history come alive for the reader.

2   These men were bringing the Civil War to its virtual finish. To be sure, other armies had yet to surrender, and for a few days the fugitive Confederate government would struggle desperately and vainly, trying to find some way to go on living now that its chief support was gone. But in effect it was all over when Grant and Lee signed the papers. And the little room where they wrote out the terms was the scene of one of the poignant, dramatic contrasts in American history.

3   They were two strong men, these oddly different generals, and they represented the strengths of two conflicting currents that, through them, had come into final collision.

4   Back of Robert E. Lee was the notion that the old aristocratic concept might somehow survive and be dominant in American life.

General Robert E. Lee (left) and Ulysses S. Grant (right).

5   Lee was tidewater Virginia, and in his background were family, culture, and tradition . . . the age of chivalry transplanted to a New World which was making its own legends and its own myths. He embodied a way of life that had come down through the age of knighthood and the English country squire. America was a land that was beginning all over again, dedicated to nothing much more complicated than the rather hazy belief that all men had equal rights and should have an equal chance in the world. In such a land Lee stood for the feeling that it was somehow of advantage to human society to have a pronounced inequality in the social structure. There should be a leisure class, backed by ownership of land; in turn, society itself should be keyed to the land as the chief source of wealth and influence. It would bring forth (according to this ideal) a class of men with a strong sense of obligation to the community; men who lived not to gain advantage for themselves, but to meet the solemn obligations which had been laid on them by the very fact that they were privileged. From them the country would get its leadership; to them it could look for the higher values—of thought, of conduct, of personal deportment—to give it strength and virtue.

6   Lee embodied the noblest elements of this aristocratic ideal. Through him, the landed nobility justified itself. For four years, the Southern states had fought a desperate war to uphold the ideals for which Lee stood. In the end, it almost seemed as if the Confederacy fought for Lee; as if he himself was the Confederacy . . . the best thing that the way of life for which the Confederacy stood could ever have to offer. He had passed into legend before Appomattox. Thousands of tired, underfed, poorly clothed Confederate soldiers, long since past the simple enthusiasm of the early days of the struggle, somehow considered Lee the symbol of everything for which they had been willing to die. But they could not quite put this feeling into words. If the Lost Cause, sanctified by so much heroism and so many deaths, had a living justification, its justification was General Lee.

7   Grant, the son of a tanner on the Western frontier, was everything Lee was not. He had come up the hard way and embodied nothing in particular except the eternal toughness and sinewy fiber of the men who grew up beyond the mountains. He was one of a body of men who owed reverence and obeisance to no one, who were self-reliant to a fault, who cared hardly anything for the past but who had a sharp eye for the future.

8   These frontier men were the precise opposite of the tidewater aristocrats. Back of them, in the great surge that had taken people over the Alleghenies and into the opening Western country, there was a deep, implicit dissatisfaction with a past that had settled into grooves. They stood for democracy, not from any reasoned conclusion about the proper ordering of human society, but simply because they had grown up in the middle of democracy and knew how it worked. Their society might have privileges, but they would be privileges each man had won for himself. Forms and patterns meant nothing. No man was born to anything, except perhaps to a chance to show how far he could rise. Life was competition.

9   Yet along with this feeling had come a deep sense of belonging to a national community. The Westerner who developed a farm, opened a shop, or set up in business as a trader, could hope to prosper only as his own community prospered—and his community ran from the Atlantic to the Pacific and from Canada down to Mexico. If the land was settled, with towns and highways and accessible markets, he could better himself. He saw his fate in terms of the nation's own destiny. As its horizons expanded, so did his. He had, in other words, an acute dollars-and-cents stake in the continued growth and development of his country.

10   And that, perhaps, is where the contrast between Grant and Lee becomes most striking. The Virginia aristocrat, inevitably, saw himself in relation to his own region. He lived in a static society which could endure almost anything except change. Instinctively, his first loyalty would go to the locality in which that society existed. He would fight to the limit of endurance to defend it, because in defending it he was defending everything that gave his own life its deepest meaning.

11   The Westerner, on the other hand, would fight with an equal tenacity for the broader concept of society. He fought so because everything he lived by was tied to growth, expansion, and a constantly widening horizon. What he lived by would survive or fall with the nation itself. He could not possibly stand by unmoved in the face of an attempt to destroy the Union. He would combat it with everything

he had, because he could only see it as an effort to cut the ground out from under his feet.

12 So Grant and Lee were in complete contrast, representing two diametrically opposed elements in American life. Grant was the modern man emerging; beyond him, ready to come on the stage, was the great age of steel and machinery, of crowded cities and a restless burgeoning vitality. Lee might have ridden down from the old age of chivalry, lance in hand, silken banner fluttering over his head. Each man was the perfect champion of his cause, drawing both his strengths and his weaknesses from the people he led.

13 Yet it was not all contrast, after all. Different as they were—in background, in personality, in underlying aspiration—these two great soldiers had much in common. Under everything else, they were marvelous fighters. Furthermore, their fighting qualities were really very much alike.

14 Each man had, to begin with, the great virtue of utter tenacity and fidelity. Grant fought his way down the Mississippi Valley in spite of acute personal discouragement and profound military handicaps. Lee hung on in the trenches of Petersburg after hope itself had died. In each man there was an indomitable quality . . . the born fighter's refusal to give up as long as he can still remain on his feet and lift his two fists.

15 Daring and resourcefulness they had, too; the ability to think faster and move faster than the enemy. These were the qualities which gave Lee the dazzling campaigns of Second Manassas and Chancellorsville and won Vicksburg for Grant.

16 Lastly, and perhaps greatest of all, there was the ability, at the end, to turn quickly from war to peace once the fighting was over. Out of the way these two men behaved at Appomattox came the possibility of a peace of reconciliation. It was a possibility not wholly realized, in the years to come, but which did, in the end, help the two sections to become one nation again . . . after a war whose bitterness might have seemed to make such a reunion wholly impossible. No part of either man's life became him more than the part he played in their brief meeting in the McLean house at Appomattox. Their behavior there put all succeeding generations of Americans in their debt. Two great Americans, Grant and Lee—very different, yet under everything very much alike. Their encounter at Appomattox was one of the great moments of American history.

READING CLOSELY AND THINKING CRITICALLY

1. According to Catton, how were Grant and Lee different and how were they similar? What is the most significant point of contrast between the generals? What is the most significant point of similarity?

2. According to Catton, why do Americans owe a debt to Grant and Lee?

3. Catton says that Grant and Lee represented conflicting forces in American society. What were those forces?

4. What do you think Catton's attitude toward the generals is? Does he admire one more than the other? Explain.

5. Why doesn't Catton contrast the two generals' conflicting views on slavery? Do you think he should have? Explain.

EXAMINING STRUCTURE AND STRATEGY

1. Bruce Catton was a historian. Do you think his essay was written for an audience of historians or for a different audience? How do you know?

2. Which sentence states Catton's thesis? What words in the thesis indicate that Catton will compare and contrast his subjects?

3. Catton organizes details with both block and alternating patterns. Which paragraphs include the block pattern, and which include the alternating pattern?

4. Why does Catton discuss the differences between Grant and Lee before he discusses the similarities?

5. How does Catton use description to make history come alive for the reader?

CONSIDERING LANGUAGE AND STYLE

1. What metaphor appears in paragraph 1? (See page 110 on metaphors.) Why is that metaphor appropriate? Explain.

2. Catton uses transitions effectively. Cite three examples of transitions in the essay and explain how they contribute to the coherence of the essay.

3. Consult a dictionary if you are unsure of the meaning of any of these words: *poignant* (paragraph 2), *tidewater* (paragraph 5), *chivalry* (paragraph 5), *squire* (paragraph 5), *deportment* (paragraph 5), *sinewy* (paragraph 7), *obeisance* (paragraph 7), *static* (paragraph 10), *diametrically* (paragraph 12), *burgeoning* (paragraph 12), *tenacity* (paragraph 14), *fidelity* (paragraph 14), *indomitable* (paragraph 14).

FOR DISCUSSION IN CLASS OR ONLINE

Catton closes by saying that Grant and Lee's "encounter at Appomattox was one of the great moments of American history." What do you think Catton means by "great"? According to that definition, what other moments in American history do you consider great? Why? If your instructor directs you to do so, post your response to your class Web site.

WRITING ASSIGNMENTS

1. **In your journal.** In a page or so write out what you learned about Grant, Lee, and the Civil War as a result of reading "Grant and Lee: A Study in Contrasts." Would you like to learn more? Why or why not?

2. **Using comparison-contrast for a purpose.** The purposes in the assignments are possibilities. You may establish whatever purposes you like, within your instructor's guidelines.

   • To inform, compare and contrast (or just contrast) two people who do the same thing, such as two teachers, two coaches, two rock musicians, two baseball players, or two actors.

- To inform and perhaps persuade, compare and contrast (or just contrast) two people who represent two value systems or philosophies of life. You might consider a coach who believes that winning is everything and a coach who does not, a liberal politician and a conservative politician, or a micromanager and someone who delegates.

- To entertain and perhaps inform, compare and contrast (or just contrast) the way men and women do something. You might consider the way men and women communicate, argue, diet, work out, or watch football.

3. **Combining patterns.** Are Grant and Lee heroes? Answer this question by defining a hero and comparing or contrasting a hero with Grant and Lee. (Definition is discussed in Chapter 11.)

4. **Connecting the readings.** Consider to what extent contrasting value systems, like those represented in "Grant and Lee: A Study in Contrasts," are responsible for human suffering. In addition to your own thinking, you can draw on ideas in Catton's essay as well as those in "On Being the Target of Discrimination" (page 234), and "Untouchables" (page 248).

5. **Drawing on sources.** Grant and Lee each represented a force in American society. Pick someone who represents a force in contemporary society (for example, Madonna, Oprah Winfrey, George W. Bush, Rush Limbaugh, Jesse Jackson) and explain what the force is and how the person's behavior represents the force. For help, use the search engine of your choice and type in the person's name as keywords, or look up the person's name in your library in the *New York Times Index, Proquest,* or the *Reader's Guide to Periodical Literature.*

BACKGROUND: Born in North Carolina, Suzanne Britt is a poet, essayist, teacher, and textbook author. She graduated from Salem Academy and College with majors in English and Latin and earned her master's degree in English from Washington University in St. Louis. She has taught at North Carolina State University, Pace College, and Duke Divinity School and is now teaching at Meredith College. Her poems have appeared in the literary magazines *Denver Quarterly, Lake Superior Review, Greensboro Review,* and *Southern Poetry Review.* Her essays and articles have appeared in many newspapers and magazines, including *Newsweek, Books and Religion,* the *Boston Globe,* the *Cleveland Plain Dealer,* the *Charlotte Observer,* and *Newsday.* If you enjoy Britt's humor, you might want to read some of her other essays, which have been collected in *Skinny People Are Dull and Crunchy Like Carrots* (1982) and *Show and Tell* (1982). "Neat People vs. Sloppy People" is from her collection *Show and Tell.*

COMBINED PATTERNS AND THEIR PURPOSE: In "Neat People vs. Sloppy People," an **entertaining** essay, Britt *contrasts* neat and sloppy people using *examples* and *description* to help make her points.

Neat People vs. Sloppy People
SUZANNE BRITT

I've finally figured out the difference between neat people and sloppy people. The distinction is, as always, moral. Neat people are lazier and meaner than sloppy people.

2   Sloppy people, you see, are not really sloppy. Their sloppiness is merely the unfortunate consequence of their extreme moral rectitude. Sloppy people carry in their mind's eye a heavenly vision, a precise plan, that is so stupendous, so perfect, it can't be achieved in this world or the next.

As you read Determine whether Britt means everything she says, or whether she is just going for laughs.

3   Sloppy people live in Never-Never Land. Someday is their métier. Someday they are planning to alphabetize all their books and set up home catalogs. Someday they will go through their wardrobes and mark certain items for tentative mending and certain items for passing on to relatives of similar shape and size. Someday sloppy people will make family scrapbooks into which they will put newspaper clippings, postcards, locks of hair, and the dried corsage from their senior prom. Someday they will file everything on the surface of their desks, including the cash receipts from coffee purchases at the snack shop. Someday they will sit down and read all the back issues of *The New Yorker.*

4   For all these noble reasons and more, sloppy people never get neat. They aim too high and wide. They save everything, planning someday to file, order, and straighten out the world. But while these ambitious plans take clearer and clearer shape in their heads, the books spill from the shelves onto the floor, the clothes pile up in the hamper and closet, the family mementos accumulate in every drawer, the surface of the desk is buried under mounds of paper and the unread magazines threaten to reach the ceiling.₁

5   Sloppy people can't bear to part with anything. They give loving attention to every detail. When sloppy people say they're going to tackle the surface of the desk,

they really mean it. Not a paper will go unturned; not a rubber band will go unboxed. Four hours or two weeks into the excavation, the desk looks exactly the same, primarily because the sloppy person is meticulously creating new piles of papers with new headings and scrupulously stopping to read all the old book catalogs before he throws them away. A neat person would just bulldoze the desk.

6   Neat people are bums and clods at heart. They have cavalier attitudes toward possessions, including family heirlooms. Everything is just another dustcatcher to them. If anything collects dust, it's got to go and that's that. Neat people will toy with the idea of throwing the children out of the house just to cut down on the clutter.

7   Neat people don't care about process. They like results. What they want to do is get the whole thing over with so they can sit down and watch the rasslin' on TV. Neat people operate on two unvarying principles: Never handle any item twice, and throw everything away.

8   The only thing messy in a neat person's house is the trash can. The minute something comes to a neat person's hand, he will look at it, try to decide if it has immediate use and, finding none, throw it in the trash.

9   Neat people are especially vicious with mail. They never go through their mail unless they are standing directly over a trash can. If the trash can is beside the mailbox, even better. All ads, catalogs, pleas for charitable contributions, church bulletins and money-saving coupons go straight into the trash can without being opened. All letters from home, postcards from Europe, bills and paychecks are opened, immediately responded to, then dropped in the trash can. Neat people keep their receipts only for tax purposes. That's it. No sentimental salvaging of birthday cards or the last letter a dying relative ever wrote. Into the trash it goes.

10   Neat people place neatness above everything, even economics. They are incredibly wasteful. Neat people throw away several toys every time they walk through the den. I knew a neat person once who threw away a perfectly good dish drainer because it had mold on it. The drainer was too much trouble to wash. And neat people sell their furniture when they move. They will sell a La-Z-Boy recliner while you are reclining in it.

11   Neat people are no good to borrow from. Neat people buy everything in expensive little single portions. They get their flour and sugar in two-pound bags. They wouldn't consider clipping a coupon, saving a leftover, reusing plastic nondairy whipped cream containers or rinsing off tin foil and draping it over the unmoldy dish drainer. You can never borrow a neat person's newspaper to see what's playing at the movies. Neat people have the paper all wadded up and in the trash by 7:05 A.M.

12   Neat people cut a clean swath through the organic as well as the inorganic world. People, animals, and things are all one to them. They are so insensitive. After they've finished with the pantry, the medicine cabinet, and the attic, they will throw out the red geranium (too many leaves), sell the dog (too many fleas), and send the children off to boarding school (too many scuffmarks on the hardwood floors).

1. Is Britt serious when she claims, in paragraph 1, that the distinction between neat and sloppy people is a moral one? Explain.
2. Britt says that neat people are insensitive, that they are bums and clods. How serious is she in this assessment? If she cannot be taken literally, then how would you describe her attitude toward neat people?
3. Do you think that Britt is being fair to neat people? To sloppy people? Explain.
4. What kind of audience do you think Britt had in mind? Does it include neat people or sloppy people?

EXAMINING STRUCTURE AND STRATEGY

1. Does Britt use an alternating or block pattern to organize her details?
2. Does Britt achieve balance by treating the same points about both of her subjects? If not, is the lack of balance a problem? Explain.
3. Why does Britt wait until the end of her essay to discuss how neat people treat living things?

NOTING COMBINED PATTERNS

1. In which paragraphs does Britt use examples to clarify a point of contrast?
2. Three paragraphs describe sloppy people and seven paragraphs describe neat people. How does the description help Britt achieve her purpose for writing? Why does she have more description about neat people than sloppy people?

CONSIDERING LANGUAGE AND STYLE

1. How does Britt's tone contribute to the humor of the essay? (Tone is discussed on page ••). Cite at least two examples to illustrate your view.
2. Almost all of Britt's paragraphs begin with the words "Neat people" or the words "Sloppy people." Why?
3. Consult a dictionary if you are unsure of the meaning of any of these words: *rectitude* (paragraph 2), *métier* (paragraph 3), *meticulously* (paragraph 5), *scrupulously* (paragraph 5), *cavalier* (paragraph 6), *swath* (paragraph 12).

FOR DISCUSSION IN CLASS OR ONLINE

Consider Britt's word choice, examples, detail selection, and tone, and then explain how Britt achieves humor. If your instructor directs you to do so, post your response to your class Web site.

WRITING ASSIGNMENTS

1. **In your journal.** Are you a neat person or a sloppy person? Identify yourself as one or the other and go on to explain whether any of Britt's characterizations are true of you. Also, note to what extent you are happy to be either neat or sloppy.

2. **Using comparison-contrast for a purpose.** The purposes in the assignments are possibilities. You may establish whatever purposes you like, within your instructor's guidelines.

   - To entertain, turn the tables on Britt and write a contrast that proclaims the superiority of neat people.

   - To entertain, contrast those who plan ahead and those who are impulsive. As an alternative contrast those who procrastinate and those who do not put things off.

   - To entertain and perhaps inform, contrast those who are technologically savvy and those who know little about technology.

3. **Combining patterns.** Contrast any of these campus types, drawing on description (explained in Chapter 4) and examples (explained in Chapter 6) to help make your points: professors and deans; commuter students and residential students; adult learners and younger students.

4. **Connecting the readings.** Humorous essays entertain, but humor can also make serious points as well consider the humor in "Neat People vs. Sloppy People," "Lost at C" (page 189), and "How I'll Become an American" (page 281). Explain how the authors use humor both to entertain and to make serious points. How does humor help the authors achieve persuasive and informative purposes?

5. **Drawing on sources.** Interview one student, one teacher, one business or professional person, and one other person of your choice. Ask each of these people the following questions:

   - Are there times when neatness is important in your life or work? If so, explain when and why.

   - Are there times when neatness is not important in your life or work? If so, explain when and why.

   - Are there times when sloppiness is acceptable? If so explain when.

   Using the information from the interviews along with your own experience and observation, write an essay that proves either that neatness counts or that neatness does not count.

BACKGROUND: Born in Chicago in 1959 and raised in Oregon, Nicholas D. Kristof is a seasoned foreign correspondent. He became bureau chief at the *New York Times* Tokyo bureau in 1994 after serving as Beijing bureau chief and Hong Kong bureau chief. In 1990, Kristof and his wife Sheryl WuDunn, who is also a *Times* foreign correspondent, jointly won the Pulitzer Prize for international reporting for their coverage of the democracy movement in China. Kristof's books include *China Wakes: The Struggle for the Soul of a Rising Power* (1994) and *Thunder from the East: Portrait of a Rising Asia* (2000), which he wrote with his wife. "In Japan, Nice Guys (and Girls) Finish Together" first appeared in the *New York Times Magazine* in 1997.

COMBINED PATTERNS AND THEIR PURPOSES: In "In Japan, Nice Guys (and Girls) Finish Together," Nicholas Kristof *contrasts* the competitive spirit of Americans with the cooperative spirit of Japanese in order to **inform** readers about the different orientations of the two cultures. In addition, he **expresses his feelings** about these orientations. To help achieve his purposes, Kristoff draws on *exemplification* and *cause-and-effect analysis.*

IN JAPAN, NICE GUYS (AND GIRLS) FINISH TOGETHER

NICHOLAS D. KRISTOF

My intention, honest, was not to scar these Japanese kids for life. I just wanted to give them a fun game to play.

2 It was the fifth birthday party last year for my son Gregory, and he had invited all his Japanese friends over from the Tokyo kindergarten that he attended. My wife and I explained the rules of musical chairs, and we started the music.

As you read
Think about aspects of the Japanese orientation that appeal to you.

3 It was not so awful for the Japanese boys. They managed to fight for seats, albeit a bit lamely. But the girls were at sea.

4 The first time I stopped the music, Gregory's 5-year-old girlfriend, Chitose-chan, was next to him, right in front of a chair. But she stood politely and waited for him to be seated first.

5 So Gregory scrambled into her seat, and Chitose-chan beamed proudly at her own good manners. Then I walked over and told her that she had just lost the game and would have to sit out. She gazed up at me, her luminous eyes full of shocked disbelief, looking like Bambi might after a discussion of venison burgers.

6 "You mean I lose because I'm polite?" Chitose-chan's eyes asked. "You mean the point of the game is to be rude?"

7 Well, now that I think of it, I guess that is the point. American kids are taught to be winners, to seize their opportunities and maybe the next kid's as well. Japanese children are taught to be good citizens, to be team players, to obey rules, to be content to be a mosaic tile in some larger design.

8 One can have an intelligent debate about which approach is better. The Japanese emphasis on consideration and teamwork perhaps explains why Japan has few armed robbers but also so few entrepreneurs. The American emphasis on winning may help explain why the United States consistently racks up Olympic gold medals but also why its hockey players trashed their rooms in Nagano.[1]

9 The civility that still lingers in Japan is the most charming and delightful

---

[1]Nagano, Japan was the site of the 1998 Winter Olympic games.

aspect of life here today. Taxi drivers wear white gloves, take pride in the cleanliness of their vehicles, and sometimes give a discount if they mistakenly take a long route. When they are sick, Japanese wear surgical face masks so they will not infect others. The Japanese language has almost no curses, and high school baseball teams bow to each other at the beginning of each game.

10   One can go years here without hearing a voice raised in anger, for when Japanese are furious they sometimes show it by becoming incredibly formal and polite. Compared with New York, it's rather quaint.

11   The conundrum is that Japan is perhaps too civilized for the 1990's. To revive its economy, mired in a seven-year slump, the country now needs an infusion of economic ruthlessness, a dose of the law of the jungle. Japan desperately needs to restructure itself, which is to say that it needs to create losers—companies need to lay off excess workers, Mom-and-Pop rice shops need to be replaced by more efficient supermarkets and failing banks need to go bankrupt.

12   But Japan is deeply uncomfortable with the idea of failures or losers. The social and economic basis of modern Japan is egalitarianism, and that does not leave much room for either winners or losers. In Japan, winning isn't everything, and it isn't the only thing, in elementary schools it isn't even a thing at all.

13   When Gregory and his brother Geoffrey went to Sports Day at their Japanese kindergarten, everybody told us that this was the big event of the year. So my wife and I went to cheer, but it wasn't really necessary. There were three-legged races and team basketball shoots and all kinds of games, but somehow at the end of the day no one won and no one lost.

There were no blue ribbons, no prizes for the fastest runner, no cheers for the best basketball shooter, or anything else; instead, every child got a small prize.

14   The point of Sports Day was not to divide students by recognizing individual excellence but to unite them by giving them a shared experience. Likewise, schools do not normally break up children into "fast reading classes" and "slow reading classes," because that would stigmatize the slower ones. During recess or phys ed, there is no system of having a few captains take turns picking teams, because the last-picked might be upset; instead kids divide by class or by the Japanese equivalent of alphabetical order. When drama teachers select a play to perform, they choose one in which there is no star, just a lot of equal parts—which makes for first-rate student harmony and second-rate drama.

15   Of course, competition is inevitable in any society, and in Japan it is introduced in junior high schools, when children must compete intensely to pass high school and college entrance examinations. But the emphasis remains on "wa," or harmony, on being one with the group.

16   Ask a traditional Japanese housewife what she wants for her child, and you will sometimes hear an answer like: "I just want my kid to grow up so as not to be a nuisance to other people." Hmmm. Not a dream often heard in America.

17   Even in business, the obsession with egalitarian wa goes to astonishing lengths. One Tokyo bank executive told me how he envied the Japanese subsidiary of Citibank, which waives certain fees for customers who keep a large minimum balance. That would never be tolerated in a Japanese bank, he said, because it would be regarded as

discriminatory against the poor. Likewise, he said, his bank cannot easily close unprofitable branches in remote areas, because then it would be criticized for abandoning the people there.

18 The emphasis on wa perhaps arises because 125 million Japanese, almost half of America's population, are squeezed into an area the size of California. How else could they survive but with a passion for protocol and a web of picayune rules dictating consideration for others? If 125 million Americans were jammed into such a small space, we might have torn each other to shreds by now.

19 Building teamwork in Japan starts from birth. When our third child, Caroline, was born in Tokyo last fall, the hospital explained that the mothers were to nurse their babies all together in the same room at particular meal times. So on her first day of life, Caroline was effectively told to discipline her appetites to adjust to a larger scheme with others.

20 This civility and egalitarianism shape just about every aspect of life. When the Japanese translation of a book that my wife and I wrote was published, we were pleased that the first reviews were positive. But we were frankly surprised when every single Japanese review was positive, and I remarked on that to a Japanese friend. "Oh, that's the only kind of book review there is in Japan," he explained. "There are no bad book reviews. Just nice ones."

21 And insipid ones, of course. Indeed, Japan itself is so polite as to be a bit bland, rather like "Mr. Rogers' Neighborhood"[2] on a national scale. And of course Mr. Rogers' Neighborhood was never known for its hustle or economic vibrancy.

"Japan itself is so polite as to be a bit bland, rather like 'Mr. Rogers' Neighborhood' on a national scale."

22 So now, Japan is trying to become nastier. Workers are being pushed out of their jobs, occasionally even laid off. Employees are no longer being automatically promoted by seniority. Pay differentials are widening. Companies are becoming more concerned with efficiency and share prices, less concerned with employee welfare.

23 All this will make Japan a more prosperous country, but perhaps a less civil one. The changes certainly rub against the grain here, particularly of older people.

24 They rub just a bit against my grain, too. I bought a long scroll of calligraphy with the character "wa," in hopes that my kids will learn harmony, instead of clubbing each other over toys. Yet on the other hand I still want them to win—at musical chairs and everything else.

25 That is getting tougher, because young Japanese are adapting to greater competition, and they seem to be a bit more aggressive and individualist than their parents. Some young Japanese are even getting pretty good at musical chairs.

26 And little Chitose-chan, Gregory's girlfriend—well, she may be polite, but

---

[2]"Mr. Rogers' Neighborhood," hosted by Fred Rogers (1928–2003), was America's longest running children's show. From 1967–2001, the program dealt with issues important to children in the characteristic soft-spoken, gentle manner of the host.

don't underestimate her generation's ability to catch on quickly. Thirty minutes after the game of musical chairs, Chitose-chan and her friend Naoko-chan got into an argument over a party favor. Chitose-chan slugged Naoko-chan in the mouth and grabbed the toy.

27 Perhaps that's globalization.

READING CLOSELY AND THINKING CRITICALLY

1. What is the primary difference between American and Japanese styles?

2. What reason does Kristof give for the difference between American and Japanese styles?

3. According to Kristof, why is the Japanese style of civility hurting Japan?

4. In paragraph 16, Kristof notes what a Japanese mother wants for her child: "to grow up so as not to be a nuisance to other people." What might an American mother say she wants for her child? How do you explain the difference?

5. Explain what Kristof means in paragraph 27 when he says, "Perhaps that's globalization."

EXAMINING STRUCTURE AND STRATEGY

1. The sentence that best expresses Kristof's thesis is delayed for several paragraphs. Where is that sentence? What is the purpose of the paragraphs before the thesis?

2. At times, Kristof implies rather than states his contrasts. For example, in paragraph 9, he notes the effects of Japanese civility, but he does not state the contrasting point about Americans. Is this strategy a problem? Why or why not? Cite another paragraph where contrast is implied rather than stated.

3. Does Kristof maintain balance between his discussion of Japanese and American styles? Explain.

4. How does Kristof convey his attitude about Japan's increasing competitiveness?

NOTING COMBINED PATTERNS

1. Kristof uses exemplification in paragraphs 8, 9, 13, 14, 17, and 20. (Exemplification is explained in Chapter 6.) How does exemplification help him achieve his writing purpose?

2. What cause-and-effect analysis appears in the essay? (Cause-and-effect analysis is explained in Chapter 9.) Why does Kristof include this cause-and-effect analysis?

CONSIDERING LANGUAGE AND STYLE

1. Explain the metaphor in paragraph 7. (**Metaphors** are explained on page 110.)

2. So their writing has a pleasing flow and rhythm, authors often alternate long and short sentences, the way Kristof does in paragraph 19. Cite another example of this technique in the essay.

3. Consult a dictionary if you are unsure of the meaning of any of these words: *conundrum* (paragraph 11), *egalitarian* (paragraph 12), *picayune* (paragraph 18), *insipid* (paragraph 21), *globalization* (paragraph 27).

Is the environment in your classrooms predominantly cooperative or competitive? Is this the best classroom environment? Why or why not? If your instructor so directs, post your response to your class Web site.

WRITING ASSIGNMENTS

1. **In your journal.** Is there anything about Japanese style that you would like to incorporate into American style? Explain in a page or two.

2. **Using comparison-contrast for a purpose.** The purposes in the assignments are possibilities. You may establish whatever purposes you like, within your instructor's guidelines.

    *   To relate experience, express feelings, and inform, compare and contrast a time you worked cooperatively and a time you worked competitively in a similar context. Explain which situation you preferred and why. For example, you can compare and contrast a time in school when you worked on a group project where everyone received the same grade and a time when you prepared for an exam that was graded on a curve. Or you can compare and contrast a time at work when you prepared a committee report with colleagues and a time you participated in a sales contest.

    *   Compare and contrast some aspect of life with competition with what that aspect would be like without competition. For example, you could compare the competitive classroom with one where students did not compete for teachers' attention or grades. Or you could compare television programming when networks compete for ratings with when ratings do not matter. Your purpose is to convince readers that one way is better than the other.

    *   Kristof likes the civility of Japan's culture, and he finds competition "nastier" than harmonious teamwork (paragraph 22). To convince readers that one way is better than the other, compare and contrast the spirit of competition and the spirit of cooperation.

3. **Combining patterns.** Throughout the essay, Kristof refers to the civility of the Japanese people. What word describes the behavior of Americans? Write a definition of that word, and compare and contrast it with civility. (Definition is explained in Chapter 11.)

4. **Connecting the readings.** Retell all or part of the story narrated in "Lost at C" (page 189) so that it conveys the Japanese spirit of harmony and teamwork.

5. **Drawing on sources.** Ask ten people to complete the following questionnaire:

    *   In the last year, what endeavors have you participated in that required teamwork? The endeavors can be related to family, school, work, or aspects of your social and community life.

    *   How successful were your teamwork projects?

    *   In the last year, what endeavors have you participated in that required you to work individually and competitively? The endeavors can be related to family, school, work, or aspects of your social and community life.

    *   How successful were these competitive endeavors?

    *   Which of the endeavors did you find the most pleasant? Why?

    Study the questionnaire results and use them, along with your own experience and observation, to discuss the role of teamwork and competition in our society.

www.mhhe.com/patterns

For more information on this author, go to

More resources > Chapter 8 > Alice Walker

C O M B I N E D   P A T T E R N S   A N D   T H E I R   P U R P O S E S : In "Am I Blue?" Walker *narrates* a story that includes both *description* and *comparison-contrast* to **inform** the reader about the oneness of animals and humans and to **persuade** the reader to treat animals well and, perhaps, become a vegetarian. Her story also allows her to **express her feelings and relate her experience.** The title of the piece is the same as a great old blues song.

AM I BLUE? | ALICE WALKER

"Ain't these tears in these eyes tellin' you?"[1]

2   For about three years my companion and I rented a small house in the country that stood on the edge of a large meadow that appeared to run from the end of our deck straight into the mountains. The mountains, however, were quite far away, and between us and them there was, in fact, a town. It was one of the many pleasant aspects of the house that you never really were aware of this.

3   It was a house of many windows, low, wide, nearly floor to ceiling in the living room, which faced the meadow, and it was from one of these that I first saw our closest neighbor, a large white horse, cropping grass, flipping its mane, and ambling about—not over the entire meadow, which stretched well out of sight of the house, but over the five or so fenced-in acres that were next to the twenty-odd that we had rented. I soon

As you read Ask yourself why the title is so appropriate.

[1]From "Am I Blue?" by Grant Clarke and Harry Akst. Copyright 1929 Warner Bros. Inc. (renewed).

learned that the horse, whose name was Blue, belonged to a man who lived in another town, but was boarded by our neighbors next door. Occasionally, one of the children, usually a stocky teenager, but sometimes a much younger girl or boy, could be seen riding Blue. They would appear in the meadow, climb up on his back, ride furiously for ten or fifteen minutes, then get off, slap Blue on the flanks, and not be seen again for a month or more.

4   There were many apple trees in our yard, and one by the fence that Blue could almost reach. We were soon in the habit of feeding him apples, which he relished, especially because by the middle of summer the meadow grasses— so green and succulent since January— had dried out from lack of rain, and Blue stumbled about munching the dried stalks halfheartedly. Sometimes he would stand very still just by the apple tree, and when one of us came out he would whinny, snort loudly, or stamp the ground. This meant, of course: I want an apple.

> "Sometimes he would stand very still just by the apple tree, and when one of us came out he would whinny, snort loudly, or stamp the ground."

5   It was quite wonderful to pick a few apples, or collect those that had fallen to the ground overnight, and patiently hold them, one by one, up to his large, toothy mouth. I remained as thrilled as a child by his flexible dark lips, huge, cubelike teeth that crunched the apples, core and all, with such finality, and his high, broad-breasted *enormity*; beside which, I felt small indeed. When I was a child, I used to ride horses, and was especially friendly with one named Nan until the day I was riding and my brother deliberately spooked her and I was thrown, head first, against the trunk of a tree. When I came to, I was in bed and my mother was bending worriedly over me; we silently agreed that perhaps horseback riding was not the safest sport for me. Since then I have walked, and prefer walking to horseback riding—but I had forgotten the depth of feeling one could see in horses' eyes.

6   I was therefore unprepared for the expression in Blue's. Blue was lonely. Blue was horribly lonely and bored. I was not shocked that this should be the case; five acres to tramp by yourself, endlessly, even in the most beautiful of meadows—and his was—cannot provide many interesting events, and once rainy season turned to dry that was about it. No, I was shocked that I had forgotten that human animals and nonhuman animals can communicate quite well; if we are brought up around animals as children we take this for granted. By the time we are adults we no longer remember. However, the animals have not changed. They are in fact *completed* creations (at least they seem to be, so much more than we) who are not likely *to* change; it is their nature to express themselves. What else are they going to express? And they do. And, generally speaking, they are ignored.

7   After giving Blue the apples, I would wander back to the house, aware that he was observing me. Were more apples not forthcoming then? Was that to be his sole entertainment for the day? My partner's small son had decided he

wanted to learn how to piece a quilt; we worked in silence on our respective squares as I thought . . .

8   Well, about slavery: about white children, who were raised by black people, who knew their first all-accepting love from black women, and then, when they were twelve or so, were told they must "forget" the deep levels of communication between themselves and "mammy" that they knew. Later they would be able to relate quite calmly, "My old mammy was sold to another good family." "My old mammy was _____." Fill in the blank. Many more years later a white woman would say: "I can't understand these Negroes, these blacks. What do they want? They're so different from us."

9   And about the Indians, considered to be "like animals" by the "settlers" (a very benign euphemism for what they actually were), who did not understand their description as a compliment.

10   And about the thousands of American men who marry Japanese, Korean, Filipina, and other non-English-speaking women and of how happy they report they are, "blissfully," until their brides learn to speak English, at which point the marriages tend to fall apart. What then did the men see, when they looked into the eyes of the women they married, before they could speak English? Apparently only their own reflections.

11   I thought of society's impatience with the young. "Why are they playing the music so loud?" Perhaps the children have listened to much of the music of oppressed people their parents danced to before they were born, with its passionate but soft cries for acceptance and love, and they have wondered why their parents failed to hear.

12   I do not know how long Blue had inhabited his five beautiful, boring acres before we moved into our house; a year after we had arrived—and had also traveled to other valleys, other cities, other worlds—he was still there.

13   But then, in our second year at the house, something happened in Blue's life. One morning, looking out the window at the fog that lay like a ribbon over the meadow, I saw another horse, a brown one, at the other end of Blue's field. Blue appeared to be afraid of it,

"I saw another horse, a brown one, at the end of Blue's field."

and for several days made no attempt to go near. We went away for a week. When we returned, Blue had decided to make friends and the two horses ambled or galloped along together, and Blue did not come nearly as often to the fence underneath the apple tree.

14   When he did, bringing his new friend with him, there was a different look in his eyes. A look of independence, of self-possession, of inalienable horseness. His friend eventually became pregnant. For months and months there was, it seemed to me, a mutual feeling between me and the horses of justice, of peace. I fed apples to them both. The look in Blue's eyes was one of unabashed "this is itness."

15   It did not, however, last forever. One day, after a visit to the city, I went out to give Blue some apples. He stood waiting, or so I thought, though not beneath the tree. When I shook the tree and jumped back from the shower of apples, he made no move. I carried some over to him. He managed to half-crunch one.

The rest he let fall to the ground. I dreaded looking into his eyes—because I had of course noticed that Brown, his partner, had gone—but I did look. If I had been born into slavery, and my partner had been sold or killed, my eyes would have looked like that. The children next door explained that Blue's partner had been "put with him" (the same expression that old people used, I had noticed, when speaking of an ancestor during slavery who had been impregnated by her owner) so that they would mate and she conceive. Since that was accomplished, she had been taken back by her owner, who lived somewhere else.

16 Will she be back? I asked.

17 They didn't know.

18 Blue was like a crazed person. Blue *was*, to me, a crazed person. He galloped furiously, as if he were being ridden, around and around his five beautiful

> "He looked always and always toward the road down which his partner had gone."

acres. He whinnied until he couldn't. He tore at the ground with his hooves. He butted himself against his single shade tree. He looked always and always toward the road down which his partner had gone. And then, occasionally, when he came up for apples, or I took apples to him, he looked at me. It was a look so piercing, so full of grief, a look so *human,* I almost laughed (I felt too sad to cry) to think there are people who do not know that animals suffer. People like me who have forgotten, and daily forget, all that animals try to tell us. "Everything you do to us will happen to you; we are your teachers, as you are ours. We are one lesson" is essentially it, I think. There are those who never once have even considered animals' rights: those who have been taught that animals actually want to be used and abused by us, as small children "love" to be frightened, or women "love" to be mutilated and raped . . . They are the great-grandchildren of those who honestly thought, because someone taught them this: "Women can't think," and "niggers can't faint." But most disturbing of all, in Blue's large brown eyes was a new look, more painful than the look of despair: the look of disgust with human beings, with life; the look of hatred. And it was odd what the look of hatred did. It gave him, for the first time, the look of a beast. And what that meant was that he had put up a barrier within to protect himself from further violence; all the apples in the world wouldn't change that fact.

19 And so Blue remained, a beautiful part of our landscape, very peaceful to look at from the window, white against the grass. Once a friend came to visit and said, looking out on the soothing view: "And it *would* have to be a *white* horse; the very image of freedom." And I thought, yes, the animals are forced to become for us merely "images" of what they once so beautifully expressed. And we are used to drinking milk from containers showing "contented" cows, whose real lives we want to hear nothing about, eating eggs and drumsticks from "happy" hens, and munching hamburgers advertised by bulls of integrity who seem to command their fate.

20 As we talked of freedom and justice one day for all, we sat down to steaks. I am eating misery, I thought, as I took the first bite. And spit it out.

READING CLOSELY AND THINKING CRITICALLY

1. Walker compares Blue to a human being. In what ways are the horse and a person similar?
2. In paragraphs 8 through 11, Blue's relationship with people is compared to a number of other human relationships. What are those relationships? What is the common element in each of these comparisons?
3. Specifically, what messages do you think Walker is trying to communicate to her reader?
4. Blue is given human qualities throughout most of the essay. However, in paragraph 18, he becomes a "beast." Why? When he becomes beastlike, is he less like a human and more like an animal? Explain.
5. Walker says that Blue has feelings and the ability to communicate those feelings. Do you agree? Explain.

EXAMINING STRUCTURE AND STRATEGY

1. Which paragraph best presents Walker's focus and the ideas she wants to convey to her reader? Why does she wait so long to present her focus?
2. Do you think Walker's title is a good one? Why or why not?
3. "Am I Blue?" appeared in *Ms.* in 1986. What kind of audience was Walker reaching? Is the essay suited to that kind of audience? Explain.

NOTING COMBINED PATTERNS

1. Which paragraphs include description? How does the description help Walker achieve her purpose?
2. To what extent is "Am I Blue?" a narrative essay (an essay that tells a story)?

CONSIDERING LANGUAGE AND STYLE

1. **Verbal irony** occurs when a speaker or writer says one thing but clearly means the opposite or nearly the opposite. Explain the irony of the images of "'contented' cows," "'happy' hens," and bulls "who seem to command their fate" (paragraph 19).
2. Walker opens paragraph 18 with this simile: "Blue was like a crazed person." (Similes are explained on page 109) Then she follows with the more literal "Blue *was*, to me, a crazed person." Explain this movement from a simile to a more literal statement.
3. Consult a dictionary if you are unsure of the meaning of either of these words: *inalienable* (paragraph 14) and *unabashed* (paragraph 14).

FOR DISCUSSION IN CLASS OR ONLINE

In paragraph 18, Walker notes that animals say to people, "Everything you do to us will happen to you; we are your teachers, as you are ours. We are one lesson." Discuss what this quote means and indicate whether you agree or disagree with it. If your instructor directs you to do so, post your response to your class Web site.

1. **In your journal.** Should people show respect for animals by not eating meat? What about wearing leather and fur? Should people wear only material not made from animals? Explore your feelings on these matters.

2. **Using comparison-contrast for a purpose.** The purposes in the assignments are possibilities. You may establish whatever purposes you like, within your instructor's guidelines.

    -   In paragraph 10, Walker refers to "the thousands of American men who marry Japanese, Korean, Filipina, and other non-English-speaking women" who are happy "until their brides learn to speak English, at which point the marriages tend to fall apart." The marriages may have fallen apart because once the wives could express themselves, conflict ensued. To relate your experience and express your feelings, compare and contrast some aspect of your life before and after you spoke up about something and created conflict.

    -   Blue's existence changed dramatically after the other horse entered his life. To relate experience, express feelings, and perhaps inform, compare and contrast your life before and after someone entered it.

    -   Blue's existence changed dramatically again after the other horse was taken away. To relate experience, express feelings, and perhaps inform, compare and contrast your life before and after someone left it.

3. **Combining patterns.** Walker compares Blue to a human being because he can feel and express emotions. If you have a pet and believe that the pet has something in common with humans, compare the pet and a human being. Use description (explained in Chapter 4) and narration (explained in Chapter 5) to help make your points. Be careful to avoid obvious comparisons, such as "My cat, like people, must eat and drink daily."

4. **Connecting the readings.** In paragraphs 18 and 19, Walker makes a case for vegetarianism. Explain her view, and drawing on the ideas in the essay, those in "The Deer at Providencia" (page 135), and your own ideas, agree or disagree with her.

5. **Drawing on sources.** State and defend your view on one or more of these questions: Are our food production techniques cruel to animals? If they are, can anything be done to eliminate that cruelty? Is the cruelty an unfortunate but necessary component of food production? If you need ideas, check the *Social Sciences Index* under the heading "Animals, treatment of." You can also type in the phrase "animal rights" at *www.yahoo.com*.

BACKGROUND: Born in 1945 and raised in Brooklyn, New York, linguist Deborah Tannen is a professor at Georgetown University. An authority on communication between the genders, Tannen has reported her research findings in many scholarly publications and in numerous newspaper and magazine articles. She has appeared on television programs including "Today," "Good Morning, America," "20/20," "48 Hours," "CBS News," "ABC World News Tonight," "Oprah," and "Larry King Live." Tannen has lectured all over the world to audiences that have included corporations such as Corning, Chevron, Motorola, and Delta Air Lines. Her lectures often include videotaped footage of office interaction to help audiences understand what happens in conversations both in the workplace and at home. Tannen's books include *That's Not What I Meant: How Conversational Style Makes or Breaks Relationships* (1986); *You Just Don't Understand: Men and Women in Conversation* (1990), which was on the *New York Times* best-seller list for almost four years; *Gender and Discourse* (1994); and *I Only Say This Because I Love You: How the Way We Talk Can Make or Break Family Relationships Throughout Our Lives* (2001). She has also published poetry, short stories, and personal essays. This essay first appeared in the *New York Times Magazine* in August 1994.

www.mhhe.com/patterns

For more information on this author, go to

More resources > Chapter 8 > Deborah Tannen

COMBINED PATTERNS AND THEIR PURPOSES: In "Squeaky Wheels and Protruding Nails: Direct and Indirect Speech," Deborah Tannen *defines* and *contrasts* direct and indirect forms of speech in order to **inform** her audience about the nature of each communication style and to **persuade** readers that despite what they may think, one style is not better than the other. Tannen's conclusions are not just opinion, however; they are rooted in research findings, some of which appear in the essay.

SQUEAKY WHEELS AND PROTRUDING NAILS: DIRECT AND INDIRECT SPEECH

DEBORAH TANNEN

A university president was expecting a visit from a member of the board of trustees. When her secretary buzzed to tell her that the board member had arrived, she left her office and entered the reception area to greet him. Before ushering him into her office, she handed her secretary a sheet of paper and said: "I've just finished drafting this letter. Do you think you could type it right away? I'd like to get it out before lunch.

As you read
Think how the research findings given in the essay are likely to affect readers.

And would you please do me a favor and hold all calls while I'm meeting with Mr. Smith?"

2   When they sat down behind the closed door of her office, Mr. Smith began by telling her that he thought she had spoken inappropriately to her secretary. "Don't forget," he said. *"You're* the president!"

3   Putting aside the question of the appropriateness of his admonishing the president on her way of speaking, it is revealing—and representative of many

Americans' assumptions—that the indirect way in which the university president told her secretary what to do struck him as self-deprecating. He took it as evidence that she didn't think she had the right to make demands of her secretary. He probably thought he was giving her a needed pep talk, bolstering her self-confidence.

4   I challenge the assumption that talking in an indirect way necessarily reveals powerlessness, lack of self-confidence or anything else about the character of the speaker. Indirectness is a fundamental element in human communication. It is also one of the elements that varies most from one culture to another, and one that can cause confusion and misunderstanding when speakers have different habits with regard to using it. I also want to dispel the assumption that American women tend to be more indirect than American men. Women and men are both indirect, but in addition to differences associated with their backgrounds—regional, ethnic and class—they tend to be indirect in different situations and in different ways.

5   At work, we need to get others to do things, and we all have different ways of accomplishing this. Any individual's ways will vary depending on who is being addressed—a boss, a peer or a subordinate. At one extreme are bald commands. At the other are requests so indirect that they don't sound like requests at all, but are just a statement of need or a description of a situation. People with direct styles of asking others to do things perceive indirect requests—if they perceive them as requests at all—as manipulative. But this is often just a way of blaming others for our discomfort with their styles.

6   The indirect style is no more manipulative than making a telephone call,

asking "Is Rachel there?" and expecting whoever answers the phone to put Rachel on. Only a child is likely to answer "Yes" and continue holding the phone—not out of orneriness but because of inexperience with the conventional meaning of the question. (A mischievous adult might do it to tease.) Those who feel that indirect orders are illogical or manipulative do not recognize the conventional nature of indirect requests.

7   Issuing orders indirectly can be the prerogative of those in power. Imagine, for example, a master who says "It's cold in here" and expects a servant to make a move to close a window, while a servant who says the same thing is not likely to see his employer rise to correct the situation and make him more comfortable. Indeed, a Frenchman raised in Brittany tells me that his family never gave bald commands to their servants but always communicated orders in indirect and highly polite ways. This pattern renders less surprising the finding of David Bellinger and Jean Berko Gleason that fathers' speech to their young children had a higher incidence than mothers' of both direct imperatives like "Turn the bolt with the wrench" *and* indirect orders like "The wheel is going to fall off."

8   The use of indirectness can hardly be understood without the cross-cultural perspective. Many Americans find it self-evident that directness is logical and aligned with power while indirectness is akin to dishonesty and reflects subservience. But for speakers raised in most of the world's cultures, varieties of indirectness are the norm in communication. This is the pattern found by a Japanese sociolinguist, Kunihiko Harada, in his analysis of a conversation he recorded between a Japanese boss and a subordinate.

9   The markers of superior status were clear. One speaker was a Japanese man in his late 40's who managed the local branch of a Japanese private school in the United States. His conversational partner was a Japanese-American woman in her early 20's who worked at the school. By virtue of his job, his age and his native fluency in the language being taught, the man was in the superior position. Yet when he addressed the woman, he frequently used polite language and almost always used indirectness. For example, he had tried and failed to find a photography store that would make a black-and-white print from a color negative for a brochure they were producing. He let her know that he wanted her to take over the task by stating the situation and allowed her to volunteer to do it: (This is a translation of the Japanese conversation.)

> On this matter, that, that, on the leaflet? This photo, I'm thinking of changing it to black-and-white and making it clearer . . .
> I went to a photo shop and asked them. They said they didn't do black-and-white. I asked if they knew any place that did. They said they didn't know. They weren't very helpful, but anyway, a place must be found, the negative brought to it, the picture developed.

10   Harada observes, "Given the fact that there are some duties to be performed and that there are two parties present, the subordinate is supposed to assume that those are his or her obligation." It was precisely because of his higher status that the boss was free to choose whether to speak formally or informally, to assert his power or to play it down and build rapport—an option not available to the subordinate, who would have seemed cheeky if she had chosen a style that enhanced friendliness and closeness.

11   The same pattern was found by a Chinese sociolinguist, Yuling Pan, in a meeting of officials involved in a neighborhood youth program. All spoke in ways that reflected their place in the hierarchy. A subordinate addressing a superior always spoke in a deferential way, but a superior addressing a subordinate could either be authoritarian, demonstrating his power, or friendly, establishing rapport. The ones in power had the option of choosing which style to use. In this spirit, I have been told by people who prefer their bosses to give orders indirectly that those who issue bald commands must be pretty insecure; otherwise why would they have to bolster their egos by throwing their weight around?

12   I am not inclined to accept that those who give orders directly are really insecure and powerless, any more than I want to accept that judgment of those who give indirect orders. The conclusion to be drawn is that ways of talking should not be taken as obvious evidence of inner psychological states like insecurity or lack of confidence. Considering the many influences on conversational style, individuals have a wide range of ways of getting things done and expressing their emotional states. Personality characteristics like insecurity cannot be linked to ways of speaking in an automatic, self-evident way.

13   Those who expect orders to be given indirectly are offended when they come unadorned. One woman said that when her boss gives her instructions, she feels she should click her heels, salute,

and say "Yes, boss!" His directions strike her as so imperious as to border on the militaristic. Yet I received a letter from a man telling me that indirect orders were a fundamental part of his military training. He wrote:

> Many years ago, when I was in the Navy, I was training to be a radio technician. One class I was in was taught by a chief radioman, a regular Navy man who had been to sea, and who was then in his third hitch. The students, about 20 of us, were fresh out of boot camp, with no sea duty and little knowledge of real Navy life. One day in class the chief said it was hot in the room. The students didn't react, except perhaps to nod in agreement. The chief repeated himself: "It's hot in this room." Again there was no reaction from the students.
>
> Then the chief explained. He wasn't looking for agreement or discussion from us. When he said that the room was hot, he expected us to do something about it—like opening the window. He tried it one more time, and this time all of us left our workbenches and headed for the windows. We had learned. And we had many opportunities to apply what we had learned.

14 This letter especially intrigued me because "It's cold in here" is the standard sentence used by linguists to illustrate an indirect way of getting someone to do something—as I used it earlier. In this example, it is the very obviousness and rigidity of the military hierarchy that makes the statement of a problem sufficient to trigger corrective action on the part of subordinates.

15 A man who had worked at the Pentagon reinforced the view that the burden of interpretation is on subordinates in the military—and he noticed the difference when he moved to a position in the private sector. He was frustrated when he'd say to his new secretary, for example, "Do we have a list of invitees?" and be told, "I don't know; we probably do" rather than "I'll get it for you." Indeed, he explained, at the Pentagon, such a question would likely be heard as a reproach that the list was not already on his desk.

16 The suggestion that indirectness is associated with the military must come as a surprise to many. But everyone is indirect, meaning more than is put into words and deriving meaning from words that are never actually said. It's a matter of where, when and how we each tend to be indirect and look for hidden meanings. But indirectness has a built-in liability. There is a risk that the other will either miss or choose to ignore your meaning.

17 On January 13, 1982, a freezing cold, snowy day in Washington, Air Florida Flight 90 took off from National Airport, but could not get the lift it needed to keep climbing. It crashed into a bridge linking Washington to the state of Virginia and plunged into the Potomac. Of the 79 people on board, all but 5 perished, many floundering and drowning in the icy water while horror-stricken bystanders watched helplessly from the river's edge and millions more watched, aghast, on their television screens. Experts later concluded that the plane had waited too long after deicing to take off. Fresh buildup of ice on the wings and engine brought the plane down.

How could the pilot and co-pilot have made such a blunder? Didn't at least one of them realize it was dangerous to take off under these conditions?

18 Charlotte Linde, a linguist at the Institute for Research on Learning in Palo Alto, Calif., has studied the "black box" recordings of cockpit conversations that preceded crashes as well as tape recordings of conversations that took place among crews during flight simulations in which problems were presented. Among the black box conversations she studied was the one between the pilot and co-pilot just before the Air Florida crash. The pilot, it turned out, had little experience flying in icy weather. The co-pilot had a bit more, and it became heartbreakingly clear on analysis that he had tried to warn the pilot, but he did so indirectly.

19 The co-pilot repeatedly called attention to the bad weather and to ice building up on other planes:

Co-pilot:
> Look how the ice is just hanging on his, ah, back, back there, see that?

> . . .

Co-pilot:
> See all those icicles on the back there and everything?

Captain:
> Yeah.

20 He expressed concern early on about the long waiting time between deicing:

Co-pilot:
> Boy, this is a, this is a losing battle here on trying to de-ice those things, it [gives] you a false feeling of security, that's all that does.

21 Shortly after they were given clearance to take off, he again expressed concern:

Co-pilot:
> Let's check these tops again since we been setting here awhile.

Captain:
> I think we get to go here in a minute.

22 When they were about to take off, the co-pilot called attention to the engine instrument readings, which were not normal:

Co-pilot:
> That don't seem right, does it? [three-second pause] Ah, that's not right . . .

Captain:
> Yes, it is, there's 80.

Co-pilot:
> Naw, I don't think that's right. [seven-second pause] Ah, maybe it is.

Captain:
> Hundred and twenty.

Co-pilot:
> I don't know.

23 The takeoff proceeded, and 37 seconds later the pilot and co-pilot exchanged their last words.

24 The co-pilot had repeatedly called the pilot's attention to dangerous conditions but did not directly suggest they abort the takeoff. In Linde's judgment, he was expressing his concern indirectly, and the captain didn't pick up on it—with tragic results.

25 That the co-pilot was trying to warn the captain indirectly is supported by evidence from another airline accident—a relatively minor one—investigated by Linde that also involved the unsuccessful use of indirectness.

26 On July 9, 1978, Allegheny Airlines Flight 453 was landing at Monroe County Airport in Rochester, when it overran the runway by 728 feet. Everyone survived. This meant that the captain and co-pilot could be interviewed. It turned out that the plane had been flying too fast for a safe landing. The captain should have realized this and flown around a second time, decreasing his speed before trying to land. The captain said he simply had not been aware that he was going too fast. But the co-pilot told interviewers that he "tried to warn the captain in subtle ways, like mentioning the possibility of a tail wind and the slowness of flap extension." His exact words were recorded in the black box. The crosshatches indicate words deleted by the National Transportation Safety Board and were probably expletives:

Co-pilot:
Yeah, it looks like you got a tail wind here.

Captain:
Yeah.
[?]: Yeah [it] moves awfully # slow.

Co-pilot:
Yeah the # flaps are slower than a #.

Captain:
We'll make it, gonna have to add power.

Co-pilot:
I know.

27 The co-pilot thought the captain would understand that if there was a tail wind, it would result in the plane going too fast, and if the flaps were slow, they would be inadequate to break the speed sufficiently for a safe landing. He thought the captain would then correct for the error by not trying to land. But the captain said he didn't interpret the co-pilot's remarks to mean they were going too fast.

28 Linde believes it is not a coincidence that the people being indirect in these conversations were the co-pilots. In her analyses of flight-crew conversations she found it was typical for the speech of subordinates to be more mitigated—polite, tentative or indirect. She also found that topics broached in a mitigated way were more likely to fail, and that captains were more likely to ignore hints from their crew members than the other way around. These findings are evidence that not only can indirectness and other forms of mitigation be misunderstood, but they are also easier to ignore.

29 In the Air Florida case, it is doubtful that the captain did not realize what the co-pilot was suggesting when he said, "Let's check these tops again since we been setting here awhile" (though it seems safe to assume he did not realize the gravity of the co-pilot's concern). But the indirectness of the co-pilot's phrasing certainly made it easier for the pilot to ignore it. In this sense, the captain's response, "I think we get to go here in a minute," was an indirect way of saying, "I'd rather not." In view of these patterns, the flight crews of some airlines are now given training to express their concerns, even to superiors, in more direct ways.

30 The conclusion that people should learn to express themselves more directly has a ring of truth to it—especially for Americans. But direct communication is not necessarily always preferable. If more direct expression is better communication, then the most direct-speaking crews should be the best ones. Linde was surprised to find in her research that

crews that used the most mitigated speech were often judged the best crews. As part of the study of talk among cockpit crews in flight simulations, the trainers observed and rated the performances of the simulation crews. The crews they rated top in performance had a higher rate of mitigation than crews they judged to be poor.

31 This finding seems at odds with the role played by indirectness in the examples of crashes that we just saw. Linde concluded that since every utterance functions on two levels—the referential (what it says) and the relational (what it implies about the speaker's relationships)—crews that attend to the relational level will be better crews. A similar explanation was suggested by Kunihiko Harada. He believes that the secret of successful communication lies not in teaching subordinates to be more direct, but in teaching higher-ups to be more sensitive to indirect meaning. In other words, the crashes resulted not only because the co-pilots tried to alert the captains to danger indirectly but also because the captains were not attuned to the co-pilots' hints. What made for successful performance among the best crews might have been the ability—or willingness—of listeners to pick up on hints, just as members of families or longstanding couples come to understand each other's meaning without anyone being particularly explicit.

32 It is not surprising that a Japanese sociolinguist came up with this explanation; what he described is the Japanese system, by which good communication is believed to take place when meaning is gleaned without being stated directly—or at all.

33 While Americans believe that "the squeaky wheel gets the grease" (so it's best to speak up), the Japanese say, "The nail that sticks out gets hammered back in" (so it's best to remain silent if you don't want to be hit on the head). Many Japanese scholars writing in English have tried to explain to bewildered Americans the ethics of a culture in which silence is often given greater value than speech, and ideas are believed to be best communicated without being explicitly stated. Key concepts in Japanese give a flavor of the attitudes toward language that they reveal—and set in relief the strategies that Americans encounter at work when talking to other Americans.

34 Takie Sugiyama Lebra, a Japanese-born anthropologist, explains that one of the most basic values in Japanese culture is *omoiyari*, which she translates as "empathy." Because of *omoiyari*, it should not be necessary to state one's meaning explicitly; people should be able to sense each other's meaning intuitively. Lebra explains that it is typical for a Japanese speaker to let sentences trail off rather than complete them because expressing ideas before knowing how they will be received seems intrusive. "Only an insensitive, uncouth person needs a direct, verbal, complete message," Lebra says.

35 *Sasshi*, the anticipation of another's message through insightful guesswork, is considered an indication of maturity.

36 Considering the value placed on direct communication by Americans in general, and especially by American business people, it is easy to imagine that many American readers may scoff at such conversational habits. But the success of Japanese businesses makes it impossible to continue to maintain that there is anything inherently inefficient about such conversational conventions.

With indirectness, as with all aspects of conversational style, our own habitual style seems to make sense—seems polite, right and good. The light cast by the habits and assumptions of another culture can help us see our way to the flexibility and respect for other styles that is the only best way of speaking.

READING CLOSELY AND THINKING CRITICALLY

1. Why did the male board member criticize the female university president? Was his criticism either appropriate or helpful? Explain.
2. What determines whether an individual uses direct or indirect speech?
3. What problems are associated with indirect speech? With direct speech?
4. Explain why indirect speech is suited to spoken communication in the military.
5. Explain the communication problems that contributed to the airplane accidents mentioned in the essay. What problem with indirect communication do the accidents highlight? How can that problem be addressed?

EXAMINING STRUCTURE AND STRATEGY

1. Tannen opens her essay with an **anecdote** (a brief story). How does the anecdote help her achieve her purpose?
2. Tannen contrasts direct and indirect communication, but she also contrasts the cultural orientations of Americans and some Asians. Why does she include the latter contrast?
3. Throughout the essay, Tannen cites the research findings of others (in paragraphs 7, 9, and 10, for example). What do these citations contribute to the essay?

NOTING COMBINED PATTERNS

1. How does Tannen use cause-and-effect analysis and exemplification to achieve her purpose?
2. How does Tannen use definition in the essay?

CONSIDERING LANGUAGE AND STYLE

1. Although Tannen is a professor, a linguist, a scholar, and a researcher, she keeps her essay accessible and interesting for the typical reader of the *New York Times Magazine,* where the essay first appeared. Explain how Tannen's word choice helps make the essay accessible to a broad audience.
2. Why do linguists use "It's cold in here" as a standard sentence for illustrating indirect communication?
3. Consult a dictionary if you are unsure of the meaning of any of these words: *admonishing* (paragraph 3), *self-deprecating* (paragraph 3), *prerogative* (paragraph 7), *rapport* (paragraph 10), *cheeky* (paragraph 10), *imperious* (paragraph 13), *mitigated* (paragraph 28), *broached* (paragraph 28), *relief* (paragraph 33).

Explain the meaning of the last sentence of the essay. Do you agree with the statement? Why or why not? If your instructor directs you to do so, post your response to your class Web site.

WRITING ASSIGNMENTS

1. **In your journal.** Do you typically use direct or indirect speech when you make a request? Will you alter your style as a result of reading "Squeaky Wheels and Protruding Nails"? Why or why not?

2. **Using comparison-contrast for a purpose.** The purposes in the assignments are possibilities. You may establish whatever purposes you like, within your instructor's guidelines.

   - To inform and perhaps persuade that one style is better than the other, contrast the communication styles of two people in similar positions, such as two friends, two teachers, two supervisors, two coaches, or two talk show hosts.

   - To inform and perhaps persuade that one style is better than the other, contrast the communication styles of two different groups, such as physicians and patients, teachers and students, parents and teenagers, or East and West Coast residents.

   - For several days, observe the communication styles of men and women as you go about your routine. Take note of any similarities and differences you observe. Then to inform your reader, compare and contrast the way men and women talk.

3. **Combining patterns.** Consider your communication with people you interact with—teachers, bosses, coaches, friends, family, co-workers, and classmates, for example. Give examples of the direct and indirect speech you were part of, and using comparison-contrast, explain whether your experiences with direct and indirect speech conform to the principles explained in Tannen's essay. Using cause-and-effect analysis (explained in Chapter 9), tell how you reacted to the examples of direct and indirect speech you cite. Were there any misunderstandings?

4. **Connecting the readings.** Based on the information in "Squeaky Wheels and Protruding Nails" and "What I've Learned from Men" (page 242) and your own experience and observation, do you think women should change the way they communicate? If so, explain how. If not, explain why not.

5. **Drawing on sources.** Now that the world is a global community, we must all gain a greater understanding of the communication styles in different cultures. For example, businesspeople traveling in Japan must understand the subtleties of indirect communication that Tannen touches on. Because much communication is nonverbal, we must also understand the gestures used in different cultures. In Mexico, for instance, a person might finger the lapel of another's suit as a sign of friendliness. Explain the importance of understanding the gestures used in other cultures by citing examples of those gestures, their meaning, and what could happen if that meaning were misunderstood. To research, you can check the *Social Sciences Index* under the heading "nonverbal communication." On the Internet, go to the Internet Public Library at *www.ipl.org* and click on "Subject Collections" and then "Social Science" and then on "Ethnicity, Culture, & Race." Type in the phrase "body language" or the keyword "gestures."

BACKGROUND: Arthur L. Campa (1905–1978), born in Mexico to American missionary parents, studied at the University of New Mexico and Columbia University. He was the chair of the Department of Modern Languages at the University of Denver, the director of the Center of Latin American Studies, and a cultural attaché at several U.S. embassies. Considered an authority on Hispanic-American culture, Campa wrote a number of books on the subject, including *Treasure of the Sangre de Cristos* (1963), *Hispanic Folklore Studies of Arthur L. Campa* (1976), and *Hispanic Culture in the Southwest* (1978). "Anglo vs. Chicano: Why?" was first published in *Western Review* in 1972.

COMBINED PATTERNS AND THEIR PURPOSE: In "Anglo vs. Chicano: Why?" Arthur L. Campa uses *contrast* to **inform** the reader of several differences between two cultures that meet—and sometimes conflict—in the southwestern United States. In addition, he uses *cause-and-effect analysis* to **inform** by explaining the origins of these differences.

ANGLO VS. CHICANO: WHY? | ARTHUR L. CAMPA

The cultural differences between Hispanic and Anglo-American people have been dwelt upon by so many writers that we should all be well informed about the values of both. But audiences are usually of the same persuasion as the speakers, and those who consult published works are for the most part specialists looking for affirmation of what they believe. So, let us consider the same subject, exploring briefly some of the basic cultural differences that cause conflict in the Southwest, where Hispanic and Anglo-American cultures meet.

As you read Notice that Campa provides considerable historical background. Ask yourself how that background helps him achieve his purpose.

2   Cultural differences are implicit in the conceptual content of the languages of these two civilizations, and their value systems stem from a long series of historical circumstances. Therefore, it may be well to consider some of the English and Spanish cultural configurations before these Europeans set foot on American soil. English culture was basically insular, geographically and ideologically; was more integrated on the whole, except for some strong theological differences; and was particularly zealous of its racial purity. Spanish culture was peninsular, a geographical circumstance that made it a catchall of Mediterranean, central European and north African peoples. The composite nature of the population produced a marked regionalism that prevented close integration, except for religion, and led to a strong sense of individualism. These differences were reflected in the colonizing enterprise of the two cultures. The English isolated themselves from the Indians physically and culturally; the Spanish, who had strong notions about *pureza de sangre* [purity of blood] among the nobility, were not collectively averse to adding one more strain to their racial cocktail. Cortés led the way by siring the first *mestizo*[1] in North America, and the rest of the conquistadores followed suit. The ultimate products of these two orientations meet today in the Southwest.

---

[1]A person of mixed blood; specifically, a person of mixed European and Native American ancestry.

> "The ultimate products of these two orientations meet today in the Southwest."

3   Anglo-American culture was absolutist at the onset; that is, all the dominant values were considered identical for all, regardless of time and place. Such values as justice, charity, honesty were considered the superior social order for all men and were later embodied in the American Constitution. The Spaniard brought with him a relativistic viewpoint and saw fewer moral implications in man's actions. Values were looked upon as the result of social and economic conditions.

4   The motives that brought Spaniards and Englishmen to America also differed. The former came on an enterprise of discovery, searching for a new route to India initially, and later for new lands to conquer, the fountain of youth, minerals, the Seven Cities of Cibola and, in the case of the missionaries, new souls to win for the Kingdom of Heaven. The English came to escape religious persecution, and once having found a haven, they settled down to cultivate the soil and establish their homes. Since the Spaniards were not seeking a refuge or running away from anything, they continued their explorations and circled the globe 25 years after the discovery of the New World.

5   This peripatetic tendency of the Spaniard may be accounted for in part by the fact that he was the product of an equestrian culture. Men on foot do not venture far into the unknown. It was almost a century after the landing on Plymouth Rock that Governor Alexander Spotswood of Virginia crossed the Blue Ridge Mountains, and it was not until the nineteenth century that the Anglo-Americans began to move west of the Mississippi.

6   The Spaniard's equestrian role meant that he was not close to the soil, as was the Anglo-American pioneer, who tilled the land and built the greatest agricultural industry in history. The Spaniard cultivated the land only when he had Indians available to do it for him.

> "The Spaniard cultivated the land only when he had Indians available to do it for him."

The uses to which the horse was put also varied. The Spanish horse was essentially a mount, while the more robust English horse was used in cultivating the soil. It is therefore not surprising that the viewpoints of these two cultures should differ when we consider that the pioneer is looking at the world at the level of his eyes while the *caballero* [horseman] is looking beyond and down at the rest of the world.

7   One of the most commonly quoted, and often misinterpreted, characteristics of Hispanic peoples is the deeply ingrained individualism in all walks of life. Hispanic individualism is a revolt against the incursion of collectivity, strongly asserted when it is felt that the ego is being fenced in. This attitude leads to a deficiency in those social qualities based on collective standards, an attitude that Hispanos do not consider negative because it manifests a measure of resistance to standardization in order to achieve a measure of individual freedom. Naturally, such an attitude has no *reglas fijas* [fixed rules].

8   Anglo-Americans who achieve a measure of success and security through

institutional guidance not only do not mind a few fixed rules but demand them. The lack of a concerted plan of action, whether in business or in politics, appears unreasonable to Anglo-Americans. They have a sense of individualism, but they achieve it through action and self-determination. Spanish individualism is based on feeling, on something that is the result not of rules and collective standards but of a person's momentary, emotional reaction. And it is subject to change when the mood changes. In contrast to Spanish emotional individualism, the Anglo-American strives for objectivity when choosing a course of action or making a decision.

9   The Southwestern Hispanos voiced strong objections to the lack of courtesy of the Anglo-Americans when they first met them in the early days of the Santa Fe trade. The same accusation is leveled at the *Americanos* today in many quarters of the Hispanic world. Some of this results from their different conceptions of polite behavior. Here too one can say that the Spanish have no *reglas fijas* because for them courtesy is simply an expression of the way one person feels toward another. To some they extend the hand, to some they bow and for the more *intimos* there is the well-known *abrazo*?[2] The concepts of "good or bad" or "right and wrong" in polite behavior are moral considerations of an absolutist culture.

10   Another cultural contrast appears in the way both cultures share part of their material substance with others. The pragmatic Anglo-American contributes regularly to such institutions as the Red Cross, the United Fund and a myriad of

"Another cultural contrast appears in the way both cultures share part of their material substance with others."

associations. He also establishes foundations and quite often leaves millions to such institutions. The Hispano prefers to give his contribution directly to the recipient so he can see the person he is helping.

11   A century of association has inevitably acculturated both Hispanos and Anglo-Americans to some extent, but there still persist a number of culture traits that neither group has relinquished altogether. Nothing is more disquieting to an Anglo-American who believes that time is money than the time perspective of Hispanos. They usually refer to this attitude as the *"mañana*[3] psychology." Actually, it is more of a "today psychology," because Hispanos cultivate the present to the exclusion of the future; because the latter has not arrived yet, it is not a reality. They are reluctant to relinquish the present, so they hold on to it until it becomes the past. To an Hispano, nine is nine until it is ten, so when he arrives at nine-thirty, he jubilantly exclaims: *"¡Justo!"* [right on time]. This may be why the clock is slowed down to a walk in Spanish while in English it runs. In the United States, our future-oriented civilization plans our lives so far in advance the present loses its meaning. January magazine issues are out in December; 1973 cars have been out since October; cemetery plots and even funeral

---

[2]Hug.

[3]Tomorrow.

arrangements are bought on the install-ment plan. To a person engrossed in living today the very idea of planning his funeral sounds like the tolling of the bells.

12   It is a natural corollary that a person who is present oriented should be compensated by being good at improvising. An Anglo-American is told in advance to prepare for an "impromptu speech," but an Hispano usually can improvise a speech because "*Nosotros la improvisamos todo*" [we improvise everything].

13   Another source of cultural conflict arises from the difference between *being* and *doing.* Even when trying to be individualistic, the Anglo-American achieves it by what he does. Today's young generation decided to be themselves, to get away from standardization, so they let their hair grow, wore ragged clothes and even went barefoot in order to be different from the Establishment. As a result they all ended up doing the same things and created another stereotype. The freedom enjoyed by the individuality of *being* makes it unnecessary for Hispanos to strive to be different.

14   In 1963 a team of psychologists from the University of Guadalajara in Mexico and the University of Michigan compared 74 upper-middle-class students from each university. Individualism and personalism were found to be central values for the Mexican students. This was explained by saying that a Mexican's value as a person lies in his *being* rather than, as is the case of the Anglo-Americans, in concrete accomplishments. Efficiency and accomplishments are derived characteristics that do not affect worthiness in the Mexican, whereas in the American it is equated with success, a value of highest priority in American culture. Hispanic people disassociate themselves from material things or from actions that may impugn a person's

sense of being, but the Anglo-American shows great concern for material things and assumes responsibility for his actions. This is expressed in the language of each culture. In Spanish one says, "*Se me cayó la taza*" [the cup fell away from me] instead of "I dropped the cup."

15   In English, one speaks of money, cash and all related transactions with frankness because material things of this high order do not trouble Anglo-Americans. In Spanish such materialistic concepts are circumvented by referring to cash as *efectivo* [effective] and when buying or selling as something *al contado* [counted out], and when without it by saying *No tengo fondos* [I have no funds]. This disassociation from material things is what produces *sobriedad* [sobriety] in the Spaniard according to Miguel de Unamuno, but in the Southwest the disassociation from materialism leads to *dejadez* [lassitude] and *desprendimiento* [disinterestedness]. A man may lose his life defending his honor but is unconcerned about the lack of material things. *Desprendimiento* causes a man to spend his last cent on a friend, which when added to lack of concern for the future may mean that tomorrow he will eat beans as a result of today's binge.

16   The implicit differences in words that appear to be identical in meaning are astonishing. Versatile is a compliment in English and an insult in Spanish.

"Versatile is a compliment in English and an insult in Spanish."

An Hispano student who is told to apologize cannot do it, because the word doesn't exist in Spanish. *Apología* means words in praise of a person. The Anglo-American either apologizes, which is a form of retraction abhorrent in Spanish, or compromises, another concept foreign to Hispanic culture. *Compromiso* means a date, not a compromise. In colonial Mexico City, two hidalgos once entered a narrow street from opposite sides, and when they could not go around, they sat in their coaches for three days until the viceroy ordered them to back out. All this because they could not work out a compromise.

17   It was that way then and to some extent now. Many of today's conflicts in the Southwest have their roots in polarized cultural differences, which need not be irreconcilable when approached with mutual respect and understanding.

READING CLOSELY AND THINKING CRITICALLY

1. In your own words write out the thesis of the essay.
2. Campa says that ideologically the English were insular, while the Spanish were peninsular. Explain what Campa means. What are the effects of the different orientations?
3. Explain a possible relationship between Hispanic individualism and the "Spaniard's equestrian role" (paragraph 6). How did the horse contribute to the cultural differences between Chicanos and Anglo-Americans?
4. Explain the different views of courtesy held by Hispanics and Anglo-Americans. How does the view of courtesy relate to concepts of individualism?
5. According to Campa, what values are important to Hispanics? To Anglo-Americans?

EXAMINING STRUCTURE AND STRATEGY

1. In what pattern does Campa arrange his contrasts, alternating or block?
2. If you were to pick an audience for the essay, what would it be like? How is the essay suited to that audience?
3. Does Campa maintain balance among his supporting details? Explain.
4. A number of times, Campa discusses historical backgrounds. How does the historical information help Campa fulfill his purpose?
5. What approach does Campa take to his conclusion? What do you think of his conclusion?

NOTING COMBINED PATTERNS

What cause-and-effect analysis is used in the essay? (Cause-and-effect is explained in Chapter 9.) What purpose does the cause-and-effect analysis serve?

CONSIDERING LANGUAGE AND STYLE

1. What can you learn about the relationship between language and culture from "Anglo vs. Chicano: Why?"
2. In paragraph 9, Campa calls Anglo culture "absolutist." What does he mean?

3. Consult a dictionary if you are unsure of the meaning of any of these words: *implicit* (paragraphs 2, 16), *configurations* (paragraph 2), *insular* (paragraph 2), *equestrian* (paragraph 5), *incursion* (paragraph 7), *pragmatic* (paragraph 10), *myriad* (paragraph 10), *acculturated* (paragraph 11), *impugn* (paragraph 14).

FOR DISCUSSION IN CLASS OR ONLINE

Campa concludes by saying that cultural differences "need not be irreconcilable when approached with mutual respect and understanding" (paragraph 17). Discuss one or more ways people can resolve conflict through increased understanding. If your instructor directs you to do so, post your response to your class Web site.

WRITING ASSIGNMENTS

1. **In your journal.** Campa explains that Anglo-Americans are future-oriented, while Chicanos are now-oriented. Do you agree? Discuss the advantages and disadvantages of each orientation.

2. **Using comparison-contrast for a purpose.** The purposes in the assignments are possibilities. You may establish whatever purposes you like, within your instructor's guidelines.
   - To inform and perhaps relate experience and express feelings, contrast your values or beliefs with those of someone else you know. Try to explain the differences by examining your ethnic backgrounds, family situations, religious upbringing, schooling, or other relevant factors.
   - To inform and perhaps persuade that one style is better than the other, contrast your view of money and spending practices with those of a friend, relative, or acquaintance. Try to explain the reasons for the differences.
   - If you and someone you know behave differently because one of you is future-oriented and one of you is focused on the present, contrast your different behaviors and attitudes. Your purpose can be to relate experience, express feelings, inform, and perhaps convince your reader that one approach is better than the other. If you want to use humor, your essay can also entertain.

3. **Combining patterns.** Select one of the following pairs: the control freak and the collaborator, the optimist and the pessimist, the dominant person and the submissive person, the noncompetitive person and the competitive person, the courteous person and the rude person. Use definition (explained in Chapter 11) as part of a comparison-contrast of the types of people. You can also use narration and exemplification to support your points.

4. **Connecting the readings.** Conflict between two groups of people is discussed in "On Being the Target of Discrimination" (page 234), "What I've Learned from Men" (page 242), and "Grant and Lee: A Study in Contrasts" (page 338). Using any of the ideas in those essays, along with ideas from "Anglo vs. Chicano: Why?" and your own thinking, explain why so much conflict exists. If you like, you can also note something that can be done to lessen some of that conflict.

5. **Drawing on sources.** Devise a grade school, middle school, or high school program that could help foster respect and understanding for different cultures. For help with ideas, search "multicultural education" at www.google.com or look up "multicultural education" in *Education Index*.

BACKGROUND: Three-time Pulitzer Prize winner Robert Frost (1874–1963) is an important 20th century poet whose works are among the most frequently read American poems. By the time he was 40, Frost had tried a variety of jobs, attempted and abandoned college twice, and buried two children. Grief-stricken and discouraged, Frost turned his full attention to writing poetry and enjoyed considerable success. Although associated with New England culture and experience, Frost's poems consider universal ideas. They are deceptively simple, however, for they often include complex images and symbolism. First published in 1932, "Fire and Ice" is one of Frost's most frequently reprinted poems.

THE PATTERN AND ITS PURPOSE: In "Fire and Ice," Robert Frost uses *comparison-contrast* to **inform** and warn the reader about the dangers of desire and hate. Like many of Frost's poems, "Fire and Ice" is more complex than it may at first appear.

Fire and Ice
ROBERT FROST

Some say the world will end in fire;
Some say in ice.
From what I've tasted of desire
I hold with those who favor fire.

As you read Determine what fire and ice represent.

But if it had to perish twice,
I think I know enough of hate
To know that for destruction ice
Is also great
And would suffice.

CONSIDERING THE POEM

1. In the poem, what does fire represent, and what does ice represent?
2. How are fire and ice—and the things fire and ice represent—similar, and how are they different?
3. In a sentence or two, tell what point Frost is making.
4. Why is desire like fire, and why is hate like ice?
5. How can desire and hate end the world?

WRITING ASSIGNMENTS

1. **In your journal.** In a page or two, discuss whether or not you like the poem, being sure to explain why you react the way you do.
2. **Using comparison-contrast for a purpose.** To inform and perhaps convince your reader that one sentiment or movement is superior, compare and contrast two sentiments or

movements on your campus that could be represented by fire and ice. Consider, for example, campus activism and apathy, censorship of the school newspaper and free speech, or school spirit and lack of support for athletic teams. The purposes in the assignment are possibilities. You may establish whatever purpose you like, within your instructor's guidelines.

3.   **Connecting the readings.** Is Frost correct about the destructive potential of desire and hate? To respond, consider the poem, "The Lottery" (page 169), "On Being the Target of Discrimination" (page 234), and "Lullaby" (page 432), along with your own ideas.

See pages 331 and 333 for strategies for writing comparison-contrast and for a revising checklist.

1. Compare and/or contrast a place on campus at two different times of the day. For example, you can compare and/or contrast a campus eating spot at the noon rush hour and again at the 3:00 lull, the football stadium during and after a game, or the library before and after finals week. Use description for vividness.

2. Compare and/or contrast two close friends, illustrating their traits with example or narration.

3. Compare and/or contrast two similar television shows (two situation comedies, two news broadcasts, two police dramas, and so on) to persuade your reader that one is better than the other.

4. Contrast two celebrations of the same holiday, such as Christmas before and after children, Independence Day as a child and as an adult, or Thanksgiving at different grandparents' houses.

5. Contrast the way a group of people (for example, mothers, police officers, fathers, or teens) is portrayed on television with the way the group is in real life.

6. Consider your circumstances before and after some change in your life: getting married, having children, going to college, getting a job, or joining an athletic team, for example. If you wish, make your details humorous and entertain your reader.

7. In your campus library, look up advertisements in *Life* and *Look* magazines from the 1950s and compare and contrast one or two of these ads with ads for similar products in contemporary magazines to inform your reader of the changes. Use cause-and-effect analysis to explain the cause and/or the effects of the changes. (See Chapter 9.)

8. Contrast the right and wrong ways to do something, such as choose a major, study for an exam, write an essay, select an adviser, buy a car, or plan a first date. Make your details humorous and entertain your reader.

9. Compare and contrast the styles of two comedians, actors, or musicians to inform your reader about the characteristics of each one.

10. Compare and contrast the chief arguments on both sides of a controversial issue (for example, abortion, capital punishment, euthanasia, animal rights, distributing condoms in schools, or bilingual education) to inform your reader of the thinking on both sides. If necessary, research the issue in your campus library or on the Internet.

11. Compare and/or contrast the toys of your youth with those that are popular today. Explain what those similarities and/or differences mean.

12. If you have lived in more than one place, compare and contrast life in two of those places.

13. If you or someone close to you has lived with chronic illness, contrast life as a healthy and sick person to heighten your reader's awareness of what it is like to be ill.

14. Contrast your view of an event at two different times in your life. For example, you could contrast your view of Christmas before and after becoming a parent or your view of yoga classes before and after enrolling in one.

15. Using vivid description, compare and/or contrast your current view of a particular place and the view you held as a child. For example, you could compare and/or contrast your views of your elementary school, a family vacation spot, your old bedroom, or your old neighborhood.

16. Compare and/or contrast the attitudes of youth and maturity. Use examples to clarify your points. Also indicate which of the attitudes is better and why.

17. Contrast your view of a parent now with your view at some point in the past.

18. Compare and/or contrast your life today with what you once thought your life would be like. If there are striking contrasts, try to explain what accounts for those contrasts.

19. Compare and/or contrast the ways men are portrayed on television with the ways women are portrayed. Use specific examples from shows and commercials to clarify and support your points. If possible, explain the effects these portrayals have on the viewer.

20. **Comparison-contrast in context.** For a humor column for your student newspaper, compare and contrast the food in your campus dining halls or other campus eatery and the food you grew up on.

The first photo below shows tennis champion Helen Wills Moody shaking hands with Elizabeth Ryan after Moody won Wimbledon in 1930. The second photo shows Venus and Serena Williams at Wimbledon in 2002. Study the photographs, and then write about the similarities and differences in clothing styles. Explain what the clothing styles suggest about the culture and values of the times. Consider what the styles say about women's tennis and what they say about women and society in general.

Cause-and-Effect Analysis

CONSIDER THE PATTERN

Movie studios use movie posters like the one on the facing page to generate interest in a film, but the poster alone does not get most people into the theater. In a paragraph, explain what causes you to see a particular movie.

THE PATTERN

Human beings need to make sense of the world by understanding why events occur and how they affect us. Thus, we examine the causes of earthquakes, try to determine how a presidential candidate's victory will change the economy, work to figure out why the car does not get the gas mileage it should, struggle to understand why our best friend suddenly seems distant, and so on. An understanding of causes and effects is important to our sense of security and our need to deal with forces in our environment. Thus, we often use **cause-and-effect analysis** to examine causes, effects, or both. When you explore causes, you identify the reasons for an event; when you explore effects, you identify the results of an event; when you look at both causes and effects, you examine reasons *and* results.

For more help with cause-and-effect analysis, click on

Writing > Paragraph Patterns
Writing > Writing Tutor > Causal Analysis

USING CAUSE-AND-EFFECT ANALYSIS FOR A PURPOSE

Cause-and-effect analysis can entertain, inform, persuade, or express feelings and relate experience. For example, you could *entertain* with a funny account of the causes and effects of your attempt to throw a surprise party—which was ultimately a disaster. If you were to explain the causes of inflation, you would *inform* a reader about an economic force, or if you explained the effects of computers on reading instruction, you would *inform* your reader about a trend in education. Similarly, if you explained the causes of math anxiety, you could do so to *persuade* your reader that women are often conditioned by our culture to avoid math, and if you explained the possible effects of failure to pass a school levy, you might do so to *persuade* your reader to vote for the levy. Cause-and-effect analysis can also allow you to *express feelings* and *relate experience,* as when you explain the causes and effects of your decision to leave home and move to another state.

While an essay is often developed solely with cause-and-effect analysis, the pattern can also form part of an essay developed primarily with another pattern. For example, if you wrote a process analysis to explain how heat lightning works, part of the essay might include a discussion of the effects of heat lightning. Similarly, if you told the story of the time you were involved in a serious car accident, the narration could also include a discussion of what caused the accident.

Cause-and-Effect Analysis in College, at Work, and in the Community

Cause-and-effect analysis is a frequent component of writing in many college classes. For instance, in a mathematics class, you might be asked to write a journal entry explaining how math affects your life. In history and political science classes, you will often be asked to explain the causes and effects of important events. For example, you could be asked on an essay exam to explain the causes of the Teapot Dome scandal, or you could be asked to write a report evaluating the causes and effects of manifest destiny. In a sociology class, you could be asked to explain the effects of the AIDS crisis on dating practices, and in a physics, chemistry, or biology class you will likely be asked to write lab reports explaining the effects of experiments. In an education class, you could detail the causes of teacher burnout or the effects of whole language instruction, and in a marketing class, you could write a paper on the effects of telemarketing.

Cause-and-effect analysis is one of the most frequently occurring patterns in college textbooks. Here, for example, is a paragraph from a business textbook that explains causes—specifically, some of the reasons for loss of American manufacturing jobs:

> Today manufacturers in countries such as China, India, South Korea, and Mexico can produce high-quality goods at low prices because their workers are paid less money than U.S. workers and they've learned quality concepts from Japanese, German, and U.S. producers. Late in 1997, however, Thailand, Malaysia, Hong Kong, Japan, South Korea, and other countries had banking problems that caused a major upheaval in global markets. These problems affected all nations, showing the interdependence of countries today. (Nickels, McHugh, and McHugh, *Understanding Business*)

The textbook authors could have simply said the global business environment affects U.S. business and employment, but by including the analysis of cause, they help students understand *how* the global environment affects U.S. business.

Here is another paragraph from the same textbook. This paragraph explains effects—specifically, the effects of the North American Free Trade Agreement (NAFTA):

> Since NAFTA was passed, the United States has created some 2.5 million jobs a year and unemployment has dropped to 4.6 percent. Many of the new jobs pay high wages because export industries pay about 13 percent more than those in manufacturing generally. Mexico's economy has been up and down since the passage of the agreement, but much of that fluctuation has been due to conditions not related to NAFTA. In general, one can say that NAFTA has been neither the success imagined by some nor the disaster proposed by others and that the more open borders may lead to better economies for all three countries [the United States, Canada, and Mexico]. (Nickels, McHugh, and McHugh, *Understanding Business*)

The explanation of the specific effects of NAFTA will help students understand that the treaty has had some positive effects.

On the job, people frequently use cause-and-effect analysis. Teachers write explanations of the causes of declining test scores, and social workers write reports for social service agencies explaining the positive effects of services on a family or community. Marketing managers write reports noting the reasons for a decline in sales, and dieticians give their clients a written explanation of the effects of sugar on insulin production. A police officer will fill out a report explaining the causes of an accident, and an official with the Environmental Protection Agency may write a study of the effects of a dam on river ecology.

Outside the classroom and workplace, cause-and-effect analysis is likely to be an important component of your writing. For example, when you write a letter of complaint to a company about a faulty product, you will describe what went wrong with the product and the damaging effects of that fault. If you ever deliver a eulogy, you will explain the positive ways the deceased affected you and others.

SUPPORTING DETAILS

A number of patterns can help you achieve your purpose. In particular, narration, exemplification, description, and process analysis can be very useful. For an essay explaining reasons people graduate from high school without being able to read, you might cite one cause as social promotions. You can help establish this point by narrating the story of Stella, a nonreader you know who was frequently passed on from grade to grade because she was a troublemaker, and teachers did not want to have her in their classrooms another year. You could also give several examples of other people who have been promoted without knowing how to read. Description can also contribute to cause-and-effect analysis. For example, if you want to explain the effects of littering, you can clarify the problem by describing a section of roadside that has been heavily littered. Sometimes, process analysis helps make a point. For example, if you want to explain the effects of tax reduction, you can note the process whereby lowering taxes creates more disposable income, which leads to increased spending, which spurs manufacturing, which ultimately creates jobs.

Events typically have more than one cause and more than one effect. Say, for example, that you are looking at the causes and effects of an enrollment decline at your college. The causes are likely to be many and might include these: a weak economy that means fewer people have the money to go to college, the creation of two new colleges in a hundred-mile radius, lack of a recruitment drive, and less financial aid available for prospective students. Similarly, the effects of the enrollment decline are likely to be many, including loss of revenue, loss of prestige, low employee morale, and fewer course offerings. When an event has multiple causes and effects, you do not want to omit any significant ones, or you will give your reader an incomplete picture. At the same time, the multiple causes and effects may not be of equal significance, so you need not develop them all in the same detail. If the primary reasons for the enrollment decline are the weak economy and the two new colleges, you should discuss those causes in considerably more detail than the reduced financial aid and lack of recruitment.

When an event has more than one cause, you may need to distinguish between causes that are *immediate* and those that are *remote*. Say, for example, that you are explaining why AIDS has reached epidemic proportions. Obviously, there are many reasons, but you may cite as one *immediate* cause the laws prohibiting notification of those exposed to the disease through their HIV-positive partners without the consent of those partners. To explain the lack of laws, you can cite a more *remote* cause: Gay and HIV activists successfully lobbied against such legislation because they feared discrimination against those publicly identified as gay and/or infected.

Sometimes cause-and-effect details include an explanation of causal chains. In a **causal chain,** a cause leads to an effect; that effect becomes a cause that leads to another effect; then that effect becomes a cause, and so on. For example, if you wanted to explain the effects of being very tall, you might reproduce a causal chain like this one: being tall made you feel awkward (effect); feeling awkward (cause) reduced your self-confidence (effect); your reduced self-confidence (cause) made it hard for you to date (effect); not dating (cause) made you depressed (effect).

In addition to reproducing causal chains, you may want to point out something that is *not*, despite popular belief, a cause or an effect. This strategy is especially effective if you need to correct your reader's understanding. For example, assume that you are explaining the effects of sex education in the schools, and you think your reader mistakenly believes that sex education leads to increased sexual activity. You can note that increased sexual activity has not been proven to be an effect of sex education.

To identify causes and effects, ask yourself the questions "Why?" and "Then what?" as you develop your details. For example, say you are explaining the causes of your shyness, and you give as one reason the fact that you do not feel comfortable around people. If you ask why you do not feel comfortable, you may remember that your family moved so frequently that you never got to know anyone very well. A new cause for your discussion, then, is those frequent moves. In a different essay, you might explain the effects of your parents' divorce on you, indicating that the divorce meant you saw less of your father. Ask "Then what?" and you might answer that you and your father drifted apart, so you never got to know him well—that is another effect you can write about.

Avoiding Errors in Logic

Two errors in logic can occur when you write cause-and-effect analysis. The first error is *oversimplifying*. Most cause-and-effect relationships are complex; they often involve multiple causes and effects. If you fail to consider important causes or effects, you are oversimplifying. Thus, to state that

Using *Affect* and *Effect* Correctly

If you have trouble understanding the difference between *affect* and *effect*, remember the following:

- *Affect* is a verb meaning "to influence" as in "Explain how football affects American culture."

- *Effect* is most often a noun meaning "result," as in "Explain the effects of football on American culture."

violence against women is solely the result of pornography is to ignore an array of other factors that contribute to the problem.

The second error in logic is *post hoc, ergo propter hoc* ("after this, therefore because of this"), which is automatically assuming that an earlier event caused a later one. Thus, you cannot assume that an increase in traffic accidents at a street corner after a traffic light was installed is necessarily a result of that traffic light. Other factors must be considered, such as a change in the speed limit and an increase in the number of cars along the route as a result of a new shopping plaza. Taken to its extreme, *post hoc, ergo propter hoc* can lead to superstitious thinking. For example, it can cause a person who sprains an ankle after breaking a mirror to assume that breaking a mirror causes bad luck.

ORGANIZING DETAILS

The thesis for your cause-and-effect analysis can indicate your topic, and whether you will explain causes, effects, or both. In addition, your thesis can suggest your purpose by noting the point your cause-and-effect analysis is making. Here is an example:

THESIS   It is certainly wrong for athletes to use drugs, but the reasons they do so are understandable.

This thesis indicates that the essay will explain the causes of drug use among athletes and that the purpose is to inform the reader that these causes are understandable.

For a clear organization, use topic sentences to introduce your discussion of each cause or effect. Here are the sample thesis and some topic sentences that could appear in an essay about the causes of drug abuse among athletes.

THESIS   It is certainly wrong for athletes to use drugs, but the reasons they do so are understandable.

TOPIC
SENTENCE   The pressure for professional athletes to justify their huge salaries is so great that they often see performance-enhancing drugs as the answer. (*Topic sentence presents the first cause: pressure on professional athletes.*)

TOPIC
SENTENCE   Furthermore, athletes may feel that they must take the drugs in order to be competitive, since so many other athletes are taking them. (*Topic sentence presents second cause: others take drugs.*)

TOPIC
SENTENCE   Finally, some athletes get hooked on drugs because their coaches and trainers administer them. (*Topic sentence presents third reason: coaches and trainers give out the drugs.*)

If you are explaining both causes and effects, you may want to discuss causes first and then move on to effects. Otherwise, a particular order may be called for. If your purpose is persuasive, you may want a progressive order so you can save your most dramatic, compelling, or significant cause

or effect for the end. If you are reproducing causal chains, you need a chrono
logical order, so you can cite the causes and effects in the order they occur.
Chronological order is also called for when you are discussing causes and
effects as they occurred across time. For example, a discussion of the effects
of your musical talent could begin with your first music lessons, then discuss increasing commitment to practicing as you grew up, and conclude with
your decision to become a music teacher. At times, you may want to arrange
your details in categories. If, for example, you are explaining the effects of
the passage of a school levy, you can discuss together all the effects on teachers, then the effects on students, and finally the effects on curriculum.

Two kinds of transitions can help you signal cause-and-effect relationships to your reader. First, the following transitions signal that one thing is
the effect of another: *as a result, consequently, thus, hence, therefore,* and *for
this reason.* Here are two examples:

> The midterm grades were very low. *For this reason,* Professor Werner
> reviewed the material with the class.

> The storm damage was extensive. *As a result,* the tourist trade in the
> coastal town declined.

Transitions of addition (*also, in addition, additionally, furthermore,* and
another) can also signal cause-and-effect analysis, as in the following
examples:

> *Another* effect of MTV is . . .

> *In addition,* stress fractures can be caused by . . .

VISUALIZING A CAUSE-AND-EFFECT ANALYSIS

The chart on page 388 can help you visualize the structure for a cause-and-
effect analysis. Like all good models, however, this one can be altered as
needed.

PROCESS GUIDELINES: STRATEGIES FOR WRITING CAUSE-AND-EFFECT ANALYSIS

1. **Selecting a Topic.** Consider writing about the causes and/or effects
   of some aspect of your life or personality. Possible topics include
   shyness, math anxiety, birth order, fear of heights, your parents'
   divorce, or living on a farm.
2. **Generating Ideas.** To generate ideas,
   - List every cause and/or effect of your topic that you can think of,
     without pausing to evaluate whether your ideas are good or not.
   - Ask "why?" and/or "then what?" of every item on your list to
     explore additional causes and effects.
   - Consider whether you can tell a story, provide an example, describe,
     or explain a process to clarify any of the points on your list.

Introduction

- Creates interest in the essay
- States the thesis, which can indicate your topic, whether you will explain causes, effects, or both, and the point the cause-and-effect analysis will make

First Body Paragraph

- Gives the first cause or effect, which can be stated in a topic sentence
- Can be developed with any patterns of development
- May reproduce causal chains
- May indicate something that is not a cause or effect
- May arrange causes before effects
- May arrange details in a progressive order or in order events in causal chain occur

Next Body Paragraph

- Gives the next cause or effect, which can be stated in a topic sentence
- Can be developed with any patterns of development
- May reproduce causal chains
- May indicate something that is not a cause or effect
- May arrange causes before effects
- May arrange details in a progressive order or in order events in causal chain occur

Next Body Paragraphs

- Continue until all the causes and /or effects are given
- Can be developed with any patterns of development
- May reproduce causal chains
- May indicate something that is not a cause or effect
- May arrange causes before effects
- May arrange details in a progressive order or in order events in causal chain occur

Conclusion

- Provides a satisfying finish
- Leaves the reader with a positive final impression

Avoiding "the Reason Is Because"

If you have trouble avoiding "the reason is because," remember that this expression is redundant because "the reason" means "because." Two alternatives are *the reason is that* and *because*.

NO	Economic development on the west side has lagged behind other areas of the city. The reason is because the Route 7 connector bridge has not been completed.
YES	Economic development on the west side has lagged behind other areas of the city. The reason is that the Route 7 connector bridge has not been completed.
YES	Economic development on the west side has lagged behind other areas of the city because the Route 7 connector bridge has not been completed.

- Consider whether your audience needs to be told whether something is not a cause or effect, even though some people mistakenly believe it to be.
- Review your list of ideas. Based on your audience and purpose, is there anything you should cross off?

3. **Organizing.** Number the remaining ideas on your list in the order you will treat them in your first draft. Consider causal chains and remote and immediate causes.

Checklist for Revising Cause-and-Effect Analysis

Be sure

_____ The thesis indicates whether you are explaining causes, effects, or both—and, perhaps, the point your analysis will make.

_____ Topic sentences introduce the discussion of each cause and effect.

_____ You have noted all significant causes and effects.

_____ You have clarified all causes and effects, as needed, with explanation, description, narration, examples, or process analysis.

_____ You have reproduced causal chains, where appropriate.

_____ You have accounted for both immediate and remote causes, without going further back than necessary.

_____ You have avoided oversimplifying and *post hoc, ergo propter hoc* errors in logic.

_____ You have used transitions, as needed, to introduce causes and effects.

Student writer Carl Benedict informs his reader by explaining the causes of steroid use among athletes. As you read, notice how carefully each cause is presented and explained. After you read, you will have an opportunity to evaluate this essay.

Why Athletes Use Steroids

Paragraph 1
The introduction gives background information. The thesis (the last sentence) indicates that the subject is steroid use and the essay will present causes.

One of the most heated controversies in athletics centers is the use 1 of anabolic steroids. Behind the dispute is the evidence that steroids pose a health hazard. They are linked to cardiovascular disease, liver disorders, and cancerous tumors. In addition, there is evidence that they cause personality aberrations. Still, an alarming number of athletes are willing to risk their health for the enhanced performance steroids provide— and it is not hard to understand why.

Paragraph 2
Sentence 1 is the topic sentence. It begins with a transition of addition and presents the first cause under consideration.

First of all, many athletes are so blinded by the obvious benefits 2 of steroid use that they fail to note their adverse effects. They are so focused on the increased strength, stamina, and size that result from steroid use, they may overlook the abuse their bodies are sustaining— often until it is too late. That is, athletes who are delighting in turning in the best performance of their lives are not likely to think about future deleterious effects. This is the same psychology that keeps the nicotine addict smoking three packs a day, until the x-ray shows the lung cancer is so advanced that nothing can be done.

Paragraph 3
The second cause is presented in the first two sentences. The paragraph also presents an effect: Contact sports become more dangerous.

Some athletes rationalize steroid use another way. They claim 3 that anabolic steroids pose no greater health hazard than participation in such contact sports as football, boxing, and wrestling. However, these athletes fail to understand that in addition to harming the body, steroids also heighten the danger of contact sports by making the par- ticipants larger and stronger, thereby increasing their momentum and impact.

Paragraph 4
This paragraph explains something that is not a cause, then goes on to give a real cause. Note the transition *instead.*

Some people think steroid use continues despite the life-threatening 4 effects because athletes are just "dumb jocks" who are not smart enough to appreciate the risks. I don't accept that explanation. Instead, I suspect that steroid use continues partly because most athletes are young, and young people never feel threatened. Part of being young is feeling invulnerable. That is why young people drive too fast, drink too much, and bungee jump. They just do not believe that anything can happen to them. The same psychology is at work with athletes. They are young people who feel they will live forever.

In addition, athletes assume that because their bodies are so physically conditioned they can withstand more punishment than the average person, so they feel even less at risk by steroid use. They think, "The average person should not do this, but I can because my body is finely tuned." 5

Perhaps the biggest reason athletes use steroids can be explained by the spirit that lies at the heart of all athletes: competition. Once a handful of athletes enhance their performance artificially, then others follow in order to stay competitive. Eventually, steroid users dominate a sport, and anyone who wants to compete at the highest levels is forced to use steroids or lose out. This fact explains why unscrupulous coaches and trainers who want to win at any cost have contributed to the problem by offering steroids to their players and urging them to use them. Sadly, this practice has even filtered down to the high school level in some cases. 6

Competition for the thrill of winning is only part of the explanation, however. Big-time athletics means big-time money. As the financial rewards rise in a given sport, so does the pressure to win at any cost. Huge salaries, enormous purses, big bonuses, and incredibly lucrative commercial endorsements all tempt athletes to enhance their performances any way they can. 7

Despite drug testing before competition and dissemination of information about the dangers of anabolic steroids, athletes still use steroids because the pressures to do so are so compelling. The truth is, too many athletes think steroids only hurt the other person, or else they think using steroids is worth the risk. 8

Paragraph 5
The first sentence is the topic sentence. It begins with a transition and presents the next cause. Does this paragraph need more detail?

Paragraph 6
The first sentence is the topic sentence. "The biggest reason" notes that detail is in a progressive order. The paragraph presents a causal chain.

Paragraph 7
This paragraph presents a cause that is an extension of the one given in the previous paragraph.

Paragraph 8
The conclusion summarizes the main causes.

Responding to "Why Athletes Use Steroids"

Evaluate "Why Athletes Use Steroids" by responding to these questions:

1. Does the essay hold your interest? Why or why not?
2. Are the introduction and conclusion effective? Why or why not?
3. Are causes and effects explained in sufficient detail? Explain.
4. Has the author accounted for both immediate and remote causes? If not, is that a problem? Explain.
5. Are there any errors in logic?
6. What do you like best about the essay?
7. Name one revision that would make the essay better.

- What cause-and-effect relationship does the advertisement express?
- For what purpose is the cause-and-effect relationship depicted?
- Who is the target audience?
- How do the words and image work together to achieve the advertisement's purpose?

BACKGROUND: Child psychologist Dorothy Siegel is vice president emeritus for student services at Towson State University, Towson, Maryland, and founder of the Campus Violence Prevention Center at Towson, which has carried out significant research on issues related to campus violence. An authority on campus crime, Siegel has testified before Congress on the subject. The first director of Maryland's Institute against Prejudice, Siegel also lectures and leads workshops about student services and campus violence and is a consultant to the U.S. Department of Justice and Education. Siegel has written *Campuses Respond to Violent Tragedy* (1994), which discusses campus responses to assaults, deaths, and disasters and suggests how college officials can respond to crises. "What Is behind the Growth of Violence on College Campuses?" first appeared in *USA Today Magazine* in 1994.

THE PATTERN AND ITS PURPOSE: "What Is Behind the Growth of Violence on College Campuses?" examines the *causes* of campus violence to **inform** the reader. To make her points, Siegel often draws on statistics, some of which may surprise you.

WHAT IS BEHIND THE GROWTH OF VIOLENCE ON COLLEGE CAMPUSES?

DOROTHY SIEGEL

America's college campuses are not the war zones newspaper and magazine articles would lead the public to believe. Those crimes committed against students get major attention from the media probably because campuses are expected to be serene and safe. What is perhaps most troubling about campus crime is that the majority of the incidents, excluding theft, but including rape and other sexual asaults, are impulsive acts committed by students themselves, according to nationwide studies conducted by Towson State University's Campus Violence Prevention Center. Students are responsible for 80 percent of campus crime, although rarely with weapons.

As you read Think why Siegel wrote for the broad readership of *USA Today Magazine* rather than a publication aimed primarily at college students.

"Students are responsible for 80 percent of campus crime, although rarely with weapons."

2   It is an uphill battle to ensure student safety. Schools provide escort services, tamper-proof windows, and continually upgraded state-of-the-art exterior lighting and electronic alarm systems. These institutional efforts frequently are undone by the immortal feelings of college-age men and women. That "it-can't-happen-to-me" attitude leads to lax security behaviors that literally leave the door open for an outside threat. Universities are challenged to help students develop and keep that awareness, except for the two weeks following an on-campus assault, when caution prevails.

3   The same students who sponsor night walks to check the lighting and grounds to increase safety will hold the door open for a stranger entering their residence hall. Despite frequent warnings, students—and even faculty, administrators, and other campus personnel—act less judiciously than they would elsewhere.

4   The mind-set of the students and probably of most of us is that crime is

going to happen at night. Following a daylight abduction at one school, students demanded better lighting and evening patrols. They are loathe to follow the cautions about garages and out-of-the-way places during the day. They have trouble acknowledging, as we all probably do, that current criminal acts require new precautions, more appropriate to what is happening now.

5 Today, as part of the orientation programs at campuses across the nation, most administrators welcome students with information about crime on campus and ways they better can ensure their own safety. Because The Higher Education Security Act requires schools to report their previous year's crime statistics to the campus [community], colleges greet many new students and their parents with the previous year's count of violations and wise warnings. They are united in their efforts to command students' attention and enlist them as active partners in prevention. They use theater, video, discussions, posters, and circulars to inform students. Police statistics and reports are disseminated widely.

6 Despite this, if a stranger is seen entering a building, it is unlikely that any observers will notify the police, even if the potential assailant is dressed strangely and/or behaving oddly. If that stranger attacks someone the community will demand more protection. A series of seminars will produce good ideas and vigilant behavior for about two weeks, after which much of the more casual behavior about safety reappears.

7 When students discuss safety, it always is about dangers from outside the campus. Students are both the perpetrators and victims of most campus crime, yet it still is protection from trespassers that motivates most safety programs

and is most in demand. It is an arduous and mostly unsuccessful process to convince students that they are more likely to be a victim of crime perpetrated by a member of their class or athletic team than by a stranger. It appears unthinkable that they themselves may become assailants. Although this message is

> "It appears unthinkable that they themselves may become assailants."

included in many orientation programs for new students, it is nearly impossible to alert them to the potential danger from people they trust simply because they are members of the same community. Yet, eight percent of students report that they have been perpetrators and approximately 12 percent say they have been victims of assault.

8 Visitors to a campus during the day will see a reasonably civil society. Students will congregate in various common areas and study, talk, laugh, or even sleep. The homeless may gather on the campus benches while a non-student stands and shouts what he or she maintains is God's will. Literally thousands of people will pass without incident. If campus police are writing citations, it is likely to be for parking violations.

9 Yet, on any night from Thursday to Saturday on the same campus, the majority of students will be drinking, some excessively, and fights will erupt over seemingly trival issues—who can have the bedroom, the keys, the boyfriend or girlfriend, the Nintendo. Small differences may escalate into brawls when combined with drug and alcohol abuse. Student assistants in residence halls may write up hundreds of classmates for

violation of the campus alcohol policy. These reports are forwarded for administrative action. Few, if any, students will be arrested. Other drunk students will be returning from town where similar incidents may have occurred. Police rarely are called for fear of endangering the bar's liquor license. Still other students are on their way to parties, where recreational drinking is the featured attraction.

10   My first experience with campus violence came after I had spent two years in my current position as vice president for student services at Towson State University. One Friday evening, a drunk student trying to enter a residence hall to visit a friend beat the student worker who denied him access. The employee was hospitalized overnight. Although the student was criminally charged, the university immediately had to create procedures for an on-campus hearing to determine how the institution should respond. He was the first student suspended from the university because of assault charges stemming from a campus incident.

11   In the late 1970s, some students on campuses around the country reported being victims of assaults by fellow students. Residence directors observed increases in vandalism. Personnel at different schools thought they were experiencing situations unique to their own campuses. Rural and urban, large and small schools noted the existence of violent incidents, quantified in Towson State's surveys of over 1,000 colleges. Those studies became the nation's first national data on student-perpetrated violence. It documented that students were both victims and perpetrators of rape, other sexual violence, and physical assault.

UNITED STATES OF VIOLENCE

12   When sexual assaults and rapes are reported, an interviewer most frequently will learn that the two students have known each other, sometimes meeting at a party earlier that evening. Typically, they both will have been drinking. One may have accepted the other's invitation to share a room because a roommate was entertaining someone. He may make advances. She says she only will accept the offer of the room (or extend the offer) if it is a non-sexual relationship. He accepts the terms, but believes her accompanying him means she is willing. She thinks she has communicated effectively. He thinks he has understood. Such misunderstandings make one appreciate the clear consent to sex that Antioch College demands of its students as set forth in its most recent handbook.

13   One percent of students reported more physically brutal rapes. Four percent of female students stated that they had been raped, predominantly by other students. Researchers report that 74 percent of sexually related crimes were committed by fellow students. More than 30 percent of these sexual crimes were committed by fraternity members, while 14 percent were committed by athletes, some by friends of friends.

14   The majority of perpetrators indicated that they were drunk, high, or in need of drugs when the crimes were committed. Substance abuse is a direct correlate of violent campus behavior. Researchers from Towson State's Campus

"The majority of perpetrators indicated that they were drunk, high or in need of drugs when the crimes were committed."

Violence Prevention Center reported in a study of responses from 1,800 college students nationwide that abuse of alcohol was heavier among victims and perpetrators than the rest of the campus population. A later study of more than 13,000 students corroborated those results, adding that students who used drugs were likely to be among the perpetrators and the victims. Perpetrators reported using intoxicants more often than did victims. In turn, the victims reported heavier drinking habits than those who were neither victims nor assailants. Whether drunk or not, a substantial majority of victims and perpetrators said that, on the day of the crime, they had been drinking and/or using drugs. It is a logical conclusion that students usually will not become victims or perpetrators in student-to-student violence if they do not use drugs or abuse alcohol.

15   In spite of all the messages of abstinence that are drilled into the nation's youth from elementary school years on, many students come to higher education with histories of excessive drinking. Against the backdrop of violence that exists in American society, the loss of control heightened by substance abuse, including alcohol, often is accompanied by violent outbursts. The various preventive efforts such as mediation and conflict resolution offered by some schools are not effective techniques for preventing the acts fueled by the presence of alcohol.

16   Universities formerly had acted *in loco parentis*. When the national age of majority was lowered to 18, college administrators had to alter their relationship with students because institutions no longer could behave as substitute parents for youths who now could vote,

drink, and go to war. While it is not documented how effective such supervision of students was, it is clear that those who wished to violate the rules had to work harder to do so. The current relationship is adult-to-adult, even though the institutions recognize that many students are not fully mature. That poses a continuing dilemma for campus personnel in helping students to develop control over their behavior, thus assuring their own safety and that of their peers.

17   Although the legal drinking age has been raised to 21 in each state, the national community of 18- to 20-year-olds simply does not accept this constraint. Some estimates are that as many as 80 percent of underage students carry fake proof-of-age identification. Drinking has become a standard pastime, and binge drinking—five or more drinks at a sitting—is condoned by 85 percent of college freshmen. The number of students who report excessive drinking is less in the sophomore year and decreases in each of the subsequent years. It has not been determined if the excessive drinkers have dropped out or changed their ways. It probably is some of both.

"It has not been determined if the excessive drinkers have dropped out or changed their ways."

The people who have been most responsive to the substance abuse education programs are the casual users who reportedly are abstaining totally now. The laws are not effective despite substantial efforts. No way has been found to govern a population by laws they do not accept.

SEEKING UNDERSTANDING

18 College students are among the nation's brightest and most successful people. In general, they come from higher socioeconomic backgrounds than the non-college-attending members of their age group. Although there has been no formal study of their behavior after university attendance, it is unlikely that perpetrators of college incidents will commit other violent crimes later. Most do not repeat offenses on campus. A contributing factor may be that many schools require those responsible to attend substance abuse intervention programs as a condition of returning to or continuing to attend the university.

19 Administrators are at a loss to understand why such an increase in student violence has emerged in the past two decades. They have tried to study the problem from several approaches, but the only factor that remains the same in the majority of cases is alcohol abuse. It is not known if as many students in the past drank as much as current ones do. Research shows, though, that almost 50 percent of freshmen had been drunk within two weeks preceding the study.

20 Behaviors that lead to violence usually are tolerated by students. Resident students are reluctant to complain, even in cases where their rights and their living space are violated by the conduct of others. They may ask for alternate housing, but are not apt to make a formal complaint. Only victims report crimes. Most actions that lead to assaultive behaviors are tolerated by the student community. Students who dislike the rowdiness are more apt to move away than to assert their rights to a more appropriate living environment.

21 On more and more campuses, housing options available to students include alcohol-free residence halls. Those who choose them have quieter and less disruptive lives. Such an option is not successful when someone other than the students themselves makes those choices.

22 It is easy to prevent violence if each student is kept under lock and key. It is a more challenging problem in a society that values freedom. The message to students is that a safe community requires their participation. The role of police is to facilitate safety, not assure it. It is a challenge to have an environment appropriate for growth and learning and safety in today's society.

23 Student society evolves and changes. For instance, women increasingly are the assaulters. Though still in the single-digit numbers and not nearly as high as the amount of incidents with male perpetrators, the total is going up. More students are participating in communal efforts to help others, which may indicate that they are assuming more membership in the campus community. They increasingly are riding the escort vans that for so long were available, but appeared inconvenient. More are working actively for a civil environment. Although they continue to prop open doors for the pizza man, we are seeing some effort to make the school safer. More are complaining about the amount of drinking on campus, but they still are not willing to say that a roommate drinks too much. Many student governments, fraternities, and sororities have supported the efforts, but continue alcohol-dominated parties. Students at many colleges no longer sponsor dances because of the enforcement of alcohol laws by the institutions. More students

are walking with others at night. Nevertheless, the struggle remains to help students pursue safer ways.

24   In our community of 10,000 full-time students, we held administrative hearings for 11 cases of physical assault in 1992. No sexual assaults were reported. Other years, the number of assaults was as high as 35, and the highest number of sexual assaults in any year was six. When colleges were required by the 1992 National Higher Education Security Act to inform their faculty, staff, and students about crime statistics on campuses, several reporters were sure that the colleges were hiding numbers. However, the amount of crimes on campuses never has been large. Still, even a single violent act requires that everyone become more discerning.

READING CLOSELY AND THINKING CRITICALLY

1.   According to Siegel, what are the causes of campus violence?

2.   One cause of campus violence, according to Siegel, is the fact that students fail to report suspicious people and behavior. How do you explain this failure?

3.   According to Siegel, why do students assume that the source of danger is outside campus, rather than within?

4.   Explain the cause-and-effect relationship Siegel maintains between sexual assaults, including rapes, and ineffective communication.

5.   Do you think that a return to *in loco parentis* would reduce the amount of crime on campus? Explain.

6.   As a college student, how do you react to Siegel's message? Do you think most college students would react the way you do? Would they be surprised by any of the information or moved to alter their behavior in any way? Explain.

EXAMINING STRUCTURE AND STRATEGY

1.   Why does Siegel mention her position as vice president for student services at Towson State University?

2.   What are the sources of Siegel's details (personal experience, observation, research, television, etc.)?

3.   Which paragraphs include statistics? How do those statistics help the author achieve her purpose? Should she have included the sources of her statistics? Explain.

4.   Evaluate the effectiveness of the concluding paragraphs (paragraphs 23 and 24).

5.   Why would the readers of *USA Today Magazine* be interested in Siegel's essay?

CONSIDERING LANGUAGE AND STYLE

1.   In paragraph 16, Siegel says, "Universities formerly acted *in loco parentis*." What does *in loco parentis* mean?

2.   Paragraphs 1 and 2 open with metaphors. What are they? What effect do they create? (Metaphors are explained on page 110.)

3. Consult a dictionary if you are unsure of the meaning of any of these words: *perpetrators* (paragraph 7), *arduous* (paragraph 7), *corroborated* (paragraph 14).

FOR DISCUSSION IN CLASS OR ONLINE

If what Siegel says about the relationship between alcohol and violence is correct, do you think colleges should ban drinking on campus? Why or why not? If your campus already has a zero-tolerance policy toward alcohol, discuss its effectiveness. If your instructor directs you to do so, post your response to your class Web site.

WRITING ASSIGNMENTS

1. **In your journal.** In a page or so, explain whether or not you feel safe on your campus and why you feel the way you do. Also note whether or not you plan to change your behavior as a result of reading the essay. If so, explain how; if not, explain why not.

2. **Using cause-and-effect analysis for a purpose.** The purposes in the assignments are possibilities. You may establish whatever purposes you like, within your instructor's guidelines.
    -   Siegel says that "students usually will not become victims or perpetrators in student-to-student violence if they do not use drugs or abuse alcohol" (paragraph 14). With that in mind, explain what would happen if your school—in cooperation with city officials—initiated a policy making the college and surrounding area completely substance-free. Your purpose can be to inform and perhaps convince your reader that such a policy is or is not a good idea.
    -   To inform, explain why "many students come to higher education with histories of excessive drinking" (paragraph 15). You can also offer solutions to the problem.
    -   To inform, explain the causes or effects of another campus problem, such as cheating, declining enrollment, failure to graduate, or plagiarizing.
    -   Violence is not limited to college campuses. In general, our country tends to have a higher level of violence than Canada or the countries of Western Europe. Explain why we are so violent. You can also consider a solution to the problem. Your purpose can be to inform and perhaps convince your reader that your solution should be adopted.

3. **Combining patterns.** Using process analysis (explained in Chapter 7), write a procedure that you think will reduce campus violence. Then, using cause-and-effect analysis, explain how the process will affect students and their interactions. You might consider such campus activities as dating, attending sporting events, working in the library, walking across campus at night, and visiting members of the opposite sex in their residence halls or apartments.

4. **Connecting the readings.** Discuss to what extent miscommunication between women and men could be responsible for sexual harassment and sexual assault. In addition to the ideas in "What Is Behind the Growth of Violence on College Campuses?" ideas in "What I've Learned from Men" (page 242) may help you.

5. **Drawing on sources.** Visit the appropriate offices on your campus to learn how much and what kind of crime exists at your school. Also learn what measures are being taken to make your campus as safe as possible. Report your findings and whether or not you think more needs to be done. If so, state what. If not, explain why not.

BACKGROUND: A native of England, Andrew Sullivan earned a Ph.D. in political science from Harvard's John F. Kennedy School of Government. A political and social commentator, Sullivan is a regular columnist for *Time* magazine and the *Sunday Times of London*. He was also the editor-in-chief of *The New Republic* magazine—the youngest editor in its history. A frequent lecturer on college campuses, Sullivan has also appeared on a number of radio and television programs, including *Nightline, CBS Evening News, Larry King Live* and National Public Radio's *Fresh Air*. His books include *Virtually Normal: An Argument about Homosexuality* (1996), *Love Undetectable: Notes on Friendship, Sex, and Survival* (1998), *Same-Sex Marriage, Pro and Con: A Reader* (2004). "Why the *M* Word Matters to Me" first appeared in *Time* in 2004.

www.mhhe.com/patterns

For more information on this author, go to

More resources > Chapter 9 > Andrew Sullivan

THE PATTERN AND ITS PURPOSES: Andrew Sullivan uses *cause-and-effect analysis* for multiple purposes: He **relates his experience** as a gay man and **expresses his feelings** about the importance of gay marriage in order to **persuade** readers that such unions should be allowed.

WHY THE *M* WORD MATTERS TO ME

ANDREW SULLIVAN

As a child, I had no idea what homosexuality was. I grew up in a traditional home—Catholic, conservative, middle class. Life was relatively simple: education, work, family. I was raised to aim high in life, even though my parents hadn't gone to college. But one thing was instilled in me. What mattered was not how far you went in life, how much money you earned, how big a name you made for yourself. What really mattered was family and the love you had for one another. The most important day of your life was not graduation from college or your first day at work or a raise or even your first house. The most important day of your life was when you got married. It was on that day that all your friends and all your family got together to celebrate the most

As you read Pay attention to the way Sullivan uses both reason and emotion.

"The most important day of your life was when you got married."

important thing in life: your happiness—your ability to make a new home, to form a new but connected family, to find love that put everything else into perspective.

2   But as I grew older, I found that this was somehow not available to me. I didn't feel the things for girls that my peers did. All the emotions and social rituals and bonding of teenage heterosexual life eluded me. I didn't know why. No one explained it. My emotional bonds to other boys were one-sided; each time I felt myself falling in love, they sensed it, pushed it away. I didn't and couldn't blame them. I got along fine with my buds in a nonemotional context, but

something was awry, something not right. I came to know almost instinctively that I would never be a part of my family the way my siblings might one day be. The love I had inside me was unmentionable, anathema. I remember writing in my teenage journal one day, "I'm a professional human being. But what do I do in my private life?"

3   I never discussed my real life. I couldn't date girls and so immersed myself in schoolwork, the debate team, school plays, anything to give me an excuse not to confront reality. When I looked toward the years ahead, I couldn't see a future. There was just a void. Was I going to be alone my whole life? Would I ever have a most important day in my life? It seemed impossible, a negation, an undoing. To be a full part of my family, I had to somehow not be me. So,

"To be fully part of my family, I had to somehow not be me."

like many other gay teens, I withdrew, became neurotic, depressed, at times close to suicidal. I shut myself in my room with my books night after night while my peers developed the skills needed to form real relationships and loves. In wounded pride, I even voiced a rejection of family and marriage. It was the only way I could explain my isolation.

4   It took years for me to realize that I was gay, years more to tell others and more time yet to form any kind of stable emotional bond with another man. Because my sexuality had emerged in solitude—and without any link to the idea of an actual relationship—it was hard later to reconnect sex to love and self-esteem. It still is. But I persevered, each relationship slowly growing longer than the last, learning in my 20s and 30s what

my straight friends had found out in their teens. But even then my parents and friends never asked the question they would have asked automatically if I were straight: So, when are you going to get married? When will we be able to celebrate it and affirm it and support it? In fact, no one—no one—has yet asked me that question.

5   When people talk about gay marriage, they miss the point. This isn't about gay marriage. It's about marriage.

"This isn't about gay marriage. It's about marriage."

It's about family. It's about love. It isn't about religion. It's about *civil* marriage licenses. Churches can and should have the right to say no to marriage for gays in their congregations, just as Catholics say no to divorce, but divorce is still a civil option. These family values are not options for a happy and stable life. They are necessities. Putting gay relationships in some other category—civil unions, domestic partnerships, whatever—may alleviate real human needs, but by their very euphemism, by their very separateness, they actually build a wall between gay people and their families. They put back the barrier many of us have spent a lifetime trying to erase.

6   It's too late for me to undo my past. But I want above everything else to remember a young kid out there who may even be reading this now. I want to let him know that he doesn't have to choose between himself and his family anymore. I want him to know that his love has dignity, that he does indeed have a future as a full and equal part of the human race. Only marriage will do that. Only marriage can bring him home.

1. Why does Sullivan believe that gays should be allowed to marry?
2. Why is it significant that Sullivan grew up "in a traditional home—Catholic, conservative, middle class" (paragraph 1)?
3. Those who favor gay marriage often point to the fact that unless couples are legally married, they are denied many rights and benefits. For example, unmarried partners cannot refuse to testify against each other in court; one partner is not always covered under the other partner's insurance policy; and partners who bequeath estates to each other can have the wills contested by family members. Why didn't Sullivan make this point? Should he have?
4. Is the essay convincing? Do you think it is likely to change readers' minds? Explain.

EXAMINING STRUCTURE AND STRATEGY

1. In paragraph 1, Sullivan describes his childhood background. Why does he begin the essay with this information? How does the first paragraph help Sullivan achieve his writing purpose?
2. Sullivan relates a painful part of his personal experience as a teenager and young man. What purpose does sharing personal experience serve?
3. What cause-and-effect relationship does the essay explain?
4. Which paragraphs are intended to move readers' emotions? Which paragraphs are intended to appeal to readers' intellect? Does Sullivan rely more on appeals to readers' emotions or appeals to their intellect? Why?

CONSIDERING LANGUAGE AND STYLE

1. In the title, why does Sullivan use "the *M* word" rather than "marriage"?
2. In paragraph 5, Sullivan repeats the phrases "It isn't about" and "It's about." What does he achieve with that repetition?
3. Consult a dictionary if you do not know the meaning of these words: *anathema* (paragraph 2), *euphemism* (paragraph 5).

FOR DISCUSSION IN CLASS OR ONLINE

Gay marriage is an issue that arouses strong reactions—both for and against. Why is gay marriage such a "hot button" topic? If your instructor so directs, post your response on your class Web site.

WRITING ASSIGNMENTS

1. **In your journal.** In a page or two describe how society reacts to homosexuals.
2. **Using cause-and-effect analysis for a purpose.** The purposes in the assignments are possibilities. You may establish whatever purposes you like, within your instructor's guidelines.

- As a gay teenager, Sullivan did not feel like he fit in. To inform your reader, explain what else causes young people to feel like they do not fit in.
- For a variety of reasons, many high school students feel like they don't fit in. To inform your readers and perhaps convince them to take action, explain the effects of not fitting in high school.
- If you have ever felt different—like you did not fit in—explain the causes and effects of the feeling in order to relate your experience and express your feelings.
- To inform readers and perhaps convince them that legalizing gay marriage is either a good or bad idea, explain what would happen if gay marriage were legalized across the country. If you like, you can focus on the family values mentioned in paragraph 5.

3. **Combining patterns.** In the last paragraph, Sullivan says, "Only marriage can bring [a young gay male] home." Define *home* (see Chapter 11 on definition), and use cause-and-effect analysis to explain how marriage can cause a person to be home.

4. **Connecting the readings.** Sullivan notes that his adolescence was a difficult, troubled time, as adolescence is for most people. Discuss one or more of the factors that cause teenage angst (anguish, anxiety). You can also discuss what can be done to make adolescence a less difficult time. For ideas, you can draw on your own experience and observation as well as on one or more of these readings: "Lost at C" (page 189), "It's Just Too Late" (page 422), and "Complexion" (page 657).

5. **Drawing on sources.** Read the arguments of those who favor and of those who oppose gay marriage by typing "gay marriage" into your favorite search engine or by looking up "gay marriage" in *ProQuest* or *Reader's Guide to Periodical Literature* (both located in your campus library's reference room). Then write a summary of the chief arguments for and against gay marriage.

BACKGROUND: James Surowiecki is the financial columnist for *The New Yorker* and a regular contributor to other publications, including *Salon* and *New York* magazine. He has written on a variety of financial and business topics, including bank mergers, the stock market, and the music industry. He has also edited *Best Crime Writing of the Year* (2002) and written *The Wisdom of Crowds: Why the Many Are Smarter Than the Few and How Collective Wisdom Shapes Business, Economies, Societies, and Nations* (2004). "Paying to Play" first appeared in *The New Yorker* (2004).

COMBINED PATTERNS AND THEIR PURPOSES: Hundreds of CDs come out each week, and radio stations cannot possibly play them all. Using *cause-and-effect analysis* and *exemplification,* James Surowiecki **informs** the reader about one way stations decide what to play: Music publishers buy air time for their recordings. Surowiecki also has a **persuasive** purpose, as he aims to convince the reader (in part, with *comparison-contrast*) that pay-for-play is a flawed system.

PAYING TO PLAY

| JAMES SUROWIECKI

Pop music thrives on repetition. You know a song's a hit when you've heard it so often that you'll be happy never to hear it again. Even by Top 40 standards, though, the playlist adopted a few weeks ago by the Nashville radio station WQZQ was extreme. On May 23rd, *Billboard*[1] reported, the station played "Don't Tell Me," the new single by Avril Lavigne, three times an hour, every hour, between midnight and 6 A.M. This didn't have much to do with the tastes of WQZQ's d.j.s or listeners. Instead, an independent promoter working for Lavigne's record label had effectively paid the station to play the song. "Don't Tell Me" had been hovering just outside *Billboard's* list of the country's ten most frequently played songs, which radio programmers use to decide what singles get airtime. The extra spins the promoter

bought—sometimes called "spot buys," because what's really being bought are blocks of ad time, as with an infomercial—were meant to bump "Don't Tell Me" up the list. By early June, Lavigne had a Top 10 hit.

> "By early June, Lavigne had a Top 10 hit. She also had a lot of angry music fans to contend with."

2 She also had a lot of angry music fans to contend with. Spot buys may be legal, but to most people they're the "new payola," a modern-day equivalent of Alan Freed's[2] taking money under the table to play rock-and-roll records. (Freed called the payments "consulting fees.") It's an obvious comparison, but a misplaced one. Spot buys aren't the

---

[1] *Billboard* is an international news weekly about the music industry. Among its features are charts of music sales and airplay.

[2] Alan Freed (1922–1965) was a disc jockey and rock-and-roll promoter. In 1962, he plead guilty to accepting money to play records. Some say he was a scapegoat, punished because he played records by black artists for white audiences.

same as old-fashioned payola. They're worse.

3   "Payola" became a household word in the fifties, when a host of d.j.s were found to be playing songs in exchange for favors and money, but the practice is as old as pop music itself. A century ago, songwriters routinely paid vaudeville singers to perform their tunes, hoping to goose demand for sheet music. In the thirties, music publishers paid off radio bandleaders. And although some forms of payola were outlawed after the mid-century scandals, various loopholes allowed other incarnations to thrive, under the guise of independent promotion. With money from the record companies, promoters used oblique tactics—subsidies, gifts, "research funds"—to encourage radio stations to add new singles to their playlists. By 2000, tens of millions of dollars a year were being spent on what you might call legal payola, and although bad publicity has severely curtailed the promotion business, paying to play is still integral to the way radio works.

4   Despite its sleazy reputation, payola has a certain rationale. In a typical year, upward of seven or eight hundred CDs are issued each week. Not even the most dedicated program director can hope to sift through all the new songs. So stations need a way to filter the possible hits from the certain bombs. Pay-for-play schemes provide one rough-and-ready way to do this, because they involve what economists call signalling. By putting money behind a record, a label signals its belief that the record has a chance to be a hit; no company will spend a lot of money trying to sell something it doesn't have high hopes for. And hits, of course, are the only thing that radio cares about.

"And hits, of course, are the only thing that radio cares about."

5   You can see the same process at work in many other businesses, too. Supermarkets and drugstores accept billions of dollars a year in "slotting fees" to position products at the end of an aisle or at eye level. Book chains sell space on the tables at the front of their stores. And record stores accept advertising dollars from labels to push certain albums. Here, too, being willing to shell out for a good space on the shelf is a statement about how much you think people will want your product.

6   This is, at best, a flawed way to find hits. Unless a record label has a good sense of what people want to hear, it could be buying airtime for flops. And labels that don't have the cash to promote their records are out of luck. But the surprising truth is that, historically speaking, payola has often fostered musical diversity, rather than squelching it. In the fifties, the music industry was dominated by a few giant labels, much as it is today; because of payola (and payola-takers, like Alan Freed), the smaller labels that revolutionized the industry—including Atlantic, Chess, and King Records—were able to get their music on the air. In retail, too, paying for space hasn't necessarily hindered innovation. Even as slotting fees have become more common in supermarkets, for instance, the number of new products that reach the shelves each year has exploded. And the same is true with books. We tend to assume that payola favors the big players because they are the ones with the big money. But the big players also have big sales forces, big

brand names, and big connections. They'd win without having to ante up to get in on the action. Paying to play, then, creates a rough marketplace democracy: if you can come up with the cash, you get a shot. But that's all. Labels can buy themselves exposure; they can't buy themselves a hit. If people don't want to hear a record, radio stations won't keep playing it of their won accord.

7   And that's where spot buys come in. Unlike conventional pay-for-play deals, spot buys like the one that propelled Avril Lavigne into the Top 10 aren't meant to introduce listeners to songs; they're meant to game the playlist system. It's a salient feature of modern me-dia that being thought to be popular can make you more popular. Best-selling books and records are discounted more than slow-selling ones and are positioned more prominently. Songs in *Billboard's* Top 10 automatically end up being spun more. And if you invest lots of money in creating an illusion of popularity—by, say, buying hours of airplay on the radio—you may end up making yourself more popular. In the process, what real listeners want matters less than it ever did. In "Payola Blues," Neil Young[3] sang to Alan Freed, "The things they're doing today/Will make a saint out of you." He didn't know the half of it.

------

[3]Neil Young is an influential singer-songwriter who was particularly prominent during the 1970s and 1980s.

READING CLOSELY AND THINKING CRITICALLY

1.   What is the thesis of the essay?
2.   Why does Surowiecki believe that spot buys are worse than payola? Do you agree? Why or why not?
3.   What are the negative effects of pay-for-play?
4.   Do you think record sales would decline if more people knew about pay-for-play? Why or why not?

EXAMINING STRUCTURE AND STRATEGY

1.   What approach does Surowiecki use for his introduction? Why does he use this approach?
2.   In paragraph 3, Surowiecki gives the history of pay-for-play. Why does he include this information? How does it help him achieve his purpose for writing?
3.   Which paragraphs have topic sentences that introduce a discussion of a cause or effect of pay-for-play?
4.   How does Surowiecki achieve coherence between paragraphs 1 and 2? Between paragraphs 2 and 3? Between paragraphs 3 and 4? Between paragraphs 4 and 5? (See page 69 on coherence.)
5.   How does the repetition of *Avril Lavigne* in the conclusion help achieve coherence?

NOTING COMBINED PATTERNS

1. How does Surowiecki use comparison-contrast to help achieve his writing purpose?
2. Why does Surowiecki compare spot buying of radio time to paying slotting fees in retail stores?
3. The opening paragraph includes an extended example, and examples appear in paragraphs 3, 5, and 6. How does this exemplification help the author achieve his writing purpose?

CONSIDERING LANGUAGE AND STYLE

1. In paragraph 6, Surowiecki says that paying to play creates a "marketplace democracy." In your opinion, is this phrase accurate? Why or why not?
2. Surowiecki uses informal language, including "goose" (paragraph 3), "shell out" (paragraph 5), and "game the playlist" (paragraph 7). What effect does this informal usage create? Is the informal usage appropriate? Explain.
3. Consult a dictionary if you do not know the meaning of any of these words and phrases: *under-the-table* (paragraph 2), *incarnations* (paragraph 3), *guise* (paragraph 3), *salient* (paragraph 7).

FOR DISCUSSION IN CLASS OR ONLINE

Is signalling (paragraph 4) a valid way to filter "possible hits from the certain bombs"? Why or why not? Can you think of a better alternative to signalling and pay-for-play? If your instructor so directs, post your response on your class Web site.

WRITING ASSIGNMENTS

1. **In your journal.** What do you think of the manipulation of the marketplace revealed in the essay? In what other ways are consumers' choices and preferences manipulated? Who benefits, and how does that make you feel? Answer one or more of these questions in a page or so.
2. **Using cause-and-effect analysis for a purpose.** The purposes in the assignments are possibilities. You may establish whatever purposes you like, within your instructor's guidelines.
   - To express your feelings and inform, explain what causes you to like one of the following: a song, a movie, a television show, a video game, a music video, or a book. How much of the title's appeal is the result of how often you see or hear it?
   - Explain why you buy particular items in the grocery store, pharmacy, book store, or from a Web site. Are you influenced by the location of the product in the store or on the Web site? Your purpose can be to inform and perhaps persuade that positioning does or does not influence buyers.
   - To inform and perhaps relate experience, explain the causes and effects of the illusions we create. You can consider such illusions as those we create in chat rooms, on résumés, and in the classroom with such artifices as posturing, lying, makeup, hair dye, wigs, and plastic surgery.

3. **Combining patterns.** In paragraph 7, Surowiecki says that "if you invest lots of money in creating an illusion of popularity . . . you may end up making yourself more popular." Use definition (explained in Chapter 11) to explain what popularity is in a particular context, such as high school, politics, the media, or athletics. In addition, use cause-and-effect analysis to explain how money can create the "illusion of popularity" in that context. You can also use process analysis (explained in Chapter 7) to track the process whereby popularity is achieved.

4. **Connecting the readings.** Surowiecki says that "being thought to be popular can make you more popular" (paragraph 7). Explain what he means and whether or not you agree with him. For ideas, you can draw on your own experience and observation as well as one or more of these readings: "Ring Leader" (page 183), "Lifosuction" (page 223), and "How I'll Become an American" (page 281).

5. **Drawing on sources.** Research the payola scandal of the 1950s and Alan Freed's alleged role in it. Then write a brief summary of what happened. For information, you can type "Alan Freed payola" into your favorite search engine or look up "Alan Freed" and "payola" in *Infotrac* or *Social Sciences Index*.

BACKGROUND: Eyal Press is a journalist and freelance writer based in New York. A one-time contributing editor at *Lingua Franca,* he has written for that publication and many others, including *The Atlantic Monthly, The American Prospect, The Nation,* the *New York Times,* and *Mother Jones.* Press's specialty is investigative reporting on a range of subjects, including global labor abuses, conditions in institutions for the mentally retarded, civil liberties, human rights violations, corporate influences in higher education, online learning, and distance education. From 1999 to 2000, he was a project fellow at Open Society Institute, where he examined privatization of public organizations, including the effort to transfer government programs to for-profit companies. "Fouled Out" first appeared in *The Atlantic Monthly* in 2001.

After reading the essay, you may wonder where Bobby Knight and Murray Sperber are now. Six months after being fired from Indiana University in 2000 for allegedly grabbing and swearing at a student player, Knight became head coach at Texas Tech, where he remains at the time of this writing. Sperber is still a professor of English and American Studies at Indiana University. He has written several books about athletics, including *Beer and Circus. How Big-Time College Sports Is Crippling Undergraduate Education* (2000).

COMBINED PATTERNS AND THEIR PURPOSES: English Professor Murray Sperber became a marked man at Indiana University. In "Fouled Out," Eyal Press uses *cause-and-effect analysis* and *exemplification to* **inform** the reader why that happened and what the results were. Could he also have a **persuasive** purpose?

FOULED OUT

EYAL PRESS

When spring-term classes began at Indiana University last January, Murray Sperber was understandably on edge. Sperber has taught English and American studies at the university for nearly three decades, and until recently his life followed the generally peaceful contours of a scholarly existence. Dropping in on one of his classes, one might find him analyzing the language in Arthur Miller's *Death of a Salesman* or discussing the social impact of Jack Kerouac's *On the Road.* Owing to his role in a recent campus controversy, however, Sperber has lately been feeling less like a professor of literature than like a man on a hit list.

As you read Determine where the author's sympathies lie.

"Sperber has lately been feeling less like a professor of literature than a man on a hit list."

2   On the advice of campus security, Sperber carries a cell phone programmed to contact the police at the touch of a single button. He was urged to enroll in a self-defense course at the local police academy (he is taking judo) and was also trained by the police in "verbal judo"—methods for defusing verbal confrontations so that they don't turn into physical ones. He was advised to avoid letting his whereabouts be known. His spring-term courses—one on post–World War II American literature, and one on the modern media—were listed in the university catalogue under other faculty members' names. (Students who enrolled were baffled on the first day of class by the sight of him; many thought they had misread the room number.) Sperber declines to hold office hours and will meet with students only in public places.

3   Sperber's troubles began on March 15 of last year, when he appeared on a CNN/Sports Illustrated television exposé about Bobby Knight, the legendary basketball coach whose success on the court (three National Collegiate Athletic Association championships and eleven Big Ten titles since joining Indiana University, in 1971) had led virtually everyone at the school to overlook his tyrannical behavior. But Sperber also happens to be one of the country's most outspoken critics of college sports, a subject he has examined in several books. So he had welcomed the opportunity to speak to CNN/SI about the now famous complaints about Knight: that he had a penchant for wild, expletive-filled tirades, and that he had once tried to choke a player.

4   Asked what would happen if he himself were to behave this way in a classroom, Sperber said that he would almost certainly lose his tenure. What would happen to Knight? Bobby Knight was "the emperor of Indiana," Sperber replied; no one would hold him accountable. Indeed, the day before, Indiana University had held a press conference to defend Knight in advance.

5   In Indiana, of course, few things are taken more seriously than basketball, and Sperber's remarks constituted a transgression that many considered unforgivable. The following morning he awoke to a torrent of irate and obscene telephone calls and e-mails. "Shame on you for giving such a wonderful university a black eye . . . You should resign!" read one e-mail, from an Indiana University alumnus. "You are a vile and pathetic little worm," another said. Anonymous callers flooded Sperber's answering machine with vituperative messages. Disparaging letters began appearing in the local paper.

6   Initially, Sperber was right about Bobby Knight's inviolability. Even after CNN/SI obtained and aired footage of the choking incident, the university allowed Knight to keep his job, although it fined him $30,000, suspended him for three games, and imposed a "zero tolerance" policy with respect to any future incidents. Sperber continued to speak out on the issue, and the angry missives from Indiana fans took on an increasingly threatening tone. "If you don't shut up, I'll shut you up," one caller warned. Sperber soon noticed that the schedule for his fall classes had been posted on a Web site for Indiana University basketball fans. "I see dead bodies," a heading on the site declared; it was followed by a list that included Sperber's name and those of two newspaper columnists who had also been critical of Knight.

7   Strangers began approaching Sperber in supermarkets and coffee shops and warning him to stop talking about Knight. Others shouted at him as they drove by his house or passed him on the street. "You're that [f_____] professor who won't keep his mouth shut!" a student yelled from across a parking lot one day; Sperber changed direction in order to avoid a physical confrontation. Another man rolled down his car window and swore at Sperber as he stood on a street corner with his ten-year-old foster daughter, waiting for the light to change. Sperber began fearing for the safety of his family. They stopped going to restaurants, tired of the icy, intimidating glares they drew from other diners. His wife stopped using her credit card after a store clerk, recognizing her last name, verbally harassed her.

8 Sperber started having nightmares and losing sleep. He could barely concentrate on his work. Arriving at his office one day, he was greeted by a message on his answering machine from a man who listed the days and times of Sperber's classes and warned, "I know how to find you." The campus police offered to post an armed guard in Sperber's lecture rooms. But, exhausted by the threats and the pressure, and feeling that he could not teach under such conditions, Sperber decided to take an unpaid leave. On June 20 he left Bloomington for Montreal, where he was born and raised, and where nobody much cared about Bobby Knight.

9 A few months ago I met Sperber for dinner in Bloomington. He was back because Knight was gone: last September, after Knight upbraided a student and committed other violations, he was fired. (He has since been hired by Texas Tech University.) His dismissal sparked an uproar on campus, but that eventually died down, and Sperber decided it was more or less safe to return.

10 When we got together, he seemed relieved by Knight's departure but was visibly worn by events. "The diehard Knight fans are still out there," he told me wearily. "They still post messages whenever I speak publicly." Several times each day he logs onto various Indiana-fan Web sites to see if any new threats have been posted. "There were some denunciations today," he said.

"The usual low-level 'I hate this guy, why doesn't he shut up?'"

11 Dressed in jeans, sneakers, and a San Francisco 49ers cap, Sperber looked nothing like the pointy-headed professor his critics often portray him as. Before becoming a professor he spent two years playing semi-professional basketball in Europe, and although an injured knee has kept him off the courts for years, he remains a fairly avid sports fan. He began writing about college athletics because of an interest in NCAA soccer.

12 Not surprisingly, however, Sperber's investigations of amateur athletics and especially the past year's experience have given him a somewhat jaundiced view of college sports. Again and again over the past year, he told me, people e-mailed or called him to ask, "Don't you understand that the purpose of Indiana University is the basketball team? That's what pays your salary as an English teacher!"

13 In fact, as Sperber points out in his latest book, *Beer and Circus: How Big-Time College Sports Is Crippling Undergraduate Education* (2000), the vast majority of athletic programs actually lose money, because expenditures for

equipment, facilities, and travel generally outstrip revenues from ticket sales and TV contracts. Although a few universities have seen enrollment rise following athletic success, Sperber argues that the disproportionate focus on college sports is partly responsible for swelling class sizes and a declining emphasis on undergraduate education. A graduate of Purdue University, where, he says, he obtained an excellent education forty years ago, Sperber believes that the problem is particularly bad at public universities, where the beer-soaked, sports-oriented party scene prevails.

14 Some fellow critics of college sports would debate this proposition. In their provocative book *The Game of Life: College Sports and Educational Values* (2001), James Shulman and William Bowen argue that the impact of sports is in some ways greater at Ivy League universities and small liberal-arts schools, where the proportion of athletes in the student population is higher than at big public universities. Sperber is unconvinced. At schools like Swarthmore and Williams, he says, most students still receive a quality education, and sports do not play a remotely comparable role in shaping the culture.

15 The day after our dinner I sat in on one of Sperber's classes. Toward the end he left the room, and the conversation turned to his situation. Several students told me that their friends still express horror at even the mention of their professor's name. A few admitted that at the start of the semester they had shared this reaction and had considered dropping the course. (Only one student actually did so.) But for all his public outspokenness, the students said, Sperber almost never mentioned Knight or his own role in the controversy during class. They seemed to appreciate this. They had come to think of Sperber not as Bobby Knight's critic but as an ordinary professor—which is, of course, what he is hoping to become once again.

READING CLOSELY AND THINKING CRITICALLY

1. What double standard does Press point out in the essay?

2. Why did Sperber decide to take an unpaid leave from Indiana University? Do you think taking the leave was the right thing to do? Why or why not?

3. Can you tell what Press thinks about the controversy surrounding Sperber? If so, how can you tell? If not, why not?

4. Does the reaction to Sperber by members of the Indiana University and Bloomington, Indiana, communities surprise you? Why or why not?

EXAMINING STRUCTURE AND STRATEGY

1. Which sentence is the thesis of "Fouled Out"? What does the thesis indicate about the topic and the aspects of the topic that will be covered?

2. Why does Press mention that Sperber played semiprofessional basketball and that he is a "fairly avid sports fan" (paragraph 11)? Why does he mention that Sperber has studied college athletics and written a book on the subject?

3. Other than noting campus security's efforts to protect Sperber, Press does not mention university or community support for Sperber. Why?

1. What cause-and-effect relationships does Press examine in "Fouled Out"?
2. How does Press arrange his cause-and-effect details?
3. Where does Press use exemplification in "Fouled Out"? How does the exemplification help Press achieve his purpose?

CONSIDERING LANGUAGE AND STYLE

1. In paragraph 1, Press describes Sperber's life before his CNN/SI interview as following "the generally peaceful contours of a scholarly existence." What phrase would you use to describe Sperber's life after the interview?
2. What is the "zero tolerance" policy that Sperber refers to in paragraph 6?
3. Consult a dictionary if you do not know the meaning of these words: *exposé* (paragraph 3), *expletive* (paragraph 3), *tirade* (paragraph 3), *transgression* (paragraph 5), *vituperative* (paragraph 5), *inviolability* (paragraph 6), *missives* (paragraph 6), *jaundiced* (paragraph 12).

FOR DISCUSSION IN CLASS OR ONLINE

Should Professor Sperber have given the CNN/SI interview? Why or why not? If your instructor directs you to do so, post your response to your class Web site.

WRITING ASSIGNMENTS

1. **In your journal.** What role do you think athletics should play in college life? Explain why you believe as you do.
2. **Using cause-and-effect analysis for a purpose.** The purposes in the assignments are possibilities. You may establish whatever purpose you like, within your instructor's guidelines.
   - To inform readers and perhaps persuade, write about another controversial sports figure and examine the effect of the controversy on the reputation of the particular sport, or sports in general.
   - Explain the role of athletics on your campus and the effect they have on campus life. Your purpose can be to inform and perhaps persuade your reader that athletics are a positive or negative influence on campus life.
   - Select a sport and explain the role it plays in American society and its effects on society. Your purpose can be to inform and perhaps persuade your reader that the sport is a positive or negative influence.
   - To relate experience and express feelings, explain the effect on you of some aspect of sports. You can consider your role as a player, as a fan, as a member of a sports-crazed family, as the parent of an athlete, or as a non-fan in a sports-conscious society or on a sports-conscious campus.

3. **Combining patterns.** Sperber spoke out and paid a price as a result. Using exemplification (explained in Chapter 6), cite other examples of people voicing unpopular views and note what happened when these people spoke out. What conclusions can you draw about voicing unpopular views?

4. **Connecting the readings.** Many people would say that Sperber displayed courage when he spoke out against Bobby Knight. Discuss the ways people can display courage. For ideas, you can draw on one or more of these selections: "Fouled Out," "Struck by Lightning" (page 141), and "Shoot to Kill" (page 299).

5. **Drawing on sources.** Paragraphs 13 and 14 consider some of the effects of college sports. Those paragraphs make it clear that people do not agree about what the effects are. In an essay, consider one or more of the effects of college sports. For ideas, try visiting the National Collegiate Athletics Association Web site (*www2.ncaa.org*) and click on "Legislation and Governance" to read about some of the problems faced by college athletes and the rules to which they must adhere. You can also look in the *Social Sciences Index* or *Psychological Abstracts* under the heading "college athletes."

BACKGROUND: Born in 1951 in Chester, Pennsylvania, Brent Staples was the oldest of nine children. He grew up in poverty, but a college scholarship rescued him from a life on the streets. One of his brothers, a cocaine dealer, was killed at 22. Staples ultimately earned his Ph.D. in psychology from the University of Chicago. A member of the *New York Times* editorial board, he writes on education, politics, and culture for the newspaper. Before joining the *Times,* he was a reporter for the *Chicago Sun Times.* He has also written for the *New York Times Magazine, Harper's,* and *New York Woman.* His memoir *Parallel Time: Growing Up in Black and White* (1994) recalls his childhood in Chester and the death of his younger brother. It was a finalist for the *Los Angeles Times* Book Award. "Just Walk on By" appeared in *Ms.* in 1986 and in a revised form in *Harper's* (1987) as "Black Men and Public Space."

www.mhhe.com/patterns

For more information on this author, go to

More resources > Chapter 9 > Brent Staples

COMBINED PATTERNS AND THEIR PURPOSES: In "Just Walk on By," Brent Staples uses *cause-and-effect analysis* to **inform** his reader that black men are at risk because they are "perceived as dangerous." To illustrate the point, he includes *narration.* He also **shares his feelings** on this issue and **relates his experience** as a black man viewed as threatening.

JUST WALK ON BY: A BLACK MAN PONDERS HIS POWER TO ALTER PUBLIC SPACE

BRENT STAPLES

My first victim was a woman—white, well dressed, probably in her early twenties. I came upon her late one evening on a deserted street in Hyde Park, a relatively affluent neighborhood in an otherwise mean, impoverished section of Chicago. As I swung onto the avenue behind her, there seemed to be a discreet uninflammatory distance between us. Not so. She cast back a worried glance. To her, the youngish black man— a broad six feet two inches with a beard and billowing hair, both hands shoved into the pockets of a bulky military jacket—seemed menacingly close. After a few more quick glimpses, she picked up her pace and was soon running in

As you read
Think about how you react to people on the basis of their appearance.

earnest. Within seconds she disappeared into a cross street.

"After a few more quick glimpses, she picked up her pace and was soon running in earnest."

2   That was more than a decade ago. I was 22 years old, a graduate student newly arrived at the University of Chicago. It was in the echo of that terrified woman's footfalls that I first began to know the unwieldy inheritance I'd come into—the ability to alter public space in ugly ways. It was clear that she thought herself the quarry of a mugger, a rapist, or worse. Suffering a bout of

insomnia, however, I was stalking sleep, not defenseless wayfarers. As a softy who is scarcely able to take a knife to a raw chicken—let alone hold it to a person's throat—I was surprised, embarrassed, and dismayed all at once. Her flight made me feel like an accomplice in tyranny. It also made it clear that I was indistinguishable from the muggers who occasionally seeped into the area from the surrounding ghetto. That first encounter, and those that followed, signified that a vast, unnerving gulf lay between nighttime pedestrians—particularly women—and me. And I soon gathered that being perceived as dangerous is a hazard in itself. I only needed to turn a corner into a dicey situation, or crowd some frightened, armed person in a foyer somewhere, or make an errant move after being pulled over by policeman. Where fear and weapons meet—and they often do in urban America—there is always the possibility of death.

3   In that first year, my first away from my hometown, I was to become thoroughly familiar with the language of fear. At dark, shadowy intersections in Chicago, I could cross in front of a car stopped at a traffic light and elicit the *thunk, thunk, thunk, thunk* of the driver—black, white, male, or female—hammering down the door locks. On less traveled streets after dark, I grew accustomed to but never comfortable with people who crossed to the other side of the street rather than pass me. Then there were the standard unpleasantries with police, doormen, bouncers, cab drivers, and others whose business it is to screen out troublesome individuals *before* there is any nastiness.

4   I moved to New York nearly two years ago and I have remained an avid night walker. In central Manhattan, the near-constant crowd cover minimizes tense one-on-one street encounters. Elsewhere—visiting friends in SoHo, where sidewalks are narrow and tightly spaced buildings shut out the sky—things can get very taut indeed.

5   Black men have a firm place in New York mugging literature. Norman

> "Black men have a firm place in New York mugging literature."

Podhoretz in his famed (or infamous) 1963 essay, "My Negro Problem—And Ours," recalls growing up in terror of black males; they "were tougher than we were, more ruthless," he writes—and as an adult on the Upper West Side of Manhattan, he continues, he cannot constrain his nervousness when he meets black men on certain streets. Similarly, a decade later, the essayist and novelist Edward Hoagland extols a New York where once "Negro bitterness bore down mainly on other Negroes." Where some see mere panhandlers, Hoagland sees "a mugger who is clearly screwing up his nerve to do more than just *ask* for money." But Hoagland has "the New Yorker's quick-hunch posture for broken-field maneuvering," and the bad guy swerves away.

6   I often witness that "hunch posture," from women after dark on the warrenlike streets of Brooklyn where I live. They seem to set their faces on neutral and, with their purse straps strung across their chests bandolier style, they forge ahead as though bracing themselves against being tackled. I understand, of course, that the danger they

perceive is not a hallucination. Women are particularly vulnerable to street violence, and young black males are drastically overrepresented among the perpetrators of that violence. Yet these truths are no solace against the kind of alienation that comes of being ever the suspect, against being set apart, a fearsome entity with whom pedestrians avoid making eye contact.

7   It is not altogether clear to me how I reached the ripe old age of 22 without being conscious of the lethality nighttime pedestrians attributed to me. Perhaps it was because in Chester, Pennsylvania, the small angry industrial town where I came of age in the 1960s, I was scarcely noticeable against a backdrop of gang warfare, street knifings, and murders. I grew up one of the good boys, had perhaps a half-dozen fist fights. In retrospect, my shyness of combat has clear sources.

8   Many things go into the making of a young thug. One of those things is the consummation of the male romance with the power to intimidate. An infant discovers that random flailings send the baby bottle flying out of the crib and crashing to the floor. Delighted, the joyful babe repeats those motions again and again, seeking to duplicate the feat. Just so, I recall the points at which some of my boyhood friends were finally seduced by the perception of themselves as tough guys. When a mark cowered and surrendered his money without resistance, myth and reality merged—and paid off. It is, after all, only manly to embrace the power to frighten and intimidate. We, as men, are not supposed to give an inch of our lane on the highway; we are to seize the fighter's edge in work and in play and even in love; we are to be valiant in the face of hostile forces.

9   Unfortunately, poor and powerless young men seem to take all this nonsense literally. As a boy, I saw countless tough guys locked away; I have since buried several, too. They were babies, really—a teenage cousin, a brother of 22, a childhood friend in his mid-twenties—all gone down in episodes of bravado played out in the streets. I came to doubt the virtues of intimidation early on. I chose, perhaps even unconsciously, to remain a shadow—timid, but a survivor.

10   The fearsomeness mistakenly attributed to me in public places often has a perilous flavor. The most frightening of these confusions occurred in the late 1970s and early 1980s when I worked as a journalist in Chicago. One day, rushing into the office of a magazine I was writing for with a deadline story in hand, I was mistaken for a burglar. The office manager called security and, with an ad hoc posse, pursued me through the labyrinthine halls, nearly to my editor's door. I had no way of proving who I was.

"I had no way of proving who I was."

I could only move briskly toward the company of someone who knew me.

11   Another time I was on assignment for a local paper and killing time before an interview. I entered a jewelry store on the city's affluent Near North Side. The proprietor excused herself and returned with an enormous red Doberman pinscher straining at the end of a leash. She stood, the dog extended toward me, silent to my questions, her eyes bulging nearly out of her head. I took a cursory look around, nodded, and bade her good night. Relatively speaking, however, I never fared as badly as another black male journalist. He went to nearby Waukegan, Illinois, a

couple of summers ago to work on a story about a murderer who was born there. Mistaking the reporter for the killer, police hauled him from his car at gunpoint and but for his press credentials would probably have tried to book him. Such episodes are not uncommon. Black men trade tales like this all the time.

12   In "My Negro Problem—And Ours," Podhoretz writes that the hatred he feels for blacks makes itself known to him through a variety of avenues—one being his discomfort with that "special brand of paranoid touchiness" to which he says blacks are prone. No doubt he is speaking here of black men. In time, I learned to smother the rage I felt at so often being taken for a criminal. Not to do so would surely have led to madness— via that special "paranoid touchiness" that so annoyed Podhoretz at the time he wrote the essay.

13   I began to take precautions to make myself less threatening. I move about with care, particularly late in the evening. I give a wide berth to nervous people on subway platforms during the wee hours, particularly when I have exchanged business clothes for jeans. If I happen to be entering a building behind some people who appear skittish, I may walk by, letting them clear the lobby before I return, so as not to seem to be following them. I have been calm and extremely congenial on those rare occasions when I've been pulled over by the police.

14   And on late-evening constitutionals along streets less traveled by, I employ what has proved to be an excellent tension-reducing measure: I whistle melodies from Beethoven and Vivaldi and the more popular classical composers. Even steely New Yorkers hunching toward night-time destinations seem to relax, and occasionally they even join in the tune. Virtually everybody seems to sense that a mugger wouldn't be warbling bright, sunny selections from Vivaldi's *Four Seasons*. It is my equivalent of the cowbell that hikers wear when they know they are in bear country.

READING CLOSELY AND THINKING CRITICALLY

1. When Staples walks at night, what effect does he have on people? What do people do when they see him?

2. Although Staples is often viewed as a threat, he is the one at risk. Why?

3. Staples explains that his effect on people—particularly women—is understandable. Why does he think so?

4. According to Staples, what causes a young man to become a thug? What do you think prompts a black male to become a thug? How did Staples escape becoming a thug?

5. In paragraphs 5 and 12, Staples refers to essays by Norman Podhoretz and Edward Hoagland. What point do you think Staples is trying to make with these references?

6. Staple's essay first appeared in *Ms.* and *Harper's*. *Ms.* is a magazine about women's issues and takes a politically progressive stand; *Harper's* is one of the oldest and most prestigious American magazines, publishing literature, commentary, arts reviews, and in-depth reporting with a liberal view point. Do the readers of these magazines make the best audience for the piece? Explain.

1. What approach does Staples take to his introduction? Does the introduction engage your interest? Explain.
2. The essay is not about what the opening sentences lead you to believe it will be about. Is that a problem? Explain.
3. In your own words, write out the thesis of "Just Walk on By." Which sentence in the essay comes closest to expressing that idea?
4. What approach does Staples take to his conclusion? Do you think the conclusion brings the essay to a satisfying close? Why or why not?

NOTING COMBINED PATTERNS

1. Staples discusses both causes and effects in his essay. What causes and effects are explained?
2. Which paragraphs include brief narrations? How do they help Staples achieve his writing purpose?

CONSIDERING LANGUAGE AND STYLE

1. What is "public space"? What does it mean to possess the power to alter public space? Name groups of people that have the power to alter public space.
2. Consult a dictionary if you are unsure of the meaning of any of these words: *quarry* (paragraph 2), *wayfarers* (paragraph 2), *errant* (paragraph 2), *extols* (paragraph 5), *warrenlike* (paragraph 6), *bandolier* (paragraph 6), *bravado* (paragraph 9), *ad hoc* (paragraph 10), *labyrinthine* (paragraph 10), *cursory* (paragraph 11), *constitutionals* (paragraph 14).

FOR DISCUSSION IN CLASS OR ONLINE

What causes a person to be perceived as threatening? If your instructor directs you to do so, post your response to your class Web site.

WRITING ASSIGNMENTS

1. **In your journal.** Although we admit that appearances can be deceiving, we often are influenced by the way others look. How do appearances affect the judgments we make about people? For example, how did the attacks on the World Trade Center and the Pentagon in September 2001 affect the way Arab Americans are sometimes perceived?
2. **Using cause-and-effect analysis for a purpose.** The purposes in the assignments are possibilities. You may establish whatever purposes you like, within your instructor's guidelines.
   - How safe do you feel walking alone on your campus or in your neighborhood? To relate experience, express feelings, and inform, explain why you feel the way you do and the effects of your feeling of security or insecurity.

- To relate experience, express feelings, and inform, explain how you think you are perceived by others and explain why you think you are perceived that way. Consider how one or more factors such as your size, gender, skin color, age, manner of dress, and degree of attractiveness affect how people judge your social class, economic level, degree of intelligence, occupation, and such. Then go on to explain how you are affected by the way you are perceived.
- If you have ever been perceived as a threat or if you have perceived someone else as a threat, explain what caused the perception and what its effects were in order to relate experience and express feelings.

3. **Combining patterns.** In paragraph 8, Staples comments on men and power: "It is, after all, only manly to embrace the power to frighten and intimidate." Do you agree that our concept of manliness is linked to the sense of power and the ability to intimidate? Agree or disagree by defining *manliness* (see Chapter 11) and explaining how men and women are affected by the concept.

4. **Connecting the readings.** Explain how people react to those they perceive as "different." Also explain why you think people react the way they do. The ideas in "Just Walk on By" and "Untouchables" (page 248) may give you some ideas.

5. **Drawing on sources.** Racial profiling occurs when the police make decisions based solely on race. For example, police officers who automatically stop and question young black males are practicing racial profiling. Summarize the arguments used to defend racial profiling and the arguments used to attack it. You can find information by typing in the phrase "racial profiling" at *www.findarticles.com* or by looking up "racial profiling" in *The Reader's Guide to Periodical Literature* or the *New York Times Index*.

BACKGROUND: A journalist and prolific author who has also performed a number of one-man shows, Calvin Trillin was born in 1935 in Kansas City, Missouri. He graduated from Yale University in 1957 and went on to write investigative pieces, humor columns, short stories, novels, and commentary for a number of magazines. He wrote a series for *The New Yorker* called "U.S. Journal," for which he contributed a 3,000-word article every three weeks from somewhere in the United States, and another series of long narratives called the "American Chronicles." Trillin's syndicated column, "Uncivil Liberties," is distributed weekly to newspapers, and he writes a weekly comic verse for *The Nation.* His many books include *An Education in Georgia: Charlayne Hunter, Hamilton Holmes and the Integration of the University of Georgia* (1964), an account of the experiences of the first two black undergraduates at the University of Georgia; *U.S. Journal* (1971), a collection from the first three years of *The New Yorker* series; *Uncivil Liberties* (1982), another collection of columns; *Killings* (1984), a look at the way Americans get killed; *Remembering Denny* (1993), a memoir that attempts to explain the 1991 suicide of a college friend, and *Family Man* (1998). "It's Just Too Late" first appeared as part of the "U.S. Journal" series and later was reprinted in *Killings.*

COMBINED PATTERNS AND THEIR PURPOSE: In "It's Just Too Late," Calvin Trillin uses *cause and effect analysis* and *narration* to **inform** the reader about the events surrounding the death of a teenager.

IT'S JUST TOO LATE | CALVIN TRILLIN

Knoxville, Tennessee
March 1979

Until she was sixteen, FaNee Cooper was what her parents sometimes called an ideal child. "You'd never have to correct her," FaNee's mother has said. In sixth grade, FaNee won a spelling contest. She played the piano and the flute. She seemed to believe what she heard every Sunday at the Beaver Dam Baptist Church about good and evil and the hereafter. FaNee was not an outgoing child. Even as a baby, she was uncomfortable when she was held and cuddled. She found it easy to tell her parents she loved them but difficult to confide in them. Particu-

> **As you read**
> Think why Trillin wants readers to know what happened.

"She found it easy to tell her parents she loved them but difficult to confide in them."

larly compared to her sister, Kristy, a cheerful, open little girl two and a half years younger, she was reserved and introspective. The thoughts she kept to herself, though, were apparently happy thoughts. Her eighth-grade essay on Christmas—written in a remarkably neat hand—talked of the joys of helping put together toys for her little brother, Leo, Jr., and the importance of her parents' reminder that Christmas is the birthday of Jesus. Her parents were the sort of people who might have been expected to have an ideal child. As a boy, Leo Cooper had been called "one of the greatest high-school basketball players ever developed in Knox County." He went on to play basketball at East Tennessee State, and he married the homecoming queen, JoAnn Henson. After college, Cooper became a high-school basketball coach and teacher and, eventually, an administrator. By the time FaNee turned thirteen, in 1973, he was in his third year as the principal of Gresham Junior High School, in Fountain City—a small Knox County town that had been swallowed up by Knoxville when the suburbs began to move north. A tall man with curly black hair going on gray, Leo Cooper has an elaborate way of talking ("Unless I'm very badly mistaken, he has never related to me totally the content of his conversation") and a manner that may come from years of trying to leave errant junior-high-school students with the impression that a responsible adult is magnanimous, even humble, about invariably being in the right. His wife, a high-school art teacher, paints and does batik, and created the name FaNee because she liked the way it looked and sounded—it sounds like "Fawnee" when the Coopers say it—but the impression she gives is not artiness but of soft-spoken small-town gentility. When she found, in the course of cleaning up FaNee's room, that her ideal thirteen-year-old had been smoking cigarettes, she was, in her words, crushed. "FaNee was such a perfect child before that," JoAnn Cooper said some time later. "She was angry that we found out. She knew we knew that she had done something we didn't approve of, and then the rebellion started. I was hurt. I was very hurt. I guess it came through as disappointment."

2 Several months later, FaNee's grandmother died. FaNee had been devoted to her grandmother. She wrote a poem in her memory—an almost joyous poem, filled with Christian faith in the afterlife ("Please don't grieve over my happiness/Rejoice with me in the presence of the Angels of Heaven"). She also took some keepsakes from her grandmother's house and was apparently mortified when her parents found them

and explained that they would have to be returned. By then, the Coopers were aware that FaNee was going to have a difficult time as a teenager. They thought

"By then, the Coopers were aware that FaNee was going to have a difficult time as a teenager."

she might be self-conscious about the double affliction of glasses and braces. They thought she might be uncomfortable in the role of the principal's daughter at Gresham. In ninth grade, she entered Halls High School, where JoAnn Cooper was teaching art. FaNee was a loner at first. Then she fell in with what could only be considered a bad crowd.

3 Halls, a few miles to the north of Fountain City, used to be known as Halls Crossroads. It is what Knoxville people call "over the ridge"—on the side of Black Oak Ridge that has always been thought of as rural. When FaNee entered Halls High, the Coopers were already in the process of building a house on several acres of land they had bought in Halls, in a sparsely settled area along Brown Gap Road. Like two or three other houses along the road, it was to be constructed basically of huge logs taken from old buildings—a house that Leo Cooper describes as being, like the name FaNee, "just a little bit different." Ten years ago, Halls Crossroads was literally a crossroads. Then some of the Knoxville expansion that had swollen Fountain City spilled over the ridge, planting subdivisions here and there on roads that still went for long stretches with nothing but an occasional house with a cow or two next to it. The increase in population did not create a town. Halls has no center. Its

commercial area is a series of two or three shopping centers strung together on the Maynardville Highway, the four-lane that leads north into Union Country—a place almost synonymous in east Tennessee with mountain poverty. Its restaurant is the Halls Freezo Drive-In. The gathering place for the group FaNee Cooper eventually found herself in was the Maynardville Highway Exxon station.

4 At Halls High School, the social poles were represented by the Jocks and the Freaks. FaNee found her friends among the Freaks. "I am truly enlighted upon irregular trains of thought aimed at strange depots of mental wards," she wrote when she was fifteen. "Yes! Crazed farms for the mental off—Oh! I walked through the halls screams & loud laughter fill my ears—Orderlys try to reason with me—but I am unreasonable! The joys of being a FREAK in circus of imagination." The little crowd of eight or ten young people that FaNee joined has been referred to by her mother as "the Union County group." A couple of the girls were from backgrounds similar to FaNee's, but all the boys had the characteristics, if not the precise addresses, that Knoxville people associate with the poor whites of Union County. They were the sort of boys who didn't bother to finish high school, or finished it in a special program for slow learners, or get ejected from it for taking a swing at the principal.

5 "I guess you can say they more or less dragged us down to their level with the drugs," a girl who was in the group—a girl who can be called Marcia—said recently. "And somehow we settled for it. It seems like we had to get ourselves in the pit before we could look out." People in the group used marijuana and Valium and LSD. They sneered at the Jocks and the "Prim and proper little ladies" who went with Jocks. "We set ourselves aside," Marcia now says. "We put ourselves above everyone. How we did that I don't know." In a Knox County high school, teenagers who want to get themselves in the pit need no mainline heroin. The Jocks they mean to be compared to do not merely show up regularly for classes and practice football and wear clean clothes; they watch their language and preach temperance and go to prayer meetings on Wednesday nights and talk about having a real good Christian witness. Around Knoxville, people who speak of well-behaved high-school kids often seem to use words like "perfect," or even "angels." For FaNee's group, the

"Around Knoxville, people who speak of well-behaved high-school kids often seem to use words like "perfect" or even "angels." "

opposite was not difficult to figure out. "We were into wicked things, strange things," Marcia says. "It was like we were on some kind of devil trip." FaNee wrote about demons and vultures and rats. "Slithering serpents eat my sanity and bite my ass," she wrote in an essay called "The Lovely Road of Life," just after she turned sixteen, "while tornadoes derail and ever so swiftly destroy every car in my train of thought." She wrote a lot about death.

6 FaNee's girl friends spoke of her as "super-intelligent." Her English teacher found some of her writing profound—and disturbing. She was thought to be

not just super-intelligent but super-mysterious, and even, at times, super-weird—an introverted girl who stared straight ahead with deep-brown, nearly black eyes and seemed to have thoughts she couldn't share. Nobody really knew why she had chosen to run with the Freaks—whether it was loneliness or rebellion or simple boredom. Marcia thought it might have had something to do with a feeling that her parents had settled on Kristy as their perfect child. "I guess she figured she couldn't be the best," Marcia said recently. "So she decided she might as well be the worst."

7   Toward the spring of FaNee's junior year at Halls, her problems seemed to deepen. Despite her intelligence, her grades were sliding. She was what her mother called "a mental dropout." Leo Cooper had to visit Halls twice because of minor suspensions. Once, FaNee had been caught smoking. Once, having ducked out of a required assembly, she was spotted by a favorite teacher, who turned her in. At home, she exchanged little more than short, strained formalities with Kristy, who shared their parent's opinion of FaNee's choice of friends. The Coopers had finished their house—a large house, its size accentuated by the huge old logs and a great stone fireplace and outsize "Paul Bunyan"-style furniture—but FaNee spent most of her time there in her own room, sleeping or listening to rock music through earphones. One night, there was a terrible scene when FaNee returned from a concert in a condition that Leo Cooper knew had to be the result of marijuana. JoAnn Cooper, who ordinarily strikes people as too gentle to raise her voice, found herself losing her temper regularly. Finally, Leo Cooper asked a counsellor he knew, Jim Griffin, to stop in at Halls High School and have a talk with FaNee—unofficially.

8   Griffin—a young man with a warm, informal manner—worked for the Juvenile Court of Knox County. He had a reputation for being able to reach teenagers who wouldn't talk to their parents or to school administrators. One Friday in March of 1977, he spent an hour and a half talking to FaNee Cooper. As Griffin recalls the interview, FaNee didn't seem alarmed by his presence. She seemed to him calm and controlled—Griffin thought it was something like talking to another adult—and, unlike most of the teenagers he dealt with, she looked him in the eye the entire time. Griffin, like some of FaNee's friends, found her eyes unsettling—"the coldest, most distant, but, at the same time, the most knowing eyes I'd ever seen." She expressed affection for her parents, but she didn't seem interested in exploring ways of getting along better with them. The impression she gave Griffin was that they were who they were, and she was who she was, and there didn't happen to be any connection. Several times, she made the same response to Griffin's suggestions: "It's too late."

9   That weekend, neither FaNee nor her parents brought up the subject of Griffin's visit. Leo Cooper has spoken of the weekend as being particularly happy; a friend of FaNee's who stayed over remembers it as particularly strained. FaNee stayed home from school on Monday because of a bad headache—she often had bad headaches—but felt well enough on Monday evening to drive to the library. She was to be home at nine. When she wasn't, Mrs. Cooper began to phone her friends. Finally, around ten, Leo Cooper got into his other car and took a swing around Halls—past the

teenage hangouts like the Exxon station and the Pizza Hut and the Smoky Mountain Market. Then he took a second swing. At eleven, FaNee was still not home.

> "At eleven, FaNee was still not home."

10   She hadn't gone to the library. She had picked up two girl friends and driven to the home of a third, where everyone took five Valium tablets. Then the four girls drove over to the Exxon station, where they met four boys from the crowd. After a while, the group bought some beer and some marijuana and reassembled at Charlie Stevens's trailer. Charlie Stevens was five or six years older than everyone else in the group—a skinny, slow-thinking young man with long black hair and a sparse beard. He was married and had a child, but he and his wife had separated; she was back in Union County with the baby. Stevens had remained in their trailer—parked in the yard near his mother's house, in a back-road area of Knox County dominated by decrepit, unpainted sheds and run-down trailers and rusted-out automobiles. Stevens had picked up FaNee at home once or twice—apparently, more as a driver for the group than as a date—and the Coopers, having learned that his unsuitability extended to being married, had asked her not to see him.

11   In Charlie's trailer, which had no heat or electricity, the group drank beer and passed around joints, keeping warm with blankets. By eleven or so, FaNee was what one of her friends has called "super-mess-up." Her speech was slurred. She was having trouble keeping her balance. She had decided not to go home. She had apparently persuaded herself that her parents intended to send her away to some sort of home for incorrigibles. "It's too late," She said to one of her friends. "It's just too late." It was decided that one of the boys, David Munsey, who was more or less the leader of the group, would drive the Coopers' car to FaNee's house, where FaNee and Charlie Stevens would pick him up in Stevens's car—a worn Pinto with four bald tires, one light, and a dragging muffler. FaNee wrote a note to her parents, and then, perhaps because her handwriting was suffering the effects of beer and marijuana and Valium, asked Stevens to rewrite it on a large piece of paper, which would be left on the seat of the Coopers' car. The Stevens version was just about the same as FaNee's, except that Stevens left out a couple of sentences about trying to work things out ("I'm willing to try") and, not having won any spelling championship himself, he misspelled a few words, like "tomorrow." The note said, "Dear Mom and Dad. Sorry I'm late. Very late. I left your car because I thought you might need it tomorrow. I love you all, but this is something I just had to do, but don't worry. I'm with a very good friend. Love you all. FaNee. P.S. Please try to understand I love you all very much, really I do. Love me if you have a chance."

12   At eleven-thirty or so, Leo Cooper was sitting in his living room, looking out the window at his driveway—a long gravel road that runs almost four hundred feet from the house to Brown Gap Road. He saw the car that FaNee had been driving pull into the driveway. "She's home," he called to his wife, who had just left the room. Cooper walked out on the deck over the garage. The car had stopped at the end of the driveway,

> "The car had stopped at the end of the driveway, and the lights had gone out."

and the lights had gone out. He got into his other car and drove to the end of the driveway. David Munsey had already joined Charlie Stevens and FaNee, and the Pinto was just leaving, travelling at a normal rate of speed. Leo Cooper pulled out on the road behind them.

13   Stevens turned left on Crippen Road, a road that has a field on one side and two or three small houses on the other, and there Cooper pulled his car in front of the Pinto and stopped, blocking the way. He got out and walked toward the Pinto. Suddenly, Stevens put the car in reverse, backed into a driveway a hundred yards behind him, and sped off. Cooper jumped in his car and gave chase. Stevens raced back to Brown Gap Road, ran a stop sign there, ran another stop sign at Maynardville Highway, turned north, veered off onto the old Andersonville Pike, a nearly abandoned road that runs parallel to the highway, and then crossed back over the highway to the narrow, dark country roads on the other side. Stevens sometimes drove with his lights out. He took some of the corners by suddenly applying his hand brake to make the car swerve around in a ninety-degree turn. He was in familiar territory—he actually passed his trailer—and Cooper had difficulty keeping up. Past the trailer, Stevens swept down a hill into a sharp left turn that took him onto Foust Hollow Road, a winding, hilly road not much wider than one car.

14   At a fork, Cooper thought he had lost the Pinto. He started to go right and then saw what seemed to be a spark from Stevens's dragging muffler off to the left, in the darkness. Cooper took the left fork, down Salem Church Road. He went down a hill and then up a long, curving hill to a crest, where he saw the Stevens car ahead. "I saw the car airborne. Up in the air," he later testified. "It was up in the air. And then it completely rolled over one more time. It started to make another flip forward, and just as it started to flip to the other side it flipped back this way, and my daughter's body came out."

15   Cooper slammed on his brakes and skidded to a stop up against the Pinto. "Book!" Stevens shouted—the group's equivalent of "Scram!" Stevens and Munsey disappeared into the darkness. "It was dark, no one around, and

> "Stevens and Munsey disappeared into the darkness."

so I started yelling for FaNee," Cooper had testified. "I thought it was an eternity before I could find her body, wedged under the back end of that car . . . I tried everything I could, and saw that I couldn't get her loose. So I ran to a trailer back up to the top of the hill back up there to try to get that lady to call to get me some help, and then apparently she didn't think that I was serious . . . I took the jack out of my car and got under, and it was dark, still couldn't see too much what was going on . . . and started prying and got her loose, and I don't know how. And then I dragged her over to the side, and, of course, at the time I felt reasonably assured that she was gone, because her head was completely—on one side just as if you had taken a sledgehammer and just hit it and bashed it in. And I did have the pleasure of one thing. I had the pleasure of listening to her breathe about the last three times she ever breathed in her life."

16 David Munsey did not return to the wreck that night, but Charlie Stevens did. Leo Cooper was kneeling next to his daughter's body. Cooper insisted that Stevens come close enough to see FaNee. "He was kneeling down next to her," Stevens later testified. "And he said, 'Do you know what you've done? Do you really know what you've done?' Like that. And I just looked at her, and I said, 'Yes,' and just stood there. Because I couldn't say nothing." There was, of course, a legal decision to be made about who was responsible for FaNee Cooper's death. In a deposition, Stevens said he had been fleeing for his life. He testified that when Leo Cooper blocked Crippen Road, FaNee had said that her father had a gun and intended to hurt them. Stevens was bound over and eventually indicted for involuntary manslaughter. Leo Cooper testified that when he approached the Pinto on Crippen Road, FaNee had a strange expression that he had never seen before. "It wasn't like FaNee, and I knew something was wrong," he said. "My concern was to get FaNee out of the car." The district attorney's office asked that Cooper be bound over for reckless driving, but the judge declined to do so. "Any father would have done what he did," the judge said. "I can see no criminal act on the part of Mr. Cooper."

17 Almost two years passed before Charlie Stevens was brought to trial. Part of the problem was assuring the presence of David Munsey, who had joined the Navy but seemed inclined to assign his own leaves. In the meantime, the Coopers went to court with a civil suit—they had "uninsured-motorist coverage," which requires their insurance company to cover any defendant who has no insurance of his own—and they won a judgment. There were ways of assigning responsibility, of course, which had nothing to do with the law, civil or criminal. A lot of people in Knoxville thought that Leo Cooper had, in the words of his lawyer, "done what any daddy worth his salt would have done." There were others who believed that FaNee Cooper had lost her life because Leo Cooper had lost his temper. Leo Cooper was not among those who expressed any doubts about his actions. Unlike his wife, whose eyes filled with tears at almost any mention of FaNee, Cooper seemed able, even eager to go over the details of the accident again and again. With the help of a school-board security man, he conducted his own investigation. He drove over the route dozens of times. "I've thought about it every day, and I guess I will the rest of my life," he said as he and his lawyer and the prosecuting attorney went over the route again the day before Charlie Stevens's trial finally began. "But I can't tell any alternative for a father. I simply wanted her out of that car. I'd have done the same thing again, even at the risk of losing her."

18 Tennessee law permits the family of a victim to hire a special prosecutor to assist the district attorney. The lawyer who acted for the Coopers in the civil case helped prosecute Charlie Stevens. Both he and the district attorney assured the jurors that the presence of a special prosecutor was not to be construed to

"Almost two years passed before Charlie Stevens was brought to trial."

mean that the Coopers were vindictive. Outside the courtroom, Leo Cooper said that the verdict was of no importance to him—that he felt sorry, in a way, for Charlie Stevens. But there were people in Knoxville who thought Cooper had a lot riding on the prosecution of Charlie Stevens. If Stevens was not guilty of FaNee Cooper's death—found so by twelve of his peers—who was?

19   At the trial, Cooper testified emotionally and remarkably graphically about pulling FaNee out from under the car and watching her die in his arms. Charlie Stevens had shaved his beard and cut his hair, but the effort did not transform him into an impressive witness. His lawyer—trying to argue that it would have been impossible for Stevens to concoct the story about FaNee's having mentioned a gun, as the prosecution strongly implied—said, "His mind is such that if you ask him a question you can hear his mind go around, like an old mill creaking." Stevens did not deny the recklessness of his driving or the sorry condition of his car. It happened to be the only car he had available to flee in, he said, and he had fled in fear for his life.

20   The prosecution said that Stevens could have let FaNee out of the car when her father stopped them, or could have gone to the commercial strip on the Maynardville Highway for protection. The prosecution said that Leo Cooper had done what he might have been expected to do under the circumstances—alone, late at night, his daughter in danger. The defense said precisely the same about Stevens: he had done what he might have been expected to do when being pursued by a man he had reason to be afraid of. "I don't fault Mr. Cooper for what he did, but I'm sorry he did it,"

the defense attorney said. "I'm sorry the girl said what she said." The jury deliberated for eighteen minutes. Charlie Stevens was found guilty. The jury recommended a sentence of from two to five years in the state penitentiary. At the announcement, Leo Cooper broke down and cried, JoAnn Cooper's eyes filled with tears; she blinked them back and continued to stare straight ahead.

21   In a way, the Coopers might still strike a casual visitor as an ideal family—handsome parents, a bright and bubbly teenage daughter, a little boy learning the hook shot from his father, a warm house with some land around it. FaNee's presence is there, of course. A picture of her, with a small bouquet of flowers over it, hangs in the living room. One of her poems is displayed in a frame on a table. Even if Leo Cooper continues to think about that night for the rest of his life, there are questions he can never answer. Was there a way that Leo and JoAnn Cooper could have prevented FaNee from choosing the path she chose? Would she still be alive if Leo Cooper had not jumped into his car and driven to the end of the driveway to investigate? Did she in fact tell Charlie Stevens that her father would hurt them—or even that her father had a gun? Did she want to get away from her family even at the risk of tearing around dark country roads in Charlie Stevens's dismal Pinto? Or did she welcome the risk? The poem of FaNee's that the Coopers have displayed is one she wrote a week before her death.

> I think I'm going to die
> And I really don't know why.
> But look in my eye
> When I tell you good-bye.
> I think I'm going to die.

READING CLOSELY AND THINKING CRITICALLY

1. What does Trillin note are effects of being a Freak?
2. Was the fact that FaNee was a Freak a remote or an immediate cause of her death?
3. In what ways were FaNee's parents a factor in her downward spiral? Were her parents a remote or an immediate cause of FaNee's death?
4. FaNee remarks twice, "It's too late" (paragraph 8 and 11). Explain the significance of this remark.
5. Why does Cooper consider it a "pleasure" that he heard FaNee breathe her final breaths?
6. In paragraph 17, Trillin says, "There were ways of assigning responsibility, of course, which had nothing to do with the law, civil or criminal." What does Trillin mean?

EXAMINING STRUCTURE AND STRATEGY

1. What do you think of the opening paragraph? How does it create interest? In addition to creating interest, the paragraph suggests that FaNee was really not the ideal child mentioned in the first sentence. How does Trillin suggest that?
2. In what order does Trillin arrange his details?
3. Evaluate the effectiveness of the title.
4. Trillin's purpose is to inform. Why do you think Trillin wants the reader to know the details of FaNee's death?
5. How does Trillin convey his own opinion about who is responsible for FaNee's death?

NOTING COMBINED PATTERNS

1. Trillin combines cause-and-effect analysis and narration. How does the cause-and-effect analysis help him achieve his writing purpose?
2. How does the narration help Trillin achieve his writing purpose?

CONSIDERING LANGUAGE AND STYLE

1. How would you describe Trillin's writing style? Is that style well suited to his purpose? Explain.
2. How does Trillen use **verbal irony** (saying one thing but suggesting another) in paragraph 1?
3. Consult a dictionary if you are unsure of the meaning of any of these words: *magnanimous* (paragraph 1), *batik* (paragraph 1), *Valium* (paragraph 10), *decrepit* (paragraph 10), *incorrigible* (paragraph 11), *deposition* (paragraph 16).

FOR DISCUSSION IN CLASS OR ONLINE

Stevens was found guilty of involuntary manslaughter (the killing of someone as a result of criminal negligence or as a result of committing another crime). Do you agree with the verdict? Are FaNee's father and mother responsible in any way? Explain. If your instructor directs you to do so, post your responses to your class website.

1. **In your journal.** Explain the meaning of the note that FaNee wrote and left in the car (paragraph 11). For example, what do you think she meant when she said, "Love me if you have a chance"?

2. **Using cause-and-effect analysis for a purpose.** The purposes in the assignments are possibilities. You may establish whatever purposes you like, within your instructor's guidelines.

   - To relate experience and express feelings, explain how you are affected by your membership in a particular group, such as runners, weight lifters, musicians, vegetarians, or feminists.

   - To relate experience and express feelings, discuss the effects of the death of someone you knew on those who knew the deceased.

   - Many teenagers are emotionally troubled. Are schools part of the problem or part of the solution? To inform and perhaps persuade your reader that schools are (or are not) doing enough to help, answer this question.

3. **Combining patterns.** At FaNee's high school, the social poles were the Jocks and the Freaks. Describe and contrast the social poles at your high school (Description is explained in Chapter 4; comparison-contrast is explained in Chapter 8.) Explain how these groups affected the student body.

4. **Connecting the readings.** Teenagers often engage in potentially harmful behavior. Drawing on your own experience and observation, as well as the ideas in "It's Just Too Late" and "Seeking Justice after a Fatal Spin of the Cylinder" (page 177), explain why adolescents put themselves at risk.

5. **Drawing on sources.** Substance abuse among teenagers is a serious problem. Write an article with an anti-drug message suitable for high school newspapers. Your goal is to communicate information that will persuade students to avoid drugs. Remember to keep your audience clearly in mind, so you stand a chance of convincing your reader. For information, check *Social Sciences Index* under the heading "Substance Abuse and Youth" in your campus library. On the Internet, you can use the search engine *www.yahoo.com* and click on "health," then "teen health," and then "teen substance abuse."

BACKGROUND: Poet, screenwriter, fiction writer, and teacher, Leslie Marmon Silko was born in Albuquerque, New Mexico, in 1948. Part Native American, part Mexican, and part Caucasian, she grew up on the Laguna Pueblo reservation. She graduated from the University of New Mexico in 1969 and was admitted to law school, but she decided instead to pursue graduate studies in English and a literary career. The dominant theme in Silko's work is the importance of preserving Native American traditions and ways of life. Her works include *Laguna Woman* (1974), which is a collection of poetry, and the novels *Ceremony* (1988), and *Storyteller* (1981). Her writing tells tales that convey the richness and unique qualities of the Native American heritage. Silko also uses prose and poetry to retell her own family's story. Her recent works include *Yellow Woman and A Beauty of the Spirit: Essays on Native American Life Today* (1996) and *Gardens in the Dunes* (1999). "Lullaby" is taken from *Storyteller*.

COMBINED PATTERNS AND THEIR PURPOSES: "Lullaby" is a dark *narration* in which Leslie Marmon Silko **informs** readers of the *effects* on a Navajo family of the treatment they receive from individual whites and the American government. The story demonstrates how government policies and white racism *cause* the destruction of the family, alcoholism, loss of cultural identity, and despair. Much of this is revealed through the *contrast* of Ayah and Chato. Because much of Silko's writing draws on her own family history, "Lullaby" also **relates some of the experience** that is part of the author's background.

Lullaby
LESLIE MARMON SILKO

The sun had gone down but the snow in the wind gave off its own light. It came in thick tufts like new wool—washed before the weaver spins it. Ayah reached out for it like her own babies had, and she smiled when she remembered how she had laughed at them. She was an old woman now, and her life had become memories.

As you read
Try to identify the differences between the two main characters, Ayah and Chato.

She sat down with her back against the wide cottonwood tree, feeling the rough bark on her back bones; she faced east and listened to the wind and snow sing a high-pitched Yeibechei song. Out of the wind she felt warmer, and she could watch the wide fluffy snow fill in her tracks, steadily, until the direction she had come from was gone. By the light of the snow she could see the dark outline of the big arroyo[1] a few feet away. She was sitting on the edge of Cebolleta Creek, where in the springtime the thin cows would graze on grass already chewed flat to the ground. In the wide deep creek bed where only a trickle of water flowed in the summer, the skinny cows would wander, looking for new grass along winding paths splashed with manure.

2 Ayah pulled the old Army blanket over her head like a shawl. Jimmie's blanket—the one he had sent to her. That was a long time ago and the green wool was faded, and it was unraveling on the edges. She did not want to think about Jimmie. So she thought about the weaving and the way her mother had done it.

---

[1] A gully or ditch.

On the tall wooden loom set into the sand under a tamarack tree for shade. She could see it clearly. She had been only a little girl when her grandma gave her the wooden combs to pull the twigs and burrs from the raw, freshly washed wool. And while she combed the wool, her grandma sat beside her, spinning a silvery strand of yarn around the smooth cedar spindle. Her mother worked at the loom with yarns dyed bright yellow and red and gold. She watched them dye the yarn in boiling black pots full of beeweed petals, juniper berries, and sage. The blankets her mother made were soft and woven so tight that rain rolled off them like birds' feathers. Ayah remembered sleeping warm on cold windy nights, wrapped in her mother's blankets on the hogan's[2] sandy floor.

3   The snow drifted now, with the northwest wind hurling it in gusts. It drifted up around her black overshoes—old ones with little metal buckles. She smiled at the snow which was trying to cover her little by little. She could remember when they had no black rubber overshoes; only the high buckskin leggings that they wrapped over their elkhide moccasins. If the snow was dry or frozen, a person could walk all day and not get wet; and in the evenings the beams of the ceiling would hang with lengths of pale buckskin leggings, drying out slowly.

4   She felt peaceful remembering. She didn't feel cold any more. Jimmie's blanket seemed warmer than it had ever been. And she could remember the morning he was born. She could remember whispering to her mother, who was sleeping on the other side of the hogan, to tell her it was time now. She did not want to wake the others. The second time she called to her, her mother stood up and pulled on her shoes; she knew. They walked to the old stone hogan together, Ayah walking a step behind her mother. She waited alone, learning the rhythms of the pains while her mother went to call the old woman to help them. The morning was already warm even before dawn and Ayah smelled the bee flowers blooming and the young willow growing at the springs. She could remember that so clearly, but his birth merged into the births of the other children and to her it became all the same birth. They named him for the summer morning and in English they called him Jimmie.

5   It wasn't like Jimmie died. He just never came back, and one day a dark blue sedan with white writing on its doors pulled up in front of the boxcar shack where the rancher let the Indians live. A man in a khaki uniform trimmed in gold gave them a yellow piece of paper and told them that Jimmie was dead. He said the Army would try to get the body back and then it would be shipped to them; but it wasn't likely because the helicopter had burned after it crashed. All of this was told to Chato because he could understand English. She stood inside the doorway holding the baby while Chato listened. Chato spoke English like a white man and he spoke Spanish too. He was taller than the white man and he stood straighter too. Chato didn't explain why; he just told the military man they could keep the body if they found it. The white man looked bewildered; he nodded his head and he left. Then Chato looked at her and shook his head, and then he told her, "Jimmie isn't coming home anymore," and when he spoke, he used the words to speak of the dead. She didn't

---

[2]An earth-covered Navajo dwelling.

cry then, but she hurt inside with anger. And she mourned him as the years passed, when a horse fell with Chato and broke his leg, and the white rancher told them he wouldn't pay Chato until he could work again. She mourned Jimmie because he would have worked for his father then; he would have saddled the big bag horse and ridden the fence lines each day, with wire cutters and heavy gloves, fixing the breaks in the barbed wire and putting the stray cattle back inside again.

6 She mourned him after the white doctors came to take Danny and Ella away. She was at the shack alone that day they came. It was back in the days before they hired Navajo women to go with them as interpreters. She recognized one of the doctors. She had seen him at the children's clinic at Cañoncito about a month ago. They were wearing khaki uniforms and they waved papers at her and a black ball-point pen, trying to make her understand their English words. She was frightened by the way they looked at the children, like the lizard watches the fly. Danny was swinging on the tire swing on the elm tree behind the rancher's house, and Ella was around the front door, dragging the broomstick horse Chato made for her. Ayah could see they wanted her to sign the papers, and Chato had taught her to sign her name. It was something she was proud of. She only wanted them to go, and to take their eyes away from her children.

7 She took the pen from the man without looking at his face and she signed the papers in three different places he pointed to. She stared at the ground by their feet and waited for them to leave. But they stood there and began to point and gesture at the children. Danny stopped swinging. Ayah could see his fear. She moved suddenly and grabbed Ella into her arms; the child squirmed, trying to get back to her toys. Ayah ran with the baby toward Danny; she screamed for him to run and then she grabbed him around his chest and carried him too. She ran south into the foothills of juniper trees and black lava rock. Behind her she heard the doctors running, but they had been taken by surprise, and as the hills became steeper and the cholla cactus were thicker, they stopped. When she reached the top of the hill, she stopped to listen in case they were circling around her. But in a few minutes she heard a car engine start and they drove away. The children had been too surprised to cry while she ran with them. Danny was shaking and Ella's little fingers were gripping Ayah's blouse.

8 She stayed up in the hills for the rest of the day, sitting on a black lava boulder in the sunshine where she could see for miles all around her. The sky was light blue and cloudless, and it was warm for late April. The sun warmth relaxed her and took the fear and anger away. She lay back on the rock and watched the sky. It seemed to her that she could walk into the sky, stepping through clouds endlessly. Danny played with little pebbles and stones, pretending they were birds eggs and then little rabbits. Ella sat at her feet and dropped fistfuls of dirt into the breeze, watching the dust and particles of sand intently. Ayah watched a hawk soar high above them, dark wings gliding; hunting or only watching, she did not know. The hawk was patient and he circled all afternoon before he disappeared around the high volcanic peak the Mexicans called Guadalupe.

9 Late in the afternoon, Ayah looked down at the gray boxcar shack with the paint all peeled from the wood; the stove pipe on the roof was rusted and crooked.

The fire she had built that morning in the oil drum stove had burned out. Ella was asleep in her lap now and Danny sat close to her, complaining that he was hungry; he asked when they would go to the house. "We will stay up here until your father comes," she told him, "because those white men were chasing us." The boy remembered then and he nodded at her silently.

10   If Jimmie had been there he could have read those papers and explained to her what they said. Ayah would have known then, never to sign them. The doctors came back the next day and they brought a BIA policeman[3] with them. They told Chato they had her signature and that was all they needed. Except for the kids. She listened to Chato sullenly; she hated him when he told her it was the old woman who died in the winter, spitting blood; it was her old grandma who had given the children this disease. "They don't spit blood," she said coldly. "The whites lie. "She held Ella and Danny close to her, ready to run to the hills again. "I want a medicine man first," she said to Chato, not looking at him. He shook his head. "It's too late now. The policeman is with them. You signed the paper." His voice was gentle.

11   It was worse than if they had died: to lose the children and to know that somewhere, in a place called Colorado, in a place full of sick and dying strangers, her children were without her. There had been babies that died soon after they were born, and one that died before he could walk. She had carried them herself, up to the boulders and great pieces of the cliff that long ago crashed down from Long Mesa; she laid them in the crevices of sandstone and buried them in fine brown sand with round quartz pebbles that washed down the hills in the rain. She had endured it because they had been with her. But she could not bear this pain. She did not sleep for a long time after they took her children. She stayed on the hill where they had fled the first time, and she slept rolled up in the blanket Jimmie had sent her. She carried the pain in her belly and it was fed by everything she saw: the blue sky of their last day together and the dust and pebbles they played with; the swing in the elm tree and broomstick horse choked life from her. The pain filled her stomach and there was no room for food or for her lungs to fill with air. The air and the food would have been theirs.

12   She hated Chato, not because he let the policeman and doctors put the screaming children in the government car, but because he had taught her to sign her name. Because it was like the old ones always told her about learning their language or any of their ways: it endangered you. She slept alone on the hill until the middle of November when the first snows came. Then she made a bed for herself where the children had slept. She did not lie down beside Chato again until many years later, when he was sick and shivering and only her body could keep him warm. The illness came after the white rancher told Chato he was too old to work for him anymore, and Chato and his old woman should be out of the shack by the next afternoon because the rancher had hired new people to work there. That had satisfied her. To see how the white man repaid Chato's years of loyalty and work. All of Chato's fine-sounding English talk didn't change things.

---

[3]Bureau of Indian Affairs officer.

13   It snowed steadily and the luminous light from the snow gradually diminished into the darkness. Somewhere in Cebolleta a dog barked and other village dogs joined with it. Ayah looked in the direction she had come, from the bar where Chato was buying the wine. Sometimes he told her to go on ahead and wait; and then he never came. And when she finally went back looking for him, she would find him passed out at the bottom of the wooden steps to Azzie's Bar. All the wine would be gone and most of the money too, from the pale blue check that came to them once a month in a government envelope. It was then that she would look at his face and his hands, scarred by ropes and the barbed wire of all those years, and she would think, this man is a stranger; for forty years she had smiled at him and cooked his food, but he remained a stranger. She stood up again, with the snow almost to her knees, and she walked back to find Chato.

14   It was hard to walk in the deep snow and she felt the air burn in her lungs. She stopped a short distance from the bar to rest and readjust the blanket. But this time he wasn't waiting for her on the bottom step with his old Stetson hat[4] pulled down and his shoulders hunched up in his long wool overcoat.

15   She was careful not to slip on the wooden steps. When she pushed the door open, warm air and cigarette smoke hit her face. She looked around slowly and deliberately, in every corner, in every dark place that the old man might find to sleep. The bar owner didn't like Indians in there, especially Navajos, but he let Chato come in because he could talk Spanish like he was one of them. The men at the bar stared at her, and the bartender saw that she left the door open wide. Snowflakes were flying inside like moths and melting into a puddle on the oiled wood floor. He motioned to her to close the door, but she did not see him. She held herself straight and walked across the room slowly, searching the room with every step. The snow in her hair melted and she could feel it on her forehead. At the far corner of the room, she saw red flames at the mica window of the old stove door; she looked behind the stove just to make sure. The bar got quiet except for the Spanish polka-music playing on the jukebox. She stood by the stove and shook the snow from her blanket and held it near the stove to dry. The wet wool smell reminded her of new-born goats in early March, brought inside to warm near the fire. She felt calm.

16   In past years they would have told her to get out. But her hair was white now and her face was wrinkled. They looked at her like she was a spider crawling slowly across the room. They were afraid; she could feel the fear. She looked at their faces steadily. They reminded her of the first time the white people brought her children back to her that winter. Danny had been shy and hid behind the thin white woman who brought them. And the baby had not known her until Ayah took her into her arms, and then Ella had nuzzled close to her as she had when she was nursing. The blonde woman was nervous and kept looking at a dainty gold watch on her wrist. She sat on the bench near the small window and watched the dark snow clouds gather around the mountains; she was worrying about the unpaved road. She was frightened by what she saw inside too: the strips of venison drying on a rope across

---

[4]A high, wide-brimmed "ten-gallon" hat.

the ceiling and the children jabbering excitedly in a language she did not know. So they stayed for only a few hours. Ayah watched the government car disappear down the road and she knew they were already being weaned from these lava hills and from this sky. The last time they came was in early June, and Ella stared at her the way the men in the bar were now staring. Ayah did not try to pick her up; she smiled at her instead and spoke cheerfully to Danny. When he tried to answer her, he could not seem to remember and he spoke English words with the Navajo. But he gave her a scrap of paper that he had found somewhere and carried in his pocket; it was folded in half, and he shyly looked up at her and said it was a bird. She asked Chato if they were home for good this time. He spoke to the white woman and she shook her head. "How much longer?" he asked, and she said she didn't know; but Chato saw how she stared at the boxcar shack. Ayah turned away then. She did not say good-bye.

17   She felt satisfied that the men in the bar feared her. Maybe it was her face and the way she held her mouth with teeth clenched tight, like there was nothing anyone could do to her now. She walked north down the road, searching for the old man. She did this because she had the blanket, and there would be no place for him except with her and the blanket in the old adobe barn near the arroyo. They always slept there when they came to Cebolleta. If the money and the wine were gone, she would be relieved because then they could go home again; back to the old hogan with a dirt roof and rock walls where she herself had been born. And the next day the old man could go back to the few sheep they still had, to follow along behind them, guiding them, into dry sandy arroyos where sparse grass grew. She knew he did not like walking behind old ewes when for so many years he rode big quarter horses and worked with cattle. But she wasn't sorry for him; he should have known all along what would happen.

18   There had not been enough rain for their garden in five years; and that was when Chato finally hitched a ride into the town and brought back brown boxes of rice and sugar and big tin cans of welfare peaches. After that, at the first of the month they went to Cebolleta to ask the postmaster for the check; and then Chato would go to the bar and cash it. They did this as they planted the garden every May, not because anything would survive the summer dust, but because it was time to do this. The journey passed the days that smelled silent and dry like the caves above the canyon with yellow painted buffaloes on their walls.

19   He was walking along the pavement when she found him. He did not stop or turn around when he heard her behind him. She walked beside him and she noticed how slowly he moved now. He smelled strong of woodsmoke and urine. Lately he had been forgetting. Sometimes he called her by his sister's name and she had been gone for a long time. Once she had found him wandering on the road to the white man's ranch, and she asked him why he was going that way; he laughed at her and said, "You know they can't run that ranch without me," and he walked on determined, limping on the leg that had been crushed many years before. Now he looked at her curiously, as if for the first time, but he kept shuffling along, moving slowly along the side of the highway. His gray hair had grown long and spread out on the shoulders of the long overcoat. He wore the old felt hat pulled down over his ears. His boots were worn out at the toes and he had stuffed pieces of an old red shirt

in the holes. The rags made his feet look like little animals up to their ears in snow. She laughed at his feet; the snow muffled the sound of her laugh. He stopped and looked at her again. The wind had quit blowing and the snow was falling straight down; the southeast sky was beginning to clear and Ayah could see a star.

20 "Let's rest awhile," she said to him. They walked away from the road and up the slope to the giant boulders that had tumbled down from the red sandrock mesa throughout the centuries of rainstorms and earth tremors. In a place where the boulders shut out the wind, they sat down with their backs against the rock. She offered half of the blanket to him and they sat wrapped together.

21 The storm passed swiftly. The clouds moved east. They were massive and full, crowding together across the sky. She watched them with the feeling of horses—steely blue-gray horses startled across the sky. The powerful haunches pushed into the distances and the tail hairs streamed white mist behind them. The sky cleared. Ayah saw that there was nothing between her and the stars. The light was crystalline. There was no shimmer, no distortion through earth haze. She breathed the clarity of the night sky; she smelled the purity of the half moon and the stars. He was lying on his side with his knees pulled up near his belly for warmth. His eyes were closed now, and in the light from the stars and the moon, he looked young again.

22 She could see it descend out of the night sky: an icy stillness from the edge of the thin moon. She recognized the freezing. It came gradually, sinking snowflake by snowflake until the crust was heavy and deep. It had the strength of the stars in Orion, and its journey was endless. Ayah knew that with the wine he would sleep. He would not feel it. She tucked the blanket around him, remembering how it was when Ella had been with her; and she felt the rush so big inside her heart for the babies. And she sang the only song she knew to sing for babies. She could not remember if she had ever sung it to her children, but she knew that her grandmother had sung it and her mother had sung it:

The earth is your mother,
    she holds you.
The sky is your father,
    he protects you.
Sleep,
sleep.
Rainbow is your sister,
    she loves you.
The winds are your brothers,
    they sing to you.
Sleep,
sleep.
We are together always
We are together always
There never was a time
when this
was not so.

CONSIDERING THE SHORT STORY

1. How are whites depicted in "Lullaby"? What specific criticisms of whites does Silko imply? How can you tell?

2. What caused Ayah to sign the paper turning her children over to the white doctors? What was the effect of her action?

3. What effect does the way whites have treated them have on Ayah and Chato's relationship?

4. Explain the causes and effects of Chato's heavy drinking.

5. Twice in the story, Ayah is satisfied, once when she and Chato lose their home and once when she is feared in the bar. Why is she satisfied?

6. What are the chief differences between Ayah and Chato? Why are those differences important?

WRITING ASSIGNMENTS

1. **In your journal.**
   - What kind of woman is Ayah? What are her chief characteristics? How can you tell?
   - Explain the meaning of the lullaby at the end of the story. Do you find it comforting? Why or why not?

2. **Using cause-and-effect analysis for a purpose.** "Lullaby," in part, is about cultural clash—about what can happen when cultures fail to understand each other's traditions, history, and beliefs. To inform, explain the causes and/or effects of a cultural clash that exists in society today. The purpose in the assignment is a possibility. You may establish whatever purpose you like, within your instructor's guidelines.

3. **Combining patterns.** "Lullaby," in part, is a story about what happens when change is forced on people. Narrate a story about a time you experienced a change that you did not initiate or welcome. (See Chapter 5 on narration.) What were the effects of the experience?

See pages 387 and 389 for strategies for writing cause-and-effect analysis and for a revising checklist.

1. Analyze the causes or effects of stress in college or high school students.

2. If you have difficulty with a particular subject (English, math, science, etc.), explain why the subject causes you problems and/or the effect of having difficulty with that subject.

3. Select a popular movie, television program, song, or book and explain why it is popular. As an alternative, explain the popularity of an actor, comedian, or singer.

4. Select an unpopular movie, television program, song, or book and explain why it is not popular. As an alternative, explain the unpopularity of an actor, comedian, or singer.

5. Explain the effects on people or society of some aspect of the Internet, such as chat rooms, online shopping, access to information, online gambling, or online games.

6. Explain the techniques television commercials (or magazine ads) use to influence consumers. As an alternative, explain the effects of commercials (or magazine ads) on us.

7. Select a bad habit you have (for example, procrastinating, smoking, overeating, or nail biting) and explain its causes and effects.

8. Explain the effects of something that happened to you in school (for example, getting cut from the basketball team, being elected class president, becoming homecoming queen, or failing a course).

9. Select a problem on your campus (for example, inadequate student housing, high tuition, or limited course offerings) and analyze the effects on students to persuade those in authority to remedy the problem.

10. Analyze how the neighborhood in which you grew up affected you.

11. Explain why students cheat and the effects cheating has on students.

12. If you have a particular fear (of heights, of math, of failure, and so on), explain the causes and/or effects of that fear.

13. Pick a harmless human characteristic or behavior (for example, checking the alarm even though we know it is set, habitually choosing the wrong bank or supermarket line, losing car keys, and so on). Then write a humorous essay that explains the causes and/or effects of this behavior or characteristic.

14. Select something inconsequential that Americans can no longer do, such as cook without a microwave, walk places, or change channels without a remote control. Then write a humorous account of the causes and effects of the "problem."

15. If you ever moved to a new town, explain how the move affected you.

16. If you have children, explain the effects of becoming a parent. If you want, you can make this essay humorous.

17. If you are an international student, explain how you have been affected by living and attending school in this country.

18. Explain why football (or baseball or basketball) is so popular in this country and how the sport affects American culture.

19. Select a person who has had a significant impact on you (for example, a coach, a clergyperson, a teacher, or a friend) and explain the effects this individual has had on you.

20. **Cause-and-effect analysis in context:** Assume you are a member of a consumer affairs panel that has secured a grant to study violence in the media. Write a report that explains why some people enjoy violent movies. Your audience is other members of the panel, and your purpose is to provide them with information.

You may be so accustomed to air-conditioned homes, stores, restaurants, offices, and schools that you fail to realize what a significant invention air-conditioning was. Think about life without air-conditioning and write about the effects air-conditioning has on our health, on how and where we live, on recreation, on transportation, and on other aspects of life. For example, would shopping malls exist without air-conditioning? What about Las Vegas casinos?

Classification and Division

CONSIDER THE PATTERN

You have encountered many kinds of students, some like those in the photograph. Name three of those types. Then identify three characteristics of one of the types you named.

THE PATTERN

Both classification and division are methods of grouping and ordering. **Classification** takes a number of items and groups them into categories; **division** takes one entity and breaks it down into its parts. Consider your college, for example. It orders courses in the catalog by placing them into groups according to the departments that offer those courses (English, biology, mathematics, and so on)—this is *classifying*. In addition, your college organizes itself by breaking into components (the School of Education, the School of Arts and Sciences, the School of Engineering, and so on)—this is *division*.

You do not have to look very far to find examples of classification. The Yellow Pages of your phone book groups telephone numbers according to the kinds of businesses; your biology textbook classifies animals according to whether they are mammals, reptiles, and so on; your local grocery store arranges items in aisles by classifying them according to whether they are canned goods, cleaning products, pet products, meats, produce, or frozen foods.

443

Division is also common. The medical laboratory examines your blood by breaking it down into its components and studying each of them (the red cells, the white cells, the plasma, and so on), a movie reviewer evaluates different parts of a film (the actors, the director, the script, the cinematography, and so on); and a real estate appraisal analyzes the separate components of your property (the location, the size, the condition, and so on). Classification and division are common because they help us order items or pieces of information to study them or to retrieve them more efficiently. Imagine a world without categories or divisions. How hard would it be to locate a book in the library or to study plant and animal life?

Sometimes classification and division are each performed alone, but often they are companion operations performed together for a specific purpose. For example, the manager of a video store can use both classification and division to organize all the tapes and DVDs so customers can locate titles easily. First the manager would use *division* to establish a breakdown into categories or parts, such as westerns, musicals, science fiction, romance, horror films, and adventure movies. Then he or she would use *classification* to sort the videos into the appropriate categories—*Star Wars* into the science fiction area, *Friday the 13th* into the horror movie area, and so on.

www.mhhe.com/patterns

For more help with classification, click on

Writing > Paragraph Patterns
Writing > Writing Tutors: Classification

USING CLASSIFICATION AND DIVISION FOR A PURPOSE

Writers often classify or divide in order to *inform*. Sometimes a writer wants to inform a reader of the relative merits of the items classified so the reader can choose one wisely. For example, you can classify various health clubs according to expense and variety of equipment and classes to help exercisers decide which club to join. Sometimes a writer wants to inform a reader of the characteristics of the parts that have been divided. For example, to inform people about how to write grant proposals more successfully, a writer could divide the effective grant proposal into its parts and explain how to write each of those parts. Sometimes a writer classifies or divides to give the reader a fresh appreciation of the familiar. In "White Lies" (page 455), Sissela Bok classifies the variety of white lies in order to help readers more carefully consider them and their moral significance. Sometimes a writer wants to help a reader understand something unfamiliar. For example, in "Territorial Behaviour" (page 477), Desmond Morris classifies the kinds of human territory for readers who know little about anthropology.

Classification and division can also allow you to *express feelings and relate experience*. This would be the case if you classified various ways to celebrate Halloween in order to relate your own childhood experiences with the holiday or if you divided your best Halloween celebration into its components.

Very often, classification and division can have a *persuasive* purpose, as is the case with "The Ways of Meeting Oppression" (page 459). In this essay, Dr. Martin Luther King, Jr., classifies the ways to deal with oppression in order to convince the average reader that one of those ways is more effective than the rest and should be employed.

Finally, classification and division can *entertain* a reader. For example, to amuse your audience, you could classify all your eccentric relatives according to their funny traits and behaviors, or you could examine your most eccentric relative by dividing that person's behavior and personality into their most amusing parts.

Classification and division can function alone or with other patterns as well. For example, in an essay explaining the causes and effects of age discrimination in the workplace, you could include a classification of the most common kinds of age discrimination.

Classification and Division in College, at Work, and in the Community

You will have many occasions to use classification and division in your college classes. For example, in an education class, you may need to divide a lesson plan into its components and explain the characteristics of effective components to demonstrate that you can write a useful plan. Similarly, a business class might require you to note the components of a sound business plan to demonstrate that you could develop such a plan, and a marketing class may require you to give the components of an effective survey to show that you know how to construct one.

At times, you will write classification and division to show that you understand the relative merits and uses of various categories of something. For example, in an advertising class, you could write a paper that classifies the kinds of direct mail campaigns, noting what kind of audience each approach appeals to and what kind of product each approach is best suited for. Such a paper would demonstrate that you knew when to use each kind of campaign.

Perhaps most frequently, you will write classification and division to demonstrate your comprehension of information. This would be the case in a biology class that required you to classify the mating behavior of birds or in a communications class that required you to divide political rhetoric into its components.

Classification and division are found in many textbooks. In the following excerpt from *The World of Music*, for example, classification and division help inform students about kinds of American folk music and explain what each of those kinds is like.

> The broad spectrum of American traditional folk music includes the following types of songs: narrative ballads, broadside ballads, lyric songs, work songs, children's songs, rally and protest songs, spirituals, and blues songs. Spirituals and the blues, however, are discussed in a later section of this chapter.

Narrative Ballads (Story Songs)

These songs originally came from New England, having been brought to America in the seventeenth, eighteenth, and nineteenth centuries by immigrants from the British Isles, particularly Scotland and Ireland. A ballad singer is a storyteller. The story has a beginning, a middle, and an end and may convey a romantic and sentimental mood or heroic action. Occasionally, dialogue between two characters in the story is inserted.

A narrative ballad may have many stanzas, each frequently comprised of four lines of poetry with a consistent rhyme scheme. The music often is strophic (the same music for each stanza regardless of the meaning and mood of the text).

Broadsides

These ballads are "folk songs" composed by professinal songwriters. They flourished during the eighteenth and nineteenth centuries in western Europe and the United States. A broadside was a narrative accounting of current events and functioned somewhat as a newspaper in communities and regions. It was published on one large sheet of paper called a broadside. It may or may not have been published with musical notation. If only the words were published, sometimes instructions were included to sing them to a well-known tune. Broadsides were sold widely and cheaply and were considered popular songs of the day. Hundreds of British and American broadsides were published.

The origin of many folk songs has been traced to broadsides. Thus, we see a case where songs originally written down were eventually passed on by word of mouth; thus, they became part of the oral tradition we associate with traditional folk songs. . . . (Willoughby, *The World of Music*)

Outlining that you do for any writing, no matter where it occurs, involves classification and division because you divide your topic into ideas and group those ideas together according to the point they develop. In addition, when you write to-do-lists, whether at home, at school, or at work, you engage in classification and division if you divide your tasks into their parts and then group the parts according to their deadlines and importance so you can decide how to proceed.

On the job, classification and division are essential. For example, to develop a solid business plan, you must group elements of the plan according to categories such as marketing, acquisition of capital, management structure, and growth potential. You may need to classify kinds of customer-incentive programs or group insurance plans to decide which one to use. Even before you get your job, you use classification and division to write a résumé, where you must divide and group your skills, education, and experience.

In your life outside school and work, you may also draw on classification and division. For example, if you were planning a large party, such as a wedding reception or retirement dinner, and needed place cards, you might classify the people on your guest list according to friendships or compatibility in order to draw up a seating chart. If you were apartment hunting, you could divide your ideal place into its components (location, size, rent, whether it has air-conditioning, furnishings, and so on). When you look at places, you could check off whether each apartment has the features.

THE ORDERING PRINCIPLE FOR CLASSIFICATION AND DIVISION

Most things can be classified or divided more than one way, depending on the ordering principle used. For example, you could classify colleges according to their cost, their location, the degrees they offer, their faculty, or prestige. Cost, location, degrees offered, faculty, prestige—each of these is an *ordering principle*.

When you decide which principle you will use to group or divide the items under consideration, keep your purpose in mind and choose a principle compatible with that purpose. For example, if you were classifying white lies to entertain your reader, your ordering principle would not be the degree of hurtfulness of the lies; however, it might be the degree of inventiveness of the lies. If your purpose were to inform, then degree of hurtfulness would be an acceptable ordering principle.

SUPPORTING DETAILS

When you select details, do not omit any categories or parts, or your classification or division will be incomplete. Say, for example, that you are classifying the forms of financial aid to inform students of ways to get help paying for college. You could include these categories: loans, grants, and scholarships. However, by omitting work-study programs, your essay is less helpful than it could—and should—be. Or say that you were analyzing the components of an effective political campaign. You could break the campaign down into these parts: grassroots support, publicity, and the focus on issues. However, you would be omitting an important component—financing.

On the other hand, you should avoid including groups and parts that are not compatible with your ordering principle. For example, if you are classifying coaches according to how important winning is to them, you might have these categories: coaches who think winning is everything; coaches who think winning is less important than learning and having fun; coaches who think winning is completely unimportant. In such a classification, you could not include coaches who are inexperienced, because that group is unrelated to the ordering principle.

Your supporting detail can include a wide range of patterns of development meant to explain the characteristics of each category or part. Say, for example, that you are classifying Halloween celebrations into three types: the sedate, the jolly, and the scary. You could use *examples* to illustrate the kinds of harmless pranks people play for a jolly celebration; you could *describe* the frightening costumes people wear for a scary celebration; you could *narrate* the story of your last Halloween celebration, which was sedate. In addition, you could use *process analysis* to tell how to prepare for a scary Halloween celebration; you could use *cause-and-effect analysis* to explain the effects of the pranks played during the jolly celebration; you could use *definition* to explain the meaning of a sedate celebration; you could use *comparison-contrast* to show the similarities and differences among the three kinds of celebrations. Of course, you will not use all these patterns in a single essay, but they are all available for your consideration as ways to achieve your writing purpose.

ORGANIZING DETAILS

The thesis for classification or division can be handled a variety of ways. First, you can indicate what you are classifying or dividing and the ordering principle you will use:

> The current crop of television talk shows can be classified according to the kinds of guests that appear. (*Television talk shows will be classified; the ordering principle is the guests that appear.*)

Another way to handle the thesis is to indicate what you are classifying or dividing, without mentioning the ordering principle:

> Although more talk shows are on television than ever before, all of these shows are one of three types. (*The thesis makes it clear that television talk shows will be classified but the ordering principle is not given.*)

A third way to handle the thesis is to indicate what will be classified or divided, along with the specific groupings that will be discussed:

> Television talk shows can be distinguished according to whether the guests are primarily entertainers, politicians, or oddballs. (*The thesis indicates that television talk shows will be classified and the categories will be those with guests who are entertainers, those with guests who are politicians, and those with guests who are oddballs.*)

Organizing a classification or division essay can be easier when topic sentences introduce the discussion of each grouping. For example, if you were classifying talk shows, you might have topic sentences like these:

> In the most common variety of talk show the guests are entertainers. (*A discussion of talk shows with entertainers as guests would follow.*)

> Somewhat more intellectual than the first type, another common variety of show has politicians for guests. (*A discussion of talk shows with politicians as guests would follow.*)

Increasingly popular is the talk show that showcases oddballs. (A discussion of talk shows with oddballs as guests would follow.)

To move smoothly from one grouping to another, you can include transitional phrases in your topic sentences:

Another category . . .

A more significant group . . .

A more common kind . . .

A second division of . . .

When you order your details, consider your thesis. If it includes categories or divisions, then you should present them in the same order they appear in the thesis. Otherwise, order is not much of an issue, unless your purpose is persuasive. Then you are likely to present the recommended category or the most important division last. In "The Ways of Meeting Oppression," for example, Dr. Martin Luther King, Jr., presents the method he wants people to adopt last.

When you are discussing the same characteristics for each category or division, you should present those characteristics in the same order each time. Thus, if you group Halloween celebrations and discuss decorations, costumes, and degree of scariness for each kind of celebration, then you should discuss these features in the same order for each one.

Maintaining Parallelism

If you have trouble expressing categories or divisions smoothly in your thesis, state them in the same grammatical form to maintain parallel structure. Here is a thesis that lacks parallelism:

Television talk shows can be divided into three types: shows with entertainers for guests, those with guests who are politicians, and shows with oddballs for guests.

Notice that the following revision is much more pleasing because of the parallel structure:

Television talk shows can be divided into three types: shows with entertainers for guests, shows with politicians for guests, and shows with oddballs for guests.

www.mhhe.com/patterns

For more help with maintaining parallelism, click on
Editing > Parallelism

VISUALIZING A CLASSIFICATION AND DIVISION ESSAY

The following chart can help you visualize the structure for a classification and division essay. Like all good models, however, this one can be altered as needed.

Introduction

- Creates interest in the essay
- States the thesis, which can indicate what you are classifying or dividing, the ordering principle, why you are classifying or dividing, and the groupings

First Body Paragraph

- Gives the first grouping, which can be stated in a topic sentence
- May include explanation and any patterns of development
- May arrange details in a progressive or other suitable order

Next Body Paragraph

- Gives the next grouping, which can be stated in a topic sentence
- May include explanation and any patterns of development
- May arrange details in a progressive or other suitable order

Next Body Paragraphs

- Continue until all the groupings are given
- May include explanation and any patterns of development
- May arrange details in a progressive or other suitable order

Conclusion

- Provides a satisfying finish
- Leaves the reader with a positive final impression

PROCESS GUIDELINES: STRATEGIES FOR WRITING CLASSIFICATION AND DIVISION

1. **Planning.** Write your ordering principle at the top of a sheet of paper or your computer screen. Below that, write each of your categories or divisions at the top of a column. Three categories or divisions will give you three columns, four will give you four columns, and so on. Under each column list the elements in the category or the characteristics of the division.

2. **Generating Supporting Details.** Ask yourself these questions of every element or characteristic in your columns. Make notes of the answers on your planning sheet.
   - Can I narrate a story to develop this element or characteristic?
   - Can I describe something to develop this element or characteristic?
   - Can I analyze causes or effects to develop this element or characteristic?
   - Can I give an example to develop this element or characteristic?
   - Can I define something to develop this element or characteristic?
   - Can I compare or contrast to develop this element or characteristic?
   - Can I use process analysis to develop this element or characteristic?

3. **Organizing.** Number the columns on your sheet in the order you want to treat them. You now have an outline to guide your draft.

4. **Revising.** As you evaluate your draft, consider everything in light of your audience and purpose. Be sure you have included all relevant categories and divisions and that they are compatible with your ordering principle.

Checklist for Revising Classification and Division

Be sure

_____ To include all relevant categories or divisions.

_____ To omit categories or division unrelated to your ordering principle.

_____ Your thesis indicates whether you are classifying or dividing and, if appropriate, your ordering principle.

_____ Transitions help you move smoothly from one category or division to the next.

_____ If you have discussed the same characteristics for each category or division, they appear in the same order.

Student-author David Wolfe uses classification to inform his reader about the origins of some common expressions. Be sure to notice how the author uses examples to help make his point. After you read, you will have an opportunity to evaluate this essay.

Strictly Speaking

Paragraph 1
This is the introduction. The thesis (the last sentence) indicates that Wolfe will use classification. It also indicates that expressions derived from outdoor life will be classified according to their sporting origins.

Expressions derived from outdoor life are so ingrained in everyday 1 English that we fail to notice them or consider their origins. However, it is interesting to pause and think about these terms, and one way to do that is to look at three basic categories of expressions: those derived from the use of firearms, those derived from hunting, and those derived from the characteristics of wildlife or game.

Paragraph 2
The first sentence is the topic sentence. It presents the first category given in the thesis. The supporting details are examples of expressions in the category.

Some common sayings come directly from the use of firearms. For 2 example, if we buy something "lock, stock, and barrel," we have purchased the whole object or believed the whole story. This expression originally meant to buy the whole gun by purchasing its three parts: the "lock" as in the flintlock, the wooden "stock," and the metal "barrel." We also talk about "going off half-cocked," which means taking action or setting out without being fully prepared. This expression goes back to having a gun on "half-cock." In the half-cocked position, the hammer is between the relaxed position and the fully cocked position, which means the gun is halfway between unready and fully ready for firing. Often we say we had our "sights set on" something or had a goal "in our sights." Both of these expressions refer to aiming a gun at something. Also, we can be "primed and ready," or fully prepared, as when a flintlock rifle is fully primed or prepared and ready to fire.

Paragraph 3
The topic sentence is the first sentence. It presents the second category. The supporting details are examples. Note the transition provided by *a second group, for example, another example, and similarly.*

A second group of expressions is derived from hunting. For exam- 3 ple, the word "hello" has its origins there. It comes from hunters calling out "hulloa" or "haloo" when they saw other hunters in the woods in order to attract attention and avoid being accidentally hurt. "Stop beating around the bush" is another example of a hunting expression. It comes from the European practice of using "beaters" or people to drive game out of the brush for the hunter to shoot at. To do the job properly, beaters had to get into the middle of the bush where the game was. Otherwise, they were not getting the job done because they were beating around the bush. If we "make tracks," we hurry. Originally, this expression referred to an animal going in a hurry and thus leaving behind a set of tracks that were easy to follow. Being on "the right trail" refers to doing something properly or going in the right direction, but its original meaning referred to a hunter being on the right trail while tracking game. Similarly, if we are "barking up the wrong tree," we are as mistaken as the hunting dogs that are howling up one tree when the raccoon is out on the limb of a different tree.

Sayings related to wildlife or game are also interesting. We brag 4 about saving money when we are "feathering our nests" or "building up our nest eggs," the way a bird does in the spring. We may be called "owl-eyed" for wearing glasses or be "wise as an owl" for knowing the right answers. If we are "blind as a bat," we can't see very well, just as a bat has poor vision. If we have a bad disposition, we are "grouchy as a bear" or told "don't be such a bear," since bears have angry temperaments. In addition, there are two ways we can get "skunked." We can actually get sprayed by a skunk, or we can lose a game of some kind very badly—in either case, we lose.

Paragraph 4
The first sentence is the topic sentence. It includes the transition also and presents the final category. The supporting details are examples.

Expressions from the outdoors are so common that even those of 5 us who never hunt, shoot, or get close to animals will find ourselves drawing on vocabulary derived from these sources, a fact you may be more aware of from now on.

Paragraph 5
The conclusion repeats the idea in the introduction that these expressions are ingrained in English.

PEER REVIEW

Responding to "Strictly Speaking"

Evaluate "Strictly Speaking" by responding to these questions:

1. Does the essay hold your interest? Why or why not?
2. Is the thesis effective? Why or why not?
3. Are the supporting details adequate? Explain.
4. Is the organization effective? Why or why not?
5. What do you like best about the essay?
6. What single change do you think would make the essay better?

- What ordering principle is used for the division depicted in the advertisement?
- What kind of details explain the parts?
- Why is this kind of explanatory detail included?
- How do the words and image work together to achieve the advertisement's purpose?

BACKGROUND: Born in 1934 in Sweden, writer and philosopher Sissela Bok was educated in Switzerland and France before coming to the United States. She earned her Ph.D. in philosophy from Harvard University. Bok is currently a senior fellow at the Harvard Center for Population and Development Studies. She is a frequent writer on ethics in medicine and government and has lectured on medical ethics at Harvard and the Massachusetts Institute of Technology. Bok won the Orwell Award for her book *Lying: Moral Choice in Private and Public Life* (1978, reissued in 1999), from which "White Lies" is taken. Her other books include *Secrets: On the Ethics of Concealment and Revelation* (1982); *A Strategy for Peace: Human Values and the Threat of War* (1989); *Alva Myrdal: A Daughter's Memoir* (1991), for which Bok received the Melcher Book Award; *Common Values* (1996); and *Mayhem: Violence as Public Entertainment* (1998). Bok is also a former member of the Pulitzer Prize Board and a member of the Academic Advisory Council of the National Campaign Against Youth Violence.

COMBINED PATTERNS AND THEIR PURPOSES: In "White Lies," Sissela Bok *classifies* and *defines* white lies to **inform** her reader of the various kinds. She also makes a **persuasive point** about the harm these lies cause, drawing on *examples* and *cause-and-effect analysis*.

White Lies
SISSELA BOK

White lies are at the other end of the spectrum of deception from lies in a serious crisis. They are the most common and the most trivial forms that duplicity can take. The fact that they are so common provides their protective coloring. And their very triviality, when compared to more threatening lies, makes it seem unnecessary or even absurd to condemn them. Some consider *all* well-intentioned lies, however momentous, to be white; in this book, I shall adhere to the narrower usage: a white lie, in this sense, is a falsehood not meant to injure anyone, and of little moral import. I want to ask whether there *are* such lies; and if there are, whether their cumulative consequences are still without harm; and, finally whether many lies are defended as "white" which are in fact harmful in their own right.

As you read Think about what life would be like if people did not tell white lies.

2   Many small subterfuges may not even be intended to mislead. They are only "white lies" in the most marginal sense. Take, for example, the many social exchanges. "How nice to see you!" or "Cordially Yours." These and a thousand other polite expressions are so much taken for granted that if someone decided, in the name of total honesty, not to employ them, he might well give the impression of an indifference he did not possess. The justification for continuing to use such accepted formulations is that they deceive no one, except possibly those unfamiliar with the language.

3   A social practice more clearly deceptive is that of giving a false excuse so as not to hurt the feelings of someone making an invitation or request: to say one "can't" do what in reality one may not *want* to do. Once again, the false excuse may prevent unwarranted inferences of greater hostility to the undertaking than one may well feel. Merely to say that one can't do something, moreover, is not deceptive in the sense that an elaborately concocted story can be.

4   Still other white lies are told in an effort to flatter, to throw a cheerful interpretation on depressing circumstances, or to show gratitude for unwanted gifts. In the eyes of many, such white lies do not harm, provide needed support and cheer, and help dispel gloom and boredom. They preserve the equilibrium and often the humaneness of social relationships, and are usually accepted as excusable so long as they do not become excessive. Many argue, moreover, that such deception is so helpful and at times so necessary that it must be tolerated as an exception to a general policy against lying. Thus Bacon[1] observed:

> Doth any man doubt, that if there were taken out of men's minds vain opinions, flattering hopes, false valuations, imaginations as one would, and the like, but it would leave the minds of a number of men poor shrunken things, full of melancholy and indisposition, and unpleasing to themselves?

5   Another kind of lie may actually be advocated as bringing a more substantial benefit, or avoiding a real harm, while seeming quite innocuous to those who tell the lies. Such are the placebos given for innumerable common ailments, and the pervasive use of inflated grades and recommendations for employment and promotion.

6   A large number of lies without such redeeming features are nevertheless often regarded as so trivial that they should be grouped with white lies. They are the lies told on the spur of the moment, for want of reflection, or to get out of a scrape, or even simply to pass the time. Such are the lies told to boast or exaggerate, or on the contrary to deprecate and understate; the many lies told or repeated in gossip; Rousseau's[2] lies told simply "in order to say something"; the embroidering on facts that seem too tedious in their own right; and the substitution of a quick lie for the lengthy explanations one might otherwise have to provide for something not worth spending time on.

7   Utilitarians often cite white lies as the *kind* of deception where their theory shows the benefits of common sense and clear thinking. A white lie, they hold, is trivial; it is either completely harmless, or so marginally harmful that the cost of detecting and evaluating the harm is much greater than the minute harm itself. In addition, the white lie can often actually be beneficial, thus further tipping the scales of utility. In a world with so many difficult problems, utilitarians might ask: Why take the time to weigh the minute pros and cons in telling someone that his tie is attractive when it is an abomination, or of saying to a guest that a broken vase was worthless? Why bother even to define such insignificant distortions or make mountains out of molehills by seeking to justify them?

8   Triviality surely does set limits to when moral inquiry is reasonable. But when we look more closely at practices such as placebo-giving, it becomes clear that all lies defended as "white" cannot be so easily dismissed. In the first place, the harmlessness of lies is notoriously disputable. What the liar perceives as harmless or even

---

[1]Francis Bacon (1561–1626), British philosopher and statesman.

[2]Jean-Jacques Rousseau (1712–1778), a French philosopher and author.

beneficial may not be so in the eyes of the deceived. Second, the failure to look at an entire practice rather than at their own isolated case often blinds liars to cumulative harm and expanding deceptive activities. Those who begin with white lies can come to resort to more frequent and more serious ones. Where some tell a few white lies, others may tell more. Because lines are so hard to draw, the indiscriminate use of such lies can lead to other deceptive practices. The aggregate harm from a large number of marginally harmful instances may, therefore, be highly undesirable in the end—for liars, those deceived, and honesty and trust more generally.

READING CLOSELY AND THINKING CRITICALLY

1. What does Bok mean when she says in paragraph 1, "The fact that [white lies] are so common provides their protective coloring"?
2. What kinds of white lies does Bok classify? What are the justifications for each of these kinds of white lies?
3. Who are the utilitarians that Bok refers to in paragraph 7? What is their view of white lies?
4. What is Bok's view of the white lie?
5. Is there any kind of white lie that Bok might find acceptable? Cite evidence from the selection to support your view.

EXAMINING STRUCTURE AND STRATEGY

1. What is Bok's ordering principle?
2. In what kind of order does Bok arrange her categories?
3. Bok introduces her categories with topic sentences. What are those topic sentences? What transitions appear in the topic sentences in paragraphs 4 and 5? What purpose do these transitions serve?

NOTING COMBINED PATTERNS

1. In paragraph 2, Bok gives examples of items in one of her categories. How do these examples help Bok achieve her purpose? Would any other paragraphs benefit from the addition of examples? Explain.
2. How does Bok use cause-and-effect analysis?
3. Is it possible to think of "White Lies" as a definition? Explain.

CONSIDERING LANGUAGE AND STYLE

1. What is a *placebo* (paragraphs 5 and 8) and how is it a form of lie?
2. Consult a dictionary if you are unsure of the meaning of any of these words: *spectrum* (paragraph 1), *duplicity* (paragraph 1), *innocuous* (paragraph 5), *utilitarians* (paragraph 7), *aggregrate* (paragraph 8).

Discuss what day-to-day living would be like if people never told white lies. Would some kinds of lies be missed more than others? If your instructor directs you to do so, post your responses to your class Web site.

WRITING ASSIGNMENTS

1. **In your journal.** In a page or two, respond to these questions: How often do you tell white lies? What kinds of white lies do you usually tell? Have you ever told a white lie that has hurt someone? Have you ever been hurt by a white lie?

2. **Using classification-division for a purpose.** The purposes in the assignments are possibilities. You may establish whatever purposes you like, within your instructor's guidelines.

   • Rather than focus on white lies as Bok does, inform your reader with a classification of all lies. If you want, you can also persuade your reader that one kind of lie is more or less serious than the others. As an alternative, use division to break down one kind of lie into its components.

   • To inform and perhaps persuade your reader of the seriousness of the lies, classify the lies told in some specific context, such as in school, on a date, at family gatherings, or in the workplace.

   • To inform and perhaps persuade, classify the types of one kind of undesirable behavior, such as cheating, disloyalty, or procrastination. As an alternative, use division to break down one type of undesirable behavior into its components and evaluate its degree of harm.

3. **Combining patterns.** Classify the lies parents tell their children or the lies that teenagers tell their parents. Use exemplification to illustrate the lies and cause-and-effect analysis to explain the causes and effects of the lies. (Exemplification is explained in Chapter 6, and cause-and-effect analysis is explained in Chapter 9.)

4. **Connecting the readings.** White lies are a common—and even accepted—form of deception. Do you think that deception is so common that it is woven into the fabric of our society? Or do you think people are honest for the most part? Be sure to cite examples to support your assertion. You can draw on "White Lies," "Salvation" (page 173) and "Behind the Formaldehyde Curtain" (page 307) for ideas.

5. **Drawing on sources.** Select a kind of product frequently advertised, such as toothpaste, soft drinks, or cleaning products. Examine advertisements for the product type on television and/or in print and write a classification of the ways the product is advertised. Draw a conclusion about how deceptive or truthful the advertising is.

BACKGROUND: Dr. Martin Luther King, Jr., (1929–1968) was a Baptist minister and the most prominent civil rights leader of the 1950s and 1960s. He founded the Southern Christian Leadership Conference in 1957 and worked tirelessly to achieve racial integration through nonviolent means, especially peaceful demonstrations. Named *Time* magazine's Man of the Year in 1963, King became the youngest winner ever of the Nobel Peace Prize in 1964. King graduated from Morehouse College and went on to Crozer Theological Seminary to continue preparing for the ministry. In 1955, he received his doctorate from Boston University. While at Crozer, King attended a lecture on Indian pacifist Mahatma Gandhi. The lecture charted the course of King's philosophy of nonviolent resistance: "His message was so profound and electrifying," King later said, "that I left the meeting and bought a half dozen books on Gandhi's life and works." On April 4, 1968, King was assassinated in Memphis, Tennessee. King's writings include *Letter from Birmingham City Jail* (1963) and *Where Do We Go from Here: Chaos or Community* (1967). "The Ways of Meeting Oppression" is taken from *Stride toward Freedom* (1958).

www.mhhe.com/patterns

For more information on this author, go to

More resources > Chapter 10 > Martin Luther King, Jr.

COMBINED PATTERNS AND THEIR PURPOSES: Using *classification* combined with *cause-and-effect analysis* and *definition,* Martin Luther King, Jr. **informs** his reader of the options oppressed people have and works to **persuade** them that nonviolent resistance is the best way to oppose oppression.

The Ways of Meeting Oppression
MARTIN LUTHER KING, JR.

Oppressed people deal with their oppression in three characteristic ways. One way is acquiescence: the oppressed resign themselves to their doom. They tacitly adjust themselves to oppression, and thereby become conditioned to it. In every movement toward freedom some of the oppressed prefer to remain oppressed. Almost 2800 years ago Moses set out to lead the children of Israel from the slavery of Egypt to the freedom of the promised land. He soon discovered that slaves do not always welcome their deliverers. They become accustomed to being slaves. They would rather bear those ills they have, as Shakespeare pointed out, than flee to others that they know not of. They prefer the "fleshpots of Egypt" to the ordeals of emancipation.

As you read Notice the biblical references and imagery.

2   There is such a thing as the freedom of exhaustion. Some people are so worn down by the yoke of oppression that they give up. A few years ago in the slum areas of Atlanta, a Negro guitarist used to sing almost daily: "Been down so long that down don't bother me." This is the type of negative freedom and resignation that often engulfs the life of the oppressed.

3   But this is not the way out. To accept passively an unjust system is to cooperate with that system; thereby the oppressed become as evil as the oppressor. Noncooperation with evil is as much a moral obligation as is cooperation with good.

The oppressed must never allow the conscience of the oppressor to slumber. Religion reminds every man that he is his brother's keeper. To accept injustice or segregation passively is to say to the oppressor that his actions are morally right. It is a way of allowing his conscience to fall asleep. At this moment the oppressed fails to be his brother's keeper. So acquiescence—while often the easier way—is not the moral way. It is the way of the coward. The Negro cannot win the respect of his oppressor by acquiescing; he merely increases the oppressor's arrogance and contempt. Acquiescence is interpreted as proof of the Negro's inferiority. The Negro cannot win the respect of the white people of the South or the peoples of the world if he is willing to sell the future of his children for his personal and immediate comfort and safety.

4   A second way that oppressed people sometimes deal with oppression is to resort to physical violence and corroding hatred. Violence often brings about momentary results. Nations have frequently won their independence in battle. But in spite of temporary victories, violence never brings permanent peace. It solves no social problem; it merely creates new and more complicated ones.

5   Violence as a way of achieving racial justice is both impractical and immoral. It is impractical because it is a descending spiral ending in destruction for all. The old law of an eye for an eye leaves everybody blind. It is immoral because it seeks to humiliate the opponent rather than win his understanding; it seeks to annihilate rather than to convert. Violence is immoral because it thrives on hatred rather than love. It destroys community and makes brotherhood impossible. It leaves society in monologue rather than dialogue. Violence ends by defeating itself. It creates bitterness in the survivors and brutality in the destroyers. A voice echoes through time saying to every potential Peter, "Put up your sword."[1] History is cluttered with the wreckage of nations that failed to follow this command.

6   If the American Negro and other victims of oppression succumb to the temptation of using violence in the struggle for freedom, future generations will be the recipients of a desolate night of bitterness, and our chief legacy to them will be an endless reign of meaningless chaos. Violence is not the way.

7   The third way open to oppressed people in their quest for freedom is the way of nonviolent resistance. Like the synthesis in Hegelian philosophy,[2] the principle of nonviolent resistance seeks to reconcile the truths of two opposites—the acquiescence and violence—while avoiding the extremes and immoralities of both. The nonviolent resister agrees with the person who acquiesces that one should not be physically aggressive toward his opponent; but he balances the equation by agreeing with the person of violence that evil must be resisted. He avoids the nonresistance of the former and the violent resistance of the latter. With nonviolent resistance, no individual or group need submit to any wrong, nor need anyone resort to violence in order to right a wrong.

---

[1]The apostle Peter had drawn his sword to defend Christ from arrest. The voice was Christ's, who surrendered himself for trial and crucifixion (John 18:11).

[2]Georg Wilhelm Hegel (1770–1831) was a German philosopher who said that contradictions could be synthesized to achieve truth.

8   It seems to me that this is the method that must guide the actions of the Negro in the present crisis in race relations. Through nonviolent resistance the Negro will be able to rise to the noble height of opposing the unjust system while loving the perpetrators of the system. The Negro must work passionately and unrelentingly for full stature as a citizen, but he must not use inferior methods to gain it. He must never come to terms with falsehood, malice, hate, or destruction.

9   Nonviolent resistance makes it possible for the Negro to remain in the South and struggle for his rights. The Negro's problem will not be solved by running away. He cannot listen to the glib suggestion of those who would urge him to migrate en masse to other sections of the country. By grasping his great opportunity in the South he can make a lasting contribution to the moral strength of the nation and set a sublime example of courage for generations yet unborn.

10   By nonviolent resistance, the Negro can also enlist all men of good will in his struggle for equality. The problem is not a purely racial one, with Negroes set against whites. In the end, it is not a struggle between people at all, but a tension between justice and injustice. Nonviolent resistance is not aimed against oppressors but against oppression. Under its banner consciences, not racial groups, are enlisted.

READING CLOSELY AND THINKING CRITICALLY

1. According to King, what are the problems with acquiescence? With physical violence?
2. In paragraph 2, King refers to the "freedom of exhaustion." What does this phrase mean?
3. In paragraph 1, King says that some "would rather bear those ills they have . . . than flee to others they know not of." What does King mean? Why do you think that he makes this point?
4. According to King, how does nonviolent resistance balance the approaches of those who acquiesce and those who engage in physical violence?
5. Why does King advocate nonviolent resistance?

EXAMINING STRUCTURE AND STRATEGY

1. What ordering principle does King use? What are his categories?
2. Which sentence is the thesis of "The Ways of Meeting Oppression"?
3. King presents his categories in topic sentences. What are those topic sentences?
4. Where in the essay does King make his persuasive purpose clear? Why do you think he establishes his persuasive point at this stage of his essay?

NOTING COMBINED PATTERNS

1. Cause-and-effect analysis appears in paragraphs 5 and 6, and 8 through 10. (Cause-and-effect analysis, the explanation of the causes or the effects of something, is discussed in Chapter 9.) How does the analysis help advance the classification?

2. Which paragraph includes definition? (Definition, an explanation of what something means, is discussed in Chapter 11.) What purpose does that definition serve? What paragraphs include examples? What purpose do those examples serve?

CONSIDERING LANGUAGE AND STYLE

1. Paragraph 5 includes two biblical references: the mention of "an eye for an eye" and the mention of Peter. Explain these references and evaluate their appropriateness. Why is it natural for King to use biblical references?
2. "The Ways of Meeting Oppression" comes from King's 1958 book *Stride toward Freedom.* What elements of King's language are clues to the era in which King was writing? Do these dated elements in any way detract from the essay? Explain.
3. Consult a dictionary if you are unsure of the meaning of any of these words: *tacitly* (paragraph 1), *fleshpots* (paragraph 1), *desolate* (paragraph 6), *legacy* (paragraph 6), *perpetrators* (paragraph 8), *glib* (paragraph 9), *en masse* (paragraph 9).

FOR DISCUSSION IN CLASS OR ONLINE

Martin Luther King's birthday is a national holiday celebrated in January. Do Americans celebrate King's birthday as it should be celebrated? Explain. If your instructor directs you to do so, post your response to your class Web site.

WRITING ASSIGNMENTS

1. **In your journal.** Write about a time when you witnessed, experienced, or heard about some form of oppression or discrimination. Describe the incident and how it made you feel.
2. **Using classification-division for a purpose.** The purposes in the assignments are possibilities. You may establish whatever purposes you like, within your instructor's guidelines.
   - To inform readers and persuade them that one way is better than the others, classify the ways of dealing with a bully. Give the chief advantages and/or disadvantages of each technique.
   - To inform readers and persuade them that one way is better than the others, classify the ways of dealing with either stress or depression. Give the chief advantages and disadvantages of each way.
   - To inform readers and persuade them that one way is better than the others, classify the ways of dealing with gender discrimination, age discrimination, or sexual harassment. Give the advantages and disadvantages of each way.
3. **Combining patterns.** Using definition (explained in Chapter 11), explain what a *bully* is and classify ways of dealing with one, being sure to indicate the methods that are most effective. As an alternative, classify kinds of bullying behavior, indicating which are the most harmful.
4. **Connecting the readings.** Read "Untouchables" on page 248 and "What Is Poverty?" on page 511. Then write an essay that explains to what extent the homeless and poor are

victims of oppression. Indicate whether or not you think King's policy of nonviolent resistance would help the homeless and poor and explain why you believe as you do.

5. **Drawing on sources.** On April 8, 1968, four days after Martin Luther King, Jr., was assassinated, U.S. Representative John Conyers, a Michigan Democrat, introduced legislation to make King's birthday a national holiday. However, it was not until Aug. 2, 1983, that the House of Representatives approved legislation to commemorate King in this way. Research the events leading up to the creation of Martin Luther King Day and classify the ways we celebrate it. How appropriate are these celebrations? For information, use the phrase "Martin Luther King Day" in your favorite search engine, or look under the entry "Martin Luther King, Jr." in *Africana* in your library.

BACKGROUND: Chicago native David Bodanis studied mathematics, physics, and economics at the University of Chicago. He has had a multifaceted professional life, with a number of parallel careers. In 1977, Bodanis moved to France as a reporter for the *International Herald Tribune,* and in the late 1980s he moved to England, where he became a faculty member at St. Anthony's College in Oxford. In the business world, Bodanis has worked for The People's Republic of China, Shell Oil, and General Motors as an analyst of business opportunities in the energy industry. In addition to his careers as a journalist, academic, and business consultant, Bodanis is a writer. His books include the best-selling *The Secret House* (1986), from which "What's in Your Toothpaste?" is taken, *The Ideas behind Politics* (1989), and *The Secret Family* (1997), which was the basis of an award-winning documentary for the Discovery Channel. His most recent book is $E = MC^2$: *A Biography of the World's Most Famous Equation* (2000).

COMBINED PATTERNS AND THEIR PURPOSES: In "What's in Your Toothpaste?" David Bodanis uses *division* and *process analysis* to **inform** readers about the ingredients in toothpaste and what those ingredients do. You will notice that Bodanis also has a **persuasive** purpose—that he wants to convince readers that toothpaste is not an appealing or necessary product. Notice how the author uses *description* to achieve that persuasive purpose.

What's in Your Toothpaste?
DAVID BODANIS

Into the bathroom goes our male resident, and after the most pressing need is satisfied it's time to brush the teeth. The tube of toothpaste is squeezed, its pinched metal seams are splayed, pressure waves are generated inside, and the paste begins to flow. But what's in this toothpaste, so carefully being extruded out?

As you read Think about what assumptions Bodanis makes about his audience.

2   Water mostly, 30 to 45 percent in most brands: ordinary, everyday simple tap water. It's there because people like to have a big gob of toothpaste to spread on the brush, and water is the cheapest stuff there is when it comes to making big gobs. Dripping a bit from the tap onto your brush would cost virtually nothing; whipped in with the rest of the toothpaste the manufacturers can sell it at a neat and accountant-pleasing $2 per pound equivalent. Toothpaste manufacture is a very lucrative occupation.

3   Second to water in quantity is chalk: exactly the same material that school-teachers use to write on blackboards. It is collected from the crushed remains of long-dead ocean creatures. In the Cretaceous[1] seas chalk particles served as part of the wickedly sharp outer skeleton that these creatures had to wrap around themselves to keep from getting chomped by all the slightly larger other ocean creatures they met. Their massed graves are our present chalk deposits.

4   The individual chalk particles—the size of the smallest mud particles in your garden—have kept their toughness over the aeons, and now on the toothbrush they'll need it. The enamel outer coating of the tooth they'll have to face is the

---

[1]A time 135 million years ago.

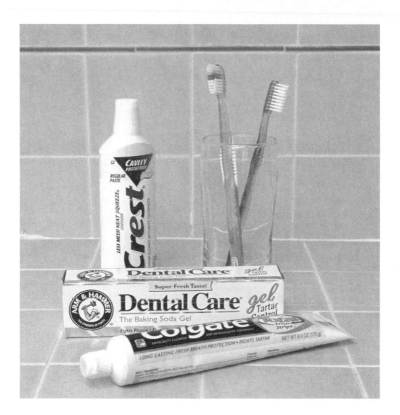

hardest substance in the body—tougher than skull, or bone, or nail. Only the chalk particles in toothpaste can successfully grind into the teeth during brushing, ripping off the surface layers like an abrading wheel grinding down a boulder in a quarry.

5   The craters, slashes, and channels that the chalk tears into the teeth will also remove a certain amount of build-up yellow in the carnage, and it is for that polishing function that it's there. A certain amount of unduly enlarged extra-abrasive chalk fragments tear such cavernous pits into the teeth that future decay bacteria will be able to bunker down there and thrive; the quality control people find it almost impossible to screen out these errant super-chalk pieces, and government regulations allow them to stay in.

6   In case even the gouging doesn't get all the yellow off, another substance is worked into the toothpaste cream. This is titanium dioxide. It comes in tiny spheres, and it's the stuff bobbing around in white wall paint to make it come out white. Splashed around onto your teeth during the brushing it coats much of the yellow that remains. Being water soluble it leaks off in the next few hours and is swallowed, but at least for the quick glance up in the mirror after finishing it will make the user think his teeth are truly white. Some manufacturers add optical whitening dyes—the stuff more commonly found in washing machine bleach—to make extra sure that that glance in the mirror shows reassuring white.

7   These ingredients alone would not make a very attractive concoction. They would stick in the tube like a sloppy white plastic lump, hard to squeeze out as well as revolting to the touch. Few consumers would savor rubbing in a mixture of water, groundup blackboard chalk, and the whitener from latex paint first thing in the morning. To get around that finicky distaste the manufacturers have mixed in a host of other goodies.

8   To keep the glop from drying out, a mixture including glycerine glycol—related to the most common car antifreeze ingredient—is whipped in with the chalk and water, and to give *that* concoction a bit of substance (all we really have so far is wet colored chalk) a large helping is added of gummy molecules from the seaweed *Chondrus Crispus*. This seaweed ooze spreads in among the chalk, paint, and antifreeze, then stretches itself in all directions to hold the whole mass together. A bit of paraffin oil (the fuel that flickers in camping lamps) is pumped in with it to help the moss ooze keep the whole substance smooth.

9   With the glycol, ooze, and paraffin we're almost there. Only two major chemicals are left to make the refreshing, cleansing substance we know as toothpaste. The ingredients so far are fine for cleaning, but they wouldn't make much of the satisfying foam we have come to expect in the morning brushing.

10   To remedy that every toothpaste on the market has a big dollop of detergent added too. You've seen the suds detergent will make in a washing machine. The same substance added here will duplicate that inside the mouth. It's not particularly necessary, but it sells.

11   The only problem is that by itself this ingredient tastes, well, too like detergent. It's horribly bitter and harsh. The chalk put in toothpaste is pretty foul-tasting too for that matter. It's to get around that gustatory discomfort that the manufacturers put in the ingredient they tout perhaps the most of all. This is the flavoring, and it has to be strong. Double rectified peppermint oil is used—a flavorer so powerful that chemists know better than to sniff it in the raw state in the laboratory. Menthol crystals and saccharin or other sugar simulators are added to complete the camouflage operation.

12   Is that it? Chalk, water, paint, seaweed, antifreeze, paraffin oil, detergent, and peppermint? Not quite. A mix like that would be irresistible to the hundreds of thousands of individual bacteria lying on the surface of even an immaculately cleaned bathroom sink. They would get in, float in the water bubbles, ingest the ooze and paraffin, maybe even spray out enzymes to break down the chalk. The result would be an uninviting mess. The way manufacturers avoid that final obstacle

is by putting something in to kill the bacteria. Something good and strong is needed, something that will zap any accidentally intrudant bacteria into oblivion. And that something is formaldehyde—the disinfectant used in anatomy labs.

13   So it's chalk, water, paint, seaweed, antifreeze, paraffin oil, detergent, peppermint, formaldehyde, and fluoride (which can go some way towards preserving children's teeth)—that's the usual mixture raised to the mouth on the toothbrush for a fresh morning's clean. If it sounds too unfortunate, take heart. Studies show that a thorough brushing with just plain water will often do as good a job.

READING CLOSELY AND THINKING CRITICALLY

1. Is the thesis of "What's in Your Toothpaste?" stated or implied? What is the thesis?
2. Bodanis uses division to inform readers of the components of toothpaste. Is his explanation similar to the kind one might find in a science textbook or reference book? Explain.
3. Using Bodanis's details and language as evidence, explain how the author views his audience.
4. After reading the essay, are you inclined to brush your teeth with toothpaste or with water? Why?

EXAMINING STRUCTURE AND STRATEGY

1. What ordering principle does Bodanis use for his division?
2. In what order does Bodanis present the toothpaste ingredients? What other orders could he have used?
3. Which paragraphs begin with topic sentences that present a division to be considered?
4. Bodanis sometimes mentions how toothpaste ingredients are used in other products. Why does he do that? How does the information help him achieve his purpose?
5. How does the conclusion help Bodanis achieve his purpose?

NOTING COMBINED PATTERNS

1. Bodanis uses a great deal of description. Is that description expressive or objective? (See page 105 on objective and expressive description.) How does the description help the author achieve his writing purpose?
2. How does Bodanis use process analysis to achieve his writing purpose?

CONSIDERING LANGUAGE AND STYLE

1. What is the tone of the essay? (See page 71 on tone.) How can you tell what the tone is?
2. Consult a dictionary if you are unsure of the meaning of any of these words: *splayed* (paragraph 1), *extruded* (paragraph 1), *aeons* (paragraph 4), *carnage* (paragraph 5), *gustatory* (paragraph 11), *tout* (paragraph 11).

Using the information in "What's in Your Toothpaste?" write an objective one-paragraph explanation of the ingredients in toothpaste. Then discuss how your paragraph compares and contrasts with Bodanis's essay. If your instructor directs you to do so, post your response to your class Web site.

WRITING ASSIGNMENTS

1. **In your journal.** How do you react to what you learned about the contents of toothpaste? Why do you react that way? Has your opinion of toothpaste changed? Why or why not? Answer these questions in a page or so.

2. **Using classification-division for a purpose.** The purposes in the assignments are possibilities. You may establish whatever purposes you like, within your instructor's guidelines.

    *   Toothpaste is widely advertised on television and in print media. These advertisements, even when they are for different brands, have much in common. To inform readers, use division to analyze the typical components of toothpaste advertisements.

    *   Like Bodanis, analyze the components of a common product or food, such as Twinkies, frozen pizza, a particular child's toy, or cigarettes. Be sure your division conveys your opinion of the product or food.

3. **Combining patterns.** Bodanis aims to convince readers that a commonly used product is unnecessary and undesirable. Try to convince readers that a product or activity they consider unappealing is really desirable. You can use division to show the product or activity's parts, process analysis (explained in Chapter 7) to show how the product or activity works, and/or description (explained in Chapter 4) to help the reader visualize the product or activity. Consider products and activities some people are resistant to, such as tofu, soy milk, weight lifting, donating blood, or car pooling.

4. **Connecting the readings.** Description can entertain readers and help them visualize things. However, description can also be used for persuasive ends and to advance a particular attitude about a subject. Drawing on "What's in Your Toothpaste?" "Behind the Formaldehyde Curtain" (page 307), and "What Is Poverty?" (page 511), explain how description can serve these purposes.

5. **Drawing on sources.** Personal care products such as toothpaste are not the only products containing chemical additives. Most of our food products do as well. Read the labels on several kinds of packaged food; for example, canned and frozen vegetables, breakfast cereals, lunch meat, bottled salad dressing, and cookies. List the most frequently occurring additives, and then look those additives up to learn what purpose they serve. You can check *Social Sciences Index* under "food additives" or visit the Web site of the U.S. Food and Drug Administration (*http://vm.cfsan.fda.gov/list.html*), and look under the heading "Program Areas." Write a classification of some of the most frequently occurring additives you found, using their purpose as your ordering principle.

BACKGROUND: William Zinsser was born in New York City. A 1944 graduate of Princeton University, he has been a writer and film critic. He has written for the New York *Herald Tribune,* the *New York Times,* and *Life* magazine. He has also been an English teacher at Yale University, where, as mentioned in the essay, he was master of Branford College. He has also taught at the New School in New York. From 1979 to 1987, he was the general editor of the Book-of-the-Month Club. An astute observer of American culture, Zinsser has written 15 books on topics ranging from jazz to baseball, including the influential books on writing, *On Writing Well* (1980) and *Writing to Learn* (1988), and *American Places: A Writer's Pilgrimage to 15 of This Country's Most Visited and Cherished Sites* (1992). "College Pressures," first published in *Blair & Ketchum's Country Journal* in 1979, still resonates with today's college students.

www.mhhe.com/patterns

For more information on this author, go to

More resources > Chapter 10 > William Zinsser

COMBINED PATTERNS AND THEIR PURPOSES: In "College Pressures," William Zinsser combines *classification-division, exemplification,* and *cause-and-effect analysis* to **inform** his reader of the nature and extent of the pressures Yale students face. However, you will notice that Zinsser's remarks speak to a wider audience as well. In addition to informing, the author has a **persuasive** purpose: He argues that students themselves must eliminate the pressures they face.

COLLEGE PRESSURES | WILLIAM ZINSSER

Dear Carlos: I desperately need a dean's excuse for my chem midterm which will begin in about 1 hour. All I can say is that I totally blew it this week. I've fallen incredibly, inconceivably behind.

As you read Decide whether or not you agree with Zinsser.

2   Carlos: Help! I'm anxious to hear from you. I'll be in my room and won't leave it until I hear from you. Tomorrow is the last day for . . .

3   Carlos: I left town because I started bugging out again. I stayed up all night to finish a take home make-up exam & am typing it to hand in on the 10th. It was due on the 5th. P.S. I'm going to the dentist. Pain is pretty bad.

4   Carlos: Probably by Friday I'll be able to get back to my studies. Right now I'm going to take a long walk. This whole thing has taken a lot out of me.

"Carlos: Probably by Friday I'll be able to get back to my studies. Right now I'm going to take a long walk. This whole thing has taken a lot out of me."

5   Carlos: I'm really up the proverbial creek. The problem is I really *bombed* the history final. Since I need that course for my major . . .

6   Carlos: Here follows a tale of woe. I went home this weekend, had to help my Mom, & caught a fever so didn't have much time to study. My professor . . .

7   Carlos: Aargh! Nothing original but everything's piling up at once. To be brief, my job interview . . .

8 Hey Carlos, good news! I've got mononucleosis.

9 Who are these wretched supplicants, scribbling notes so laden with anxiety, seeking such miracles of postponement and balm? They are men and women who belong to Branford College, one of the twelve residential colleges at Yale University, and the messages are just a few of the hundreds that they left for their dean, Carlos Hortas—often slipped under his door at 4 A.M.—last year.

10 But students like the ones who wrote those notes can also be found on campuses from coast to coast—especially in New England and at many other private colleges across the country that have high academic standards and highly motivated students. Nobody could doubt that the notes are real. In their urgency and their gallows humor they are authentic voices of a generation that is panicky to succeed.

11 My own connection with the message writers is that I am master of Branford College. I live in its Gothic quadrangle and know the students well. (We have 485 of them.) I am privy to their hopes and fears—and also to their stereo music and their piercing cries in the dead of night ("Does anybody *ca-a-are?*"). If they went to Carlos to ask how to get through tomorrow, they come to me to ask how to get through the rest of their lives.

12 Mainly I try to remind them that the road ahead is a long one and that it will have more unexpected turns than they think. There will be plenty of time to change jobs, change careers, change whole attitudes and approaches. They don't want to hear such liberating news. They want a map—right now—that they can follow unswervingly to career security, financial security, Social Security and, presumably, a prepaid grave.

13 What I wish for all students is some release from the clammy grip of the future. I wish them a chance to savor each

> "What I wish for all students is some release from the clammy grip of the future."

segment of their education as an experience in itself and not as a grim preparation for the next step. I wish them the right to experiment, to trip and fall, to learn that defeat is as instructive as victory and is not the end of the world.

14 My wish, of course, is naive. One of the few rights that America does not proclaim is the right to fail. Achievement is the national god, venerated in our media—the million-dollar athlete, the wealthy executive—and glorified in our praise of possessions. In the presence of such a potent state religion, the young are growing up old.

15 I see four kinds of pressure working on college students today: economic pressure, parental pressure, peer pressure, and self-induced pressure. It is easy to look around for villains—to blame the colleges for charging too much money, the professors for assigning too much work, the parents for pushing their children too far, the students for driving themselves too hard. But there are no villains, only victims.

16 "In the late 1960s," one dean told me, "the typical question that I got from students was 'Why is there so much suffering in the world?' or 'How can I make a contribution?' Today it's 'Do you think it would look better for getting into law school if I did a double major in history and political science, or just majored in one of them?'" Many other deans confirmed this pattern. One said: "They're trying to find an edge—the intangible something that will look better on paper if two students are about equal."

17   Note the emphasis on looking better. The transcript has become a sacred document, the passport to security. How one appears on paper is more important than how one appears in person. *A* is for Admirable and *B* is for Borderline, even though, in Yale's official system of grading, *A* means "excellent" and *B* means "very good." Today, looking very good is no longer good enough, especially for students who hope to go on to law school or medical school. They know that entrance into the better schools will be an entrance into the better law firms and better medical practices where they will make a lot of money. They also know that the odds are harsh. Yale Law School, for instance, matriculates 170 students from an applicant pool of 3,700; Harvard enrolls 550 from a pool of 7,000.

18   It's all very well for those of us who write letters of recommendation for our students to stress the qualities of humanity that will make them good lawyers or doctors. And it's nice to think that admission officers are really reading our letters and looking for the extra dimension of commitment or concern. Still, it would be hard for a student not to visualize these officers shuffling so many transcripts studded with *A*s that they regard a *B* as positively shameful.

19   The pressure is almost as heavy on students who just want to graduate and get a job. Long gone are the days of the "gentleman's *C*," when students journeyed through college with a certain relaxation, sampling a wide variety of courses—music, art, philosophy, classics, anthropology, poetry, religion—that would send them out as liberally educated men and women. If I were an employer I would rather employ graduates who have this range and curiosity than those who narrowly pursued safe subjects and high grades. I know countless students whose inquiring minds exhilarate me. I like to hear the play of their ideas. I don't know if they are getting *A*s or *C*s, and I don't care. I also like them as people. The country needs them, and they will find satisfying jobs. I tell them to relax. They can't.

20   Nor can I blame them. They live in a brutal economy. Tuition, room, and board at most private colleges now comes to at least $7,000,[1] not counting books and fees. This might seem to suggest that the colleges are getting rich. But they are equally battered by inflation. Tuition covers only 60 percent of what it costs to educate a student, and ordinarily the remainder comes from what colleges receive in endowments, grants, and gifts. Now the remainder keeps being swallowed by the cruel costs—higher every year—of just opening the doors. Heating oil is up. Insurance is up. Postage is up. Health-premium costs are up. Everything is up. Deficits are up. We are witnessing in America the creation of a brotherhood of paupers—colleges, parents, and students, joined by the common bond of debt.

21   Today it is not unusual for a student, even if he works part time at college and full time during the summer, to accrue $5,000 in loans after four years—loans that he must start to repay within one year after graduation. Exhorted at commencement to go forth into the

---

[1]In 2004, tuition, room, and board average $12,000 a year for public schools and $27,000 for private schools.

world, he is already behind as he goes forth. How could he not feel under pressure throughout college to prepare for this day of reckoning? I have used "he," incidentally, only for brevity. Women at Yale are under no less pressure to justify their expensive education to themselves, their parents, and society. In fact, they are probably under more pressure. For although they leave college superbly equipped to bring fresh leadership to traditionally male jobs, society hasn't yet caught up with this fact.

22   Along with economic pressure goes parental pressure. Inevitably, the two are deeply intertwined.

23   I see many students taking premedical courses with joyless tenacity. They go off to their labs as if they were going to the dentist. It saddens me because I know them in other corners of their life as cheerful people.

24   "Do you want to go to medical school?" I ask them.

25   "I guess so," they say, without conviction, or "Not really."

26   "Then why are you going?"

27   "Well, my parents want me to be a doctor. They're paying all this money and . . ."

28   Poor students, poor parents. They are caught in one of the oldest webs of love and duty and guilt. The parents mean well; they are trying to steer their sons and daughters toward a secure future. But the sons and daughters want to major in history or classics or philosophy—subjects with no "practical" value. Where's the payoff on the humanities? It's not easy to persuade such loving parents that the humanities do indeed pay off. The intellectual faculties developed by studying subjects like history and classics—an ability to synthesize and relate, to weigh cause and effect, to

"It's not easy to persuade such loving parents that the humanities do indeed pay off."

see events in perspective—are just the faculties that make creative leaders in business or almost any general field. Still, many fathers would rather put their money on courses that point toward a specific profession—courses that are pre-law, pre-medical, pre-business, or, as I sometimes heard it put, "pre-rich."

29   But the pressure on students is severe. They are truly torn. One part of them feels obligated to fulfill their parents' expectations, after all, their parents are older and presumably wiser. Another part tells them that the expectations that are right for their parents are not right for them.

30   I know a student who wants to be an artist. She is very obviously an artist and will be a good one—she has already had several modest exhibits. Meanwhile she is growing as a well-rounded person and taking humanistic subjects that will enrich the inner resources out of which her art will grow. But her father is strongly opposed. He thinks that an artist is a "dumb" thing to be. The student vacillates and tries to please everybody. She keeps up with her art somewhat furtively and takes some of the "dumb" courses her father wants her to take—at least they are dumb courses for her. She is a free spirit on a campus of tense students—no small achievement in itself—and she deserves to follow her muse.

31   Peer pressure and self-induced pressure are also intertwined, and they begin almost at the beginning of freshman year.

32   "I had a freshman student I'll call Linda," one dean told me, "who came in and said she was under terrible pressure because her roommate, Barbara, was much brighter and studied all the time. I couldn't tell her that Barbara had come in two hours earlier to say the same thing about Linda."

33   The story is almost funny—except that it's not. It's symptomatic of all the pressure put together. When every student thinks every other student is working harder and doing better, the only solution is to study harder still. I see students going off to the library every night after dinner and coming back when it closes at midnight. I wish they could sometimes forget about their peers and go to a movie. I hear the clacking of typewriters in the hours before dawn. I see the tension in their eyes when exams are approaching and papers are due: *"Will I get everything done?"*

34   Probably they won't. They will get sick. They will get "blocked." They will sleep. They will oversleep. They will bug out. *Hey Carlos, help!*

35   Part of the problem is that they do more than they are expected to do. A

"Part of the problem is that they do more than they are expected to do."

professor will assign five-page papers Several students will start writing ten-page papers to impress him. Then more students will write ten-page papers, and a few will raise the ante to fifteen. Pity the poor student who is still just doing the assignment.

36   "Once you have twenty or thirty percent of the student population deliberately overexerting," one dean points out, "it's bad for everybody. When a teacher gets more and more effort from his class, the student who is doing normal work can be perceived as not doing well. The tactic works, psychologically."

37   Why can't the professor just cut back and not accept longer papers? He can, and he probably will. But by then the term will be half over and the damage done. Grade fever is highly contagious and not easily reversed. Besides, the professor's main concern is with his course. He knows his students only in relation to the course and doesn't know that they are also overexerting in their other courses. Nor is it really his business. He didn't sign up for dealing with the student as a whole person and with all the emotional baggage the student brought along from home. That's what deans, masters, chaplains, and psychiatrists are for.

38   To some extent this is nothing new: a certain number of professors have always been self-contained islands of scholarship and shyness, more comfortable with books than with people. But the new pauperism has widened the gap still further, for professors who actually like to spend time with students don't have as much time to spend. They also are overexerting. If they are young, they are busy trying to publish in order not to perish, hanging by their fingernails onto a shrinking profession. If they are old and tenured, they are buried under the duties of administering departments— as departmental chairmen or members of committees—that have been thinned out by the budgetary axe.

39   Ultimately it will be the students' own business to break the circles in which they are trapped. They are too young to be prisoners of their parents' dreams and their classmates' fears. They must be

jolted into believing in themselves as unique men and women who have the power to shape their own future.

40 "Violence is being done to the undergraduate experience," says Carlos Hortas. "College should be open-ended:

> "Violence is being done to the undergraduate experience," says Carlos Hortas.

at the end it should open many, many roads. Instead, students are choosing their goal in advance, and their choices narrow as they go along. It's almost as if they think that the country has been codified in the type of jobs that exist—that they've got to fit into certain slots. Therefore, fit into the best-paying slot.

41 "They ought to take chances. Not taking chances will lead to a life of colorless mediocrity. They'll be comfortable. But comething in the spirit will be missing."

42 I have painted too drab a portrait of today's students, making them seem a solemn lot. That is only half of their story; if they were so dreary I wouldn't so thoroughly enjoy their company. The other half is that they are easy to like. They are quick to laugh and to offer friendship. They are not introverts. They are usually kind and are more considerate of one another than any student generation I have known.

43 Nor are they so obsessed with their studies that they avoid sports and extracurricular activities. On the contrary, they juggle their crowded hours to play on a variety of teams, perform with musical and dramatic groups, and write for campus publications. But this in turn is one more cause of anxiety. There are too many choices. Academically, they have 1,300 courses to select from; outside class they have to decide how much spare time they can spare and how to spend it.

44 This means that they engage in fewer extracurricular pursuits than their predecessors did. If they want to row on the crew and play in the symphony they will eliminate one; in the '60s they would have done both. They also tend to choose activities that are self-limiting. Drama, for instance, is flourishing in all twelve of Yale's residential colleges as it never has before. Students hurl themselves into these productions—as actors, directors, carpenters, and technicians—with a dedication to create the best possible play, knowing that the day will come when the run will end and they can get back to their studies.

45 They also can't afford to be the willing slave of organizations like the *Yale Daily News*. Last spring at the one-hundredth anniversary banquet of that paper—whose past chairmen include such once and future kings as Potter Stewart, Kingman Brewster, and William F. Buckley, Jr.[2]—much was made of the fact that the editorial staff used to be small and totally committed and that "newsies" routinely worked fifty hours a week. In effect they belonged to a club; Newsies is how they defined themselves at Yale. Today's student will write one or two articles a week, when he can, and he defines himself as a student. I've never heard the word Newsie except at the banquet.

46 If I have described the modern undergraduate primarily as a driven creature who is largely ignoring the blithe

---

[2]Stewart was a U.S. Supreme Court justice; Brewster was a president of Yale; and Buckley is a conservative editor and columnist.

spirit inside who keeps trying to come out and play, it's because that's where the crunch is, not only at Yale but throughout American education. It's why I think we should all be worried about the values that are nurturing a generation so fearful of risk and so goal-obsessed at such an early age.

47 I tell students that there is no one "right" way to get ahead—that each of them is a different person, starting from a different point and bound for a different destination. I tell them that change is a tonic and that all the slots are not codified nor the frontiers closed. One of my ways of telling them is to invite men and women who have achieved success outside the academic world to come and talk informally with my students during the year. They are heads of companies or ad agencies, editors of magazines, politicians, public officials, television magnates, labor leaders, business executives, Broadway producers, artists, writers, economists, photographers, scientists, historians—a mixed bag of achievers.

48 I ask them to say a few words about how they got started. The students assume that they started in their present profession and knew all along that is was what they wanted to do. Luckily for me, most of them got into their field by a circuitous route, to their surprise, after many detours. The students are startled. They can hardly conceive of a career that was not pre-planned. They can hardly imagine allowing the hand of God or chance to nudge them down some unforeseen trail.

READING CLOSELY AND THINKING CRITICALLY

1. According to Zinsser, what factors cause the pressure that college students experience?
2. Make a list of at least five words or phrases Zinsser uses to describe the contemporary college student.
3. In a sentence or two, summarize Zinsser's advice to college students. What do you think of this advice?
4. According to Zinsser, how can college pressures be eliminated?
5. Are the author's description of Yale students and his classification of the pressures they face representative of students and their pressures in general? Explain.

EXAMINING STRUCTURE AND STRATEGY

1. In your own words, write out Zinsser's thesis.
2. In which paragraph does Zinsser's classification begin, and in which paragraph does it end?
3. What is Zinsser classifying? What does the classification contribute to the essay? That is, what purpose does it serve?

NOTING COMBINED PATTERNS

1. What element of cause-and-effect analysis appears in the essay? What does the analysis contribute to the essay?
2. What is the purpose of the opening examples of notes written to Carlos Hortas?

1. Zinsser uses *he* to refer to college students and professors. He says, however, in paragraph 21 that he uses this pronoun for "brevity"; he recognizes that women, too, are under pressure. Do you think Zinsser should have used language that includes women? Explain.
2. What metaphor appears in paragraph 9? Do you find the metaphor appropriate? Explain. (Metaphors are explained on page 110.)
3. Consult a dictionary if you are unsure of the meaning of any of these words: *supplicants* (paragraph 9), *gallows humor* (paragraph 10), *privy* (paragraph 11), *venerated* (paragraph 14), *matriculates* (paragraph 17), *accrue* (paragraph 21), *exhorted* (paragraph 21), *muse* (paragraph 30), *blithe* (paragraph 46), *circuitous* (paragraph 48).

FOR DISCUSSION IN CLASS OR ONLINE

In paragraph 47, Zinsser tells of inviting people to speak to his students. Do you think these classroom visits changed the attitudes of many students? Why or why not? If your instructor so directs, post your responses to your class Web site.

WRITING ASSIGNMENTS

1. **In your journal.** In two or three pages, describe the kinds and amount of pressure you experience as a college student. Then explain the effects this pressure has on you.
2. **Using classification-division for a purpose.** The purposes in the assignments are possibilities. You may establish whatever purposes you like, within your instructor's guidelines.
    *   To inform readers, write a classification of the kinds of college students. Use examples from your own experience and observation to illustrate your categories. As an alternative, use division to explain the aspects of a typical college student.
    *   To inform, classify the pressures in some nonacademic setting, such as the pressures of parenthood, of being an only child, of working as a table server, of being a lifeguard, or of being a student athlete. Like Zinsser, offer some advice for overcoming the pressures.
    *   In paragraph 41, Zinsser notes that Carlos Hortas says students "ought to take chances. Not taking chances will lead to a life of colorless mediocrity." To inform, classify the kinds of risks people should take.
3. **Combining patterns.** In paragraph 12, Zinsser says that students "want a map—right now—that they can follow unswervingly to career security, financial security, Social Security and, presumably, a prepaid grave." If you disagree, or if you think students want more than a map, inform and persuade your reader with your classification of things students want. Use cause-and-effect analysis (discussed in Chapter 9) to explain why students want what they do.
4. **Connecting the readings.** How do the pressures that college students face create situations conducive to the panic and choking explained in "The Art of Failure" (p. 516)? What, if anything, can be done to prevent panic and choking among college students?
5. **Drawing on sources.** Interview 10 students, either in person or by e-mail, to learn about the pressures characteristic of students on your campus. Then classify those pressures. Explain how your classification compares to Zinsser's. Have college pressures changed since Zinsser wrote his essay?

BACKGROUND: Born in England in 1929, zoologist, artist, and writer Desmond Morris earned his Ph.D. from Oxford University. After graduation, he was first an animal behavior researcher in Oxford's zoology department and then head of Granada TV's Film Unit at the London Zoo and a curator of mammals at the Zoological Society of London. He became keenly interested in explaining animal and human behavior to the public and published his findings about human behavior in his well-received books. *The Naked Ape* (1967) became a best seller, popularizing sociology and zoology. Morris followed it with numerous television programs about animal behavior. His other books include *The Human Zoo* (1969), *Manwatching* (1977), *The Soccer Tribe* (1981), *Animal-Watching* (1990), and *The Human Sexes* (1997). "Territorial Behaviour" is an excerpt from *Manwatching*.

COMBINED PATTERNS AND THEIR PURPOSE: People behave the way they do for a variety of reasons. In "Territorial Behaviour," Desmond Morris *classifies* the kinds of human territory and uses *cause-and-effect analysis* and *exemplification* to **inform** the reader that we often act the way we do as a result of our efforts to mark or protect our space.

Territorial Behaviour
DESMOND MORRIS

A territory is a defended space. In the broadest sense, there are three kinds of human territory: tribal, family and personal.

2   It is rare for people to be driven to physical fighting in defence of these "owned" spaces, but fight they will, if pushed to the limit. The invading army encroaching on national territory, the gang moving into a rival district, the trespasser climbing into an orchard, the burglar breaking into a house, the bully pushing to the front of a queue, the driver trying to steal a parking space, all of these intruders are liable to be met with resistance varying from the vigorous to the savagely violent. Even if the law is on the side of the intruder, the urge to protect a territory may be so strong that otherwise peaceful citizens abandon all their usual controls and inhibitions. Attempts to evict families from their homes, no matter how socially valid the reasons, can lead to siege conditions reminiscent of the defence of a medieval fortress.

As you read
Be on the alert for a category that includes two classifications of its own.

3   The fact that these upheavals are so rare is a measure of the success of Territorial Signals as a system of dispute prevention. It is sometimes cynically stated that "all property is theft," but in reality it is the opposite. Property, as owned space which is *displayed* as owned space, is a special kind of sharing system which reduces fighting much more than it causes it. Man is a co-operative species, but he is also competitive, and his struggle for dominance has to be structured in some way if chaos is to be avoided. The establishment of territorial rights is one such structure. It limits dominance geographically. I am dominant in my territory and you are dominant in yours. In other words, dominance is shared out spatially, and we all have some. Even if I am weak and unintelligent and you can dominate me when we meet on neutral ground, I can still enjoy a thoroughly dominant role as soon as I retreat to my private base. Be it ever so humble, there is no place like a home territory.

4   Of course, I can still be intimidated by a particularly dominant individual who enters my home base, but his encroachment will be dangerous for him and he will think twice about it, because he will know that here my urge to resist will be dramatically magnified and my usual subservience banished. Insulted at the heart of my own territory, I may easily explode into battle—either symbolic or real—with a result that may be damaging to both of us.

5   In order for this to work, each territory has to be plainly advertised as such. Just as a dog cocks its leg to deposit its personal scent on the trees in its locality, so the human animal cocks its leg symbolically all over his home base. But because we are predominantly visual animals, we employ mostly visual signals, and it is worth asking how we do this at the three levels: tribal, family and personal.

6   First, the Tribal Territory. We evolved as tribal animals, living in comparatively small groups, probably of less than a hundred, and we existed like that for millions of years. It is our basic social unit, a group in which everyone knows everyone else. Essentially the tribal territory consisted of a home base surrounded by extended hunting grounds. Any neighbouring tribe intruding on our social space would be repelled and driven away. As these early tribes swelled into agricultural supertribes, and eventually into industrial nations, their territorial defence systems became increasingly elaborate. The tiny, ancient home base of the hunting tribe became the great capital city, the primitive war-paint became the flags, emblems, uniforms and regalia of the specialized military, and the war-chants became national anthems, marching songs and bugle calls. Territorial boundary-lines hardened into fixed borders, often conspicuously patrolled and punctuated with defensive structures—forts and look-out posts, checkpoints and great walls, and, today, customs barriers.

7   Today each nation flies its own flag, a symbolic embodiment of its territorial status. But patriotism is not enough. The ancient tribal hunter lurking inside each citizen finds himself unsatisfied by membership in such a vast conglomeration of individuals, most of whom are totally unknown to him personally. He does his best to feel that he shares a common territorial defence with them all, but the scale of the operation has become inhuman. It is hard to feel a sense of belonging with a tribe of fifty million or more. His answer is to form subgroups, nearer to his ancient pattern, smaller and more personally known to him—the local club, the teenage gang, the union, the specialist society, the sports association, the political party, the college fraternity, the social clique, the protest group, and the rest. Rare indeed is the individual who does not belong to at least one of these splinter groups, and take from it a sense of tribal allegiance and brotherhood. Typical of all these groups is the development of Territorial Signals—badges, costumes, headquarters, banners, slogans, and all the other displays of group identity. This is where the action is, in terms of tribal territorialism, and only when a major war breaks out does the emphasis shift upwards to the higher group level of the nation.

8   Each of these modern pseudo-tribes sets up its own special kind of home base. In extreme cases non-members are totally excluded, in others they are allowed in as visitors with limited rights and under a control system of special rules. In many ways they are like miniature nations, with their own flags and emblems and their own border guards. The exclusive club has its own "customs barrier": the doorman

who checks your "passport" (your membership card) and prevents strangers from passing in unchallenged. There is a government: the club committee; and often special displays of the tribal elders: the photographs or portraits of previous officials on the walls. At the heart of the specialized territories there is a powerful feeling of security and importance, a sense of shared defence against the outside world. Much of the club chatter, both serious and joking, directs itself against the rottenness of everything outside the club boundaries—in that "other world" beyond the protected portals.

9   In social organizations which embody a strong class system, such as military units and large business concerns, there are many territorial rules, often unspoken, which interfere with the official hierarchy. High-status individuals, such as officers or managers, could in theory enter any of the regions occupied by the lower levels in the pecking order, but they limit this power in a striking way. An officer seldom enters a sergeant's mess or a barrack room unless it is for a formal inspection. He respects those regions as alien territories even though he has the power to go there by virtue of his dominant role. And in businesses, part of the appeal of unions, over and above their obvious functions, is that with their officials, headquarters and meetings they add a sense of territorial power for the staff workers. It is almost as if each military organization and business concern consists of two warring tribes, the officers versus the other ranks, and the management versus the workers. Each has its special home base within the system, and the territorial defence pattern thrusts itself into what, on the surface, is a pure social hierarchy. Negotiations between managements and unions are tribal battles fought out over the neutral ground of a board-room table, and are as much concerned with territorial displays as they are with resolving problems of wages and conditions. Indeed, if one side gives in too quickly and accepts the other's demands, the victors feel strangely cheated and deeply suspicious that it may be a trick. What they are missing is the protracted sequence of ritual and counter-ritual that keeps alive their group territorial identity.

10   Likewise, many of the hostile displays of sports fans and teenage gangs are primarily concerned with displaying their group image to rival fan-clubs and gangs. Except in rare cases, they do not attack one another's headquarters, drive out the occupants, and reduce them to a submissive, subordinate condition. It is enough to have scuffles on the borderlands between the two rival territories. This is particularly clear at football matches, where the fan-club headquarters becomes temporarily shifted from the club-house to a section of the stands, and where minor fighting breaks out at the unofficial boundary line between the massed groups of rival supporters. Newspaper reports play up the few accidents and injuries which do occur on such occasions, but when they are studied in relation to the total numbers of displaying fans involved, it is clear that the serious incidents represent only a tiny fraction of the overall group behaviour. For every actual punch or kick there are a thousand war-cries, war-dances, chants and gestures.

11   Second: the Family Territory. Essentially, the family is a breeding unit and the family territory is a breeding ground. At the centre of this space, there is the nest— the bedroom—where, tucked up in bed, we feel at our most territorially secure. In a typical house the bedroom is upstairs, where a safe nest should be. This puts it

farther away from the entrance hall, the area where contact is made, intermittently, with the outside world. The less private reception rooms, where intruders are allowed access, are the next line of defence. Beyond them, outside the walls of the building, there is often a symbolic remnant of the ancient feeding grounds—a garden. Its symbolism often extends to the plants and animals it contains, which cease to be nutritional and become merely decorative—flowers and pets. But like a true territorial space it has a conspicuously displayed boundary-line, the garden fence, wall, or railings. Often no more than a token barrier, this is the outer territorial demarcation, separating the private world of the family from the public world beyond. To cross it puts any visitor or intruder at an immediate disadvantage. As he crosses the threshold, his dominance wanes, slightly but unmistakably. He is entering an area where he senses that he must ask permission to do simple things that he would consider a right elsewhere. Without lifting a finger, the territorial owners exert their dominance. This is done by all the hundreds of small ownership "markers" they have deposited on their family territory: the ornaments, the "possessed" objects positioned in the rooms and on the walls; the furnishings, the furniture, the colours, the patterns, all owner-chosen and all making this particular home base unique to them.

12   It is one of the tragedies of modern architecture that there has been a standardization of these vital territorial living units. One of the most important aspects of a home is that it should be similar to other homes only in a general way, and that in detail it should have many differences, making it a *particular* home. Unfortunately, it is cheaper to build a row of houses, or a block of flats, so that all the family living-units are identical, but the territorial urge rebels against this trend and house-owners struggle as best they can to make their mark on their mass-produced properties. They do this with garden-design, with front-door colours, with curtain patterns, with wallpaper and all the other decorative elements that together create a unique and different family environment. Only when they have completed this nest-building do they feel truly "at home" and secure.

13   When they venture forth as a family unit, they repeat the process in a minor way. On a day-trip to the seaside, they load the car with personal belongings and it becomes their temporary, portable territory. Arriving at the beach, they stake out a small territorial claim, marking it with rugs, towels, baskets and other belongings to which they can return from their seaboard wanderings. Even if they all leave it at once to bathe, it retains a characteristic territorial quality and other family groups arriving will recognize this by setting up their own "home" bases at a respectful distance. Only when the whole beach has filled up with these marked spaces will newcomers start to position themselves in such a way that the inter-base distance becomes reduced. Forced to pitch between several existing beach territories, they will feel a momentary sensation of intrusion, and the established "owners" will feel a similar sensation of invasion, even though they are not being directly inconvenienced.

14   The same territorial scene is being played out in parks and fields and on riverbanks, wherever family groups gather in their clustered units. But if rivalry for spaces creates mild feelings of hostility, it is true to say that without the territorial system of sharing and space-limited dominance, there would be chaotic disorder.

15   Third: the Personal Space. If a man enters a waiting-room and sits at one end of a long row of empty chairs, it is possible to predict where the next man to enter will seat himself. He will not sit next to the first man, nor will he sit at the far end, right away from him. He will choose a position about halfway between these two points. The next man to enter will take the largest gap left, and sit roughly in the middle of that, and so on, until eventually the latest newcomer will be forced to select a seat that places him right next to one of the already seated men. Similar patterns can be observed in cinemas, public urinals, airplanes, trains and buses. This is a reflection of the fact that we all carry with us, everywhere we go, a portable territory called a Personal Space. If people move inside this space, we feel threatened. If they keep too far outside it, we feel rejected. The result is a subtle series of spatial adjustments, usually operating quite unconsciously and producing ideal compromises as far as this is possible. If a situation becomes too crowded, then we adjust our reactions accordingly and allow our personal space to shrink. Jammed into an elevator, a rush-hour compartment, or a packed room, we give up altogether and allow body-to-body contact, but when we relinquish our Personal Space in this way, we adopt certain special techniques. In essence, what we do is to convert these other bodies into "nonpersons." We studiously ignore them, and they us. We try not to face them if we can possibly avoid it. We wipe all expressiveness from our faces, letting them go blank. We may look up at the ceiling or down at the floor, and we reduce body movements to a minimum. Packed together like sardines in a tin, we stand dumbly still, sending out as few social signals as possible.

16   Even if the crowding is less severe, we still tend to cut down our social interactions in the presence of large numbers. Careful observations of children in play groups revealed that if they are high-density groupings there is less social interaction between the individual children, even though there is theoretically more opportunity for such contacts. At the same time, the high-density groups show a higher frequency of aggressive and destructive behaviour patterns in their play. Personal Space—"elbow room"—is a vital commodity for the human animal, and one that cannot be ignored without risking serious trouble.

17   Of course, we all enjoy the excitement of being in a crowd, and this reaction cannot be ignored. But there are crowds and crowds. It is pleasant enough to be in a "spectator crowd," but not also appealing to find yourself in the middle of a rush-hour crush. The difference between the two is that the spectator crowd is all facing in the same direction and concentrating on a distant point of interest. Attending a theatre, there are twinges of rising hostility towards the stranger who sits down immediately in front of you or the one who squeezes into the seat next to you. The shared armrest can become a polite, but distinct, territorial boundary-dispute region. However, as soon as the show begins, these invasions of Personal Space are forgotten and the attention is focused beyond the small space where the crowding is taking place. Now, each member of the audience feels himself spatially related, not to his cramped neighbours, but to the actor on the stage, and this distance is, if anything, too great. In the rush-hour crowd, by contrast, each member of the pushing throng is competing with his neighbours all the time. There is no escape to a spatial relation with a distant actor, only the pushing, shoving bodies all around.

18   Those of us who have to spend a great deal of time in crowded conditions become gradually better able to adjust, but no one can ever become completely immune to invasions of Personal Space. This is because they remain forever associated with either powerful hostile or equally powerful loving feelings. All through our childhood we will have been held to be loved and held to be hurt, and anyone who invades our Personal Space when we are adults is, in effect, threatening to extend this behaviour into one of these two highly charged areas of human interaction. Even if his motives are clearly neither hostile nor sexual, we still find it hard to suppress our reactions to his close approach. Unfortunately, different countries have different ideas about exactly how close is close. It is easy enough to test your own "space reaction": when you are talking to someone in the street or in any open space, reach out with your arm and see where the nearest point on his body comes. If you hail from western Europe, you will find that he is at roughly fingertip distance from you. In other words, as you reach out, your fingertips will just about make contact with his shoulder. If you come from eastern Europe, you will find you are standing at "wrist distance." If you come from the Mediterranean region, you will find that you are much closer to your companion, a little more than "elbow distance."

19   Trouble begins when a member of one of these cultures meets and talks to one from another. Say a British diplomat meets an Italian or an Arab diplomat at an embassy function. They start talking in a friendly way, but soon the fingertips man begins to feel uneasy. Without knowing quite why, he starts to back away gently from his companion. The companion edges forward again. Each tries in his way to set up a Personal Space relationship that suits his own background. But it is impossible to do. Every time the Mediterranean dipomat advances to a distance that feels comfortable for him, the British diplomat feels threatened. Every time the Briton moves back, the other feels rejected. Attempts to adjust this situation often lead to a talking pair shifting slowly across a room, and many an embassy reception is dotted with western-European fingertip-distance men pinned against the walls by eager elbow-distance men. Until such differences are fully understood and allowances made, these minor differences in "body territories" will continue to act as an alienation factor which may interfere in a subtle way with diplomatic harmony and other forms of international transaction.

20   If there are distance problems when engaged in conversation, then there are clearly going to be even bigger difficulties where people must work privately in a shared space. Close proximity of others, pressing against the invisible boundaries of our personal body-territory, makes it difficult to concentrate on non-social matters. Flat-mates, students sharing a study, sailors in the cramped quarters of a ship, and office staff in crowded work-places, all have to face this problem. They solve it by "cocooning." They use a variety of devices to shut themselves off from the others present. The best possible cocoon, of course, is a small private room—a den, a private office, a study or a studio—which physically obscures the presence of other nearby territory-owners. This is the ideal situation for non-social work, but the space-sharer cannot enjoy this luxury. Their cocooning must be symbolic. They may, in certain cases, be able to erect small physical barriers, such as screens and

partitions, which give substance to their invisible Personal Space boundaries, but when this cannot be done, other means must be sought. One of these is the "favoured object." Each space-sharer develops a preference, repeatedly expressed until it becomes a fixed pattern, for a particular chair, or table, or alcove. Others come to respect this, and friction is reduced. This system is often formally arranged (this is my desk, that is yours), but even where it is not, favoured places soon develop. Professor Smith has a favourite chair in the library. It is not formally his, but he always uses it and others avoid it. Seats around a messroom table, or a board-room table, become almost personal property for specific individuals. Even in the home, father has his favourite chair for reading the newspaper or watching television. Another device is the blinkers-posture. Just as a horse that over-reacts to other horses and the distractions of the noisy race-course is given a pair of blinkers to shield its eyes, so people studying privately in a public place put on pseudo-blinkers in the form of shielding hands. Resting their elbows on the table, they sit with their hands screening their eyes from the scene on either side.

21   A third method of reinforcing the body-territory is to use personal markers. Books, papers and other personal belongings are scattered around the favoured site to render it more privately owned in the eyes of companions. Spreading out one's belongings is a well-known trick in public-transport situations, where a traveller tries to give the impression that seats next to him are taken. In many contexts care-fully arranged personal markers can act as an effective territorial display, even in the absence of the territory owner. Experiments in a library revealed that placing a pile of magazines on the table in one seating position successfully reserved that place for an average of 77 minutes. If a sports-jacket was added, draped over the chair, then the "reservation effect" lasted for over two hours.

22   In these ways, we strengthen the defences of our Personal Spaces, keeping out intruders with the minimum of open hostility. As with all territorial behaviour, the object is to defend space with signals rather than with fists and at all three levels— the tribal, the family and the personal—it is a remarkably efficient system of space-sharing. It does not always seem so, because newspapers and newscasts inevitably magnify the exceptions and dwell on those cases where the signals have failed and wars have broken out, gangs have fought, neighbouring families have feuded, or colleagues have clashed, but for every territorial signal that has failed, there are millions of others that have not. They do not rate a mention in the news, but they nevertheless constitute a dominant feature of human society—the society of a remarkably territorial animal.

READING CLOSELY AND THINKING CRITICALLY

1.   In paragraph 2, Morris says that "it is rare for people to be driven to physical fighting in defense of these 'owned' spaces, but fight they will, if pushed to the limit." Agree or disagree with this statement and explain why you think the way you do.

2.   How does territorial behavior reconcile the seemingly conflicting cooperative and competitive aspects of human beings?

3. Why are people uncomfortable with membership in large tribal groups and what do they do to alleviate that discomfort?

4. Why does Morris define family as a "breeding unit" and family territory as a "breeding ground"? Do you find these definitions insulting or inappropriate? Explain.

5. What happens when people have their personal space invaded? What happened the last time your own personal space was invaded?

6. What does Morris explain is the purpose of territorial behavior? That is, why do we need a territorial system of dominance?

EXAMINING STRUCTURE AND STRATEGY

1. Where does Morris best express his thesis?

2. Morris does not begin the classification until paragraph 6. What purpose do the first five paragraphs serve?

3. Morris's third category is personal space. Within that category, he includes two other classifications. What are those classifications, and what categories do they include?

4. What transitions does Morris use to move from one category to another? Evaluate the effectiveness of these transitions.

NOTING COMBINED PATTERNS

1. Which paragraphs include particularly strong examples? What would be lost if those examples were not there?

2. What elements of cause-and-effect analysis appear?

CONSIDERING LANGUAGE AND STYLE

1. Why does Morris spell the following words the way he does: *behaviour, defence, centre, colours, favoured?*

2. The tone of "Territorial Behaviour" is formal and academic, yet it is not stuffy or stiff. In fact, you likely found the selection very readable. What strategies does Morris use to keep his writing accessible to a general reader?

3. Consult a dictionary if you are unsure of the meaning of any of these words: *encroachment* (paragraph 4), *regalia* (paragraph 6), *clique* (paragraph 7), *pseudo* (paragraph 8), *portals* (paragraph 8), *pecking order* (paragraph 9), *demarcation* (paragraph 11), *render* (paragraph 21).

DISCUSSION IN CLASS OR ONLINE

With some classmates, identify the kinds of territorial behavior evident on college campuses. Also consider what purposes these behaviors serve. If your instructor directs you to do so, post your responses on your class Web site.

1. **In your journal.** In paragraph 7, Morris discusses subgroups and why people belong to them. List the subgroups that you belong to and note what you get out of each of these groups.

2. **Using classification-division for a purpose.** The purposes in the assignments are possibilities. You may establish whatever purposes you like, within your instructor's guidelines.

   - In paragraph 4, Morris refers to the "home base." To inform, classify the kinds of home bases and give examples of each.

   - To inform and perhaps relate experience and express feelings, classify the "specialized territories" that create "a powerful feeling of security and importance" (paragraph 8) for you or for people in general.

   - In paragraph 11, Morris says that "we feel at our most territorially secure" in the bedroom. Where else do we feel secure? To inform your reader, classify these places and explain why we feel secure there.

3. **Combining patterns.** Define *cocooning* and classify the kinds of cocooning that you and your family engage in. (Definition is discussed in Chapter 11.) As an alternative, classify the kinds of cocooning that you and your co-workers or classmates engage in and provide examples.

4. **Connecting the readings.** Read "Just Walk on By: A Black Man Ponders His Power to Alter Public Space" (page 416) and explain what principles of territorial behavior the author illustrates. Then go on to suggest how the author can deal with his problem using some of the sociological principles pointed out in "Territorial Behavior."

5. **Drawing on sources.** *Proxemics* is the study of how space is used and how people react to the use of space. It includes the study of personal space, which Morris discusses in "Territorial Behaviour." Write a classification of the ways people are affected by personal space. As an alternative, classify cultural differences in the use of personal space. For information, type *proxemics* in your favorite search engine, or look up "personal space" in the *Social Sciences Index* in your library's reference room.

BACKGROUND: Welsh poet Dylan Thomas (1914–1953) made a living in various ways—as an actor, a reporter, a reviewer, a scriptwriter, and a handyman. During World War II, he was an anti-aircraft gunner, and after the war, he was a poetry commentator for the British Broadcasting Company (BBC). He published his first book of poetry, *Eighteen Poems* (1934), when he was only 19 years old. Thomas's second and third volumes were *Twenty-five Poems* (1936) and *The Map of Love* (1939). The poems of his first three volumes were collected in *The World I Breathe* (1939). He also wrote *A Portrait of the Artist as a Young Dog* (1940), a collection of humorous autobiographical sketches; *Deaths and Entrances* (1946); and *In Country Sleep* (1951). *Collected Poems, 1934–1953* (1953) contains all of his poetry that he wished to preserve. The dominant themes of Thomas's poetry are divine purpose and the cycle of birth and death. "Do Not Go Gentle into That Good Night" comes from *Poems of Dylan Thomas* (1952).

THE PATTERN AND ITS PURPOSES: In "Do Not Go Gentle into That Good Night," Dylan Thomas *classifies* the ways different men face death to **persuade** his dying father to resist his own death. The poem also allows Thomas to **express his feelings.**

Do Not Go Gentle into That Good Night
DYLAN THOMAS

Do not go gentle into that good night,
Old age should burn and rave at close of day;
Rage, rage against the dying of the light.

Though wise men at their end know dark is right,
Because their words had forked no lightning they   5
Do not go gentle into that good night.

As you read
Look for the different metaphors Thomas uses to refer to death.

Good men, the last wave by, crying how bright
Their frail deeds might have danced in a green bay,
Rage, rage against the dying of the light.

Wild men who caught and sang the sun in flight,   10
And learn, too late, they grieved it on its way
Do not go gentle into that good night.

Grave men, near death, who see with blinding sight
Blind eyes could blaze like meteors and be gay,
Rage, rage against the dying of the light.   15

And you, my father, there on the sad height,
Curse, bless, me now with your fierce tears, I pray.
Do not go gentle into that good night.
Rage, rage against the dying of the light.

CONSIDERING THE POEM

1. What are Thomas's categories? What is his ordering principle?
2. How does the classification help Thomas achieve his purpose?

3. What metaphors does Thomas use to refer to death? (Metaphors are explained on page 110.)

4. What is Thomas asking of his father in the last stanza? Why does he ask to be cursed *and* blessed?

5. Why do the men of the poem "rage against the dying of the light"?

6. Explain the double meaning of "grave" in the fifth stanza.

WRITING ASSIGNMENTS

1. In your journal.

- In a page or two, give your specific reactions to the poem. Do you enjoy it? Why or why not?

- In a page or two, relate your own views about death.

- Write your own poem about death or loss. This is not for sharing, so feel free to experiment and be bold.

2. Using classification-division for a purpose. The purposes in the assignments are possibilities. You may establish whatever purposes you like, within your instructor's guidelines.

- To inform, classify approaches to death or serious illness.

- To inform, classify approaches to a particular life cycle event, such as graduation, marriage, birth, confirmation, or bar or bat mitzvah.

See page 451 for strategies for writing classification and division and for a revising checklist.

1. Classify popular music to inform people who do not know much about this music.

2. Classify either television talk shows or situation comedies to explain the nature of these forms of entertainment. As an alternative, use division to break down one of these shows into its various parts.

3. Classify teachers you have had.

4. Classify baseball pitchers, football quarterbacks, basketball forwards, or others who play a particular position on an athletic team.

5. Classify movie superstars to explain what their appeal is. As an alternative, use division to break down the typical superstar into his or her components.

6. Classify kinds of shoppers.

7. Classify radio disc jockeys or television newscasters or talk show hosts.

8. Classify sources of frustration.

9. Classify kinds of dishonesty.

10. Classify types of inner strength or types of courage.

11. To help explain their appeal, classify horror movies or break them down into their various parts.

12. Classify parenting styles. If you wish, your purpose can be to persuade your reader that a particular style is the best.

13. Classify types of drivers. If you like, your purpose can be to entertain.

14. Classify soft drink advertisements on television or makeup advertisements in magazines to inform your reader of the persuasive strategies that are employed. As an alternative, analyze the components of a typical advertisement for one of these products.

15. Classify the kinds of parties college students attend. As an alternative, use division to present the various aspects of a college party.

16. Classify football, baseball, or basketball fans.

17. Classify the kinds of neighbors people can have.

18. Write a classification of the kinds of good luck or bad luck.

19. Classify the different kinds of theme parks or roller coasters.

20. *Classification and division in context:* Assume you are the entertainment editor for your campus newspaper. For the first issue of the fall term, write an article that classifies the kinds of entertainment available to students at your school. Your purpose is to inform first-year students of the options available to them and the chief features of each kind of entertainment in order to help them adjust to your compus.

The following graphic is a Venn diagram. A Venn diagram, composed of overlapping circles, is often used for examining how items relate to each other. This particular Venn diagram divides a criminal event into its components. Analyze the diagram for the following information:

- What do the overlaps mean?
- What elements are generally present when a crime is committed?
- Define a "suitable target," "likely offender," and "capable guardian."
- What does this diagram suggest about how crime can be prevented?

After analyzing the diagram, read a newspaper account of a crime and explain what took place and whether the crime conforms to the division given in the diagram.

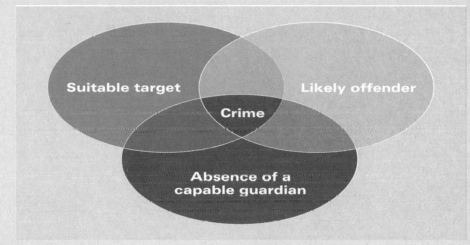

From Freda Adler, Gerhard O. W. Mueller, and William S. Laufer, *Criminology,* 4th ed., New York: McGraw-Hill, 2001, p. 241. Copyright © 2001 The McGraw-Hill Companies. Reprinted by permission of The McGraw-Hill Companies, Inc.

11

Definition

We often associate courage with dramatic acts of bravery such as rescuing a child from a burning building. Yet courage is displayed in other ways as well. For example, consider the courage of a fearful child (like the one on the facing page) walking into a new classroom on the first day of school. In a paragraph or two, write your own definition of *courage*.

THE PATTERN

Except for the phone book, the dictionary may be the most frequently consulted reference book. Since grade school, we have gone to the dictionary to check the meaning of a word we don't know, and now when we work on the computer, we can strike a key or two and consult an online dictionary even faster. When we consult a dictionary, we get a **formal definition,** which often explains a term by giving the class it belongs to and how it differs from other members of that class.

term	class	differentiation
A formula is	a set of words	that indicates a procedure to be followed.

Formal definitions often include synonyms, so a formula may be defined as a "method" or a "procedure." Textbooks often include formal definitions to help students understand new terminology.

Another kind of definition is the **stipulative definition,** which states a particular, special way a term is being used. Writers who want to use a term in a way a reader might not expect can include a stipulative definition. For example, if you were writing an essay to convince the dean of student services to offer more night classes for adult learners, you might write something like this:

> By adult learner, I mean any student over twenty-five who has been out of school for at least five years. The adult learner typically works full-time and helps support a family.

You can use a stipulative definition to ensure that your reader understands precisely how you are using a term.

Sometimes you want to go beyond a word's literal dictionary meaning to explain the significance, associations, private meanings, and personal experiences associated with the word. This information can only come from an **extended definition,** the kind of essay this chapter treats. For example, consider the word *sled.* A dictionary will tell a reader that it is a vehicle on runners used for coasting on snow. However, an extended definition can tell the reader that a sled contributed to the happiest times you shared with your brother and father. Now consider the word *prejudice,* which can mean different things to different people. An extended definition allows you to explain the meaning and significance *you* ascribe to the word. Thus, an extended definition affords a writer the opportunity to go beyond the formal or stipulative meaning to express feelings, opinions, knowledge, unusual views, and personal experiences associated with a word.

---

www.mhhe.com/patterns

For more help with definition, click on
Writing > Paragraph Patterns
Writing > Writing Tutor: Definition

USING DEFINITION FOR A PURPOSE

More often than not, an extended definition *informs.* Sometimes you inform by clarifying something that is complex. For example, an essay that defines *freedom* can help the reader understand this very difficult concept. A definition can also inform by bringing the reader to a fresh appreciation of something familiar or taken for granted. For example, if you think that Americans do not sufficiently appreciate free speech, you could define *free speech* to help readers renew their appreciation for this important liberty. A definition can also bring a reader to an understanding of something unfamiliar. In "What Is Poverty?" (page 511), for example, the author defines poverty for an audience who has not experienced it and hence does not fully understand what it means.

In addition to informing, an extended definition can allow you to *express feelings and relate experiences.* For example, you could define *teenager* by explaining what your own teenage years were like and in this way relate part of your experience with adolescence.

A definition can also entertain, as when you write a humorous definition of *freshman*, to amuse your reader. Finally, an extended definition can serve a *persuasive* purpose, particularly when it points to a conclusion about a controversial issue. For example, Jo Goodwin Parker presents a powerful, graphic definition of *poverty* in "What Is Poverty?" in order to move the reader to take steps to end this social condition. Similarly, Judy Brady defines *wife* in "I Want a Wife" (page 502) to convince the reader that the traditional wifely role is unfair to women.

In addition to using definition to develop entire essays, you will often use this pattern with other methods of development. For example, if you classify kinds of folk art, you might first define what folk art is; if you provide examples of courage, you might begin with your personal definition of courage; and if you explain the causes and effects of anorexia nervosa, you will probably define anorexia nervosa early on.

Definition in College, at Work, and in the Community

College work requires you to learn the meaning of terms and concepts, and a good way to demonstrate your understanding of these terms and concepts is to write definitions. Sometimes these definitions will be extended, as when you define *existentialism* in a paper for a philosophy class or when you define *naturalism* for an essay for an American literature class. You might also write an extended definition of *natural selection* for a biology class, of *the enclosure movement* for an economics class, or of *cultural relativity* for an anthropology class.

Many times, you will incorporate formal definition with other patterns of development. For example, a history paper might require you to define the *chivalric code* and then go on to explain its effects. Similarly, a paper for an introductory to psychology course might require you to define and classify *defense mechanisms* and then go on to give examples of each kind.

Definition is an important part of college textbooks. Here is one example, taken from the introductory textbook *Sociology*.

> It is tempting to evaluate the practices of other cultures on the basis of our own perspectives. Sociologist William Graham Sumner (1906) coined the term *ethnocentrism* to refer to the tendency to assume that one's culture and way of life constitute the norm or are superior to all others. The ethnocentric person sees his or her own group as the center or defining point of culture and views all other cultures as deviations from what is "normal."
>
> Those westerners who are contemptuous of India's Hindu religion and culture because of its view of cattle as sacred are engaged in ethnocentrism. As another manifestation of ethnocentrism, people in one culture may dismiss as unthinkable the mate selection or child rearing practices of another culture . . . (Schaefer, *Sociology*).

To clarify unfamiliar terms and concepts, textbooks often follow definitions with examples. In the above excerpt, notice that the definition of ethnocentrism comes in the first paragraph and examples of ethnocentrism come in the second paragraph to help students grasp the concept and remember the definition.

On the job, definition is also important. A teacher might write a stipulative definition of "competency testing" in a memo to parents in order to help them understand how the tests are used in their children's classrooms. A dietician might write formal definitions of "good cholesterol" and "bad cholesterol" to help clients make better food choices. A human resources manager might combine formal, stipulative, and extended definitions of "mutual gains bargaining" to persuade a labor union to adopt this negotiating practice.

Outside the classroom, writers have many occasions to use definition. As editor of your religious congregation's newsletter, you might write an editorial that is an extended definition of *charity* to encourage congregants to give more generously. In a letter to the editor of your local newspaper, you might define *good citizen* to encourage readers to vote.

SUPPORTING DETAILS

In general, an extended definition presents the characteristics of what is being defined. Thus, to define *courage,* you might note that its characteristics include doing what needs to be done without regard to personal cost and even when afraid.

Often when you present the characteristics, you rely on other patterns. For example, if you define *sinus headache* to relate your own experiences with this misery, you could *describe* the pain. To define *math anxiety* to inform the reader of what this condition is like, part of your essay could *narrate* an account of a time you experienced this anxiety. To define a *good teacher* to inform your reader of what a teacher should be like, you could include examples of good teachers from your past. To define *maturity* to clarify this concept, you could include a *contrast* of maturity with immaturity. To define *sexual harassment* to convince people to take action against this practice, part of your piece could analyze the *causes and effects* of sexual harassment to show why it is such a problem.

Sometimes you should explain what your subject is *not,* especially if you need to correct a misconception. For example, if you were defining *poverty,* you could note that poverty is not necessarily something that people can escape if they just try hard enough.

When you write your definition, avoid stating the obvious, and avoid using a dictionary style unless you are writing a formal definition. If you state the obvious, you will bore your reader. Thus, if you are defining *mother,* you need not state that a mother is a female parent. Similarly, a dictionary style in an extended definition is likely to bore a reader because it is stiff and unlike your own natural style. Thus, avoid defining *teenager* as "a person in that developmental period of hormonal and social change marking the transition from childhood to adulthood."

Avoiding Circular Definitions

If you have trouble avoiding circular definitions, remember to avoid repeating the words you are defining or merely using synonyms for those words.

CIRCULAR   **Male liberation is the liberation of men.**

CIRCULAR   **Male liberation involves freeing men.**

BETTER   **Male liberation allows men to relinquish their historical roles to assume roles formerly held only by women.**

As you can see, circular definitions communicate very little, so they are not helpful.

ORGANIZING DETAILS

The thesis for an extended definition can state what will be defined and your assertion about what will be defined, like this:

> Adolescence is not the happy time many people remember it to be.

This thesis indicates you will define *adolescence* and show that it can be a difficult period.

You can also shape a thesis by noting what will be defined and why it is important to understand the term, like this:

> If we do not understand the meaning of free speech, we will be in danger of losing it.

To create interest in your essay, your introduction can explain the significance of the definition. Thus, if you are defining *homelessness*, you can note the extent of homelessness in this country to show why readers need to understand it. You can also tell a story related to what you are defining. In addition, if the meaning of your term has changed over the years, you can explain what your term used to mean before going on to give a current definition. For example, if you are defining *dating*, you could open by noting that dating used to mean sitting in the parlor with a girl's parents or attending a church social together.

Since definition often includes other patterns, the order of details will be influenced by these patterns. Thus, narrations will use chronological order, cause-and-effect analysis will reproduce causal chains, and so on. Purpose, too, can influence order. Thus, if your purpose is persuasive, you may want to place the characteristics of what you are defining in a progressive order to save the most important points for last.

VISUALIZING A DEFINITION ESSAY

The following chart can help you visualize the structure for a definition essay. Like all good models, however, this one can be altered as needed.

Introduction

- Creates interest in the essay, perhaps by explaining the significance of the definition, explaining how its meaning has changed over the years, or telling a story related to the term
- States the thesis, which can state what will be defined and your assertion about what will be defined or why it is important to understand the term

First Body Paragraph

- Gives and explains the first characteristic of the term
- May include any patterns of development
- May explain what the term is not
- Avoids stating the obvious, circular definitions, and dictionary style
- Arranges details according to the patterns used

Next Body Paragraph

- Gives and explains the next characteristic of the term
- May include any patterns of development
- May explain what the term is not
- Avoids stating the obvious, circular definitions, and dictionary style
- Arranges details according to the patterns used

Next Body Paragraphs

- Continue until all the characteristics are given and explained
- May include any patterns of development
- May explain what the term is not
- Avoids stating the obvious, circular definitions, and dictionary style
- Arranges details according to the patterns used

Conclusion

- Provides a satisfying finish
- Leaves the reader with a positive final impression

PROCESS GUIDELINES: STRATEGIES FOR WRITING DEFINITION

1. **Selecting a Topic.** Consider the roles you play in your life and the aspects of those roles. For example, if you are an athlete, you can define *student athlete* or *competition.* Or consider the emotions and moods you have experienced lately and define one of them: *love, anger, anxiety, anticipation, jealousy,* and so forth.

2. **Generating Ideas.** List all the characteristics of what you are defining. Then circle the ones you want to treat.

   a. For each circled characteristic, ask these questions:
   - Can I tell a story to reveal or illustrate the characteristic?
   - What examples illustrate the characteristic?
   - Can I describe the characteristic?
   - Can I compare or contrast the characteristic with something?
   - Can I explain how the characteristic works?
   - What are the causes and effects of the characteristic?

   b. Decide whether you need to clear up any reader misconceptions by explaining what your subject is not.

   c. Write a statement of the significance of your term and why it is important to define it. You can use a version of this statement in your introduction, as your thesis, or in your conclusion.

Checklist for Revising Definition

Be sure

_____ Your thesis notes what you are defining.

_____ You have avoided stating the obvious.

_____ You have avoided an inappropriate dictionary style.

_____ You have developed all the relevant characteristics of your term.

_____ You have used appropriate patterns of development and organized accordingly.

_____ You have explained what your term is *not,* as needed.

_____ You have stated or strongly implied the significance of your definition.

_____ You have avoided "is when" constructions and circular definitions.

Student writer Nick Hickman defines a technical term for a nontechnical reader in order to inform and—surprisingly—entertain. To address the needs of his audience, Nick uses process analysis, exemplification, and an image. After you read, you will have an opportunity to evaluate the essay.

Why Did the Chicken Cross the Möbius Strip?
(Or Babysitting for Dummies)

Paragraph 1
The introduction creates interest with a twist on a children's riddle. The thesis is the last two sentences. It combines a formal technical definition with the intriguing notion (that also creates interest) that the the Möbius strip is "seemingly impossible."

Ask anyone over the age of three why the chicken crossed the road, and you will immediately get the response: "to get to the other side." Ask the question in the title (Why did the chicken cross the Möbius strip?), and you will get a far different response: "What is a Möbius strip?" The answer is that the *Möbius strip* is an example of a nonorientable surface. It is a seemingly impossible object of great interest to mathematicians, yet a person can hold it in the palm of one hand.

Paragraph 2
The paragraph opens with a topic sentence that notes a necessary background definition will be given (of *surface*). The supporting details give a characteristic of the term being defined and explain the characteristic with examples.

To understand the Möbius strip, a person must know what a nonorientable surface is, which means first knowing the definition of a surface. Think of a *surface* as anything that can be created by taping together sheets of paper. The only restriction is that the sheets must be taped flat-side-to-flat side or edge-to-edge. In other words, long strips of paper are surfaces, and an L-shape made by two sheets taped at their edges is a surface. A cylinder can be thought of as a surface in two different ways—by putting two pieces of paper together or by connecting the opposite edges of one sheet. A person who gets really creative can even build a pair of pants or a shirt this way but not a set of bookshelves. Bookshelves cannot be a surface because the edges and back of each shelf make a T-shape with the outer casing.

Paragraph 3
The topic sentence is the last sentence. It notes that another background definition (*orientable surface*) is given. The supporting details give a characteristic of the term, which is explained with examples.

In addition to all of them being surfaces, a cylinder, a pair of pants, and a shirt have something else in common. They all have a clearly distinguishable inside and outside. That is, a person who touches a pair of pants with a finger can readily tell whether the outside or the inside of the object is being touched. The same is true for a tabletop, a drinking glass, or a funhouse mirror because all of these are surfaces with a well-defined front and back, inside and outside, or top and bottom. This is what it means to be an *orientable surface*.

Obviously, that means that a *nonorientable surface* must be a sur-4 face with only one side! Orientable surfaces are boring everyday objects—certainly no fun at parties—but a one-sided object could really be something to show off to a crowd!

The best way to demonstrate that a Möbius strip is a nonorientable 5 surface is to construct one. Take a standard pants belt, unbuckled. Bring the tip around toward the buckle, just as if you were putting the belt around your waist, but do not buckle it. Notice that if you buckled the belt normally it would clearly have two sides, an inside and an outside. Now take the tip and give it half a twist so the "inside" is facing out, and buckle it in this position. This is a Möbius strip, a one-sided surface right in your own home that looks like this:

To test for nonorientability, take your finger and place it by the 6 buckle. Now trace the belt around until it gets back to the buckle again. Your finger should be on the "other side" of the belt. Without lifting your finger, keep tracing. When you get back to the buckle a second time, your finger will have returned to the "correct side" of the belt. You have now touched every part of the surface, but you changed sides without lifting your finger!

To mathematicians, a nonorientable surface is a two-dimensional 7 manifold with no consistent choice of fundamental class in its second homology group. The Möbius strip, which was discovered by German mathematician August Ferdinand Möbius in 1868, can be thought of as one of two canonical vector bundles over the circle or as a topological quotient space of the closed unit square. At heart, though, a Möbius strip

Paragraph 4
This is a transitional paragraph, linking the definitions of orientable and nonorientable surfaces. Notice the touch of humor. How is it likely to appeal to the author's intended audience?

Paragraph 5
The paragraph opens with a topic sentence that notes the paragraph will be about how to make a Möbius strip. Knowing how to make the strip helps the reader understand its nature. The detail is process analysis.

The drawing helps the reader visualize the strip. How important is the drawing?

Paragraph 6
The process analysis further clarifies the nature of the term.

Paragraph 7
This paragraph contrasts a technical definition with a nontechnical one and brings the technical down to the everyday level for the average reader. Notice the energetic, nonscientific tone.

is just a twisted belt. Advanced abstract mathematics is actually that close to our boring everyday lives, and if you don't think a twisted belt is really all that exciting, give one to a child and explain how the finger-tracing works. Imagine a house cat trying to come to terms with a holo-gram of a mouse, and you will understand how the Möbius strip can be an amazing babysitting tool.

So, why did the chicken cross the Möbius strip? You should have 8 figured that out by now: to get to the same side.

Paragraph 8
The conclusion provides closure by connecting to the introduction and cleverly playing on the opening riddle.

PEER REVIEW

Responding to "Why Did the Chicken Cross the Möbius Strip? (Or Babysitting for Dummies)"

Evaluate "Why Did the Chicken Cross the Möbius Strip? (Or Babysitting for Dummies)" by responding to these questions:

1. Does the essay hold your interest? Why or why not?
2. Is the thesis effective? Why or why not?
3. Is there enough of the right kind of detail to define the term adequately? Explain.
4. Is the organization effective? Why or why not?
5. Is the drawing effective and helpful? Explain.
6. What do you like best about the essay?
7. What single change do you think would make the essay better?

- Why does The Statue of Liberty mean different things to different people?
- Why are recent immigrants, long-time citizens, those longing to move to the United States, and anti-American extremists likely to define the Statue differently?
- Select two of the above groups. How might their definitions of the Statue of Liberty differ?

BACKGROUND: Born in San Francisco in 1937, Judy Brady earned a degree in painting from the University of Iowa in 1962. She is a political activist, feminist, and freelance writer who has written on abortion, education, the labor movement, and the women's movement. In 1973, she traveled to Cuba to learn about the relationship between social class and change. Brady writes a column for the Women's Cancer Research Center and has also edited *Women and Cancer* (1990) and *One in Three: Women with Cancer Confront an Epidemic* (1991), a collection of writings by women. Involved in women's issues since 1969, Brady published "I Want a Wife" in 1972 for the first issue of *Ms.* magazine, and it quickly became a classic piece of satire.

www.mhhe.com/patterns

For more information on this author, go to

More resources > Chapter 11 > Judy Brady

THE PATTERN AND ITS PURPOSES: In "I Want a Wife," Judy Brady *defines* the traditional wifely role to **inform** the reader of its servile nature. While the typical reader of *Ms.* does not need to be persuaded of the fundamental injustice of that role, the essay also works to **persuade** other readers of that injustice.

I WANT A WIFE | JUDY BRADY

I belong to that classification of people known as wives. I am A Wife. And, not altogether incidentally, I am a mother.

2   Not too long ago a male friend appeared on the scene from the Midwest fresh from a recent divorce. He had one child, who is, of course, with his ex-wife. He is obviously looking for another wife. As I thought about him while I was ironing one evening, it suddenly occurred to me that I, too, would like to have a wife. Why do I want a wife?

As you read Decide whether much of what the author says is still true today.

3   I would like to go back to school so that I can become economically independent, support myself, and, if need be, support those dependent upon me. I want a wife who will work and send me to school. And while I am going to

"I want a wife who will work and send me to school."

school I want a wife to take care of my children. I want a wife to keep track of the children's doctor and dentist appointments. And to keep track of mine, too. I want a wife to make sure my children eat properly and are kept clean. I want a wife who will wash the children's clothes and keep them mended. I want a wife who is a good nurturant attendant to my children, arranges for their schooling, makes sure that they have an adequate social life with their peers, takes them to the park, the zoo, etc. I want a wife who takes care of the children when they are sick, a wife who arranges to be around when the children need special care, because, of course, I cannot miss classes at school. My wife must arrange to lose time at work and not lose the job. It may mean a small cut in my wife's income from time to time, but I guess I can tolerate that. Needless to say, my wife will arrange and pay for the care of the children while my wife is working.

4   I want a wife who will take care of *my* physical needs. I want a wife who will keep my house clean. A wife who will pick up after my children, a wife who will pick up after me. I want a wife who will keep my clothes clean, ironed, mended, replaced when need be, and who will see to it that my personal things are kept in their proper place so that I can find what I need the minute I need it. I want a wife who cooks the meals, a wife who is a *good* cook. I want a wife who will plan the menus, do the necessary grocery shopping, prepare the meals, serve them pleasantly, and then do the cleaning up while I do my studying. I want a wife who will care for me when I am sick and sympathize with my pain and loss of time from school. I want a wife to go along when our family takes a vacation so that someone can continue to care for me and my children when I need a rest and a change of scene.

> "I want a wife who will not bother me with rambling complaints about a wife's duties."

5   I want a wife who will not bother me with rambling complaints about a wife's duties. But I want a wife who will listen to me when I feel the need to explain a rather difficult point I have come across in my course of studies. And I want a wife who will type my papers for me when I have written them.

6   I want a wife who will take care of the details of my social life. When my wife and I are invited out by my friends, I want a wife who will take care of the babysitting arrangements. When I meet people at school that I like and want to entertain, I want a wife who will have the house clean, will prepare a special meal, serve it to me and my friends, and not interrupt when I talk about the things that interest me and my friends. I want a wife who will have arranged that the children are fed and ready for bed before my guests arrive so that the children do not bother us. I want a wife who takes care of the needs of my guests so that they feel comfortable, who makes sure that they have an ashtray, that they are passed the hors d'oeuvres, that they are offered a second helping of the food, that their wine glasses are replenished when necessary, that their coffee is served to them as they like it. And I want a wife who knows that sometimes I need a night out by myself.

7   I want a wife who is sensitive to my sexual needs, a wife who makes love passionately and eagerly when I feel like it, a wife who makes sure that I am satisfied. And, of course, I want a wife who will not demand sexual attention when I am not in the mood for it. I want a wife who assumes the complete responsibility for birth control, because I do not want more children. I want a wife who will remain sexually faithful to me so that I do not have to clutter up my intellectual life with jealousies. And I want a wife who understands that *my* sexual needs may entail more than strict adherence to monogamy. I must, after all, be able to relate to people as fully as possible.

8   If, by chance, I find another person more suitable as a wife than the wife I already have, I want the liberty to replace my present wife with another one. Naturally, I will expect a fresh, new life; my wife will take the children and be

solely responsible for them so that I am left free.

9   When I am through with school and have acquired a job, I want my wife to quit working and remain at home so that my wife can more fully and completely take care of a wife's duties.

10   My God, who *wouldn't* want a wife?

READING CLOSELY AND THINKING CRITICALLY

1.   What is Brady's attitude toward the wifely role she depicts in the essay?
2.   What view of men does Brady present in her essay? Do you think she is being fair to men? Explain.
3.   Why does Brady say she wants a wife? Does she imply more reasons than she gives? Explain.
4.   Can Brady be taken literally? That is, does she mean *exactly* what she says? Explain.

EXAMINING STRUCTURE AND STRATEGY

1.   Paragraphs 1 and 2 form the introduction of "I Want a Wife." What strategy does Brady use in that introduction?
2.   In your own words, state the thesis of "I Want a Wife."
3.   Brady uses classification and division to help develop her definition. (Classification and division, discussed in Chapter 10, sort items into categories and divide them into parts.) What categories does Brady establish for the wife's duties?
4.   Why does Brady open with a statement that she is a wife and mother?

CONSIDERING LANGUAGE AND STYLE

1.   Brady frequently repeats the words "I want." What is the effect of this repetition?
2.   A speaker or writer who asks a *rhetorical question* does not expect an answer. Brady closes "I Want a Wife" with a rhetorical question. Do you think it creates an effective conclusion? Explain.
3.   Consult a dictionary if you are unsure of the meaning of any of these words: *nurturant* (paragraph 3), *hors d'oeuvres* (paragraph 6), *entail* (paragraph 7), *monogamy* (paragraph 7).

FOR DISCUSSION IN CLASS OR ONLINE

Is "I Want a Wife" as relevant today as it was when it was first published in 1972? Explain. If your instructor directs you to do so, post your response to your class Web site.

1. **In your journal.** Write a description of the ideal spouse.
2. **Using definition for a purpose.** The purposes in the assignments are possibilities. You may establish whatever purposes you like, within your instructor's guidelines.

    *   Write an essay entitled "I Want a _____." Fill in the blank with some family role (husband, child, older brother, younger sister, mother, father, grandparent, and so on). To inform and persuade your reader that the role can be difficult, define that role and point out its difficulty and/or unfairness. If you like, you can borrow Brady's technique and repeat the words "I want a _____ who. . . ."
    *   To inform and perhaps persuade, define what you think the role of a *wife* should be. As an alternative, define what the role of *husband* should be.
    *   To inform and convince your reader that the role is unjust, define the role of someone who has traditionally been exploited, such as a table server, a babysitter, or a cleaning person.
    *   Write a definition of one of the roles you currently play or have played in the past: wife, husband, mother, father, child, friend, soldier, student, track star, musician, younger brother, older sister, student athlete, nontraditional student, international student, coach, and so on. Like Brady, let your definition convey how you feel about the role.

3. **Combining patterns.** Brady's definition of the ideal wife depicts a stereotype as it existed in 1972. Write your own definition of the ideal wife or husband to depict today's stereotype. Use cause-and-effect analysis (discussed in Chapter 9) to explain what factors are responsible for that stereotype (such as television, movies, the women's movement, or advertisements).

4. **Connecting the readings.** Compare and contrast the wife that Judy Brady depicts with Gretel Ehrlich, as she depicts herself in "Struck by Lightning" (page 141). Is either woman typical of women today?

5. **Drawing on sources.** In your library, examine the advertisements and articles in magazines from a specific decade of the twentieth century. Based on what you see, define the image of women in that decade.

BACKGROUND: Former contributing editor and economic policy correspondent to the *National Journal,* a nonpartisan journal on government and public policy, political writer and journalist Jonathan Rauch is currently the publication's opinion columnist. He is also a correspondent for *The Atlantic Monthly.* A 1982 graduate of Yale, Rauch writes on a range of topics, including American politics, economic issues, and animal rights. He has written for many periodicals, including London's *The Economist,* the *Winston-Salem* (North Carolina) *Journal,* and *The New Republic.* Rauch's books include *Kindly Inquisitors: The New Attacks on Free Thought* (1993), *Government's End: Why Washington Stopped Working* (1999), and *Gay Marriage: Why It Is Good for Gays, Good for Straights, and Good for America* (2004). "Caring for Your Introvert" first appeared in *The Atlantic Monthly* (2003).

COMBINED PATTERNS AND THEIR PURPOSES: In "Caring for Your Introvert," Jonathan Rauch combines a *definition* of *introvert* with *contrast* to **inform** readers of the characteristics of a little-understood personality type. In addition, Rauch works to **persuade** readers that although introverts are an oppressed group, they are superior to extroverts. You will, no doubt, notice elements of humor in the essay that **entertain** readers.

CARING FOR YOUR INTROVERT | JONATHAN RAUCH

Do you know someone who needs hours alone every day? Who loves quiet conversations about feelings or ideas, and can give a dynamite presentation to a big audience, but seems awkward in groups and maladroit at small talk? Who has to be dragged to parties and then needs the rest of the day to recuperate? Who growls or scowls or grunts or winces when accosted with pleasantries by people who are just trying to be nice?

As you read Consider why Rauch organizes part of his essay with a question-and-answer format.

2   If so, do you tell this person he is "too serious," or ask if he is okay? Regard him as aloof, arrogant, rude? Redouble your efforts to draw him out?

3   If you answered yes to these questions, chances are that you have an introvert on your hands—and that you aren't caring for him properly. Science has learned a good deal in recent years about the habits and requirements of introverts. It has even learned, by means of brain scans, that introverts process information differently from other people (I am not making this up). If you are behind the curve on this important matter, be reassured that you are not alone. Introverts may be common, but they are also among the most misunderstood and aggrieved groups in America, possibly the world.

> "My name is Jonathan, and I am an introvert."

4   I know. My name is Jonathan, and I am an introvert.

5   Oh, for years I denied it. After all, I have good social skills. I am not morose or misanthropic. Usually. I am far from shy. I love long conversations that explore intimate thoughts or passionate interests. But at last I have self-identified and come out to my friends and colleagues. In doing so, I have found myself liberated from any number of damaging misconceptions and stereotypes. Now I am here to tell you what you need to know in order to

respond sensitively and supportively to your own introverted family members, friends, and colleagues. Remember, someone you know, respect, and interact with every day is an introvert, and you are probably driving this person nuts. It pays to learn the warning signs.

What is introversion?

6   In its modern sense, the concept goes back to the 1920s and the psychologist Carl Jung. Today it is a mainstay of personality tests, including the widely used Myers-Briggs Type Indicator. Introverts are not necessarily shy. Shy people are anxious or frightened or self-excoriating in social settings; introverts generally are not. Introverts are also not misanthropic, though some of us do go along with Sartre[1] as far as to say "Hell is other people at breakfast." Rather, introverts are people who find other people tiring.

7   Extroverts are energized by people, and wilt or fade when alone. They often seem bored by themselves, in both senses of the expression. Leave an extrovert alone for two minutes and he will reach for his cell phone. In contrast, after an hour or two of being socially "on," we introverts need to turn off and recharge. My own formula is roughly two hours alone for every hour of socializing. This isn't antisocial. It isn't a sign of depression. It does not call for medication. For introverts, to be alone with our thoughts is as restorative as sleeping, as nourishing as eating. Our motto: "I'm okay, you're okay—in small doses."[2]

How many people are introverts?

8   I performed exhaustive research on this question, in the form of a quick Google search. The answer: About 25 percent. Or: Just under half. Or—my favorite—"a minority in the regular population but a majority in the gifted population."

Are introverts misunderstood?

9   Wildly. That, it appears, is our lot in life. "It is very difficult for an extrovert to understand an introvert," write the education experts Jill D. Burruss and Lisa Kaenzig. (They are also the source of the quotation in the previous paragraph.) Extroverts are easy for introverts to understand, because extroverts spend so much of their time working out who they are in voluble, and frequently inescapable, interaction with other people. They are as inscrutable as puppy dogs. But the street does not run both ways. Extroverts have little or no grasp of introversion. They assume that company, especially their own, is always welcome. They cannot imagine why someone would need to be alone; indeed, they often take umbrage at the suggestion. As often as I have tried to explain the matter to extroverts, I have never sensed that any of them really understood. They listen for a moment and then go back to barking and yipping.

Are introverts oppressed?

10   I would have to say so. For one thing, extroverts are overrepresented in politics, a profession in which only the

---

[1] Jean-Paul Satre (1905–1980), A French philosopher; "hell is other people" is a quotation from his 1947 play No Exit.

[2] I'm OK—You're ok (1967), a self-help book by Thomas Harris, M.D.

garrulous are really comfortable. Look at George W. Bush. Look at Bill Clinton. They seem to come fully to life only around other people. To think of the few introverts who did rise to the top in politics—Calvin Coolidge, Richard Nixon—is merely to drive home the point. With the possible exception of Ronald Reagan, whose fabled aloofness and privateness were probably signs of a deep introverted streak (many actors, I've read, are introverts, and many introverts, when socializing, feel like actors), introverts are not considered "naturals" in politics.

11   Extroverts therefore dominate public life. This is a pity. If we introverts ran the world, it would no doubt be a calmer, saner, more peaceful sort of place. As Coolidge is supposed to have said, "Don't you know that four fifths of all our troubles in this life would disappear if we would just sit down and keep still?" (He is also supposed to have said, "If you don't say anything, you won't be called on to repeat it." The only thing a true introvert dislikes more than talking about himself is repeating himself.)

12   With their endless appetite for talk and attention, extroverts also dominate social life, so they tend to set expectations. In our extrovertist society, being outgoing is considered normal and therefore desirable, a mark of happiness, confidence, leadership. Extroverts are seen as big-hearted, vibrant, warm, empathic. "People person" is a compliment. Introverts are described with words like "guarded," "loner," "reserved," "taciturn," "self-contained," "private"—narrow, ungenerous words, words that suggest emotional parsimony and smallness of personality. Female introverts, I suspect, must suffer especially. In certain circles, particularly in the Midwest, a man can still some-

times get away with being what they used to call a strong and silent type; introverted women, lacking that alternative, are even more likely than men to be perceived as timid, withdrawn, haughty.

Are introverts arrogant?

13   Hardly. I suppose this common misconception has to do with our being more intelligent, more reflective, more independent, more level-headed, more refined, and more sensitive than extroverts. Also, it is probably due to our lack of small talk, a lack that extroverts often mistake for disdain. We tend to think before talking, whereas extroverts tend to think *by* talking, which is why their meetings never last less than six hours. "Introverts," writes a perceptive fellow named Thomas P. Crouser, in an online review of a recent book called *Why Should Extroverts Make All the Money?* (I'm not making *that* up, either), "are driven to distraction by the semi-internal dialogue extroverts tend to conduct. Introverts don't outwardly complain, instead roll their eyes and silently curse the darkness." Just so.

14   The worst of it is that extroverts have no idea of the torment they put us through. Sometimes, as we gasp for air amid the fog of their 98-percent-content-free talk, we wonder if extroverts even bother to listen to themselves. Still, we endure stoically, because the etiquette books—written, no doubt, by extroverts—regard declining to banter as rude and gaps in conversation as awkward. We can only dream that someday, when our condition is more widely understood, when perhaps an Introverts' Rights movement has blossomed and borne fruit, it will not be impolite to say "I'm an introvert. You are a wonderful person and I like you. But now please shush."

How can I let the introvert in my life know that I support him and respect his choice?

15   First, recognize that it's not a choice. It's not a lifestyle. It's an *orientation*.

16   Second, when you see an introvert lost in thought, don't say "What's the matter?" or "Are you all right?"

17   Third, don't say anything else, either.

READING CLOSELY AND THINKING CRITICALLY

1.   Which sentence is the thesis of the essay?

2.   Why does Rauch want readers to understand what introverts are like? That is, what is the significance of the definition?

3.   Some of the essay is humorous, and some of the points are exaggerated. Cite one humorous detail and one exaggerated detail. Given the humor and exaggeration, how serious is Rauch?

4.   According to Rauch, what misconceptions do people have about introverts?

5.   Rauch says the fact that Calvin Coolidge and Richard Nixon were introverts helps make the point that introverts are not natural politicians. Explain what Rauch means.

EXAMINING STRUCTURE AND STRATEGY

1.   Why does Rauch open his essay with questions that include the characteristics of an introvert rather than state the introvert's characteristics in declarative sentences?

2.   Rauch cites scientific and other sources throughout the essay. (See, for example, paragraphs 3 and 6). How does this material help the author achieve his purpose?

3.   Why does Rauch use the question-and-answer format in paragraphs 6–15? Do you think this format provides an effective organizational structure? Explain.

4.   What techniques does Rauch use to create humor and entertain his reader?

NOTING COMBINED PATTERNS

1.   What is the purpose of the contrast in paragraphs 6 and 7?

2.   What is the purpose of the contrast in paragraphs 10–12?

3.   What is the purpose of the contrast in paragraph 13?

CONSIDERING LANGUAGE AND STYLE

1.   At times, Rauch uses exaggeration and mock seriousness. For example, in paragraph 3, he exaggerates by saying that introverts are one of the "most misunderstood and aggrieved groups in America, possibly the world." Cite three other examples of exaggeration or mock seriousness.

2. At times, Rauch adopts the language of sexual orientation. He even uses introversion as a metaphor for being gay. Cite two examples of this use of language.

3. Consult a dictionary if you are unsure of the meaning of these words: *maladroit* (paragraph 1), *misanthropic* (paragraph 5, 6), *self-excoriating* (paragraph 6), *garrulous* (paragraph 10), *parsimony* (paragraph 12).

FOR DISCUSSION IN CLASS OR ONLINE

Rauch says that extroverts "dominate public life" (paragraph 11). Is it possible for introverts to dominate public life? Why or why not? If your instructor directs you to do so, post your response to your class Web site.

WRITING ASSIGNMENTS

1. **In your journal.** In a page or so, explain whether you are an introvert or an extrovert. Cite examples to illustrate your characterization.

2. **Using definition for a purpose.** The purposes in the assignments are possibilities. You may establish whatever purposes you like, within your instructor's guidelines.
   - To inform and perhaps entertain, write your own definition of *introvert.*
   - To inform and perhaps entertain, define *extrovert.* You can also try to convince readers that extroverts are superior to introverts.
   - Rauch says that introverts are oppressed. To entertain your reader, define another such oppressed group, perhaps impulsive people, procrastinators, the fashion-challenged, or clumsy people.
   - In paragraph 12, Rauch says that "being outgoing is considered normal." To inform, and perhaps persuade or entertain, define *normal.*

3. **Combining patterns.** Define some characteristic or condition that you have, such as shyness, self-consciousness, attention deficit disorder, dyslexia, or hearing impairment. Using narration (explained in Chapter 5), tell one or more brief stories to illustrate how you are affected by the characteristic or condition.

4. **Connecting the readings.** In "Neat People vs. Sloppy People" (page 344), Suzanne Britt contrasts those who are neat and sloppy, and she argues that sloppy people are better than neat ones. Using the ideas in that essay along with those in "Caring for Your Introvert," explain the advantages of being either a sloppy extrovert or neat introvert.

5. **Drawing on sources.** Observe people in gatherings you are regularly a part of, such as those that occur in the classroom, at social functions with your friends, at the gym, in houses of worship, and in grocery stores. What differences do you notice between introverts and extroverts? Do you agree with Rauch's characterizations of introverts and extroverts? Do you agree with his conclusion that extroverts "dominate public life" (paragraph 11)? Support your responses with examples of the people you observe.

BACKGROUND: When University of Oklahoma professor George Henderson was gathering material for his book *America's Other Children: Public Schools Outside Suburbia* (1971), "What Is Poverty?" was mailed to him from West Virginia. Henderson, who included the essay in his book, says it was a speech delivered in De Land, Florida, in 1965. We do not know for sure whether Parker is writing of herself or acting as a spokesperson for others. Either way, her definition of poverty is so startlingly vivid that it has become a frequently reprinted example of definition.

COMBINED PATTERNS AND THEIR PURPOSES: In addition to **informing** her audience about the nature of poverty, Parker's *definition* works to **persuade** the reader to help solve the problem. As you read, you will notice a great deal of *description,* some *cause-and-effect analysis,* and *exemplification.*

What Is Poverty?

JO GOODWIN PARKER

You ask me what is poverty? Listen to me. Here I am, dirty, smelly, and with no "proper" underwear on and the stench of my rotting teeth near you. I will tell you. Listen to me. Listen without pity. I cannot use your pity. Listen with understanding. Put yourself in my dirty, worn out, ill-fitting shoes, and hear me.

As you read
Notice that many paragraphs begin "Poverty is ...." What effect does the repetition of those words have on you?

2   Poverty is getting up every morning from a dirt- and illness-stained mattress. The sheets have long since been used for diapers. Poverty is living in a smell that never leaves. This is a smell of urine, sour milk, and spoiling food sometimes joined with the strong smell of long-cooked onions. Onions are cheap. If you have smelled this smell, you did not know how it came. It is the smell of the outdoor privy. It is the smell of young children who cannot walk the long dark way in the night. It is the smell of the mattresses where years of "accidents" have happened. It is the smell of the milk which has gone sour because the refrigerator long has not worked, and it costs money to get it fixed. It is the smell of rotting garbage. I could bury it, but where is the shovel? Shovels cost money.

3   Poverty is being tired. I have always been tired. They told me at the hospital when the baby came that I had chronic anemia caused from poor diet, a bad case of worms, and that I needed a corrective operation. I listened politely—the poor are always polite. The poor always listen. They don't say that there is no money for iron pills, or better food, or worm medicine. The idea of an operation is frightening and costs so much that, if I had dared, I would have laughed. Who takes care of my children? Recovery from an operation takes a long time. I have three children. When I left them with "Granny" the last time I had a job, I came home to find the baby covered with fly specks, and a diaper that had not been changed since I left. When the dried diaper came off, bits of my baby's flesh came with it. My other child was playing with a sharp bit of broken glass, and my oldest was playing alone at the edge of a lake. I made twenty-two dollars a week, and a good nursery school costs twenty dollars a week for my three children. I quit my job.

4   Poverty is dirt. You say in your clean clothes coming from your clean house, "Anybody can be clean." Let me explain about housekeeping with no money. For

breakfast I give my children grits with no oleo[1] or cornbread without eggs and oleo. This does not use up many dishes. What dishes there are, I wash in cold water and with no soap. Even the cheapest soap has to be saved for the baby's diapers. Look at my hands, so cracked and red. Once I save for two months to buy a jar of Vaseline for my hands and the baby's diaper rash. When I had saved enough, I went to buy it and the price had gone up two cents. The baby and I suffered on. I have to decide every day if I can bear to put my cracked, sore hands into the cold water and strong soap. But you ask, why not hot water? Fuel costs money. If you have a wood fire it costs money. If you burn electricity, it costs money. Hot water is a luxury. I do not have luxuries. I know you will be surprised when I tell you how young I am. I look so much older. My back has been bent over the wash tubs for so long, I cannot remember when I ever did anything else. Every night I wash every stitch my school-age child has on and just hope her clothes will be dry by morning.

5   Poverty is staying up all night on cold nights to watch the fire, knowing one spark on the newspaper covering the walls means your sleeping children die in flames. In summer poverty is watching gnats and flies devour your baby's tears when he cries. The screens are torn and you pay so little rent you know they will never be fixed. Poverty means insects in your food, in your nose, in your eyes, and crawling over you when you sleep. Poverty is hoping it never rains because diapers won't dry when it rains and soon you are using newspapers. Poverty is seeing your children forever with runny noses. Paper handkerchiefs cost money and all your rags you need for other things. Even more costly are antihistamines. Poverty is cooking without food and cleaning without soap.

6   Poverty is asking for help. Have you ever had to ask for help, knowing your children will suffer unless you get it? Think about asking for a loan from a relative, if this is the only way you can imagine asking for help. I will tell you how it feels. You find out where the office is that you are supposed to visit. You circle that block four or five times. Thinking of your children, you go in. Everybody is very busy. Finally, someone comes out and you tell her that you need help. That never is the person you need to see. You go see another person, and after spilling the whole shame of your poverty all over the desk between you, you find that this isn't the right office after all—you must repeat the whole process, and it never is any easier at the next place.

7   You have asked for help, and after all it has a cost. You are again told to wait. You are told why, but you don't really hear because of the red cloud of shame and the rising black cloud of despair.

8   Poverty is remembering. It is remembering quitting school in junior high because "nice" children had been so cruel about my clothes and my smell. The attendance officer came. My mother told him I was pregnant. I wasn't but she thought that I could get a job and help out. I had jobs off and on, but never long enough to learn anything. Mostly I remember being married. I was so young then. I am still young. For a time, we had all the things you have. There was a little house

---

[1]Oleo is short for oleomargarine, more frequently abbreviated to margarine.

in another town, with hot water and everything. Then my husband lost his job. There was unemployment insurance for a while and what few jobs I could get. Soon, all our nice things were repossessed and we moved back here. I was pregnant then. This house didn't look so bad when we first moved in. Every week it gets worse. Nothing is ever fixed. We now had no money. There were a few odd jobs for my husband, but everything went for food then, as it does now. I don't know how we lived through three years and three babies, but we did. I'll tell you something, after the last baby I destroyed my marriage. It had been a good one, but could you keep on bringing children in this dirt? Did you ever think how much it costs for any kind of birth control? I knew my husband was leaving the day he left, but there were no good-byes between us. I hope he has been able to climb out of this mess somewhere. He never could hope with us to drag him down.

9   That's when I asked for help. When I got it, you know how much it was? It was, and is, seventy-eight dollars a month for the four of us; that is all I ever can get. Now you know why there is no soap, no needles and thread, no hot water, no aspirin, no worm medicine, no hand cream, no shampoo. None of these things forever and ever and ever. So that you can see clearly, I pay twenty dollars a month rent, and most of the rest goes for food. For grits and cornmeal, and rice and milk and beans. I try my best to use only the minimum electricity. If I use more, there is that much less for food.

10   Poverty is looking into a black future. Your children won't play with my boys. They will turn to other boys who steal to get what they want. I can already see them behind the bars of their prison instead of behind the bars of my poverty. Or they will turn to the freedom of alcohol or drugs, and find themselves enslaved. And my daughter? At best, there is for her life like mine.

11   But you say to me, there are schools. Yes, there are schools. My children have no extra books, no magazines, no extra pencils, or crayons, or paper and the most important of all, they do not have health. They have worms, they have infections, they have pink-eye all summer. They do not sleep well on the floor, or with me in my one bed. They do not suffer from hunger, my seventy-eight dollars keeps us alive, but they do suffer malnutrition. Oh yes, I do remember what I was taught about health in school. It doesn't do much good. In some places there is a surplus commodities program. Not here. The county said it cost too much. There is a school lunch program. But I have two children who will already be damaged by the time they get to school.

12   But, you say to me, there are health clinics. Yes, there are health clinics and they are in the towns. I live out here eight miles from town. I can walk that far (even if it is sixteen miles both ways), but can my little children? My neighbor will take me when he goes; but he expects to get paid, *one way or another*. I bet you know my neighbor. He is that large man who spends his time at the gas station, the barbershop, and the corner store complaining about the government spending money on the immoral mothers of illegitimate children.

13   Poverty is an acid that drips on pride until all pride is worn away. Poverty is a chisel that chips on honor until honor is worn away. Some of you say that you would do *something* in my situation, and maybe you would, for the first week or the first month, but for year after year?

14   Even the poor can dream. A dream of a time when there is money. Money for the right kinds of food, for worm medicine, for iron pills, for toothbrushes, for hand cream, for a hammer and nails and a bit of screening, for a shovel, for a bit of paint, for some sheeting, for needles and thread. Money to pay *in money* for a trip to town. And, oh, money for hot water and money for soap. A dream of when asking for help does not eat away the last bit of pride. When the office you visit is as nice as the offices of other governmental agencies, when there are enough workers to help you quickly, when workers do not quit in defeat and despair. When you have to tell your story to only one person, and that person can send you for other help and you don't have to prove your poverty over and over and over again.

15   I have come out of my despair to tell you this, Remember I did not come from another place or another time. Others like me are all around you. Look at us with an angry heart, anger that will help you help me. Anger that will let you tell of me. The poor are always silent. Can you be silent too?

READING CLOSELY AND THINKING CRITICALLY

1. According to Parker, what are the chief characteristics of poverty?

2. What are the effects of poverty on children?

3. According to the author, why doesn't education provide a way out of poverty for children?

4. In paragraphs 11, 12, and 13, Parker addresses people who say that schools, health clinics, and the poor themselves can help alleviate poverty. How does she counter the argument these people make? Why does she bother to address this argument?

5. Paragraph 8 describes a vicious cycle that is part of poverty. What other vicious cycles can you detect as a result of reading the essay?

6. Who do you think would make the best audience for "What Is Poverty?" Why?

EXAMINING STRUCTURE AND STRATEGY

1. "What Is Poverty?" was originally delivered as a speech. Is the opening question equally appropriate for speech and writing? Explain. What approach does Parker take to the rest of the introduction?

2. Parker addresses her audience directly with frequent use of "you." Why does she do so?

3. What approach does the author take to the conclusion?

NOTING COMBINED PATTERNS

1. Parker uses a great deal of description. Is this description objective or expressive? (See page 105 on objective and expressive details.) How does the descriptive detail help Parker achieve her purpose?

2. In which paragraph does Parker use examples? What do these examples contribute?
3. In which paragraph does Parker use cause-and-effect analysis? What does the analysis contribute?

CONSIDERING LANGUAGE AND STYLE

1. Many of Parker's paragraphs begin with the words "Poverty is . . ." Is this technique effective? Explain.
2. Consult a dictionary if you are unsure of the meaning of any of these words: *privy* (paragraph 2), *antihistamines* (paragraph 5), *repossessed* (paragraph 8).

FOR DISCUSSION IN CLASS OR ONLINE

Discuss your reactions to "What Is Poverty?" What does Parker do to cause your reaction? If your instructor directs you to do so, post your responses to your class Web site.

WRITING ASSIGNMENTS

1. **In your journal.** Compare and contrast your understanding of poverty before and after you read "What Is Poverty?" How has your understanding changed?
2. **Using definition for a purpose.** The purposes in the assignments are possibilities. You may establish whatever purposes you like, within your instructor's guidelines.
   - To relate your experience, inform, and persuade, define a social problem you have firsthand knowledge of, such as drug use, alcohol use, peer pressure, sexual harassment, or greed. Like Parker, try to arouse your audience to take action to help solve the problem.
   - To relate experience, express feelings, and inform, define a school problem, such as pressure for grades, cheating, competition, exam anxiety, or math anxiety. If you like, you can use description and exemplification, as Parker does.
   - To relate experience and express feelings, draw on personal experience to define one of the following: fear, ambition, pride, jealousy, satisfaction, depression, or serenity.
3. *Combining patterns.* Write a definition of wealth, drawing on description and exemplification to help make your points. If you like, you can also include cause-and-effect analysis.
4. **Connecting the readings.** Using information from "What Is Poverty?" and "Untouchables" (page 248), write an essay to persuade legislators to increase their effort to aid the poor and homeless.
5. **Drawing on sources.** Poverty is a problem both in the United States and worldwide. In an essay, define one aspect of poverty, such as hunger, despair, uncertainty, or chronic illness. Then go on to suggest something college students can do to help alleviate the problem. You can find information in your library by looking up the heading "poor" in the *Reader's Guide to Periodical Literature* or "poverty" in the *Social Sciences Index*. On the Internet, go to *http://www.worldbank.org/poverty,* or click on "people" and "poverty" at *http://www.census.gov.*

BACKGROUND: Born in 1963 in England to a Jamaican mother and an English father, Malcolm Gladwell grew up in Canada and graduated with a degree in history from the University of Toronto in 1984. He is a former business and science writer and New York City bureau chief for the *Washington Post*. Since 1996, he has been a staff writer for *The New Yorker* magazine. His *New Yorker* essays have been on a wide range of topics, including risk theory, the drop in New York City's crime rate in the 1990s, advertising for hair dye, a Chicago grandmother who seems to know everybody, and physical genius. His book *The Tipping Point: How Little Things Can Make a Difference* (2000) has been on both the *New York Times* best-seller list and the business best-seller list of *The Wall Street Journal*. His most recent book, *Blink* (2005), analyzes social intuition. "The Art of Failure" was originally published in *The New Yorker* in 2000.

COMBINED PATTERNS AND THEIR PURPOSE: In "The Art of Failure," Malcolm Gladwell *defines* several things, including panicking, choking, and stereotype threat. He ties the definitions together to **inform** the reader about why people—even ones who usually succeed—fail. To clarify his definitions, the author uses many patterns of development, including *narration*, *process analysis*, *comparison-contrast*, and *cause-and-effect analysis*.

THE ART OF FAILURE | MALCOLM GLADWELL

There was a moment, in the third and deciding set of the 1993 Wimbledon final, when Jana Novotna seemed invincible. She was leading 4–1 and serving at 40–30, meaning that she was one point from winning the game, and just five points from the most coveted championship in tennis. She had just hit a backhand to her opponent, Steffi Graf,

As you read Decide whether the distinction between panicking and choking is an important one.

"Jana Novotna seemed invincible."

that skimmed the net and landed so abruptly on the far side of the court that Graf could only watch, in flat-footed frustration. The stands at Center Court were packed. The Duke and Duchess of Kent were in their customary place in the royal box. Novotna was in white, poised and confident, her blond hair held back with a headband—and then something happened. She served the ball straight into the net. She stopped and steadied herself for the second serve—the toss, the

arch of the back—but this time it was worse. Her swing seemed halfhearted, all arm and no legs and torso. Double fault. On the next point, she was slow to react to a high shot by Graf, and badly missed on a forehand volley. At game point, she hit an overhead straight into the net. Instead of 5–1, it was now 4–2. Graf to serve: an easy victory, 4–3. Novotna to serve. She wasn't tossing the ball high enough. Her head was down. Her movements had slowed markedly. She double-faulted once, twice, three times. Pulled wide by a Graf forehand, Novotna inexplicably hit a low, flat shot directly at Graf, instead of a high crosscourt forehand that would have given her time to get back into position: 4–4. Did she suddenly realize how terrifyingly close she was to victory? Did she remember that she had never won a major tournament before? Did she look across the net and see Steffi Graf—Steffi Graf!—the greatest player of her generation?

2   On the baseline, awaiting Graf's serve, Novotna was now visibly agitated, rocking back and forth, jumping

up and down. She talked to herself under her breath. Her eyes darted around the court. Graf took the game at love; Novotna, moving as if in slow motion, did not win a single point: 5–4, Graf. On the sidelines, Novotna wiped her racquet and her face with a towel, and then each finger individually. It was her turn to serve. She missed a routine volley wide, shook her head, talked to herself. She missed her first serve, made the second, then, in the resulting rally, mis-hit a backhand so badly that it sailed off her racquet as if launched into flight. Novotna was unrecognizable, not an elite tennis player but a beginner again. She was crumbling under pressure, but exactly why was as baffling to her as it was to all those looking on. Isn't pressure supposed to bring out the best in us? We try harder. We concentrate harder. We get a boost of adrenaline. We care more about how well we perform. So what was happening to her?

3   At championship point, Novotna hit a low, cautious, and shallow lob to Graf. Graf answered with an unreturnable overhead smash, and, mercifully, it was over. Stunned, Novotna moved to the net. Graf kissed her twice. At the awards ceremony, the Duchess of Kent handed Novotna the runner-up's trophy, a small silver plate, and whispered something in her ear, and what Novotna had done finally caught up with her. There she was, sweaty and exhausted, looming over the delicate white-haired Duchess in her pearl necklace. The Duchess reached up and pulled her head down onto her shoulder, and Novotna started to sob.

4   Human beings sometimes falter under pressure. Pilots crash and divers drown. Under the glare of competition, basketball players cannot find the basket and golfers cannot find the pin. When that happens, we say variously that people have "panicked" or, to use the sports colloquialism, "choked." But what do those words mean? Both are pejoratives. To choke or panic is considered to be as bad as to quit. But are all forms of failure

> "To choke or to panic is considered to be as bad as to quit."

equal? And what do the forms in which we fail say about who we are and how we think? We live in an age obsessed with success, with documenting the myriad ways by which talented people overcome challenges and obstacles. There is as much to be learned, though, from documenting the myriad ways in which talented people sometimes fail.

5   "Choking" sounds like a vague and all-encompassing term, yet it describes a very specific kind of failure. For example, psychologists often use a primitive video game to test motor skills. They'll sit you in front of a computer with a screen that shows four boxes in a row, and a keyboard that has four corresponding buttons in a row. One at a time, x's start to appear in the boxes on the screen, and you are told that every time this happens you are to push the key corresponding to the box. According to Daniel Willingham, a psychologist at the University of Virginia, if you're told ahead of time about the pattern in which those x's will appear, your reaction time in hitting the right key will improve dramatically. You'll play the game very carefully for a few rounds, until you've learned the sequence, and then you'll get faster and faster. Willingham calls this "explicit learning." But suppose you're

not told that the x's appear in a regular sequence, and even after playing the game for a while you're not aware that there is a pattern. You'll *still* get faster: you'll learn the sequence unconsciously. Willingham calls that "implicit learning"—learning that takes place outside of awareness. These two learning systems are quite separate, based in different parts of the brain. Willingham says that when you are first taught something—say, how to hit a backhand or an overhead forehand—you think it through in a very deliberate, mechanical manner. But as you get better the implicit system takes over: you start to hit a backhand fluidly, without thinking. The basal ganglia, where implicit learning partially resides, are concerned with force and timing, and when that system kicks in you begin to develop touch and accuracy, the ability to hit a drop shot or place a serve at a hundred miles per hour. "This is something that is going to happen gradually," Willingham says. "You hit several thousand forehands, after a while you may still be attending to it. But not very much. In the end, you don't really notice what your hand is doing at all."

6   Under conditions of stress, however, the explicit system sometimes takes over. That's what it means to choke. When Jana Novotna faltered at Wimbledon, it was because she began thinking about her shots again. She lost her fluidity, her touch. She double-

"She lost her fluidity, her touch."

faulted on her serves and mis-hit her overheads, the shots that demand the greatest sensitivity in force and timing. She seemed like a different person—playing with the slow, cautious deliberation of a beginner—because, in a sense,

she *was* a beginner again: she was relying on a learning system that she hadn't used to hit serves and overhead forehands and volleys since she was first taught tennis, as a child. The same thing has happened to Chuck Knoblauch, the New York Yankees' second baseman, who inexplicably has had trouble throwing the ball to first base. Under the stress of playing in front of forty thousand fans at Yankee Stadium, Knoblauch finds himself reverting to explicit mode, throwing like a Little Leaguer again.

7   Panic is something else altogether. Consider the following account of a scuba-diving accident, recounted to me by Ephimia Morphew, a human-factors specialist at NASA: "It was an open-water certification dive, Monterey Bay, California, about ten years ago. I was nineteen. I'd been diving for two weeks. This was my first time in the open ocean without the instructor. Just my buddy and I. We had to go about forty feet down, to the bottom of the ocean, and do an exercise where we took our regulators out of our mouth, picked up a spare one that we had on our vest, and practiced breathing out of the spare. My buddy did hers. Then it was my turn. I removed my regulator. I lifted up my secondary regulator. I put it in my mouth, exhaled, to clear the lines, and then I inhaled, and, to my surprise, it was water. I inhaled water. Then the hose that connected that mouthpiece to my tank, my air source, came unlatched and air from the hose came exploding into my face.

8   "Right away, my hand reached out for my partner's air supply, as if I was going to rip it out. It was without thought. It was a physiological response. My eyes are seeing my hand do something irresponsible. I'm fighting with

myself. *Don't do it.* Then I searched my mind for what I could do. And nothing came to mind. All I could remember was one thing: If you can't take care of yourself, let your buddy take care of you. I let my hand fall back to my side, and I just stood there."

9   This is a textbook example of panic. In that moment, Morphew stopped thinking. She forgot that she had another source of air, one that worked perfectly well and that, moments before, she had taken out of her mouth. She forgot that her partner had a working air supply as well, which could easily be shared, and she forgot that grabbing her partner's regulator would imperil both of them. All she had was her most basic instinct: *get air.* Stress wipes out short-term memory. People with lots of experience tend

"Stress wipes out short-term memory."

not to panic, because when the stress suppresses their short-term memory they still have some residue of experience to draw on. But what did a novice like Morphew have? *I searched my mind for what I could do. And nothing came to mind.*

10   Panic also causes what psychologists call perceptual narrowing. In one study, from the early seventies, a group of subjects were asked to perform a visual-acuity task while undergoing what they thought was a sixty-foot dive in a pressure chamber. At the same time, they were asked to push a button whenever they saw a small light flash on and off in their peripheral vision. The subjects in the pressure chamber had much higher heart rates than the control group, indicating that they were under stress. That stress didn't affect their ac-

curacy at the visual-acuity task, but they were only half as good as the control group at picking up the peripheral light. "You tend to focus or obsess on one thing," Morphew says. "There's a famous airplane example, where the landing light went off, and the pilots had no way of knowing if the landing gear was down. The pilots were so focussed on that light that no one noticed the autopilot had been disengaged, and they crashed the plane." Morphew reached for her buddy's air supply because it was the only air supply she could see.

11   Panic, in this sense, is the opposite of choking. Choking is about thinking too much. Panic is about thinking too little. Choking is about loss of instinct. Panic is reversion to instinct. They may look the same, but they are worlds apart.

12   Why does this distinction matter? In some instances, it doesn't much. If you lose a close tennis match, it's of little moment whether you choked or panicked; either way, you lost. But there are clearly cases when *how* failure happens is central to understanding *why* failure happens.

13   Take the plane crash in which John F. Kennedy, Jr., was killed last summer. The details of the flight are well known. On a Friday evening last July, Kennedy took off with his wife and sister-in-law for Martha's Vineyard. The night was hazy, and Kennedy flew along the Connecticut coastline, using the trail of lights below him as a guide. At Westerly, Rhode Island, he left the shoreline, heading straight out over Rhode Island Sound, and at that point, apparently disoriented by the darkness and haze, he began a series of curious maneuvers: He banked his plane to the right, farther out into the ocean, and then to the left. He climbed and descended. He sped up and

slowed down. Just a few miles from his destination, Kennedy lost control of the plane, and it crashed into the ocean.

"Just a few miles from his destination, Kennedy lost control of the plane, and it crashed into the ocean."

14   Kennedy's mistake, in technical terms, was that he failed to keep his wings level. That was critical, because when a plane banks to one side it begins to turn and its wings lose some of their vertical lift. Left unchecked, this process accelerates. The angle of the bank increases, the turn gets sharper and sharper, and the plane starts to dive toward the ground in an ever-narrowing corkscrew. Pilots call this the graveyard spiral. And why didn't Kennedy stop the dive? Because, in times of low visibility and high stress, keeping your wings level—indeed, even knowing whether you are in a graveyard spiral—turns out to be surprisingly difficult. Kennedy failed under pressure.

15   Had Kennedy been flying during the day or with a clear moon, he would have been fine. If you are the pilot, looking straight ahead from the cockpit, the angle of your wings will be obvious from the straight line of the horizon in front of you. But when it's dark outside the horizon disappears. There is no external measure of the plane's bank. On the ground, we know whether we are level even when it's dark, because of the motion-sensing mechanisms in the inner ear. In a spiral dive, though, the effect of the plane's G-force on the inner ear means that the pilot *feels* perfectly level even if his plane is not. Similarly, when you are in a jetliner that is banking at thirty degrees after takeoff, the book on your neighbor's lap does not slide into your lap, nor will a pen on the floor roll toward the "down" side of the plane. The physics of flying is such that an airplane in the midst of a turn always feels perfectly level to someone inside the cabin.

16   This is a difficult notion, and to understand it I went flying with William Langewiesche, the author of a superb book on flying, "Inside the Sky." We met at San Jose Airport, in the jet center where the Silicon Valley billionaires keep their private planes. Langewiesche is a

"We met at San Jose Airport, in the jet center where the Silicon Valley billionaires keep their private planes."

rugged man in his forties, deeply tanned, and handsome in the way that pilots (at least since the movie "The Right Stuff") are supposed to be. We took off at dusk, heading out toward Monterey Bay, until we had left the lights of the coast behind and night had erased the horizon. Langewiesche let the plane bank gently to the left. He took his hands off the stick. The sky told me nothing now, so I concentrated on the instruments. The nose of the plane was dropping. The gyroscope told me that we were banking, first fifteen, then thirty, then forty-five degrees. "We're in a spiral dive," Langewiesche said calmly. Our airspeed was steadily accelerating, from a hundred and eighty to a hundred and ninety to two hundred knots. The needle on the altimeter was moving down. The plane was dropping like a stone, at three thousand feet per minute. I could hear, faintly, a slight increase in the hum of the engine, and the wind noise as we picked up speed. But if

Langwiesche and I had been talking I would have caught none of that. Had the cabin been unpressurized, my ears might have popped, particularly as we went into the steep part of the dive. But beyond that? Nothing at all. In a spiral dive, the G-load—the force of inertia—is normal. As Langewiesche puts it, the plane *likes* to spiral-dive. The total time elapsed since we started diving was no more than six or seven seconds. Suddenly, Langewiesche straightened the wings and pulled back on the stick to get the nose of the plane up, breaking out of the dive. Only now did I feel the full force of the G-load, pushing me back in my seat. "You feel no G-load in a bank," Langewiesche said. "There's nothing more confusing for the uninitiated."

17 I asked Langewiesche how much longer we could have fallen. "Within five seconds, we would have exceeded the limits of the airplane," he replied, by which he meant that the force of trying to pull out of the dive would have broken the plane into pieces. I looked away from the instruments and asked Langewiesche to spiral-dive again, this time without telling me. I sat and waited. I was about to tell Langewiesche that he could start diving anytime, when, suddenly, I was thrown back in my chair. "We just lost a thousand feet," he said.

18 This inability to sense, experientially, what your plane is doing is what makes night flying so stressful. And this was the stress that Kennedy must have felt when he turned out across the water at West-

"This inability to sense, experientially, what your plan is doing is what makes night flying so stressful."

erly, leaving the guiding lights of the Connecticut coastline behind him. A pilot who flew into Nantucket that night told the National Transportation Safety Board that when he descended over Martha's Vineyard he looked down and there was "nothing to see. There was no horizon and no light . . . I thought the island might [have] suffered a power failure." Kennedy was now blind, in every sense, and he must have known the danger he was in. He had very little experience in flying strictly by instruments. Most of the time when he had flown up to the Vineyard the horizon or lights had still been visible. That strange, final sequence of maneuvers was Kennedy's frantic search for a clearing in the haze. He was trying to pick up the lights of Martha's Vineyard, to restore the lost horizon. Between the lines of the National Transportation Safety Board's report on the crash, you can almost feel his desperation:

19 About 2138 the target began a right turn in a southerly direction. About 30 seconds later, the target stopped its descent at 2200 feet and began a climb that lasted another 30 seconds. During this period of time, the target stopped the turn, and the airspeed decreased to about 153 KIAS. About 2139, the target leveled off at 2500 feet and flew in a southeasterly direction. About 50 seconds later, the target entered a left turn and climbed to 2600 feet. As the target continued in the left turn, it began a descent that reached a rate of about 900 fpm.

20 But was he choking or panicking? Here the distinction between those two states is critical. Had he choked, he would have reverted to the mode of explicit

learning. His movements in the cockpit would have become markedly slower and less fluid. He would have gone back to the mechanical, self-conscious application of the lessons he had first received as a pilot—and that might have been a good thing. Kennedy *needed* to think, to concentrate on his instruments, to break away from the instinctive flying that served him when he had a visible horizon.

21   But instead, from all appearances, he panicked. At the moment when he needed to remember the lessons he had been taught about instrument flying, his mind—like Morphew's when she was underwater—must have gone blank. Instead of reviewing the instruments, he seems to have been focussed on one question: Where are the lights of Martha's Vineyard? His gyroscope and his other instruments may well have become as invisible as the peripheral lights in the underwater-panic experiments. He had fallen back on his instincts—on the way the plane *felt*—and in the dark, of course, instinct can tell you nothing. The N.T.S.B. report says that the last time the Piper's wings were level was seven seconds past 9:40, and the plane hit the water at about 9:41, so the critical period here was less than sixty seconds. At twenty-five seconds past the minute, the plane was tilted at an angle greater than forty-five degrees. Inside the cockpit it would have felt normal. At some point, Kennedy must have heard the rising wind outside, or the roar of the engine as it picked up speed. Again, relying on instinct, he might have pulled back on the stick, trying to raise the nose of the plane. But pulling back on the stick without first levelling the wings only makes the spiral tighter and the problem worse. It's also possible that Kennedy did nothing at all, and that he was frozen at the controls, still frantically searching for the lights of the Vineyard, when his plane hit the water. Sometimes pilots don't even try to make it out of a spiral dive. Langewiesche calls that "one G all the way down."

22   What happened to Kennedy that night illustrates a second major difference between panicking and choking. Panicking is conventional failure, of the sort we tacitly understand. Kennedy panicked because he didn't know enough about instrument flying. If he'd had another year in the air, he might not have panicked, and that fits with what we believe—that performance ought to improve with experience, and that pressure is an obstacle that the diligent can overcome. But choking makes little intuitive sense. Novotna's problem wasn't lack of diligence; she was as superbly conditioned and schooled as anyone on the tennis tour. And what did experience do for her? In 1995, in the third round of the French Open, Novotna choked even more spectacularly than she had against Graf, losing to Chanda Rubin after surrendering a 5–0 lead in the third set. There seems little doubt that part of the reason for her collapse against Rubin was her collapse against Graf—that the second failure built on the first, making it possible for her to be up 5–0 in the third set and yet entertain the thought *I can still lose*. If panicking is conventional failure, choking is paradoxical failure.

23   Claude Steele, a psychologist at Stanford University, and his colleagues have done a number of experiments in recent years looking at how certain groups perform under pressure, and their findings go to the heart of what is so strange about choking. Steele and Joshua Aronson found that when they gave a group of Stanford undergradu-

ates a standardized test and told them that it was a measure of their intellectual ability, the white students did much better than their black counterparts. But when the same test was presented simply as an abstract laboratory tool, with no relevance to ability, the scores of blacks and whites were virtually identical. Steele and Aronson attribute this disparity to what they call "stereotype threat": when black students are put into a situation where they are directly confronted with a stereotype about their group—in this case, one having to do with intelligence—the resulting pressure causes their performance to suffer.

24   Steele and others have found stereotype threat at work in any situation where groups are depicted in negative ways. Give a group of qualified women a math test and tell them it will measure their quantitative ability and they'll do much worse than equally skilled men will; present the same test simply as a research tool and they'll do just as well as the men. Or consider a handful of experiments conducted by one of Steele's former graduate students, Julio Garcia, a professor at Tufts University. Garcia gathered together a group of white, athletic students and had a white instructor lead them through a series of physical tests: to jump as high as they could, to do a standing broad jump, and to see how many pushups they could do in twenty seconds. The instructor then asked them to do the tests a second time, and, as you'd expect, Garcia found that the students did a little better on each of the tasks the second time around. Then Garcia ran a second group of students through the tests, this time replacing the instructor between the first and second trials with an African-American. Now the white students ceased to improve on their vertical leaps. He did the experiment again, only this time he replaced the white instructor with a black instructor who was much taller and heavier than the previous black instructor. In this trial, the white students actually jumped less high than they had the first time around. Their performance on the pushups, though, was unchanged in each of the conditions. There is no stereotype, after all, that suggests that whites can't do as many pushups as blacks. The task that was affected was the vertical leap, because of what our culture says: *white men can't jump.*

25   It doesn't come as news, of course, that black students aren't as good at test-taking as white students, or that white students aren't as good at jumping as black students. The problem is that we've always assumed that this kind of failure under pressure is panic. What is it we tell underperforming athletes and students? The same thing we tell novice pilots or scuba divers: to work harder, to buckle down, to take the tests of their ability more seriously. But Steele says that when you look at the way black or female students perform under stereotype threat you don't see the wild guessing of a panicked test taker. "What you tend to see is carefulness and second-guessing," he explains. "When you go and interview them, you have the sense that when they are in the stereotype-threat condition they say to themselves, 'Look, I'm going to be careful here. I'm not going to mess things up.' Then, after having decided to take that strategy, they calm down and go through the test. But that's not the way to succeed on a standardized test. The more you do that, the more you will get away from the intuitions that help you, the quick processing. They think they did well, and they are trying to do well. But

they are not." This is choking, not panicking. Garcia's athletes and Steele's students are like Novotna, not Kennedy. They failed because they were good at what they did: only those who care about how well they perform ever feel the pressure of stereotype threat. The usual prescription for failure—to work harder and take the test more seriously—would only make their problems worse.

26   That is a hard lesson to grasp, but harder still is the fact that choking requires us to concern ourselves less with the performer and more with the situation in which the performance occurs. Novotna herself could do nothing to prevent her collapse against Graf. The only thing that could have saved her is if—at that critical moment in the third set—the television cameras had been turned off, the Duke and Duchess had gone home, and the spectators had been told to wait outside. In sports, of course, you can't do that. Choking is a central part of the drama of athletic competition because the spectators *have* to be there—and the ability to overcome the pressure of the spectators is part of what it means to be a champion. But the same ruthless inflexibility need not govern the rest of our lives. We have to learn that sometimes a poor performance reflects not the innate ability of the performer but the complexion of the audience; and that sometimes a poor test score is the sign not of a poor student but of a good one.

27   Through the first three rounds of the 1996 Masters golf tournament, Greg Norman held a seemingly insurmountable lead over his nearest rival, the Englishman Nick Faldo. He was the best player in the world. His nickname was the Shark. He didn't saunter down the fairways; he stalked the course, blond and broad-shouldered, his caddy behind

him, struggling to keep up. But then came the ninth hole on the tournament's final day. Norman was paired with Faldo, and the two hit their first shots well. They were now facing the green. In front of the pin, there was a steep slope, so that any ball hit short would come rolling back down the hill into oblivion. Faldo shot first, and the ball landed safely long, well past the cup.

28   Norman was next. He stood over the ball. "The one thing you guard against here is short," the announcer said, stating the obvious. Norman swung and then froze, his club in midair, following the ball in flight. It was short. Norman watched, stone-faced, as the ball rolled thirty yards back down the hill, and with that error something inside of him broke.

29   At the tenth hole, he hooked the ball to the left, hit his third shot well past the cup, and missed a makable putt. At eleven, Norman had a three-and-a-half-foot putt for par—the kind he had been making all week. He shook out his hands and legs before grasping the club, trying to relax. He missed: his third straight bogey. At twelve, Norman hit the ball straight into the water. At thirteen, he hit it into a patch of pine needles. At sixteen, his movements were so mechanical and out of synch that, when he swung, his hips spun out ahead of his body and the ball sailed into another pond. At that, he took his club and made a frustrated scythelike motion through the grass, because what had been obvious for twenty minutes was now official: he had fumbled away the chance of a lifetime.

30   Faldo had begun the day six strokes behind Norman. By the time the two started their slow walk to the eighteenth hole, through the throng of spectators, Faldo had a four-stroke lead. But he took those final steps quietly, giving only the

smallest of nods, keeping his head low. He understood what had happened on the greens and fairways that day. And he was bound by the particular etiquette of choking, the understanding that what he had earned was something less than a victory and what Norman had suffered was something less than a defeat.

31   When it was all over, Faldo wrapped his arms around Norman. "I don't know what to say—I just want to give you a hug," he whispered, and then he said the only thing you can say to a choker. "I feel horrible about what happened. I'm so sorry." With that, the two men began to cry.

READING CLOSELY AND THINKING CRITICALLY

1.   What is implicit learning, and what is explicit learning?

2.   According to Gladwell, what is choking? What is panicking? How are choking and panicking alike, and how are they different?

3.   What caused Jana Novotna to choke at Wimbledon? What caused Ephimia Morphew to panic during her dive? How is Novotna's experience an example of choking? How is Morphew's experience an example of panicking?

4.   Gladwell says that it doesn't matter whether Novotna panicked or choked, but it *does* matter that John F. Kennedy, Jr., panicked rather than choked. Why does the distinction matter in one situation but not the other?

5.   What is stereotype threat, and how is it related to choking?

EXAMINING STRUCTURE AND STRATEGY

1.   How does Gladwell achieve transition between paragraphs 3 and 4? Between paragraphs 5 and 6? Between paragraphs 7 and 8? Between paragraphs 9 and 10? Between paragraphs 11 and 12? Between paragraphs 15 and 16?

2.   Where does Gladwell give the significance of his definitions of *choking* and *panic*?

3.   Why does Gladwell close his essay with the narration of what happened between Greg Norman and Nick Faldo?

NOTING COMBINED PATTERNS

1.   How does the comparison-contrast in paragraphs 5 and 11 help Gladwell achieve his purpose?

2.   How does the cause-and-effect analysis in paragraphs 6, 10, and 15 help Gladwell achieve his purpose?

3.   Gladwell includes a number of narrations for specific reasons. Explain the purpose of each of the following narrations, what concept each narration describes, and how each contributes to the definition:

    a. Jana Novotna's deciding set against Steffi Graf (paragraphs 1–3).

    b. Ephimia Morphew's diving experience (paragraphs 7–8).

    c. Gladwell's experience flying with Langewiesche (paragraphs 16–18).

    d. Greg Norman's experience at the 1996 Masters (paragraphs 27–31).

4. Gladwell includes process analysis in paragraph 5 and in paragraphs 14–15. How does that process analysis help him achieve his purpose?

CONSIDERING LANGUAGE AND STYLE

1. Gladwell often uses descriptive language. For example, in paragraph 1, he writes that Novotna "had just hit a backhand . . . that skimmed the net and landed so abruptly on the far side of the court that Graf could only watch, in flat-footed frustration." Cite three other examples of descriptive language. How does the description help Gladwell achieve his purpose?

2. A *rhetorical question* requires no answer from the reader or listener. Explain the purpose of the rhetorical questions in paragraphs 1, 2, and 4.

3. Consult a dictionary if you do not know the meaning of these words: *invincible* (paragraph 1), *coveted* (paragraph 1), *inexplicably* (paragraph 1), *colloquialism* (paragraph 4), *pejoratives* (paragraph 4), *myriad* (paragraph 4), *acuity* (paragraph 10), *inertia* (paragraph 16).

FOR DISCUSSION IN CLASS OR ONLINE

What implications does stereotype threat have for teachers? Should educators take specific steps to deal with stereotype threat? Explain. If your instructor directs you to do so, post your responses to your class Web site.

WRITING ASSIGNMENTS

1. **In your journal.** Write about a time when you choked or panicked. Does anything in the essay help you better understand your experience? Explain.

2. **Using definition for a purpose.** The purposes in the assignments are possibilities. You may establish whatever purposes you like, within your instructor's guidelines.

- To inform, define *failure*. Try to illustrate aspects of your definition with narrations.

- To inform, define *pressure* or *stress*. Try to illustrate aspects of your definition with narration.

- To inform and perhaps relate experience and express feelings, define *good sport*. Try to illustrate aspects of your definition with narration.

3. **Combining Patterns.** In paragraph 4, Gladwell says, "We live in an age obsessed with success. . . ." Define *success* and agree or disagree with Gladwell, using exemplification (explained in Chapter 6) to support your assertion.

4. **Connecting the readings.** The account of her struggle to stay alive in "Struck by Lightning" (page 141) shows that Gretel Ehrlich neither choked nor panicked. Contrast Ehrlich's actions with those of Novotna, Kennedy, Norman, or Morphew.

5. **Drawing on sources.** Read accounts of the death of John F. Kennedy, Jr., in four different newspapers, magazines, or online sources. Drawing on the accounts that you read for examples, define *responsible reporting*.

BACKGROUND: Born in 1928 in what is now part of Romania, Elie Wiesel is a survivor of the Holocaust, which claimed the lives of his parents and youngest sister. He was at both Auschwitz and Buchenwald concentration camps, experiences he has written and lectured on. When he was liberated from Buchenwald by Allied troops, Wiesel was taken to Paris, where he studied at the Sorbonne and worked as a journalist. His writings, although ultimately very successful, were initially met with skepticism because people resisted hearing the dark truths he tells. His frequent efforts to examine human suffering and injustice associated with the Holocaust won Wiesel the Nobel Peace Prize in 1986 and the Ellis Island Medal of Honor in 1992. Wiesel has written over 40 works of fiction and nonfiction, including *Night* (1958), a memoir of his experiences in the concentration camps; with John O'Connor, the late Roman Catholic Cardinal, *A Journey of Faith* (1990); *After the Darkness* (2002); and *Wise Men and Their Tales* (2003). Wiesel currently lives in New York City and is now a U.S. citizen. "To Be a Jew" is an excerpt from *A Jew Today* (1979).

www.mhhe.com/patterns

For more information on this author, go to

More resources > Chapter 11 > Elie Wiesel

COMBINED PATTERNS AND THEIR PURPOSES: In "To Be a Jew," Elie Wiesel combines *definition* with *narration* and *cause-and-effect analysis* to **inform** the reader of what it means to be a Jew and to **relate his experiences and express his feelings** as a Jew before and during the Holocaust.

To Be a Jew

ELIE WIESEL

Once upon a time, in a distant town surrounded by mountains, there lived a small Jewish boy who believed himself capable of seeing good in evil, of discovering dawn within dusk and, in general, of deciphering the symbols, both visible and invisible, lavished upon him by destiny.

As you read
Consider how
Wiesel feels
about being
Jewish.

2   To him, all things seemed simple and miraculous: life and death, love and hatred. On one side were the righteous, on the other the wicked. The just were always handsome and generous, the miscreants always ugly and cruel. And God in His heaven kept the accounts in a book only He could consult. In that book each people had its own page, and the Jewish people had the most beautiful page of all.

3   Naturally, this little boy felt at ease only among his own people, his own setting. Everything alien frightened me. And alien meant not Moslem or Hindu, but Christian. The priest dressed in black, the woodcutter and his ax, the teacher and his ruler, old peasant women crossing themselves as their husbands uttered oath upon oath, constables looking gruff and merely preoccupied—all of them exuded a hostility I understood and considered normal, and therefore without remedy.

4   I *understood* that all these people, young and old, rich and poor, powerful and oppressed, exploiters and exploited, should want my undoing, even my death. True,

we inhabited the same landscape, but that was yet another reason for them to hate me. Such is man's nature: he hates what disturbs him, what eludes him. We depended on the more or less unselfish tolerance of the "others," yet our life followed its own course independently of theirs, a fact they clearly resented. Our determination to maintain and enrich our separate history, our separate society, confused them as much as did that history itself. A living Jew, a believing Jew, proud of his faith, was for them a contradiction, a denial, an aberration. According to their calculations, this chosen and accursed people should long ago have ceased to haunt a mankind whose salvation was linked to the bloodstained symbol of the cross. They could not accept the idea of a Jew celebrating his Holy Days with song, just as they celebrated their own. That was inadmissible, illogical, even unjust. And the less they understood us, the more I understood them.

5   I felt no animosity. I did not even hate them at Christmas or Easter time when they imposed a climate of terror upon our frightened community. I told myself: They envy us, they persecute us because they envy us, and rightly so; surely *they* were the ones to be pitied. Their tormenting us was but an admission of weakness, of inner insecurity. If God's truth subsists on earth in the hearts of mortals, it is our doing. It is through us that God has chosen to manifest His will and outline His designs, and it is through us that He has chosen to sanctify His name. Were I in their place I, too, would feel rejected. How could they not be envious? In an odd way, the more they hunted me, the more I rationalized their behavior. Today I recognize my feelings for what they were: a mixture of pride, distrust and pity.

6   Yet I felt no curiosity. Not of any kind, or at any moment. We seemed to intrigue them, but they left me indifferent. I knew nothing of their catechism, and cared less. I made no attempt to comprehend the rites and canons of their faith. Their rituals held no interest for me; quite the contrary, I turned away from them. Whenever I met a priest I would avert my gaze and think of something else. Rather than walk in front of a church with its pointed and threatening belfry, I would cross the street. To see was as frightening as to be seen; I worried that a visual, physical link might somehow be created between us. So ignorant was I of their world that I had no idea that Judaism and Christianity claimed the same roots. Nor did I know that Christians who believe in the eternity and in the divinity of Christ also believe in those of God, *our* God. Though our universes existed side by side, I avoided penetrating theirs, whereas they sought to dominate ours by force. I had heard enough tales about the Crusades and the pogroms, and I had repeated enough litanies dedicated to their victims, to know where I stood. I had read and reread descriptions of what inquisitors, grand and small, had inflicted on Jews in Catholic kingdoms; how they had preached God's love to them even as they were leading them to the stake. All I knew of Christianity was its hate for my people. Christians were more present in my imagination than in my life. What did a Christian do when he was alone? What were his dreams made of? How did he use his time when he was not engaged in plotting against us? But none of this really troubled me. Beyond our immediate contacts, our public and hereditary confrontations, he simply did not exist.

7 My knowledge of the Jew, on the other hand, sprang from an inexhaustible source: the more I learned, the more I wanted to know. There was inside me a thirst for knowledge that was all-enveloping, all-pervasive, a veritable obsession.

8 I knew what it meant to be a Jew in day-to-day life as well as in the absolute. What was required was to obey the Law; thus one needed first to learn it, then to remember it. What was required was to love God and that which in His creation bears His seal. And His will would be done.

9 Abraham's covenant, Isaac's suspended sacrifice, Jacob's fiery dreams, the revelation at Sinai, the long march through the desert, Moses' blessings, the conquest of Canaan, the pilgrimages to the Temple in Jerusalem, Isaiah's and Habakkuk's beautiful but harsh words, Jeremiah's lamentations, the Talmudic legends: my head was abuzz with ancient memories and debates, with tales teeming with kings and prophets, tragedies and miracles. Every story contained victims, always victims, and survivors, always survivors. To be a Jew meant to live with memory.

10 Nothing could have been easier. One needed only to follow tradition, to reproduce the gestures and sounds transmitted through generations whose end product I was. On the morning of Shavuoth[1] there I was with Moses receiving the Law. On the eve of Tishah b'Av,[2] seated on the floor, my head covered with ashes, I wept, together with Rabbi Yohanan Ben Zakkai, over the destruction of the city that had been thought indestructible. During the week of Hanukkah,[3] I rushed to the aid of the Maccabees,[4] and on Purim,[5] I laughed, how I laughed, with Mordecai, celebrating his victory over Haman. And week after week, as we blessed the wine during Shabbat meals, I accompanied the Jews out of Egypt—yes, I was forever leaving Egypt, freeing myself from bondage. To be a Jew meant creating links, a network of continuity.

11 With the years I learned a more "sophisticated," more modern vocabulary. I was told that to be a Jew means to place the accent simultaneously and equally on verb and noun, on the secular and the eternal, to prevent the one from excluding the other or succeeding at the expense of the other. That it means to serve God by espousing man's cause, to plead for man while recognizing his need of God. And to opt for the Creator *and* His creation, refusing to pit one against the other.

12 Of course, man must interrogate God, as did Abraham; articulate his anger, as did Moses; and shout his sorrow, as did Job. But only the Jew opts for Abraham—who questions—*and* for God—who is questioned. He claims every role and assumes every destiny: he is both sum and synthesis.

13 I shall long, perhaps forever, remember my Master, the one with the yellowish beard, telling me, "Only the Jew knows that he may oppose God as long as he

---

[1]A festival celebrating the giving of the Ten Commandments.

[2]A Fast day in memory of the destruction of the First and Second Temples.

[3]A holiday celebrating the rededication of the Temple following the victory of the Maccabees over the Syrians.

[4]A group of Jewish leaders around 167–137 BC.

[5]A holiday celebrating the saving of Jews from destruction in Persia.

does so in defense of His creation." Another time he told me, "God gave the Law, but it is up to man to interpret It—and his interpretation is binding on God and commits Him."

14 Surely this is an idealized concept of the Jew. And of man. And yet it is one that is tested every day, at every moment, in every circumstance.

15 At school I read in the Talmud:[6] Why did God create only one man? The answer: All men have the same ancestor. So that no man, later, could claim superiority over another.

16 And also: A criminal who sets fire to the Temple, the most sacred, the most revered edifice in the world, is punishable with only thirty-nine lashes of the whip; let a fanatic kill him and *his* punishment would be death. For all the temples and all the sanctuaries are not worth the life of a single human being, be he arsonist, profanator, enemy of God and shame of God.

17 Painful irony: We were chased from country to country, our Houses of Study were burned, our sages assassinated, our schoolchildren massacred, and still we went on tirelessly, fiercely, praising the inviolate sanctity of life and proclaiming faith in man, any man.

18 An extraordinary contradiction? Perhaps. But to be a Jew is precisely to reveal oneself within one's contradictions by accepting them. It means safeguarding one's past at a time when mankind aspires only to conquer the future; it means observing Shabbat when the official day of rest is Sunday or Friday; it means fervently exploring the Talmud, with its seemingly antiquated laws and discussions, while outside, not two steps away from the hedel[7] or the yeshiva[8] one's friends and parents are rounded up or beaten in a pogrom; it means asserting the right of spirituality in a world that denies spirituality; it means singing and singing again, louder and louder, when all around everything heralds the end of the world, the end of man.

19 All this was really so. The small Jewish boy is telling only what he heard and saw, what he lived himself, long ago. He vouches for its truth.

20 Yes, long ago in distant places it all seemed so simple to me, so real, so throbbing with truth. Like God, I looked at the world and found it good, fertile, full of meaning. Even in exile, every creature was in its place and every encounter was charged with promise. And with the advent of Shabbat, the town changed into a kingdom whose madmen and beggars became the princes of Shabbat.

21 I shall never forget Shabbat in my town. When I shall have forgotten everything else, my memory will still retain the atmosphere of holiday, of serenity pervading even the poorest houses: the white tablecloth, the candles, the meticulously combed little girls, the men on their way to synagogue. When my town shall fade into the abyss of time, I will continue to remember the light and the warmth it radiated on Shabbat. The exalting prayers, the wordless songs of the Hasidim,[8] the fire and radiance of their Masters.

---

[6]A collection of Jewish law.

[7]Both the hedel and the yeshiva are Jewish schools.

[8]Members of a Jewish sect founded in the eighteen century that emphasizes religious zeal, mysticism, and joy.

22   On that day of days, past and future suffering and anguish faded into the distance. Appeased man called on the divine presence to express his gratitude.

23   The jealousies and grudges, the petty rancors between neighbors could wait. As could the debts and worries, the dangers. Everything could wait. As it enveloped the universe, the Shabbat conferred on it a dimension of peace, and aura of love.

24   Those who were hungry came and ate; and those who felt abandoned seized the outstretched hand; and those who were alone, and those who were sad, the strangers, the refugees, the wanderers, as they left the synagogue were invited to share the meal in any home; and the grieving were urged to contain their tears and come draw on the collective joy of Shabbat.

25   The difference between us and the others? The others, how I pitied them. They did not even know what they were missing; they were unmoved by the beauty, the eternal splendor of Shabbat.

26   And then came the Holocaust, which shook history and by its dimensions and goals marked the end of a civilization. Concentration-camp man discovered the anti-savior.

27   We became witnesses to a huge simplification. On the one side there were the executioners and on the other the victims. What about the onlookers, those who remained neutral, those who served the executioner simply by not interfering? To be a Jew then meant to fight both the complacency of the neutral and the hate of the killers. And to resist—in any way, with any means. And not only with weapons. The Jew who refused death, who refused to believe in death, who chose to marry in the ghetto, to circumcise his son, to teach him the sacred language, to bind him to the threatened and weakened lineage of Israel—that Jew was resisting. The professor or shopkeeper who disregarded facts and warnings and clung to illusion, refusing to admit that people could so succumb to degradation—he, too, was resisting. There was no essential difference between the Warsaw ghetto fighters and the old men getting off the train in Treblinka[9] because they were Jewish, they were all doomed to hate, and death.

28   In those days, more than ever, to be Jewish signified *refusal*. Above all, it was a refusal to see reality and life through the enemy's eyes—a refusal to resemble him, to grant him that victory, too.

29   Yet his victory seemed solid and, in the beginning, definitive. All those uprooted communities, ravaged and dissolved in smoke; all those trains that crossed the nocturnal Polish landscapes; all those men, all those women, stripped of their language, their names, their faces, compelled to live and die according to the laws of the enemy, in anonymity and darkness. All those kingdoms of barbed wire where everyone looked alike and all words carried the same weight. Day followed day and hour followed hour, while thoughts, numb and bleak, groped their way among the corpses, through the mire and the blood.

30   And the adolescent in me, yearning for faith, questioned: Where was God in all this? Was this another test, one more? Or a punishment? And if so, for what sins?

---

[9]A concentration camp in Poland.

What crimes were being punished? Was there a misdeed that deserved so many mass graves? Would it ever again be possible to speak of justice, of truth, of divine charity, after the murder of one million Jewish children?

31   I did not understand, I was afraid to understand. Was this the end of the Jewish people, or the end perhaps of the human adventure? Surely it was the end of an era, the end of a world. That I knew, that was all I knew.

32   As for the rest, I accumulated uncertainties. The faith of some, the lack of faith of others added to my perplexity. How could one believe, how could one not believe, in God as one faced those mountains of ashes? Who would symbolize the concentration-camp experience—the killer or the victim? Their confrontation was so striking, so gigantic that it had to include a metaphysical, ontological aspect: would we ever penetrate its mystery?

33   Questions, doubts. I moved through the fog like a sleepwalker. Why did the God of Israel manifest such hostility toward the descendants of Israel? I did not know. Why did free men, liberals and humanists, remain untouched by Jewish suffering? I did not know.

34   I remember the midnight arrival at Birkenau. Shouts. Dogs barking. Families together for the last time, families about to be torn asunder. A young Jewish boy walks at his father's side in the convoy of men; they walk and they walk and night walks with them toward a place spewing monstrous flames, flames devouring the sky. Suddenly an inmate crosses the ranks and explains to the men what they are seeing, the truth of the night: the future, the absence of future; the key to the secret, the power of evil. As he speaks, the young boy touches his father's arm as though to reassure him, and whispers, "This is impossible, isn't it? Don't listen to what he is telling us, he only wants to frighten us. What he says is impossible, unthinkable, it is all part of another age, the Middle Ages, not the twentieth century, not modern history. The world, Father, the civilized world would not allow such things to happen."

35   And yet the civilized world did know, and remained silent. Where was man in all this? And culture, how did it reach this nadir? All those spiritual leaders, those thinkers, those philosophers enamored of truth, those moralists drunk with justice—how was one to reconcile their teachings with Josef Mengele,[10] the great master of selections in Auschwitz? I told myself that a grave, a horrible error had been committed somewhere—only, I knew neither its nature nor its author. When and where had history taken so bad a turn?

36   I remember the words of a young Talmudist whose face was that of an old man. He and I worked as a team, carrying boulders weighing more than the two of us.

37   "Let us suppose," he whispered, "let us suppose that our people had not transmitted the Law to other nations. Let us forget Abraham and his example, Moses and his justice, the prophets and their message. Let us suppose that our contributions to philosophy, to science, to literature are negligible or even nonexistent. Maimonides, Nahmanides, Rashi: nothing. Spinoza, Bergson, Einstein, Freud: nothing. Let us suppose that we have in no way added to progress, to the well-being of

---

[10]A Nazi doctor who performed hideous experiments on concentration camp inmates at Auschwitz, another concentration camp in Poland.

mankind. One thing cannot be contested: the great killers, history's great assassins—Pharaoh, Nero, Chmelnitzky, Hitler—not one was formed in our midst "

38   Which brings us back to where we started: to the relations between Jews and Christians, which, of course, we had been forced to revise. For we have been struck by a harsh truth: in Auschwitz all the Jews were victims, all the killers were Christian.

39   I mention this here neither to score points nor to embarrass anyone. I believe that no religion, people or nation is inferior or superior to another; I dislike facile triumphalism, for us and for others. I dislike self-righteousness. And I feel closer to certain Christians—as long as they do not try to convert me to their faith—than to certain Jews. I felt closer to John XXIII and to Francois Mauriac[11] than to self-hating Jews. I have more in common with an authentic and tolerant Christian than with a Jew who is neither authentic nor tolerant. I stress this because what I am about to say will surely hurt my Christian friends. Yet I have no right to hold back.

40   How is one to explain that neither Hitler nor Himmler was ever excommunicated by the church? That Pius XII never thought it necessary, not to say indispensable, to condemn Auschwitz and Treblinka? That among the S.S. a large proportion were believers who remained faithful to their Christian ties to the end? That there were killers who went to confession between massacres? And that they all came from Christian families and had received a Christian education?

41   In Poland, a stronghold of Christianity, it often happened that Jews who had escaped from the ghettos returned inside their walls, so hostile did they find the outside world; they feared the Poles as much as the Germans. This was also true in Lithuania, in the Ukraine, in White Russia and in Hungary. How is one to explain the passivity of the population as it watched the persecution of its Jews? How explain the cruelty of the killers? How explain that the Christian in them did not make their arms tremble as they shot at children or their conscience bridle as they shoved their naked, beaten victims into the factories of death? Of course, here and there, brave Christians came to the aid of Jews, but they were few: several dozen bishops and priests, a few hundred men and women in all of Europe.

42   It is a painful statement to make, but we cannot ignore it: as surely as the victims are a problem for the Jews, the killers are a problem for the Christians.

43   Yes, the victims remain a serious and troubling problem for us. No use covering it up. What was there about the Jew that he could be reduced so quickly, so easily to the status of victim? I have read all the answers, all the explanations. They are all inadequate. It is difficult to imagine the silent processions marching toward the pits. And the crowds that let themselves be duped. And the condemned who, inside the sealed wagons and sometimes on the very ramp at Birkenau, continued not to see. I do not understand. I understand neither the killers nor the victims.

44   To be a Jew during the Holocaust may have meant not to understand. Having rejected murder as a means of survival and death as a solution, men and women agreed to live and die without understanding.

---

[11]A French novelist whose work explored the conflict between human behavior and religious ideals.

45 For the survivor, the question presented itself differently: to remain or not to remain a Jew. I remember our tumultuous, anguished debates in France after the liberation. Should one leave for Palestine and fight in the name of Jewish nationalism, or should one, on the contrary, join the Communist movement and promulgate the ideal of internationalism? Should one delve deeper into tradition, or turn one's back on it? The options were extreme: total commitment or total alienation, unconditional loyalty or repudiation. There was no returning to the earlier ways and principles. The Jew could say: I have suffered, I have been made to suffer, all I can do is draw closer to my own people. And that was understandable. Or else: I have suffered too much, I have no strength left, I withdraw, I do not wish my children to inherit this suffering. And that, too, was understandable.

46 And yet, as in the past, the ordeal brought not a decline but a renascence of Jewish consciousness and a flourishing of Jewish history. Rather than break his ties, the Jew strengthened them. Auschwitz made him stronger. Even he among us who espouses so-called universal causes outside his community is motivated by the Jew in him trying to reform man even as he despairs of mankind. Though he may be in a position to become something else, the Jew remains a Jew.

47 Throughout a world in flux, young Jews, speaking every tongue, products of every social class, join in the adventure that Judaism represents for them, a phenomenon that reached its apex in Israel and Soviet Russia. Following different roads, these pilgrims take part in the same project and express the same defiance: "They want us to founder, but we will let our joy explode; they want to make us hard, closed to solidarity and love, well, we will be obstinate but filled with compassion." This is the challenge that justifies the hopes the Jew places in Judaism and explains the singular marks he leaves on his destiny.

48 Thus there would seem to be more than one way for the Jew to assume his condition. There is a time to question oneself and a time to act; there is a time to tell stories and a time to pray; there is a time to build and a time to rebuild. Whatever he chooses to do, the Jew becomes a spokesman for all Jews, dead and yet to be born, for all the beings who live through him and inside him.

49 His mission was never to make the world Jewish but, rather, to make it more human.

READING CLOSELY AND THINKING CRITICALLY

1. Make a list of words and phrases that describe Wiesel as a boy.
2. How does Wiesel say his non-Jewish neighbors viewed him? Why did they view him that way? Was Wiesel troubled by the view? Explain.
3. According to Wiesel's definition, what are the characteristics of a Jew?
4. Wiesel says that to be a Jew is "to live with memory" (paragraph 9). What do you think Wiesel means?
5. Why was Shabbat (Sabbath) so important to Wiesel when he was a boy?

6. For what kind of audience is "To Be a Jew" well suited? Do you think the intended audience is non-Jewish? Explain.

7. Using the evidence in the essay, explain how Wiesel feels about being Jewish.

EXAMINING STRUCTURE AND STRATEGY

1. What is the effect of the dialogue in paragraph 34?

2. Like transitional words and phrases, transitional paragraphs connect ideas to move the reader smoothly from the discussion of one point to a discussion of the next. Which paragraphs are transitional paragraphs, and what ideas do they connect?

3. Wiesel often asks questions in the essay. What purposes do these questions serve? Are they an effective strategy? Explain.

NOTING COMBINED PATTERNS

1. Wiesel narrates an account of his childhood, he provides a definition of a Jew, and he gives an account of the Holocaust. How do these elements relate to each other? That is, how is it possible to include all three in the same essay?

2. What cause-and-effect analysis does Wiesel include in the essay?

CONSIDERING LANGUAGE AND STYLE

1. Why does Wiesel switch from the third person pronouns *he/him* in paragraphs 1 and 2 to the first person pronouns *I/me* in paragraph 3? Is the switch a problem for you? Explain.

2. "To Be a Jew" includes many historical and religious references some readers may not be familiar with. Are these references too obscure? Explain.

3. Consult a dictionary if you are unfamiliar with any of these words: *miscreants* (paragraph 2), *catechism* (paragraph 6), *canons* (paragraph 6), *pogroms* (paragraph 6), *inquisitors* (paragraph 6), *Talmud* (paragraph 9), *espousing* (paragraph 11), *Hasidim* (paragraph 21), *metaphysical* (paragraph 32), *ontological* (paragraph 32), *nadir* (paragraph 35), *excommunicated* (paragraph 40), *promulgate* (paragraph 45), *renascence* (paragraph 46).

FOR DISCUSSION IN CLASS OR ONLINE

Wiesel points out a number of contradictions. For example, he notes that Christians and Jews of his childhood believed in the same God, but they lacked knowledge of each other. What other contradictions are noted, and what is their significance? If your instructor directs you to do so, post your response to your class Web site.

WRITING ASSIGNMENTS

1. **In your journal.** In a page or two, tell what you know about the Holocaust and how you came to know it.

2. **Using definition for a purpose.** The purposes in the assignments are possibilities. You may establish whatever purposes you like, within your instructor's guidelines.

- Write a definition with the title "To Be a _____." (Fill in the blank with a noun that indicates your religious affiliation.) Like Wiesel, use definition to inform readers of the chief characteristics of a person with the affiliation. As an alternative, write an essay with the title "To Be an Atheist" or "To Be an Agnostic."

- To inform readers and express your feelings, define *Sabbath* or another religious day or ceremony, such as confirmation, Ramadan, Holy Communion, Easter, or Chanukah. Include the chief characteristics of the event, including how it is celebrated and its significance to you.

- In paragraph 32, Wiesel writes about faith. To express your feelings and perhaps inform, define *faith*.

- In paragraph 49, Wiesel says that a Jew's mission is "to make [the world] more human." To inform, write a definition that explains what it means to be "human." You may also work to persuade readers to behave in ways that are more human.

3. **Combining patterns.** Each year, Jews commemorate the Holocaust, its victims, and survivors, with a day of remembrance called Yom Hashoah. If a Holocaust remembrance day were to become a national day of observance, how do you think it should be observed? Define "day of remembrance" and write a process analysis (explained in Chapter 7) that explains how to observe the day. As an alternative write a process analysis that explains how another event should be remembered or celebrated.

4. **Connecting the readings.** Write an essay that explains what a single individual can do to help make the world "more human" (paragraph 49). The ideas in "To Be a Jew," "Untouchables" (page 248), and "What Is Poverty?" (page 511) may help you.

5. **Drawing on sources.** Write a definition of the *Holocaust* and explain whether or not you think high schools should include courses that study it. For information, look up *Holocaust* in *Social Sciences Index* and *Education Index,* or on the Internet go to the United States Holocaust Memorial Museum site at *www.ushmm.org.*

BACKGROUND: El Paso, Texas, native Pat Mora was born in 1942. Both sets of her grand-parents left Mexico for El Paso to escape the turmoil of the Mexican revolution of the early twentieth century. Mora earned her M.A. from the University of Texas at El Paso and then became a teacher, a college administrator, and a public radio host for a show called "Voices: The Mexican-American in Perspective." Her many awards include a Kellogg National Fellowship to study ways of pre-serving cultures and a National Endowment for the Arts Fellowship. A prolific author of children's stories, poetry, and essays, Mora often bases her material on family members and personal expe-rience. Much of her poetry treats her Chicana heritage and Southwestern experience. Of her work, the *El Paso Herald Post* says, "Mora's poems reflect vividly the Mexican-American culture and life in the Southwest. Pat Mora can evoke the desert and its features and creatures better than any other poet." Mora's children's books include *A Birthday Basket for Tia* (1992) and *Pablo's Tree* (1994). Her poetry collections include *Borders* (1986), in which "Immigrants" appears, *Chants* (1994), and *My Own True Name* (2000).

COMBINED PATTERNS AND THEIR PURPOSES: In "Immigrants," Pat Mora *defines* Americans from the perspective of people new to the United States. She also explains a *process* some immigrants employ to help their children assimilate into American cul-ture. While the poem **informs,** Mora also uses it to **express her feelings** about assimilation and conformity.

Immigrants
PAT MORA

As you read
Try to determine how Mora feels about assimilation and conformity.

wrap their babies in the American flag,
feed them mashed hot dogs and apple pie,
name them Bill and Daisy,
buy them blonde dolls that blink blue
eyes or a football and tiny cleats
before the baby can even walk,
speak to them in thick English,
    hallo, babee, hallo,
whisper in Spanish or Polish
when the babies sleep, whisper
in a dark parent bed, that dark
parent fear, "Will they like
our boy, our girl, our fine american
boy, our fine american girl?"

CONSIDERING THE POEM

1. How are Americans defined in the poem? Whose definition is given? Is that definition accurate? Explain.
2. What is ironic about the definition of Americans in the poem?
3. Is Mora suggesting that some immigrants literally "wrap their babies in the American flag" (line 1)? Explain.

4. According to the poem, what do immigrant parents fear?
5. In the last two lines, *american* appears in lower case. Why?
6. What does the poem imply about Mora's view of conformity and assimilation?

WRITING ASSIGNMENTS

1. **In your journal.**
   - Why do you think immigrants attempt to "Americanize" their children? Should they do so?
   - Write a page or two of advice for the international students at your school to help them adjust to life on your campus.
2. **Using definition for a purpose.** The purposes in the assignments are possibilities. You may establish whatever purposes you like, within your instructor's guidelines.
   - Some people use "melting pot" as a metaphor to describe the United States and its diversity; others say that "salad" is a more accurate term. Briefly define each of these metaphors and then argue which term is more accurate.
   - To inform, write a definition of *American*.
3. **Combining patterns.** Define your ethnic heritage and use cause-and-effect analysis (discussed in Chapter 9) to explain how your heritage has influenced you.

See page 497 for strategies for writing definition and for a revising checklist.

1. Define *stereotype* to help your readers recognize stereotypes and their dangers.
2. To give your readers a fresh appreciation of the familiar, define *friend* or *family*.
3. Define something that can be positive but that has the potential to tyrannize a person: aerobics, running, weight training, video games, getting As, vegetarianism, and so forth.
4. To convince your reader that it is either good or bad, define *censorship*.
5. Define *science fiction movie* to help your reader appreciate the appeal of this genre.
6. Define *power* in a way that expresses an opinion.
7. If you have a hobby or special interest, define it to help your reader appreciate its appeal.
8. Define and illustrate *politically correct* to help your reader better understand this concept and its affect on society.
9. If you have a job, define your role to help your reader appreciate what you do. For example, you could define *nurse, lifeguard, camp counselor,* or *security guard*.
10. Define something that helps you simplify your life: an answering machine, a microwave oven, a computer, inline skates, and so forth.
11. Define *bureaucracy* to show the frustrations that can be associated with it. If you like, you can make this a humorous definition.
12. Write a definition of a news source: your local paper, your campus paper, the national news on TV, a website. Your goal is to convince your reader that the source is or is not a useful one.
13. Define *peer pressure* to help your reader understand what a potent force it is.
14. To clarify something not well understood, define *creativity*.
15. To entertain and/or to inform, define *style*.
16. To entertain and/or to inform, define *tacky*.
17. To express your own thoughts and feelings, define *Christmas spirit*.
18. Define *frustration*. If you want to make the piece amusing, your purpose can be to entertain.
19. Define a custom or concept unique to your ethnic heritage so someone who does not share your heritage will understand it.
20. **Definition in context:** Assume you are a tutor in your campus writing center and the director has asked you to develop a pamphlet on writer's block to be given to students who come to the center. Write a definition of *writer's block* and its effects, suitable for inclusion in the pamphlet. You may also include narrations about experiencing writer's block if those narrations help illustrate its characteristics.

Clowns have delighted children and adults at the circus, in television shows, and at birth-day parties. Some clowns are even spokespeople and trademarks for products, including McDonald's. The appearance of clowns varies, so the picture here by no means reflects the full range of clown dress and makeup. And just as their appearance varies, so do their demeanor and performance styles. In an essay, write a definition of a clown, being sure to explain the reasons for the clown's appeal.

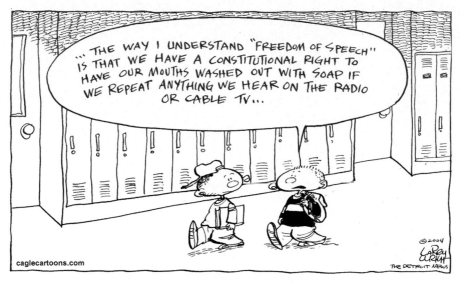

The Law and Society:
A Casebook for Argumentation-Persuasion

CONSIDER THE PATTERN

The cartoon on the facing page satirizes the fact that speech is not *completely* free—some restrictions apply. In a paragraph, mention one restriction on speech and argue that the restriction is or is not necessary.

THE DIFFERENCE BETWEEN ARGUMENTATION AND PERSUASION

Both **argumentation** and **persuasion** aim to convince a reader to adopt a particular view or to take a particular action. In the purest sense, argumentation relies on sound reasoning and logic to move the reader, while persuasion employs appeals to emotion, values, and beliefs. Say, for example, that you want to convince a female friend to vote for a particular candidate for governor. You would employ argumentation if you noted the candidate's prior experience in the state legislature and strong political ties to Washington; you would employ persuasion if you noted the need for more women in high political office. Although argumentation and persuasion are technically different, in practice, the distinction is blurred because reason and logic are usually combined with appeals to emotions, values, and beliefs. Thus, to convince your friend to vote for your candidate, you might mention her political credentials *and* her gender.

Already in this book, you have dealt with a number of essays with a persuasive purpose because each chapter of readings has included one or more selections meant to move the reader to think or act a particular way. In this chapter, however, you will study argumentative-persuasive technique in greater detail.

PURPOSE AND AUDIENCE

As explained, argumentation-persuasion works to convince the reader to think or act a particular way. For example, a newspaper editorial argues that the city's layoff of municipal employees is unnecessary in order to convince readers that the layoffs are a mistake. An advertisement extols the virtues of a car to persuade people to buy it.

Sometimes you have no hope of convincing your reader, so you must establish a less ambitious goal, such as softening your reader's objection or convincing your reader that your view has some merit. Say, for example, that you are arguing that the governor should increase the sales tax to support public education. If your reader has children in school, you can reasonably aim to convince your audience to agree with you. However, if your reader is a retired person on a fixed income, expecting agreement may be unreasonable. In this case, a more suitable goal is to convince your reader that there are some good reasons to raise the sales tax—even if he or she does not fully support the idea. Perhaps you are wondering what good it is to soften a reader's objection or convince that person that your view has some merit. The answer is that if you can lessen a reader's resistance to your view, he or she may come around to your thinking eventually or work less hard to oppose you. Thus, if you convince a retired person that there are some valid reasons for the sales tax, he or she still might not vote for it but also might not campaign actively against it.

Audience assessment is particularly important in argumentation-persuasion. You must assess your reader's interest in order to establish a reasonable purpose for your writing, and you must understand the characteristics of your audience so you know which points need to be stated and proven, what kind of evidence will be the most effective, how hard you must work to convince your reader, and how your audience will respond to emotional appeals.

Argumentation-Persuasion in College, at Work, and in the Community

Argumentation will be a considerable part of your college writing. While you often will be tested on your ability to recall information, at other times you will need to do more than restate what you have read in a text or heard in a lecture. To show that you have thoughtfully considered that information, you will be asked to analyze it, consider different points of view, and then draw your own conclusions, which your instructors will ask you to present and defend with argumentation that relies on reason.

For example, in a political science or American studies class, you may be asked to do more that just explain affirmative action initiatives and their history; you may also have to argue whether or not such initiatives have hurt or helped minority populations. In an ethics class, you may need to do more than explain what is possible with genetic engineering; you may have to develop guidelines governing genetic screening and argue for their acceptance. In a history class, you may need to explain why the atomic bomb was dropped during World War II and then argue that it should or should not have been used to end the war with Japan; in a business course, you may need to define inflation, explain how to combat it, and then go on to argue which combative strategy is the best. In an environmental science course, you may need to argue that the government should or should not sponsor legislation to control global warming.

Argumentation-persuasion is not frequently seen in college textbooks because their emphasis is on an objective presentation of facts. When a controversy does surround an issue covered by a textbook, the author generally covers all sides of the issue evenhandedly. However, at times, a text may include an opinion backed up with an element of argumentation-persuasion. Here is an example of such a passage, taken from the education textbook *Teachers, Schools, and Society* by Myra and David Sadker.

> There is an important difference between *teaching about* religion and *promoting* religion. Today's texts fail to discuss adequately many religious issues that are intellectually complex and socially controversial. Columnist Ellen Goodman suggests that as publishers retreat from controversy, they also retreat from many important lessons. Goodman points out that the strength of our nation, what children really need to learn, is that our history has not always had happy endings, and that we have not yet resolved all our differences. In fact, Americans may never resolve all of their differences. The lesson to be taught to children is that we can live together as a people and not agree on everything.

In this excerpt, the authors state the opinion that textbooks do not do a good job of discussing some religious issues, a view they support by quoting Ellen Goodman. When a textbook—or any other material—argues an opinion or attempts to persuade its audience, you must recognize what is going on and accept or reject the idea advanced on the basis of its merit, how well it is argued, and your own reasoning.

Argumentation-persuasion is also frequently required in the workplace. For example, copywriters compose advertisements to persuade consumers to buy products. Attorneys write briefs to convince judges of the merits of their case. Public health officials draw on research to persuade people to improve their eating habits or to promote no-smoking legislation. Artists write proposals to convince art councils to fund their projects. Contractors write project proposals to persuade builders to hire them. Managers write reports to convince co-workers and supervisors of many things: which phone service to purchase, which contract to accept, how to reorganize an office, what investment to make, which property to buy, and so forth.

Outside of the workplace and classroom, you will use argumentation-persuasion frequently in your personal writing, such as in a letter to the editor to persuade others to share your view on an issue important to you, an e-mail to convince a friend to join you on a cross-country trip, a letter to a customer service representative to persuade a business to give you a refund for a faulty product, a grant proposal to convince the state arts council to fund a community theater, or a speech to convince school board members to change a school bus route.

SUPPORTING DETAILS

Our system of logic was formulated by the ancient Greeks, who identified three elements of a successful argument: *logos, pathos,* and *ethos.* **Logos** (from which our word *logical* derives) refers to the sound reasoning of the argument. It includes the evidence, facts, statistics, examples, authoritative statements, and so forth that you supply to back up your position. **Pathos** (from which our word *pathetic* derives) refers to the emotional component of language and its ability to appeal to the reader's feelings, values, attitudes, and beliefs. Say you want to persuade your reader to buy a particular stock. If you said that failure to buy the stock could mean missing the opportunity of a lifetime, that part of your argument would use pathos because it appeals to the reader's fear of passing up an opportunity. However, if you explained that the stock was undervalued and part of a growing market sector, that part of your argument would use logos because it appealed to the reader's intellect. **Ethos** (from which our word *ethical* derives) refers to establishing your honesty, integrity, and reliability so your reader will trust you and, therefore, believe what you say. You must present yourself as knowledgeable and thoughtful, as one who carefully weighs all evidence before drawing conclusions. If your reader thinks you are impetuous, careless, or biased, he or she may not accept your position no matter how well argued it is.

Logos

To present your argument soundly, you must reason logically. Be careful, then, to avoid the errors in logic discussed on pages 5–7.

For the most part, your argumentative detail will be the reasons you hold your view. Thus, if you want to convince your reader that the federal government should pay day care expenses for working parents, you would give all the reasons this is a good idea. However, supplying reasons for your stand is not enough; you must also back up those reasons with support. Say you argue that the family unit is in trouble and you give the high divorce rate as one reason to support your view. You must then go on to back up this reason, perhaps by giving a statistic about how high the divorce rate is and by explaining the specific negative effects of divorce on the family.

To back up your reasons, you can rely on a number of sources and strategies, including personal experience and observation, facts and statistics, quotations and paraphrases, interviews, speculation about the effects of adopting or not adopting your view, and the patterns of development.

Draw on Personal Experience and Observation

Say that you are in favor of federally funded day care, and you cite as one reason the fact that children of working parents do not always get satisfactory care without it. To back up this claim, you could rely on observation by telling about your neighbor, who cannot afford decent care for her child while she is at work. If your own experience as a working parent supports the point, you could also write about that experience to back up your claim.

Use Facts and Statistics

Say that you want to convince your reader that we need a fresh approach to solving the problem of juvenile crime. You could show that our current approach is not working by citing Linda J. Collier's claim in "Adult Crime, Adult Time" (page 591) that since 1965, there has been a twofold increase in arrests of 12-year-olds for crimes of violence and a threefold increase in arrests of 13- and 14-year-olds for crimes of violence. If you do use facts and statistics from sources, be sure to document this information according to the conventions explained in Chapter 14.

Use Quotations and Paraphrases

If you want to argue that racist speech should not be protected by the first amendment, you could quote or paraphrase Charles R. Lawrence III, who says in "The Debate over Placing Limits on Racist Speech Must Not Ignore the Damage It Does to Its Victims" (page 612), "Whenever we decide that racist speech must be tolerated because of the importance of maintaining societal tolerance for all unpopular speech, we are asking blacks and other subordinated groups to bear the burden for the good of all." If you do use quotations or paraphrases, be sure to follow the guidelines given in Chapter 14.

www.mhhe.com/patterns

For more help with incorporating quotes and paraphrases, click on
Research > Incorporating Source Information

Conduct Interviews

Say that to argue for federally funded day care you note that the day care fees are too high for some individuals. To support this reason, you can interview the owners of local day care centers to learn the cost of enrollment. You could then interview parents searching for day care and report their thoughts on the enrollment fees you discovered.

Speculate about What Would Happen If Your Thesis Were or Were Not Adopted

Sometimes you can argue your case by explaining the good that would result if your thesis were adopted or the bad that would result if your thesis were not adopted. Say, for example, that you want to argue for the elimination of the foreign language requirement for mathematics and science majors. You could argue that if your thesis is adopted, science and math majors will have more time to participate in valuable internship programs. As an alternative, you could argue that if the requirement is not abolished, many prospective math and science students will attend school at the nearby colleges that do not require a foreign language.

Use the Patterns of Development

To explain and back up the reasons for your stand, you can use any of the patterns discussed in this book. If, for instance, you want to convince your reader that couples should marry rather than just live together, you can *narrate* an account of what happened when your brother and his girlfriend lived together. You can also *provide examples* of the problems couples face when they do not marry. You can *contrast* the benefits of marriage with the drawbacks of living together. You can *classify* the benefits of marriage, you can *describe* the embarrassment of older relatives of the unmarried couple, and so on.

---

www.mhhe.com/patterns

For more help with patterns of paragraph development, click on

Writing > Paragraph Patterns

Pathos

In addition to appealing to your reader's intellect with sound reasons, you can be convincing by appealing to your reader's emotions, needs, values, beliefs, and concerns. For example, to persuade your reader to support assisted suicide, you can move the reader to compassion by describing the agony of a patient who must linger in pain with no hope of recovery.

Similarly, to convince your reader that the federal government should fund day care, you can stir up the reader's emotions with a graphic explanation of the substandard care the child next door is getting. Persuasive detail, then, uses emotionally charged language to move a reader to a particular view or action.

Appealing to your reader's emotions is a valid technique, but do not overdo. Emotional appeal should be restrained. It is fine to move your reader's emotions by arousing compassion for a homosexual couple who wants to marry, but it is unfair to charge that tens of thousands of people are despondent and totally unfulfilled because they cannot marry. Further, the number of emotional appeals should be reasonable. They should appear *in addition to* logical reasons—not *instead of* them. Rely mostly on logical reasons, and supplement those reasons with emotional appeal when appropriate.

Ethos

You can do a number of things to earn your reader's trust. Perhaps most important, you can present a well-reasoned argument, restrained emotional appeals, and a logical progression of ideas. In addition, if you have particular knowledge or experiences that make you authoritative on a relevant issue, mention them to establish your credentials. For example, if you are arguing that your community should update its zoning laws, note that you were on the zoning board for five years; if you are arguing for improved safety guidelines for playground equipment, mention that your child was injured on a piece of unsafe equipment. Finally, you can present yourself as a thoughtful person who weighs all sides of an issue before forming an opinion. The best way to show your reader that you have done that is by *raising and countering objections,* a technique that is discussed on page 551.

How Logos, Pathos, and Ethos Relate to Purpose and Audience

When you write argumentation-persuasion, you will usually use some combination of logos, pathos, and ethos. To determine the proportions of these elements, consider your purpose and audience. Of what do you want to persuade your reader? Do you want to convince your audience to think a particular way, perhaps agree that additional campaign finance reform is a good idea? Then you can emphasize sound reasons (logos) and your own trustworthiness (ethos). Or do you want your reader to take action and write members of Congress to encourage them to vote for campaign finance reform? That purpose may require the addition of emotional appeal (pathos), perhaps by moving your reader to anger over the current method for financing campaigns.

To determine the appropriate blend of logos, pathos, and ethos, assess your audience in light of your purpose to determine whether your reader is *supportive*, *wavering*, or *hostile*.

- A *supportive reader* is already on your side. This reader trusts you and shares some or all of your positions. If you were arguing for strengthening the sex education curriculum in local schools, a supportive audience would include members of Planned Parenthood. Although you will still use sound reasoning to support your argument, you can also draw on your trustworthiness to establish your bond with the reader and rely more heavily on emotional appeals to tap into shared beliefs, attitudes, and emotions and solidify support for your assertion. You may want to use some elements of logos to remind the reader of certain facts and thereby reaffirm agreement. Alter your purpose, however, and the balance of appeals changes. For example, to convince members of Planned Parenthood to contribute to the campaign of a school board candidate, you will need to rely much more on sound reasoning—including information about the candidate's views, qualifications, and commitment to sex education.

- A *wavering reader* can be brought to your side but is currently not committed to your assertion. Such a reader may be insufficiently informed about the issue, may not have made up his or her mind, or may not have a reason to care. If you were arguing for strengthening the sex education curriculum in local schools, a wavering audience might be parents with very young children, parents who have not yet turned their attention to this issue, or parents who are uncertain about what will be best for their children. For a wavering audience, you must draw on reliable evidence and sound reasoning to convince your readers of the validity of your position and of your own trustworthiness (perhaps as a parent yourself) to incline readers to trust what you say. Emotional appeals (pathos) can be used, but they must be very restrained, or you can alienate your readers by giving them the impression that you are trying to manipulate them.

- A *hostile reader* is the most difficult audience to persuade. This reader is strongly opposed to your assertion or difficult to reach for some other reason—perhaps because of lack of interest, anger, or reluctance to consider opposing viewpoints. With a hostile audience, you must shape your purpose realistically. You may not have a chance of changing a reader's mind, but you may be able to soften that person's objection a bit or earn some respect for your assertion. For example, if your reader has strong moral beliefs that sex education belongs in the home and not in schools, you will not be able to convince that person to support a stronger sex education curriculum. However, you may be able to help that person see that sex education has some positive aspects. With a hostile reader, emphasize logos. Give your audience your best facts and reasoning and hope they have some impact.

RAISING AND COUNTERING OBJECTIONS

No matter what stand you take on an issue, some reasonable people will disagree with you, and those people will have valid points to support their view. Ignoring this opposition will weaken your argumentation or persuasion because you will not come across as someone who has carefully examined all sides before arriving at a position. Furthermore, even if you ignore the opposition, your reader will not. Your audience will be thinking about the points that work against your assertion, and if you do not deal with those points, you may fail to convince your reader. Thus, you must recognize the opposing arguments and find a way to make them less compelling. Recognizing and making opposition points less compelling is called *raising and countering objections*.

To raise and counter objections, you first acknowledge the objection to your stand by stating it. This is *raising the objection*. Then you make the objection less compelling. This is *countering the objection*. In general, you can raise and counter objections three ways, as illustrated below.

1. *State that the opposition has a point, but so do you.*

   Many people are concerned because federally funded day care will raise taxes [objection raised]. However, children who are currently given substandard care because we lack a comprehensive, federally funded program will not thrive. Children who do not thrive fail to realize their potential or they develop problems, both of which end up costing society more money than day care [*objection countered*].

2. *State that the opposition has a point, but your point is better.*

   Although some are concerned about the cost of federally funded day care [objection raised], we cannot put a price tag on the well-being of our children because they are our hope for a better future [*objection countered*].

3. *State that the opposition's point is untrue.*

   There are those who maintain that we do not need federally funded day care [objection raised]. However, the number of mothers who must work outside the home is very high, and many of these working mothers are the sole support of their children and could not stay home even if they wanted to. As a result, many parents are forced into substandard, or even downright dangerous, child care arrangements [*objection countered*].

Raising and countering objections helps strengthen your case, but you need not deal with every opposition point. Instead, identify the most compelling objections and deal with those.

THE TOULMIN MODEL

In his book *The Uses of Argument* (1958), Stephen Toulmin identifies three parts of an argument. An adaptation of his division is given here. You may find it helpful as you analyze the arguments of others and write your own arguments.

In the Toulmin model, you can think of argumentation-persuasion as having three parts: the claim, the support, and the assumption.

The *claim* is the point you are arguing; it is what you are trying to convince your reader of. Here are some examples of claims.

> CLAIM   This university should switch from its current quarter system to the semester system.

> CLAIM   Teachers should not be permitted to engage in labor strikes.

> CLAIM   The United States's immigration policy creates many problems.

In argumentation-persuasion, the claim appears in the thesis.

The *support* is the ideas and information you include to convince the reader. The support can be evidence based on logical reasoning—statistics and facts, for example—or it can be appeals to emotions, values, and beliefs. Here are examples of both kinds of support.

> CLAIM   This university should switch from its current quarter system to the semester system.

> SUPPORT (BASED ON REASON)   The administration says that the switch would save the university money because fewer terms would reduce the cost of registration and advisement.

> SUPPORT (APPEAL TO BELIEF)   Semesters allow students to study subjects at a more leisurely pace. (An appeal to the belief that it is better to study something for 15 weeks than for 10.)

In argumentation-persuasion, the support will be the supporting details.

The third part of argumentation-persuasion is the *assumption*, which is the inference or belief that connects the claim and the support. To see how the assumption connects the claim and support, study this example.

> CLAIM   This university should switch from its current quarter system to the semester system.

> SUPPORT (REASON)   The administration says that the switch would save the university money because fewer terms would reduce the cost of registration and advisement.

UNSTATED ASSUMPTIONS	The administration is trustworthy, so it can be believed when it says that money will be saved. Saving the administration money is a good thing.

If the reader trusts the administration, the assumption is accepted and the support is convincing. However, if the reader does not trust the administration, then the assumption is not accepted and the support fails to convince. When a reader might not accept an assumption automatically, you must support the assumption to make it convincing.

STATED ASSUMPTION WITH SUPPORT	The administration says that the switch would save the university money because fewer terms would reduce the cost of registration and advisement. They arrived at this conclusion after surveying 200 schools that have switched from the quarter to the semester system.

Sometimes an assumption is a value or belief.

CLAIM	Teachers should not be allowed to engage in labor strikes.
SUPPORT	When teachers strike, they cause a great deal of harm.
ASSUMPTION	Teachers are different from other workers who engage in strikes that create problems.

This example shows that the assumption is very much at the heart of an argument because it is what will or will not incline the reader to move from the support to accepting the claim. To prove that teachers should not strike, you would have to prove the assumption and show how teachers are different from others who strike: steelworkers, truck drivers, television writers, and so forth.

Sometimes the assumption is self-evident, so it need not be written out. Say, for example, that you want to argue that we should censor the Internet to protect children from predatory adults. The assumption that we do not want children harmed is so obvious that it need not be stated. Now say that you want to argue that teenagers who commit murder should be tried as adults. In this case, the assumption that some teenagers are emotionally and intellectually mature needs to be stated and proven. Otherwise, your reader may have difficulty moving from your support to accepting your claim.

INDUCTIVE AND DEDUCTIVE REASONING

Induction and deduction are two methods of reasoning especially helpful for supporting a claim.

Induction

Induction is a form of reasoning that moves from specific evidence to a general conclusion. That is, when you reason inductively, you examine specific facts, cases, examples, and other available evidence and then draw a reasonable conclusion based on that information. Induction is used all the time: A doctor ponders a patient's symptoms and test results and reasons inductively to reach a diagnosis; a jury considers the evidence presented at the trial and reasons inductively to reach a verdict; a police officer studies the crime scene, examines clues, and reasons inductively to establish a list of suspects.

When you write argumentation-persuasion, induction can serve you well. Assume, for example, that you wish to argue the need for a traffic light at the corner of First Street and Third Avenue. You can first present your specific evidence: In the last year, traffic accidents at that intersection have increased 80 percent; five people have died there, including two children; traffic at that intersection has increased since the shopping mall opened a mile away; the State Highway Patrol has said a traffic light there could reduce the number of accidents. After offering this evidence, you can present your view in the form of a generalization that follows from the evidence: We need a traffic light installed at the corner of First Street and Third Avenue. This generalization would be your thesis.

No matter how compelling your evidence seems to be, you cannot always be certain of the reliability of the generalization you conclude from it. Thus, it may well be true that a traffic light would solve the problem at First Street and Third Avenue, but it could also be true that the real problem is the speed limit and a better solution is to reduce it from 55 mph to 35 mph. Because the conclusion drawn in inductive reasoning is rarely certain beyond a doubt, that conclusion is called an *inference*. To increase the likelihood that your inferences are accurate, be sure that your evidence is sound. Be careful to supply enough evidence and to verify that the evidence is accurate, recent, specific, and representative. For help with supplying sound evidence, review the information on avoiding errors in logic on pages 5–7.

Deduction

In a broad sense, deduction involves reasoning from the general to the specific, but you should not think of deduction as the opposite of induction. Instead, **deduction** moves from a generalization (called a *major premise*) to a specific case (called a *minor premise*) and on to a conclusion, like this:

MAJOR PREMISE (GENERALIZATION)	Because of compulsory attendance laws, a number of students who do not want to be in school disrupt the educational process.
MINOR PREMISE (SPECIFIC CASE)	Many students in this state do not want to be in school, and they disrupt the educational process for those who do want to learn.
CONCLUSION	If we abolish compulsory attendance laws in this state, students who do not want to be in school can leave and make it easier for others to learn.

Recall that with inductive reasoning, the conclusion is an inference rather than a certainty. In deductive reasoning, however, if the two premises are accurate, then the conclusion will follow inescapably. If one or both of the premises are wrong, then the conclusion will not follow, as is the case in this example:

MAJOR PREMISE   All college students drink beer.

MINOR PREMISE   Chris is a college student.

CONCLUSION   Chris drinks beer.

In this example, the conclusion cannot be accepted because the major premise is an overgeneralization. (See page 6.) Not all college students drink beer; therefore, we cannot conclude inescapably that college-student Chris drinks beer. To be sure your major and minor premises meet the test of logic, refer to page 5 on avoiding errors in logic.

Deductive reasoning can provide a very useful framework for argumentation-persuasion. You can set up your essay so that your supporting details present the evidence demonstrating the truth of each premise. With the premises proven, your reader will accept your thesis, which is the point you are arguing.

ORGANIZING ARGUMENTATION-PERSUASION

The introduction of argumentation-persuasion can be handled many ways. Explaining why the issue is important can be effective because it helps the reader understand the seriousness of your purpose. Thus, if you are arguing that high schools should have day care centers for teenage mothers, your introduction can note the large number of teen mothers who drop out of school because they have no child care. This figure should help your reader appreciate the urgency of the issue. If your reader needs certain background information in order to appreciate your argument, the introduction can be a good place to provide that information. Thus, if you are arguing the need to return to homogeneous groupings in classrooms, you should explain what a homogeneous grouping is if your reader is not likely to know. The introduction can also be a good place to establish your ethos. Thus, if you are arguing in favor of increasing the city sales tax, you can note that you have worked in the city's finance department for three years and can confirm the recent claims of shortfalls.

Your thesis, whether it appears in the opening paragraphs or elsewhere, should state the issue and your assertion about that issue, like one of the following:

The United States desperately needs federally funded day care. (*issue:* federally funded day care; *stand:* in favor of it)

Federally funded day care would create more problems than it solves. (*issue:* federally funded day care; *stand:* against it)

Be sure that the issue you are arguing is genuinely debatable. There is no reason to argue that parents should love their children because no one will disagree with you. Similarly, avoid matters of taste. For example, arguing that basketball is a better sport than football is not productive because the issue is a matter of personal preference.

In general, arranging your points in a progressive order (from least to most compelling) is effective. This way, you can save your most convincing arguments for the end so your reader leaves your essay with them fresh in mind. Or you can place your strongest arguments first and last for a big opening and finish. Remember, the points at the end of an essay are in the most emphatic position and therefore likely to have the biggest impact.

If you are reasoning inductively, you can place your thesis at the end of your essay, after you have presented all the specific evidence pointing to the inference that stands as your thesis. Placing the thesis at the end can work well for a hostile reader. You can build your case and then present your assertion about the issue. If you are reasoning deductively, you can first present the evidence to support your major premise, and then present the evidence to support your minor premise.

You will probably find topic sentences helpful when you structure argumentation-persuasion. You can place each reason for your thesis in its own topic sentence and follow each topic sentence with the appropriate support. Thus, an essay arguing that we should pay college athletes rather than give them scholarships could have these topic sentences:

> If we pay college athletes, the players can use the money for whatever they like—including tuition and books.
>
> If we pay college athletes, we can finally dispel the myth that the players are always students first.
>
> Finally, once we pay college athletes, we can allow colleges to openly acknowledge that they are farm clubs for professional teams.

If you raise and counter objections, you can do this throughout the essay, wherever a point to be countered logically emerges. However, if you are dealing with very few objections, you can raise and counter them together in one or two paragraphs at the beginning or end of the essay.

To conclude, you can reaffirm your assertion for emphasis, summarize your chief arguments if your reader is likely to appreciate the reminder, or present your most persuasive point. In addition, you can call your audience to action by explaining what you want your reader to do. Or you can recommend a particular solution to a problem. Finally, explaining what would happen if your thesis were or were not adopted can be an effective closing.

---

www.mhhe.com/patterns

For more help with writing an argument essay, click on

Writing > Writing Tutor: Arguments

VISUALIZING AN ARGUMENTATION-PERSUASION ESSAY

The following chart can help you visualize the structure for an argumentation-persuasion essay. Like all good models, however, this one can be altered as needed.

Introduction

- Creates interest in the essay, perhaps by explaining why the issue is important, providing background information, or establishing your reliability
- States the thesis, which gives the debatable issue and your assertion

First Body Paragraph

- Gives and explains the first point to support your assertion
- May rely on logos, pathos, and /or ethos
- May raise and counter objections
- Relies on inductive or deductive reasoning
- Arranges details in progressive order

Next Body Paragraph

- Gives and explains the next point to support your assertion
- May rely on logos, pathos, and /or ethos
- May raise and counter objections
- Relies on inductive or deductive reasoning
- Arranges details in progressive order

Next Body Paragraphs

- Continue until all the points to support the assertion are made
- May rely on logos, pathos, and/or ethos
- May raise and counter objections
- Rely on inductive or deductive reasoning
- Arrange details in progressive order

Conclusion

- Can reaffirm your position or present your most persuasive point
- Can call your reader to action or recommend a solution to a problem
- Can explain what would happen if your thesis were or were not adopted

PROCESS GUIDELINES: STRATEGIES FOR WRITING ARGUMENTATION-PERSUASION

1. **Selecting a Topic.** If you need help discovering a topic, try one of these strategies.
   - Review the essays in this book for ideas. Or review local and campus newspapers to learn about controversial issues of importance.
   - Fill in the blank in one of these sentences:

     It is unfair that _____.

     It makes me angry that _____.

     I disagree with people who believe that _____.

     The quality of life in my community would be better if _____.

     People of my generation would be more confident about our future if _____.

     Opportunities for children would be enhanced if _____.

2. **Determining Purpose and Assessing Audience.** Answer these questions:
   - Do you want to convince your reader to think a particular way about an issue? If so, what do you want your reader to think?
   - Do you want your reader to take a particular action? If so, what do you want your reader to do?
   - Is your reader supportive, wavering, or hostile? Is your purpose reasonable for such an audience?

3. **Generating Ideas.** Answering the following questions can help you generate ideas:
   - Based on your purpose and audience, how will you balance logos, pathos, and ethos?

Avoiding Errors in Logic

If you have trouble avoiding errors in logic, review pages 5–7 on "Detecting Errors in Logic." Being able to detect errors in the logic of others should help you, during revision, to avoid faulty reasoning in your own writing as well.

TROUBLESHOOTING GUIDE

- Why is your issue important? To whom is it important?
- What would happen if your thesis were adopted? If it were not adopted?
- What are the chief objections to your thesis? How can you logically and constructively counter those objections?
- How can you appeal to your reader's emotions?
- How can you present yourself as trustworthy?

4. **Revising.** Ask two reliable readers to review your draft to be sure you have avoided errors in logic (see page 5) and that you have countered important objections.

Checklist for Revising Argumentation-Persuasion

Be sure

_____ Your thesis is genuinely debatable.

_____ Your introduction provides background, explains why your topic is important, or otherwise engages readers' interest.

_____ Your thesis notes the issue and your assertion.

_____ All your points are clarified and supported.

_____ Logos, pathos, and ethos are appropriately balanced.

_____ You have avoided "as any fool can see" phrasings.

_____ If necessary, you have stated and supported the assumptions that connect your claims and support.

_____ You have appealed to emotion, values, and beliefs with appropriate restraint.

_____ You have avoided problems with logic.

_____ You have raised and countered compelling objections.

_____ Paraphrases and quotations are documented according to the conventions given in Chapter 14.

_____ Your conclusion brings the essay to a satisfying close.

Student-author Hannah Scheels uses argumentation to convince readers that the Kansas attorney general's rejection of 1,600 free CDs is a serious form of censorship. She also works to move readers to take action against this censorship. After you read the essay, you will have an opportunity to evaluate it.

Title
Notice the word play: "Cast Out" is a clever reference to OutKast.

Paragraph 1
This introductory paragraph gives background information—the details of the settlement. The thesis is the last sentence. The issue is the action of the Kansas attorney general; the assertion is that the action undermines the first amendment. Notice the use of quotation.

Paragraph 2
The topic sentence idea (library patrons are denied access to important music) is implied. The details establish that the rejected music is important, which helps support the idea that the attorney general did the wrong thing. Notice that the source of information is acknowledged.

Cast Out of Kansas: Music Censorship in Public Libraries

In the summer of 2004, Kansas was one of forty states nationwide [1] to receive several thousand free compact disks as part of a settlement to resolve charges that the music industry had fixed prices for recordings. The disks were intended to be given, free of charge, to public libraries in these forty states, where they would be made available to anyone who wished to listen to them. However, library patrons in Kansas will not be able to listen to more than 1,600 of these recordings (out of a total 51,000) because the Kansas attorney general found that they "did not mesh with the values of a majority of Kansans" (CNN.com). This chilling example of state-sponsored censorship interferes with the ability of Kansas citizens—and their librarians—to determine their own "values" for themselves. Left unchallenged, the actions of the Kansas attorney general set a dangerous precedent that undermines First Amendment rights to free speech guaranteed to all by the U.S. Constitution.

According to an article on CNN.com, the rejected disks include [2] works by the rap artists OutKast and Notorious B.I.G., the popular alternative rock bands Stone Temple Pilots and Rage Against the Machine, and classic alternative voices ranging from Lou Reed to Devo. All of these artists have well-earned reputations for the quality and expressiveness of their lyrics as well as their innovative music. Another quality these artists share is their status as "alternative." Even though many of these artists are Grammy winners (a testament to their popularity and the enormous sales of their music), they are more importantly critically acclaimed. Rap artists OutKast have merged funk, rhythm and blues, and hip-hop in a significantly creative fashion. At the same time, their music videos brilliantly send up stereotypical images of black musicians. Notorious B.I.G.'s lyrics capture the very real violence that defines the lives of so many urban Americans. Lou Reed's deadpan lyrics describe the alternative lifestyles of the 1960s and 1970s in unforgettable images.

And both the Stone Temple Pilots and Rage Against the Machine evoke, in both their lyrics and their musical arrangements, the frustration and lack of opportunity felt by so many young people in an age of increasing cultural and economic conformity.

It is true that these artists, in their desire to tell the truth as they see it and express the realities they believe we should all at least acknowledge, often use explicit language and create images that can be disturbing. Sometimes, as in the work of OutKast, the sexual language and imagery can be pornographic. This is why the recording industry puts parental advisory stickers on disks that contain violent or explicit language, and why many artists (including OutKast) also release "clean" versions of their albums that digitally remove the potentially offensive language without interfering with the overall integrity of the music.

What is most disturbing about the decision of the Kansas attorney general is that he has made his decision based on "Internet databases of lyrics" (CNN.com). In other words, these artists are being censored as writers, not just as musicians. If these musicians published their lyrics as poetry or short stories instead of albums, this decision would seem to set a precedent that would allow a state attorney general to remove books from a library—or, as in this case, prevent some books from ever even reaching a library's shelves.

The actions of the Kansas attorney general also override the expertise, experience, and responsibilities of local librarians. Even though the executive director of the Kansas Library Association is quoted in the CNN.com article as saying that the attorney general "did libraries a big favor by selecting these CDs because there's no way libraries could have said what they wanted," the fact is that librarians had no say at all in this decision. Local librarians are trained to be sensitive to the needs and "values" of their particular neighborhoods and communities. By abdicating their responsibility to a state attorney general—an elected official with a political agenda—the librarians of Kansas have damaged the First Amendment rights of Kansas citizens. Further, they have violated the Code of Ethics of the American Library Association, which states that

3

Paragraph 3
The topic sentence (the first sentence) presents an objection, and the rest of the paragraph counters that objection.

4

Paragraph 4
The topic sentence (the second sentence) gives the next reason supporting the assertion. The rest of the paragraph relies on sound reasoning (logos) for support. Notice that transition is achieved with the synonym "decision." Also notice the quotation, which is credited in parentheses.

5

Paragraph 5
The topic sentence (the first sentence) gives the next reason supporting the assertion. The rest of the paragraph relies on sound reasoning (logos) for support. Notice the quotation and that the source is given.

librarians must "uphold the principles of intellectual freedom and resist all efforts to censor library resources" (American Library Association).

Paragraph 6
The topic sentence (the first sentence) gives the next reason supporting the assertion. The rest of the paragraph relies on sound reasoning (logos) for support. Notice the transition, "furthermore."

Furthermore, this decision is grossly unfair to those citizens who 6 either cannot afford to purchase CDs, or who wish to sample a recording before purchasing it (or allowing their children to purchase it). Paradoxically, in an age where major retailers such as Wal-Mart are themselves curtailing (based on "values") the kinds of music, DVDs, books, and magazines they make available to consumers, public libraries may in some communities be the *only* place people can turn to for a genuinely diverse and fair selection of media.

Paragraph 7
This is the conclusion. The essay ends with a call to action.

Patrons of libraries nationwide should actively protest what is happening in Kansas, unless they want their acquisitions and holdings to be managed by lawyers rather than librarians. The issue here is not about the "decency" of certain musicians, but about the freedom of Americans to determine their values for themselves. 7

Works Cited
For information on how to document paraphrases and quotations, including how to write a works cited citation, see Chapter 14.

Works Cited

American Library Association. "Code of Ethics." 28 June 1995. 12 Sept. 2004 http://www.ala.org/ala/oif/statementspols/codeofethics/codeethics.htm.

"'OutKast' Not Allowed in Kansas Libraries." CNN.com. 6 Aug. 2004. 12 Sept. 2004 http://www.cnn.com/2004/SHOWBIZ/Music/08/06/library.cdsettlement.ap/index.html.

Responding to "Cast Out of Kansas: Music Censorship in Public Libraries"

Evaluate "Cast Out of Kansas: Music Censorship in Public Libraries" by responding to these questions:

1. Is the essay persuasive? Why or why not?
2. Should the essay include more logos, ethos, or pathos? Explain.
3. Are significant objections raised and countered effectively? Explain.
4. Are there any problems with logic?
5. Do paraphrases and quotations help the writer achieve her persuasive purpose?
6. What do you like best about the essay?
7. What single change do you think would improve the essay?

SHOULD THE LAW ALLOW CLONING OF EMBRYONIC STEM CELLS?

Biomedical researchers say that embryonic stem cell research can one day produce cures for many catastrophic diseases. However, the same research might also produce clonal babies one day—a possibility that terrifies almost everyone. Those who favor stem cell research cite its potential medical and scientific benefits. Those who oppose it fear it will send us down a "slippery slope" to human cloning—that is, it will lead incrementally but inevitably to a world populated by human clones.

In the next selections, you will read a debate between Jeremy Rifkin and Raymond Barglow that appeared in *Tikkun* in 2002. *Tikkun,* a magazine of Jewish and interfaith social, political, and cultural commentary, has a progressive, reform-minded editorial policy, which inclines it to the political left. Since the magazine paired these essays, you are reading the perspectives of two progressives who do not attempt to represent the views of the religious right or social conservatives, who condemn stem cell research for many of the same reasons that they condemn abortion. But opposition to cloning is not limited to conservatives, as the essay by Rifkin reveals. Barglow responds with an argument in support of cloning for medical research.

Any debate about stem cell research and therapeutic cloning touches on deep-seated beliefs about the sanctity of life, the definition of life, divine will, human suffering, and the

Cloning is an asexual form of reproduction. All the child's genes would come from a *body cell* of a *single* individual:

Cloning or Asexual Reproduction

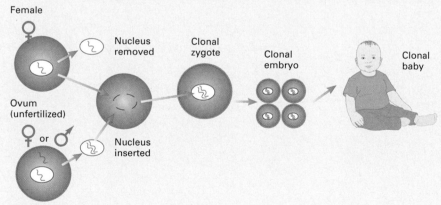

Who is the clonal child's genetic mother or father? As we understand those terms, a clonal child wouldn't have a genetic mother or father, it would have a single 'nuclear donor.'

purpose and dangers of scientific advances. Thus, it is not surprising that debates on this subject are carried out with great intensity.

Stem Cells

Stem cells are primordial cells capable of developing into a variety of types of cells. Some stem cells are found in the adult body. Others are found in very early embryos. These stem cells can be cultured in petri dishes and potentially used to generate "therapeutic tissues" or "spare organs":

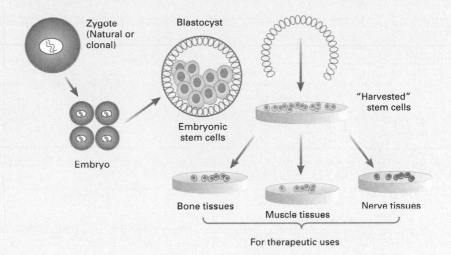

Many people support the use of stem cells of both types for such therapeutic purposes. Many others support the use of *adult* stem cells for this purpose but oppose the use of *embryonic* stem cells, because they oppose the destruction or manipulation of human embryos.

BACKGROUND: Founder and president of the Foundation on Economic Trends in Washington, DC, which studies the impact of new technologies on the global economy, Jeremy Rifkin has shaped policy around the world. He is cited by *The National Journal* as one of 150 people in the United States with the greatest influence on federal government policy. A frequent advisor to heads of state, Rifkin is an advisor to Romano Prodi, President of the European Commission, which is the governing body of the European Union. He has also lectured at more than 500 universities in 20 countries. A frequent lecturer to corporate leaders around the world on the impact of science and technology, Rifkin also writes a newspaper column on global issues that appears in papers in the United Kingdom, Germany, Spain, Italy, France, and the United Arab Emirates. His books include *The Biotech Century: Harnessing the Gene and Remaking the World* (1999), *The Age of Access: The New Culture of Hypercapitalism, Where All of Life Is a Paid-for Experience* (2001), and *The End of Work: The Decline of the Global Labor Force and the Dawn of the Post-Market Era* (2004). "Why I Oppose Human Cloning" first appeared in *Tikkun,* which calls itself a "Bimonthly Jewish and Interfaith Critique of Politics, Culture, & Society," in 2002.

COMBINED PATTERNS AND THEIR PURPOSE: In "Why I Oppose Human Cloning," Jeremy Rifkin writes to **persuade** readers that cloning embryos for research into disease cures, a process called therapeutic cloning, is not just wrong—it is dangerous because of where it could lead us. To support his assertion, Rifkin draws on several patterns of development, including *cause-and-effect analysis, comparison-contrast,* and *narration.*

WHY I OPPOSE HUMAN CLONING

JEREMY RIFKIN

Up to now, the cloning and stem cell debate has been viewed in Washington and the media as a classic Right vs. Left struggle, pitting social conservatives, right-to-life activists, and the Catholic Church against the scientific community and progressive forces, with Republicans lined up on one side and Democrats on the other. In reality, however, many of us in the progressive Left are also opposed to cloning, although our reasons differ in some respects from those of the social conservatives. Earlier this year, sixty-seven leading progressives lent their support to legislation that would outlaw both therapeutic and full-birth (also called reproductive) cloning. The signatories of the anti-cloning petition included many of the best-known intellectuals and activists in left circles today.

As you read Notice to what extent Rifkin relies on logical reasoning and to what extent he relies on emotional appeals.

"The signatories of the anticloning petition included many of the best-known intellectuals and activists in left circles today."

2   While the social conservatives' opposition to cloning is well understood, little or no attention has been given in the media or public debate as to why some of us on the Left oppose cloning. We worry that the market for women's eggs that would be created by this research will provide unethical incentives for women to undergo health-threatening hormone treatment and surgery. We are also concerned about the increasing bio-

industrialization of life by the scientific community and life science companies; we are shocked and dismayed that clonal human embryos have been patented and declared to be human "inventions." We oppose efforts to reduce human life and its various parts and processes to the status of mere research tools, manufactured products, and utilities.

3   To the argument that medical science needs embryonic stem cells for research purposes, we answer that adult stem cells, which can be taken from individuals after birth, have proved promising in both animal studies and clinical trials. This "soft path" approach to using the new science poses none of the ethical, social, and economic risks of strategies using embryo stem cells.

4   Moreover, many, if not most, of the diseases researchers hope to cure by using embryonic stem cells are the result of a complex choreography acted out between genetic predispositions and environmental triggers. By concentrating research almost exclusively on magic bullets in the form of gene replacements, the medical community forecloses the less invasive option of prevention—that is, using the sophisticated new scientific understanding of the relationship between genes and environments to develop medical therapies that keep people well.

5   We are also concerned about the slippery slope advocates of embryo cloning have started down. If using a twelve-day-old cloned embryo for producing cells and tissues is morally acceptable, what would preclude advocates in the future from championing the harvesting of more developed cells from, say, an eight-week-old embryo, or from harvesting organs from a five-month-old cloned fetus if it were found

to be a more useful medical therapy? One doesn't have to be a right-to-lifer to feel squeamish about harvesting organs from a second-trimester fetus.

"What about the question of cloning a full-birth human being?"

6   What about the question of cloning a full-birth human being? Today, almost no one supports full-birth cloning. Certainly, most members of Congress, on both sides of the aisle, would oppose a clonal birth. But what some supporters of therapeutic cloning don't realize is that for many in Congress, the scientific community, and the biotech industry, opposition to full-birth cloning is solely based on the fact that the cloning technique is still unsafe and could pose a risk of producing a malformed baby. Far fewer members of either party would be opposed to cloning a human baby were the procedure to become safe and reliable. After all, argue proponents, if an infertile couple desires to pass on their genetic inheritance by producing clones of one or both partners, shouldn't they be able to exercise their right of choice in the newly emerging biotech marketplace? We need not worry about the possibility of producing truly identical people, proponents argue, since, even though the clone will have the exact same genetic makeup as the original, he or she will develop differently because his or her life will unfold in a different social and environmental context than the donor's.

7   In all the technical and economic talk what both liberals and market libertarians miss is that the cloning of a human raises fundamental questions that go to

the very nature of what it means to be a human being. From time immemorial we have thought of the birth of our progeny as a gift bestowed by God and/or a beneficent nature. We celebrate our generativity and revel in being participants in an act of creation. The coming together of sperm and egg represents a moment of utter surrender to forces outside of our control. We give part of ourselves up to another and the fusing of our maleness and femaleness results in a unique and finite new creation.

8   The reason most people have an almost instinctual revulsion to cloning is that deep down, they sense that it signals the beginning of a new journey where the "gift of life" is steadily marginalized and eventually abandoned all together. In its place, the new progeny becomes the ultimate shopping experience—designed in advance, produced to specification, and purchased in the biological marketplace.

"Cloning is, first and foremost, an act of 'production,' not creation."

9   Cloning is, first and foremost, an act of "production," not creation. Using the new biotechnologies, a living being is produced with the same degree of engineering as we have come to expect on an assembly line. When we think of engineering standards, what immediately comes to mind is quality controls and predictable outcomes. That's exactly what cloning a human being is all about.

For the first time in the history of our species, we can dictate, in advance, the final genetic constitution of the offspring. The child is no longer a unique creation—one of a kind—but rather an engineered reproduction.

10   Human cloning opens the door wide to the dawn of a commercial Brave New World.[1] Already life science companies have leaped ahead of the political game being played out in Congress and the media by patenting both human embryos and stem cells, giving them upfront ownership and control of a new form of reproductive commerce. Many in the Left worry that the advent of human cloning, embryonic stem cell research, and, soon, designer babies, lays the groundwork for a new form of bio-colonialism in which global life science companies become the ultimate arbiters over the evolutionary process itself.

11   We have good reason to be concerned. While heads of state and parliamentarians wrestle with the escalating struggle between right to life advocates and researchers, a far more menacing tale is unfolding behind the scenes with enormous potential consequences for society. U.S. and British scientists and biotech companies are using embryo and stem cell technology to develop the framework for a commercial eugenics civilization with profound long-term implications for the human race.

12   "Eugenics" is a term coined by Sir Francis Galton, the British philosopher, in the nineteenth century. It means to use breeding to both eliminate undesirable genetic traits and add desirable

---

[1]A reference to *Brave New World*, a science fiction novel published by Aldous Huxley in 1932. In the book, reproduction is automated and occurs on a conveyor belt, where workers manipulate embryos to produce a variety of human beings with different characteristics.

traits to improve the characteristics of an organism or species. When we think of eugenics, we think of Adolf Hitler's ghoulish plan to create the "master" race. Today, however, a new commercial eugenics movement is being meticulously prepared in corporate boardrooms, far away from public scrutiny, and far different in nature from the kind of social eugenics hysteria that engulfed the world in the first half of the twentieth century.

13   Our story begins with a small biotech company, Roslin Bio-Med. The company was created in April 1998 by the Roslin Institute, a government-funded research institution outside Edinburgh, Scotland, where Dolly the sheep was cloned. The company was given an exclusive license to all the Roslin Institute's cloning technology for biomedical research. A year later, Roslin Bio-Med was sold to Geron, a U.S. firm headquartered in Menlo Park, California. Then, in January 2000, the British Patent Office granted a patent to Dr. Ian Wilmut for his cloning technology. The patent—now owned by Geron—covers the cloning process and all the animals produced by the cloning process. What the public doesn't know—because it has received so little attention—is that the British Patent Office granted Wilmut and his company a patent on all cloned human embryos up to the blastocyst stage of development—that's the stage where pluripotent stem cells emerge. The British government, in effect, became the first in the world to recognize a human embryo as a form of intellectual property. The United Kingdom was also the first country to sanction the use of embryos, and even cloned embryos, for the harvesting of stem cells.

14   Despite British success in creating a favorable regulatory and commercial regime for the new research, it was the American company Geron that was quick to lock up the cloning technology. Even before securing the embryo patent, Geron had been quietly financing stem cell research conducted by two U.S. researchers, Dr. James A. Thomson of the University of Wisconsin and Dr. John Gearhart of Johns Hopkins University in Baltimore, Maryland. In November of 1998 both scientists announced that they had independently isolated and identified human stem cells. The breakthrough opened the door to the era of stem cell experimentation in medicine.

"The breakthrough opened the door to the era of stem cell experimentation in medicine."

The researchers' academic institutions immediately applied for patents and sold the exclusive licenses to use the patents to Geron. According to the terms of the Johns Hopkins agreement, Gearhart receives a share of the royalties collected on his patent. Gearhart and Johns Hopkins also own stock in Geron, and Gearhart serves as a consultant to the company. Geron, once alone in the field, is now being challenged by a competitor. Geron's founder, Michael West, broke away from the company and now heads up Advanced Cell Technology in Massachusetts. West's new company has secured its own patents on nonhuman embryo cloning and is experimenting on alternative ways to create human stem cells.

15   By securing patents on the cloning process, as well as on cloned human

embryos and stem cells, companies like Geron and Advanced Cell Technology are in a position to dictate the terms for further advances in medical research using stem cells. The mass production of cloned human embryos provides an unlimited source of stem cells. The stem cells, in turn, are the progenitors of all of the 200 or so differentiated cell types that make up the biology of human life. Researchers, institutes, and other companies from around the world will have to pay Geron and Advanced Cell Technology to access either the use of the embryos or the stem cells they produce, giving the companies unprecedented market advantage. If other researchers or companies actually succeed in making specific body cells from the stem cells, they will likely have to enter into commercial licensing agreements of various kinds with Geron and Advanced Cell Technology for the right to produce the products.

16 What does this portend for the future? To begin with, the granting of a patent for cloned human embryos raises a formidable political question. Can commercial institutions lay claim to a potential individual human life, in the form of intellectual property, at its early stage of development? The British Patent Office has said yes. In the nineteenth century, we fought over the question of whether human beings after birth could be held as commercial property and eventually every nation abolished slavery. Now, however, we have technology that allows companies like Geron to claim potential human beings as intellectual property, at the developmental stage, between conception and birth. The question of whether commercial enterprises will be allowed to own potential human life at the developmental stage, will

likely be one of the seminal political issues of the Biotech Century.

17 Secondly, should companies like Geron and Advanced Cell Technology be allowed to own—in the form of intellectual property—the primary human cells that are the gateway to the entire biological composition that constitutes human life? Do we risk the dawn of a new era in human history where the creation of human life itself will increasingly fall under the control of commercial forces? Will global biotech companies own the designs, the parts, and the processes that produce a human life?

"Will global biotech companies own the designs, the parts, and the processes that produce a human life?"

18 The commercial implications of embryo and stem cell research need to be examined in their entirety. Failure to do so could trap all of us into a commercial eugenics future we neither anticipated nor willingly chose.

19 A Personal Note: As a Jew and a progressive, I was shocked at the news that the Union of Orthodox Jewish Congregations of America and The Rabbinical Council of America had announced their support of so-called therapeutic cloning. The very notion that Rabbis would support legislation that authorized the creation of cloned human embryos for the sole and specific purpose of medical experimentation and research, with a legal requirement that they then be destroyed, is aberrant to everything I believed our religious teachings and heritage stood for. As to the argument that the end justifies the means—that is, that valuable medical advances might flow

from the research—I would argue that such thinking is an anathema to Jewish teachings. Who would have believed that just half a century after the Holocaust, our own religious leaders would give their blessing to a new kind of medical research with commercial eugenics implications that are likely to be every bit as evil in the long run as the social eugenics dogma of an earlier era?

READING CLOSELY AND THINKING CRITICALLY

1. In paragraph 1, how does Rifkin position his argument?
2. Why does Rifkin oppose the cloning of human embryos?
3. What does Rifkin mean when he says he is concerned about "the increasing bio-industrialization of life" (paragraph 2). What exactly is he concerned about?
4. Rifkin fears that embryo cloning will lead to "a commercial eugenics civilization" (paragraph 11). What does he mean? How realistic is this fear?
5. In paragraph 12, Rifkin states that "a new commercial eugenics movement is being meticulously prepared in corporate boardrooms, far away from public scrutiny, and far different in nature from the kind of social eugenics hysteria that engulfed the world in the first half of the twentieth century." Does he prove this to be so? Explain.
6. Why does Rifkin bring up the Holocaust at the end of the essay? (See the headnote that describes the publication the essay first appeared in.) What point is he making, and how is it relevant to his original audience? How does the point help him achieve his persuasive purpose?

EXAMINING STRUCTURE AND STRATEGY

1. What element of ethos appears in paragraph 1? Does the element of ethos contribute to an effective opening? Explain.
2. For the following paragraphs, indicate whether Rifkin relies on logos, pathos, ethos, or a combination: paragraphs 2–4, paragraphs 5–8.
3. Overall, what does Rifkin rely on the most—logical reasoning, emotional appeals, or ethical appeals? How convincing is the argument as a result of the reliance on this approach?
4. What objections does Rifkin raise and counter? How effective are the counters? Does he raise and counter all the most compelling objections? Explain.

NOTING COMBINED PATTERNS

1. Rifkin's principal pattern of development is cause-and-effect analysis. How does he use this pattern to achieve his persuasive purpose?
2. In paragraph 9, Rifkin contrasts cloning as an act of *production*, rather than as an act of *creation*. How does the contrast help him achieve his persuasive purpose?
3. How does Rifkin use narration?

1. Cloning embryos in order to use their cells in research for cures for disease is called "therapeutic cloning." After paragraph 1, Rifkin stops using that term and instead just refers to the process as "cloning." Why?

2. How does Rifkin use questions in paragraphs 5 and 19? In paragraphs 6 and 16?

3. Consult a dictionary if you are unsure of the meaning of any of these words and phrases: *slippery slope* (paragraph 5), *preclude* (paragraph 5), *progeny* (paragraph 7), *beneficent* (paragraph 7), *seminal* (paragraph 16), *anathema* (paragraph 19).

For writing assignments based on "Why I Oppose Human Cloning," see page 578.

BACKGROUND: Raymond Barglow, who has a Ph.D in psychology, is a psychologist, political activist, and computer programmer. He cares passionately about the debate concerning embryonic cloning and works actively to promote embryonic stem cell research. Barglow often writes about the problems and promise of technology. His works include *The Crisis of the Self in the Age of Information: Computers, Dolphins, and Dreams* (1994). "A Reply to Rifkin" first appeared in *Tikkun* (2004).

COMBINED PATTERNS AND THEIR PURPOSE: In "A Reply to Rifkin," Raymond Barglow rebuts the arguments Jeremy Rifkin makes against embryonic stem cell research in "Why I Oppose Human Cloning." To **persuade** readers that he is right and Rifkin is wrong, Barglow relies most heavily on *cause-and-effect analysis*, but he also draws on *comparison-contrast*.

A REPLY TO RIFKIN | RAYMOND BARGLOW

In his essay, "Why I Oppose Human Cloning," Jeremy Rifkin proposes that his view is widely shared within the progressive community: "many of us in the progressive Left are equally opposed to both therapeutic and full birth cloning . . . Earlier this year, sixty-seven leading progressives lent their support to legislation that would outlaw therapeutic and full birth cloning. The signatories of the anti-cloning petition included many of the best-known intellectuals and activists in left circles today." In fact, the petition came from Mr. Rifkin himself (the document became known as "the Rifkin petition"), and two of the petition's signers, Stanley Aronowitz and Quentin Young, have since withdrawn their support from the petition.

As you read This essay was paired with "Why I Oppose Human Cloning" by the editor of *Tikkun* magazine in a debate format. Consider how that fact affects the structure of Barglow's argument.

2   Some of Jeremy Rifkin's criticisms of reproductive cloning are well taken; I do not have the space here to discuss his argument in detail. But his campaign against therapeutic cloning (known by scientists as Somatic Cell Nuclear Transfer, or SCNT, which is explained below) is not equally justified.

3   In the domain of biomedicine, progressives can readily identify with Rifkin's opposition to "efforts to reduce human life and its various parts and processes to the status of mere research tools, manufactured products, and utilities." But despite his assertions to the contrary, few among us can see the link he assumes between the research cloning of embryonic stems cells for therapeutic purposes and the larger doomsday scenario that he lays out. The stem cell issue—which is receiving a lot of attention from the national media—has provided Rifkin with a wedge for introducing his anti-biotechnology agenda to a wide audience at the cost of neglecting the specific intentions and prospects of scientists working with embryonic stem cells to better understand disease processes and to develop new therapies based on that understanding.

4   In its campaign to discredit embryonic stem cell research, the religious right has blurred the differences between therapeutic and reproductive cloning, creating in the popular imagination nightmare visions of cloned babies born into brave new worlds[1] (evoked as well in popular entertainment like the

----

[1]See note on page 568.

movie *Attack of the Clones*). But therapeutic cloning provides scant supplies for these science fiction scenarios. This research is already subject to federal regulation, does not involve significant health risks to cell donors, does not alter existing genomes, and takes place in a laboratory setting with a handful of embryonic stem cells that will not be implanted in a womb.

> "Therapeutic cloning provides scant supplies for these science fiction scenarios."

5   Our task as progressives should be to expose the way that anti-abortion spokespersons twist the facts about this kind of research. Instead, Rifkin has allied himself with these very forces. He rightly points out that biomedical research needs careful ethical evaluation. And in his book *The Biotech Century*, he elaborated a fairly reasonable dialectical approach to such research, recognizing its enormous potential for good, while pointing out also the dangers. But now his blanket opposition to the cloning of human embryos abandons that balance in favor of dubious assumptions and misleading arguments. Banning therapeutic cloning would obstruct research paths that could lead to effective remedies for major illnesses such as childhood leukemia, diabetes, Alzheimer's, and Parkinson's disease.

6   Rifkin argues that "By concentrating research almost exclusively on magic bullets in the form of gene replacements, the medical community forecloses the less invasive option of prevention . . ." This is erroneous on two counts. First, it overlooks what may be the most valuable result of research cloning: A better understanding of disease processes. Researchers can take a diseased cell from an adult (the disease in question could be cancer, cardiovascular disease, Alzheimer's, or another disease in which genetic inheritance or mutation plays a role) and use embryonic cloning to create a stem cell line from it. (The line's originating cells are harvested from the cloned embryo.) Studying a stem cell line of this kind—seeing how the disease develops as the stem cells differentiate—will help us understand that development and find remedies for it. For example, the way in which embryonic stem cells, which have been cloned using adult cells from an Alzheimer's patient, differentiate into brain cells can be compared with the normal formation of brain cells, thereby providing new information that might help us cure this disease. If SCNT research is criminalized, this entire domain of investigation will be shut down.

7   Second, research of this kind needn't be counterposed to preventive measures (which indeed should be medicine's highest priority, as I've argued in an essay published in *Tikkun*, March/April 2002). Consider diabetes for instance. Certainly we need to address the social/environmental factors that may be contributing to its increase over the past two decades. But anyone who has seen a child suffering from diabetes surely hopes also that a medical remedy will be found.

> "But anyone who has seen a child suffering from diabetes surely hopes also that a medical remedy will be found."

8   Rifkin is right, however, to ask basic questions about the priorities and governance of biomedical research. Stem cell experimentation, for example, is a complex, multifaceted enterprise that advances at the cutting edge of scientific understanding. How can it be made to conform to democratically arrived-at norms of social responsibility? How can lay persons, lacking expertise in specialized scientific/technological domains, intelligently evaluate the research approaches that scientists come up with?

9   Progressives have faced this quandary many times before—in our opposition to the nuclear power industry, for instance. In arriving at our judgments about the advisability of using complex technologies, we rely a lot upon the views of authorities who are respected within progressive/environmentalist circles—upon "our" experts, whom we take to be more conscientious and less aligned with profit-seeking interests than are the advocates on "the other side."

10   In the domain of biotechnology, which deploys methods of cellular and molecular investigation that most of us know little or nothing about, how are we to figure out which pathways are ethically and politically acceptable? We may accept the guidance of people like Jeremy Rifkin who have considerable specialized knowledge. Rifkin himself would probably agree, however, that we cannot blindly trust the "experts," even when they espouse values that we believe in.

11   Here are responses to some of the questions that have been raised about therapeutic cloning research:

12   What is therapeutic cloning and why do we need it?

"What is therapeutic cloning and why do we need it?"

13   . . . Therapeutic cloning places the genetic material from an adult cell inside an egg, in order to grow therapeutically beneficial stem cells, not to produce a baby. These cells can be used in scientific research to deepen our comprehension of disease origins and development, and to develop new medical therapies.

14   Many debilitating medical conditions are caused by cell damage. Therapeutic cloning (SCNT), could allow a patient's own genetic material to be used to repair that damage. Replacement cells—neurons, blood cells, pancreatic cells, etc.—generated from cloned stem cells would be much less likely to be rejected by a patient's immune system, since they would be genetically identical to the debilitated tissue they were replacing.

15   Forty Nobel Laureates recently issued a statement that finds this research promising. They cite the prospect of developing cell-replacement therapies, and also of advancing our understanding of fundamental disease processes: "it may be possible to use nuclear transplantation technology to produce patient-specific embryonic stem cells that could overcome the rejection normally associated with tissue and organ transplantation. Nuclear transplantation technology might also permit the creation of embryonic stem cells with defined genetic constitution, permitting a new and powerful approach to understanding how inherited predispositions lead to a variety of cancers and neurological diseases such as Parkinson's and Alzheimer's diseases."

16   Among biomedical researchers in the United States, there is a broad

consensus that the research cloning of embryonic stem cells may lead to new remedies for severe childhood and adult illnesses that afflict millions of people. On February 8 of this year, the National Academy of Sciences concluded that therapeutic cloning "offers great promise for treating diseases . . . closing these avenues of research may have real costs for millions of people who now have these diseases."

17 Are embryonic stem cells really needed for this therapeutic research? Can't scientists use only adult stem cells instead?

18 Rifkin suggests that "few, if any, on the Left oppose research on adult stem cells, which can be taken from individuals after birth and have proved promising in both animal studies and clinical trials. This 'soft path' approach poses none of the ethical, social, and economic risks of strategies using embryo stem cells." Most scientists working in this area, however, believe that adult stem cells are less promising for research purposes than embryonic ones. Embryonic stem cells haven't been damaged by aging, and they show a much greater plasticity—the potential for developing into a variety of specialized cells that could be used in life-saving therapies—than adult ones do. Two recent studies published in *Nature* (March 13, 2002), one of them conducted at the University of Florida and the other by researchers at the University of Edinburgh, cast doubt on previous claims that adult stem cells could revert to an earlier stage of development. In any event, researchers in this domain need to study and work with both embryonic and adult stem cells. We do not yet know which particular path of investigation will lead to useful therapies.

19 There is an additional and very important use of cloned embryonic stem cells in medical research that adult stem cells cannot serve. As explained

"There is an additional and very important use of cloned embryonic stem cells that adult stem cells cannot serve."

above, stem cell lines that result from the embryonic cloning of diseased cells can help us better understand the inception and development of major diseases.

20 Will therapeutic cloning inevitably lead us onto a slippery slope to the production of cloned human babies?

21 No. Federal authority can make it illegal to implant a cloned embryo into a uterus. Our model for regulatory oversight should be the English Fertilisation and Embryology Act of 1990, which limits any experimentation with embryos to the first fourteen days. It is at fourteen days that an embryo first begins to develop the primitive streak, the first indication of a nervous system. It is also at fourteen days that, in all but the most extreme case, an embryo loses the ability to split into two and become twins. The oversight mandated by the English Act has prevented any "slippery slope" in the United Kingdom and there is no reason to assume that a similar approach would not work as well in this country.

22 Will therapeutic cloning lead to unethical incentives being offered for women's eggs, as Rifkin suggests?

23 The prospect of an increased market for women's eggs is a legitimate concern. But our aim should be to regulate,

not to criminalize, the procedures whereby scientists obtain egg cells for research purposes. Moreover, there are clearly some cases where the concern for improper incentives or risk of egg donation would not be relevant—when a mother wishes to donate an egg to help her child, for example, or to create stem cells that could be used to save her own life. If a person can agree to participate, for example, in a dangerous malaria vaccine study to help prevent or cure this disease, why should she be prevented from donating eggs for similar (but much safer) lifesaving research?

24   All of the constituencies that have a stake in the benefits of this research need to devise effective regulations for its continuation. We agree with Jeremy Rifkin that we ought not to trust blindly the scientific community or biotech industry. Legislative bodies—with the participation of scientists, medical practitioners, patients' groups, and other interested parties—need to improve already existing statutes regarding egg donation for any purpose: in vitro fertilization, surrogate motherhood, or therapeutic cloning. This is the democratic way to address the relevant social and ethical concerns.

"This is the democratic way to address the relevant social and ethical concerns."

25   It is also important to note that by researching therapeutic cloning, scientists hope to understand the biological properties of a cloned egg cell that induce it to generate stem cells. Once they learn how this cell "reprogramming" occurs, they may no longer need to use egg cells.

26   Irving Weissman, a biology professor at Stanford, compares the current debate over stem cell research to the 1970s controversy over recombinant DNA technology, which now produces a broad range of medicines, including cancer and diabetes treatments. He points out that "the lives of hundred of thousands of Americans each year are saved or made better by such recombinant DNA products . . . I believe the kind of medical research that can follow from nuclear transplantation will have a similar magnitude of medical benefits."

27   Because of its therapeutic potential, research that clones stem cells for medical purposes deserves our support. It should be publicly funded and better regulated, not outlawed.

READING CLOSELY AND THINKING CRITICALLY

1.   What is Barglow's thesis, and where is that thesis expressed?

2.   Why is Barglow in favor of stem cell research that involves embryonic cloning?

3.   What is Barglow's objection to using adult stem cells?

4.   Barglow says that some who oppose embryonic stem cell research fail to distinguish between therapeutic and reproductive cloning (paragraph 4). What is the difference? Why is the distinction important to Barglow's argument?

5.   In paragraphs 5 and 9, Barglow uses "our" to include himself as a member of the audience he is addressing. How does identifying with his audience in this way contribute to the ethos of this essay?

EXAMINING STRUCTURE AND STRATEGY

1. What approach does Barglow take to the opening paragraph? How does this approach help the author achieve his persuasive purpose?
2. Barglow raises and counters Rifkin's objections in paragraphs 2, 4, 6–7, 8, and 17–23. Why does he devote so much of his argument to raising and countering Rifkin's objections? Does he do so because his essay was paired with Rifkin's in *Tikkun* as a debate? Explain.
3. Paragraphs 12–23 are written in a question-and-answer format. How does this strategy help Barglow achieve his persuasive purpose? Paragraph 11 is a transition to Barglow's question-and-answer format. Do you find the shift a smooth one or an abrupt one? Why?
4. For the following paragraphs, indicate whether Barglow relies on logos, pathos, ethos, or a combination: paragraph 7, paragraph 8, paragraphs 15–16, paragraph 24, paragraph 25.
5. Overall, what does Barglow rely on most: logos, pathos, or ethos?
6. At times, Barglow acknowledges that Rifkin has a valid point (in paragraph 8, for example). Why does he do so?

NOTING COMBINED PATTERNS

1. Explain how Barglow uses cause-and-effect analysis.
2. How does the comparison in paragraphs 9 and 26 help Barglow achieve his persuasive purpose?

CONSIDERING LANGUAGE AND STYLE

1. In paragraph 3, Barglow accuses Rifkin of creating a "doomsday scenario." What does Barglow mean, and why does he think Rifkin creates a doomsday scenario? Do you agree that Rifkin creates such a scenario? Why or why not?
2. Consult a dictionary if you are unsure of the meaning of any of these words: *genome* (paragraph 4), *dialectical* (paragraph 5), *constituencies* (paragraph 24), *recombinant DNA* (paragraph 26).

ASSIGNMENTS FOR DISCUSSION AND WRITING

"Why I Oppose Human Cloning" and "A Reply to Rifkin"

1. **For discussion in class or online.** In paragraph 2, Raymond Barglow says, "Some of Jeremy Rifkin's criticisms of reproductive cloning are well taken." In the embryonic cloning debate, as in most debates, reasonable people disagree. What are the best arguments for the side of the debate with which you *disagree*. Why are the these arguments compelling? If your instructor so directs, post your response to your class Web site.
2. **In your journal.** In about two pages, discuss your view of the stem cell research/embryonic cloning debate. Have you made up your mind? Do you need more information?

3. **Using argumentation for a purpose.** The purposes in the assignments are possibilities. You may establish whatever purposes you like, within your instructor's guidelines.

- Barglow had an advantage over Rifkin because he was rebutting an argument rather than launching his own. Now give the same advantage to Rifkin: Take the side of Rifkin and respond to Barglow. What would Rifkin say? How might he consider and reject Barglow, as Barglow considered and rejected him? Your purpose is to convince readers that Rifkin has the more compelling argument. As an alternative, rewrite Barglow's essay as a stand-alone argumentation essay rather than a rebuttal.

- To convince your writing instructor that you have thoroughly studied both "Why I Oppose Human Cloning" and "A Reply to Rifkin," write an essay arguing that one of the essays presents a better argument than the other. Consider all the aspects of argumentation you have been studying: audience, purpose, logos, pathos, ethos, kind and quality of supporting detail, raising and countering objections, and so on.

- To convince a reader who is undecided about the wisdom of embryonic stem cell research, argue for or against the validity of Rifkin's fears that cloning "opens the door wide to the dawn of a commercial Brave New World" (paragraph 10).

- Every advance has its dark side. Jeremy Rifkin presents what he sees as the potential dark side of stem cell research involving embryonic cloning. Give examples of other technologies, discoveries, or inventions that have their dark side, explain what the dark side is, and argue whether the problems associated with an advance should dissuade us from making use of it. You might consider such advances, discoveries, and inventions as nuclear power, medical narcotics, chemical pesticides, and gasoline-powered engines. Your purpose is to convince the average reader to agree with your assertion.

- In paragraph 21, Barglow gives one legal safeguard associated with embryonic cloning. If you were a federal legislator, what safeguards would you propose to govern stem cell research? State the safeguard and argue for its passage into law.

4. **Connecting the readings.** Reread Dylan Thomas's poem "Do Not Go Gentle into That Good Night" on page 486. Is supporting embryonic stem cell research consonant with what Thomas means by "rage, rage against the dying of the light"? What about surgery and organ transplants? Explain your view.

5. **Drawing on sources.**

- In your campus library or on the Internet, seek out alternate opinions on embryonic stem cell research. In the library you can use *InfoTrac, The Reader's Guide to Periodical Literature,* or *The New York Times Index* to find information. On the Internet, you can use your favorite search engine. Read the opinions you discover, consider them, and then write an essay that expresses what you believe after weighing out the ideas in this chapter and the ones you research.

- President Reagan's son, Ron Reagan, delivered a speech in favor of stem cell research at the 2004 Democratic Convention that nominated John Kerry. Locate that speech using *The New York Times Index* in your library's reference room or by typing "transcript Ron Reagan speech Democratic Convention" into your favorite search engine. Read the speech, summarize its contents, and evaluate how convincing it is. What grade would you give it? Why?

IS JUSTICE SERVED BY TRYING JUVENILE OFFENDERS AS ADULTS?

In the early twentieth century, a new awareness of adolescent psychology prompted reforms in education, child labor, and criminal law, including the development of a juvenile justice system. By 1925, most states had established a separate legal system for juveniles that emphasized prevention and rehabilitation instead of punishment. However, outbreaks of violence in schools, such as multiple killings at Columbine High School by two teenagers, have caused many to question whether justice is served when juveniles who commit murder are not tried as adults.

What should we do with our most violent juvenile offenders? Is the juvenile justice system adequate to handle murder, or should young murderers be placed in the adult system? How do we prevent violence in the future? Some believe that answers do not come from treating juveniles as adults. This view is expressed in the *New York Times* editorial, "Little Adult Criminals." Some, like Laurence Steinberg in "Should Juvenile Offenders Be Tried as Adults?" believe that some juveniles can be tried as adults, but others cannot. Still others believe we need a get-tough policy that tries juveniles in the adult justice system. This view is advanced by Linda Collier in "Adult Crime, Adult Time." As you consider the issue and weigh out principles of rehabilitation, retribution, punishment, and accountability, you may find Timothy Roche and Amanda Bower's essay, "Young Voices from the Cell" helpful for learning how some young offenders fare in adult prisons.

Copyright © 2002 by Mike Keefe. The Denver Post, 10/25/2002.

BACKGROUND: In 2000, Nathaniel Brazill was sentenced to the minimum of 25 years for shooting his seventh-grade teacher, Barry Grunow, with a semiautomatic pistol. Brazill was 13 at the time of the shooting and could have received a life sentence without parole. At 14, Lionel Tate became the youngest person sentenced to life in prison. He was convicted of stomping a 6-year-old playmate to death. Three years later, in 2004, an appeals court ruled that his mental competency should have been evaluated before the trial, and he was granted bond and released. Both children were tried as adults. After these Florida murder trials made particularly visible the trend toward trying minors as adults, public debate about how to deal with violent juvenile offenders heated up. Some of that debate took place on the editorial pages of our nation's newspapers. In fact, "Little Adult Criminals" first appeared on the editorial page of the *New York Times* in May 2001.

COMBINED PATTERNS AND THEIR PURPOSE: "Little Adult Criminals" advances the argument that children of 12 or 14 have insufficient emotional maturity to control their impulses or to comprehend the consequences of their actions. To achieve its **persuasive** purpose, the editorial includes *cause-and-effect analysis* and *exemplification*.

Little Adult Criminals

NEW YORK TIMES EDITORIAL

Spurred by news of teenagers with easy access to guns and other weapons committing increasingly violent crimes, all but three states have made it easier in recent years to try minors as adults. The idea was that certain types of violent crime are so serious that they do not belong in a juvenile court system designed not only to punish delinquents but to rehabilitate them before they reach adulthood. Two high-profile murder trials in Florida this year have sounded a warning that the trend may have gone too far.

As you read Notice that the author offers a compromise. Determine whether that compromise adds to the persuasive quality of the editorial.

2   In the first case, Lionel Tate, a 14-year-old, was convicted in January of first-degree murder for beating to death a 6-year-old playmate when he was 12. He was sentenced in March to life without parole. His mother had foolishly refused to accept a plea bargain that would have carried only a three-year sentence in a youth facility followed by 10 years of probation.

3   Then this month, a jury convicted Nathaniel Brazill, also 14, of second-degree murder. When he was 13 he shot and killed a teacher who would not allow him back into class after he had been suspended for throwing water balloons. "Not too bad," was the youth's reaction to the verdict, which carries a sentence of 25 years to life in prison. In his case we are again left wondering whether the disciplinary troubles of a teenager would have escalated into a crime if he had lived in a place where guns were not so readily available.

4   A civilized society must not easily give up hope of rehabilitating a

child who commits a crime. While a 17-year-old repeat offender may warrant trial as an adult criminal, children who are 12 or 14 do not possess the emotional maturity to control their impulses, or to fully understand the consequences of their actions. It is more than social development; recent medical research has found that the brain continues to develop into one's teenage years. In no instance does a juvenile belong in adult prisons.

5   In Florida, it was evident that the two defendants did not fully grasp the significance of the proceedings. Some of the jurors in each case later questioned the wisdom of trying the boys in an adult court, and even Gov. Jeb Bush said that Nathaniel should not have been tried as an adult. "There should be a sensitivity to the fact that a 14-year-old is not a little adult," he said.

6   The governor can act upon this belief in reviewing the clemency petitions of both boys. He should also press for review of whether juvenile court judges, instead of prosecutors or state legislatures, should determine whether a particular minor ought to be tried in an adult criminal system whose procedures, sentencing guidelines and prisons make no allowances for minors. Florida, like many other states, has wrongly granted prosecutors too much discretion in making that call.

7   Reasserting the role of the juvenile criminal system, traditionally charged with acting in the best interests of a minor, does not mean society's interest in public safety is shortchanged. Juvenile courts have rarely hesitated to transfer minors to adult court where necessary, such as when a 17-year-old with a history of violent behavior commits a heinous, premeditated crime.

8   Moreover, studies have shown that minors who have gone through the juvenile system, with its emphasis on rehabilitation through counseling, mentoring, education and vocational training, are less likely to be arrested again after being released than those who have served time in ordinary prisons. A sensible approach is to have minors convicted in criminal court serve time in juvenile detention facilities, and have their sentences reviewed when they come of age. The criminal justice system is charged with determining an individual's level of culpability, and it must factor a minor's age into that equation.

9   To send 14-year-olds directly to adult prisons for a quarter-century is to give up on them. It may even ensure that they become lifetime criminals.

READING CLOSELY AND THINKING CRITICALLY

1. According to the editorial, why have so many states made it easier to try juveniles in adult courts?
2. For what reasons is the author opposed to trying juveniles as adults?
3. What is the author's position on gun ownership? How can you tell?
4. What compromise solution does the author offer to resolve the question of whether to try juveniles as adults? Does the compromise help achieve the author's persuasive purpose? Explain.

EXAMINING STRUCTURE AND STRATEGY

1. Why does the author mention that Lionel Tate's mother refused a plea bargain? How does that information contribute to the author's persuasive purpose?
2. What objections does the author raise and counter? Are the counterarguments effective? Explain.
3. Does the author support points to your satisfaction? Explain.
4. What does the editorial's conclusion contribute to its persuasive purpose?

NOTING COMBINED PATTERNS

1. How does the editorial writer use cause-and-effect analysis as part of the editorial's introduction?
2. How does the editorial writer use cause-and-effect analysis in paragraphs 8 and 9 as part of the argument?
3. How do examples in paragraphs 2, 3, and 5 help support the argument?

1. In paragraph 1, sentence 2, why did the author include the phrase "designed not only to punish delinquents but to rehabilitate them before they reach adulthood"?

2. Consult your dictionary if you do not know the meaning of these words: *clemency* (paragraph 6), *heinous* (paragraph 7), *premeditated* (paragraph 7), *mentoring* (paragraph 8), *culpability* (paragraph 8)

For writing assignments based on "Little Adult Criminals," see page 603.

BACKGROUND: Laurence Steinberg attended Vassar and earned his Ph.D. from Cornell University. He is the Distinguished University Professor of Psychology at Temple University and the director of the John D. and Catherine T. MacArthur Foundation Research Network on Adolescent Development and Juvenile Justice. He has also taught at Cornell University, the University of California at Irvine, and the University of Wisconsin at Madison. Steinberg is an expert on the psychological development of adolescents, parent-child relationships, high school reform, and juvenile justice. He is a member of the National Academy of Science's Panel on the Health Implications of Child Labor and a consultant to federal agencies on child labor and juvenile justice policy. The author of more than 150 scholarly articles, he is also the author or editor of ten books, including *You and Your Adolescent: A Parent's Guide for Ages 10–20* (1997), *Handbook of Adolescent Psychology* (2004), *The Ten Basic Principles of Good Parenting* (2004), and the best-selling textbook *Adolescence*, now in its seventh edition (2005). "Should Juvenile Offenders Be Tried as Adults?" first appeared in *USA Today Magazine* in January 2001.

COMBINED PATTERNS AND THEIR PURPOSES: In "Should Juvenile Offenders Be Tried as Adults?" Laurence Steinberg draws on several patterns of development, including *definition, contrast,* and *cause-and-effect analysis* to **inform** readers about the nature of the juvenile justice system and how it differs from the adult system. He also **argues** that children of a certain age should not be tried as adults unless they are assessed and judged to be sufficiently competent to enter the adult system.

SHOULD JUVENILE OFFENDERS BE TRIED AS ADULTS?

| LAURENCE STEINBERG

Few issues challenge a society's ideas about the natures of human development and justice as much as serious juvenile crime. Because people neither expect children to be criminals nor expect crimes to be committed by them, the unforeseen intersection between childhood and criminality creates a dilemma that most of us find difficult to resolve. The only way out of this dilemma is either to redefine the offense as something less serious than a crime or to redefine the offender as someone who is not really a child.

2   For the past 100 years, American society has most often chosen the first approach. It has redefined juvenile offenses by treating most of them as delinquent acts to be adjudicated within a separate juvenile justice system that is theoretically designed to recognize the special

As you read
Pay attention to where Steinberg raises and counters an objection and determine why he does so at that point.

needs and immature status of young people and emphasize rehabilitation over punishment. Two guiding beliefs about young people have prevailed: first, that juveniles have different competencies than adults (and therefore need to be adjudicated in a different type of venue); and second, that they have different potential for change than adults (and therefore merit a second chance and an attempt at rehabilitation). States have recognized that conduct alone—that is, the alleged criminal act—should not by itself determine whether to invoke the heavy hand of the adult criminal justice system.

"States have determined that conduct alone should not by itself determine whether to invoke the heavy hand of the adult criminal justice system."

3   In recent years, though, there has been a dramatic shift in the way juvenile crime is viewed by policymakers and the general public, one that has led to widespread changes in policies and practices concerning the treatment of juvenile offenders. Rather than choosing to define offenses committed by youth as delinquent, society increasingly is opting to redefine them as adults and transfer them to the adult court and criminal justice system.

4   Most reasonable people agree that a small number of young offenders should be transferred to the adult system because they pose a genuine threat to the safety of other juveniles, the severity of their offense merits a relatively more severe punishment, or their history of repeated offending bodes poorly for their ultimate rehabilitation. However, this does not describe the tens of thousands of young people who currently are being prosecuted in the adult system, a large proportion of whom have been charged with nonviolent crimes. When the wholesale transfer to criminal court of various categories of juvenile offenders starts to become the rule rather than the exception, this represents a fundamental challenge to the very premise that the juvenile court was founded on—that adolescents and adults are different.

5   There are many lenses through which one can view debates about transfer policies. As a developmental psychologist, I ask whether the distinctions we draw between people of different ages under the law are sensible in light of what we know about age differences in various aspects of intellectual, emotional, or social functioning. More specifically, on the basis of what we know about development, should a boundary be drawn between juveniles and adults

in criminal matters and, if so, at what age should we draw it?

6   Developmental psychology, broadly defined, concerns the scientific study of changes in physical, intellectual, emotional, and social development over the life cycle. Developmental psychologists are mainly interested in the study of "normative" development. My concern is whether the study of normative development indicates that there are scientific reasons to warrant the differential treatment of young people and adults within the legal system, especially with regard to the age period most under current political scrutiny—the years between 12 and 17.

7   First, this age range is an inherently transitional time. There are rapid and dramatic changes in individuals' physical, intellectual, emotional, and social capabilities. If there is a period in the life span during which one might choose to draw a line between incompetent and competent individuals, this is it.

" . . . Adolescence is a period of potential malleability."

8   Second, adolescence is a period of potential malleability. Experiences in the family, peer group, school, and other settings still have a chance to influence the course of development. To the extent that malleability is likely, transferring juveniles into a criminal justice system that precludes a rehabilitative response may not be very sensible public policy. However, to the extent that amenability is limited, their transfer to the adult system is less worrisome.

9   Finally, adolescence is a formative period during which a number of developmental trajectories become firmly established and increasingly difficult to

alter. Many adolescent experiences have a tremendous cumulative impact. Bad decisions or poorly formulated policies pertaining to juvenile offenders may have unforeseen and harmful consequences that are very hard to undo.

10   It is only fair to ask whether or why a developmental perspective is even relevant to contemporary discussions of trying juvenile offenders in the adult criminal system. After all, current discussions about trying juveniles in adult court are typically not about the characteristics of the offender, but about the seriousness and harmfulness of the offense—factors independent of the offender's age or maturity. "Adult time for adult crime"—the mantra of the get-tough-on-juvenile-crime lobby—says nothing about the age of the offender, except for the fact that it ought to be considered irrelevant.

11   I believe that it is logically impossible to make the age of the offender irrelevant in discussions of criminal justice policy. A fair punishment to an adult is unfair when applied to a child who did not understand the consequences of his or her actions. The ways we interpret and apply laws should rightfully vary when the case at hand involves a defendant whose understanding of the law is limited by intellectual immaturity or whose judgment is impaired by emotional immaturity. Moreover, the implications and consequences of administering a long and harsh punishment are very different when the offender is young than when he or she is an adult.

12   Transferring juveniles to criminal court has three sets of implications that need to be considered in discussions about whether they should be tried as adults. First, transfer to adult court alters the legal process by which a minor is tried. Criminal court is based on an adversarial model, while juvenile court is based, at least in theory, on a more cooperative model. This difference in the climates of juvenile vs. adult courts is significant because it is unclear at what age individuals have sufficient understanding of the ramifications of the adversarial process and the different vested interests of prosecutors, defense attorneys, and judges. Young defendants may simply not have what it takes—by the standards established in the Constitution—to be able to defend themselves in criminal court.

"Transfer to adult court alters the legal process by which a minor is tried."

13   Second, the legal standards applied in adult and juvenile courts are different. For example, competence to stand trial is presumed among adult defendants unless they suffer from a serious mental illness or substantial mental retardation. We do not know if the presumption of competence holds for juveniles, who, even in the absence of mental retardation or mental illness, may lack sufficient competence to participate in the adjudicative process. Standards for judging culpability may be different in juvenile and adult courts as well. In the absence of mental illness or substantial deficiency, adults are presumed to be responsible for their own behavior. We do not know the extent to which this presumption applies to juveniles, or whether the validity of this presumption differs as a function of the juvenile's age.

14   Finally, the choice of trying a young offender in adult vs. juvenile court determines the possible outcomes of the adjudication. In adult court, the outcome

of being found guilty of a serious crime is nearly always some sort of punishment. In juvenile court, the outcome of being found delinquent may be some sort of punishment, but juvenile courts typically retain the option of a rehabilitative disposition, in and of itself or in combination with some sort of punishment. This has two significant ramifications: the stakes of the adjudication are substantially greater and, in juvenile court, offenders generally are presumed amenable unless the prosecutor demonstrates otherwise. In adult court, amenability is not presumed, and must instead be shown by the defendant's counsel.

15 In other words, decisionmakers within the juvenile and criminal justice systems bring different presumptions to the table. The juvenile court operates under the presumption that offenders are immature, in three different senses of the word: Their development is incomplete; their judgment is less than mature; and their character is still developing. The adult court, in contrast, presumes that defendants are mature, competent, responsible, and unlikely to change.

16 Which of these presumptions best characterizes individuals between the ages of 12 and 17? Is there an approximate age where the presumptions of the criminal court become more applicable to an offender than the presumptions of the juvenile court? Although developmental psychology does not point to any one age that politicians and practitioners should use in formulating transfer policies or practices, it does point to age-related trends in certain legally relevant attributes, such as the intellectual or emotional capabilities that affect decisionmaking in court and on the street.

17 It is appropriate, based on developmental research, to raise serious concerns about the transfer of individuals 12 and under to adult court, because of their limited adjudicative competence as well as the very real possibility that most children this young will not prove to be sufficiently blameworthy to warrant exposure to the harsh consequences of a criminal court adjudication. For this reason, individuals 12 and under should continue to be viewed as juveniles, regardless of the nature of their offense. This does not mean that we should let them off the hook or fail to punish them. It merely means that they should be punished and held responsible within a system designed to treat children, not fully mature adults.

"This does not mean that we should let them off the hook or fail to punish them."

18 At the other end of the continuum, it appears appropriate to conclude that the vast majority of individuals older than 16 are not appreciably different from adults in ways that would prohibit their fair adjudication within the criminal justice system. My view is that variability among individuals older than 12, but younger than 16, requires that some sort of individualized assessment of an offender's competence to stand trial, blameworthiness, and likely amenability to treatment be made before reaching a transfer decision. The relevant decisionmakers (e.g., judges, prosecutors, and defense attorneys) should be permitted to exercise judgment about individual offenders' maturity and eligibility for transfer.

19 It is true that a bullet wound hurts just as much when the weapon is fired by a child as when it is fired by an adult,

but this argument is a red herring, since we comfortably acknowledge that there are numerous situations where mitigating factors should be taken into account when trying a defendant, such as insanity, emotional duress, or self-defense. Immaturity is another mitigating factor. People may differ in their opinions about the extent to which, the ways in which, and the age at which an offender's maturity should be considered in court decisions. One person might believe that a boundary should be drawn at 18, another at 15, and yet another at 13. Nevertheless, ignoring the offender's age entirely is like trying to ignore an elephant

> "Ignoring the offender's age entirely is like trying to ignore an elephant that has wandered into the courtroom."

that has wandered into the courtroom. You can do it, but most people will notice that something smells foul.

READING CLOSELY AND THINKING CRITICALLY

1. What is Steinberg arguing? What are the issues and his assertion?
2. Steinberg says that we have two ways to deal with children who commit crimes. What are they? Which option has American society chosen most often in the past 100 years?
3. How is the American juvenile justice system designed to treat the youthful offender?
4. Steinberg notes a recent change in the nation's handling of juvenile crime. What is the change? How extensive is it?
5. Why does Steinberg consider the age span 12 to 17 so significant? Why is it important to handle properly the juvenile offenders in this group?
6. Some people believe the age of the offender is irrelevant. Instead, the nature of the crime should determine the punishment. Does Steinberg agree? Explain.

EXAMINING STRUCTURE AND STRATEGY

1. In paragraph 5, the author identifies himself as a developmental psychologist. In what way is that information a form of ethos? (See page 549 on ethos.) How does it help the author achieve his persuasive purpose?
2. How does the author develop his ethos in paragraphs 10 and 11?
3. In paragraph 19, what objection does Steinberg raise? How does he counter that objection? Why does he raise and counter the objection at the end of the essay?

NOTING COMBINED PATTERNS

1. Paragraph 6 includes definition. How does that definition help Steinberg achieve his persuasive purpose?
2. What is contrasted in paragraphs 12 through 14? Where does cause-and-effect analysis appear in the essay?

3. How do the contrast and cause-and-effect analysis help Steinberg achieve his persuasive purpose?

CONSIDERING LANGUAGE AND STYLE

1. In paragraph 19, Steinberg refers to an argument as a "red herring." What does he mean?
2. Paragraph 4 opens with the words, "Most reasonable people agree." What is the effect of that clause?
3. Consult a dictionary if you are unsure of these words: *adjudicate* (paragraph 2), *venue* (paragraph 2), *malleability* (paragraph 8), *amenability* (paragraph 8), *trajectories* (paragraph 9), *mantra* (paragraph 10), *culpability* (paragraph 13).

For writing assignments based on this essay, see page 603.

BACKGROUND: Linda J. Collier is an attorney who has worked in juvenile courts. Currently the dean of public services and social sciences at Delaware County Community College, she earned her Bachelor of Arts and Juris Doctorate degrees from Howard University and her Master of Science in criminal justice from St. Joseph's University. Collier has been a special assistant for legal affairs to the presidents at both Cheyney and Lincoln universities and has taught courses in English, political justice, sociology, and criminal justice. She has also been the director of student legal services at Penn State University. "Adult Crime, Adult Time" originally appeared in the *Washington Post* in 1998 as "Adult Crime, Adult Time: Outdated Juvenile Laws Thwart Justice."

COMBINED PATTERNS AND THEIR PURPOSES: In "Adult Crime, Adult Time," Linda Collier uses *process analysis* to **inform** readers about how the juvenile justice system works, and she discusses the *effects* of those procedures in part with *exemplification*. Her goal is to **persuade** readers that the current system is inadequate and that we should be trying juveniles as adults if they commit violent crimes.

Adult Crime, Adult Time

LINDA J. COLLIER

When prosecutor Brent Davis said he wasn't sure if he could charge 11-year-old Andrew Golden and 13-year-old Mitchell Johnson as adults after Tuesday afternoon's slaughter in Jonesboro, Ark.,[1] I cringed. But not for the reasons you might think.

As you read Evaluate how compelling Collier's supporting detail is.

2   I knew he was formulating a judgment based on laws that have not had a major overhaul for more than 100 years. I knew his hands were tied by the long-standing creed that juvenile offenders, generally defined as those under the age of 18, are to be treated rather than punished. I knew he would have to do legal cartwheels to get the case out of the juvenile system. But most of all, I cringed because today's juvenile suspects—even those who are accused of committing the most violent crimes—are still regarded by the law as children first and criminals second.

3   As astonishing as the Jonesboro events were, this is hardly the first time that children with access to guns and other weapons have brought tragedy to a school. Only weeks before the Jonesboro shootings, three girls in Paducah, Ky., were killed in their school lobby when a 14-year-old classmate allegedly opened fire on them. Authorities said he had several guns with him, and the alleged murder weapon was one of seven stolen from a neighbor's garage. And the day after the Jonesboro shootings, a 14-year-old in Daly City, Calif., was charged

[1]Fourteen-year-old Mitchell Johnson and 12-year-old Andrew Golden were convicted of shooting four classmates and a teacher in Jonesboro, Arkansas in 1998. After the article was written, the two boys were sentenced to the maximum penalty allowed by Arkansas law—confinement in a juvenile center until they turn 21.

as a juvenile after he allegedly fired at his middle-school principal with a semiautomatic handgun.

4   It's not a new or unusual phenomenon for children to commit violent crimes at younger and younger ages, but it often takes a shocking incident to draw our attention to a trend already in progress. According to the U.S. Department of Justice, crimes committed by juveniles have increased by 60 percent since 1984. Where juvenile delinquency was once limited to truancy or vandalism, juveniles now are more likely to be the perpetrators of serious and deadly crimes such as arson, aggravated assault, rape and murder. And these violent offenders increasingly include those as young as the Jonesboro suspects. Since 1965, the number of 12-year-olds arrested for violent crimes has doubled and the number of 13- and 14-year-olds has tripled, according to government statistics.

5   Those statistics are a major reason why we need to revamp our antiquated juvenile justice system. Nearly every state, including Arkansas, has laws that send most youthful violent offenders to the juvenile courts, where they can only be found "delin-quent" and confined in a juvenile facility (typically not past age 21). In recent years, many states have enacted changes in their juvenile crime laws, and some have lowered the age at which a juvenile can be tried as an adult for certain violent crimes. Virginia, for example, has reduced its minimum age to 14, and suspects accused of murder and aggravated malicious wounding are automatically waived to adult court. Illinois is now sending some 13-year-olds to adult court after a hearing in juvenile court. In Kansas, a 1996 law allows juveniles as young as 10 to be prosecuted as adults in some cases. These are steps in the right direction, but too many states still treat violent offenders under 16 as juveniles who belong in the juvenile system.

6   My views are not those of a frustrated prosecutor. I have represented children as a court-appointed guardian ad litem, or temporary guardian, in the Philadelphia juvenile justice system. Loosely defined, a guardian ad litem is responsible for looking after the best interest of a neglected or rebellious child who has come into the juvenile courts. It is often a humbling experience as I try to help children whose lives have gone awry, sometimes because of circumstances beyond their control.

7   My experience has made me believe that the system is doing a poor job at treatment as well as punishment. One of my "girls," a chronic truant, was a foster child who longed to be adopted. She often talked of how she wanted a pink room, a frilly bunk bed and sisters with whom she could share her dreams. She languished in foster care from ages 2 to 13 because her drug-ravaged mother would not relinquish her parental rights. Initially, the girl refused to tolerate the half-life that the state had maintained was in her best interest. But as it became clear that we would never convince her mother to give up her rights, the girl became a frequent runaway. Eventually she ended up pregnant, wandering from place to place and committing adult crimes to survive. No longer a child, not quite a woman, she is the kind of teenage offender for whom the juvenile system has little or nothing to offer.

8   A brief history: Proceedings in juvenile justice began in 1890 in

Chicago, where the original mandate was to save wayward children and protect them from the ravages of society. The system called for children to be processed through an appendage of the family court By design, juveniles were to be kept away from the court's criminal side, the district attorney and adult correctional institutions.

9   Typically, initial procedures are informal, non-threatening and not open to public scrutiny. A juvenile suspect is interviewed by an "intake" officer who determines the child's fate. The intake officer may issue a warning, lecture and release; he may detain the suspect; or, he may decide to file a petition, subjecting the child to juvenile "adjudication" proceedings. If the law allows, the intake officer may make a recommendation that the juvenile be transferred to adult criminal court.

10   An adjudication is similar to a hearing, rather than a trial, although the juvenile may be represented by counsel and a juvenile prosecutor will represent the interests of the community. It is important to note that throughout the proceedings, no matter which side of the fence the parties are on, the operating principle is that everyone is working in the best interests of the child. Juvenile court judges do not issue findings of guilt, but decide whether a child is delinquent. If delinquency is found, the judge must decide the child's fate. Should the child be sent back to the family—assuming there is one? Declare him or her "in need of supervision," which brings in the intense help of social services? Remove the child from the family and place him or her in foster care? Confine the child to a state institution for juvenile offenders?

11   This system was developed with truants, vandals and petty thieves in mind. But this model is not appropriate for the violent juvenile offender of

today. Detaining a rapist or murderer in a juvenile facility until the age of 18 or 21 isn't even a slap on the hand. If a juvenile is accused of murdering, raping or assaulting someone with a deadly weapon, the suspect should automatically be sent to adult criminal court. What's to ponder?

12 With violent crime becoming more prevalent among the junior set, it's a mystery why there hasn't been a major overhaul of juvenile justice laws long before now. Will the Jonesboro shootings be the incident that makes us take a hard look at the current system? When it became evident that the early release of Jesse Timmendequas—whose murder of 7-year-old Megan Kanka in New Jersey sparked national outrage—had caused unwarranted tragedy, legislative action was swift. Now New Jersey has Megan's Law, which requires the advance notification of a sexual predator's release into a neighborhood. Other states have followed suit.

13 It is unequivocally clear that the same type of mandate is needed to establish a uniform minimum age for trying juveniles as adults. As it stands now, there is no consistency in state laws governing waivers to adult court. One reason for this lack of uniformity is the absence of direction from the federal government or Congress. The Bureau of Justice Statistics reports that adjacent states such as New York and Pennsylvania respond differently to 16-year-old criminals, with New York tending to treat offenders of that age as adults and Pennsylvania handling them in the juvenile justice system.

14 Federal prosecution of juveniles is not totally unheard of, but it is uncommon. The Bureau of Justice Statistics estimates that during 1994, at least 65 juveniles were referred to the attorney general for transfer to adult status. In such cases, the U.S. attorney's office must certify a substantial federal interest in the case and show that one of the following is true: The state does not have jurisdiction; the state refuses to assume jurisdiction or the state does not have adequate services for juvenile offenders; the offense is a violent felony, drug trafficking or firearm offense as defined by the U.S. Code.

15 Exacting hurdles, but not insurmountable. In the Jonesboro case, prosecutor Davis has been exploring ways to enlist the federal court's jurisdiction. Whatever happens, federal prosecutions of young offenders are clearly not the long-term answer. The states must act. So as far as I can see, the next step is clear: Children who knowingly engage in adult conduct and adult crimes should automatically be subject to adult rules and adult prison time.

READING CLOSELY AND THINKING CRITICALLY

1. Which sentence is the thesis of "Adult Crime, Adult Time"?

2. Collier says that she cringed—but not for the reasons the reader might think—when she heard that the prosecutor "wasn't sure if he could charge" Andrew Golden and Mitchell Johnson as adults. Why did she cringe? For what reasons does she think her readers will cringe?

3. In paragraph 7, Collier cites the example of a girl who began committing adult crimes. Does this example effectively support the author's view? Explain.

4. Can the example of the girl in paragraph 7 be used to argue *against* trying juveniles as adults? Why or why not?

5. What reasons does Collier give for her assertion? Does she provide sufficient support for her stand? Explain.

EXAMINING STRUCTURE AND STRATEGY

1. In paragraph 4, Collier includes government statistics. How do these statistics help her achieve her purpose?

2. In paragraph 6, Collier identifies herself as a person who has been a court-appointed guardian for juveniles. She also says that she is not a frustrated prosecutor. Why does she make these points?

3. In paragraph 8, Collier gives a brief history of the juvenile justice system. Does this information help her achieve her purpose? Explain.

4. A *rhetorical question* is not meant to elicit a reply. Does the rhetorical question in paragraph 11 help Collier achieve her persuasive purpose? Why or why not?

5. Is Collier's reasoning inductive or deductive? How do you know?

NOTING COMBINED PATTERNS

1. What purpose do the examples in paragraphs 3 and 5 serve?

2. How does the process analysis in paragraphs 9 and 10 help Collier support her thesis?

3. In what way is cause-and-effect analysis important to Collier's persuasive strategy?

CONSIDERING LANGUAGE AND STYLE

1. Explain the metaphor *legal cartwheels* in paragraph 2. What does it mean? Is it effective? (Metaphors are explained on page 110.)

2. Paragraph 15 opens with a sentence fragment rather than with a sentence. How is the fragment used? Would a sentence have been more effective? Explain.

3. Consult a dictionary if you are unsure of the meaning of these words: *creed* (paragraph 2), *truancy* (paragraph 4), *awry* (paragraph 6), *languished* (paragraph 7), *ravages* (paragraph 8), *appendage* (paragraph 8).

For writing assignments based on this essay, see page 603.

BACKGROUND: Timothy Roche and Amanda Bower both write frequently for *Time* magazine. Roche has written on a wide range of national issues including the controversy surrounding the painkiller OxyContin, the murder in Georgia of sheriff-elect Derwin Brown, the crisis of foster care, the controversy surrounding the election of George W. Bush, segregation, and school prayer. Bower frequently writes the "Milestones" section of the magazine, which notes important events in the lives of famous people, and articles on health issues. In addition, she has written articles on Mother Teresa and the 2001 disappearance of Washington intern Chandra Levy. "Young Voices from the Cell" first appeared in *Time* in May 2001.

COMBINED PATTERNS AND THEIR PURPOSE: In "Young Voices from the Cell," Timothy Roche and Amanda Bower use *cause-and-effect analysis* to **inform** the reader of why young boys go on killing rampages at their schools and what happens when they are incarcerated in adult prisons. To make their points, the authors use *exemplification* by describing the lives of 12 teenagers who opened fire on students and teachers at their schools.

YOUNG VOICES FROM THE CELL

TIMOTHY ROCHE AND AMANDA BOWER

"Not too bad," that's what the boy killer murmured to his lawyer when the verdict came in. He was right that it could have been worse. The Florida jury might have gone for murder one but instead convicted Nathaniel Brazill, 14, of murder in the second degree for pointing a gun between the eyes of his favorite teacher and pulling the trigger a year ago. "I'm O.K.," he mouthed to his mother Polly, seated in the courtroom's second row. Then he gave a little wave to a young cousin, sitting nearby.

As you read Consider how the authors use direct quotation to help them achieve their persuasive purpose.

2 If Brazill didn't at that instant grasp the grim future that awaits him, it probably won't take him long. Next month the judge will mete out a sentence that could mean a lifetime in prison.[1] And if Brazill needs a clearer picture of what's in store for him, the prison life of other school shooters will give him an idea. These young gunmen, at the moment of their wrathful outbursts, were often filled with a sense of potency and triumph or at least relief that whatever or whoever was troubling them had been exorcised. But those sensations generally prove fleeting. As they settle into the monotony and isolation of prison life, these boys tend to experience feelings of profound regret, remorse and loss as they come to terms with what they have done to their victims and what they have done to themselves.

3 For eight weeks, *Time* delved into the lives of 12 convicted school shooters—who had terrified their classmates and periodically traumatized the nation since 1997. Among them, they fired 135 shots, killing 21 people and wounding 62. If they were not suffering overtly from mental illness before their crimes, many clearly are now, with varying degrees of treatment available. Psychologists say they are likely to be suicidal for much of their lives and suffer repeated

---

[1]Brazill was sentenced to 25 years in prison, the minimum term.

flashbacks to the single day when everything changed, when they killed beloved teachers or gunned down schoolmates they did not know, when they went from good sons to the young terrorists among us.

4   Within the system and in their own personal circles, these boys engender a wide range of reactions. Prosecutors label many of them unredeemable sociopaths; defenders say that with education and counseling, they can be restored. Even loved ones take varying positions. Some offer support, while others abandon their own.

"To this day, a few of the boys refuse to explain themselves."

5   To this day, a few of the boys refuse to explain themselves. And it is fair to ask why we would want to hear from any of them anyway or have sympathy for what they have to say. But many have developed, sometimes with the help of psychologists, a better understanding of what led them to murderous fury—an understanding that could help others avoid such atrocities in the future. Almost all the shooters were expressing rage, either against a particular person for a particular affront or, more often, against a whole cohort of bullying classmates. Some of their stories confirm the notion that school shootings are a contagion, that the perpetrators are imitating the gross acts of carnage they've seen reported in other places. On the day that he brought to school a .25-cal. semiautomatic handgun that he had stolen from his grandfather's desk drawer, Brazill boasted to a classmate that he would be "all over the news."

6   If these kids felt empowered by the notorious shooters who came before them, however, at least some—the most self-aware of the group—now want to set a new example for students tempted to perpetuate the cycle. Don't look to Columbine's Dylan Klebold and Eric Harris, the most notorious of the school avengers, this group is saying. Those boys killed themselves and never had to face the aftermath of their rampage. Instead, this group says, look to us, who are living the postscript, and don't let it happen to you. Even Brazill, in an interview with *Time* six weeks before his conviction, had come that far. Asked what he would like to tell the student groups who sometimes tour his jail, he replied, "Don't pick up a gun. You don't know what's going to happen."

THE PRICE

7 Even Ramsey knows. Four years ago, he brought a pump-action shotgun to his Alaska high school and opened up, killing the principal and one student. Now he is serving a 210-year term in a maximum-security prison in the Alaskan mountains. Every night, before crashing in the tiny cell he shares with a fellow murderer, he mops the prison floors, a job that earns him $21 a month, just enough to buy soap, shampoo and stationery, which the Spring Creek Correctional Center does not supply for free. His face pasty white from lack of sun, Ramsey told *Time* his biggest complaint is the total absence of privacy. The light is always on in his cell, and the toilet sits in the open at the end of his bunk.

8   A school shooter with one of the longest sentences, Ramsey has encountered some of the harder edges of prison life. He spent six months in solitary confinement after beating a fellow inmate with a sock packed with batteries when

the prisoner reneged on a gambling debt of four candy bars. Ramsey has heard that an uncle of the student he killed is in the same prison and that the man "wants to do a bunch of different things to me."

9   Ramsey says he committed his rampage because he was sick of being picked on in school, where he was nicknamed "Screech'" after the geeky character in the TV show 'Saved by the Bell.' "Nobody liked me, and I could never understand why," he says. "It was pretty bad then, but it's a lot worse now." Sometimes Ramsey will be starkly reminded of the shooting, for instance, when he recently received papers on a civil suit his victims' families have filed against the school district. "I sit there, and I wish, I wish, I wish, I wish I didn't do what I did," he says. "I wish I would have known the things that I know now."

10   Among Ramsey's wishes is that one of the two friends to whom he confided his lethal plan would have turned him in. Last week a blue-ribbon panel that studied the Columbine massacre criticized police, school officials and the killers' parents for not intervening to stop Klebold and Harris, after being given signs of their murderous intent. "That would have been one of the best things a person could have done," says Ramsey of his own case. Instead, Ramsey's buddies egged him on.

11   Maintaining relationships from within prison walls is a trial. Some of these kids have devoted parents and friends. A number have attracted admirers. Ramsey has a pen-pal fiancée. Kip Kinkel, who is serving a 112-year term for killing his parents and then two students in his Oregon high school in 1998, has received money in the mail from strangers. Charles (Andy) Williams, who is in prison on charges of killing two students in his Santee, Calif., school in March, gets more letters than he can answer—as many as 40 a week, according to his lawyer. There are five different clubs on Yahoo! dedicated to him, as well as a dozen homemade websites. But the real, deepest ties these kids have to their communities are often shredded. Ramsey's family visits only once a year. At one point, they went nine months without even calling.

"There are five different clubs on Yahoo! dedicated to him, as well as a dozen homemade websites."

12   The father of Mitchell Johnson, who with buddy Andrew Golden killed four kids and a teacher when they attacked their Jonesboro, Ark., school with an arsenal of weapons in 1998, has severed contact with him. Mitchell told his mother that his father said to him on the phone, "You're the reason I quit praying" and hung up. After T. J. Solomon of Conyers, Ga., shot and wounded six classmates with a sawed-off shotgun in 1999, his mother demanded to know why he hadn't blasted himself. "You were going to kill yourself, I understand. How did that not happen?" she asked him just after his arrest. "I don't understand how you took innocent children, but you were too afraid to do anything to you. That really has me puzzled. You didn't think twice about doing it to them."

13   Luke Woodham, who killed two classmates in Pearl, Miss., in 1997 after beating and stabbing his mother to death, gets very few visitors. The school friends of Michael Carneal, who killed

three classmates in West Paducah, Ky., in 1997, largely shun him. From jail, Brazill continued to write love letters to Dinora Rosales, one of the girls he wanted to see when the teacher he killed, Barry Grunow, refused to allow Brazill inside the classroom because he had been suspended for throwing water balloons. But the 14-year-old Rosales, feeling threatened, turned the mash notes over to the police.

THE REMORSE

14 After Jacob Davis used a magnum bolt-action rifle to mow down his girlfriend's ex-lover at his Tennessee high school in 1998, he dropped down beside the bleeding body. A friend came over and said to Davis, "Man, you just flushed your life down the toilet." Davis replied, "Yes, but it's been fun." The fun didn't last. Today Davis is serving a 52-year term at a medium-security correctional facility in Clifton, Tenn. Before the shooting, he had received an academic scholarship to study computer science at Mississippi State University. Instead, he takes a prison course to learn the low-tech skill of computer refurbishment. Dressed in prison blues, Davis spoke to *Time* while seated at a small wooden table in a visitor's room, with a security guard standing watch in the corner.

15 "When you got someone else's blood on your hands, it's not an easy thing to deal with," Davis says, looking downward. "I will suffer my own personal hell the rest of my life. There's nothing you can do to make it go away. I'm truly remorseful for what happened. He's gone," Davis says of Nick Creson, the 18-year-old boy he killed, "and I can't do anything to change it and bring him back."

16 Davis is plagued by nightmares and insomnia, as are many of the other gunmen. And when he awakens each day, he often confronts anew the calamitous effects of his act on Creson's family and his own. "It's kind of hard not to when you wake up every morning in a prison cell," he says. If Johnson didn't understand at the time the consequences of his murders, he does now, says his mother Gretchen Woodard. "He's older. He knows now the permanence of it," she says. "If words from him would not hurt those families, he'd write them."

"David is plagued by nightmares and insomnia, as are many of the other gunmen."

17 For many of the young shooters, news of another school rampage sets off bouts of emotional turmoil. Carneal became "seriously depressed" after the Columbine attack, according to Kentucky juvenile-justice commissioner Ralph Kelly. "He really took a setback from that. He felt a lot of responsibility for that happening." Kinkel also blamed himself for Columbine. On hearing the news, Kinkel told a psychologist, "I flipped out, started blaming myself." According to a friend, the March school shooting in Santee also disturbed Kinkel. Victor Cordova, incarcerated in a juvenile-treatment facility in New Mexico for shooting a schoolmate in the head, was so upset by a TV report on the Santee case that he asked to be released from the requirement that residents watch the evening news each day. Brazill, the night of his conviction, couldn't stomach even an episode of "Law & Order" that featured a school shooting; he retreated from the common room to his cell.

18 Woodham, whom many investigators believe started the chain of recent school shootings with his killing spree in 1997, is haunted by that burden. "If there's any way that I can, I would like to help stop these shootings," he wrote in a letter to *Time*. Davis has the same idea and a plan. He's writing a book about his experiences. "I want somebody to learn from the mistakes I've gone through," he says. "I want to be a part of changing all this crap that's going on."

19 One way to do that is to try to understand the triggers for these crimes. Davis says for him the proximate cause was jealous rage. After his girlfriend, Tonya Bishop, confided that she had had sex with Creson, Davis became increasingly obsessed over a period of three months with hatred for Creson. Davis' stepmother Phyllis thought this was "just like any other" teen-romance drama and assumed that "just like everybody else, he'd get over it." He didn't. He was besotted with Bishop but didn't trust her. He started sleeping just a few hours a night. His grades fell from A's to D's and F's. One day, after a glaring match with Creson in a hallway, Davis recalls, "it was just like something clicked in my head. I had been going downhill for so long. I got stuck thinking about all the pain I'd suffered. And I couldn't put all that out of my head." He went home, got his hunting rifle and ambushed Creson in the school parking lot.

20 With the benefit of antidepressant medication, Davis now believes that mental illness was at the root of his behavior. The psychiatrists who examined him agree, having determined that at the time of the shooting, Davis was suffering from serious depression with psychotic features. Eight of the other 11 convicted kids that *Time* reviewed have had some sort of mental disorder diagnosed since their crimes, mostly depression but also personality disorders and schizophrenia or its precursors. Six of the kids have had behavior-altering psychotropic drugs prescribed.

21 The presence of mental illness may help explain why some kids snap when faced with the usual torments of adolescence and others don't. Of course, some kids consider their vexations extraordinary. Carneal, who at the time of his crime was a freshman who got picked on for his small stature and quiet manner, told a psychiatrist that he felt going to prison would be better than continuing to endure the bullying in school.

"Carneal told a psychiatrist that he felt going to prison would be better than continuing to endure the bullying at school."

22 Psychiatrist Stuart Twemlow, director of the Erik H. Erikson Institute for Education and Research in Stockbridge, Mass., notes that a significant subgroup of the school shooters consists of kids who come from relatively affluent families, who are academically above average, if not gifted, and who rarely have the qualities expected of violent offenders—such as a history of substance abuse or mental disorder. In Twemlow's view, this is no coincidence. "Bullying is more common in affluent schools probably than in the low-income schools," he says. It is spurred, he believes, by "the dynamics that come out of our typical hard-nosed, competitive" middle class.

23 Park Dietz, a forensic psychiatrist who has interviewed numerous school

shooters, says they tend to have in common "some degree of depression, considerable anger, access to weapons that they aren't ready to have, and a role model salient in their memory. So far," he told a *Time* reporter, "it's always been a mass murderer who has been given ample coverage in your magazine." Describing his pre-rampage mind-set, Solomon once wrote, "I felt the next thing left to release my anger would be through violence. I had just gotten the idea from the shooting at Columbine High School on April 20." Solomon opened fire precisely one month after that date. Seth Trickey, who in 1999 shot and wounded five classmates in Fort Gibson, Okla., told a psychiatrist he had become preoccupied with previous school shooters and wondered how he would hold up in their shoes. Woodham told the cops who took his confession, "I guess everyone is going to remember me now."

THE REHABILITATION

24 Though Woodham has since expressed remorse, prison authorities aren't especially interested in his redemption. Woodham receives no schooling or counseling. "We don't make any pretense about trying to rehabilitate someone who is going to spend their natural life in prison," says Robert Johnson, commissioner of Mississippi's Department of Corrections. "What's the use?"

25 Most of the rest of the boys are working toward high school diplomas. A couple hope to move on to college correspondence courses. Seven of the shooters are offered regular psychological counseling, ranging from daily to weekly sessions. However, some lawyers and relatives have begun to question the treatment and challenge the qualifications of prison psychologists, who increasingly are overburdened and underfunded as overall inmate populations grow.

26 In Pennsylvania, the mother of Andrew Wurst, who opened fire on his middle-school dance in 1998, killing a teacher, has battled prison officials to upgrade her son's therapy. She has been rebuffed. So Wurst remains totally delusional, according to psychiatrist Robert Sadoff, who examined him. Sadoff wrote that Wurst believes "he is real but everyone else is unreal." That includes the teacher he killed, John Gilette, who in Wurst's mind "was already dead or unreal." Wurst told Sadoff that, excepting himself, everyone has been programmed by the government by means of "time tablets" that control people's thoughts.

"Wurst believes 'he is real but everyone else is unreal.'"

27 There are other kids lost in their own worlds. Trickey, according to a report of the Oklahoma Office of Juvenile Affairs, "does not show any remorse for his crime and has little insight into his problems." Father John Kiernan, who used to visit Solomon regularly, says he seemed unaware of the consequences of his rampage. But in 1999, Solomon carved an X across his chest, apparently with a fingernail, and last January he attempted suicide by swallowing 22 pills of the antidepressant Elavil that he had bought from another inmate.

28 Many years will pass before most of the shooters come up for possible release. Three of them expect never to be paroled. Others will be men of 50 or even 70 before they have that option. But a handful of these boys, sentenced in more lenient states, will be released during the next five to seven years.

Trickey's continued detention is reviewed every six months, and he will certainly go free by the time he turns 19. Cordova gets out at age 21. So do Johnson and Golden.

29 For his part, Solomon is in for 40 years. He's likely to be haunted by nightmares for much of that duration. "I've been having dreams and many flashbacks, and most recently, I have been hearing screams," he wrote after his arrest. "I know that it's just in my mind, [but] it's like I'm really hearing them, as if someone were screaming in

> "For his part, Solomon is in for 40 years. He's likely to be haunted by nightmares for much of that duration."

my face. Usually when it's time to go to sleep and everything is quiet is when my thoughts get worst, because it's all I can hear." Of a dream, he said, "I see myself standing there, shooting me." In his sleep, he is his own victim. And when he wakes up, he is too.

READING CLOSELY AND THINKING CRITICALLY

1. How do family, friends, and others react to the 12 boys in the essay who gunned down teachers and schoolmates?

2. What prompted the boys in the essay to kill? How are they responding to their incarceration in adult prisons?

3. The authors indicate that some young killers may have been mentally ill at the time they committed their crimes. Should mental illness influence whether juveniles are tried in the adult system? Why or why not?

4. Why do some affluent young people become school shooters?

5. In paragraph 23, the authors present evidence that the publicity surrounding school shootings contributes to other school shootings. Should media coverage of these events be limited? Why or why not?

6. Do the authors advance a particular point of view, or is the essay unbiased? Explain.

EXAMINING STRUCTURE AND STRATEGY

1. Do the opening paragraphs of the essay engage your interest? Why or why not?

2. The authors include direct quotations of the words of the jailed boys. What is the effect of those quotations? Do they help the authors achieve their purpose? Explain.

3. In paragraph 8, the authors suggest a little about the exploitation and abuse experienced by juveniles in the adult system. Should they have included more information about the horror of prison life? Why or why not?

4. In paragraph 3, the authors tell how many prisoners they studied, how long they studied them, how many people the prisoners killed, and how many they wounded. Why do they provide this information?

5. The authors conclude by mentioning Solomon's nightmares. What effect does that conclusion create?

1. The authors use cause-and-effect analysis for more than one informational purpose. What informational purposes does the cause-and-effect analysis serve?
2. The authors use exemplification for more than one informational purpose. What informational purposes does the exemplification serve?

CONSIDERING LANGUAGE AND STYLE

1. In the first sentence, the authors refer to Nathaniel Brazill as "the boy killer." Why do they use that phrase?
2. Consult your dictionary if you do not know the meaning of these words and phrases: *mete out* (paragraph 2), *engender* (paragraph 4), *sociopaths* (paragraph 4), *cohort* (paragraph 5), *contagion* (paragraph 5), *reneged* (paragraph 8), *affluent* (paragraph 22), *salient* (paragraph 23).

ASSIGNMENTS FOR DISCUSSION AND WRITING

"Little Adult Criminals," "Should Juvenile Offenders Be Tried as Adults?" "Adult Crime, Adult Time," and "Young Voices from the Cell"

1. **For discussion in class or online.** Answer any or all of the following questions: How much bullying goes on in schools? Have you witnessed or experienced bullying? If so, how did you deal with the experience? How can schools deal with bullying? If your instructor directs you to do so, post your responses to your class Web site.
2. **In your journal.** In "Young Voices from the Cell," the authors describe life in prison. How do you react to that description?
3. **Using argumentation for a purpose.** The purposes in the assignments are possibilities. You may establish whatever purposes you like, within your instructor's guidelines.

   - Write a guest editorial for your local newspaper arguing for instituting conflict resolution classes and initiatives to deal with bullying in elementary and middle schools. Your purpose can be to convince readers to write members of the state board of education to petition for these changes.

   - In paragraph 10 of "Young Voices from the Cell," the authors note that Evan Ramsey's friends encouraged him to commit murder and that parents and school officials were criticized for not trying to stop the Columbine shooters. Should we prosecute those who have reason to believe a shooting might occur but fail to report their knowledge to police? Argue your assertion to soften the objections of a hostile reader. (See page 550 on hostile readers.)

   - Paragraph 24 of "Young Voices from the Cell" quotes Robert Johnson, commissioner of Mississippi's Department of Corrections, as saying, "We don't make any pretense about trying to rehabilitate someone who is going to spend their natural life in prison." Agree or disagree with this position to convince a wavering reader. (See page 550 on wavering readers.)

- Write a speech suitable for a middle school assembly to be held at the beginning of the school year. Your purpose is to convince students not to engage in bullying and to show students how to behave if they are the targets of or witnesses to bullying.
- To convince students not to bully others, create a poster for a middle school newspaper that argues against bullying.

4. **Connecting the readings.**
   - Discuss immaturity, insecurity, and other characteristics of adolescence as a cause of teenage violence. Is there more we can do to prevent violence committed by teenagers? In addition to the readings in this section, consider, "Seeking Justice after a Fatal Spin of the Cylinder" (page 177) and "It's Just Too Late" (page 422).
   - Summarize the main points made in "Little Adult Criminals," "Should Juvenile Offenders Be Tried as Adults?" "Adult Crime, Adult Time," and "Young Voices from the Cell." Indicate which of the points are the most compelling and explain why.

5. **Drawing on sources.** Agree or disagree with the concept "adult time for adult crime." Be sure to raise and counter significant objections to your view. If you would like to read more on the subject, visit the Public Broadcasting System's "*Frontline*" Web site at *http://www.pbs.org/wgbh/pages/frontline/shows/juvenile* or look up "juvenile justice" in the *Social Sciences Index* in your library reference room.

WHAT SPEECH DOES THE FIRST AMENDMENT PROTECT ON COLLEGE CAMPUSES?

The freedom most central to a viable democracy is freedom of speech, which is protected by the First Amendment. However, our First Amendment rights do not extend to injurious speech. Thus, the first Amendment does not allow us to yell "Fire!" in a crowded theater when there is no fire because doing so will create panic and cause harm. First Amendment matters are not always this clear cut, and the readings in this section consider some of the complex free speech issues on today's college campuses.

First, Nat Hentoff and Charles R. Lawrence III weigh in on whether colleges should restrict and punish virulent hate speech. Hentoff's view, articulated in "Free Speech on Campus," is that suppressing speech—even hate speech—violates the First Amendment and principles of academic freedom. Lawrence, on the other hand, argues in "The Debate over Placing Limits on Racist Speech Must Not Ignore the Damage It Does to Its Victims" that hate speech does not deserve First Amendment protection. In their related essay, "Speech Codes: Alive and Well at Colleges," Harvey A. Silverglate and Greg Lukianoff argue that when colleges write guidelines stipulating "acceptable" and "unacceptable" speech on campus, they are engaged in a harmful form of censorship.

Howard M. Wasserman and Robert O'Neil consider two other free speech issues. In "Fan Profanity," Wasserman examines an often-vexing matter: fans who use profanity at college sporting events to taunt—and even attack—members of both the home and opposing teams. In "What Limits Should Campus Networks Place on Pornography?" O'Neil considers whether First Amendment rights extend to downloading pornography that becomes visible to those on campus who find it offensive.

BACKGROUND: Born in 1925 in Boston, free speech advocate and civil libertarian Nat Hentoff attended Northeastern University and Harvard. He was awarded a Guggenheim Fellowship in education and an American Bar Association Silver Gavel Award in 1980 for his coverage of the law and criminal justice in his columns. He has been a columnist for the *Village Voice, Commonweal, The Atlantic Monthly,* the *Washington Post,* and *The New Yorker,* where he has been a staff writer for more than 25 years. A prolific author of both fiction and nonfiction, he has published books on jazz, biographies, novels, and books for children. Among his works are *The First Freedom: The Tumultuous History of Free Speech in America* (1989), *Speech for Me—But Not for Thee* (1993), and *The War on the Bill of Rights and the Gathering Resistance* (2003). Hentoff is considered an authority on First Amendment defense, the Bill of Rights, the Supreme Court, student rights, and education. "Free Speech on Campus" was first published in 1989 in the *Progressive,* a magazine with a politically liberal viewpoint.

COMBINED PATTERNS AND THEIR PURPOSE: Although Nat Hentoff usually defends the political left, in "Free Speech on Campus" he **argues** that the left's commitment to politically correct language comes at the expense of free speech on college campuses. To make his point, Hentoff uses *cause-and-effect analysis* and *exemplification.*

FREE SPEECH ON CAMPUS | NAT HENTOFF

A flier distributed at the University of Michigan some months ago proclaimed that blacks "don't belong in classrooms, they belong hanging from trees."

2 At other campuses around the country, manifestations of racism are becoming commonplace. At Yale, a swastika and the words WHITE POWER! were painted on the building housing the University's Afro-American Cultural Center. At Temple University, a White Students Union has been formed with some 130 members.

3 Swastikas are not directed only at black students. The Nazi symbol has been spray-painted on the Jewish Student Union at Memphis State University. And on a number of campuses, women have been singled out as targets of wounding and sometimes frightening speech. At the law school of the State University of New York at Buffalo, several women students have received anonymous letters characterized by one professor as venomously sexist.

"What is to be done, . . . about speech alone—however disgusting, inflammatory, and rawly divisive that speech may be?"

4 These and many more such signs of the resurgence of bigotry and know-nothingism throughout the society—as well as on campus—have to do solely with speech, including symbolic speech. There have also been physical assaults on black students and on black, white, and Asian women students, but the way to deal with physical attacks is clear: call the police and file a criminal complaint. What is to be done, however, about speech alone—however disgusting, inflammatory, and rawly divisive that speech may be?

5 At more and more colleges, administrators—with the enthusiastic support of black students, women students, and liberal students—have been answering that question by preventing or punishing speech. In public universities, this is a clear violation of the First Amendment. In private colleges and universities, suppression of speech mocks the secular religion of academic freedom and free inquiry.

6 The Student Press Law Center in Washington, D.C.—a vital source of legal support for student editors around the country—reports, for example, that at the University of Kansas, the student host and producer of a radio news program was forbidden by school officials from interviewing a leader of the Ku Klux Klan. So much for free inquiry on that campus.

7 In Madison, Wisconsin, the *Capital Times* ran a story in January about Chancellor Sheila Kaplan of the University of Wisconsin branch at Parkside, who ordered her campus to be scoured of "some anonymously placed white supremacist hate literature." Sounding like the legendary Mayor Frank ("I am the law") Hague of Jersey City, who booted "bad speech" out of town, Chancellor Kaplan said, "This institution is not a lamppost standing on the street corner. It doesn't belong to everyone."

8 Who decides what speech can be heard or read by everyone? Why, the Chancellor, of course. That's what George III[1] used to say, too.

9 University of Wisconsin political science professor Carol Tebben thinks otherwise. She believes university administra-

tors "are getting confused when they are acting as censors and trying to protect students from bad ideas. I don't think students need to be protected from bad ideas. I think they can determine for themselves what ideas are bad."

10 After all, if students are to be "protected" from bad ideas, how are they going to learn to identify and cope with them? Sending such ideas underground simply makes them stronger and more dangerous.

11 Professor Tebben's conviction that free speech means just that has become a decidedly minority view on many campuses. At the University of Buffalo Law School, the faculty unanimously adopted a "Statement Regarding Intellectual Freedom, Tolerance, and Political Harassment." Its title implies support of intellectual freedom, but the statement warned students that once they enter "this legal community," their right to free speech must become tempered "by the responsibility to promote equality and justice."

12 Accordingly, swift condemnation will befall anyone who engages in "remarks directed at another's race, sex, religion, national origin, age, or sex preference." Also forbidden are "other remarks based on prejudice and group stereotype."

13 This ukase is so broad that enforcement has to be alarmingly subjective. Yet the University of Buffalo Law School provides no due-process procedures for a student booked for making any of these prohibited remarks. Conceivably, a student caught playing a Lenny Bruce, Richard Pryor, or Sam Kinison album in

---

[1]King of England from 1760–1820 who attempted to suppress American revolutionaries.

this room could be tried for aggravated insensitivity by association.

"Conceivably, a student caught playing a Lenny Bruce, Richard Pryor, or Sam Kinison album in this room could be tried for aggravated insensitivity by association."

14   When I looked into this wholesale cleansing of bad speech at Buffalo, I found it had encountered scant opposition. One protester was David Gerald Jay, a graduate of the law school and a cooperating attorney for the New York Civil Liberties Union. Said the appalled graduate: "Content-based prohibitions constitute prior restraint and should not be tolerated."

15   You would think that the law professors and administration at this public university might have known that. But hardly any professors dissented, and among the students only members of the conservative Federalist Society spoke up for free speech. The fifty-strong chapter of the National Lawyers Guild was on the other side. After all, it was more important to go on record as vigorously opposing racism and sexism than to expose oneself to charges of insensitivity to these malignancies.

16   The pressures to have the "right" attitude—as proved by having the "right" language in and out of class—can be stifling. A student who opposes affirmative action, for instance, can be branded a racist.

17   At the University of California at Los Angeles, the student newspaper ran an editorial cartoon satirizing affirmative action. (A student stops a rooster on campus and asks how the rooster got into UCLA. "Affirmative action," is the answer.) After outraged complaints from various minority groups, the editor was suspended for violating a publication policy against running "articles that perpetuate derogatory or cultural stereotypes." The art director was also suspended.

18   When the opinion editor of the student newspaper at California State University at Northridge wrote an article asserting that the sanctions against the editor and art director at UCLA amounted to censorship, he was suspended too.

19   At New York University Law School, a student was so disturbed by the pall of orthodoxy at that prestigious institution that he wrote to the school newspaper even though, as he said, he expected his letter to make him a pariah among his fellow students.

20   Barry Endick described the atmosphere at NYU created by "a host of watchdog committees and a generally hostile classroom reception regarding any student comment right of center." This "can be arguably viewed as symptomatic of a prevailing spirit of academic and social intolerance of . . . any idea which is not 'politically correct.'"

21   He went on to say something that might well be posted on campus bulletin boards around the country, though it would probably be torn down at many of them: "We ought to examine why students, so anxious to wield the Fourteenth Amendment, give short shrift to the First. Yes, Virginia, there are racist assholes. And you know what, the Constitution protects them, too."

22   Not when they engage in violence or vandalism. But when they speak or write, racist assholes fall right into this Oliver Wendell Holmes definition—highly unpopular among bigots, liberals, radicals, feminists, sexists, and college administrators: "If there is any principle of the Constitution that more imperatively calls for attachment than any other, it is the principle of free thought—not free only for those who agree with us, but freedom for the thought we hate."

23   The language sounds like a pietistic Sunday sermon, but if it ever falls wholly into disuse, neither this publication nor any other journal of opinion—right or left—will survive.

24   Sometimes, college presidents and administrators sound as if they fully understand what Holmes was saying. Last year, for example, when the *Daily Pennsylvanian*—speaking for many at the University of Pennsylvania—urged that a speaking invitation to Louis Farrakhan be withdrawn, University President Sheldon Hackney disagreed.

"If any story distills the essence of the current decline of free speech on college campuses, it is the Ballad of Murray Dolfman."

25   "Open expression," said Hackney, "is the fundamental principle of a university." Yet consider what the same Sheldon Hackney did to the free-speech rights of a teacher at his own university. If any story distills the essence of the current decline of free speech on college campuses, it is the Ballad of Murray Dolfman.

26   For twenty-two years, Dolfman, a practicing lawyer in Philadelphia, had been a part-time lecturer in the Legal Studies Department of the University of Pennsylvania's Wharton School. For twenty-two years, no complaint had ever been made against him; indeed his student course evaluations had been outstanding. Each year students competed to get into his class.

27   On a November afternoon in 1984, Dolfman was lecturing about personal-service contracts. His style somewhat resembles that of Professor Charles Kingsfield in *The Paper Chase*.[2] Dolfman insists that students he calls on be prepared—or suffer the consequences. He treats all students this way—regardless of race, creed, or sex.

28   This day, Dolfman was pointing out that no one can be forced to work against his or her will—even if a contract has been signed. A court may prevent the resister from working for someone else so long as the contract is in effect but, Dolfman said, there can "be nothing that smacks of involuntary servitude."

29   Where does this concept come from? Dolfman looked around the room. Finally, a cautious hand was raised: "The Constitution?"

30   "Where in the Constitution?" No hands. "The Thirteenth Amendment," said the teacher. So, what does *it* say? The students were looking everywhere but at Dolfman.

31   "We will lose our liberties," Dolfman often told his classes, "if we don't know what they are."

32   On this occasion, he told them that he and other Jews, as ex-slaves, spoke at Passover of the time when they were

---

[2]A popular 1974 film and later television series starring John Houseman as a stern Harvard law professor.

Copyright © 2001 Larry Wright, *The Detroit News.*

slaves under the Pharaohs so that they would remember every year what it was like not to be free.

33 "We have ex-slaves here," Dolfman continued, "who should know about the Thirteenth Amendment." He asked black students in the class if they could tell him what was in that amendment.

34 "I wanted them to really think about it," Dolfman told me recently, "and know its history. You're better equipped to fight racism if you know all about those post–Civil War amendments and civil rights laws."

35 The Thirteenth Amendment provides that "neither slavery nor involuntary servitude . . . shall exist within the United States."

36 The black students in his class did not know what was in the amendment, and Dolfman had them read it aloud. Later, they complained to university of-ficials that they had been hurt and humiliated by having been referred to as ex-slaves. Moreover, they said, they had no reason to be grateful for a constitutional amendment which gave them rights which should never have been denied them—and gave them precious little else. They had not made these points in class, although Dolfman—unlike Professor Kingsfield—encourages rebuttal.

" . . . Dolfman told the black students he had intended no offense, and he apologized if they had been offended."

37 Informed of the complaint, Dolfman told the black students he had intended no offense, and he apologized if they had been offended.

38   That would not do—either for the black students or for the administration. Furthermore, there were mounting black-Jewish tensions on campus, and someone had to be sacrificed. Who better than a part-time Jewish teacher with no contract and no union? He was sentenced by—George Orwell would have loved this—the Committee on Academic Freedom and Responsibility.

39   On his way to the stocks, Dolfman told President Sheldon Hackney that if a part-time instructor "can be punished on this kind of charge, a tenured professor can eventually be booted out, then a dean, and then a president."

40   Hackney was unmoved. Dolfman was banished from the campus for what came to be a year. But first he was forced to make a public apology to the entire university and then he was compelled to attend a "sensitivity and racial awareness" session. Sort of like a Vietnamese reeducation camp.

41   A few conservative professors objected to the stigmatization of Murray Dolfman. I know of no student dissent. Indeed, those students most concerned with making the campus more "sensitive" to diversity exulted in Dolfman's humiliation. So did most liberals on the faculty.

42   If my children were still of college age and wanted to attend the University of Pennsylvania, I would tell them this story. But where else could I encourage them to go?

READING CLOSELY AND THINKING CRITICALLY

1.   What issue is Hentoff arguing, and what is his assertion about the issue?
2.   According to Hentoff, how have college administrators been reacting to hate speech? What does Hentoff think of this reaction?
3.   Do you think that students should be protected from bad ideas (paragraph 9)? Why or why not? How would you define a "bad idea"?
4.   Why do you think there was so little opposition to the University of Buffalo's "Statement Regarding Intellectual Freedom, Tolerance, and Political Harassment"?
5.   Explain the double meaning of the essay's title.
6.   What assumptions connect Hentoff's claim and support? (See page 552 on claims, support, and assumptions.)

EXAMINING STRUCTURE AND STRATEGY

1.   Which paragraphs form the introduction? What approach does Hentoff take to this introduction? Do you find it effective? Explain.
2.   Where does Hentoff state the issue and his assertion about the issue?
3.   What specific evidence does Hentoff give to support his assertion about the issue? Is this evidence adequate and convincing? Explain.
4.   Does Hentoff use emotional appeal as a persuasive strategy? Explain.
5.   To what extent does Hentoff raise and counter objections? Are there any compelling objections he did not deal with but should have? Explain.

NOTING COMBINED PATTERNS

1. Cause-and-effect analysis is the dominant pattern in the essay. How does Hentoff use this pattern?
2. Hentoff uses quite a few examples in his essay. Do these examples add to the persuasiveness of the essay? Explain.
3. Why is the example of Murray Dolfman developed in such detail?

CONSIDERING LANGUAGE AND STYLE

1. In paragraph 5, Hentoff refers to "the secular religion of academic freedom and free inquiry." How can a religion be secular? How can academic freedom and free inquiry be a religion? Explain this use of language and its meaning.
2. Hentoff refers to George Orwell in paragraph 38. Explain the significance of this reference.
3. Consult a dictionary if you are unfamiliar with any of these words: *know-nothingism* (paragraph 4), *ukase* (paragraph 13), *pall* (paragraph 19), *pariah* (paragraph 19), *rebuttal* (paragraph 36), *stocks* (paragraph 39).

For writing assignments based on "Free Speech on Campus," see page 636.

BACKGROUND: An award-winning professor, Charles R. Lawrence began his teaching career at the University of San Francisco and went on to teach at Stanford University. Currently, he is law professor at Georgetown University. He is an expert on antidiscrimination law, equal protection, and theories of race. He has written two books with Mari Matsuda, *Words That Wound: Critical Race Theory, Assaultive Speech, and the First Amendment* (1993) and *We Won't Go Back: Making the Case for Affirmative Action* (1997). Lawrence adapted the following essay from a speech he delivered to the American Civil Liberties Union. This written version was first published in the *Chronicle of Higher Education* (1989), which is read primarily by college faculty and administrators.

THE PATTERN AND ITS PURPOSE: In his essay, Charles R. Lawrence uses *cause-and-effect analysis to* **persuade** readers that hate speech on college campuses should not be protected.

The Debate over Placing Limits on Racist Speech Must Not Ignore the Damage It Does to Its Victims

CHARLES R. LAWRENCE III

I have spent the better part of my life as a dissenter. As a high school student, I was threatened with suspension for my refusal to participate in a civil-defense drill, and I have been a conspicuous consumer of my First Amendment liberties ever since. There are very strong reasons for protecting even racist speech. Perhaps the most important of these is that such protection reinforces our society's commitment to tolerance as a value, and that by protecting bad speech from government regulation, we will be forced to combat it as a community.

As you read Consider whether Lawrence relies more on logic (logos) or emotional appeal (pathos) to convince his audience.

2   But I also have a deeply felt apprehension about the resurgence of racial violence and the corresponding rise in the incidence of verbal and symbolic assault and harassment to which blacks and other traditionally subjugated and excluded groups are subjected. I am troubled by the way the debate has been framed in response to the recent surge of racist incidents on college and university campuses and in response to some universities' attempts to regulate harassing speech. The problem has been framed as one in which the liberty of free speech is in conflict with the elimination of racism. I believe this has placed the bigot on the moral high ground and fanned the rising flames of racism.

3   Above all, I am troubled that we have not listened to the real victims, that we have shown so little understanding of their injury, and that we have abandoned those whose race, gender, or sexual preference continues to make them second-class citizens. It seems to me a

very sad irony that the first instinct of civil libertarians has been to challenge even the smallest, most narrowly framed efforts by universities to provide black and other minority students with the protection the Constitution guarantees them.

4   The landmark case of *Brown* v. *Board of Education* is not a case that we normally think of as a case about speech. But *Brown* can be broadly read as articulating the principle of equal citizenship. *Brown* held that segregated schools were inherently unequal because of the *message* that segregation conveyed—that black children were an untouchable caste, unfit to go to school with white children. If we understand the necessity of eliminating the system of signs and symbols that signal the inferiority of blacks, then we should hesitate before proclaiming that all racist speech that stops short of physical violence must be defended.

5   University officials who have formulated policies to respond to incidents of racial harassment have been characterized in the press as "thought police," but such policies generally do nothing more than impose sanctions against intentional face-to-face insults. When racist speech takes the form of face-to-face insults, catcalls, or other assaultive speech aimed at an individual or small group of persons, it falls directly within the "fighting words" exception to First Amendment protection. The Supreme Court has held that words which "by their very utterance inflict injury or tend to incite an immediate breach of the peace" are not protected by the First Amendment.

6   If the purpose of the First Amendment is to foster the greatest amount of speech, racial insults disserve that purpose. Assaultive racist speech functions as a preemptive strike. The invective is experienced as a blow, not as a proffered idea, and once the blow is struck, it is unlikely that a dialogue will follow. Racial insults are particularly undeserving of First Amendment protection because the perpetuator's intention is not to discover truth or initiate dialogue but to injure the victim. In most situations, members of minority groups realize that they are likely to lose if they respond to epithets by fighting and are forced to remain silent and submissive.

7   Courts have held that offensive speech may not be regulated in public forums such as streets where the listener may avoid the speech by moving on, but the regulation of otherwise protected speech has been permitted when the speech invades the privacy of the unwilling listener's home or when the unwilling listener cannot avoid the speech. Racist posters, fliers, and graffiti in dormitories, bathrooms, and other common living spaces would seem to clearly fall within the reasoning of these cases. Minority students should not be required to remain in their rooms in order to avoid racial assault. Minimally, they should find a safe haven in their dorms and in all other common rooms that are a part of their daily routine.

8   I would also argue that the university's responsibility for ensuring that these students receive an equal educational opportunity provides a compelling justification for regulations that ensure them safe passage in all common areas. A minority student should not have to risk becoming the target of racially assaulting speech every time he or she chooses to walk

across campus. Regulating vilifying speech that cannot be anticipated or avoided would not preclude announced speeches and rallies—situations that would give minority-group members and their allies the chance to organize counterdemonstrations or avoid the speech altogether.

9   The most commonly advanced argument against the regulation of racist speech proceeds something like this: We recognize that minority groups suffer pain and injury as the result of racist speech, but we must allow this hate mongering for the benefit of society as a whole. Freedom of speech is the lifeblood of our democratic system. It is especially important for minorities because often it is their only vehicle for rallying support for the redress of their grievances. It will be impossible to formulate a prohibition so precise that it will prevent the racist speech you want to suppress without catching in the same net all kinds of speech that it would be unconscionable for a democratic society to suppress.

10   Whenever we make such arguments, we are striking a balance on the one hand between our concern for the continued free flow of ideas and the democratic process dependent on that flow, and, on the other, our desire to further the cause of equality. There can be no meaningful discussion of how we should reconcile our commitment to equality and our commitment to free speech until it is acknowledged that there is real harm inflicted by racist speech and that this harm is far from trivial.

11   To engage in a debate about the First Amendment and racist speech without a full understanding of the nature and extent of that harm is to risk making the First Amendment an instrument of domination rather than a vehicle of liberation. We have not all known the experience of victimization by racist, misogynist, and homophobic speech, nor do we equally share the burden of the societal harm it inflicts. We are often quick to say that we have heard the cry of the victims when we have not.

12   The *Brown* case is again instructive because it speaks directly to the psychic injury inflicted by racist speech by noting that the symbolic message of segregation affected "the hearts and minds" of negro children "in a way unlikely ever to be undone." Racial epithets and harassment often cause deep emotional scarring and feelings of anxiety and fear that pervade every aspect of a victim's life.

13   *Brown* also recognized that black children did not have an equal opportunity to learn and participate in the school community if they bore the additional burden of being subjected to the humiliation and psychic assault contained in the message of segregation. University students bear an analogous burden when they are forced to live and work in an environment where at any moment they may be subjected to denigrating verbal harassment and assault. The same injury was addressed by the Supreme Court when it held that sexual harassment that creates a hostile or abusive work environment violates the ban on sex discrimination in employment of Title VII of the Civil Rights Act of 1964.

14   Carefully drafted university regulations would bar the use of words as

assault weapons and leave unregulated even the most heinous of ideas when those ideas are presented at times and places and in manners that provide an opportunity for reasoned rebuttal or escape from immediate injury. The history of the development of the right to free speech has been one of carefully evaluating the importance of free expression and its effects on other important societal interests. We have drawn the line between protected and unprotected speech before without dire results. (Courts have, for example, exempted from the protection of the First Amendment obscene speech and speech that disseminates official secrets, that defames or libels another person, or that is used to form a conspiracy or monopoly.)

15 Blacks and other people of color are skeptical about the argument that even the most injurious speech must remain unregulated because, in an unregulated marketplace of ideas, the best ones will rise to the top and gain acceptance. Our experience tells us quite the opposite. We have seen too many demagogues elected by appealing to America's racism. We have seen too many good liberal politicians shy away from the issues that might brand them as being too closely allied with us.

16 Whenever we decide that racist speech must be tolerated because of the importance of maintaining societal tolerance for all unpopular speech, we are asking blacks and other subordinated groups to bear the burden for the good of all. We must be careful that the ease with which we strike the balance against the regulation of racist speech is in no way influenced by the fact that the cost will be borne by others. We must be certain that those who will pay that price are fairly represented in our deliberations and that they are heard.

17 At the core of the argument that we should resist all government regulation of speech is the ideal that the best cure for bad speech is good, that ideas that affirm equality and the worth of all individuals will ultimately prevail. This is an empty ideal unless those of us who would fight racism are vigilant and unequivocal in that fight. We must look for ways to offer assistance and support to students whose speech and political participation are chilled in a climate of racial harassment.

18 Civil-rights lawyers might consider suing on behalf of blacks whose right to an equal education is denied by a university's failure to ensure a nondiscriminatory educational climate or conditions of employment. We must embark upon the development of a First Amendment jurisprudence grounded in the reality of our history and our contemporary experience. We must think hard about how best to launch legal attacks against the most indefensible forms of hate speech. Good lawyers can create exceptions and narrow interpretations that limit the harm of hate speech without opening the floodgates of censorship.

19 Everyone concerned with these issues must find ways to engage actively in actions that resist and counter the racist ideas that we would have the First Amendment protect. If we fail in this, the victims of hate speech must rightly assume that we are on the oppressors' side.

READING CLOSELY AND THINKING CRITICALLY

1. Lawrence expresses discomfort with the way the debate over hate speech has been framed. What problems does he see?
2. What irony does Lawrence identify in the debate over hate speech? (See page 175 on irony.)
3. Lawrence offers the landmark Supreme Court decision in *Brown* v. *The Board of Education* as one reason to punish hate speech. Explain his reasoning. Do you agree with his reasoning? Why or why not?
4. Why does Lawrence believe that racial insults do not deserve first amendment protection?
5. What support and assumption does Lawrence use for his argument in paragraph 12? (See page 552 on support and assumptions.)
6. Lawrence delivered an earlier version of the essay as a speech before members of the American Civil Liberties Union. Characterize the audience for the speech and consider how that audience was likely to react to Lawrence's thesis. What kind of persuasive goal do you think Lawrence could reasonably have established for the speech?

EXAMINING STRUCTURE AND STRATEGY

1. Lawrence opens by noting that he has been a longtime dissenter. Why does he make this opening remark? What does this statement suggest about Lawrence's view of his audience?
2. What objections does Lawrence raise, and how does he counter them?
3. Does Lawrence rely more on logical reasoning or emotional appeal to persuade his reader?
4. In paragraph 14, Lawrence notes historical exemptions to free speech. Does that information contribute to the persuasive quality of the essay? Explain.
5. Lawrence uses deductive reasoning to present his argument. What are his major and minor premises? (See page 554 on deductive reasoning.)
6. Which paragraphs form the conclusion of the essay? What approach does Lawrence take to that conclusion?

CONSIDERING LANGUAGE AND STYLE

1. In paragraph 2, Lawrence mentions symbolic assaults. Cite examples of symbolic (nonverbal) language that is threatening to some people.
2. Consult a dictionary if you are unfamiliar with any of these words: *catcalls* (paragraph 5), *preemptive strike* (paragraph 6), *invective* (paragraph 6), *epithets* (paragraph 6), *vilifying* (paragraph 8), *hate mongering* (paragraph 9), *unconscionable* (paragraph 9), *misogynist* (paragraph 11), *heinous* (paragraph 14), *demagogues* (paragraph 15).

For writing assignments based on this essay, see page 636.

BACKGROUND: Harvey A. Silverglate is a Boston attorney who specializes in civil liberties, academic freedom, and student rights law. He is also a director of the Foundation for Individual Rights for Education (FIRE), an organization mentioned in the essay that monitors and advocates for free speech issues on college campuses. A three-decade member of the Massachusetts American Civil Liberties Union (ACLU), Silverglate has taught at Harvard Law School. With Alan Charles Kors, he wrote *The Shadow University* (1999). He has also written for *The National Law Journal, The Wall Street Journal, The Boston Globe,* and *Media Studies Journal.* Attorney Greg Lukianoff is the director of legal and public advocacy for FIRE. A frequent guest on local and national radio and television programs, he has also testified before Congress about free speech issues on college campuses. Lukianoff has written for several publications, including *The Stanford Technology Law Review* and the *Daily Journal of Los Angeles and of San Francisco.* "Speech Codes: Alive and Well at Colleges" was published in 2003 in *The Chronicle of Higher Education,* a periodical for university faculty and administrators.

COMBINED PATTERNS AND THEIR PURPOSE: To **persuade** readers that campus speech codes are a harmful form of censorship, Silverglate and Lukianoff rely heavily on *exemplification* and *cause-and-effect analysis.* An element of *definition* also appears because the meaning of important terms must be clarified.

Speech Codes: Alive and Well at Colleges

HARVEY A. SILVERGLATE AND GREG LUKIANOFF

Five years ago, a higher-education editor for *The New York Times* informed one of us, Harvey Silverglate, that Neil L. Rudenstine—then president of Harvard University—had insisted that Harvard did not have, much less enforce, any "speech codes." Silverglate suggested the editor

As you read
Ask yourself why colleges adopt speech codes.

dig deeper, because virtually any undergraduate could contest the president's claim.

2   A mere three years earlier, the faculty of the Harvard Law School had adopted "Sexual Harassment Guidelines" targeted at "seriously offensive" speech. The guidelines

were passed in response to a heated campus controversy involving a law-student parody of an expletive-filled *Harvard Law Review* article that promoted a postmodernist, gender-related view of the nature of law. In response to an outcry by outraged campus feminists and their allies, a law professor lodged a formal complaint against the parodists

plaint against the parodists with the college's administrative board.

3   When the board dismissed the charge on the technicality that the law school had no speech code that would specifically outlaw such a parody, the dean at the time appointed a faculty committee to draft the guidelines, which remain in force today. The intention was to prevent, or punish if necessary, future offensive gender-related speech that might create a "hostile environment" for female law students at Harvard. As far as Silverglate (who lives and works near the

Harvard campus and follows events there closely) has observed, there has not been a truly biting parody on hot-button issues related to gender politics at the law school since.

4   Last fall, officials at Harvard Business School admonished and threatened with punishment an editor of the school's student-run newspaper for publishing a cartoon critical of the administration. He resigned in protest over the administration's assault on the paper's editorial independence.

5   At virtually the same time, after a controversy in which a law student was accused of racially insensitive speech, a cry went up for adopting "Discriminatory Harassment Guidelines" to parallel the code that outlawed gender-based insults. As the controversy progressed, some students accused two professors of insensitivity for trying to discuss the issues in class. Soon after the Black Law Students Association demanded that one of those professors be disciplined and banned from teaching required first-year classes,

he announced that he would not teach his course for the rest of the semester. The other professor insisted on continuing to teach, but the dean's office announced that all of his classes had to be tape-recorded so that any students who felt offended being in his presence could instead listen to the recorded lecture.

6   All of that at a university that, as President Rudenstine supposedly assured *The New York Times*, did not have, much less enforce, a speech code.

7   Today, many in higher education still share Rudenstine's apparent belief that a speech code exists only if it is prominently stamped SPEECH CODE in the student handbook. To them, any speech code is an anachronism, a failed relic of the 1980s that has disappeared from all but the most repressive backwaters of academe.

8   But speech codes are alive and well, if one is realistic about what makes a campus regulation a speech code. The Foundation for Individual Rights in Education defines a speech code as *any campus*

regulation that punishes, forbids, heavily regulates, or restricts a substantial amount of protected speech.[1] Thus defined, speech codes are the rule rather than the exception in higher education.

9   Why does virtually no college call its speech code by that name? For one thing, in the 1980s and 90s, every legal challenge of a clearly identified speech code at a public institution was successful. To maintain a weapon against speech that is "offensive" or "uncivil" (or merely too robust), the authors of the current stealthier generation of speech codes have adopted highly restrictive "speech zone" policies, e-mail policies that ban "offensive" speech, "diversity statements" with provisions that punish those uttering any "intolerant expression," and, of course, the ubiquitous "harassment policies" aimed at "hostile" viewpoints and words that operate by redefining speech as a form of conduct.

10   FIRE initiated, in April, a litigation project aimed at abolishing such codes at public colleges and universities, begin-

---

[1]Protected speech is the communication guaranteed free—and hence unregulated—by the First Amendment to the Constitution.

ning with a lawsuit charging that various policies at Shippensburg University are unconstitutional. Shippensburg promises only to protect speech that does not "provoke, harass, demean, intimidate, or harm another." Shippensburg's "Racism and Cultural Diversity" statement (modified by the university after FIRE filed suit) defined harassment as "unsolicited, unwanted conduct which annoys, threatens, or alarms a person or group." Shippensburg also has "speech zones" that restrict protests to only two areas on the campus.

11   In a recent *Chronicle* article, Shippensburg's president, Anthony F. Ceddia, complained that FIRE had "cobbled together words and expressions of different policies and procedures." That is true; it found unconstitutional provisions in many different places—the student handbook and the university's Web site, to cite just two—and is challenging all of them.

12   FIRE has been developing an online database of policies that restrict speech on both private and public campuses. Given the longstanding assumption that academic freedom at liberal-arts col-leges protects offensive and unpopular speech, the number and variety of such policies are startling. FIRE's still-in-progress survey and analysis demonstrates that a clear majority of higher-education institutions have substantial speech restrictions and many others have lesser restrictions that still, arguably, infringe on academic freedom.

13   Some codes, of course, are worse than others. Some are patently unconstitutional; others, artfully written by offices of general counsels, seek to obfuscate their intention to prohibit or discourage certain speech. However, there is no excuse for a liberal-arts institution, public or private, to punish speech, no matter how impolite, impolitic, unpopular, or ornery.

14   No one denies that a college can and should ban true harassment—but a code that *calls* itself a "racial-harassment code" does not thereby magically inoculate itself against free-speech and academic-freedom obligations. The recent controversy over "racial harassment" at Harvard Law School has been replicated on campuses across the country, often with outcomes as perilous to aca-demic freedom. For example, in 1999, a professor at the Columbia University School of Law administered a criminal-law exam posing a complex question concerning the issues of feticide, abortion, violence against women, and consent to violence. Some women in the class complained to two faculty members, who then told the law-school dean that the professor's exam was so insensitive to the women in the class that it may have constituted harassment. The dean brought the case to Columbia's general counsel before concluding—correctly of course—after a dialogue with FIRE that academic freedom absolutely protected the professor.

15   Such examples demonstrate the persistence of the notion that administrators may muzzle speech that some students find "offensive," in the name of protecting civil rights. Further, the continuing existence of these codes relies on people's unwillingness to criticize any restriction that sports the "progressive" veneer of preventing racial or sexual "harassment"—even when the codes themselves go far beyond the traditional boundaries of academic and

Copyright © John Pritchett.

constitutional freedom. Fortunately, some see these codes for what they are and recognize that there is nothing progressive about censorship.

16 It should be obvious that allowing colleges to promulgate broad and amorphous rules that can punish speech, regardless of the intention, will result in self-censoring and administrative abuses. Consider the case of Mercedes Lynn de Uriarte, a professor at the University of Texas at Austin. In 1999, after filing an employment grievance, she re-ceived notice that the campus's office of equal employment opportunity had chosen to investigate her for "ethnic harassment" of another profes-sor in her department. Both de Uriarte and the accusing professor were Mexican-American. The facts suggest that the ethnic-harassment accu-sation was little more than an excuse for the univer-sity to retaliate against de Uriarte for filing the grievance. After nine months of pressing de Uriarte to answer per-sonal questions about her beliefs and why she dis-liked the other professor, the EEO office concluded that there was no evi-dence of "ethnic harass-ment" but scolded de Uriarte for "harboring personal animosity" to-ward the other professor and for not being suffi-ciently cooperative with the investigating dean.

17 In 2001 at Tufts Uni-versity, a female under-graduate filed sexual-harassment charges against a student publication, cit-ing a sexual-harassment code and claiming a satiri-cal cartoon and text made

her a "sex object." A vocal member of the Student Labor Action Movement, she was offended when the paper mocked "oh-so-tight" slam tank tops (amid other jokes about Madonna and President Bush). Hearings were initiated. FIRE successfully persuaded the hearing panel to reject the attempted censorship.

18 Those are just two examples among dozens that FIRE has seen recently where speech codes are used against students or faculty members. They illustrate not only that these codes are enforced, but that they are enforced against speech that would be clearly protected in the larger society.

19 Moreover, virtually none of the cases that FIRE has dealt with have followed the paradigm that "hate-speech codes" were supposedly crafted to combat: the intentional hurling of an epithet at a member of a racial or sexual minority. Overwhelmingly, speech codes are used against much milder expression, or even against expression of a particular unpopular or officially disfavored viewpoint.

20 The situation of Steve Hinkle, a student at California Polytechnic State University, is another case in point. In the fall of 2002, he posted fliers for a speech by C. Mason Weaver, the author of *It's OK to Leave the Plantation.* In his book, Weaver, an African-American writer, argues that government-assistance programs place many black people in a cycle of poverty and dependence similar to slavery. The flier included the place and time of the speech, the name of the book, and the author's picture. When Hinkle tried to post a flier in one public area, several students approached him and demanded that he not post the "offensive" flier. One student actually called the campus police, whose reports note that the students complained of "a suspicious white male passing out literature of an offensive racial nature." Hinkle was subjected to administrative hearings over the next half year and was found guilty of "disruption" for trying to post the flier.

21 Unless one considers posting a flier with factually accurate information a "hate crime," it is clear such speech codes are used to punish speech that administrators or students simply dislike. That should not come as a surprise to any student of history.

When broad powers and unchecked authority are granted to Officials—even for what are claimed to be the noblest of goals—those powers will be abused. Indeed, the Supreme Court has ruled unequivocally that "hate-speech laws," in contrast to "hate-crimes laws," are unconstitutional. Yet most of the speech prosecuted on college campuses does not even rise to the level of hate speech.

22 Some argue that speech codes communicate to students the kind of society to which we all *should* aspire. That is perhaps the most pernicious of all justifications, for it makes unexamined assumptions about the power of administrators to reach intrusively into the hearts and consciences of students. There is nothing ideal about a campus where protests and leaflets are quarantined to tiny, remote "speech zones," or where being inoffensive is a higher value than intellectual engagement.

23 Yet even if one agrees with such "aspirations," it is antithetical to a liberal-arts-college to coerce others into sharing them. The threat of sanctions crosses the clear line between *encouraging* such aspirations and *coercing* fealty to them, whether genuine or

affected. An administrator's employing the suasion of the bully pulpit differs crucially from using authority to bully disfavored opinions into submission.

24   Some people contend that the codes are infrequently enforced. The facts demonstrate otherwise, but even if a campus never enforced its speech code, the code would remain a palpable form of coercion. As long as the policy exists, the *threat* of enforcement remains real and will inevitably influence some people's speech. In First Amendment law, that is known as a "chilling" effect:[2] Merely by disseminating the codes in student handbooks, administrators can prevent much of the speech they disfavor. Students, seeing what is banned—or even guessing at what might be banned as they struggle with the breadth or vagueness of the definitions— will play it safe and avoid engaging in speech that, even though constitutionally protected, may offend a student or a disciplinary board.

25   In the long run, speech codes—actively enforced or not—send the message that it is OK to ban controversial or arguably ugly expressions that some do not wish to hear. Students will not forget that lesson once they get their diplomas. A whole generation of American students is learning that its members should hide their deeply held unpopular beliefs, while other students realize that they have the power, even the right, to censor opinions they dislike.

26   Take the case at Ithaca College last spring, when the College Republicans brought to campus Bay Buchanan, the sister of Patrick Buchanan, for a speech entitled "The Failures of Feminism." Instead of protesting the speech or debating Buchanan's points, several students demanded that the campus police stop the event and declare it a "bias-related incident"—a punishable offense. The "Bias-Related Incidents Committee" ultimately declared the speech protected but then announced that it would explore developing policies that could prohibit similar future speeches. Outrageous though it seems, the students' reaction is un-

derstandable. Ithaca College teaches that it is okay to ban "biased" speech. The "Bias-Related Incidents Committee" shunned free speech as a sacred value and instead sought ways to punish disagreeable viewpoints in the future.

27   FIRE generally eschews litigation in favor of reasoning with campus administrators in detailed philosophical, academic, and moral arguments made in memorandums and letters. However, speech codes have proved remarkably impervious to reasoned arguments, for while FIRE often can snatch individual students from the jaws of speech prosecutions, administrators rarely abandon the codes themselves. (A happy exception was when in 1999 the Faculty Senate of the University of Wisconsin at Madison voted to repeal the long-standing code that restricted faculty speech.) FIRE thus initiated its litigation campaign.

28   Shippensburg is the beginning. In cooperation with FIRE's Legal Network, attorney Carol Sobel in May challenged a speech code at Citrus College, in California, where

---

[2]A "chilling effect" occurs when regulations or a particular atmosphere discourage free speech.

students were allocated three remote areas—less than 1 percent of the campus—for protest activities. Even if they were to protest within the ironically named "free speech area," students had to get permission in advance, alert campus security of the intended message, and provide any printed materials that they wished to distribute, in addition to a host of other restrictions. Further, this free-speech area was open only from "8 A.M. through 6 P.M. Monday through Friday." Citrus's student-conduct code banned "lewd, indecent, obscene or offensive conduct [and] expression," and included a number of other highly restrictive provisions. Just two weeks after the lawsuit was filed, the administration yielded and rescinded all of the provisions listed above. It is unfortunate that it took a lawsuit to demonstrate that restrictions on words have no place on the modern liberal-arts campus.

29 Colleges must recognize that growth, progress, and innovation require the free and occasionally outrageous exchange of views. Without speech codes, students are more likely to interact honestly. Having one's beliefs challenged is not a regrettable side effect of openness and intellectual diversity, but an essential part of the educational process. And, in fact, liberty is more than simply a prerequisite for progress; it is, at the deepest level, a fundamental and indispensable way of being human.

READING CLOSELY AND THINKING CRITICALLY

1. Was Neil L. Rudenstine lying when he said that Harvard did not have any speech codes? Explain.
2. Why is it surprising that colleges have speech codes?
3. Why do so many colleges adopt and defend speech codes? Why is it difficult for people to object to speech codes?
4. What are speech zones? How do speech zones affect free speech on college campuses?
5. List the negative effects of speech codes. Can you think of any positive effects?

EXAMINING STRUCTURE AND STRATEGY

1. The thesis of the essay is delayed until paragraph 8. What do the paragraphs before the thesis accomplish?
2. In which paragraphs do the authors raise and counter objections?
3. Do the authors rely mostly on logos, ethos, or pathos? Why?
4. The authors write a strong conclusion. What makes it so effective?

NOTING COMBINED PATTERNS

1. Silverglate and Lukianoff use many examples throughout the essay. Cite four paragraphs that include examples. What purpose do the examples serve? Would the essay be as persuasive without them? Explain.

2. The authors use definition in paragraphs 8–10 and 24. Why?

3. How does the cause-and-effect analysis in the essay help the authors achieve their persuasive purpose?

CONSIDERING LANGUAGE AND STYLE

1. List three words or phrases that describe the authors' writing style in "Speech Codes: Alive and Well at Colleges."

2. The audience for the *Chronicle of Higher Education,* where "Speech Codes: Alive and Well at Colleges" first appeared is college professors and administrators. How would the language, style, and emphasis of the essay be different if the audience were for college students?

3. Consult a dictionary if you are unsure of the meaning of any of these words: *postmodernist* (paragraph 2), *anachronism* (paragraph 7), *ubiquitous* (paragraph 9), *obfuscate* (paragraph 10), *amorphous* (paragraph 16), *paradigm* (paragraph 19), *fealty* (paragraph 23), *suasion* (paragraph 23), *bully pulpit* (paragraph 23).

For writing assignments based on "Speech Codes: Alive and Well at Colleges," see page 636.

BACKGROUND: An assistant professor of law at Florida International University College of Law, Howard M. Wasserman is an expert on issues related to civil procedure, civil rights, and free speech. Before joining the faculty of FIU, Wasserman was an attorney in Chicago and later a clerk for a United States District Court judge and for a United States Court of Appeals judge. His many publications include pieces in the Emory, Tulane, and Kentucky law reviews and in the *William and Mary Bill of Rights Journal.* "Fan Profanity" was written for First Amendment Center's Web site. Operated by Vanderbilt University, this site offers comprehensive coverage of First Amendment issues, including research, commentary, and analysis by legal specialists. You can visit the site at *www.firstamendmentcenter.org.*

COMBINED PATTERNS AND THEIR PURPOSES: Howard M. Wasserman uses *exemplification* to **inform** readers about the kinds of profane speech used by college sports fans. To **persuade** readers that such speech is protected by the First Amendment, Wasserman draws on *comparison* and *cause-and-effect analysis.* Finally, to clarify terms, Wasserman uses *definition.*

FAN PROFANITY

HOWARD M. WASSERMAN

Many free-speech controversies, especially on college campuses, are grounded in concerns for civility, politeness, and good taste. They also tend to follow the same path and end the same way. A government entity regulates speech in an effort to elevate discourse, limit the profane and protect public and personal sensitivities; courts strike down the regulations as violating the First Amendment freedom of speech; and we end up right where we started.

As you read
Consider why university officials are concerned about fan profanity.

2   Colleges may be pursuing a similar course in trying to deal with objectionable cheering by students at sporting events. University of Maryland officials expressed anger and embarrassment following a men's basketball game against conference rival Duke University in January 2004, when fans chanted and sported T-shirts with the slogan "F--- Duke" and directed epithets at Duke players. This was one of many incidents of offensive or obnoxious cheering by students throughout the country during the 2004 college basketball season.

"This was "... fans chanted and sported T-shirts with the slogan 'F--- Duke' ... "

3   John K. Anderson, chief of the Educational Affairs Division of the Maryland Attorney General's Office, advised the university that a written code of fan conduct applicable at a university-owned and -operated athletic facility, if "carefully drafted," would be constitutionally permissible. University of Maryland Associate Athletics Director Michael Lipitz began working with a committee of students to consider rules of conduct. The committee ultimately recommended that the university promote voluntary compliance, although rules and formal punishment remain a "last resort" if a proposed standing monitoring commit-

tee determines that voluntary compliance is ineffective. Other schools, such as Western Michigan University, currently have, or are studying the need for, similar codes to restrict profanity and other abusive language. And the approach of a new academic year may bring new incidents and new university attempts at regulating fan expression.

4   One can envision guidelines restricting profanity and epithets in signs and chants, as well as imposing a general requirement that students keep things stylish, clever, clean, and classy. Presumably, the sanction would be removal from the arena. The ostensible purpose behind such guidelines is to enable the majority of fans to enjoy the game unburdened by objectionable or offensive signs, messages, and chants. But any such policy enacted and enforced at a public university such as Maryland should not and perhaps will not survive First Amendment scrutiny. On the other hand, a private college, not bound by the strictures of the First Amendment, obviously remains free to impose such restrictions.

5   The speech at issue is expression by fans related to a sporting event, to all aspects of the game and all the participants in the game—what we can call "cheering speech." Cheering speech can be directed at players, coaches, officials, executives, administrators, or other fans. It can be in support of one's own players and team, against the opposing players and team or even critical of one's own players and team. It can be about events on the field or it can target broader social and political issues surrounding the game, the players or sport in general.

6   In advising the university that it could regulate cheering speech, Anderson insisted that fans at sporting events, particularly children, are "captive auditors." The are captives in the arena or stadium; the only way to avoid being offended by the chants or sings is to leave the arena or stop coming to games. This captive status, Anderson argued, alters the ordinary First Amendment burden. Rather than requiring objecting listeners to "avert their eyes" (or ears) to avoid objectionable speech, the university can force speakers, especially students, to alter their manner of communicating to protect the sensibilities of these captive fans.

"One certainly could avert one's eyes to avoid viewing the message written on a sign or on the body of a student at a basketball game."

7   In reality, the captive-audience doctrine is far more limited than Anderson suggests. Courts have found listeners to be captives in only four places: their own homes, the workplace, public elementary and secondary schools, and inside and around abortion clinics. And even in those places, captive-audience status permits government to limit oral expression but not the same message in written form on pickets, signs, or clothing. One certainly could avert one's eyes to avoid viewing the message written on a sign or on the body of a student at a basketball game.

8   Of course, one problem with cheering speech is that much of it is oral. Fans have complained not only about signs and T-shirts, but also about chants and taunts targeting players, coaches and officials, which other fans may be unable to avoid no matter where in the arena

they sit. Objectors must perform the more difficult task of averting their ears to avoid offensive cheers, something that children may be even less able to do. It is true that courts have upheld content-neutral regulations on sound and noise levels to protect captive audiences, beginning with the Supreme Court case *Kovacs v. Cooper* in 1949. But government never has been permitted to protect captive auditors by singling out particular profane or offensive oral messages for selective restriction while leaving related messages on the same subject, uttered at the same volume, undisturbed.

9   More important, the captive-audience doctrine never has been applied to listeners in public places of recreation and entertainment, places to which people voluntarily go for the particular purpose of engaging in expressive activity, in this case cheering on their favorite college team. Fans who pay to attend a college basketball game at an on-campus arena are not captive auditors there, any more than an individual walking on a city street who stumbles across an objectionable political rally or an individual whose office sits above the route of an objectionable parade.

10   The Hobson's Choice that Anderson believes this creates for fans—leave the arena and stop attending games or tolerate offensive cheers—is precisely the choice people make in any public place at which expression occurs. It is the same choice that people in the California courthouse had to make when confronted with a jacket emblazoned with the message "F--- the Draft," a message and manner of expression that the Supreme Court found to be protected from prosecution under a disturbing-the-peace statute in the 1971 landmark case *Cohen v. California*. In fact, leaving was even less of an option there for an objecting auditor whose job required her to remain in the courthouse or an objector conducting business before the court and likely required to be there on pain of contempt or default. It is difficult to reconcile that "F--- the Draft" is a protected message in a courthouse, but "F--- Duke" is unprotected amid the cacophony of 20,000 screaming basketball fans. It is even less comprehensible that Paul Cohen's intellectual heir could be prohibited from wearing his jacket (for example, to protest the so-called "backdoor draft"[1] created by extending reservists' service) at a university sports arena governed by a fan speech code.

11   The real import of *Cohen* is the principle that a speaker's choice of words and manner of communication are essential elements of the overall message expressed and government cannot prohibit certain words or manner without also suppressing certain messages in the process. A cheering fan's point of view is bound up in the decision to formulate a particular message by telling an opponent that he "sucks" or by targeting more personal issues. Fans have created controversy by targeting a player whose girlfriend had posed in *Playboy*, chanting "rapist" at a player who had pled guilty to sexual assault and waving fake joints at a player with a history of use. "Fear the Turtle," "We Hate Duke" and "Duke Sucks" are three ways of cheering for the Maryland Terrapins, as well as cheering

_____

[1]Some say that extending the hours of duty of National Guard and reservist troops beyond their expected length of time amounts to a form of conscription.

against Duke. But each conveys a distinct message and point of view and each has ample grounds for constitutional protection within the expressive milieu of a college sports stadium.

12 Because word choice and communicative manner are essential components of free-speech protection, it becomes impossible to enforce any fan-conduct policy in a uniform, non-arbitrary way. The state cannot neutrally define what words or manner are offensive or establish any meaningful standard to measure offensiveness. Justice John Marshall Harlan's memorable phrase in *Cohen* was that "one man's vulgarity is another's lyric," and government's inability to make principled distinctions means "the Constitution leaves matters of taste and style so largely to the individual."

13 Under current doctrine, offensiveness cannot be measured from the standpoint of the most sensitive person in the crowd; the level of permissible expression cannot be reduced to what the least-tolerant listener will accept. Nor should it be measured from the standpoint of children in the crowd, because, as the Court long has insisted, the level of discourse for an adult audience cannot be reduced to what is fit or proper for children. The university sports arena exemplifies the problem of the mixed audience—how can government regulate speech in the interest of protecting children when the speech occurs before a mixed audience of children and adults? The pithy answer may be that it simply cannot do so. There is no, and can be no, baseline for oral speech before a mixed audience; either children unavoidably hear some "adult" expression or we reduce the level of speech to what is suitable for a sandbox.

"The university sports arena exemplifies the problem of the mixed audience."

14 In seeking to control abusive cheering speech, universities apparently do not distinguish among expressive forms. On one hand is blatant use of profanity; on the other hand are epithets or chants that do not employ any of the seven dirty words, but that target opposing teams, players, coaches or officials, perhaps with references to personal life or criminal difficulties. The presumption apparent in Anderson's recommendation to the University of Maryland was that a public university could serve the same interest in protecting children through a single conduct policy that banned both "F--- Duke" chants and signs and chants and signs targeting a player accused of sexual assault. One can imagine attempts to require students to keep things "polite" or "positive"— cheer for your team and your players, but do not jeer or criticize the opponent (or, for that matter, your own team). Even conceding a government interest in protecting sensitive and juvenile ears from the seven dirty words in public spaces, government goes a step beyond when it begins to restrict particular non-profane messages that bear on the game played on the field or on the participants in that game.

15 Moreover, the sexual-assault example presents an additional wrinkle. Taunting a player who has been accused of sexual assault may be, at least in part, a social or political statement, protesting or drawing attention to the problem of athlete misbehavior or to the fact that this player continues to be allowed to

play for the school despite his off-court misconduct.

16 Perhaps the level of protection turns on the subtlety of the chants. Students are obvious in their attempts to offend when they use profanity, chant "rapist," or wave fake joints. But what if Maryland students chant or wear T-shirts bearing the slogan "Duck Fuke"? This is an obvious play on the profanity that created controversy at Maryland, but it does not use (as opposed to hinting at) dirty words. Should hinting at profanity be enough to justify a restriction on protected manner of expression?

17 Or what if the offensiveness is lost on those who might otherwise be offended? Students at Allen Field House at the University of Kansas were praised for their cleverness during the 2004 season when they chanted "salad tosser" at Texas Tech Basketball Coach Bob Knight. On the surface, the taunt was a reference to Knight's infamous verbal altercation several days earlier with the Texas Tech chancellor at a salad bar in Lubbock. But the phrase also is a slang reference to a particular sexual act, a double entendre the students surely knew when they began the chant, but many listeners likely did not.

18 Dissenting in *Cohen*, Justice Harry Blackmun derided Paul Cohen's jacket as "an absurd and immature antic." By contrast, Justice Harlan insisted that the expression at issue was, in fact, of "no small constitutional consequence." Free-speech scholars laud *Cohen* for recognizing that government must leave matters of expressive taste and style to the individual. One could dismiss offensive signs, T-shirts and taunts at college basketball games as similarly absurd and immature antics. However, as in *Cohen*, skirmishes over what fan expression will be permitted at public university sporting events are of no small constitutional consequence.

19 College sport has become, for better or for worse, a central part of college life and culture. The prevailing belief among university administrators and most commentators is that successful athletic teams, particularly in high-profile football and men's basketball, can be a source of university pride, publicity, media attention, revenue and increased donations. The non-athlete students who pack the stadium provide an essential ingredient of that overall culture. Students are encouraged to attend games and make noise, to be excited and passionate about their school, to cheer for their team and players (and against the opposing team and players), and to create a playing environment that will be intimidating or distracting to the opponent and will give their team a home-court advantage. Indeed, it is somewhat ironic that Duke players were at the receiving end of the taunts that prompted Maryland to consider an arena speech code. Duke students have attained wide notoriety for their sometimes-clever, sometimes-offensive cheering speech and the headaches they cause opposing teams and players.

"The grandstand at the arena or stadium has become the central public forum for cheering speech."

20 The grandstand at the arena or stadium has become the central public forum for cheering speech. Fans are invited to the arena and encouraged to speak, loudly and in however vivid or stark terms, to support, oppose, cheer,

jeer, criticize and even taunt teams, players, coaches, and officials in that game. Having created this forum for students to express themselves, a public university has ceded control over the manner in which students do so, at least within the parameters of protected speech. Fans must remain free to jeer as well as cheer players and teams and in as blatant or profane a manner as they wish.

21 Perhaps one may not particularly enjoy sitting, or having one's children sit, in an arena where students are shouting expletives throughout the game. But commitment to a neutral free-speech principle means tolerating a great deal of speech that one personally does not like or does not wish to hear. And there is nothing wrong with hortatory efforts by the university, coaches and, most important, other students to encourage fans, especially student fans, to keep their cheering stylish, clean, classy, and creative. The "voluntary compliance" policies recommended in June by the student committee at the University of Maryland included a program under which students could exchange profane T-shirts for noncontroversial ones, contests that would encourage appropriate signs and banners, having coaches address students about the need for good sportsmanship and fan behavior and distributing newspapers at games with "creative witty cheers" for students to use.

22 The point is that a state university may not formally punish—even via non-criminal sanction such as removal from the arena—those students who depart generally accepted norms by loudly wielding a particular loaded word to inform officials or opposing players that they are not very good at what they do.

READING CLOSELY AND THINKING CRITICALLY

1. In your own words, write the thesis of "Fan Profanity." Be sure to indicate the issue and assertion being argued.
2. John K. Anderson bases his support of a speech code for fans, in part, on the captive-audience doctrine. What is that doctrine? Does Wasserman think the captive-audience doctrine applies to speech at sporting events? Explain.
3. According to Wasserman, how is *Cohen v. California* relevant to fan profanity issues?
4. Do you think the expression "Duck Fuke" should qualify as profanity? Why or why not?
5. Why you think some university officials are concerned about fan profanity?
6. How successful do you think the University of Maryland's voluntary policing policy will be? Explain your view.

EXAMINING STRUCTURE AND STRATEGY

1. What strategy does Wasserman use in the first two paragraphs?
2. Paragraph 3 has an important function in the essay. What is that function?
3. Which paragraphs raise and counter objections?

4. The topic sentence of paragraph 16 (the last sentence) is a question, as is the topic sentence of paragraph 17 (the first sentence). What does the author achieve by framing these topic sentences as questions?

NOTING COMBINED PATTERNS

1. Comparison is an important pattern in "Fan Profanity." How does Wasserman use comparison to help build his argument?
2. How does Wasserman use exemplification?
3. How does Wasserman use cause-and-effect analysis to help achieve his persuasive purpose?
4. What elements of definition appear in the essay?

CONSIDERING LANGUAGE AND STYLE

1. What characteristics of the essay reflect the fact that Wasserman is an attorney writing about a legal issue?
2. Consult a dictionary if you are unsure of the meaning of any of these words: *epithets* (paragraphs 2, 4, 14), *Hobson's choice* (paragraph 10), *cacophony* (paragraph 10), *milieu* (paragraph 11), *pithy* (paragraph 13), *double entendre* (paragraph 17), *hortatory* (paragraph 21).

For writing assignments based on "Fan Profanity," see page 636.

BACKGROUND: Former law clerk to Supreme Court Justice William J. Brennan, Jr., Robert O'Neil was president of the University of Wisconsin system and the University of Virginia, where he continues to teach in the law school, specializing in constitutional law and free speech and the Internet. The founding director of the Thomas Jefferson Center for the Protection of Free Expression and the first president of Virginia's Coalition for Open Government, O'Neil has testified before congressional committees on how proposed legislation will affect the First Amendment. O'Neil has written several books, including *Free Speech: Responsible Communication Under Law, The Rights of Public Employees* (1993) and *Free Speech in the College Community* (1997). "What Limits Should Campus Networks Place on Pornography?" first appeared in 2003 in *The Chronicle of Higher Education,* a publication for college faculty and administrators.

THE PATTERN AND ITS PURPOSES: As a former college president and as an attorney specializing in constitutional issues, Robert O'Neil is uniquely qualified to **inform** readers of the issues surrounding censorship of pornography on the Internet, which he does with the help of *cause-and-effect analysis.* He also **argues** for a compromise solution to the conflict between free speech advocates who oppose censorship and those who want to restrict pornography to avoid offending those who are troubled by the material.

What Limits Should Campus Networks Place on Pornography?

ROBERT O'NEIL

What if you were about to present a PowerPoint lecture to a large undergraduate class, but found instead on your computer a series of sexually explicit ads and material from pornographic Web sites? That's essentially what happened recently to Mary Pedersen, a nutrition-

As you read Evaluate how convincingly O'Neil argues his thesis.

science professor at California Polytechnic State University at San Luis Obispo. That incident and the increasing presence of such imagery at Cal Poly have led to a novel, although undoubtedly predictable, struggle over computer content— one that is quite likely to be replicated at countless campuses in the coming months.

2   A concerned faculty group at Cal Poly has announced its intention to bring before the Academic Senate, sometime this spring, a "Resolution to Enhance Civility and Promote a Diversity-Friendly Campus Climate." Specifically, the measure would prohibit using the university's computers or network to access or download digital material generally described as "pornography." The resolution would also forbid the "transmission" of hate literature and obscenity on the Cal Poly network.

3   The sponsoring faculty members have offered several reasons for proposing such drastic action. First and foremost, they contend that the ready availability of sexually explicit imagery can create occasional but deeply disturbing encounters like Pedersen's discovery of unwelcome and unexpected material on her classroom computer. The pervasive pres-

Copyright © 2002 by Mike Keefe. *The Denver Post*, 4/21/2002.

ence of such images, proponents of the resolution argue, is inherently demeaning to female faculty members, administrators, and students.

4 Indeed, they suggest that the university might even be legally liable for creating and maintaining a "hostile workplace environment" if it fails to take steps to check the spread of such offensive material. That concern has been heightened by a putative link to a growing number of sexual assaults in the environs of the university.

5 Those who call for tighter regulation cite several other factors to support anti-pornography measures. In their view, a college or university must maintain the highest of standards, not only in regard to the integrity of scholarship and relations between teachers and students, but also in the range of material to which it provides electronic access. The clear implication is that the ready availability of sexually explicit and deeply offensive imagery falls below "the ethical standards that the university claims to uphold."

6 Critics of easy access to such material also claim that it can divert time, talent, and resources from the university's primary mission. Kimberly Daniels, a local lawyer who is advising the resolution's sponsors, told the student newspaper that "it is offensive that Cal Poly is taking the position that it is acceptable for professors to view pornography during work hours in their work office." That risk is not entirely conjectural. In fact, one professor left the institution last year after being convicted on misdemeanor charges for misusing a state-owned computer, specifically for the purpose of downloading in his office thousands of sexually explicit images. Local newspapers have also reported that the FBI is investigating another

former Cal Poly professor who allegedly used a campus computer to view child pornography.

7   Finally, the concerned faculty group insists that the free flow of pornographic materials may expose the Cal Poly computer network to a greater risk of virus infection. They cite a student's recent experience in opening a salacious virus-bearing attachment that the student mistakenly believed had been sent by one of his professors.

8   The proposed Academic Senate resolution has touched off an intense debate. The university's existing computer-use policy presumes that access and choice of material are broadly protected, although it adds that "in exceptional cases, the university may decide that such material directed at individuals presents such a hostile environment under the law that certain restrictive actions are warranted." The new proposal would focus more sharply on sexually explicit imagery, and would require those who wish to view such material through the campus network to obtain the express permission of the university's president.

9   Defenders of the current approach, including the senior staff of the university's office of information technology, insist that a public university may not banish from its system material that is offensive, but legal, without violating First Amendment rights. Those familiar with the operations of such systems also cite practical difficulties in the enforcement of any such restrictions, given the immense volume of digital communications that circulate around the clock at such a complex institution.

10   The debate at Cal Poly echoes what occurred some six years ago in Virginia. The General Assembly enacted what remains as the nation's only ban on public employees' use of state-owned or state-leased computers to access sexually explicit material—at least without express permission of a "superior" for a "bona fide research purpose." Six state university professors immediately challenged the law on First Amendment grounds. A district judge struck down the statute, but the U.S. Court of Appeals for the Fourth Circuit reversed that ruling. The law had been modified before that judgment, and many Virginia professors have since received exemptions or dispensations, but the precedent created by the appeals-court decision remains troubling for advocates of free and open electronic communications.

11   The Virginia ruling complicates the Cal Poly situation. The First Amendment challenge of those who oppose the Academic Senate resolution is less clear than it might at first appear. Two premises underlying that resolution—the need to protect government-owned hardware and the imperative to combat sexual hostility in the public workplace—contributed both to the passage of the Virginia ban, and to its eventual success in the federal courts. What's more, the U.S. Equal Employment Opportunity Commission some months ago gave its blessing to a hostile-workplace complaint filed by Minneapolis Public Library staff members who were offended by persistent display of graphic sexual images on reading-room terminals.

12   Thus, there is more than a superficial basis for the claims of Cal Poly's pornbanishers that (in the words of one faculty member) "the First Amendment doesn't protect . . . subjecting others to inappropriate

material in the workplace." Even the information-technology consultant who has championed the current computer-use policy at the university has conceded that access to controversial material is fully protected only "as long as it isn't offending others."

13 Although the desire to reduce the potential for offense and affront to other users of a campus computer network seems unobjectionable, its implications deserve careful scrutiny. In the analogous situation of public terminals in a library reading room, it is one thing to ask a patron who wishes to access and display sexually explicit material—or racially hateful material, for that matter—to use a terminal facing away from other users and staff members. It is quite another matter to deny access to such material altogether on the plausible premise that, if it can be obtained at all, there is a palpable risk that its visible display will offend others. To invoke an analogy that is now before the U.S. Supreme Court in a challenge to the Children's Internet Protection Act: It is one thing for a library to provide—even be compelled to provide—filtered access for parents who wish it for their children, but quite another to deny all adult patrons any unfiltered access.

14 What Cal Poly should seek to do, without impairing free expression, is to protect people from being gratuitously assaulted by digital material that may be deeply offensive, without unduly restricting access of those who, for whatever reason, may wish to access and view such material without bothering others. The proposal in the resolution that permission may be obtained from the university's president, for bona-fide research purposes, is far too narrow. Among other flaws, such a precondition might well deter sensitive or conscientious scholars, whether faculty members or students, who are understandably reluctant to reveal publicly their reasons for wishing to access sexually explicit images or hate literature.

15 A responsible university, seeking to balance contending interests of a high order, might first revisit and make more explicit its policies that govern acceptable computer use and access, by which all campus users are presumably bound. Such policies could condemn the flaunting of thoughtless dissemination of sexually explicit material and digital hate literature, expressing institutional abhorrence of such postings, without seeking to ban either type of material. The computer network might also establish a better warning system through which to alert sensitive users to the occasional and inevitable presence of material that may offend. Finally, a broader disclaimer might be in order, recognizing the limited practical capacity of a university server to control (or even enable users to avoid) troubling material.

16 What is needed is a reasonable balance that avoids, as Justice William O. Douglas warned a half-century ago, "burning down the house to roast the pig." That aphorism has special felicity here; in the offensive flaunting of sexually explicit imagery, there is a "pig" that doubtless deserves to be roasted. But there is also a house of intellect that must remain free and open, even to those with aberrant tastes and interests.

READING CLOSELY AND THINKING CRITICALLY

1. What reasons do the Cal Poly concerned faculty give for supporting a resolution to restrict access to Internet pornography and hate materials?
2. What are the reasons to oppose the resolution?
3. What conflicting principles are inherent in any move to restrict Internet content?
4. Explain why the Virginia court ruling lends support for the Cal Poly resolution.
5. Why does O'Neil object to the Cal Poly resolution?
6. What do you think of O'Neil's solution to the conflict explained in the essay? Is his solution practical? Can it work?

EXAMINING STRUCTURE AND STRATEGY

1. What approach does O'Neil take to his opening paragraph? Why does he use this approach?
2. O'Neil uses a problem-solution organization. Which paragraphs explain the problem, and which offer a solution?
3. O'Neil develops the problem more than the solution. Does his emphasis undermine the essay's persuasiveness?
4. Where does O'Neil state his thesis? Why is the thesis located there?
5. How does O'Neil use cause-and-effect analysis?

CONSIDERING LANGUAGE AND STYLE

1. Explain the meaning of Justice Douglas's warning against "burning down the house to roast the pig" (paragraph 16). How is this aphorism relevant to First Amendment issues?
2. Consult a dictionary if you are unsure of the meaning of any of these words: *putative* (paragraph 4), *conjectural* (paragraph 6), *salacious* (paragraph 7), *aphorism* (paragraph 16), *aberrant* (paragraph 16).

ASSIGNMENTS FOR DISCUSSION AND WRITING

"Free Speech on Campus," "The Debate over Placing Limits on Racist Speech Must Not Ignore the Damage It Does to Its Victims," "Speech Codes: Alive and Well at Colleges," "Fan Profanity," and "What Limits Should Campus Networks Place on Pornography?"

1. **For discussion in class or online.** Should a member of the Ku Klux Klan or American Nazi party be allowed to speak at your school? What about advocates of terror or torture? Porn stars? Where do we draw the line—or should there be no line? If your instructor so directs, post your response on your class Web site.
2. **In your journal.**
   - Do you feel pressured to have the "right," politically correct attitude at school or on the job? Explain in a page or two.

- In the original version of "Fan Profanity," which appeard on the First Amendment Center's Web site *www.firstamendmentcenter.org*, author Howard Wasserman used a common obscenity for which "f---" was substituted in this book. Why do you think the reprinted essay in this book includes the change? Does the change affect the meaning of the essay or your reaction to it? Do you think such substitutions are appropriate? Why or why not?

3. **Using argumentation-persuasion for a purpose.** The purposes in the assignments are possibilities. You may establish whatever purposes you like, within your instructor's guidelines.

- Do college instructors have the right to express their opinions? For example, can they publicly express the view that homosexuals should not be allowed to marry, that abortion is a sin or a necessity to restrict population growth, or that preemptive war is unjust? Argue your view to convince members of your school's academic senate.

- Should access to Internet pornography be restricted on campus, in offices, and in libraries? State and defend your view for a wavering audience. (See page 550 on wavering audiences.)

- If the fans at athletic events on your campus often use profanity, write a letter to the editor of your campus newspaper defending or attacking this behavior.

- Write a publication policy for your campus newspaper that gives guidelines covering hate speech, profanity, and politically correct speech. Then argue for adoption of your policy on your campus, drawing on your own ideas and the readings in this section for support.

4. **Connecting the readings.**

- Discuss the way we respond to hatred. In addition to your own ideas, you can draw on "Free Speech on Campus," "The Debate over Placing Limits on Racist Speech Must Not Ignore the Damage It Does to Its Victims," "The Lottery" (page 169), "Just Walk on By" (page 416), and "The Ways of Meeting Oppression" (page 459).

- Discuss the challenges raised by technology on campus. In addition to your own ideas, you can draw on "What Limits Should Campus Networks Place on Pornography?" and "Computers Help Unite Campuses but Also Drive Some Students Apart" (page 228).

5. **Drawing on sources.** Find out what your school's policy is on public speech and argue whether or not that policy is a good one. As an alternative, argue for a specific change in your school's policy.

13

Combining Patterns
of Development

CONSIDER THE PATTERNS

A crazy quilt, like the one on the facing page, is made by sewing together fabric in patterns of different shapes, sizes, colors, and textures to create a single work of art. Although made of many different patterns, the quilt does not seem like a hodgepodge. In fact, it is attractive and has a distinct unity. In a paragraph, describe what makes the quilt attractive and what gives it a distinct unity.

PATTERNS FOR A PURPOSE

An important focus of this book is to demonstrate how you can use the patterns of development to achieve your purpose for writing. In fact, this focus is so important that it gives this book its title, *Patterns for a Purpose*.

You have probably noticed that in addition to demonstrating how individual patterns of development can help you achieve your writing purpose, *Patterns for a Purpose* also demonstrates how you can *combine* two or more patterns to achieve your purpose:

- Many readings in the book combine patterns.
- Prereading headnotes labeled "Combined Patterns and Their Purpose(s)" signal when and why patterns are combined.
- Postreading questions labeled "Noting Combined Patterns" help you study strategies for combining patterns.
- Writing assignments labeled "Combining Patterns" give you experience combining patterns in a single essay.

639

To emphasize further that you can combine patterns to achieve your writing purpose, this chapter includes six additional readings that combine patterns to achieve a range of purposes.

USING THE PATTERNS OF DEVELOPMENT IN YOUR WRITING

How do you know if your writing is successful? The best indicator of success is whether your writing achieves its purpose with its target audience. Sometimes you can achieve your purpose using a single pattern of development, and sometimes you need to combine two or more patterns. For example, assume that at work you are the editor of the company newsletter and must write an article to inform new employees about vacation and sick leave policies. For this target audience, a single pattern—process analysis—may be sufficient to explain how the policies work. However, if your audience is long-term employees and your purpose is to inform them of changes in vacation and sick leave policies, you may need two patterns—process analysis to explain how the new policies work and comparison-contrast to make sure long-term employees understand how the new policies differ from the old.

Sometimes you need more than two patterns to achieve your purpose. Let's say that in another edition of the newsletter you profile the employee-of-the-month to inspire other employees to strive for the same award. To achieve this purpose, you might use exemplification to give examples of the employee's accomplishments, narration to tell a story about a time the employee did something extraordinary, and cause-and-effect analysis to explain how the employee affects the success of the company.

When you combine patterns to achieve your writing purpose, you often draw on one pattern more heavily than the others. That is, you will have primary and secondary patterns. For example, an essay about your favorite vacation spot can rely heavily on description. However, in a paragraph or two, you might also narrate a story about something enjoyable that happened when you last visited the spot. Then, description would be your *primary pattern*, and narration would be your *secondary pattern*. Or to convince readers to practice meditation, you might use exemplification as a primary pattern to illustrate the benefits of meditation, and process analysis and classification as secondary patterns to explain how meditation works and to explain the kinds of meditation, to help readers decide which kind is best for them.

Whenever you write—in college, at work, in the community—be open to the possibility of combining patterns to achieve your purpose. Combining patterns often strengthens your writing and makes it more interesting and more likely to appeal to your audience.

PROCESS GUIDELINES: STRATEGIES FOR COMBINING PATTERNS

1. **Selecting a Topic.** If your topic has been assigned, look for combinations of patterns suggested by that topic. For example, the essay topic "What is media bias and how common is it?" suggests that you will combine a definition of media bias with examples of its occurrence. Or if you have to write about media bias and have trouble

narrowing your topic, call on the patterns to help you. Exemplification will focus your topic on examples of media bias; cause-and-effect analysis will narrow your topic to discuss the reasons for and consequences of media bias; classification will narrow the topic to types of media bias; definition will guide you toward explaining the meaning of media bias. Looking at your topic through the lens of the patterns can help you bring your ideas into focus.

2. **Achieving Your Purpose and Assessing Your Audience.** Ask yourself how multiple patterns can help you achieve your purpose with your target audience. The answer may suggest ways to combine patterns to heighten your essay's appeal.

3. **Generating Ideas.** If you have trouble discovering ideas for developing your writing topic, use the patterns. They help you generate ideas by looking at your topic from different angles. To generate ideas for a newsletter article about the employee-of-the-month, for instance, consider each pattern and the detail it can provide. Ask "What can I describe?" and you might answer "the employee's desk—for humor." Ask "What can I narrate?" and you might answer "the time the employee administered CPR to another worker."

4. **Organizing Details.** Consider whether your pattern combination suggests combining certain organizational schemes. For example, if you combine process analysis and cause-and-effect analysis, you may need to order your details with a combination of chronological and progressive orders.

5. **Revising.** For help revising an essay with multiple patterns, you can consult the revising checklists in Chapters 4–11. These checklists note the revision concerns for each pattern of development.

---

www.mhhe.com/patterns

For more help with combining patterns, click on
Writing > Writing Tutor: Blended Essay

Using Transitions and Other Coherence Devices

If you have trouble signaling the relationships among the ideas you express with combined patterns, consult the transition chart on page 69. The transitions in this chart, along with the other coherence devices explained on pages 69–70, can also help you move smoothly from pattern to pattern.

TROUBLESHOOTING GUIDE

In the following essay, student writer Mary Ann Bevilacqua combines comparison-contrast, exemplification, and cause-and-effect analysis to explain to parents of teenagers the attraction—and danger—associated with Instant Messaging (IM). After you read, you will have an opportunity to evaluate this essay.

The Telephone Is Out; IM Is In

Paragraph 1
This introduction gives background information. The thesis is the last sentence. It identifies the audience as parents of teenagers and states the informational purpose: The essay will explain why IM is so appealing to teenagers.

In the not-too-distant past, parents could not get their teenagers off 1 the telephone. So permanently was the phone glued to their teens' ears that parents, desperate for their own access to the phone, often added a second phone line exclusively for their teenagers' use. Today, teens are still chatting incessantly, but now they are using AOL Instant Messenger, America Online's chat network that enables users to "talk" to others in real time at the touch of a computer keyboard. AOL Instant Messenger (IM for short) is rapidly becoming indispensable to teenagers and young adults. As a result, parents are less likely to ask, "What can they possibly be talking about on that phone for so long?" and more likely to wonder, "What in the world are they doing on that computer for so long?" Parents, let me explain the attraction.

Paragraph 2
To fulfill the informational purpose, this paragraph **contrasts** IM with something parents understand better: the telephone. The contrast also includes clarifying **examples.**

Instant Messenger has advantages over the telephone. Unlike the 2 telephone, IM allows your teenager to chat with people all over the world without creating exorbitant bills. Your teen can talk to the Japanese exchange student who returned to Tokyo just as easily, immediately, and cheaply as to Tiffany down the street. Further, IM eliminates the need for time-consuming small talk. For example, to invite a friend to meet for dinner at six o'clock using the telephone, your teen would first have to say "hello," then inquire how the friend was doing, perhaps listen to complaints about the awful calculus quiz for fifteen minutes, and only then be able to propose dinner. With Instant Messenger, on the other hand, your teen would simply type three things: Dinner @ 6. Also unlike with the telephone, more than two people can talk at once, without arranging complicated conference calls that require special equipment and services. In fact, there is really no limit to the number of people who can participate in an IM conversation, so teens have access to all their friends at once, as long as they are all online at the same time. Imagine the possibilities in the world of incessant teenage chatter.

Another draw of IM is the "accessorizing" it offers. In particular, IM allows users to convey emotions much more simply and precisely than with any telephone. Volatile teens can "scream" over the Internet by using Caps Lock, Bold font, or a stream of exclamation points. Using emoticons, IM users can clearly indicate happiness (:->), sadness (:-<), anger (>:-/), shock (:-o), sleepiness (‡ o), boredom, (o :-l), and confusion (:-?). IM also allows teens to hide emotions, which is not so easily done on the phone. Imagine a person on the phone trying to play it cool with his or her latest crush while a quivering voice and nervous attempts at clever conversation constantly betray true emotions. In contrast, Instant Messenger and emoticons allow your teen to retain some dignity while being unceremoniously cyber-dumped ("Of course, we can still be friends ☺").

Paragraph 3
This paragraph relies heavily on **exemplification** to illustrate an important attraction of IM to help parents understand why teens are drawn to it.

While the telephone does not offer privacy when others are within earshot, IM affords privacy as long as no one is peaking over the typist's shoulder. During my first year of college, I lived in a quad with three other girls, and there was no privacy at all. If I wanted to discuss with Roommate A an issue I was having with Roommate B, our cramped quarters made it very difficult to do so. Fortunately, Instant Messenger came to the rescue and gave new meaning to the term "talking behind one's back." Often, while the four of us were at our desks attempting to write five page papers for our various intro courses, Lizzie and I would secretly type each other messages over Instant Messenger—Can you **BELIEVE** what Abby said to me?!?!

Paragraph 4
This paragraph combines **comparison-contrast** and **exemplification** to further explain the attraction and a drawback of IM (when it affords and does not afford privacy).

Instant messaging is not without its problems, however. So addictive is the technology that otherwise sane people carry their laptops everywhere because they cannot bear to be cut off from their IM buddies. Checking "away messages" can quickly turn into a dangerously obsessive pastime. While it may be useful to know that IcePrincess502 is planning a trip to the mall later in the evening, checking every fifteen minutes to learn what she is up to may be regarded as slightly unhealthy behavior. When the Instant Messenger service is down, the body of the addicted teen experiences a host of withdrawal symptoms such as depression, anxiety, moodiness, and itchy fingers.

Paragraph 5
This paragraph combines **cause-and-effect analysis,** and **exemplification** to explain a drawback of IM, so parents have a more complete understanding of the technology.

Paragraph 6
The conclusion is a restatement.

Instant Messenger is an important, useful addition to the canon of 6 modern communication, and for many teenagers it has replaced the telephone. Parents should respect the importance of IM to their teens, but they should also be aware of its addictive potential. Like all technology, IM has its dark side.

PEER REVIEW

Responding to "The Telephone Is Out; IM Is In"

Evaluate "The Telephone Is Out; IM Is In" by responding to these questions:

1. Does the essay hold your interest? Why or why not?
2. Could the author have achieved her purpose if she used only one pattern? Explain.
3. Are all the author's points adequately supported? Explain.
4. What do you like best about the essay? Why?
5. What change do you think would improve the essay? Why?

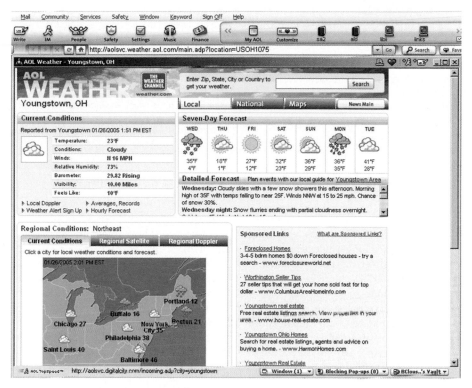

The AOL.com triangle logo and AOL are registered trademarks of America Online, Inc. The AOL.com screenshot is © 2005 by America Online, Inc. The America Online content, name, icons and Trademarks are used with permission.

- What element of description appears on this Web site reproduction?
- What element of division?
- What element of contrast?
- How do all these patterns help the Web site achieve its informational purpose?

BACKGROUND: When Brad Whetstine wrote "Augustinian Influences," he was a senior majoring in English at Indiana University. The essay was published in *The College,* which is a publication of the Indiana University Alumni Association, in its winter, 2003–2004 edition.

COMBINED PATTERNS AND THEIR PURPOSES: Brad Whetstine combines *narration, cause-and-effect analysis, comparison-contrast* and *description* to explain why he left welding to become a college student. He **relates his experience** and **expresses his feelings.** However, *The College,* which published Whetstine's essay, gives its purpose as encouraging "alumni interest in and support for Indiana University," so the essay also has a **persuasive** purpose.

AUGUSTINIAN INFLUENCES | BRAD WHETSTINE

Known for its sweet corn and community fish fries, my hometown was a farming community built along a glacial boundary where the rumpled landscape matched that of a blanket on an unmade bed. The schools in this area were small, consolidated, and known more so for their athletics than their academics. Students like me who weren't on the honor roll or the ball team soon found themselves in the vocational tracks learning a trade, and it was here I took my first welding class.

As you read Ask yourself why this essay was published in Indiana University's alumni magazine.

2   Welders were heroes in my hometown: They fixed machinery and kept the farmers farming. It was a vocation few knew well enough to master, but I was fortunate to learn the science of welding through my high school classes and to be one of two students chosen to expand our skills at a larger vocational school. The skills I acquired there landed me a job in sheet metal fabrication, where I welded for 10 years.

"Welders were heroes in my hometown."

3   The economy was up then. The shop I worked in was a small, privately owned business committed to quality rather than quantity. The hours were plentiful; the days were long; overtime was not a problem. They were days of cutting, fitting, and fusing—days of hundred-degree heat that felt clean and refreshing once I was out of the mask and heavy leathers worn to protect my face, arms, hands, and torso from hot slag, sharp sparks, and blinding light. The well-oiled steel smelled of freshly laid asphalt when heated, and the smoke that rose with the temperature proved just as black. This same blackness I washed from my hair, blew from my nose, and coughed up each night after work. Though the conditions were not the best, at the time, I still thought they fared better than farming. One evening after work while couched on the sofa, eating left-over Hamburger Helper and worn out from another 10-hour day, I began to listen carefully to the film playing on television.

4   Larry McMurtry's epic western *Lonesome Dove* was a story of chance and change, and as I listened to the retired Texas Rangers Augustus McCrae and Woodrow Call discuss leaving the dust-laden corrals of southwest Texas for a lush new ranch in northern Montana, I, too, began to wonder what life outside of welding was like. I selected portions of their discussion and cut them away as I would a piece of steel.

5   Call had heard of Montana's rolling terrain and grassy valleys where the grazing was good and the water pure, and he longed to see it. And after a decade of working in the same place at the same trade I, too, wondered after each workday, staring into my handkerchief of black, if there was something better out there—a faraway land where to believe such a place existed meant going there and seeing it for myself.

6   As Call and McCrae rounded up hundreds of cattle and horses for the big drive north, I began rounding up the pieces I had cut from their conversation and equating the moving of the stock with reasons for trying something new. Suddenly, I had hundreds of reasons cut and fitted together.

7   The most influential scene—the scene that helped me fuse it all together—was when Augustus suddenly abandoned the herd right outside of Lonesome Dove to sit, lotus style, along a little stream and cry softly into a bandanna.

8   Augustus adored this spot. He had shared, loved, proposed, and quarreled here. In all his life this place, where he once picnicked with a woman long ago, was the one place where he was the happiest. After Woodrow rode up to the stream, Augustus asked him where in his life he was the happiest. Woodrow, being Woodrow, ignored the question. But I didn't.

9   These pieces of thought I had cut, fitted, and fused formed another thought: Would I, one day, be able to recount a spot in my life where I could say I was the happiest? Choosing to live as an Augustus rather than a Woodrow, I realized that welding was keeping me from something more, reasoning that the same

"I realized that welding was keeping me from something more."

cutting, fitting, and fusing I had done in welding could apply to other things, mainly ideas. To one day tell a friend that out of all my life, here, where I stand, was where I was the happiest is a venture that will require many years and many moves. But I am happy with the moves I have made thus far, beginning with the move to higher education. Like welding, education offers promise and a way out, and I suspect it will take me places, as welding and a retired Texas Ranger once did.

READING CLOSELY AND THINKING CRITICALLY

1. How did Whetstine feel about welding during most of the time he was a welder?
2. Explain how *Lonesome Dove* affected Whetstine. Why do you think the movie affected him that way?
3. What does Whetstine mean when he says in paragraph 9 that he chose to "live as an Augustus rather than a Woodrow"?
4. "Augustinian Influences" appeared in an Indiana University magazine, whose purpose is to encourage "alumni interest in and support for Indiana University." How does the essay help the magazine fulfill its persuasive purpose?

EXAMINING STRUCTURE AND STRATEGY

1. Why does Whetstine open his essay with a description of his hometown, the schools, and himself as a student?
2. How does Whetstine achieve transition from paragraph 1 to paragraph 2? From paragraph 2 to paragraph 3? From paragraph 3 to paragraph 4?
3. How does the final sentence tie everything together for satisfying closure?

NOTING COMBINED PATTERNS

1. Stories are usually told to make a particular point. What point does Whetstine's narration make?
2. How does Whetstine use cause-and-effect analysis?
3. How does the description in paragraphs 1 and 3 help the author achieve his writing purpose?
4. What comparisons does Whetstine make in paragraphs 5 and 6? In paragraph 9?
5. Which of the patterns that Whetstine uses are primary, and which are secondary?

CONSIDERING LANGUAGE AND STYLE

1. Identify the metaphor in paragraph 1 and the simile in paragraph 4. What do you think of them? (Metaphors and similes are explained on page 109.)
2. Consult a dictionary if you do not know the meaning of *fabrication* (paragraph 2).

FOR DISCUSSION IN CLASS OR ONLINE

Whetstine began college after working as a welder for ten years. Do you think people should delay college for a year or more after high school and get some life experiences before starting college? If you instructor so directs, post your response to your class Web site.

WRITING ASSIGNMENTS

1. **In your journal.** For Whetstine, education "offers promise and a way out" (paragraph 9). What does education offer you? Respond in a page or two.
2. **Combining patterns for a purpose.** The purposes in the assignments are possibilities. You may establish whatever purposes you like, within your instructor's guidelines.
   - *Classification and description.* In paragraph 1, Whetstine refers to "students like me." To inform, relate your experience, and express your feelings, classify types of students, note which classification you fit into, and describe students like *you.*
   - *Narration and cause-and-effect analysis.* Like Whetstine, narrate an account of an event that marked a turning point for you in order to relate your experience and express your feelings. Explain how you were affected by the event.

- *Comparison-contrast and description.* Whetstine compares welding to writing. To relate experience, express feelings, and inform, explain what writing is similar to for *you.* If you like, you can discuss whether writing is like making a quilt similar to one in the image that opens this chapter.

- *Narration and cause-and-effect analysis.* Combine narration and cause-and-effect analysis to tell a story about a time a book, movie, television program, play, article, or song influenced you and to explain how it influenced you.

3. **Connecting the readings.** *Lonesome Dove* helped Whetstine realize that there was a world beyond his. The same realization is one of the points in "The Lesson" on page 257. Using the ideas in these selections, along with your own experience and observation, discuss the tensions that exist between your life and one or more worlds or contexts beyond your life. How do you become aware of other worlds?

4. **Drawing on sources.**

- The movie *Lonesome Dove* is an adaptation of the novel with the same name written by Larry McMurtry. Look up reviews of the novel using *Book Review Digest* in your library's reference room, or type "Lonesome Dove book review" into your favorite search engine. In an essay, summarize three of the reviews and go on to indicate whether you would be interested in reading the novel and why. If you have already read it, summarize the reviews and explain whether or not you agree with them and why.

- The television miniseries version of *Lonesome Dove,* starring Robert Duvall and Tommy Lee Jones, is available on video. Watch the video and write a summary and response.

www.mhhe.com/patterns

For more information on this author, go to

More resources > Chapter 13 > George Orwell

COMBINED PATTERNS AND THEIR PURPOSES: George Orwell was strongly influenced by the British colonial rule in India. Although Orwell was English, as a democratic socialist, he came to reject British imperialism, partly as a result of his experiences in Burma and with the Imperial Police, including the one narrated in "A Hanging." Orwell combines *narration* and *description* in "A Hanging" to **relate his experience** and **express his feelings** about the hanging of a prisoner. Orwell also works to **inform** his readers of the horrors of capital punishment and to **persuade** them that it is wrong.

A HANGING | GEORGE ORWELL

It was in Burma, a sodden morning of the rains. A sickly light, like yellow tinfoil, was slanting over the high walls into the jail yard. We were waiting outside the condemned cells, a row of sheds fronted with double bars, like small animal cages. Each cell measured about ten feet by ten and was quite bare within except for a plank bed and a pot for drinking water. In some of them brown, silent men were squatting at the inner bars, with their blankets draped round them. These were the condemned men, due to be hanged within the next week or two.

As you read Try to identify the point Orwell is making with his narration.

2   One prisoner had been brought out of his cell. He was a Hindu, a puny wisp of a man, with a shaven head and vague liquid eyes. He had a thick, sprouting mustache, absurdly too big for his body, rather like the mustache of a comic man on the films. Six tall Indian warders were guarding him and getting him ready for the gallows. Two of them stood by with rifles and fixed bayonets, while the others handcuffed him, passed a chain through his handcuffs and fixed it to their belts, and lashed his arms tight to his sides. They crowded very close about him, with their hands always on him in a careful, caressing grip, as though all the while feeling him to make sure he was there. It was like men handling a fish which is still alive and may jump back into the water. But he

stood quite unresisting, yielding his arms limply to the ropes, as though he hardly noticed what was happening.

3   Eight o'clock struck and a bugle call, desolately thin in the wet air, floated from the distant barracks. The superintendent of the jail, who was standing apart from the rest of us, moodily prodding the gravel with his stick, raised his head at the sound. He was an army doctor, with a gray toothbrush mustache and a gruff voice. "For God's sake, hurry up, Francis," he said irritably. "The man ought to have been dead by this time. Aren't you ready yet?"

" 'The man ought to have been dead by this time. Aren't you ready yet?' "

4   Francis, the head jailer, a fat Dravidian[1] in a white drill suit and gold spectacles, waved his black hand. "Yes sir, yes sir," he bubbled. "All is satisfactorily prepared. The hangman is waiting. We shall proceed."

5   "Well, quick march, then. The prisoners can't get their breakfast until this job's over."

6   We set out for the gallows. Two warders marched on either side of the prisoner, with their rifles at the slope; two others marched close against him, gripping him by the arm and shoulder, as though at once pushing and supporting him. The rest of us, magistrates and the like, followed behind. Suddenly, when we had gone ten yards, the procession stopped short without any order or warning. A dreadful thing had happened—a dog, come goodness knows

whence, had appeared in the yard. It came bounding among us with a loud volley of barks and leapt round us wagging its whole body, wild with glee at finding so many human beings together. It was a large woolly dog, half Airedale, half pariah. For a moment it pranced around us, and then, before anyone could stop it, it had made a dash for the prisoner, and jumping up tried to lick his face. Everybody stood aghast, too taken aback even to grab the dog.

7   "Who let that bloody brute in here?" said the superintendent angrily. "Catch it, someone!"

8   A warder detached from the escort, charged clumsily after the dog, but it danced and gamboled just out of his reach, taking everything as part of the game. A young Eurasian jailer picked up a handful of gravel and tried to stone the dog away, but it dodged the stones and came after us again. Its yaps echoed from the jail walls. The prisoner, in the grasp of the two warders, looked on incuriously, as though this was another formality of the hanging. It was several minutes before someone managed to catch the dog. Then we put my handkerchief through its collar and moved off once more, with the dog still straining and whimpering.

9   It was about forty yards to the gallows. I watched the bare brown back of the prisoner marching in front of me. He walked clumsily with his bound arms, but quite steadily, with that bobbing gait of the Indian who never straightens his knees. At each step his muscles slid neatly into place, the lock of hair on his scalp danced up and down, his feet printed themselves on the wet gravel.

---

[1] A native speaker of one of the southern Indian languages.

And once, in spite of the men who gripped him by each shoulder, he stepped lightly aside to avoid a puddle on the path.

> "This man was not dying, he was alive just as we are alive."

10   It is curious; but till that moment I had never realized what it means to destroy a healthy, conscious man. When I saw the prisoner step aside to avoid the puddle, I saw the mystery, the unspeakable wrongness, of cutting a life short when it is in full tide. This man was not dying, he was alive just as we are alive. All the organs of his body were working—bowels digesting food, skin renewing itself, nails growing, tissues forming—all toiling away in solemn foolery. His nails would still be growing when he stood on the drop, when he was falling through the air with a tenth-of-a-second to live. His eyes saw the yellow gravel and the gray walls, and his brain still remembered, foresaw, reasoned—even about puddles. He and we were a party of men walking together, seeing, hearing, feeling, understanding the same world; and in two minutes, with a sudden snap, one of us would be gone—one mind less, one world less.

11   The gallows stood in a small yard, separate from the main grounds of the prison, and overgrown with tall prickly weeds. It was a brick erection like three sides of a shed, with planking on top, and above that two beams and a crossbar with the rope dangling. The hangman, a gray-haired convict in the white uniform of the prison, was waiting beside his machine. He greeted us with a servile crouch as we entered. At a word from Francis the two warders, gripping the prisoner more closely than ever, half led, half pushed him to the gallows and helped him clumsily up the ladder. Then the hangman climbed up and fixed the rope round the prisoner's neck.

12   We stood waiting, five yards away. The warders had formed in a rough circle round the gallows. And then, when the noose was fixed, the prisoner began crying out to his god. It was a high, reiterated cry of "Ram! Ram! Ram! Ram!"[2] not urgent and fearful like a prayer or cry for help, but steady, rhythmical, almost like the tolling of a bell. The dog answered the sound with a whine. The hangman, still standing on the gallows, produced a small cotton bag like a flour bag and drew it down over the prisoner's face. But the sound, muffled by the cloth, still persisted, over and over again: "Ram! Ram! Ram! Ram! Ram!"

13   The hangman climbed down and stood ready, holding the lever. Minutes seemed to pass. The steady, muffled crying from the prisoner went on and on, "Ram! Ram! Ram!" never faltering for an instant. The superintendent, his head on his chest, was slowly poking the ground with his stick; perhaps he was counting the cries, allowing the prisoner a fixed number—fifty, perhaps, or a hundred. Everyone had changed color. The Indians had gone gray like bad coffee, and one or two of the bayonets were wavering. We looked at the lashed, hooded man on the drop, and listened to his cries—each cry another second of life; the same thought was in all our minds; oh, kill him quickly, get it over, stop that abominable noise!

---

[2]The prisoner calls upon Rama, Hindu god who sustains and preserves.

14   Suddenly the superintendent made up his mind. Throwing up his head he made a swift motion with his stick. "Chalo!"[3] he shouted almost fiercely.

15   There was a clanking noise, and then dead silence. The prisoner had vanished, and the rope was twisting on itself. I let go of the dog, and it galloped immediately to the back of the gallows; but when it got there it stopped short, barked, and then retreated into a corner of the yard, where it stood among the weeds, looking timorously out at us. We went round the gallows to inspect the prisoner's body. He was dangling with his toes pointed straight downwards, very slowly revolving, as dead as a stone.

16   The superintendent reached out with his stick and poked the bare brown body; it oscillated slightly. *"He's* all right," said the superintendent. He backed out from under the gallows, and blew out a deep breath. The moody look had gone out of his face quite suddenly. He glanced at his wristwatch. "Eight minutes past eight. Well, that's all for this morning, thank God."

17   The warders unfixed bayonets and marched away. The dog, sobered and conscious of having misbehaved itself, slipped after them. We walked out of the gallows yard, past the condemned cells with their waiting prisoners, into the big central yard of the prison. The convicts, under the command of warders armed with lathis,[4] were already receiving their breakfast. They squatted in long rows, each man holding a tin pannikin,[5] while two warders with buckets marched around ladling out rice; it seemed quite a homely, jolly scene, after the hanging. An enormous relief had come upon us now that the job was done. One felt an impulse to sing, to break into a run, to snigger. All at once everyone began chattering gaily.

18   The Eurasian boy walking beside me nodded toward the way we had come, with a knowing smile: "Do you know, sir, our friend" (he meant the dead man) "when he heard his appeal had been dismissed, he pissed on the floor of his cell. From fright. Kindly take one of my cigarettes, sir. Do you not admire my new silver case, sir? From the boxwallah, two rupees eight annas. Classy European style."

19   Several people laughed—at what, nobody seemed certain.

"Several people laughed— at what, nobody seemed certain."

20   Francis was walking by the superintendent, talking garrulously; "Well, sir, all has passed off with the utmost satisfactoriness. It was all finished—flick! Like that. It is not always so—oah, no! I have known cases where the doctor was obliged to go beneath the gallows and pull the prisoner's legs to ensure decease. Most disagreeable!"

21   "Wriggling about, eh? That's bad," said the superintendent.

22   "Ach, sir, it is worse when they become refractory! One man, I recall, clung to the bars of his cage when we went to take him out. You will scarcely

---

[3](Hindi) "Hurry up!"

[4]Policemen's wooden clubs.

[5]Small pan.

credit, sir, that it took six warders to dislodge him, three pulling at each leg. We reasoned with him, 'My dear fellow,' we said, 'think of all the pain and trouble you are causing to us!' But no, he would not listen! Ach, he was very troublesome!"

23 I found that I was laughing quite loudly. Everyone was laughing. Even the superintendent grinned in a tolerant way. "You'd better all come out and have a drink," he said quite genially. "I've got a bottle of whiskey in the car. We could do with it."

24 We went through the big double gates of the prison into the road. "Pulling at his legs!" exclaimed a Burmese magistrate suddenly, and burst into a loud chuckling. We all began laughing again. At that moment Francis' anecdote seemed extraordinarily funny. We all had a drink together, native and European alike, quite amicably. The dead man was a hundred yards away.

1. What is Orwell's attitude toward capital punishment? What is his attitude toward the condemned prisoners? How can you tell what these attitudes are?
2. Why does the superintendent say that he wants Francis and the other guards to hurry and get the prisoner to the gallows? Do you think the reason he gives is the real one? Explain.
3. Why do you think Orwell calls the entrance of the dog "a dreadful thing"?
4. What is the significance of the condemned man stepping aside "to avoid the puddle" (paragraph 9)?
5. Why are the spectators so unnerved by the prisoner's repeated calls to his God?
6. How would you describe the superintendent's attitude toward the prisoner and the execution?
7. Of what significance is the fact that "native and European alike" had a drink together after the hanging (paragraph 24)?

EXAMINING STRUCTURE AND STRATEGY

1. Orwell often uses dialogue in the essay. How does the dialogue help him achieve his purpose?
2. What is the effect of the last two sentences of the essay? Do you think they help Orwell achieve his persuasive purpose? Explain.
3. Would the narration have been more effective—that is, would Orwell have better achieved his persuasive purpose— if he had said what crime the prisoner committed? Explain.

NOTING COMBINED PATTERNS

1. Orwell uses a considerable amount of description in the essay. Cite an example and explain how it helps Orwell achieve his purpose. Is the description a primary or secondary pattern?
2. What is the point of the narration?
3. Where does Orwell pause the narration to comment on events? How does that commentary help him achieve his purpose?

CONSIDERING LANGUAGE AND STYLE

1. Paragraph 1 includes two similes (see page 109 on similes). What are they and what do they contribute?
2. What is the tone of "A Hanging"? (See page 71 on tone.) Give examples of words and phrases that help convey that tone.
3. Consult a dictionary if you are unsure of the meaning of any of these words: *sodden* (paragraph 1), *pariah* (paragraph 6), *gamboled* (paragraph 8), *incuriously* (paragraph 8), *timorously* (paragraph 15), *oscillated* (paragraph 16), *garrulously* (paragraph 20), *refractory* (paragraph 22).

How does "A Hanging" present an argument against capital punishment? Cite the specific strategies that help Orwell make his case and then go on to explain what kind of readers are likely to respond to those strategies. If your instructor so directs, post your response to your class Web site.

WRITING ASSIGNMENTS

1. **In your journal.** Do you believe in the death penalty? Explain why or why not. As an alternative, explain whether your opinion about the death penalty has changed as a result of reading "A Hanging."

2. **Combining patterns for a purpose.** The purposes in the assignments are possibilities. You may establish whatever purposes you like, within your instructor's guidelines.

   • *Narration and cause-and-effect analysis.* During the course of the events in "A Hanging," Orwell recognizes that capital punishment is wrong. To relate your experience and express your feelings, narrate an account of a time you realized something important. Explain how you were affected by the realization.

   • *Process analysis and comparison-contrast.* Orwell tells about something he thinks is wrong: capital punishment. Explain a process you think is wrong, such as hazing, Little League tryouts, spelling bees, or awarding of financial aid. To convince your reader that there is a better way, contrast that process with one you think would be better.

   • *Narration and description.* The men who witnessed and supervised the hanging were clearly uncomfortable, which helps to explain their behavior before, during, and after the execution. Tell a story about an event to which witnesses had a strong reaction, such as an accident, a death, an embarrassing moment, or an argument. Describe the reaction. Your purpose can be to inform.

   • *Definition and exemplification.* Orwell's narration tells of oppression. To inform, define *oppression* or *discrimination* and give examples that illustrate that definition.

3. **Connecting the readings.** How do you think we should punish people for committing the most serious crimes? To answer this question, you can draw on your own ideas and one or more of these readings: "A Hanging," "The Lottery" (page 169), "Seeking Justice after a Fatal Spin of the Cylinder" (page 177), and "Adult Crime, Adult Time" (page 591).

4. **Drawing on sources.** Orwell's essay titled "Shooting an Elephant" also draws on his experiences as a police officer in Burma. You can find it in your campus library as part of *Shooting an Elephant and Other Essays* or on the Internet at *http://pages. citenet.net/users/charles/shootelp.html*. Read that essay and then explain what "A Hanging" and "Shooting an Elephant" reveal about Orwell's view of government. Be sure to back up your assertions with specific references to the essays. (For help with writing a synthesis, see p. 17.)

BACKGROUND: Born in 1944 in San Francisco, Richard Rodriguez is a first-generation Mexican American who spoke only Spanish until he was six years old. He is an editor at Pacific News Service and a contributing editor for *Harper's Magazine, U.S. News & World Report,* and the Sunday "Opinion" section of the *Los Angeles Times.* A prolific author who frequently writes of his heritage, Rodriguez has published numerous articles in the *New York Times, The Wall Street Journal, The American Scholar, Time, Mother Jones,* and *The New Republic,* as well as other publications. His three autobiographical books are *Hunger of Memory* (1981), from which "Complexion" is taken, *Days of Obligation: An Argument with My Mexican Father* (1992), and *Brown: The Last Discovery of America* (2002). In 1997, Rodriguez earned the prestigious George Foster Peabody Award for his essays on American life for the PBS series "The NewsHour with Jim Lehrer." He has also received the Frankel Medal from the National Endowment for the Humanities and the International Journalism Award from the World Affairs Council of California.

www.mhhe.com/patterns

For more information on this author, go to

More resources > Chapter 13 > Richard Rodriguez

COMBINED PATTERNS AND THEIR PURPOSES: In "Complexion," Richard Rodriguez **expresses his feelings and relates his experience** by combining *contrast, narration,* and *description* with his discussion of the *effects* his skin color had on his self-concept. In doing so, he also **informs** his audience about the Mexican-American experience and reminds the reader of the adolescent struggle to feel at ease with one's physical appearance.

Complexion
RICHARD RODRIGUEZ

Complexion. My first conscious experience of sexual excitement concerns my complexion. One summer weekend, when I was around seven years old, I was at a public swimming pool with the whole family. I remember sitting on the damp pavement next to the pool and seeing my mother, in the spectator's bleachers, holding

As you read
Consider how the author defines masculinity.

my younger sister on her lap. My mother, I noticed, was watching my father as he stood on a diving board, waving to her. I watched her wave back. Then saw her radiant, bashful, astonishing smile. In that second I sensed that my mother and father had a relationship I knew nothing about. A nervous excitement encircled my stomach as I saw my mother's eyes follow my father's figure curving into the water. A second or two later, he emerged. I heard him call out. Smiling, his voice sounded, buoyant, calling me to swim to him. But turning to see him, I caught my mother's eye. I heard her shout over to me. In Spanish she called through the crowd: "Put a towel on over your shoulders." In public, she didn't want to say why. I knew.

2   That incident anticipates the shame and sexual inferiority I was to feel in later years because of my dark complexion. I was to grow up an ugly child. Or one who thought himself ugly. (*Feo.*) One night when I was eleven or twelve years old, I locked myself in the bathroom and carefully regarded my reflection in the mirror over the

sink. Without any pleasure I studied my skin. I turned on the faucet. (In my mind I heard the swirling voices of aunts, and even my mother's voice, whispering, whispering incessantly about lemon juice solutions and dark, *feo* children.) With a bar of soap, I fashioned a thick ball of lather. I began soaping my arms. I took my father's straight razor out of the medicine cabinet. Slowly, with steady deliberateness, I put the blade against my flesh, pressed it as close as I could without cutting, and moved it up and down across my skin to see if I could get out, somehow lessen, the dark. All I succeeded in doing, however, was in shaving my arms bare of their hair. For as I noted with disappointment, the dark would not come out. It remained. Trapped. Deep in the cells of my skin.

3   Throughout adolescence, I felt myself mysteriously marked. Nothing else about my appearance would concern me so much as the fact that my complexion was dark. My mother would say how sorry she was that there was not money enough to get braces to straighten my teeth. But I never bothered about my teeth. In three-way mirrors at department stores, I'd see my profile dramatically defined by a long nose, but it was really only the color of my skin that caught my attention.

4   I wasn't afraid that I would become a menial laborer because of my skin. Nor did my complexion make me feel especially vulnerable to racial abuse. (I didn't really consider my dark skin to be a racial characteristic. I would have been only too happy to look as Mexican as my light-skinned older brother.) Simply, I judged myself ugly. And, since the women in my family had been the ones who discussed it in such worried tones, I felt my dark skin made me unattractive to women.

5   Thirteen years old. Fourteen. In a grammar school art class, when the assignment was to draw a self-portrait, I tried but could not bring myself to shade in the face on the paper to anything like my actual tone. With disgust then I would come face to face with myself in mirrors. With disappointment I located myself in class photographs—my dark face undefined by the camera which had clearly described the white faces of classmates. Or I'd see my dark wrist against my long-sleeved white shirt.

6   I grew divorced from my body. Insecure, overweight, listless. On hot summer days when my rubber-soled shoes soaked up the heat from the sidewalk, I kept my head down. Or walked in the shade. My mother didn't need anymore to tell me to watch out for the sun. I denied myself a sensational life. The normal, extraordinary, animal excitement of feeling my body alive—riding shirtless on a bicycle in the warm wind created by furious self-propelled motion—the sensations that first had excited in me a sense of my maleness, I denied. I was too ashamed of my body. I wanted to forget that I had a body because I had a brown body. I was grateful that none of my classmates ever mentioned the fact.

7   I continued to see the *braceros*,[1] those men I resembled in one way and, in another way, didn't resemble at all. On the watery horizon of a Valley afternoon, I'd see them. And though I feared looking like them, it was with silent envy that I regarded them still. I envied them their physical lives, their freedom to violate the

---

[1]Mexican laborers admitted into the country temporarily to do seasonal work, such as harvesting crops.

taboo of the sun. Closer to home I would notice the shirtless construction workers, the roofers, the sweating men tarring the street in front of the house. And I'd see the Mexican gardeners. I was unwilling to admit the attraction of their lives. I tried to deny it by looking away. But what was denied became strongly desired.

8   In high school physical education classes, I withdrew, in the regular company of five or six classmates, to a distant corner of a football field where we smoked and talked. Our company was composed of bodies too short or too tall, all graceless and all—except mine—pale. Our conversation was usually witty. (In fact we were intelligent.) If we referred to the athletic contests around us, it was with sarcasm. With savage scorn I'd refer to the "animals" playing football or baseball. It would have been important for me to have joined them. Or for me to have taken off my shirt, to have let the sun burn dark on my skin, and to have run barefoot on the warm wet grass. It would have been very important. Too important. It would have been too telling a gesture—to admit the desire for sensation, the body, my body.

9   Fifteen, sixteen. I was a teenager shy in the presence of girls. Never dated. Barely could talk to a girl without stammering. In high school I went to several dances, but I never managed to ask a girl to dance. So I stopped going. I cannot remember high school years now with the parade of typical images: bright drive-ins or gliding blue shadows of a Junior Prom. At home most weekend nights, I would pass evenings reading. Like those hidden, precocious adolescents who have no real-life sexual experiences, I read a great deal of romantic fiction. "You won't find it in your books," my brother would playfully taunt me as he prepared to go to a party by freezing the crest of the wave in his hair with sticky pomade. Through my reading, however, I developed a fabulous and sophisticated sexual imagination. At seventeen, I may not have known how to engage a girl in small talk, but I had read *Lady Chatterley's Lover.*

10   It annoyed me to hear my father's teasing: that I would never know what "real work" is: that my hands were so soft. I think I knew it was his way of admitting pleasure and pride in my academic success. But I didn't smile. My mother said she was glad her children were getting their educations and would not be pushed around like *los pobres.*[2] I heard the remark ironically as a reminder of my separation from *los braceros.* At such times I suspected that education was making me effeminate. The odd thing, however, was that I did not judge my classmates so harshly. Nor did I consider my male teachers in high school effeminate. It was only myself I judged against some shadowy, mythical Mexican laborer—dark like me, yet very different.

---

[2]The poor ones.

READING CLOSELY AND THINKING CRITICALLY

1.   What effects did the color of Rodriguez's complexion have on him?
2.   In what ways did the women in Rodriguez's family make him feel self-conscious and inferior?

3. Why do you think that Rodriguez was so attracted to the lives of the Mexican gardeners and construction workers?

4. Using the information in the essay for clues, explain the author's idea of masculinity.

5. Why did Rodriguez read so much? Why do you think he was afraid that reading and education would make him effeminate?

6. "Complexion" came from Rodriguez's autobiographical *Hunger of Memory*. What kind of reader do you think would enjoy reading about Rodriguez's life?

EXAMINING STRUCTURE AND STRATEGY

1. In which paragraph does Rodriguez indicate what is *not* an effect of his reaction to his complexion?

2. In what order are the effects of Rodriguez's skin color arranged? What are the clues to this arrangement?

3. If the first paragraph omitted the initial fragment, "Complexion" and began instead with the sentence that follows, "My first conscious experience of sexual excitement concerns my complexion," how would the emphasis shift?

NOTING COMBINED PATTERNS

1. What is Rodriguez's primary pattern of development? How does he use that pattern?

2. In which paragraph does Rodriguez use narration to help develop the cause-and-effect relationship?

3. With what people does Rodriguez contrast himself? How does that element of contrast help the author achieve his purpose?

4. Cite an example of descriptive language and explain how the description helps the author achieve his purpose.

CONSIDERING LANGUAGE AND STYLE

1. Rodriguez uses sentence fragments intentionally in paragraphs 1, 2, 5, 6, 8, and 9. Ordinarily, sentence fragments are an editing error. Here, the fragments serve a purpose. What is that purpose?

2. Rodriguez uses three Spanish words: *feo, braceros,* and *los pobres*. What does this use of Spanish contribute to his essay? Explain.

3. Consult a dictionary if you are unsure of the meaning of any of these words: *buoyant* (paragraph 1), *menial* (paragraph 4), *listless* (paragraph 6), *taboo* (paragraph 7), *precocious* (paragraph 9), *pomade* (paragraph 9).

FOR DISCUSSION IN CLASS OR ONLINE

With some classmates, consider the factors that shape a person's self-concept. Discuss the influence of family, friends, teachers, coaches, television, advertisements, and anything else you can think of. If your instructor directs you to do so, post your response to your class Web site.

1. **In your journal.** Rodriguez tells about feeling self-conscious because of his skin color. Write about some aspect of your physical appearance that made you self-conscious as an adolescent and explain the reason for your feeling. As an alternative, write about some feature of your appearance that made you proud.

2. **Combining patterns for a purpose.** The purposes in the assignments are possibilities. You may establish whatever purposes you like, within your instructor's guidelines.

   - *Description and cause-and-effect analysis.* Pick one aspect of your physical appearance, such as your height, weight, nose, or skin color. To relate experience, express feelings, and inform, describe that feature of your appearance and explain the effect it has had on you. (The previous journal writing may give you some ideas.)

   - *Classification and exemplification.* Rodriguez says he was shy as an adolescent and that he withdrew from the company of family and friends because of his insecurity. To inform, classify the kinds of behaviors adolescents exhibit in response to how they feel about their looks. Give examples for each category in your classification. Then, use your classification as a basis for arguing whether or not schools should institute courses to help students feel comfortable with their looks or improve their looks.

   - *Definition and classification.* To inform, write an extended definition of *body image* and classify the most common kinds.

   - *Narration and comparison-contrast.* In paragraph 1, Rodriguez tells about his realization that his parents had a sexual relationship. Tell about a time when you came to understand something about one or both or your parents or other caregiver. To relate experience and express feelings, contrast your feelings and understanding before and after the realization. If you prefer, write about another adult in your life, such as a coach, clergy member, teacher, or grandparent.

3. **Connecting the readings.** School has a significant impact on the self-concepts of young people. Explain school's potential to affect the way we view ourselves. The ideas in "Complexion" and "Lost at C" (page 189) may give you some ideas.

4. **Drawing on sources.** Ask 10 men and 10 women this question: "If you could get free plastic surgery on one part of your body, what would you change and why?" Report your findings and discuss any conclusions you can draw from them.

BACKGROUND: Award-winning journalist, short story writer, and novelist, Pagan Kennedy is a frequent contributor to the *Boston Globe* and *New York Times*. Kennedy's writing topics are diverse, ranging from alternative fuel, to rock musicians, Boston hoodlums, roommates, profiles of a teenage female weightlifter and an Islam mystic and auto mechanic. A fan of alternative fiction, Kennedy published the 'zine, *Pagan's Head,* for six years. Kennedy's books include *Black Livingstone: A True Tale of Adventure in Nineteenth Century Congo* (2002), which is the story of early black American missionary to Africa, William Sheppard; *Exes* (1998), which is a book about the 'zine she published; and *Pagan Kennedy's Living: A Handbook for Maturing Hipsters* (1997), which is a nonfiction collection she characterizes as "a Martha Stewart for people who sleep on stained futons and have seven housemates." "One Room, 3,000 Brains" first appeared in the *Boston Globe Magazine* in June 2004.

COMBINED PATTERNS AND THEIR PURPOSES: In "One Room, 3,000 Brains," Pagan Kennedy combines *cause-and-effect analysis, description, narration,* and *process analysis* to achieve several purposes. Most apparently, she **informs** readers about the Harvard Brain Tissue Resource Center and the work done there. More subtly, she **informs** about the changing understanding of mental illness, and she aims to **persuade** readers to donate their brains to science. In addition, the story of one researcher's medical history **relates an experience** and **expresses feelings.**

ONE ROOM, 3,000 BRAINS | PAGAN KENNEDY

When I peer down into one of the buckets in a sink, I see my first human brain. It's actually half a brain, trailing some stem, and the noodlelike folds are pearly in color, rather than the gray you'd expect. "We don't want the smell to be too strong," says George Tejada, explaining the need to soak the half-brain in water. It has been preserved in formaldehyde, which gives off a powerful stench.

As you read
Give some thought to how society treats people who have a mental illness.

2   We're standing in the dissection room of the Harvard Brain Tissue Resource Center, a.k.a. the Brain Bank, which is housed on the McLean Hospital campus in Belmont. A few minutes ago, Tejada peeled off a latex glove so we could shake hands. "Don't worry, my hands are clean," he assured me. I did not doubt him. Tejada, the assistant director of tissue processing at the Brain Bank, could pass for the headmaster of a prep school, with his crisp button-down shirt and pressed khakis. The dissection room itself, where human brains arrive and get sliced up at a rate of about one per day, also appears to be disappointing spick-and-span. Aside from the buckets in the sink—and the map of the brain regions taped up above the counter—it would be hard to guess what goes on here.

3   The institution collects brains from donors and distributes tissue to researchers around the world. The Brain Bank stocks "normal" brains as well as those donated by people who had schizophrenia, bipolar disorder, Huntington's disease, and Parkinson's disease. In part, it is because of the Brain Bank—and other such repositories—that neuroscientists are finally beginning to zero in on the genes involved in such mental disabilities, a crucial step needed to speed the development of lifesaving drugs.

4   Thirty years ago, there were no brain banks in the United States—at least not officially. Now, more than 100 such repositories exist. Over the past few

decades, psychiatry has gone through a monumental transition, away from talk therapy and toward drug therapy. So scientists are sorting, storing, and examining human brains as never before, peering through microscopes at tiny slices of tissue for clues about why we go mad. This is all happening at a time when the proportion of mentally ill people worldwide who receive treatment is "woefully inadequate," according to an unprecedented new study by a World Health Organization consortium and published this month in the *Journal of the American Medical Association*.

5   Just this year, McLean researchers announced that they had pinpointed what they called energy deficiencies in the brain cells of people with bipolar disorder, an important insight that could contribute to the development of specific drugs to help the 2.3 million Americans the illness afflicts. It is this type of brain work that marks a profound shift in the way we think about our own thoughts.

> "It is this type of brain work that marks a profound shift in the way we think about our own thoughts."

6   Dr. Francine M. Benes, director of the Brain Bank, explains just how powerful this kind of analysis has proved to be. She says, "We're on the threshold of finding the markers for schizophrenia," that is, the genes that contribute to a person's susceptibility to the disease.

7   And to boost genetic research at other institutions, the Brain Bank has put a database online. It is open to researchers and the general public (it can be found on the Web at *national_databank. mclean.harvard.edu*). Benes's hope is that

scientists who receive tissue from the Brain Bank will submit the results of their research to the database, helping to create a superstorehouse of brain data for the field.

8   It all sounds very worthy and hygienic, but I must admit that I had come to the Brain Bank hoping to be grossed out, at least just a little. My ideas about what might go on at a facility that houses more than 3,000 human brains had been inflamed by an episode of the original *Star Trek* in which DayGlo-colored brains order slaves to fight battles for their amusement. And then there is an old sci-fi movie called *They Saved Hitler's Brain*, in which the Fuhrer's cut-off head, kept alive inside a glass jar, commands what's left of the Nazi empire. Something about iced brains captures the imagination—after all, no one would bother to make a movie called *They Saved Hitler's Liver.* The brain seems to contain the essence of the self. Yet, unlike so many other dear and familiar body parts—our eyes, our arms, our toes—it exists under wraps. Even as I write that sentence, I'm aware of my own brain dwelling in the loft apartment of my skull, doing who-knows-what up there. It is me, and it is also eerily remote.

9   "This is a problem that's not going to go away soon," says Benes about the complex feelings people have about their brains and, therefore, about donating that particular organ to science. "It's believed by many that the soul of their loved one resides in the brain, or they see the brain as what gives one a special connectedness in the spiritual." For years, when people donated their bodies to organ banks, brains were not part of the deal. Now, the taboo against collecting brains has begun to relax. The New England Organ Bank and the New

England Eye & Tissue Transplant Bank, for instance, have quietly begun to include brains in the roster of donations they collect. The brain is on its way to becoming just another body part.

10   While this is a great boon to the Brain Bank, in terms of recruiting donors, outreach is only one small part of what goes on here. Most of the work happens after the donor dies, at which time the cells in his or her brain immediately begin to deteriorate. Within hours of getting a call from the donor's family, the Brain Bankers must find a pathologist in the appropriate region of the country, arrange for that pathologist to extract the brain and put it in a special container, and fly the brain to McLean by same-day shipping. After that, the brain will be assigned a number, sliced up and photographed, frozen, preserved in formaldehyde, examined, entered into a database, and distributed to worthy investigators.

11   The brain in the bucket, in fact, turns out to be the only one I come across here that looks remotely brain-like. Every other piece of tissue has been so carefully preserved and processed that you'd be hard-pressed to say what it is. Tejada shows me into a room full of freezers, and opens a door to reveal plastic bags, each of which holds a brain hemisphere cut into 16 sections. Mist rolls out into the room—the freezer is kept at 80 below zero. The bags themselves appear to contain flash-frozen shrimp.

12   When a brain arrives here, usually half of it gets frozen while the other half ends up in formaldehyde—a system designed to give researchers as many options as possible. In the "Tupperware room," slices of brain tissue marinate in chemicals; each half-brain is stored in the kind of plastic container you might use to microwave leftover pasta. From the looks of the original labels, which still cling to some of the containers, the Brain Bank chose an off-brand rather than genuine Tupperware.

13   Tejada leads me back to his office and shows me a photo of one of the brains. Such mug shots are made available to researchers, along with other information, in order to help them select which tissue sample they would like to order. The brain in the photo, freshly cut out of the donor's head, gleams with blood. Unlike the brains in sci-fi movies, this one does not look up to the task of issuing commands to Nazi followers. It's just a piece of meat. I'm reminded of what William James said: "The brain itself is an excessively vascular organ, a sponge full of blood." This photo is a powerful argument for using a biological model to understand what goes on in the mind.

14   "I was part of the shift" toward seeing mental illness as an organic problem, says Benes, who is trim and wears a starched lab coat. We're sitting in her office, and she's holding research on her lap—a sheaf of papers covered with numbers that represent the gene profiles of schizophrenic, bipolar, and control-group brains.

15   In 1973, Francine Benes attended a neuroscience meeting at a ski resort in Colorado. Then a cell biologist, she had no particular expertise in mental illness. Nonetheless, she found herself in a talk

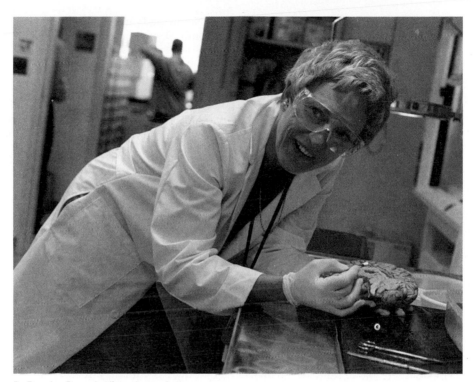

Dr. Francine Benes holding a human brain

on schizophrenia, delivered by Dr. Janice R. Stevens. "I was standing in the back of the room, and it blew me away," Benes says. Stevens proposed that schizophrenia was due to a dopamine disturbance in a part of the brain called the nucleus accumbens—a radical theory back when psychiatrists were still blaming mothers, who were presumed to have driven their children mad with Joan Crawford-like behavior. Stevens's paper helped to erase that stigma. The illness became a matter of bad wiring rather than bad mothering. "Schizophrenia could now be visualized in terms of the circuitries in the brain," Benes says.

16   The revelation changed the direction of Benes's life. She returned to medical school to get her MD, and, in 1982, established the Laboratory for Structural Neuroscience at McLean. Early on, "there was me and maybe two other people who were doing postmortem schizophrenia research," she says. By the late 1980s, however, researchers were routinely examining postmortem brain tissue in order to search for the causes of Alzheimer's and Huntington's disease. Using the same methods to investigate mental illness no longer seemed so strange. These days, Benes says, "the stigma is gone, and you have the excitement of getting inside the cells," chasing after the genes that lead to mental dysfunction.

17   Most exciting, brain scientists have begun to borrow ideas from the colleagues

who study problems that affect other parts of the body. "At this juncture, we're starting to move into alignment with cancer research and hematology research," Benes says. "That is going to prove to be the most historic step in this field." Treating the brain as just another part of the body—vulnerable to high cholesterol, secondhand smoke, and bad genes—may lead to breakthroughs that were not possible back when the brain seemed to be something special and separate.

"Most exciting, brain scientists have begun to borrow ideas from the colleagues who study problems that affect other parts of the body."

18 "I am a Brain Banker, asking for a deposit from you," Jill Bolte Taylor sings to me over the phone from her home in Bloomington, Indiana. She's sitting with a guitar in her lap and a phone receiver lying on the floor before her, strumming like a cowboy. "Find the key to unlock this thing we call insanity," she warbles. "Just dial 1-800-BRAIN-BANK for information, please." And then she ends with a whoop worthy of Hank Williams.

19 Taylor, the Brain Bank's spokeswoman for psychiatric disorders, tours the country, exhorting the public and especially those with mental illnesses to donate their brains to science. In just about every talk she gives, "there's this wonderful moment when the audience realizes, 'Oh, my gosh, she wants my brain,'" Taylor says. "The tension in the room gets really thick. Everyone's looking down like we're all in the first grade—'Don't call on me, don't call on me.' So I'll pull out my guitar and sing the Brain Bank jingle. It lightens everything up. It's been a wonderful marketing tool."

20 Taylor hooked up with the Brain Bank in 1993, a postdoc working in Benes's lab, researching the organic causes of schizophrenia. She was determined to prove they existed. Her brother had schizophrenia.

21 "The thinking in the professional community for decades was that it was a character flaw caused in part by the schizophrenogenic mother—they blamed the family," she says. Taylor fought against that stigma on two fronts: as a Harvard researcher and as a board member of the National Alliance for the Mentally Ill, a group that pioneered the effort to understand mental illness as a biological problem rather than a failure of the will. "It's only been 10 years really that it has been put out that severe mental illness, schizophrenia in particular, is a biologically based brain disorder," Taylor says. In the mid-1990s, Taylor worked in the lab from Monday through Friday, and then would often hop on a plane over the weekend to deliver lectures around the country, spreading the word about brain donation. "When I first started, we were receiving fewer than five psychiatric brains a year," she says. Now that figure has jumped to 25.

22 Taylor admits that, back then, she was something of an overachiever. "I had been driven toward excellence by very powerful anger," she says. "And that anger was related to growing up with a sibling who was not normal. You're constantly on guard. You trust him, and then he hurts you emotionally."

23 On December 10, 1996, Taylor, then 37 years old, woke up to find she had a brain disorder of her own. "Inside four

hours, I watched my mind deteriorate in its ability to process incoming information," she says. A fist-sized hemorrhage had formed in the left hemisphere of her brain, between the two centers that process language. Because the hemorrhage had also knocked out the portion of the brain that creates fear, she felt only curiosity as her mental functions shut down. "I learned as much about my brain in those four hours as I had in my whole academic career," she says. "Eventually, my right arm went completely paralyzed, and that's when my brain said, 'Oh, my gosh, I'm having a stroke. I'm having a stroke? I'm a very busy woman. Well, I can't stop this from happening, so I'll do this for a week, learn what I can learn from it, and then I'll get back to work.'"

24   In fact, recovery took years. "I was an infant in a woman's body," she says. She was unable to wiggle her toes or roll over in bed. "I couldn't understand when I heard other people making language at me. I lost my ability to read and write." It was two years before she could cook and talk on the phone at the same time, and many more before she could hop from rock to rock without planning exactly where to put her feet.

25   Last summer, year seven of her recovery, Taylor slipped into water skis for the first time since her stroke. As a girl, she'd been a slalomer, so comfortable on the water that her skis felt like part of her feet. Now, as the boat pulled away, she found her balance and began cutting through the glassy water. "All of a sudden, there was this moment when my body took its position, and every cell remembered that it was powerful. Off I went. It was pure bliss. I had recovered who I was before that hemorrhage."

26   No longer a workaholic, she enjoys a laid-back life in Indiana. She continues to spread the word about brain donations, and she also makes brains—out of stained glass. Taylor's creations are suitable for hanging against a big sunny window, where you can watch the world through the yellow and blue and green pieces of glass that represent the nuclei and gyri and limbic system.

27   Right now, in one window of my computer, I'm donating my brain to science, typing information into an online form at *www.brainbank.mclean.org/questionnaire.htm*. It's no more difficult than ordering a book from Amazon.com. You give your name, address, next of kin, and use a pull-down menu to let the Brain Bank know what kind you've got. For a moment, I linger over that list, deciding how to classify myself: normal control, schizophrenia, bipolar disorder, Parkinson's disease, Huntington's disease. I click on "normal control," knowing that designation could change. That blood-soaked sponge in my head, so soft, so frangible, could be destroyed by any of a number of diseases. I have seen them up close on a computer screen at McLean. There, a helpful man in a lab coat showed me slides of brain tissue that had been eaten away by abnormalities, from the tangles of Alzheimer's to the bloom of melanoma cells.

28   We hope, of course, that all of this study of brain tissue will lead to the discovery of new pills and treatments. But along the way, perhaps it will offer another benefit, too. The more we know about the neurological disorders, the

more likely we are to feel compassion for the people who have those disorders. I'm remembering something that Jill Taylor said about the moment when her brother was diagnosed with schizophrenia: "It was a relief. Finally, I could separate him from the disease. I could forgive him. I could love him again as my big brother."

READING CLOSELY AND THINKING CRITICALLY

1. Something about the Brain Bank disappoints the author. What is it?
2. What is the purpose of the Brain Bank?
3. Why have people been reluctant to donate their brains to science even when they are willing to donate other body parts?
4. What is the stigma associated with mental illness? Why does this stigma exist?
5. In paragraph 5, Kennedy says that brain research "marks a profound shift in the way we think about our own thoughts." What does she mean?

EXAMINING STRUCTURE AND STRATEGY

1. "One Room, 3,000 Brains" originally appeared in *The Boston Globe Magazine.* Are the title and first sentence likely to engage the interest of readers of a large metropolitan daily newspaper? Explain.
2. Part of the article is written in the present tense. See, for example, paragraphs 2, 6, and 11. Why is the present tense used?
3. How does Kennedy make a scientific subject accessible to readers of the *Boston Globe*?

NOTING COMBINED PATTERNS

1. What is the purpose of the description in paragraph 1? How does the description in paragraphs 2, 11, and 13 help Kennedy achieve her purpose?
2. What is the purpose of the process analysis in paragraphs 10 and 12? How does the process analysis in paragraph 27 help Kennedy achieve her purpose?
3. What is the purpose of the narration in paragraphs 15–16? What is the purpose of the narration in paragraphs 23–26?
4. What is the purpose of the cause-and-effect analysis in paragraphs 4–5? In paragraphs 8–9? In paragraph 22?

CONSIDERING LANGUAGE AND STYLE

1. Kennedy uses language not commonly associated with writing about scientific topics. For example, in paragraph 8, she refers to the location of the brain as being in a loft apartment, and in paragraph 12, she refers to tissue samples as being in off-brand Tupperware. Cite another example of such unusual word choice. What effect does this word choice have? Why does Kennedy use such word choice?

2. Kennedy uses simple, specific words. For example, in paragraph 2, she says the researcher "peeled off a latex glove." Give two other examples of simple, specific word choice. What effect does this word choice have?

3. Consult a dictionary if you do not know the meaning of these words: *repositories* (paragraphs 3, 4), *dopamine* (paragraph 15), *postmortem* (paragraph 16), *hematology* (paragraph 17), *exhorting* (paragraph 19), *slalomer* (paragraph 25).

FOR DISCUSSION IN CLASS OR ONLINE

Is there still a stigma associated with mental illness? Explain why or why not. If your instructor so directs, post your response to your class Web site.

WRITING ASSIGNMENTS

1. **In your journal.** Are you willing to donate your brain to science? What about other body parts, such as your heart, corneas, skin, or liver? In a page or two, explain how you feel and why.

2. **Combining patterns for a purpose.** The purposes in the assignments are possibilities. You may establish whatever purposes you like, within your instructor's guidelines.

   - *Description and process analysis.* Describe a body part and explain its function in a way that gives your reader a fresh appreciation for something that is familiar.

   - *Narration and cause-and-effect analysis.* To relate an experience and express feelings, tell about a time you or someone you know was ill or incapacitated. In addition, explain the effect of the illness or incapacitation.

   - *Cause-and-effect analysis and narration.* The director of the Brain Bank made a career change as a result of a conference she attended. To relate your experience and perhaps express your feelings, narrate an account of what caused you to make an important decision about your life, career, or schooling. How has the decision worked out?

   - *Process analysis and exemplification.* To inform your reader, explain a process you know well for someone who knows little about that process. For example, you could explain how to surf, how to train a dog, how an automobile hybrid engine works, or how cells divide. To convince your reader of the importance of the process, give examples of ways the process is useful, interesting, or significant.

3. **Connecting the readings.** Research is showing us that schizophrenia, bipolar disorder, and other forms of mental illness are brain disorders. Unfortunately, they can lead the afflicted to commit violent acts. Knowing that, do you think we need to make any changes in our criminal justice system? In addition to your own ideas, you can use the ideas in any of the following selections: "One Room, 3,000 Brains," "The Hanging" (page 650), "Seeking Justice after a Fatal Spin of the Cylinder" (page 177), and "Young Voices from the Cell" (page 596).

4. **Drawing on sources.** Write an article for your campus newspaper that explains brain donation to the campus community. Visit *http://www.brainbank.mclean.org* and click on these links: How to Make a Brain Donation and Types of Tissue collection. Summarize the main points to help people make up their minds. As an alternative, visit the National Alliance for the Mentally Ill site at *http://www.nami.org* and summarize the information about one mental illness discussed there.

BACKGROUND: A professor at the Missouri School of Journalism and associate dean of graduate studies, Esther Thorson is only the third woman to win the Distinguished Advertising Educator Award. Thorson has researched how people process information in television ads, how community news affects citizens, how people respond to television, and how health campaigns affect people. Her publications include hundreds of academic journal articles and book chapters. "Dissect an Ad," first written in 1996, is now part of the Public Broadcasting System's "By the People" Web site, which covers various aspects of the 2004 Presidential election campaign.

COMBINED PATTERNS AND THEIR PURPOSE: Using *division, cause-and-effect analysis,* and *exemplification,* Esther Thorson identifies the components of political advertisements to **inform** readers about how the ads persuade people by appealing to their emotions.

DISSECT AN AD

| ESTHER THORSON

Both pundits and citizens spend a lot of time making fun of political commercials. They're short, simple-minded, and as election day approaches, they become more obnoxiously frequent. There seems good reason to ridicule the idea that they affect how people vote and how they think about government and politicians.

As you read Determine why it's important to examine political ads carefully.

2   But a large body of studies carried out in the last 15 years shows quite clearly that political commercials have major effects on people. In Presidential elections, television commercials consume most of the money spent by candidates in their attempts to get elected. This is also true of state-level elections.

3   The bottom line, then, is that it's important for citizens to look carefully at political ads. Certainly the truth or falsity and, regardless of "truth," the deceptiveness of ad content is important to examine. Many newspapers and television analysis programs provide the citizen a good opportunity to learn more about the quality of the verbal content of political commercials. Although a majority of Americans are not aware of this, government closely controls the truth value of national product advertising on television. But because of the principle of free speech, a principle protected by the U.S. Constitution, there is no control whatsoever on the content of a political commercial. Basically, a politician can say anything she or he wishes in a political ad. The only "control" over content in a political ad is media and public response to that content.

"Basically, a politician can say anything she or he wishes in a political ad."

4   But ads communicate more than their verbal content. Like any persuasive message developed by a professional communicator, every aspect of their few-seconds duration is carefully designed to influence. Aspects of ads beyond their verbal content are called structural features.

5   This guide describes ten of the structural features that political ads use most commonly. Recognizing a persuasive tool for what it is, helps people understand the true impact of ads on themselves and others. Regardless of

what verbal content an ad uses, it will employ one or many of these persuasive tools. Recognizing them and figuring out what their intended meaning is can provide important new insight into a political ad.

CANDIDATE MYTHOLOGIES

6   When people think about a political office-holder like the President, Vice President, Governor, or Senator, they often, unbeknownst to themselves, attribute mythological features to that person. Common mythologies about the U.S. President represent him as:

a.   War hero
b.   Man of the people
c.   Father
d.   Savior
e.   Friend

7   These perceptions are "myths" in that they carry a lot of cultural baggage with them, but they are never true features of a president. They're used, however, to create emotion in viewers. If that face up on the screen asking for your vote is your "friend," you feel differently about him. If he's a "hero," he may make you feel proud or safe. If he's your "father," you may feel you can trust him.

8   Myths like these are generally not spoken, but represented in images. A candidate shown with people trying to touch him, shake his hand, or clapping for him, is being represented as a hero. Shown with his family, he's obviously a

"A candidate shown with people trying to touch him, shake his head, or clapping for him, is being represented as a hero."

father, but he's also a father when shown kissing babies or supporting laws that aid children. Probably the most common spoken myth is "friend." "Friend of the people," "the working man's friend," are popular ad phrases. Clasping a voter around the shoulders or a warm handshake visually represents "friend."

BACKGROUND LOCATIONS

9   Where the candidate is when he is shown, or where the opponent is shown to be in an attack ad, is critically important to what is being communicated. Kennedy was shown walking along the beach. Perot was almost always in a paneled den or office. Clinton was most frequently surrounded by people. Each of the backgrounds is used to communicate a variety of things about the candidate.

PROPS

10   Props are objects shown in the scenes. The most common prop is the American flag. Desks are important props. Headlines in newspapers are props used to verify statistical and factual claims ("If the newspaper said it, it must be true.") A podium is a prop and sometimes other people can serve as props. Once, a U.S. Senate candidate in Wisconsin even used a cardboard standup of Elvis as a prop.

EMOTION-COMMUNICATING FACES

11   While any scene, any piece of music, any statement can induce emotion, the most common emotional device is the human face: the fear and anger in the face of teen druggie, the admiration and enthusiasm in crowd faces, babies' faces crying, fierce, uncaring expressions on the faces of opponents. All of these faces and their expressions are carefully

planted in ads. A most common approach is to take the face of an opponent at its most unattractive and show that face as background for words written on the screen to indicate what awful things he has done. Faces are probably a candidate's most direct conduit to creating feelings in viewers.

APPEALS

12   Every ad, political or otherwise, has at its center an appeal. This is the main message of the ad and it is designed to speak to a viewer's emotions: insurance ads appeal to fears of disasters; cosmetics ads appeal to personal ego; many high-ticket products appeal to greed. Political ads are no different. Ads for candidates can appeal to positive feelings such as patriotism or pride but they can also elicit fears, especially if they are attack ads. These fears include things like war, crime, job loss or poor education. They may even imply that their opponent is untrustworthy or that he will take health benefits away from your parents or even that he will lead the country into war. Consultants are always looking for "hot button" issues—issues that will be effective with a large percentage of voters. Once found, they will include these issues in the major appeal of the ad and sometimes in several minor appeals as well.

MUSIC AND BACKGROUND SOUNDS

13   Almost all political ads use music. It's usually orchestral, stately, designed to sound inspiring to a broad spectrum of listeners. Volume of music is very important. A common approach is have a crescendo of sound at the end of an ad. Background music is borrowed from horror movies when the ad attacks an

> "Background music is borrowed from horror movies when the ad attacks an opponent."

opponent. Music is often fiercely patriotic-sounding.

14   Background noises are important and seldom consciously noticed by viewers. Sirens, traffic noise, drumbeats are commonly employed. A good way to pick up use of music and background sounds, of course, is to look away from the screen during the ad. You'll find a lot going on there that you'd otherwise be unlikely to notice.

FILM EDITING AND CAMERA USE

15   Slow-motion is commonly used to increase the salience of an image. Extreme close-ups increase our perceptions of importance. They're also used to emphasize emotion, evil, and truthfulness. Often the camera comes in closer to the candidate as he begins his pledge to us voters—whatever that pledge may be. Jump-cuts occur when scenes are edited together and the central figure moves suddenly from one location to another. Shooting from above the candidate when he's greeting a crowd provides an impression of warmth and bonding. Black and white pictures usually mean the topic is serious and, most likely, negative.

CLOTHING

16   What a candidate is wearing is carefully chosen to show the viewer something "important" about him. An expensive suit shows power, taste, authority. Shirt sleeves show hard work and empathy with ordinary people. Jacket over the shoulder shows ease, warmth, confidence. A loosened tie usually indicates the same characteristics.

DEPICTED ACTIONS

17 What the candidate is doing in a support ad and what the opponent is doing in an attack ad are important. Getting off a plane shows characteristics like international expertise and concern, familiarity and caring about the whole country, or just plain old power. Interacting with the family shows caring. Holding hands with a spouse does the same. Signing papers shows ability to get important things done. Greeting ordinary people shows popularity and caring. Speaking from a podium emphasizes power and good ideas.

18 In the opponent, the activity is sometimes representing as "silly" or weak. A good example is the 1988 ad which featured Dukakis's helmeted head popping out of the top of an army tank. The opponent is sometimes shown with an incriminating "other." Candidates are usually doing things in color. Opponents are usually doing things in black and white.

SUPERS AND CODE WORDS

19 Supers are words printed in large letters on the screen. They appear over a background that is supposed to exemplify whatever is being said by the super. A super says, "Pay attention to this factoid or claim." It is often a phrase that communicates outrage at something the opponent has said or done such as, "RAISED TAXES THREE TIMES IN THREE YEARS." A super can also emphasize the larger appeal being made in the ad such as: "WRONG FOR YESTERDAY. WRONG FOR TOMORROW." Supers can use code words, which are words that sound simple but carry significant unconscious meaning for viewers. For example, when the word "values" is used in ads, it makes the candidate sound upright and moral, but often the exact values represented by the candidate are not made clear. The implication of the ad is that the candidate featured has values, but his or her opponent does not. Many argue that "crime"

"The implication of the ad is that the candidate featured has values, but his or her opponent does not."

and "welfare" are code words that encourage viewers to look at these issues through a racial lens. Even a seemingly innocuous word like "yesterday" can be a code word if the meaning is implied to be that someone or something is too old and no longer relevant, rather than meaning it just occurred in the past.

READING CLOSELY AND THINKING CRITICALLY

1. Why is it important to examine televised political advertisements critically?
2. In paragraph 9, Thorson states that background locations "communicate a variety of things about the candidate." What do you think they communicate?
3. The components of televised political ads are calculated to appeal to emotions, not reason. Why?
4. Do you think televised political advertisements are deceptive? Explain.

EXAMINING STRUCTURE AND STRATEGY

1. What is the purpose of "Dissect an Ad"? Where is the purpose stated? Do you think the purpose is an important one? Why or why not?
2. Why does Thorson include the information in paragraphs 1 and 2? Why didn't she just begin with the information in paragraph 3?
3. Is the supporting detail adequate? Explain.

NOTING COMBINED PATTERNS

1. Most of the essay is developed with division and cause-and-effect analysis, the dominant patterns of development. Explain why these patterns are used and how they help Thorson achieve her writing purpose.
2. How does Thorson use exemplification? How important is that exemplification?

CONSIDERING LANGUAGE AND STYLE

1. Paragraph 6 explains that political advertisements can attribute "mythological features" to a candidate. What is a mythological feature?
2. Consult a dictionary if you do not know the meaning any of these words: *pundits* (paragraph 1), *conduit* (paragraph 11), *salience* (paragraph 15), *innocuous* (paragraph 19).

FOR DISCUSSION IN CLASS OR ONLINE

How do you decide which political candidates you favor? Where do you get most of your information about political candidates—-from TV ads, from newspapers, from Internet news? How reliable are these sources? If your instructor so directs, post your response to your class Web site.

WRITING ASSIGNMENTS

1. **In your journal.** What did you learn as a result of reading "Dissect an Ad"? Can you apply what you learned to nonpolitical advertisements? Explain.
2. **Combining patterns for a purpose.** The purposes in the assignments are possibilities. You may establish whatever purposes you like, within your instructor's guidelines.
   - *Description, exemplification, and cause-and-effect analysis.* With your eyes closed, listen to several television advertisements. Describe what you hear and draw conclusions about how sound is used in advertisements, using three or more ads as examples. Now repeat the exercise and watch some ads with the sound off. What is missed? Your purpose is to inform readers about how sound is used to influence people to buy products.
   - *Division and exemplification.* Study magazine advertisements for either cosmetics or some personal hygiene product, such as shampoo, mouthwash, or soap. Inform readers by dividing the ads into their components so consumers understand how the ads work. Use the components of the ads you study as examples of persuasive strategies.

- *Description, exemplification, and cause-and-effect analysis.* Paragraph 16 notes that clothing communicates certain characteristics of political candidates. In high school, too, clothing often communicates a great deal. Students often make judgments about each other based on what they wear, and sometimes they become very competitive about clothing. To persuade your reader, argue that high school students in public schools should or should not have to wear uniforms.
- *Classification and exemplification.* Political figures are not the only people with mythological features. Movie, television, and sports stars also have mythological features attributed to them. Classify these mythological features, and give examples of movie, television, and sports stars to whom these features are attributed.

3. **Connecting the readings.** Are political advertisements a form of lying? To support your assertion, you can draw on ideas in "Dissect an Ad," "Lifosuction" (page 223), and "White Lies" (page 455).

4. **Drawing on sources.** Visit the Public Broadcasting System site called "The 30 Second Candidate" at *www.pbs.org/30secondcandidate/front.html.* Click on "tricks of the trade" and there you can manipulate a political ad to make it favorable to a candidate and then unfavorable to the candidate. Compare and contrast the two ads you create and give the conclusions you form as a result of the experience.

BACKGROUND: A superb essayist whose literary accomplishments won him the Presidential Medal of Freedom in 1963, Elwyn Brooks White (1899–1985) was a reporter for the *Seattle Times* before moving to New York to become an advertising copywriter. He went on to write for *The New Yorker* for 50 years and helped establish its reputation for excellence with his "Talk of the Town" column. He soon became known for his prose style and his personal essays, which often display an ironic view of the world. White also wrote the "One Man's Meat" column for *Harper's*, where "Once More to the Lake" first appeared in 1941. You may know White as the author of the popular children's book *Charlotte's Web* (1952) or as the author, with William Strunk, Jr., of the popular and enduring writer's guide, *The Elements of Style* (1959), a reference often checked by students and professional writers alike.

COMBINED PATTERNS AND THEIR PURPOSES: In "Once More to the Lake," White uses *description* to **relate the experience** of his visits to a family vacation spot in Maine, visits he made both as a child and as an adult. Using *narration,* White recounts a visit that he made with his son. Using *comparison-contrast,* he reveals that the spot is, at once, the same and different after the passing of years. Be sure to notice that his description allows White to **express his feelings** about the vacation spot. Notice, too, how it leads the author to an unnerving conclusion.

ONCE MORE TO THE LAKE | E. B. WHITE

One summer, along about 1904, my father rented a camp on a lake in Maine and took us all there for the month of August. We all got ringworm from some kittens and had to rub Pond's Extract on our arms and legs night and morning, and my father rolled over in a canoe with all his clothes on; but outside of that the vacation was a success and from then on none of us ever thought there was any place in the world like that lake in Maine. We returned summer after summer—always on August 1 for one month. I have since become a salt-water man, but sometimes in summer there are days when the restlessness of the tides and the fearful cold of the sea water and the incessant wind that blows across the afternoon and into the evening make me wish for the placidity of a lake in the woods. A few weeks ago this feeling got so strong I bought myself a couple of bass hooks

As you read
Notice how the essay makes you feel. Do you find the essay upbeat or depressing?

and a spinner and returned to the lake where we used to go, for a week's fishing and to revisit old haunts.

"I took along my son, who had never had any fresh water up his nose and who had seen lily pads only from train windows."

2   I took along my son, who had never had any fresh water up his nose and who had seen lily pads only from train windows. On the journey over to the lake I began to wonder what it would be like. I wondered how time would have marred this unique, this holy spot—the coves and streams, the hills that the sun set behind, the camps and the paths behind the camps. I was sure that the tarred road would have found it out, and I wondered in what other ways it would be desolated. It is strange how much you can remember about places like that once you allow your mind to

return into the grooves that lead back. You remember one thing, and that suddenly reminds you of another thing. I guess I remembered clearest of all the early mornings, when the lake was cool and motionless, remembered how the bedroom smelled of the lumber it was made of and of the wet woods whose scent entered through the screen. The partitions in the camp were thin and did not extend clear to the top of the rooms, and as I was always the first up I would dress softly so as not to wake the others, and sneak out into the sweet outdoors and start out in the canoe, keeping close along the shore in the long shadows of the pines. I remembered being very careful never to rub my paddle against the gunwale for fear of disturbing the stillness of the cathedral.

3 The lake had never been what you would call a wild lake. There were cottages sprinkled around the shores, and it was in farming country although the shores of the lake were quite heavily wooded. Some of the cottages were owned by nearby farmers, and you would live at the shore and eat your meals at the farmhouse. That's what our family did. But although it wasn't wild, it was a fairly large and undisturbed lake and there were places in it that, to a child at least, seemed infinitely remote and primeval.

4 I was right about the tar: It led to within half a mile of the shore. But when I got back there, with my boy, and we settled into a camp near a farmhouse and into the kind of summertime I had known, I could tell that it was going to be pretty much the same as it had been before—I knew it, lying in bed the first morning smelling the bedroom and hearing the boy sneak quietly out and go off along the shore in a boat. I began to

sustain the illusion that he was I, and therefore, by simple transposition, that I was my father. This sensation persisted, kept cropping up all the time we were there. It was not an entirely new feeling, but in this setting it grew much stronger. I seemed to be living a dual existence. I would be in the middle of some simple act, I would be picking up a bait box or laying down a table fork, or I would be saying something and suddenly it would be not I but my father who was saying the words or making the gesture. It gave me a creepy sensation.

"I seemed to be living a dual existence."

5 We went fishing the first morning. I felt the same damp moss covering the worms in the bait can, and saw the dragonfly alight on the tip of my rod as it hovered a few inches from the surface of the water. It was the arrival of this fly that convinced me beyond any doubt that everything was as it always had been, that the years were a mirage and that there had been no years. The small waves were the same, chucking the rowboat under the chin as we fished at anchor, and the boat was the same boat, the same color green and the ribs broken in the same places, and under the floorboards the same fresh water leavings and debris—the dead hellgrammite, the wisps of moss, the rusty discarded fishhook, the dried blood from yesterday's catch. We stared silently at the tips of our rods, at the dragonflies that came and went. I lowered the tip of mine into the water, tentatively, pensively dislodging the fly, which darted two feet away, poised, darted two feet back, and came to rest again a little farther up the rod. There had been no years between the ducking of

this dragonfly and the other one—the one that was part of memory. I looked at the boy, who was silently watching his fly, and it was my hands that held his rod, my eyes watching. I felt dizzy and didn't know which rod I was at the end of.

6   We caught two bass, hauling them in briskly as though they were mackerel, pulling them over the side of the boat in a businesslike manner without any landing net, and stunning them with a blow on the back of the head. When we got back for a swim before lunch, the lake was exactly where we had left it, the same number of inches from the dock, and there was only the merest suggestion of a breeze. This seemed an utterly enchanted sea, this lake you could leave to its own devices for a few hours and come back to, and find that it had not stirred, this constant and trustworthy body of water. In the shallows, the dark, water-soaked sticks and twigs, smooth and old, were undulating in clusters on the bottom against the clean ribbed sand, and the track of the mussel was plain. A school of minnows swam by, each minnow with its small individual shadow, doubling the attendance, so clear and sharp in the sunlight. Some of the other campers were in swimming, along the shore, one of them with a cake of soap, and the water felt thin and clear and unsubstantial. Over the years there had been this person with the cake of soap, this cultist, and here he was. There had been no years.

7   Up to the farmhouse to dinner through the teeming dusty field, the road under our sneakers was only a two-track road. The middle track was missing, the one with the marks of the hooves and the splotches of dried, flaky manure. There had always been three tracks to choose from in choosing which track to walk in; now the choice was narrowed down to two. For a moment I

> "There had always been three tracks to choose from in choosing which track to walk in; now the choice was narrowed down to two."

missed terribly the middle alternative. But the way led past the tennis court, and something about the way it lay there in the sun reassured me; the tape had loosened along the backline, the alleys were green with plantains and other weeds, and the net (installed in June and removed in September) sagged in the dry noon, and the whole place steamed with midday heat and hunger and emptiness. There was a choice of pie for dessert, and one was blueberry and one was apple, and the waitresses were the same country girls, there having been no passage of time, only the illusion of it as in a dropped curtain—the waitresses were still fifteen; their hair had been washed, that was the only difference—they had been to the movies and seen the pretty girls with the clean hair.

8   Summertime, oh, summertime, pattern of life indelible with fadeproof lake, the wood unshatterable, the pasture with the sweetfern and the juniper forever and ever, summer without end; this was the background, and the life along the shore was the design, the cottages with their innocent and tranquil design, their tiny docks with the flagpole and the American flag floating against the white clouds in the blue sky, the little paths over the roots of the trees leading from camp to camp and the paths leading

back to the outhouses and the can of lime for sprinkling, and at the souvenir counters at the store the miniature birch-bark canoes and the postcards that showed things looking a little better than they looked. This was the American family at play, escaping the city heat, wondering whether the newcomers in the camp at the head of the cove were "common" or "nice," wondering whether it was true that the people who drove up for Sunday dinner at the farmhouse were turned away because there wasn't enough chicken.

9   It seemed to me, as I kept remembering all this, that those times and those summers had been infinitely precious and worth saving. There had been jollity and peace and goodness. The arriving (at the beginning of August) had been so big a business in itself, at the railway station the farm wagon drawn up, the first smell of the pine-laden air, the first glimpse of the smiling farmer, and the great importance of the trunks and your father's enormous authority in such matters, and the feel of the wagon under you for the long ten-mile haul, and at the top of the last long hill catching the first view of the lake after eleven months of not seeing this cherished body of water. The shouts and cries of the other campers when they saw you, and the trunks to be unpacked, to give up their rich burden. (Arriving was less exciting nowadays, when you sneaked up in your car and parked it under a tree near the camp and took out the bags and in five minutes it was all over, no fuss, no loud wonderful fuss about trunks.)

"The only thing that was wrong now, really, was the sound of the place."

10   Peace and goodness and jollity. The only thing that was wrong now, really, was the sound of the place, an unfamiliar nervous sound of the outboard motors. This was the note that jarred, the one thing that would sometimes break the illusion and set the years moving. In those other summertimes all motors were inboard; and when they were at a little distance, the noise they made was a sedative, an ingredient of summer sleep. They were one-cylinder and two-cylinder engines, and some were make-and-break and some were jump-spark, but they all made a sleepy sound across the lake. The one-lungers throbbed and fluttered, and the twin-cylinder ones purred and purred, and that was a quiet sound, too. But now the campers all had outboards. In the daytime, in the hot mornings, these motors made a petulant, irritable sound; at night in the still evening when the afterglow lit the water, they whined about one's ears like mosquitoes. My boy loved our rented outboard, and his great desire was to achieve single-handed mastery over it, and authority, and he soon learned the trick of choking it a little (but not too much), and the adjustment of the needle valve. Watching him I would remember the things you could do with the old one-cylinder engine with the heavy flywheel, how you could have it eating out of your hand if you got really close to it spiritually. Motorboats in those days didn't have clutches, and you would make a landing by shutting off the motor at the proper time and coasting in with a dead rudder. But there was a way of reversing them, if you learned the trick, by cutting the switch and putting it on again exactly on the final dying revolution of the flywheel, so that it would kick back against compression and begin reversing.

Approaching a dock in a strong following breeze, it was difficult to slow up sufficiently by the ordinary coasting method, and if a boy felt he had complete mastery over his motor, he was tempted to keep it running beyond its time and then reverse it a few feet from the dock. It took a cool nerve, because if you threw the switch a twentieth of a second too soon you would catch the flywheel when it still had speed enough to go up past center, and the boat would leap ahead, charging bull-fashion at the dock.

11   We had a good week at the camp. The bass were biting well and the sun shone endlessly, day after day. We would be tired at night and lie down in the accumulated heat of the little bedrooms after the long hot day and the breeze would stir almost imperceptibly outside and the smell of the swamp drift in through the rusty screens. Sleep would come easily and in the morning the red squirrel would be on the roof, tapping out his gay routine. I kept remembering everything, lying in bed in the mornings—the small steamboat that

had a long rounded stern like the lip of a Ubangi, and how quietly she ran on the moonlight sails, when the older boys played their mandolins and the girls sang and we ate doughnuts dipped in sugar, and how sweet the music was on the water in the shining night, and what it had felt like to think about girls then. After breakfast we would go up to the store and the things were in the same place— the minnows in a bottle, the plugs and spinners disarranged and pawed over by the youngsters from the boys' camp, the Fig Newtons and the Beeman's gum. Outside, the road was tarred and cars stood in front of the store. Inside, all was just as it had always been, except there was more Coca-Cola and not so much Moxie and root beer and birch beer and sarsaparilla. We would walk out with the bottle of pop apiece and sometimes the pop would backfire up our noses and hurt. We explored the streams, quietly, where the turtles slid off the sunny logs and dug their way into the soft bottom; and we lay on the town wharf and fed worms to the tame bass. Everywhere we went I had trouble making out which was I, the one walking at my side, the one walking in my pants.

> "We would walk out with the bottle of pop apiece and sometimes the pop would backfire up our noses and hurt."

12   One afternoon while we were at that lake a thunderstorm came up. It was like the revival of an old melodrama that I had seen long ago with childish awe.

The second-act climax of the drama of the electrical disturbance over a lake in America had not changed in any important respect. This was the big scene, still the big scene. The whole thing was so familiar, the first feeling of oppression and heat and a general air around camp of not wanting to go very far away. In midafternoon (it was all the same) a curious darkening of the sky, and a lull in everything that had made life tick; and then the way the boats suddenly swung the other way at their moorings with the coming of a breeze out of the new quarter, and the premonitory rumble. Then the kettle drum, then the snare, then the bass drum and cymbals, then crackling light against the dark, and the gods grinning and licking their chops in the hills. Afterward the calm, the rain steadily rustling in the calm lake, the return of light and hope and spirits, and the campers running out in joy and relief to go swimming in the rain, their bright cries perpetuating the deathless joke about how they were getting simply drenched, and the children screaming with delight at the new sensation of bathing in the rain, and the joke about getting drenched linking the generations in a strong indestructible chain. And the comedian who waded in carrying an umbrella.

13   When the others went swimming my son said he was going in, too. He pulled his dripping trunks from the line where they had hung all through the shower and wrung them out. Languidly, and with no thought of going in, I watched him, his hard little body, skinny and bare, saw him wince slightly as he pulled up around his vitals the small, soggy, icy garment. As he buckled the swollen belt, suddenly my groin felt the chill of death.

READING CLOSELY AND THINKING CRITICALLY

1. Why does White return to the lake after an absence of 40 years? Do you think the reasons the author gives are the only ones? Explain.

2. What do you think White's dominant impression of the lake is as an adult?

3. What conclusion does White draw about the passage of time? Where is that conclusion best expressed?

4. White mentions several times that he has trouble distinguishing himself from his son and that he has trouble distinguishing the present from the past. Why do you think he experiences this blurring of identities and time?

5. White believes that his past summers at the lake were "infinitely precious and worth saving" (paragraph 9). Why?

6. If White had visited the lake more regularly over the past 40 years, do you think the visit narrated and described in the essay would have prompted the same feelings and realizations? Explain.

7. Is "Once More to the Lake" upbeat or depressing? Explain.

EXAMINING STRUCTURE AND STRATEGY

1. To make the essay vivid, White appeals to the sense of smell, touch, and sound in addition to the sense of sight. Mention one example each of a description that appeals to smell, touch, and sound. Underline the specific words that appeal to the senses.

2. Cite two other descriptions that you find particularly appealing. Underline the specific words.

3. White does not refer to his son by name, nor does he describe the boy very much. Why does he not give his son more identifying characteristics?

NOTING COMBINED PATTERNS

1. Without White's vivid description, much of the essay's joy would be lost. What else would be lost? Is description a primary or secondary pattern?

2. What narration does White include? How does the narration help him achieve his purpose for writing? Is narration a primary or secondary pattern?

3. In what way does White compare and contrast? How does the comparison-contrast help White achieve his purpose for writing? Is comparison-contrast a primary or secondary pattern?

CONSIDERING LANGUAGE AND STYLE

1. Look up the meaning of *paean* in a dictionary; then read paragraph 8 aloud. How is that paragraph similar to a paean?

2. What metaphor (see page 109) does White include in paragraph 2? In paragraph 12? What do these metaphors contribute?

3. Consult a dictionary if you are unsure of the meaning of any of these words: *incessant* (paragraph 1), *gunwale* (paragraph 2), *primeval* (paragraph 3), *helgrammite* (paragraph 5), *pensively* (paragraph 5), *indelible* (paragraph 8), *petulant* (paragraph 10), *Ubangi* (paragraph 11), *premonitory* (paragraph 12), *languidly* (paragraph 13).

"Once More to the Lake" deals with issues of youth and age. With your classmates, discuss the extent to which we are concerned with issues of youth and age in our culture. Cite spe cific examples to support your view. If your instructor so directs, post your responses to your class Web site.

WRITING ASSIGNMENTS

1. **In your journal.** In paragraph 12, when he writes of the thunderstorm, White notes that "the joke about getting drenched [links] the generations in a strong indestructible chain." What events, experiences, and circumstances link the generations in your family or in your locale? Explain in a page or two.

2. **Combining the patterns for a purpose.** The purposes in the assignments are possibilities. You may establish whatever purposes you like, within your instructor's guidelines.

    - *Description and process analysis.* Paragraph 12 describes a thunderstorm. To entertain and inform your reader, write your own description of a thunderstorm or other weather event as it develops, peaks, and wanes.

    - *Description and comparison-contrast.* If you have ever returned to a place after being gone for a while, compare and contrast by describing how the place was when you returned and how it was at the earlier time. For example, you could describe your first trip home after being away at school for several months or your elementary school after seeing it for the first time as an adult. Your purpose is to relate your experience and express your feelings.

    - *Narration and description.* Narrate a story about a place that holds special significance for you, and describe that place in a way that helps the reader understand why the place is important to you. Your purpose is to express your feelings and perhaps relate experience.

    - *Narration and cause-and-effect analysis.* In the essay, White recognizes his own mortality. Tell about an event that caused you to recognize your mortality—or at least your inability to control something. To relate experience and express feelings, narrate what happened and use cause-and-effect to explain how you were affected.

3. **Connecting the readings.** In "Once More to the Lake," "The Homestead on Rainy Creek" (page 119), My Neighborhood" (page 124), and "In the Kitchen" (page 291), the authors tell about childhood places that hold special meaning to them as adults. Discuss one or more of the ways that places from our childhood can influence us as both children and adults.

4. **Drawing on sources.** American advertisers are often accused of targeting youthful populations at the expense of older ones. Decide for yourself whether this allegation is true by going to the source: Watch television commercials for at least three popular programs and review recent magazine advertisements from at least three mainstream publications: *Time, Newsweek, TV Guide,* or *People,* for example. Then write an essay arguing that advertisers either do or do not target the younger consumers and neglect older ones. Be sure to back up your points with descriptions of specific commercials and advertisements.

"Really? Someone told me it's not plagiarism if they're dead."

14

Locating, Evaluating, and Drawing on Sources

CONSIDER USING SOURCES

In a paragraph, explain what the penalties for plagiarism are in your writing classroom and on your campus. If necessary, do some research to learn about these penalties.

USING SOURCES

Writers frequently draw on the work of other writers. For example, you may use an idea from an essay in this book to back up one of your points, or another writer's idea may prompt you to write an essay of your own. That is one of the exciting things about writing—writers engage in an ongoing conversation by responding to each other's ideas and using them for support or departure points. In addition, when they take in-depth looks at subjects, writers often produce research papers that bring together authoritative facts, opinions, and speculation. To be part of the ongoing conversation and to produce credible research papers, you must learn how to locate relevant, reliable sources and draw on them fairly and responsibly.

LOCATING SOURCES

The amount of material currently available to researchers is both thrilling and daunting. To locate material in the midst of this information explosion, you need efficient strategies, like the ones explained next.

www.mhhe.com/patterns

For more help with locating sources, click on
Research > Using the Library

- **Take a tour of your campus library to learn about its resources, where they are located, and how to use them.** You may be tempted to rely solely on Internet research, but your campus library houses a considerable amount of information unavailable on the Internet. Many libraries offer self-guided tours to take at your convenience; others have regularly scheduled tours or workshops given by staff members.

- **Decide on the kind of information you need.** Perhaps you are in the earliest stages of a writing project and need an overview of a topic such as gun control in order to narrow your topic. Or perhaps you already have your topic and need a sense of the most compelling arguments for and against a ban on assault weapons. Or you may need a single piece of specific information, such as the number of registered hand guns in the country. Knowing what you want helps your research go more quickly and efficiently.

- **Consult your librarian.** He or she can direct you to print and electronic resources that will save you time. Also, if you need materials unavailable in your library, the librarian can assist you in obtaining them through interlibrary loan.

- **Use reference books.** Reference books are housed in a specific area of the library and cannot be checked out. In some cases, they are on CD-ROMs that must be read at computer terminals, or they are available as online databases linked through your library's Web page. Reference works include works like the following:

  a. General encyclopedias such as *World Book* that offer an overview of a broad spectrum of topics.
  b. Specialty encyclopedias, like *Encyclopedia of Education* and *Encyclopedia of Crime and Justice,* that give more in-depth information in a specific subject area.
  c. Discipline or genre specific works, such as *The Oxford Companion to Art, A Political Handbook of the World,* and *The Oxford Companion to American Literature.*
  d. Biographical dictionaries, such as *Who's Who in America* and *International Who's Who,* that give sketches of the lives and accomplishments of famous people.

e. Almanacs and yearbooks, such as *World Almanac, Information Please Almanac,* and *Facts on File,* that provide statistics and information on current events.

www.mhhe.com/patterns

For more help with locating sources, click on
Research > Discipline Specific Resources

- **Locate books through the catalog.** Usually computerized, the catalog includes information on every book in the library. This information can be accessed by author, title, and subject. Look up the subject you are researching by typing in key words. If you do not find your subject in the catalog, or if you find too few entries, look up your subject in the three-volume *Library of Congress Subject Headings,* which is located near the computer terminals. This work lists the subject headings used in the catalog, so you can be sure you are looking up your subject using the appropriate key words.

- **Locate magazines, journals, and newspapers with indexes.** Because they are published at regular intervals, periodicals (magazines, journals, and newspapers) offer the most up-to-date information. To discover useful periodicals, look up your subject in a print, online, or CD-ROM index, such as one in the following list. (Increasingly, online indexes include a subset of full-text titles.)

  Business Periodicals Index
  Current Index to Journals in Education
  Government Publications Indexes
  Humanities Index
  InfoTrac
  New York Times Index
  ProQuest
  Reader's Guide to Periodical Literature
  Resources in Education
  ScienceSource
  Social Sciences Index

- **Use Internet search engines.** Use at least two search engines to get a broader range of results, but remember that search engines do not tell you which sites are reliable or the most valid. You must use your judgment, and if you are unsure, ask your instructor or a librarian.

www.mhhe.com/patterns

For more help with Internet search engines, click on
Research > Using the Internet

There are two basic kinds of search engines: those that present a series of categories and subcategories, and those that scour the Web for all instances in which your keyword or phrase appears. Among the most useful search engines are the following:

Category-Based Engines

AltaVista at *www.altavista.com*

Dogpile at *www.dogpile.com*

Excite at *www.excite.com*

Yahoo at *www.yahoo.com*

Keyword-Based Engines

Google at *www.google.com*

Metacrawler at *www.metacrawler.com*

For a more academically focused search, try Google scholar at *http://scholar. google.com.*

---

www.mhhe.com/patterns

For more help with Internet search engines, click on

Research > Using the Internet

To use a category-based search engine, click on the broadest category of your interest and narrow your search with specific keywords. For example, to get information on bilingual education, first click on the category "Education" on the category-based search engine's home page. On the next screen, you'll see a "search" box where you'll type in specific keywords to find within the broader "Education" sites. Type in the keywords "bilingual education" for more specific results.

To use a keyword-based engine, knowing Boolean search logic can help you search more efficiently. Boolean logic refers to the way you phrase your keyword search and helps the search engine refine the results it delivers. Using Boolean commands such as AND, OR, and NOT can also help you refine a search. For example, this Boolean search

"bilingual education" AND "Hispanic children"

will find much more specific information than simply typing in the word *bilingual.*

- **Use other online references.** Among the many helpful online references are these:

    Reference Desk: *www.refdesk.com*

    Information Please: *www.infoplease.com*

    Biography.com: *www.biography.com*

    Online Newspapers: *www.onlinenewspapers.com*

Internet Public Library: *www.ipl.org*

World Wide Web Virtual Library: *www.vlib.org*

In addition, check the online resources your library subscribes to. They are listed on your library home page and often available via your campus network or in computer labs.

EVALUATING PRINT AND INTERNET SOURCES

After locating sources, you must evaluate the quality and suitability of those sources by answering the questions given here.

Questions for Print Sources

- **Is the source recent enough?** Your topic will determine how current the information needs to be. For example, a historic topic such as battlefield strategies of the Civil War will not be as time sensitive as an examination of new treatments for AIDS.

- **Is the source detailed enough to meet your needs?** Evaluate whether the material is written for students (elementary, secondary, college), professionals, technical experts, or the general public. Avoid material that is too simplistic, and let your purpose dictate whether to use a source aimed at a general audience or one aimed at readers with technical knowledge.

- **Is the author reliable?** Check the source or type the author's name into a search engine to learn the author's credentials. What are the person's publications, degrees, and professional affiliations? Has the author received any awards or professional acknowledgment? What professional experiences has the author had?

- **Is the author or publisher associated with a particular point of view?** For example, if you are researching gun control and encounter a piece published by the National Rifle Association, you can assume a particular point of view.

- **Can you understand the material?** If the material is too technical or specialized for you, it is not helpful.

Questions for Internet Sources

- **Have you answered the relevant questions for print sources given above?** These questions are also important for evaluating Internet sources.

- **Who is sponsoring the page?** A page sponsored by a university or research foundation may be more reliable than one sponsored by a for-profit company. Pages affiliated with major news and media organizations are also generally credible.

- **When was the site last updated?** For many topics, you will need current information.

- **Can the information be verified elsewhere?** Check other sites, reference works, books or periodicals to be sure any surprising or questionable information can be corroborated. Information that cannot be verified may not be false, but it should be scrutinized carefully. Consult with your instructor if you are unsure about a site.
- **Are there links to other credible sites?** Credible sites link to other sites that look professional (see below) and that are sponsored by news agencies, educational organizations, government agencies, nonprofit groups and other trustworthy organizations.

www.mhhe.com/patterns

For more help with evaluating sources, click on
Research > CARS Source Evaluation Tutor

- **Does the page look professional?** Is it free of grammatical and spelling errors; is it attractively designed?

DRAWING ON SOURCES: PARAPHRASING AND QUOTING

To incorporate source material into your writing, you can write a paraphrase or a direct quotation.

www.mhhe.com/patterns

For more help with paraphrasing and quoting, click on
Research > Incorporating Source Information

Paraphrasing

To **paraphrase,** you restate another author's ideas, using your own writing style and wording. Paraphrasing is useful because it helps you incorporate brief excerpts from different sources into your essays to support your own ideas. (The sample synthesis on page 19 shows how paraphrases of different sources can be brought together.)

When you paraphrase you should

- Use your own wording and style, not the wording and style in the source.
- Use quotation marks for key words and phrases that are the author's distinctive expression.
- Avoid adding meaning.
- Avoid changing meaning.

www.mhhe.com/patterns

For more help with using quotation marks, click on
Editing > Quotation Marks

Here is an example of an acceptable paraphrase and unacceptable paraphrase of part of paragraph 1 of "Fan Profanity" on page 625. Notice that
the acceptable paraphrase places the author's distinctive phrasing in quotation marks. The unacceptable paraphrase fails to alter style and wording
enough. The examples here and throughout the chapter follow the Modern
Language Association's (MLA) rules for in-text, parenthetical citations (see
page 696).

SOURCE   Many free-speech controversies, especially on college
                campuses, are grounded in concerns for civility, polite-
                ness, and good taste. They also tend to follow the same
                path and end the same way. A government entity regu-
                lates speech in an effort to elevate discourse, limit the
                profane and protect public and personal sensitivities;
                courts strike down the regulations as violating the First
                Amendment freedom of speech; and we end up right
                where we started.

ACCEPTABLE   Howard M. Wasserman sees a recurring pattern to many
                First Amendment challenges. He says that when the
                government tries to create a more mannered atmosphere
                by setting rules to reduce instances of profanity and
                "protect public and personal sensitivities," the efforts are
                struck down in court as a violation of free speech (625).

UNACCEPTABLE   Howard M. Wasserman says that many free-speech
                debates, particularly ones at colleges, are based on
                concerns for politeness and good taste. These debates
                seem to take the same course, and end the same. First a
                government agency controls speech to raise the level of
                communication. Then, the judiciary condemns the regu-
                lations for violating the Constitutional guarantee of free
                speech. Then we end up back at the beginning (625).

When you write your paraphrases, avoid plugging in synonyms. If you
merely substitute synonyms for words in the source, the paraphrase will
lack your distinctive style. Furthermore, the result is often an awkward
sounding sentence. Here is an example using "Should Juvenile Offenders
Be Tried as Adults?" on page 585 as the source.

SOURCE   Few issues challenge a society's ideas about the natures
                of human development and justice as much as serious
                juvenile crime.

UNACCEPTABLE   Steinberg believes that not very many concerns confront
                a social order's notions about the characters of people's
                growth and the legal system as much as grave crime
                committed by young people (585).

ACCEPTABLE   Steinberg believes that of all the problems facing a
                society, the problem of "serious juvenile crime" is among
                the most difficult to grapple with (585).

Quoting

To write a **direct quotation,** reproduce the author's exact words within quotation marks. You should limit the number of quotations you use because with too many quotations, your writing will lack your distinctive style. As a general guide, limit your quoting to those times when something is so well expressed that you want to preserve the original wording.

A number of conventions govern the use of quotations. These are illustrated using material from "Fan Profanity" on page 625.

- Use ellipses (three spaced periods) to indicate that something has been left out of the original text.

    SOURCE   Many free-speech controversies, especially on college campuses, are grounded in concerns for civility, politeness, and good taste.

    QUOTATION   According to Howard M. Wasserman, "Many free-speech controversies . . . are grounded in concerns for civility, politeness, and good taste" (625).

- Use brackets to add clarification or to make changes to work the quotation into your sentence.

    SOURCE   The Hobson's Choice that Anderson believes this creates for fans—leave the arena and stop attending games or tolerate offensive cheers—is precisely the choice people make in any public place at which expression occurs.

    QUOTATION   Wasserman says, "The Hobson's Choice [a seeming choice that really is no choice] that Anderson believes this creates for fans—leave the arena and stop attending games or tolerate offensive cheers—is precisely the choice people make in any public place at which expression occurs" (627).

- Use single quotation marks for a quotation within a quotation.

    SOURCE   The speech at issue is expression by fans related to a sporting event, to all aspects of the game and all the participants in the game—what we can call "cheering speech."

    QUOTATION   Wasserman explains that "the speech at issue is expression by fans related to a sporting event, to all aspects of the game and all the participants in the game—what we can call 'cheering speech'" (626).

- Underline to indicate that something appeared in italics in the source.

    SOURCE   It is true that courts have upheld content-neutral regulations on sound and noise levels to protect captive audiences, beginning with the Supreme Court case *Kovacs v. Cooper* in 1949.

QUOTATION   One attorney explains, "It is true that courts have upheld
             content-neutral regulations on sound and noise levels to
             protect captive audiences, beginning with the Supreme
             Court case <u>Kovacs v. Cooper</u> in 1949" (Wasserman 627).

- Set off long quotations (five or more lines in your paper) according
  to the following model.

SOURCE   Many free-speech controversies, especially on college
             campuses, are grounded in concerns for civility, polite-
             ness, and good taste. They also tend to follow the same
             path and end the same way. A government entity regu-
             lates speech in an effort to elevate discourse, limit the
             profane and protect public and personal sensitivities;
             courts strike down the regulations as violating the First
             Amendment freedom of speech; and we end up right
             where we started.

QUOTATION   Howard Wasserman explains the cycle that free-speech
             debates often take:

             Many free-speech controversies, especially on
             college campuses, are grounded in concerns for civility,
             politeness, and good taste. They also tend to follow
             the same path and end the same way. A government
             entity regulates speech in an effort to elevate discourse,
             limit the profane and protect public and personal
             sensitivities; courts strike down the regulations as
             violating the First Amendment freedom of speech;
             and we end up right where we started. (625)

www.mhhe.com/patterns

For more help with using quotation marks, click on
Editing > Quotation Marks

INTEGRATING PARAPHRASES AND QUOTATIONS

The following strategies will help you work paraphrases and quotations
into your paper smoothly so your paper reads well, so your reader can tell
that you are paraphrasing or quoting, and so your reader understands how
you are using the source material.

- **Use sources to help you fulfill your writing purpose.** Avoid
  letting your sources drive the content and organization of your
  writing, and avoid stringing together quotations and paraphrases,
  one after another. Instead, use source material for a reason, such
  as to establish a point, support an argument, explain an idea, or
  illustrate a concept.
- **Include the author and/or source with the paraphrase or quotation.** Most often, that information comes before the quotation or

paraphrase, but it can also come in the middle or at the end, as these examples from "Adult Crime, Adult Time" on page 591 illustrate. (The italicized material is a study aid.)

AT THE BEGINNING *Linda J. Collier explains,* "Federal prosecution of juveniles is not totally unheard of, but it is uncommon" (594).

IN THE MIDDLE "Federal prosecution of juveniles is not totally unheard of," *notes Collier,* "but it is uncommon" (594).

AT THE END "Federal prosecution of juveniles is not totally unheard of, but it is uncommon," *according to Linda J. Collier* (594).

- **Vary the present tense verbs you use to work in the paraphrase or quotation.** Rather than repeating clauses such as "Collier says," try other verbs, including

acknowledges	implies	questions
argues	insists	replies
asserts	maintains	reveals
believes	notes	suggests
contends	points out	wonders

- **Indicate the purpose of each paraphrase and quotation by choosing verbs and including language to demonstrate how the source material relates to the ideas before or after.** Here is an example using "Adult Crime, Adult Time" and "Should Juvenile Offenders Be Tried as Adults?" (page 585). (The italics are a study aid.)

  Linda J. Collier believes in treating juveniles who commit violent crimes as adults because, as she states in "Adult Crime, Adult Time," the current juvenile justice system "is not appropriate for the violent juvenile offender of today" (593–594). *Laurence Steinberg, however, takes a less simplistic view.* In "Should Juvenile Offenders Be Tried as Adults?" Steinberg seems willing to try young people 13 and older as adults, but he expresses concern about trying children under 13 as adults because of the possibility that "children this young will not prove to be sufficiently blameworthy to warrant exposure to the harsh consequences of a criminal court adjudication" (588).

The reader can tell from the second sentence of the paragraph that the paraphrase and quotation of Steinberg present a view that contrasts with the view expressed in the Collier quotation. Take out the language that shows how the borrowed material relates to other ideas, and the reader has a more difficult time connecting the two ideas:

  Linda J. Collier believes in treating juveniles who commit violent crimes as adults because as she states in "Adult Crime, Adult Time," the current juvenile justice system "is not appropriate for the violent juvenile offender of today" (593–594). In "Should Juvenile Offenders Be Tried as Adults?" Steinberg seems willing to try young people 13 and older as adults, but he expresses concern about trying children under 13 as

Using the Present Tense with Paraphrases and Quotations

If you have trouble knowing what tense to use when you integrate paraphrases and quotations, remember that the present tense is conventional. This *present tense convention* is used because printed words—even ones written long ago—exist in the present.

YES   **Linda Collier <u>maintains</u> that as it currently exists, the juvenile justice system is not suitable for children and adolescents who commit violent crimes.**

NO   **Linda Collier <u>maintained</u> that as it currently exists, the juvenile justice system is not suitable for children and adolescents who commit violent crimes.**

adults because of the possibility that "children this young will not prove to be sufficiently blameworthy to warrant exposure to the harsh consequences of a criminal court adjudication" (588).

---

www.mhhe.com/patterns

For more help with incorporating paraphrases and quotations, click on

Research > Incorporating Paraphrases and Summaries
Research > Incorporating Quotations
Research > Using Sources Accurately

AVOIDING PLAGIARISM

Plagiarism is theft. If you use another person's ideas, words, manner of expression, or research and pass that material off as your own, you are guilty of plagiarism. Whether intentional or unintentional, plagiarism can result in serious penalties, including failing an assignment, failing a course, or expulsion.

To avoid plagiarism, remember the following.

- **Never hand in another person's work as your own.** Knowingly submitting another person's work as your own—including a paper you buy on the Internet or elsewhere—is the most blatant form of intentional plagiarism.

- **Never copy material from the library and use it in a paper as if it were your own ideas.** Unless the information is common knowledge (see below on common knowledge), material taken from any library source must be credited according to the documentation conventions explained in the next section.

- **Never download material from the Internet, paste it into your paper, and use it as if it were your own.** Copying from the Internet into your paper is easily accomplished, but doing so amounts to theft of intellectual property if you do not cite the source according to the documentation conventions explained in the next section.

- **Give credit for all ideas, facts, opinions, and statistics that are not common knowledge.** Material that is common knowledge does not have to be cited. Common knowledge includes well-known facts (on the Fahrenheit scale, 32 degrees is the freezing point), undisputed historical events (Germany was defeated in World War II), common sayings (It's always darkest before the dawn), and generally agreed upon information (Not everyone approves of using the electoral college to elect a president). If you are unsure whether something is common knowledge, consult with your instructor or err on the side of caution and credit the material according to the conventions in the next section.

- **Take notes carefully.** As you take notes, be sure to distinguish between your own ideas and words or ideas you take from sources. Unintentional plagiarism can occur if you forget that you took something from a source and include it in a paper as if it were your own.

- **Always credit the source and use quotation marks around someone else's words.** Even if you only use one or two words, if they are another person's distinctive phrasing, place that phrasing in quotation marks and credit it according to the conventions explained in the next section.

- **Quote accurately.** Do not change the wording of a direct quotation without using ellipses for omissions and brackets for additions, as explained on page 692.

- **Credit all of your paraphrases and quotations according to the appropriate documentation conventions.** In this chapter, the Modern Language Association's documentation conventions are explained in the next section.

www.mhhe.com/patterns

For more help with avoiding plagiarism, click on
Research > Avoiding Plagiarism

DOCUMENTING SOURCES

For proper **documentation,** you must show your reader the source of your paraphrases and quotations. The documentation conventions given in this book are those of the sixth edition of the *Handbook for Writers of Research Papers,* published by the Modern Language Association (MLA). These conventions are often called "MLA style." However, different disciplines and different instructors favor different conventions. In the social sciences, for example, the conventions of the American Psychological Association (APA) are often preferred. When in doubt, check with your instructor to learn the conventions you should follow.

www.mhhe.com/patterns

For more help with documenting sources, click on
Research > Avoiding Plagiarism > Using Copyrighted Materials
Research > Bibliomaker
Research > Links to Documentation Sites

To document according to MLA conventions, do the following:

- **The first time you use a source, introduce it with the author's full name and the title of the source.**

  In "Fan Profanity," Howard M. Wasserman explains that "many free-speech controversies, especially on college campuses, are grounded in concerns for civility, politeness, and good taste" (625).

- **Subsequent times you use a source, you can introduce with either the author's last name or the title of the source; you do not need both.**

  Wasserman goes on to explain that when governments regulate speech, "courts strike down the regulations as violating the First Amendment" (625).

- **Follow the paraphrase or quotation with a parenthetical text citation that gives the page number where the borrowed information or wording can be found.** If the introduction does not include the author's name, the parenthetical citation should note the name along with the page number. Otherwise, only the page number is needed.

  Steinberg believes that of all the problems facing a society, the problem of "serious juvenile crime" is among the most difficult to grapple with (585).

  One psychologist believes that of all the problems facing a society, the problem of "serious juvenile crime" is among the most difficult to grapple with (Steinberg 585).

- **For online sources that do not have page numbers, place the author's name in parentheses. If the author's name is not given online, place the title in parentheses.**

  Linaman says that boys living with their mothers experience more hostility than girls do, both immediately after the divorce and far beyond (Linaman).

- If you quote or paraphrase a source that is cited in a second source, note the secondhand nature of the borrowing with *qtd.* (meaning "quoted") *in* the parenthetical citation.

  > Justice John Marshall Harlan best described the relative nature of profanity when he said, "'One man's vulgarity is another's lyric'" (qtd. in Wasserman 628).

- **Follow your writing with a Works Cited page.** A "Works Cited" page is a listing of your sources alphabetized by author. (For an example of a Works Cited page, see page 706.) It includes full bibliographic information on each source from which you quoted or paraphrased. For the correct works cited forms, consult the next section.

MLA Forms for the Works Cited Page

For correct MLA documentation, the entries on your works cited page should follow the models given below. If you use sources that do not fit these models, consult a handbook or a research paper guide.

---

www.mhhe.com/patterns

For more help with MLA documentation, click on
Research > Bibliomaker
Research > Links to Documentation Sites
Research > Sample Research Paper > Sample Paper in MLA Style

Books

Book by One Author

> Gladwell, Malcolm. Blink: The Power of Thinking without Thinking. New York: Little, Brown, 2005.

Book by Two or Three Authors

> Hallowell, Edward M., and John J. Ratey. Delivered from Distraction: Getting the Most Out of Life with Attention Deficit Disorder. New York: Ballantine, 2004.

Book by More than Three Authors

> Davidson, James West, et al. Nation of Nations: A Concise Narrative of the American Republic. 3rd ed. New York: McGraw-Hill, 2002.

Revised Edition of a Book

> Miller, Casey, and Kate Swift. The Handbook of Nonsexist Writing. 2nd ed. New York: Harper, 1988.

A Book with an Editor

Marshall, Sam A., ed. 1990 Photographer's Market. Cincinnati: Writer's Digest, 1989.

A Book by an Author with an Editor

Arnold, Matthew. Culture and Anarchy. Ed. J. Dover Wilson. Cambridge: Cambridge UP, 1961.

Encyclopedia Article

"Terrorism." Encyclopedia Britannica. 2001 ed.

More than One Book by the Same Author

Tannen, Deborah. I Only Say This because I Love You: How the Way We Talk Can Make or Break Family Relationships throughout Our Lives. New York: Random House, 2006.

---. You Just Don't Understand: Women and Men in Conversation. New York: Ballantine, 1990.

Selection from an Anthology

Baker, Russell. "The Plot against People." Patterns for a Purpose: A Rhetorical Reader. Ed. Barbara Fine Clouse. 3rd ed. New York: McGraw, 2003. 474–475

Periodicals

Article from a Weekly or Biweekly Magazine

Klein, Joe. "The Trouble with Polls and Focus Groups." Time 4 Oct. 2004: 29.
"Advice for the Asking." Newsweek 27 Sept. 2004: 60.

Article from a Monthly or Bimonthly Magazine

Rauch, Jonathan. "Divided We Stand." The Atlantic Monthly Oct. 2004: 39–40.

Newspaper Article

Oppenheimer, Andres. "Don't Ignore Corporate Corruption." The Vindicator [Youngstown, Ohio] 13 Oct. 2004: A10.

Article from a Scholarly Journal with Continuous Pagination

Knipe, Penley. "Paper Profiles: American Portrait Silhouettes." Journal of the American Institute for Conservation 41 (2002): 203–23.

Article from Scholarly Journal with Separate Pagination

Pierrous, Palmyre. "Communicating in Art Museums: Language and Concepts in Art Education." Journal of Museum Education 28.1 (2003): 3–7.

Portable Databases (CD-ROMs, Diskettes, and Magnetic Tapes)

If the portable database is a periodical that is also published in print, follow the conventions for periodicals and provide the title of the electronic source, the medium ("Diskette" or "CD-ROM," for example), the distributor's name, and the date of electronic publication. If the periodical is published as a portable database only, omit the publication information for the print version.

> "Real Facts about the Sun." The Dynamic Sun. CD-ROM. Washington, D.C.:
>
> NASA, 2000.

Online Sources

Online sources are varied. In general, your citation should include the author's name, the title of the work, the title of the online site, the date of electronic publication, the date you consulted the source, and the complete address (URL) in angle brackets (< >). When some of this information is unavailable, give as complete a citation as you can.

Material from a Professional Site

> States Covers Washington. States News Service. 3 Oct. 2001 <http://www.
>
> statesnews.com>.

Note: The date refers to date of access.

Article in a Reference Database

> "Abbott, Berenice." Women in American History. Encyclopaedia Britannica. 9 April
>
> 1998 <http://women.eb.com/women/articles/abbott_bernice.html>.

Note: The date refers to the date of access.

Magazine Article

> Leo, John. "Self-Inflicted Wounds." U.S. News and World Report. 11 Oct. 04. 14
>
> Oct. 04 <http://www.usnews.com/usnews/issue/041011/opinion/11john.htm>.

Note: The second date is the date the material was accessed.

Journal Article

> Goleman, Judith. "An 'Immensely Simplified Task': Form in Modern Composition-
>
> Rhetoric." College Composition and Communication Sept. 2004. 12 Oct. 2004
>
> <http://www.ncte.org/library/files/Publications/Journals/ccc/0561-sept04/
>
> CO0561Immensely.pdf.>.

Note: The second date is the date the material was accessed.

Material from an Electronic Source That Has Also Appeared in Print

"The End of Life." The Atlantic Unbound. 12 Nov. 1997. 14 Nov. 1997
      <http://www.theatlantic.com/unbound/citation/wc971112.htm>.

Note: The second date is the date the material was accessed.

Material from a Scholarly Site

The Labyrinth: Resource for Medieval Studies. 1977. Georgetown. 30 Apr. 1998
      <http://www.georgetown.edu/labyrinth/labyrinth-home.html>.

Online Posting to a Listserv, Newsgroup, Or Forum

Quinlan, Rob. "Biocultural Evolution." Online posting. 19 Sept. 1995. Anthro-I:
      The General Anthropology Bulletin Board. 30 Apr. 1998 <http://www.
      anatomy.usyd.edu.au/danny/anthropology/anthro-1/>.

Note: The second date is the date the material was accessed.

Other Sources

Radio or Television Program

Moyers, Bill, and Robert Bly. A Gathering of Men. PBS. WNET, New York.
      8 Jan. 1990.

Personal Interview

DeSalvo, Joy. Personal interview. 30 Sept. 1996.

A Recording

Brooks, Mel. The Producers. Orch. Doug Besterman. Perf. Nathan Lane, Matthew
      Broderick, and Gary Beach. Sony Classical, 2001.

Image of a Painting, Photograph, or Other Artwork from a Print Source

Remington, Frederic. A Dash for the Timber, 1889. Amon Carter Museum, Fort
      Worth. American Art: History and Culture. By Wayne Craven. New York:
      McGraw, 1994. 387.

Note: Provide the institution or owner and the city, as well as publication information for the source in which the painting or photograph appears.

Image of a Painting, Photograph, or Other Artwork from an Electronic Source

Cézanne, Paul. The Bather. 1885. Museum of Mod. Art, New York. 14 June 2004
      <http://www.moma.org/collection/depts/paint_sculpt/blowups/paint_sculpt_001.
      html>.

The following student paper was written after the author read "The View of Me from Mars" on page 199. It illustrates how writers can combine their own ideas with research material in an essay. The notations in the margin call your attention to some of the essay's features, including its use of MLA conventions. (For two other examples of student essays that incorporate sources, see pages 334 and 560.)

Florence David

Professor Dietz

English 551

14 November 2004

Divorce as a Violation of Trust

"The View of Me from Mars" by Lee K. Abbott is about trust, the trust between a husband and wife and the trust between a parent and child. Husbands and wives trust each other to be honest, and children trust their parents to tell the truth. However, as both the story and the story-within-a story illustrate, that trust is sometimes betrayed, and when it is, something important is lost. As I read the short story, I was at first reminded of the high divorce rate in this country, perhaps because of the main character's infidelity. Eventually, though, I realized that the theme of trust triggered my thinking about divorce because one of the most serious violations of trust occurs when spouses divorce, and children are left feeling frightened and insecure. Children trust their parents to love each other and take care of them as a unit. When parents divorce, they violate that trust and children suffer.

According to Nancy Dreger in "Divorce and the American Family," United States Census Bureau statistics show that in 1960, fifty-three percent of families consisted of a father, mother, and at least one child. In 1995, the percentage dropped about twenty percent and is still falling (2). Just in 1995 alone there were 1.2 million divorces, says Barry Frieman in "Two Parents-Two Homes" (5). The number of children affected by those divorces is staggering: over a million according to James Hopper in *The Effects of Divorce on Children* (3). The effects of these divorces are serious. In fact, they are so serious that I think couples should consider staying married for the sake of their children.

When our trust is violated, we feel stress, and children of divorce are no different. A study done on 700 junior-high students, reported by Karl Zinsmeister in "Divorce's Toll on Children," reveals that the stress

Paragraphs 1 and 2 are the introduction. The thesis is the last sentence of paragraph 2.

Paragraph 2 synthesizes paraphrases from three sources to show the prevalence of divorce and the number of children affected. The writer uses parenthetical citations.

Paragraph 3 begins with a topic sentence. The paragraph combines three paraphrases with the author's own experience to show the effects of the stress of divorce. Notice that sentences with paraphrases include words to show the source and a parenthetical citation.

of divorce ranks right beneath the stress of the death of a parent or close family member (19). The stress can lead to emotional and behavioral problems, says Hopper (3). When my parents divorced when I was twelve, for example, I became so nervous that I began to use drugs. That led to skipping school and finally getting arrested for shoplifting. I had never been in trouble before the divorce, at least not trouble that serious. Apparently my reaction is not uncommon because Zinsmeister reports that teenagers of divorced parents often abuse drugs and commit violent acts (21).

Paragraph 4 combines paraphrase and quotation. Notice that the author adds her own sentences to connect the borrowings and show how they relate to each other.

Some girls whose parents divorce become promiscuous because   4 their self-esteem is lowered. Zinsmeister calls this the "sleeper effect" of divorce (21). Boys can face a different problem, especially when they live with their mothers, because they lack a role model. As Robert Bly notes in "The Pillow and the Key," "When women, even women with the best intentions, bring up a boy alone, he may in some way have no male face, or he may have no face at all" (476). In "The Effects of Divorce on Children and Families," marriage and family therapist Todd E. Linaman reports one effect of the loss of the father figure. He says that boys living with their mothers experience more hostility than girls do, both immediately after the divorce and far beyond (Linaman). Imagine what it must be like for a young boy whose father is not on the scene. He can't help but feel hostile about the loss of trust in the dependability of his male parent.

Paragraph 5 opens with a topic sentence that is supported with three paraphrases and the author's own thinking.

After divorce, a family's finances may suffer, which can com-   5 pound the feelings of loss of trust for children. As Linaman explains, women and children can be particularly hard hit because half of divorced men required to pay child support do not do so regularly; of the remaining half, a quarter make none of their payments, and a quarter pay less than the required amount (Linaman). A study by Jennifer Gerner and Dean Lillard, reported in "The Hidden Costs of Divorce" by Mike Powers, shows that even those who graduate from high school are less likely to go to college because of financial problems (25). In fact, according to Linaman, 60 percent fewer children of divorce attend college than children of intact families (Linaman). Again, children whose standard of living is reduced or whose college plans are sidetracked are likely to feel a threat to their basic security and a loss of trust in the ability of their parents to fulfill their responsibility to care for them.

Of course, to suggest that all unhappy spouses should stay married when children are involved or that all divorces are harmful to children makes no sense. Mel Krantzler, in *Creative Divorce,* says that children are resilient and can come through a divorce just fine (192), and Linaman concedes that children in "high conflict" marriages, in which the couple "engages in hostile, aggressive and destructive fighting" may be better off if the parents do divorce (Linaman). However, Linaman also contends that most marriages ending in divorce are high conflict. He states:

> It is estimated that only 30% of divorces occur under these circumstances. Approximately 70% of all divorces end "low conflict" marriages. Many experts believe that these are marriages that could potentially be saved, and that continuing the marriage would not produce more negative stress for the child than would ending the relationship. (Linaman)

When trust is at stake, saving a marriage helps protect children. With very young children, the effects of loss of trust that divorce entails may be worse than they are for older children, who at least understand some of what is happening. Young children may not understand why one parent is gone and why the family unit is destroyed. In this case, the loss of trust can affect the child's security and ability to relate to people for all time. This is the child who may be afraid to get close to anyone for fear that the person will leave, or the child who thinks he or she is to blame for the divorce and is filled with guilt or self-loathing. The loss of trust a child of divorce experiences

6

Paragraph 6
In this paragraph, the author raises and counters some objections and suggests circumstances in which divorce may be the best option, but she also uses a source to point out that most divorces do not involve these circumstances. Notice the long quotation.

7

Paragraph 7
is the conclusion. The author draws her points together and restates her thesis.

harms the child, and it may last a lifetime. Thus, couples with children should think carefully before divorcing.

Works Cited

Bly, Robert. "The Pillow and the Key." Writing about Diversity: An Argument Reader and Guide. Ed. Irene L. Clark. 2nd ed. Fort Worth: Harcourt, 1997. 465–484.

Dreger, Nancy. "Divorce and the American Family." Current Health 2 Nov. 1996: 6–12.

Frieman, Barry B. "Two Parents-Two Homes." Educational Leadership Apr. 1997: 23–25.

Hopper, James A. The Effects of Divorce on Children: A Review of the Literature. Maryland: ERIC Clearinghouse, 1997. ERIC NO-408539.

Krantzler, Mel. Creative Divorce: A New Opportunity for Personal Growth. New York: M. Evans, 1974.

Linaman, Todd E. "The Effects of Divorce on Children and Families." Family Life Facts. 9 Sept. 2004 <http://www.flc.org/hfl/marriage/mar-flf03.htm>.

Powers, Mike. "The Hidden Costs of Divorce." Human Ecology Forum 25.1 (Winter 1997): 4–7.

Zinsmeister, Karl. "Divorce's Toll on Children." Current Health Feb. 1997, 29–33.

Parker, Jo Goodwin. "What is Poverty?" by Jo Goodwin Parker in *America's Other Children: Public Schools Outside Suburbia* by George Henderson. Reprinted by permission of University of Oklahoma Press.

Press, Eyal. "Fouled Out" originally published in *The Atlantic Monthly,* July/August 2001. Copyright © 2001 by Eyal Press. Reprinted by permission of the author.

Rauch, Jonathan. "Caring for Your Introvert." Copyright © 2003 by Jonathan Rauch. First published in *The Atlantic Monthly,* March 2003. Reprinted by permission of the author.

Rifkin, Jeremy. "Why I Oppose Human Cloning," Reprinted from *Tikkun Magazine,* a bimonthly interfaith critique of politics, culture and society. Copyright © 2002 by *Tikkun Magazine.*

Ríos, Alberto. "The Vietnam Wall" from *The Lime Orchard Woman* by Alberto Ríos. Copyright © 1988 by Alberto Ríos. Published by The Sheep Meadow Press. Reprinted by permission of the author.

Roberts, Paul. "How to Say Nothing in 500 Words" from *Understanding English* by Paul Roberts. Copyright © 1958 by Paul Roberts. Reprinted by permission of Pearson Education, Inc.

Roche, Timothy and Amanda Bower. "Young Voices from the Cell," *Time,* May 28, 2001. Copyright © 2001 Time, Inc. Reprinted by permission.

Rodriquez, Richard. "Complexion" from *Hunger of Memory* by Richard Rodriguez. Copyright © 1981 by Richard Rodriguez (Boston: David Godine, 1981). Reprinted by permission of Georges Borchardt, Inc. on behalf of the author.

Shepherd, Jean. "Lost at C." Copyright © 1973 by Playboy Enterprises, Inc. First appeared in *Playboy* Magazine, from *A Fistful of Fig Newtons* by Jean Shepherd. Used by permission of Doubleday, a division of Random House, Inc.

Siegal, Dorothy. "What Is Behind the Growth of Violence on College Campuses?" by Dorothy Siegal, *USA Today,* May 1994. Copyright © 1994 by the Society for the Advancement of Education.

Silko, Leslie Marmon. "Lullaby" from *Storyteller* by Leslie Marmon Silko. Copyright © 1981 by Leslie Marmon Silko. Published by Seaver Books, New York, NY. Reprinted by permission.

Silverglate, Harvey A. and Greg Lukianoff. "Speech Codes: Alive and Well at Colleges." *Chronicle of Higher Education,* 2003. Reprinted by permission of the authors.

Staples, Brent. "Just Walk On By: A Black Man Ponders His Power to Alter Public Space." Copyright © 1986 by Brent Staples. Brent Staples Writes for *The New York Times* and is author of the memoir *Parallel Time: Growing Up in Black and White.*

Steinberg, Laurence. "Should Juvenile Offenders Be Tried as Adults?" *USA Today Magazine,* January 2001. Copyright © 2001 by the Society for the Advancement of Education. Reprinted by permission.

Sullivan, Andrew. "Why the *M* Word Matters to Me," *Time,* February 16, 2004. Copyright © 2004 Time Inc. Reprinted by permission.

Surowiecki, James. "Paying to Play," *The New Yorker,* July 12 & 19, 2004. Copyright © 2004 by James Surowiecki. Reprinted by permission of the author.

Tannen, Deborah. "Indirectness at Work" by Deborah Tannen, *The New York Times Magazine,* August 28, 1994. Copyright © 1994 Deborah Tannen. Reprinted by permission. This article is adapted in part from the author's book, *Talking From 9 to 5* (Quill, 1994).

Thomas, Dylan. "Do Not Go Gentle Into That Good Night." Copyright © 1952 by Dylan Thomas. Reprinted by permission of New Directions Publishing Corp. and David Higham Associates.

Thorson, Esther. "Dissect an Ad," copyright © 1996 by Esther Thorson. Reprinted by permission of the author.

Trillin, Calvin. "It's Just Too Late" by Calvin Trillin. From *Killings.* Published by Ticknor & Fields. Copyright © 1979, 1984 by Calvin Trillin. Originally appeared in *The New Yorker.* Reprinted by permission of Lescher & Lescher, Ltd. All rights reserved.

Vámos, Miklós. "How I'll Become An American," *New York Times,* Op-Ed April 17, 1989.

Walker, Alice. "Am I Blue?" from *Living By the Word: Selected Writings 1973–1987.* Copyright © 1986 by Alice Walker. Reprinted by permission of Harcourt, Inc.

Wasserman, Howard. "Fan Profanity," September 25, 2004. Appeared on First Amendment Center Online, *http://www. firstamendmentcenter.org.* Reprinted with permission.

Whetstine, Brad. "Augustinian Influences," *The College*, Winter 2003–2004. Reprinted by permission of Indiana University Alumni Association.

White, E. B. "Once More to the Lake" from *One Man's Meat*, text copyright © 1941 by E. B. White. Copyright renewed. Reprinted by permission of Tilbury House, Publishers, Gardiner, Maine.

Wiesel, Elie. "To Be a Jew" from *A Jew Today* by Elie Wiesel, translated by Marion Wiesel. Copyright © 1978 by Elirion Associates, Inc. Used by permission of Random House, Inc.

Zinsser, William. "College Pressures" published in *Blair & Ketchum's Country Journal*, April 1979. Copyright © 1979 by William Zinsser. Reprinted by permission of the author.

Photo Credits:

Page 24: © Lewis Hine, photograph courtesy of NARA; **26:** Courtesy of State Farm Mutual Automobile Insurance Company, 2002; **86:** Photofest; **100:** © Alan Thornton/Stone/ Getty Images; **118:** Google; **130:** © David Johnson; **149:** © John Neubauer/PhotoEdit; **153:** Library of Congress; **154:** © AP Photo/ Tsugufumi Matsumoto; **206:** © Royalty-Free/ Corbis; **225:** © 2003 Greg Clarke; **265:** © Elliott Erwitt/Magnum Photos; **266:** from Nickels, McHugh, and McHugh, Understanding Business, 5th ed., New York, McGraw-Hill, 1999, p. 33; **280:** © Bo Bridges Photography; **320:** Courtesy of Lexmark International, Inc.; **322:** B. D. McKay cartoon © 2003 Scott McMahan, *http://cyberreviews.skwc.com/ bdmckay/*; **337:** Marvel/Sony Pictures/ The Kobal Collection/Melissa Moseley; **339:** (left) NARA, (right) Library of Congress; **378:** (left) © Corbis, (right) © Fred Mullane/ NewSport/Corbis; **380:** Photofest; **393:** Used with permission. © 2004 Mothers Against Drunk Driving. All rights reserved.; **441:** © Schenectady Museum; Hall of Electrical History Foundation/Corbis; **442:** © Royalty-Free/Corbis; **454:** Courtesy of National Search Dog Foundation. Photograph by Deborah Samuel /Makita © 2002 from PUP/ Chronicle Books.; **465:** © Bonnie Kamin/ Index Stock Imagery, Inc.; **490:** © AP Photo/ Virginia Mayo; **501:** © PhotoLink/Getty Images; **540:** © Bettmann/Corbis; **582:** © AP Photo/Gary I. Rothstein, Pool; **593:** © Don Murray/ZUMA/Corbis; **638:** Historic Costume and Textile Museum, Department of Apparel, Textiles and Interior Design, Kansas State University, Object #1987.825.1. Photography by KSU Photographic Services; **654:** © Esbin-Anderson/The Image Works; **662:** Rose Lincoln/Harvard News Office; **680:** © Diaphor Agency/Index Stock Imagery, Inc.

This glossary provides definitions of the terms set in boldface throughout the text and gives the pages where the terms are first used. Words in small capital letters are defined elsewhere in the glossary.

alternating pattern In COMPARISON-CONTRAST, the arrangement of detail whereby a point is made for one subject, and then the corresponding point is made for the other subject. This arrangement continues until all points are made for both subjects.   page 329 (See also BLOCK PATTERN.)

analogy A comparison of two elements from different categories in order to shed light on one or both elements. For example, comparing marriage to a roller-coaster ride is an analogy, as is comparing divorce to a medieval siege. page 326

anecdote A brief NARRATION often used as an example.   page 156

argumentation The use of reason and logic to persuade a reader to think or act a particular way. Argumentation employs compelling evidence and counters significant objections to the writer's view to earn the reader's agreement.   page 543 (See also PERSUASION.)

audience The readers for a particular piece of writing. For example, the audience for your campus newspaper is the students, faculty, staff, and administration of your college. Different audiences have different characteristics, and writers must be aware of those characteristics to meet the needs of their readers. page 35

block pattern In COMPARISON-CONTRAST, the arrangement of detail by first presenting all the points about one subject and then all the points about the second subject.   page 329 (See also ALTERNATING PATTERN.)

body paragraph A paragraph composed of a TOPIC SENTENCE that gives a main idea and SUPPORTING DETAILS that develop that idea. A body paragraph helps support the THESIS.   page 64

causal chain In CAUSE-AND-EFFECT ANALYSIS, a sequence that occurs when a cause leads to an effect, and that effect becomes a cause leading to another effect, and so on.   page 384

cause-and-effect analysis A pattern of essay development that examines the reasons for an event (causes), the results of an event (effects), or both. page 381

chronological order The arrangement of details in an essay according to a time sequence, usually beginning with the first event and proceeding to the second and subsequent events.   page 110 (See also FLASHBACK.)

classification A pattern of essay development that groups items into related categories according to a specific principle. In classification, items that share characteristics are grouped together.   page 443 (See also DIVISON.)

coherence The smooth connection of SUPPORTING DETAILS and BODY PARAGRAPHS in a clear, understandable way. To achieve coherence, writers use transitions, logical ordering of ideas, and repetition of keywords and ideas to show how ideas relate to each other.   page 69

comparison-contrast A pattern of essay development that notes the similarities and/or differences between two subjects. Comparison notes similarities, and contrast notes differences.   page 323 conclusion The final sentences or paragraph of an essay, meant to provide resolution and closure. An effective conclusion creates a satisfying ending and does not close abruptly.   page 72

context See WRITING CONTEXT.

critical reading Evaluating written text to draw conclusions about its significance, meaning, implications, reliability, and connections to other ideas.   page 1

deduction A form of reasoning that moves from the general to the specific, from a GENERALIZATION (the major premise) to a specific case (the minor premise) to a conclusion.   page 554 (See also INDUCTION.)

definition A pattern of essay development that gives the meaning of a term. page 491 (See also EXTENDED DEFINITION, FORMAL DEFINITION, and STIPULATIVE DEFINITION.)

description A pattern of essay development that uses words to create mental images for the reader.   page 102 (See also EXPRESSIVE DETAILS and OBJECTIVE DETAILS.)

direct quotation The reproduction of exact spoken or written words.   pages 159 and 629

directional process analysis A form of PROCESS ANALYSIS that gives the steps in a procedure so the reader can perform it.   page 267 (See also EXPLANATORY PROCESS ANALYSIS.)

division A pattern of essay development that breaks an entity down into its parts. page 443 (See also CLASSIFICATION.)

documentation The formal crediting of borrowed material (PARAPHRASE and DIRECT QUOTATION) by noting the source of the borrowing according to conventions of a particular discipline. Papers written in a literature or composition class are often documented according to the conventions of the Modern Language Association (MLA).   page 696

dominant impression In DESCRIPTION, the quality the descriptive details are meant to convey.   page 104

editing The process of finding and correcting errors in grammar, usage, punctuation, capitalization, and spelling.   page 84

errors in logic See LOGIC, ERRORS IN.

ethos One of three elements of a successful argument. (The other two elements are LOGOS and PATHOS.) Ethos refers to establishing the reliability and trustworthiness of the writer of an argument.   page 546

euphemism A polite or indirect substitute for an unpleasant expression. For example, "pass away" is a euphemism for "die."   page 314

exemplification A pattern of essay development that uses specific instances (examples) to clarify a point, to add interest, or to persuade.   page 210 (See also HYPOTHETICAL EXAMPLE.)

explanatory process analysis A form of PROCESS ANALYSIS that explains how something works, how it is made, or how it is done. The procedure explained is not meant to be carried out by the reader.   page 267 (See also DIRECTIONAL PROCESS ANALYSIS.)

expressive details In DESCRIPTION, points that give a subjective or emotional view of what is being described.   page 105 (See also OBJECTIVE DETAILS.)

extended definition A form of DEFINITION in which the writer goes beyond the literal meaning of a word to give the significance, private meanings, and personal experiences associated with that word.   page 492 (See also FORMAL DEFINITION and STIPULATIVE DEFINITION.)

fact A statement that can be proven or that has been proven. For example, it is a fact that plants manufacture oxygen from carbon dioxide.   page 2 (See also OPINION.)

first draft A writer's initial effort to get ideas down in essay form. A first draft is usually very rough and in need of REVISION.   page 61

flashback A form of CHRONOLOGICAL ORDER that involves moving from one point in time to a more distant point in the past and back again.   page 161

formal definition A definition that states the term to be defined, its class, and how it differs from other members of the class: An antibiotic is a type of drug that attacks bacteria.   page 491 (See also DEFINITION, EXTENDED DEFINITION, and STIPULATIVE DEFINITION.)

generalization A broad statement that asserts that something is true in most cases or in every case.   page 64 (See also DEDUCTION.)

hypothetical example An illustration based on something that *could* happen. page 213 (See also EXEMPLIFICATION.)

induction A form of reasoning that moves from specific evidence to a general conclusion.   page 553 (See also DEDUCTION and INFERENCE.)

inference A conclusion drawn on the basis of what a speaker or writer suggests, rather than what is specifically stated. In INDUCTION, an inference is the conclusion drawn; it is usually not certain beyond a doubt.   page 3 and 554

introduction One or more paragraphs that open an essay. The introduction is meant to engage a reader's interest; many times the introduction also presents the THESIS.   page 62

irony See SITUATIONAL IRONY and VERBAL IRONY.

journalist's questions Who? What? When? Where? Why? How? In NARRATION, the answers form much of the supporting detail.   page 158

logic, errors in Forms of faulty reasoning that lead a person to a false conclusion. page 5

logos One of the three elements of a successful argument. (The other elements are ETHOS and PATHOS.) Logos refers to sound reasoning, facts, evidence, statistics, and authoritative statements used to back up an assertion.   page 546 (See also LOGIC, ERRORS IN.)

metaphor An implied comparison made without using the words *like* or *as*: "The play's opening act was a train wreck."   page 110

narration A pattern of essay development that involves telling a story.   page 155

objective details In DESCRIPTION, points that give a factual, unemotional picture of what is described.   page 105 (See also EXPRESSIVE DETAILS.)

opinion A statement of a person's judgment, interpretation, or belief. Unlike a FACT, an opinion cannot be proven. For example, it is an opinion that the current movie rating system is inadequate.   page 2

paraphrase The restatement of an author's written ideas in your own words and style. Paraphrases are used in essays and research papers that draw on sources. page 690

pathos One of the three elements of a successful argument. (The other elements are LOGOS and ETHOS.) Pathos refers to the appeal to emotions, attitudes, beliefs, and values.   page 546

persuasion Uses appeals to emotions, values, and beliefs to convince a reader to think or act a particular way.   page 543 (See also ARGUMENTATION.)

plagiarism A form of academic dishonesty that occurs when a person submits another's words, ideas, or work as his or her own, or when a person fails to provide DOCUMENTATION of borrowed material.   page 695

process analysis A pattern of essay development that explains how something is made, how something is done, or how something works.   page 267 (See also DIRECTIONAL PROCESS ANALYSIS and EXPLANATORY PROCESS ANALYSIS.)

progressive order The arrangement of details from the least important or compelling points to the most important or compelling points.   page 50

purpose The reason a person writes, the goal the writer hopes to achieve. A writer's purpose can be to entertain, to express feelings or relate experience, to inform, and/or to persuade.   page 34

quotation See DIRECT QUOTATION.

revising The process of evaluating and making changes in a draft's content, organization, and expression of ideas in order to improve it. The revision process can involve writing multiple drafts.   page 77

role The way the writer presents himself or herself. For example, a writer can assume the role of a student, parent, average reader, concerned citizen, voter, and so forth.   page 36

sensory detail DESCRIPTION that appeals to any of the five senses (sight, sound, taste, smell, touch).   page 106 (See also EXPRESSIVE DETAILS and OBJECTIVE DETAILS.)

simile A comparison made using the word *like* or the word *as*: "The overheated radiator spewed water like a geyser."   page 109

situational irony When something happens that runs counter to what is expected to happen. An example of situational irony is a character who goes to a surprise party and discovers he is the guest of honor who is surprised.   page 175 (See also VERBAL IRONY.)

spatial order The arrangement of details across space, for example from top to bottom, near to far, front to back, or left to right.   page 50

stipulative definition Explains a special or unexpected way a term is used. The following is an example: "By spouse, I do not refer merely to the legally married partner. I also refer to a same-sex partner in a committed relationship."   page 492 (See also DEFINITION, EXTENDED DEFINITION, and FORMAL DEFINITION.)

summary The brief restatement of the main points of a piece of writing in one's own words and style, given without adding or altering meaning.   page 14

supporting details In a BODY PARAGRAPH, all the points made to prove or explain the TOPIC SENTENCE.   page 64

synthesis The process whereby a person relates new information to previously learned information.   page 4 Also, the bringing together of material from two or more sources.   page 17 thesis The central point or controlling idea of an essay, the idea that everything else in the essay relates to and that the BODY PARAGRAPHS support. page 45

tone The writer's attitude or feeling about the reader or about the subject of the writing. Tone can be neutral, angry, sympathetic, annoyed, and so on. page 71

topic sentence In a BODY PARAGRAPH, the sentence that expresses the main idea. A topic sentence can be stated or implied. page 68

verbal irony When an author says one thing but really means the opposite. An example of verbal irony is saying "Oh, that's *great!*" (Your tone indicates that something is not great at all.) page 133 (See also SITUATIONAL IRONY.)

writing context The combination of the writer's PURPOSE, AUDIENCE, and ROLE. The writing context creates the situation within which a person writes. page 34

- SOURCES OF DEMOCRATIC SUPPORT (GRAPH) Reading Graphs *p. 23*
- CHILD LABORER, ADDIE LAIRD (PHOTOGRAPH) Reading Photographs *p. 24*
- STATE FARM INSURANCE (ADVERTISEMENT) Reading Advertisements *p. 26*
- THE ROCK (POSTER) Student Essay *p. 86*
- "THE RAILWAY ENGINE" (DRAWING) "Consider the Pattern" *p. 100*
- GOOGLE LOGOS (DRAWINGS) "Examining Visuals" *p. 118*
- ICE SKATER (DRAWING) Professional Selection *p. 130*
- THE VIETNAM VETERANS MEMORIAL WALL (PHOTOGRAPH) Professional Selection *p. 150*
- THE GREAT SEAL OF THE UNITED STATES (PHOTOGRAPH) "Responding to an Image" *p. 153*
- "SCENE FROM *GORGO*" (PHOTOGRAPH) "Consider the Pattern" *p. 154*
- CURTIS (CARTOON) "Examining Visuals" *p. 168*
- "EVERYDAY MISHAPS" (PHOTOGRAPH) "Responding to an Image" *p. 206*
- FAMILY LIFE: THEY SPEND MOST OF THEIR LIFE CLICKING" (CARTOON) "Consider the Pattern" *p. 208*
- "SEVENTH GRADE READING LIST" (CARTOON) "Examining Visuals" *p. 222*
- LIFOSUCTION (DRAWING) Professional Selection *p. 225*
- SEPARATE BUT EQUAL? (PHOTOGRAPH) "Responding to an Image" *p. 265*
- "INTERNET GROWTH CHART" (CARTOON) "Consider the Pattern" *p. 266*
- SKATEBOARDER (PHOTOGRAPH) "Examining Visuals" *p. 280*
- LOADING PAPER INTO A LEXMARK PRINTER: INSTRUCTIONS (DRAWING) "Responding to an Image" *p. 320*
- "THE WAY WE REMEMBER IT. . .THE WAY IT WAS. . ." (CARTOON) "Consider the Pattern" *p. 322*
- TOBEY MAGUIRE AS SPIDERMAN (PHOTOGRAPH) "Examining Visuals" *p. 337*
- ULYSSES S. GRANT (PHOTOGRAPH) Professional Selection *p. 339*
- ROBERT E. LEE (PHOTOGRAPH) Professional Selection *p. 339*
- TENNIS FASHIONS (PHOTOGRAPH) "Responding to an Image" *p. 378*
- "THE LORD OF THE RINGS: THE TWO TOWERS: (POSTER) "Consider the Pattern" *p. 380*
- MOTHERS AGAINST DRUNK DRIVING (ADVERTISEMENT) "Examining Visuals" *p. 393*
- WOMAN WITH FAN (PHOTOGRAPH) "Responding to an Image" *p. 441*
- COLLEGE STUDENTS: A SPECTRUM (PHOTOGRAPH) "Consider the Pattern" *p. 442*
- "THE $10,000 DOG" (ADVERTISEMENT) "Examining Visuals" *p. 454*
- TOOTHPASTE AND TOOTHBRUSHES (PHOTOGRAPH) Professional Selection *p. 465*
- BECOMING A VICTIM OF CRIME (DRAWING) "Responding to an Image" *p. 489*

- THE FIRST DAY OF SCHOOL (PHOTOGRAPH) "Consider the Pattern" *p. 490*

- BELT IN SHAPE OF A MÖBIUS STRIP (DRAWING) Student Essay *p. 499*

- STATUE OF LIBERTY (PHOTOGRAPH) "Examining Visuals" *p. 501*

- EMMET KELLY: THE CLOWN (PHOTOGRAPH) "Responding to an Image" *p. 540*

- FREEDOM OF SPEECH (CARTOON) "Consider the Pattern" *p. 542*

- CLONING OR ASEXUAL REPRODUCTION (DRAWING) Professional Selection *p. 564*

- CULTURING STEM CELLS PROFESSIONAL SELECTION *p. 565*

- JUVENILE EXECUTIONS (CARTOON) Professional Selection *p. 580*

- NATE IS A CHILD (PHOTOGRAPH) Professional Selection *p. 582*

- ADULT TIME FOR ADULT CRIME (PHOTOGRAPH) Professional Selection *p. 593*

- FREEDOM OF SPEECH ON CAMPUS (CARTOON) Professional Selection *p. 609*

- POLITICAL CORRECTNESS VS THE FIRST AMENDMENT (CARTOON) Professional Selection *p. 620*

- FREEDOM OF SPEECH AND PORNOGRAPHY: A PACKAGE DEAL (CARTOON) Professional Selection *p. 633*

- CRAZY QUILT (PHOTOGRAPH) "Consider the Pattern" *p. 638*

- THE WEATHER CHANNEL (SCREEN SHOT) "Examining Visuals" *p. 645*

- GALLOWS (PHOTOGRAPH) Professional Selection *p. 654*

- DR. FRANCINE BENES (PHOTOGRAPH) Professional Selection *p. 665*

- A LAKE (PHOTOGRAPH) Professional Selection *p. 680*

- WHAT IS PLAGIARISM? (CARTOON) "Consider Using Sources" *p. 684*

Essays that Express Feelings and Relate Experience

- GAIL GODWIN   The Watcher at the Gates   *p. 58*
- N. SCOTT MOMADAY   The Homestead on Rainy Mountain Creek   *p. 119*
- RICK BASS   A Winter's Tale   *p. 129*
- ANNIE DILLARD   The Deer at Providencia   *p. 135*
- CHRIS ABANI   The Lottery   *p. 169*
- LANGSTON HUGHES   Salvation   *p. 173*
- NATALIE KUSZ   Ring Leader   *p. 183*
- JEAN SHEPHERD   Lost at C   *p. 189*
- RALPH ELLISON   On Being the Target of Discrimination   *p. 234*
- HENRY LOUIS GATES   In the Kitchen   *p. 291*
- NICHOLAS D. KRISTOF   In Japan, Nice Boys (and Girls) Finish Together   *p. 348*
- ALICE WALKER   Am I Blue?   *p. 353*
- ANDREW SULLIVAN   Why the *M* Word Matters to Me   *p. 401*
- BRENT STAPLES   Just Walk on By: A Black Man Ponders His Power to Alter Public Space   *p. 416*
- BRAD WHETSTINE   Augustinian Influences   *p. 646*
- GEORGE ORWELL   A Hanging   *p. 650*
- RICHARD RODRIGUEZ   Complexion   *p. 657*
- PAGAN KENNEDY   One Room, 3,000 Brains   *p. 662*
- E. B. WHITE   Once More to the Lake   *p. 676*

Essays that Inform

- MORTIMER ADLER   How to Mark a Book   *p. 28*
- GAIL GODWIN   The Watcher at the Gates   *p. 58*
- PAUL ROBERTS   How to Say Nothing in 500 Words   *p. 89*
- RICK BASS   A Winter's Tale   *p. 129*
- WILLIAM GLABERSON   Seeking Justice after a Fatal Spin of the Cylinder   *p. 177*
- JEAN SHEPHERD   Lost at C   *p. 189*
- CULLEN MURPHY   Liposuction   *p. 223*
- TRIP GABRIEL   Computers Help Unite Campuses but Also Drive Some Students Apart   *p. 228*
- RALPH ELLISON   On Being the Target of Discrimination   *p. 234*
- BARBARA EHRENREICH   What I've Learned from Men   *p. 242*

- DIANE COLE   Don't Just Stand There   *p. 285*

- HENRY LOUIS GATES   In the Kitchen   *p. 291*

- TIMOTHY HARPER   Shoot to Kill   *p. 299*

- JESSICA MITFORD   Behind the Formaldehyde Curtain   *p. 307*

- BRUCE CATTON   Grant and Lee: A Study in Contrasts   *p. 338*

- NICHOLAS D. KRISTOF   In Japan, Nice Boys (and Girls) Finish Together   *p. 348*

- ALICE WALKER   Am I Blue?   *p. 353*

- DEBORAH TANNEN   Squeaky Wheels and Protruding Nails: Direct and Indirect Speech   *p. 359*

- ARTHUR L. CAMPA   Anglos vs. Chicano: Why?   *p. 368*

- DOROTHY SIEGEL   What Is Behind the Growth of Campus Violence?   *p. 394*

- JAMES SUROWIECKI   Paying to Play   *p. 405*

- EYAL PRESS   Fouled Out   *p. 410*

- BRENT STAPLES   Just Walk on By: A Black Man Ponders His Power to Alter Public Space   *p. 416*

- CALVIN TRILLIN   It's Just Too Late   *p. 422*

- SISSELA BOK   White Lies   *p. 455*

- MARTIN LUTHER KING, JR.   The Ways of Meeting Oppression   *p. 459*

- DAVID BODANIS   What's in Your Toothpaste?   *p. 464*

- WILLIAM ZINSSER   College Pressures   *p. 469*

- DESMOND MORRIS   Territorial Behaviour   *p. 477*

- JUDY BRADY   I Want a Wife   *p. 502*

- JONATHAN RAUCH   Caring for Your Introvert   *p. 506*

- JO GOODWIN PARKER   What Is Poverty?   *p. 511*

- MALCOLM GLADWELL   The Art of Failure   *p. 516*

- ELIE WIESEL   To Be a Jew   *p. 527*

- TIMOTHY ROCHE AND AMANDA BOWER   Young Voices from the Cell   *p. 596*

- HOWARD WASSERMAN   Fan Profanity   *p. 625*

- ROBERT O'NEIL   What Limits Should Campus Networks Place on Pornography?   *p. 632*

- GEORGE ORWELL   A Hanging   *p. 650*

- PAGAN KENNEDY   One Room, 3,000 Brains   *p. 662*

- ESTHER THORSON   Dissect an Ad   *p. 670*

Essays that Persuade

- BARBARA EHRENREICH   What I've Learned from Men   *p. 242*

- JONATHAN KOZOL   Untouchables   *p. 248*

- MIKLÓS VÁMOS   How I'll Become an American   *p. 281*

- JESSICA MITFORD   Behind the Formaldehyde Curtain   *p. 307*

- DEBORAH TANNEN   Squeaky Wheels and Protruding Nails: Direct and Indirect Speech   *p. 359*

- ANDREW SULLIVAN   Why the *M* Word Matters to Me   *p. 401*

- JAMES SUROWIECKI   Paying to Play   *p. 405*

- SISSELA BOK   White Lies   *p. 455*

- MARTIN LUTHER KING, JR.   The Ways of Meeting Oppression   *p. 459*

- DAVID BODANIS   What's in Your Toothpaste?   *p. 464*

- JUDY BRADY   I Want a Wife   *p. 502*

- JONATHAN RAUCH   Caring for Your Introvert   *p. 506*

- JO GOODWIN PARKER   What Is Poverty?   *p. 511*

- JEREMY RIFKIN   Why I Oppose Human Cloning   *p. 566*

- RAYMOND BARGLOW   A Reply to Rifkin   *p. 573*

- *NEW YORK TIMES*   Little Adult Criminals   *p. 581*

- LAURENCE STEINBERG   Should Juvenile Offenders Be Tried as Adults?   *p. 585*

- LINDA J. COLLIER   Adult Crime, Adult Time   *p. 591*

- NET HENTOFF   Free Speech on Campus   *p. 605*

- CHARLES R. LAWRENCE III   The Debate over Placing Limits on Racist Speech Must Not Ignore the Damage It Does to Its Victims   *p. 612*

- HARVEY A. SILVERGLATE AND GREG LUKIANOFF   Speech Codes: Alive and Well at Colleges   *p. 617*

- HOWARD WASSERMAN   Fan Profanity   *p. 625*

- ROBERT O'NEIL   What Limits Should Campus Networks Place on Pornography?   *p. 632*

- GEORGE ORWELL   A Hanging   *p. 650*

- PAGAN KENNEDY   One Room, 3,000 Brains   *p. 662*

Essays that Entertain

- PAUL ROBERTS   How to Say Nothing in 500 Words   *p. 89*

- RICK BASS   A Winter's Tale   *p. 129*

- JEAN SHEPHERD   Lost at C   *p. 189*
- CULLEN MURPHY   Lifosuction   *p. 223*
- MIKLÓS VÁMOS   How I'll Become an American   *p. 281*
- SUZANNE BRITT   Neat People vs. Sloppy People   *p. 344*
- JUDY BRADY   I Want a Wife   *p. 502*
- E. B. WHITE   Once More to the Lake   *p. 676*

- The Not-So-Ideal Male   *p. 85*
- The Gendarme   *p. 114*
- The Family Reunion, Revisited   *p. 165*
- *Food for Thought   *p. 218*
- A Visit to Candyland   *p. 277*
- Teaching a New Dog Old Tricks   *p. 334*
- Why Athletes Use Steroids   *p. 390*
- Strictly Speaking   *p. 452*
- *Why Did the Chicken Cross the Möbius Strip?   *p. 498*
- *Cast Out of Kansas: Music Censorship in Public Libraries   *p. 560*
- *The Telephone Is Out: IM Is In   *p. 642*
- Divorce as a Violation of Trust   *p. 703*

INDEX OF STUDENT ESSAYS

Abani, Chris, "The Lottery," 169–170
Abbott, Lee K. "The View of Me from Mars," 199–204
Adequate detail, 64–68
Adler, Mortimer, "How to Mark a Book," 28–32
"Adult Crime, Adult Time," 591–594
Advertisements, reading, 23–25
Affect/effect, 385
Alternating pattern, 329, G-1
"Am I Blue?" 353–356
"Americanization Is Tough on 'Macho,'" 11–13
Analogy, 326, G-1
Anecdote, 156, G-1
"Anglo vs. Chicano: Why?" 368–371
Argumentation-persuasion, 543–563, G-1, G-4
　annotated student essay, 560–562
　audience, 544, 549–551
　college writing, in 544–545
　deduction, 554–555
　ethos, 549–551
　induction, 553–554
　introduction, 555
　logic, 5–7, 553–555
　logos, 546–549
　organizing, 555–557
　pathos, 546, 548–549
　process guidelines, 558–559
　purpose of, 544–546, 549–551
　raising and countering objections, 551–552
　revising checklist, 558
　strategies for writing, 558–559
　supporting detail, 546–568
　thesis, 552, 555, 556
　Toulmin model, 552–553
　visualizing, 557
"Art of Failure, The," 516–524
Audience, 35–36, 544, 549–551, G-1
　hostile reader, 550–551
　supportive reader, 550
　wavering reader, 550
"Augustinian Influences," 646–647

Bambara, Toni Cade, "The Lesson," 257–262
Barglow, Raymond, "A Reply to Rifkin," 573–577
Bass, Rick, "A Winter's Tale," 129–132
"Behind the Formaldehyde Curtain," 307–313
Benedict, Carl, "Why Athletes Use Steroids," 390–391
Bevilacqua, Mary Ann, "The Telephone Is Out; IM Is In," 642–644
Block pattern, 329, G-1
Bodanis, David, "What's in Your Toothpaste?" 464–466
Body paragraphs, 64–72, G-1
　coherence, 69–70
　paragraphing, 70–71

patterns of development, 66–68
supporting detail, 64–70
topic sentence, 64
visual material, 71–72
Bok, Sissella, "White Lies," 455–457
Bower, Amanda, and Timothy Roche, "Young Voices from the Cell," 596–602
Brady, Judy, "I Want a Wife," 502–503
Brainstorming, 38–39, 42
Britt, Suzanne, "Neat People vs. Sloppy People," 344–345

Campa, Arthur, "Anglo vs. Chicano: Why?" 368–371
"Caring for Your Introvert," 506–508
"Cast Out of Kansas: Music Censorship in Public Libraries," 560–562
Catton, Bruce, "Grant and Lee: A Study in Contrasts," 338–341
Causal chain, 384–385, G-1
Cause-and-effect analysis, 56–57, 380–393, G-1
　annotated student essay, 390–391
　causal chain, 384–385, G-1
　college writing, in, 382–383
　logic, 385–386
　organizing, 386–387, 388
　process guidelines, 387, 389
　purpose of, 382–383
　revising checklist, 389
　strategies for writing, 387, 389
　supporting detail, 384–386
　thesis, 386
　visualizing, 388
Charts, reading, 22–23
Chronological order, 50, 110, 161, 214, 273, 290, 387, G-1
Classification-division, 56–57, 442–454, G-1
　annotated student essay, 452–453
　college writing, in, 445–446
　ordering principle, 447
　organizing, 447–450
　process guidelines, 451
　purpose of, 444–447
　revising checklist, 451
　strategies for writing, 451
　supporting detail, 447–450
　thesis, 448
　topic sentences, 448–449
Clichés, 109
Clustering, 42–43, 44–45
Coherence, 69–70, 641, G-1
Cole, Diane, "Don't Just Stand There," 285–289
"College Pressures," 469–475
Collier, Linda J., "Adult Crime, Adult Time," 591–594
Combining patterns of development, 67–68, 639–644
Comparison-contrast, 322–337, G-1
　alternating pattern, 329
　analogy, 326

Comparison-contrast (*continued*)
    annotated student essay, 334–336
    college writing, in, 324–325
    organizing, 328–330
    purpose of, 324–326
    revising checklist, 333
    strategies for writing, 331–332
    supporting detail, 327–329
    thesis, 328
    visualizing, 330
"Complexion," 657–659
Computer, using a, 39, 44, 51, 53–54
"Computers Help Unite Campuses But Also
        Drive Some Students Apart,"
        228–231
Conclusion, 72–74, G-2
Context (*see* Writing context)
Critical reading (*see* Reading)
Critical thinking, 1–27, G-2
    evaluating quality, 4–5
    facts and opinions, distinguishing
        between, 2–3
    inferences, making, 3–4
    logic, detecting errors in, 5–7. 385–386
    reading journal, 13–14
    strategies for, 8–13
    summarizing, 14–17
    synthesizing, 4, 17–18
    visual material, reading, 21–27

David, Florence, "Divorce as a Violation of
        Trust," 703–706
"Debate over Placing Limits on Racist
        Speech Must Not Ignore Its
        Victims, The, 612–615
Deduction, 554–555, G-2
"Deer at Providencia, The," 135–138
Definition, 56–57, 490–500, G-2
    annotated student essay, 498–500
    circular, 495
    college writing, in, 494
    extended, 492
    formal, 491
    introduction, 495
    organizing, 495–496
    process guidelines, 497
    purpose of, 492–494
    revising checklist, 497
    stipulative, 492, G-4
    strategies for writing, 497
    supporting details, 494–496
    thesis, 495
Description, 56–57, 100–150, G-2
    annotated student essay, 114–117
    clichés, 109
    college writing, in, 103–104
    descriptive words, 107–109
    dominant impression, 104–105
    metaphors, 109–110
    objective and expressive details, 105–107
    organizing, 100–111
    process guidelines, 112

    purpose of, 102–104
    revising checklist, 112
    sensory details, 106
    similes, 109–110
    specific words, 107–108
    strategies for writing, 112
    supporting details, 105–110
    thesis, 110
    visualizing, 111
Dialect, 263
Diction
    clichés, 109
    descriptive words, 107–109
    euphemism, 314
    metaphors, 109–110
    modifiers, 332
    similes, 109–110
    specific words, 107–108
Dillard, Annie, "The Deer at Providencia,"
        135–138
Direct quotation, 159–160, 547, 692–693, 695,
        G-2
Directional process analysis, 267, G-2
Discovery draft, 42
"Dissect an Ad," 670–673
Division (*see* Classification-division)
"Divorce as a Violation of Trust," 703–706
Documenting borrowed material, 696–701,
        G-2
"Do Not Go Gentle into That Good
        Night," 486
Dominant impression, 104–105, G-2
"Don't Just Stand There," 285–289
Drafting, 42, 61–77
    essay structure, 62–77
    tips, 61–62

Editing, 83–84, G-2
    tips, 84
Effect/affect, 385
Ehrenreich, Barbara, "What I've Learned
        from Men," 242–244
Ehrlich, Gretel, "Struck by Lightning,"
        141–146
Ellison, Ralph, "On Being the Target of
        Discrimination," 234–239
Essay in progress, 76–77, 81–83, 85–88
Essay structure, 50–54, 62–77
    argumentation-persuasion, 555–557
    body paragraphs, 64–72
    classification-division, 447–450
    coherence, 69–70
    comparison-contrast, 328–330
    conclusion, 72–74
    definition, 495–496
    description, 110–111
    exemplification, 214–215
    introduction, 62–64
    narration, 160–162, 163
    patterns of development, 66–68
    process analysis, 272–274
    supporting details, 64–70

thesis, 45–49
titles, 74
topic sentence, 64, 68
transitions, 69–70
visual material, 71–72
visualizing, 74–75
Ethos, 549–551, G-2
Euphemism, 314, G-2
Evaluating sources, 689–690
Examining subject from different angles, 39–40
Exemplification, 56–57, 208–222, G-2
    annotated student essay, 218–221
    college writing, in, 211–212
    hypothetical example, 213–214
    organizing, 214–215
    process guidelines, 216
    purpose of, 210–212
    revising checklist, 217
    strategies for college writing, 216
    supporting detail, 212–214
    thesis, 214
    topic sentence, 214
    visualizing, 215
Explanatory process analysis, 267–268, G-2
Expressive details, 105–107, G-2
Extended definition, 492, G-3

Facts, 2–3, 547, G-3
"Family Reunion Revisited, The," 165–166
"Fan Profanity," 625–630
"Fire and Ice," 374
First draft, 61, G-3
Flashback, 161, G-3
Formal definition, 491, G-3
Formal outline, 52–53
"Fouled Out," 410–413
"Free Speech on Campus," 605–610
Freewriting, 39
Frost, Robert, "Fire and Ice," 374

Gabriel, Trip, "Computers Help Unite Campuses But Also Drive Some Students Apart," 228–231
Gates, Henry Louis, Jr., "In the Kitchen," 291–296
"Gendarme, The," 114–117
Generalization, 64–66, 68, 211, G-3
Generating ideas, 37–44 (See also Idea generation)
Glaberson, William, "Seeking Justice after a Fatal Spin of the Cylinder," 177–180
Gladwell, Malcolm, "The Art of Failure," 516–524
Godwin, Gail, "The Watcher at the Gates," 58–60
"Grant and Lee: A Study in Contrasts," 338–341
Graphs, reading, 22–23
Guibault, Rose Del Castillo, "Americanization Is Tough on Macho," 11–13

"Hanging, A," 650–654
Harper, Timothy, "Shoot to Kill," 299–304
Hentoff, Nat, "Free Speech on Campus," 605–610
Hickman, Nick, "Why Did the Chicken Cross the Möbius Strip," 498–500
"Homestead on Rainy Mountain Creek, The," 119–121
Hostile reader, 550–551
"How I'll Become an American," 281–283
"How to Mark a Book," 28–32
"How to Say Nothing in 500 Words," 89–98
Hughes, Langston, "Salvation," 173–174
Hypothetical example, 213–214, G-3

"I Want a Wife," 502–503
Idea generation, 39–44
    brainstorming, 38–39, 42
    checking the Internet, 43–44
    clustering, 42–43, 44–45
    developing a thesis, 45–49
    discovery draft, 42
    examining a subject from different angles, 37–40
    freewriting, 39
    narrowing a topic, 40
    patterns of development, considering, 53–57
    shaping a writing topic, 37–41
    talking to other people, 43
    using a computer, 39, 44, 51, 53–54
Imperative sentences, 268
Implied thesis, 47, 161
"In Japan, Nice Guys (and Girls) Finish Together," 348–350
"In the Kitchen," 291–296
Induction, 553–554, G-3
Inferences, 3–4, 554, G-3
Informal outline, 51–52
Integrating sources, 693–695
Internet, 44, 689–690
Introductions, 62–64, 495, 555, G-3
Irony, 175, 197, G-3
"It's Just Too Late," 422–429

Journal, reading, 13–14
Journalist's questions, 158, G-3
"Just Walk on By: A Black Man Ponders His Power to Alter Public Space," 416–419

Kazin, Alfred, "My Neighborhood," 124–126
Kennedy, Pagan, "One Room, 3000 Brains," 662–668
King, Martin Luther, Jr., "The Ways of Meeting Oppression," 459–461
Kozol, Jonathan, "Untouchables," 248–255
Kristoff, Nicholas D., "In Japan, Nice Guys (and Girls) Finish Together," 348–350
Kusz, Natalie, "Ring Leader," 183–186

Lawrence, Charles R. "The Debate Over Racist Speech Must Not Ignore Its Victims," 612–615
"Lesson, The," 257–262
"Lifosuction," 223–226
"Little Adult Criminals," 581–583
Locating sources, 686–689
Logic, 5–7, 385–386, 553–555, 558, G-3
Logos, 546–549, G-3
"Lost at C," 189–196
"Lottery, The," 169–170
Lukianoff, Greg, and Harvey A. Silverglate, "Speech Codes: Alive and Well at Colleges," 617–623
"Lullaby," 432–438

Metaphors, 109–110, G-3
Momaday, N. Scott, "The Homestead on Rainy Mountain Creek," 119–121
Mitford, Jessica, "Behind the Formaldehyde Curtain," 307–313
Modifiers, 332
Mitchell, Ralph, "The Gendarme," 114–117
Morris, Desmond, "Territorial Behaviour," 477–483
Murphy, Cullen, "Lifosuction," 223–226
"My Neighborhood," 124–126

Narration, 56–57, 154–167, G-3
    anecdote, 156
    annotated student essay, 165–166
    college writing, in, 156–157
    description in, 158
    dialogue in, 159–160
    flashback, 161
    journalist's questions, 158
    organizing, 160–162
    process guidelines, 162–163
    purpose of, 155–157
    revising checklist, 164
    strategies for writing, 162–163
    supporting detail, 158–162
    thesis, 161
    visualizing, 163
Narrowing a topic, 40
"Neat People vs. Sloppy People," 344–345
New York Times, "Little Adult Criminals," 581–583
"Not-So-Ideal Male, The," 76–77, 81–83, 85–88
Nye, Naomi Shihab, "Traveling Onion, The," 316

Objective details, 105–107, G-3
"On Being the Target of Discrimination," 234–239
"Once More to the Lake," 676–681
"One Room, 3000 Brains," 662–668
O'Neil, Robert, "What Limits Should Campus Networks Place on Pornography?" 632–635
Opinion, 2–3, G-3

Organization
    alternating, 329, G-1
    of argumentation-persuasion, 555–557
    block, 329, G-1
    body paragraphs, 64–72, G-1
    of cause-and-effect analysis, 386–387, 388
    chronological order, 50, 110, 161, 214, 273, 290, 387, G-1
    of classification and division, 447–450
    coherence, 69–70, 641
    of comparison-contrast, 328–330
    conclusion, 72–74
    of definition, 495–496
    of description, 110–111
    of exemplification, 214–215
    flashback, 161
    implied thesis, 47
    introduction, 62–64, 495, 555
    of narration, 160–162
    ordering details, 50–54
    ordering principle, 447
    outlining, 50–54
    paragraphing, 70–71, 160
    process analysis, 272–274
    progressive order, 50, 110, 214, G-4
    spatial order, 50 110, G-4
    supporting details, 55–57, 64–70, G-4
    thesis, 45–49, 110, 161, 214, 328, 386, 448, 495, 552, 555, 556, G-5
    topic sentence, 64, 68, 214, 386, 448–449, 556, G-5
    transitions, 69–70, 331, 641
Orwell, George, "A Hanging," 650–654
Outline tree, 52
Outlining, 50–54
    computer, using a, 51, 53–54
    formal outline, 52–53
    informal outline, 51–52
    outline tree, 52
    scratch outline, 51

Paragraphing, 70–71, 160
Parallelism, 449
Paraphrasing, 690–691, 695, G-3
Parker, Jo Goodwin, "What Is Poverty?" 511–514
Pathos, 546, 548–549, G-4
Patterns of Development, 55–57, 66–68, 548
    cause-and-effect analysis, 56–57, 66–68, 548
    classification-division, 56–57, 442–454
    comparison-contrast, 56–57, 322–337
    definition, 56–57, 490–500
    description, 56 57, 100–153
    exemplification, 56–57, 208–264
    narration, 56–57, 154–204
    primary, 640
    process analysis, 56–57, 267–276
    secondary, 640
"Paying to Play," 405–407
Peer review, 79–80
Person shift, 275
Persuasion (see Argumentation-persuasion)

Plagiarism, 18, 695–696, G-4
Preliminary thesis, 49
Press, Eyal, "Fouled Out," 410–413
Prewriting (*see* Idea generation)
Primary pattern of development, 640
Process analysis, 56–57, 267–320, G-4
    annotated student essay, 277–279
    college writing, in, 269
    declarative sentences, 268
    directional, 267, G-2
    explanatory, 267–268, G-2
    imperative sentences, 268
    organizing, 272–274
    process guidelines, 273–275
    purpose of, 268–270
    revising checklist, 276
    strategies for writing, 273–275
    supporting details, 270–273
    thesis, 272
    visualizing, 267, 274
Process guidelines:
    argumentation-persuasion, 558–559
    cause-and-effect analysis, 389
    classification-division, 451
    combining patterns, 640–641
    comparison-contrast, 331–332
    definition, 497
    description, 112
    exemplification, 216–217
    narration, 216–217
    process analysis, 273–275
Progressive order, 50, 110, 214, G-4
Proofreading, 85
Purpose, 34–35, G-4
    of argumentation-persuasion, 544–546,
      549–551
    of cause-and-effect analysis, 382–383
    of classification and division, 444–447
    of combined patterns, 639–640
    of comparison-contrast, 324–326
    of definition, 492–494
    of description, 102–104
    of exemplification, 210–212
    of narration, 155–157
    of process analysis, 268–270

Quoting, 159–160, 547, 692–693, 695

Raising and countering objections, 551–552
Rauch, Jonathan, "Caring for Your Introvert,"
    506–508
Reading
    facts, 2–3
    inferences, 3–4
    keeping a reading journal, 13–14
    logic, 5–7
    opinions, 2–3
    quality, evaluating, 4–5
    strategies for, 8–13
    summary, writing a, 14–17
    synthesizing, 4, 17–18
    visual material, 21–27

Reading journal, 13–14
Relevant detail, 66
"Reply to Rifkin, A," 573–577
Research:
    annotated student essay, 702–706
    documenting sources, 696–701
    evaluating sources, 689–690
    integrating, 693–695
    locating sources, 686–689
    paraphrasing, 690–691, 693–694
    plagiarism, 18, 695–696
    quoting, 692–693, 693–694
    works cited page, 698–701
Revising, 77–83, G-4
    argumentation, 559
    cause-and-effect analysis, 389
    checklist, 78, 112, 164, 217, 276, 333, 451,
      597, 558
    classification-division, 451
    comparison-contrast, 332–333
    definition, 497
    description, 112
    exemplification, 217
    narration, 163–164
    peer review, 79–80
    process analysis, 275–276
    tips, 79
Revising checklist, 78, G-4
    for argumentation-persuasion, 588
    for cause-and-effect analysis, 409
    for comparison-contrast, 354
    for classification and division, 471
    for definition, 521
    for description, 110
    for exemplification, 228
    for narration, 167
    for process analysis, 292
Rifkin, Jeremy, "Why I Oppose Human
    Cloning," 566–571
Ríos, Alberto, "The Vietnam Wall," 149–150
Roberts, Paul, "How to Say Nothing in 500
    Words," 89–98
Roche, Timothy, and Amanda Bower, "Young
    Voices from the Cell," 596–602
Rodriguez, Richard, "Complexion," 657–659
Role, writer's, 36–37, G-4

"Salvation," 173–174
Scheels, Hannah, "Cast Out of Kansas:
    Music Censorship in Public
    Libraries," 560–562
Scratch outline, 51
"Seeking Justice after a Fatal Spin of the
    Cylinder," 177–180
Sensory details, 106, G-4
Shepherd, Jean, "Lost at C," 189–196
Shift:
    in person, 275
    in tense, 164
"Shoot to Kill," 299–304
"Should Juvenile Offenders Be Tried As
    Adults?" 585–589

Siegel, Dorothy, "What Is Behind the Growth of Violence on College Campuses?" 394–398
Silko, Leslie Marmon, "Lullaby," 432–438
Silverglate, Harvey A., and Greg Lukianoff, "Speech Codes: Alive and Well at Colleges," 617–623
Similes, 109–110, G-4
Situational irony, 175, 197, G-4
Sources (*see* Research)
Spatial order, 50, 110, 214, G-4
Specific words, 107–108
"Speech Codes: Alive and Well at Colleges," 617–623
"Squeaky Wheels and Protruding Nails: Direct and Indirect Speech," 359–366
Staples, Brent, "Just Walk on By: A Black Man Ponders His Power to Alter Public Space," 416–419
Steinberg, Laurence, "Should Juvenile Offenders Be Tried as Adults?" 485–489
Stipulative definition, 492, G-4
"Strictly Speaking," 452–453
"Struck by Lightning," 141–146
Sullivan, Andrew, "Why the *M* Word Matters to Me," 401–402
Summarizing, 14–17, G-4
Supporting details, 55–57, 64–70, G-4
    adequate detail, 64–68
    for argumentation-persuasion, 546–58
    body paragraphs, 64–72, G-1
    causal chain, 384–385, G-1
    for cause-and-effect analysis, 384–386
    chronological order, 50, 100
    for classification and division, 447–450
    coherence, 69–70
    combining patterns, 67–68, 639–644
    for comparison-contrast, 327–329
    for definition, 494–496
    for description, 105–110
    dialogue, 159–160
    ethos, 549–551
    for exemplification, 212–214
    logos, 546–549
    for narration, 158–162
    objective and expressive details, 105–107
    organizing, 50–54
    pathos, 548–549
    patterns of development, 55–57, 66–68, 548
    for process analysis, 270–273
    progressive order, 50, 110
    raising and countering objections, 551–552
    relevant detail, 66
    sensory detail, 106
    source of, 66
    sources, using, 685–706
    spatial order, 50, 110
    tone, 71
    topic sentence, 64, 68

transitions, 69–71
visual material, 71–72
Surowiecki, James, "Paying to Play," 405–407
Synthesizing, 4, 17–18, G-4

Talking to people about topic, 43
Tannen, Deborah, "Squeaky Wheels and Protruding Nails: Direct and Indirect Speech," 359–366
"Teaching a New Dog Old Tricks," 334–336
"Telephone Is Out, IM Is In, The," 642–644
Tense shifts, 164
"Territorial Behaviour," 477–483
Thesis, 45–49, G-5
    for argumentation-persuasion, 552, 555, 556
    for cause-and-effect analysis, 386
    for classification and division, 448
    for comparison-contrast, 328
    composing, 48–49
    for definition, 495
    for description, 110
    for exemplification, 214
    implied, 47, 161
    location, 46–47
    for narration, 161
    preliminary, 49
    for process analysis, 272
    qualities, 47–48
Thomas, Dylan, "Do Not Go Gentle into That Good Night," 486
Thorson, Esther, "Dissect an Ad," 670–673
Titles, 74
"To Be a Jew," 527–534
Tone, 71, G-5
Topic selection, 37–41, 110, G-5
Topic sentence, 64, 68, 214, 386, 448–449, 556
Toulmin model, 552–553
Transitions, 69–71, 331, 641
"Traveling Onion, The," 316
Trillin, Calvin, "It's Just Too Late," 422–429

"Untouchables," 248–255

Vámos, Miklós, "How I'll Become an American," 281–283
Verbal irony, 133, 314, 352, 430, G-5
"Vietnam Wall, The," 149–150
"View of Me from Mars, The," 199–204
"Visit to Candyland, A," 277–279
Visual material:
    reading, 21–27
    as support, 71–72
Visualizing an essay, 74–75, 111, 163, 215, 274, 330, 388, 450, 496, 557

Walker, Alice, "Am I Blue?" 353–356
Warnock, Robbie, "The Family Reunion, Revisited," 165–166
Wasserman, Howard M. "Fan Profanity," 625–630
"Watcher at the Gates, The," 58–60

Wavering reader, 550
"Ways of Meeting Oppression, The,"
    459–461
"What Is Behind the Growth of Violence on
    College Campuses?" 394–398
"What Is Poverty?" 511–514
"What I've Learned from Men," 242–244
"What Limits Should Campus Networks
    Place on Pornography?" 632–635
"What's In Your Toothpaste?" 464–466
Whetstine, Brad, "Augustinian Influences,"
    646–647
White, E.B., "Once More to the Lake,"
    676–681
"White Lies," 455–457
"Why Athletes Use Steroids," 390–391
"Why Did the Chicken Cross the Möbius
    Strip?" 498–500
"Why I Oppose Human Cloning," 566–571

"Why the M Word Matters to Me," 401–402
Wiesel, Elie, "To Be a Jew," 527–534
"Winter's Tale, A" 129–132
Wolfe, David, "Strictly Speaking," 452–453
Word choice, (see Diction)
Works cited page, 698–701
Writing context, 34–37, G-5
    audience, 35–36, G-1
    purpose, 34–35 G-4
    role, 36–37, G-4
Writing process (See Drafting, Editing, Idea
    generation, Process guidelines,
    Proofreading, Revising)
Writing topic, 37–41

"Young Voices from the Cell," 596–602

Zinsser, William, "College Pressures,"
    469–575